Lecture Notes in Computer Science 6179

Commenced Publication in 1973
Founding and Former Series Editors:
Gerhard Goos, Juris Hartmanis, and Jan van Leeuwen

Klaus Miesenberger   Joachim Klaus
Wolfgang Zagler   Arthur Karshmer (Eds.)

Computers Helping People with Special Needs

12th International Conference, ICCHP 2010
Vienna, Austria, July 14-16, 2010
Proceedings, Part I

 Springer

Volume Editors

Klaus Miesenberger
University of Linz, Institute "Integriert Studieren"
Altenbergerstraße 49, 4040, Linz, Austria
E-mail: klaus.miesenberger@jku.at

Joachim Klaus
University of Karlsruhe (TH), Study Center for the Visually Impaired Students
Engesserstr. 4, 76131 Karlsruhe, Germany
E-mail: klaus@szs.uni-karlsruhe.de

Wolfgang Zagler
Vienna University of Technology, Institute "Integriert Studieren"
Favoritenstr. 11/029, 1040, Vienna, Austria
E-mail: zw@fortec.tuwien.ac.at

Arthur Karshmer
University of San Francisco
2130 Fulton St., San Francisco, CA 94117, USA
E-mail: arthur@lakeland.usf.edu

Library of Congress Control Number: 2010929485

CR Subject Classification (1998): H.5.2, H.5, H.4, H.3, K.4, K.4.2

LNCS Sublibrary: SL 3 – Information Systems and Application, incl. Internet/Web
and HCI

ISSN   0302-9743
ISBN-10   3-642-14096-3 Springer Berlin Heidelberg New York
ISBN-13   978-3-642-14096-9 Springer Berlin Heidelberg New York

springer.com

© Springer-Verlag Berlin Heidelberg 2010

Typesetting: Camera-ready by author, data conversion by Scientific Publishing Services, Chennai, India
Printed on acid-free paper   06/3180

Preface

Welcome to the Proceedings of ICCHP 2010!

July 14-16, 2010
Pre-conference July 12-13
International Conference on Computers
Helping People with Special Needs
Vienna University of Technology

We were proud to welcome participants from more than 40 countries from all over the world to this year's ICCHP.

Since the late 1980s, it has been ICCHP's mission to support and reflect development in the field of "Assistive Technologies," eAccessibility and eInclusion. With a focus on scientific quality, ICCHP has become an important reference in our field. The 2010 conference and this collection of papers once again fulfilled this mission.

The International Programme Committee, comprising 106 experts from all over the world, selected 147 full and 44 short papers out of 328 abstracts submitted to ICCHP. This acceptance ratio of about half of the submissions demonstrates our strict pursuit of scientific quality both of the programme and in particular of the proceedings in your hands.

An impressive number of experts agreed to organize "Special Thematic Sessions" (STS) for ICCHP 2010. These STS help to bring the meeting into sharper focus in several key areas. In turn, this deeper level of focus helps to collate a state of the art and mainstream technical, social, cultural and political developments.

Our keynote speakers highlighted issues of outstanding importance, such as *"Usable Web Accessibility,"* areas which can be seen as breakthroughs in our field, like the development of 2D Braille displays *allowing "Maintaining an Overview Through Your Fingers,"* and new and upcoming issues of interest for our field, like *"Weak and Silent Speech."* Additional keynote addresses included presentations from the *European Commission, UNESCO and ISO*.

With an interesting workshop programme, meetings, an exhibition including presentations and demonstrations of major software and assistive technology producers and vendors, ICCHP once again provided the framework for an international meeting place and a center of advanced information exchange.

ICCHP 2010 was held under the auspices of Heinz Fischer, President of the Federal Republic of Austria. We would also like to thank all supporters and sponsors.

Our special thanks go to those contributing toward putting this conference in place.

We thank the Austrian Computer Society for announcing and sponsoring the Roland Wagner Award on Computers Helping People with Special Needs.

The Austrian Computer Society decided in September 2001 to endow this award in honor of Roland Wagner, the founder of ICCHP.

The Roland Wagner Award is a biannual award in the range of €3000. It will be handed over on the occasion of ICCHP conferences.

Award Winners:

- Award 0: Roland Wagner on the occasion of his 50th birthday, 2001
- Award 1: WAI-W3C, ICCHP 2002 in Linz
- Special Award 2003: A Min Tjoa, Vienna University of Technology on the occasion of his 50th birthday
- Award 2: Paul Blenkhorn, University of Manchester, ICCHP 2004 in Paris
- Award 3: Larry Scadden, National Science Foundation, ICCHP 2006 in Linz
- Special Award 2006: Roland Traunmüller, University of Linz
- Award 4: George Kersher, Daisy Consortium

Once again we thank all those who helped in putting ICCHP in place and thereby supporting the AT field and a better quality of life for people with disabilities. Special thanks go to all our supporter and sponsors, displayed at: http://www.icchp.org/sponsors.

July 2010   Klaus Miesenberger
                                                                                                                     Joachim Klaus
                                                                                                                   Arthur Karshmer
                                                                                                                   Wolfgang Zagler

Organization

General ICCHP 2010 Chair, H.J. Murphy, Founder, Former Director and Member Advisory Board of the Centre on Disabilities, California State University, Northridge, USA.

Programme Chairs

Karshmer, A.	University of San Francisco, USA
Burger, D.	INSERM, France
Suzuki, M.	Kyushu University, Japan
Tjoa, A. M.	Vienna University of Technology, Austria
Wagner, R.	University of Linz, Austria

Publishing Chairs

Klaus, J.	Karlsruhe Institute of Technology (KIT), Germany
Miesenberger, K.	University of Linz, Austria
Zagler, W.	Vienna University of Technology, Austria

Young Researchers Consortium Chairs

Alm, N.	Dundee University, UK
Archambault, D.	Université Pierre et Marie Curie, France
Fels, D.	Ryerson University, Canada
Fitzpatrick, D.	Dublin City University, Ireland
Kobayashi, M.	Tsukuba College of Technology, Japan
Morandell, M.	AIT Austrian Institute of Technology GmbH, Austria
Pontelli, E.	New Mexico State University, USA
Sinclair, R.	Microsoft, USA
Weber, G.	Technische Universität Dresden, Germany

Programme Committee

Abascal, J.	Euskal Herriko Unibertsitatea, Spain
Abou-Zahra, S.	W3C Web Accessibility Initiative (WAI), Austria
Abu-Ali, A.	Philadelphia University, Jordan
Andrich, R.	Polo Tecnologico Fondazione Don Carlo Gnocchi Onlus, Italy
Arató, A.	KFKI-RMKI, Hungary
Arató, P.	TU Budapest, Hungary
Ariwa, E.	London Metropolitan University, UK
Azevedo, L.	Instituto Superior Tecnico, Portugal

Batusic, M.	University of Linz, Austria
Baumann, K.	FH Johaneum, Austria
Bernareggi, C.	Università degli Studi di Milano, Italy
Bothe, H.-H.	Technical University of Denmark, Denmark
Bühler, C.	TU Dortmund University, FTB, Germany
Craddock, G.	Centre for Excellence in Universal Design, Ireland
Craven, J.	CERLIM, Manchester Metropolitan University, UK
Crombie, D.	European Adaptive Content Network (EUAIN), The Netherlands
Cummins Prager, M.	California State University Northridge, USA
Darvishy, A.	Züricher Hochschule für Angewandte Wissenschaften, Switzerland
Darzentas, J.	University of the Aegean, Greece
DeRuyter, F.	Duke University Medical Center, USA
Diaz del Campo, R.	Antarq Tecnosoluciones, Mexico
Dotter, F.	Universität Klagenfurt, Austria
Edwards, A.D.N.	University of York, UK
Emiliani, P.L.	Institute of Applied Physics "Nello Carrara", Italy
Engelen, J.	Katholieke Universiteit Leuven, Belgium
Evreinov, G.	University of Tampere, Finland
Gardner, J.	Oregon State University, USA
Gupta, G.	University of Texas at Dallas, USA
Hanson, V.	University of Dundee, UK
Harper, S.	University of Manchester, UK
Holzinger, A.	Graz University Hospital, Austria
Inoue, T.	National Rehabilitation Center for Persons with Disabilities, Japan
Ioannidis, G	IN2 search interfaces development Ltd, Germany
Jemni, M.	University of Tunis, Tunisia
Kalinnikova, L.	Pomor State University, Russia
Knops, H.	NG4All, The Netherlands
Koronios, A.	University of South Australia, Australia
Kouroupetroglou, G.	University of Athens, Greece
Kremser, W.	OCG, HSM, Austria
Lauruska, V.	Siauliai University, Lithuania
Leahy, D.	Trinity College Dublin, Ireland
Lunn, D.	University of Manchester, UK
Magnussen, M.	Stockholm University, Sweden
Mathiassen, N-E.	Danish Centre for Assistive Technology, Denmark
McKenzie, N.	DEDICON, The Netherlands
McMullin, B.	Dublin City University, Ireland
Mendelova, E.	Comenius University of Bratislava, Slovak Republic
Neveryd, H.	Lund University, Sweden
Normie, L.	GeronTech - The Israeli Center for Assistive Technology & Aging, Israel
Nussbaum, G.	KI-I, Austria
Ohnabe, H.	Niigata University of Health & Welfare, Japan

Ono, T.	Tsukuba University of Technology, Japan
Otogawa, T.	National Rehabilitation Center for Persons with Disabilities, Japan
Paciello, M.	The Paciello Group, USA
Panek, P.	Vienna University of Technology, Austria
Petrie, H	University of York, UK
Petz, A.	University of Linz, Austria
Prazak, B.	Austrian Research Centres, Austria
Pühretmair, F.	KI-I, Austria
Quirchmayr, G.	University of Vienna, Austria
Raisamo, R.	University of Tampere, Finland
Rauhala, M.	Vienna University of Technology, Austria
Salminen, A.	KELA, Finland
Scadden, L.	Independent Consultant on Assistive Technology, USA
Schultz, T.	Universität Karlsruhe (TH), Germany
Sik Lányi, C.	University of Pannonia, Hungary
Snaprud, M.	University of Agder, Norway
Soede, T.	Zuyd University, The Netherlands
Steiner, D.	University of Linz, Austria
Stephanidis, C.	University of Crete, FORTH-ICS, Greece
Stoeger, B.	University of Linz, Austria
Strauss, C.	University of Vienna, Austria
Sueda, O.	University of Tokushima, Japan
Svensson, H.	National Agency for Special Needs Education and Schools, Sweden
Takahashi, Y.	Toyo University, Japan
Tauber, M.	University of Paderborn, Germany
Traunmüller, R.	University of Linz, Austria
Trehin, P.	World Autism Organisation, Belgium
Treviranus, J.	University of Toronto, Canada
Vaspöri, T.	KFKI-RMKI, Hungary
Velasco, C.A.	Fraunhofer Institute for Applied Information Technology, Germany
Vigouroux, N.	IRIT Toulouse, France
Wagner, Gerold	Upper Austria University of Applied Sciences, Austria
Weber, H.	ITA, University of Kaiserslautern, Germany
Wöß, W.	University of Linz, Austria

Organizing Committee (University of Linz, Vienna Technical University)

Bernkopf, G.	Ossmann, R.	Keim, C.
Feichtenschlager, P.	Petz, A.	Neustätter, G.
Miesenberger, K.	Schult, C.	Vomastek, C.
Morandell, M.	Fuhrmann – Ehn, M.	Zagler, W.

Table of Contents – Part I

Design for Adaptive Content Processing

Digital Access to Documents for People with Print Disabilities

HCI and Non Classical Interfaces

HCI: Software Accessibility and Social Interaction

Entertainment Software Accessibility

Accessible Tourism

Smart and Assistive Environments

Usable Web Accessibility: Editing

Usable Web Accessibility: Education and Motivation

Usable Web Accessibility: Evaluation

eGovernment Accessibility

Accessibility of Blended and E-Learning for Mature Age and Disabled Students and Staff

Successful Service Provision

Standards: A Driver for Accessibility and Usability

People with Speech Impairment: "Weak and Silent Speech": Tools to Support People with Speech Impairment

People with Speech Learning and Cognitive Problems: Easy-to-Web

Table of Contents – Part II

People with Specific Learning and Cognitive Problems: ICT, AT and HCI

People with Motor Disabilities: HCI and Rehabilitation

People with Motor Disabilities: How to Improve Text Input

Deaf and Hard of Hearing People: Accessible Information and Education

Deaf People: AT for Sign Language

Blind and Partially Sighted People: Mobility and Interaction without Sight

Blind and Partially Sighted People: Rehabilitation and Social Skills

Blind and Partially Sighted People: HCI

Blind and Partially Sighted People: Access to Mathematics

Blind and Partially Sighted People: Designing Haptic Interaction for a Collaborative World

Blind and Partially Sighted People: Three-Dimensional Tactile Models for Blind People and Recognition of 3D Objects by Touch

Ageing: HCI Usability (HCI4AGING)

Design for Adaptive Content Processing: Introduction to the Special Thematic Session

David Crombie

DEDICON
Molenpad 2, The Netherlands
dcrombie@dedicon.nl
http://www.dedicon.nl

Abstract. The Special Thematic Session (STS) on Design for Adaptive Content Processing (ACP) is intended to provide a focus for different but related activities that can be described as having an emphasis on the design *process* rather than the end product of that process. The European Accessible Information Network (EUAIN) was established to bring together the different stakeholders in the accessible content processing chain and to build on common concerns. The parallel PRO-ACCESS project sought to build on this work and provide ISO 9001 industry-faced guidelines. The mainstreaming of adaptive content processing has also been given an added spur at a European level with the establishment of a high-level stakeholders group which is examining the needs of print impaired people and significantly increasing the current levels of provision.

1 Introduction

The special thematic session on accessible content processing (ACP) attempts to cover several key areas, such as: modeling accessible content processing; content personalization and adaptation; using design as a driver of user-centered innovation; and integrating accessible processing within mainstream environments. Adaptive content processing is a complex area and requires us to consider new workflows for content creation, production and consumption and to take on board the needs of print impaired people when navigating through complex information spaces.

The results from the first phase of the **EUAIN** network clearly show that there is a lack of knowledge of accessibility related standards and formats within the publishing industry. From this work with publishers it is also clear that there is no shared understanding of the nature of 'structured information' and there is often little communication between publishers and the accessible content producing communities. There is a similar lack of knowledge of publishing workflows and standards within specialist accessible content producing communities. This lack of understanding makes it very difficult to give comprehensive suggestions to publishers in order to mainstream accessible content production processes. The PRO-ACCESS project also tackled this area and it is anticipated that a set of ISO 9001 compliant guidelines will shortly be made available. The work of the current VIP Stakeholder Group will also help to ensure that cross-border barriers do not limit the access to

K. Miesenberger et al. (Eds.): ICCHP 2010, Part I, LNCS 6179, pp. 1–4, 2010.

these adaptive materials for European citizens. So, in short, some significant changes in provision are likely in the European context over the coming years, both in terms of automation, adaptation and levels of provision.

Having said this, there is still a perception that the provision of digital files in alternative formats will compromise technical protection measures. There is a further perception that the provision of accessible format materials is expensive and time-consuming. And there is a lack of knowledge of the scale of the accessible format market. It is hard for publishers to estimate the monetary cost-benefit ratio, since there are less comprehensive statistics and market estimations for accessible content products. It is to be hoped that the work being undertaken by the VIP Stakeholder Group can offer some pointers as to how we can integrate accessible content production within mainstream environments for the benefit of all.

2   Areas Covered by STS

Many ICT-based solutions are poorly designed, poorly constructed and use hopelessly outdated notions of *"the user"*. Most of these problems stem from poor communication, a situation which arises because technologists and system users often seem to use different languages while essentially working towards common goals. Nevertheless a common language actually does exist, as the common elements in the analysis of computer programming and creative thinking are those of structure and form. At this point interfaces provide connection points for enhancing levels of communication. This involves paying greater attention to each part of the information processing chain (from creation or composition, through processing or transformation to presentation and delivery). It also requires us to consider in more depth key aspects of information granularity and addressability.

From the **system design perspective**, there has been only limited attention to information convergence. The gap in our repertoire of possible descriptions of structures of content currently lies in the description of the creative processes that yield these structures. With the availability of such description guidelines, the practical means will emerge that allow us to draw the relations between the creative processes and any kind of process that builds on this creativity explicitly. By putting *people back into these processes* at a fundamental level, we can redress the current technology-driven imbalance.

From the **content processing perspective**, this is becoming known as 'Intelligent Content' with its convergence of multimedia, web and knowledge engineering. Sometimes described as 'content that listens', intelligent content is designed for the interactive age, reaching out from linear stories to possibilities that are as vast as the web itself. This kind of content is very new, and poses challenges for authors, producers, delivery systems and business models.

From the **interface design perspective**, this involves the development of new approaches to designing interactive processes. Different users of the same content necessarily have different perspectives on that content. For example, to academics a book (even a work of fiction) is a reference source for their field. To a layman, reading a book is a leisure activity. To an author, the same book represents a means to communicate concepts. To a publisher, this versatile object is a unit of production in a wider supply chain. Given these multiple perspectives on something as familiar as a book, it is clear that one person's output medium is another's input medium. The STS features seven presentations that deal with tools and technologies for the creation and processing of adaptive content.

Dürnegger, Feilmayr and **Wöß** introduce guidelines for graphics that are characterized by high information content and report on a tool for the software-based evaluation of SVG images. It is a fact that pixel-based graphics provided without an alternative text are useless for blind people and bar charts that have similar colours for different bars are difficult to be identified by people with colour deficiencies. To overcome such problems a SVG guideline catalogue was developed, which offers users of web applications accessible graphics with improved structural and textual description quality. **Ruemer** and **Miesenberger** report on extensive work that has been carried out in Austria for the production and delivery of alternative format materials for pupils with disabilities. They describe on the one hand the improvements that have been made, but also give some insight into the needs and future work in this very special and diverse field of education. The idea is to create a technical environment that acts as enabler for pedagogues to concentrate on the adaptation of specific types of exercises and sharing of knowledge on how to adapt them for pupils with disabilities or chronic diseases. Another key area of development has been the use of OpenOffice within production workflows and **Strobbe, Engelen** and **Spiewak** report on a new tool which offers an open-source extension for producing books in the DAISY format. DAISY contains features that allow users to navigate by headings, page numbers, paragraphs, or lines, and to have a text version that is synchronised with the audio version. odt2daisy produces both Full DAISY 3 (text synchronised with audio) and DAISY 3 XML (text without audio). odt2daisy enables the production of DAISY books with only open-source software, for example Ubuntu Linux, OpenOffice.org, odt2daisy and eSpeak constitute a completely open-source software stack.

The use of Semi-Automatic META-Data recognition in the production process provides a solid base for higher quality output. The capacities in terms of workforce, that become available then can either be used for improving special types of content (e.g. mathematics, graphics, etc.) or can be returned to the user by decreasing the costs for the production. **Ruemer** and **Miesenberger** demonstrate how to improve the re-digitization process by using software with automatic metadata detection. If we can support this re-digitalisation process with comprehensive tools and implement workflows that avoid media breaks we can deliver high quality documents in an affordable time and under affordable costs. For this we need intelligent tools that are capable of recognizing structure and META-Data. Audio Tactile diagrams are addressed by **McMullen** and **Fitpatrick**, once again making use of the DAISY format. This paper provides an overview of the Audio Tactile Construction and Delivery Framework(ATCDF), an approach that is designed to make the construction of audio tactiles more efficient by providing re-usability, interoperability and producer support. It must be stressed that this research is not intended to replace or diminish the solutions provided by current incarnations of any commercial audio tactile system. The aim of the work is to assess the impact that a service based approach could have on the production and delivery of audio tactile diagrams. It is hoped that the approach would allow for multiple forms of interaction to take place using the same content, providing a multimodal learning experience for the user with limited effort on the part of the producer.

Bernier and **Burger** describe the situation in France and the advances made by the introduction of the Helene server which offers alternative format materials. BrailleNet has contracted with more than 100 publishers, providing their book source files.

Beginning 2010, more than 4800 DTBook files were available on the server. To ensure the access to copyrighted files, a secured delivery mechanism based on S/MIME and digital certificates has been set up. A collaborative wiki platform that can be used by authorized proofreaders and accessibility specialists has been established. Content edition and structuring are performed using the Extended Wikitext language. The work on PDF or scanned books is facilitated by features of the ProofreadPage extension: for each page of a book, the original image is displayed beside the OCR recognized text, so, a user has the ability to refer permanently to the original source. **Darvishy**, **Hutter** and **Dorigo** present a flexible software architecture concept that allows the automatic generation of fully accessible PDF documents originating from various authoring tools such as Adobe InDesign or Microsoft Word. The architecture can be extended with any authoring tools capable of creating PDF documents. For each authoring tool, a software accessibility Plug-in must be implemented that analyses the logical structure of the document and creates an XML representation of it.

3 Future Research Areas

It is becoming clear that a far deeper examination of *fundamental* accessibility is required if we are to mirror mainstream content provision. Given the general move towards distributed media, there is a need to develop open source frameworks to bridge the gap between original content design heuristics and intuitive multimodal interfaces required for content and communication systems. Such frameworks would provide built-in, profile-based access to information, content and services, which not only combine and extend state-of-the-art technologies for information access, but also conform to standards and guidelines available for accessibility, usability, scalability and adaptability. More information about the work of **EUAIN** and all current materials are available from the **EUAIN** portal (www.euain.org).

Generating DAISY Books from OpenOffice.org

Christophe Strobbe[1], Jan Engelen[1], and Vincent Spiewak[2]

[1] Katholieke Universitcit Leuven, Kasteelpark Arenberg 10, B-3001 Heverlee-Leuven, Belgium
{christophe.strobbe,jan.engelen}@esat.kuleuven.be
[2] 45 Boulevard Soult, 75012, Paris, France
vspiewak@gmail.com

Abstract. odt2daisy is an open-source extension for OpenOffice.org Writer that converts word processing files into digital talking books in the DAISY format (ANSI/NISO Z39.86). odt2daisy produces Full DAISY 3 (text synchronised with audio), DAISY 3 XML (text without audio) and Full DAISY 2.02 (for compatibility with older DAISY players). The extension also supports mathematical content (MathML). odt2daisy works on Microsoft Windows, Mac OS X, Linux and Solaris. For the production of audio, odt2daisy relies on the DAISY Pipeline Lite, an open-source software developed by the DAISY Consortium, the LAME MP3 encoding technology, and the operating system's text-to-speech (TTS) engine(s). The supported languages depend on the TTS engines available on the user's system. On Unix-based systems odt2daisy relies on the open-source eSpeak TTS engine, which supports 27 languages. odt2daisy enables the production of DAISY books with only open-source software. Vincent Spiewak started working on odt2daisy at the Université Pierre et Marie Curie (Paris, France) and continued the work at the Katholieke Universiteit Leuven (Leuven, Belgium) in the framework of ÆGIS, a research and development project co-financed by the European Commission's 7th Framework Programme.

Keywords: digital talking book, DAISY, OpenDocument Format, ODF, OpenOffice.org, open source.

1 Introduction

The Digital Accessible Information System (DAISY) [1] is a standard for digital talking books. The format was developed in response to dissatisfaction about analogue talking books, which were time-consuming to read. [4] Creating high-quality audio books is a labour-intensive process; DAISY books are usually produced by specialised centres and stored in repositories that protect copyrighted materials against inappropriate use (through digital rights management or DRM). Talking books were traditionally produced by recording the voice of a human reader on a storage medium (originally on phonograph records [12]). This was a costly and time-consuming process. Nowadays, audio can be produced through synthetic speech, and talking books can be distributed on CDs, memory cards or over the Internet. Software for producing digital talking books is also available under open source licences, for example, the DAISY Consortium's DAISY Pipeline [6] and the Open XML to

K. Miesenberger et al. (Eds.): ICCHP 2010, Part I, LNCS 6179, pp. 5–11, 2010.
© Springer-Verlag Berlin Heidelberg 2010

DAISY XML Translator for Microsoft Office [16]. With the latter solution, end users can create their own DAISY books. odt2daisy makes this process even cheaper by adding this functionality to OpenOffice.org, the free and open source office suite [13].

Most of the work described in this paper was undertaken in the context of the ÆGIS project, an integrated project co-funded by the European Commission's Seventh Framework Programme. One of the main goals of this project is to mainstream accessibility in document authoring and software development, and this work includes contributions to open-source projects. Technical developments in ÆGIS cover three platforms: the desktop, rich internet applications (RIAs) and mobile applications. The work described in this paper is one of several contributions to accessibility enhancements to the open-source office suite OpenOffice.org. The remainder of this paper explains the origins of odt2daisy, its design and features, and concludes with ongoing and future work.

1.1 odt2dtbook

odt2daisy is the successor of odt2dtbook, a student project at the Université Pierre et Marie Curie (Paris, France)[2]. The goal was to create an extension for OpenOffice.org Writer that could export OpenDocument Text (ODT, word processing files) as DAISY 3 books. By May 2009, this work had resulted in a cross-platform extension (Windows, Mac OS and Unix-based systems) that supported most of the ODT specification and Mathematical Markup Language (MathML). The business logic was available in a Java Archive (jar) that was reusable in other applications. It did not yet produce audio, nor DAISY 2.02 (for compatibility with older DAISY players). In the summer of 2008, the project won an Open Source Community Innovation Award [17].

2 Design and Components

2.1 Java OpenDocument Library (JODL)

JODL is a sub-project of odt2daisy that preprocesses the ODT file (which is a zip file containing several XML files, the document's image files and a few other files):

- it merges the XML files that make up the ODT format (content.xml for content, meta.xml for metadata, styles.xml for style definitions, etcetera) into a single XML file to facilitate processing at later stages,
- it extracts all images and normalizes their file names,
- it inserts <pagenum> tags to facilitate pagenumbering support, as content.xml does not contain page numbers,
- it carries out corrections, such as the removal of empty headings.

JODL can be reused as a Java library and as a command-line tool.

2.2 The odt2daisy Library

The "odt2daisy library" converts the ODT file into DAISY 3.0 XML using JODL and an XSLT stylesheet [3]. After this conversion, the XML file is validated against the DAISY 3.0 DTD to check that it is valid at a basic level.

The odt2daisy library can be reused as a Java library and as a command-line tool.

2.3 The odt2daisy Extension

The odt2daisy extension acts as a wrapper for the other components:

- It uses OpenOffice.orgs's UNO API to save the current document as a temporary ODT file.
- It uses the odt2daisy library to convert the ODT file into DAISY 3.0 XML and DAISY 2.02.
- It uses the DAISY Pipeline Lite (see below) to generate a full DAISY 3.0 book with audio.

The odt2daisy extension also includes a few other components. templates and the DAISY Pipeline Lite.

2.4 DAISY Templates

The odt2daisy extension includes a few templates with custom styles that are specifically targeted to the creation of "rich" DAISY books. These templates are added through OpenOffice.org's non-code extensions mechanism [14].

2.5 DAISY Pipeline Lite

The DAISY Pipeline Lite is a light version of the DAISY Pipeline that was specifically developed for inclusion in other programs such as the Open XML to DAISY XML Translator for Microsoft Office and the DAISY authoring tool Obi [11]. This component also uses the open-source LAME MP3 encoder [18]. LAME uses C and needs to be compiled statically in order to create a standalone Pipeline Lite that can be included in odt2daisy. odt2daisy extracts the Pipeline Lite from the OpenOffice.org extension file (the OXT file) and installs it in the user's system directory when the user uses odt2daisy for the first time. The extension also contains a remove/re-extract mechanism in order to be able to update the Pipeline Lite separately from the other components.

2.6 Unit Tests

A set of 166 ODT files that cover the whole ODT specification were manually created, and subsequently converted into DAISY XML files. The DAISY XML files were reviewed and, where necessary, corrected. These files were integrated into a testing framework with JUnit [10] and XMLUnit [22], and serve as a test suite to avoid the introduction of regression bugs.

3 odt2daisy 2.x

odt2daisy 2.0 was developed in June-November 2009 at the Katholieke Universiteit Leuven and released on 9 November 2009. Version 2.1 was released in April 2010 to ensure compatibility with OpenOffice.org 3.2 (released in February 2010) and to provide localisation in a few European languages (French, Spanish, Dutch and Hungarian). In addition to many other improvements (fixing bugs, refactoring code, etcetera), the following features have been added since odt2dtbook:

- Exporting full DAISY 2.02 for compatibility with older DAISY players.
- Generating audio by integrating the DAISY Pipeline Lite. This includes audio for multilingual documents. Since the open-source text-to-speech engine eSpeak (which covers 27 languages with varying levels of quality) is not only available on Unix-based systems but also as a SAPI 5 engine on Microsoft Windows, many users can now have very cheap access to text-to-speech.
- A suite of test files for unit testing and regression testing.
- Tutorials provided as videos[1], DAISY books and text (ODT and PDF).
- Documentation for developers (especially for NetBeans) and for translators of the user interface (localisation).
- Exporting playlists for MP3 players in various formats (since version 2.1).

The odt2daisy source code is available under the GNU Lesser General Public License (LGPL). The source code repository is available in a SourceForge project at http://sourceforge.net/projects/odt2daisy/.

4   Ongoing and Future Work

This section discusses ongoing and future work. Some of these issues are being addressed by the European project ÆGIS (see acknowledgements below), while others are being addressed by other organisations.

4.1   ODF-Related Issues

The development of odt2daisy highlighted a number of ODF characteristics that posed some problems for the production of DAISY books.

ODT files can use MathML to represent mathematical formulas. DAISY requires both alternative text (alttext attribute) and an alternative image (altimg attribute) for such formulas. These attributes provide a fallback mechanism for DAISY players that cannot render MathML [5]. ODT files don't contain an alternative image for formulas, and OpenOffice.org Writer does not provide a mechanism to add alternative images.

Page numbers in ODT files are not "visible" in the XML file that internally contain the content ("content.xml"); they are declared in various ways in the XML file that describes the formatting of the document ("styles.xml"). This makes page processing computationally intensive; page processing would be much more efficient if content.xml contained page numbers.

A somewhat similar issue is the absence of column break indicators when a section in an ODT file uses columns (i.e. columns as a page layout mechanism, as opposed to table columns): the information where a new column starts needs to be gleaned from the styles.xml file.

Tables in ODT files can have a caption (below or above the table). However, unlike HTML, the ODT XML code contains no mechanism that unambiguously links a table and its caption. It is possible to use heuristics to determine the presence and location of a caption, but an unambiguous mechanism would be preferable.

---

[1]   In the documentation section at http://odt2daisy.sourceforge.net/doc/ and as YouTube videos at http://www.youtube.com/view_play_list?p=8D08BBF489F62D0E.

Unlike HTML, ODT provides no mechanism to mark a span of text as an abbreviation or an acronym and to unambiguously link it with its definition or meaning. There is no mechanism to provide a pronunciation (this is also an unsolved issue in HTML), even though this would be very useful when generating synthetic speech. As an interim solution, this issue can be addressed by means of custom styles and OpenOffice.org's support for the Resource Description Framework (RDF) [15].

OpenOffice.org Writer enables authors to mark up the language of a document and individual spans of text. The language settings in the software's options dialogue also allow authors to define the default language of documents for three types of languages: "Western" (ranging from Germanic languages over Russian to Indonesian, Vietnamese and Zulu!), "Asian" (only Chinese, Japanese and Korean) and "complex text layout" or CTL (including right-to-left languages such as Arabic, Farsi and Hebrew, but also left-to-right scripts such as Burmese, Kannada, Tamil and Thai). When settings for more than one type of languages are active, the language of each span of text – each character even – becomes ambiguous. Even checking the Unicode code point of each individual character – and thereby guessing the script being used – would not be sufficient to reliably determine the language of a span of text because some characters, especially those from the Latin script, can be interspersed with other scripts, for example Chinese, without a language change. However, for the purpose of text-to-speech applications, language markup needs to be unambiguous and correct.

These issues have been reported to the OASIS Technical Committee that is in charge of the OpenDocument Format.

4.2 Licensing Issues

By using the DAISY Pipeline Lite, odt2daisy relies on the open-source library LAME to encode synthetic speech as MP3 files. MP3 is a format subject to patents by the Fraunhofer Institut in Germany. For this reason, software that uses Pipeline Lite needs to include a disclaimer like the following: "Using the LAME encoding engine (or other mp3 encoding technology) in your software may require a patent license in some countries." Using an open standard such Ogg Vorbis [19] instead of a patented technology would make this disclaimer a thing of the past.

When an ODT files contains formulas marked up with MathML, the Pipeline Lite throws a failure because it cannot create alternative text and images for the formulas without an additional plugin. The only plugin available for this purpose is a commercial product developed by a member organisation of the DAISY consortium [7]. The user is not given the choice to generate the DAISY book without alternative text and images for the formulas and adding them (manually or with DAISY authoring software) after the conversion process.

4.3 Quality of Synthetic Speech

odt2daisy uses the default text-to-speech engines or "voices" on the user's computer system to generate synthetic speech. If the system does not have a text-to-speech engine for a language used in the document, some parts of the document will not be "spoken" in the right language. Even when the system has text-to-speech engines for all the languages used the content, these engines do not always provide a high quality of synthetic speech. End users are not likely to buy high-quality, expensive, text-to-speech engines, even though the quality of the synthetic speech has a significant impact on the usability of a DAISY book. This issue could be solved by providing an Internet-based service that handles the complete conversion process for the user. The provider of this service would have high-quality text-to-speech engines, thereby foregoing the need for thousands of users to buy these engines individually. This type of service could also solve issues related to additional plugins, such as the plugin for mathematical content mentioned above. The PipeOnline project develops a web application for creating and running Pipeline jobs over the Internet [8, 9].

Another issue is that a user may have several speech engines for the same language on his system, for example, if he has installed the open-source eSpeak library next to a commercial engine that was already present. In that case, odt2daisy cannot give the user an opportunity to select one of these engines over the other.

4.4 Accessibility

Generating fully accessible DAISY books requires the availability of accessible source documents. Using templates and heading styles correctly, providing alternative text for images, marking up language changes, etcetera requires knowledge that is not available to everybody. Authors would be greatly helped by an accessibility checker for ODT files. This would not only benefit authors of DAISY books but also authors of other formats that OpenOffice.org can export, such as HTML and PDF. A similar checker for Microsoft Office 2010 has been announced by Microsoft [20]. Documents about creating accessible content with OpenOffice.org Writer are available, for example by WebAIM [21], but preparatory work for an accessibility checker would need to delve much deeper than these guidelines; for example, it should check the effect of text wrapping around images on the availability of text alternatives, and the effect of column layouts on text navigation. Such research cannot limit itself to Microsoft Windows, because the accessibility of OpenOffice.org is significantly lower than on Mac OS and Unix-based systems.

Acknowledgements. This work was partially funded by the EC FP7 project ÆGIS - Open Accessibility Everywhere: Groundwork, Infrastructure, Standards, Grant Agreement No. 224348.

References

1. American National Standard Developed (ANSI), National Information Standards Organization (NISO): Specifications for the Digital Talking Book - ANSI/NISO Z39.86-2005 - Revision of ANSI/NISO Z39.86-2002 (2005), http://www.niso.org/workrooms/daisy/Z39-86-2005.html
2. Archambault, Dominique, Spiewak, Vincent: odt2dtbook - OpenOffice.org Save-as-Daisy Extension. In: Emiliani, P.L., Burzagli, L., Gabbanini, F., Salminen, A.-L. (eds.) Assistive Technology from Adapted Equipment to Inclusive Environments - AAATE 2009. Assistive Technology Research Series, vol. 25, pp. 212–216. IOS Press, Amsterdam (2009)
3. Clark, J. (ed.): XSL Transformations (XSLT) Version 1.0 - W3C Recommendation (November 16, 1999), http://www.w3.org/TR/xslt

4. DAISY Consortium: History, http://www.daisy.org/history
5. DAISY Consortium: Part II (g): Mathematics. In: DAISY 3 Structure Guidelines (2008),
   http://www.daisy.org/z3986/structure/SG-DAISY3/
   part2-math.html
6. DAISY Consortium: Pipeline, http://www.daisy.org/project/pipeline
7. DAISY Consortium: Pipeline Add-ins,
   http://www.daisy.org/project/pipeline-other-add-ins
8. DAISY Consortium: The DAISY Pipeline Project,
   http://daisymfc.sourceforge.net/
9. DAISY Consortium: The PipeOnline Project,
   http://daisy-trac.cvsdude.com/pipeline/wiki/PipeOnline
10. JUnit, http://www.junit.org/
11. Obi, http://daisy-trac.cvsdude.com/obi/
12. Obterfeuer, J.: A New Read on Digital Talking Books (2007),
    http://www.speechtechmag.com/Articles/Column/The-View-from-
    AVIOS/A-New-Read-on-Digital-Talking-Books-37407.aspx
13. OpenOffice.org, http://www.openoffice.org/
14. OpenOffice.org: Non-code extensions,
    http://wiki.services.openoffice.org/wiki/Non-code_extensions
15. OpenOffice.org: RDF metadata,
    http://wiki.services.openoffice.org/wiki/Documentation/
    DevGuide/OfficeDev/RDF_metadata
16. Open XML to DAISY XML Translator,
    http://sourceforge.net/projects/openxml-daisy/
17. Sun Microsystems: Sun Honors Community Awards Winners (September 24, 2008),
    http://www.sun.com/aboutsun/media/features/2008-0924/
18. The LAME Project, http://lame.sourceforge.net/
19. Vorbis.com, http://www.vorbis.com/
20. Waldman, Larry: Office 2010: Accessibility Investments & Document Accessibility.
    Microsoft Office 2010 Engineering Blog (January 7, 2010),
    http://blogs.technet.com/office2010/archive/2010/01/07/
    office-2010-accessibility-investments-document-
    accessibility.aspx
21. WebAIM: OpenOffice.org and Accessibility,
    http://www.webaim.org/techniques/ooo/
22. XMLUnit, http://xmlunit.sourceforge.net/

Combining Web Services and DAISY for the Production and Delivery of Audio Tactile Diagrams

Declan McMullen and Donal Fitzpatrick

School of Computing,
Dublin City University,
Glasnevin, Dublin 9, Ireland
dmcmullen@computing.dcu.ie, dfitzpat@computing.dcu.ie
http://www.computing.dcu.ie/~dmcmullen

Abstract. In recent years audio tactile diagrams have emerged as a viable method of providing blind learners with access to diagrammatical material. It has proven beneficial, but obstacles remain to its widespread adoption, especially in situations where a teacher may not be skilled in tactile production. Current approaches to audio tactile production contain limitations in various areas namely reusability, producer support and interoperability.

This paper discusses the Audio Tactile Construction and Delivery Framework (ATCDF), which is a service based approach for the production and delivery of audio tactile diagrams. The approach separates audio tactile diagrams into their component parts, which are then stored independently of one another in repositories. The content in the repositories can be searched for, retrieved and reused independently of one another. Completed audio tactiles can be exported for delivery using the DAISY 3 standard, forming a *DAISY based audio tactile*. The approach has benefits in areas of reusability, interoperability and producer support.

Keywords: blind students, web services, daisy, audio tactiles, tactile graphics, e-learning.

1 Introduction

Tactile diagrams remain the primary method of providing blind learners with access to visual material. As a tactile alone is insufficient in order to explain a concept, supplementary information has always been required alongside the diagram. In the majority of situations, this information is provided by a sighted guide or the use of Braille labeling. In recent years audio tactile technology emerged that aimed to reduce the burden on the sighted guide and provide a more interactive experience to the learner. Audio tactile technology involves a touchscreen connected to a computer. The tactile diagram is placed on the touchscreen and relevant audio feedback is provided to the user when they press

K. Miesenberger et al. (Eds.): ICCHP 2010, Part I, LNCS 6179, pp. 12–19, 2010.

on different areas of the tactile. This technology has proven to be beneficial, especially in a classroom setting, but obstacles remain to its widespread adoption, especially in situations where a teacher may not be skilled in tactile production.

This paper provides an overview of the Audio Tactile Construction and Delivery Framework(ATCDF), an approach that is designed to make the construction of audio tactiles more efficient by providing reusability, interoperability and producer support. It must be stressed that this research is not intended to replace or diminish the solutions provided by current incarnations of any commercial audio tactile system. The aim of the work is to assess the impact that a service based approach could have on the production and delivery of audio tactile diagrams. If significant benefits were found, the approach could be adopted in the next generation of audio tactile systems.

2   State of the Art

There are two commercial approaches currently available for the construction of audio tactile diagrams, T3 [1] developed by Touch Graphics and IVEO® [2] developed by ViewPlus. Both systems take different approaches to their interface design, system interaction and content packaging [3][4]. When diagrams are produced in T3 and IVEO, their visual data and layer content (the information played back to the user), are stored in Macromedia Director™and SVG [5] files respectively. Packaging audio tactile content into single files produces limitations in various areas namely reusability, producer support and interoperability.

2.1   Reusability

Due to packaging, audio tactile content is not easily reusable. If a producer wishes to reuse only the diagram element of an audio tactile and add their own content, they must open the audio tactile package, delete the content that is linked to the diagram, replace the content with their own and save a new audio tactile package. This creates a scenario where an identical image is being unnecessarily replicated over and over in order to change the content that is linked to it. Packaging creates a scenario where the individual components of an audio tactile are not independently reusable.

2.2   Producer Support

Current systems do not provide a facility to search for, retrieve and reuse individual diagram components. This has a particular impact on non expert audio tactile producers. With current approaches the producer must author a tactile image or get it authored for them and then add content to that image. Thus, a certain level of audio tactile production knowledge is required for the use of either system. Functionality should be provided that allows an audio tactile producer to reuse content that already exists. This is particularly important for teachers, lecturers or parents who need to quickly create audio tactile material.

2.3 Interoperability

As each audio tactile approach to date has used a different packaging system, audio tactile content produced on one system can not be used on another. If a producer wishes to support all of the available audio tactile systems, they must author their audio tactile independently on each system. This increases the amount of time and effort a producer has to provide for audio tactile production. A method should exist where a producer can author their content once and have it delivered on multiple audio tactile systems.

2.4 Independent Usability

Each system contains barriers to its widespread adoption in an independent learning environment. Independent learning refers to a scenario where there is no sighted guide present to aid the user. Primarily, if a user does not read Braille, it is not possible for them to correctly identify a T3 or IVEO tactile diagram. If a user cannot locate the diagram they currently need to use, for example in a bundle that they may have on their desk, the ability to use either system independently is diminished.

3 Work to Date

3.1 AHVITED

The first phase of this research took place as part of the Audio Haptics for Visually Impaired Training and Education at a Distance(AHVITED) [6] project. AHVITED was an E.U funded project whose aim was to evaluate the use of audio tactile technology in an independent learning scenario. Through a series of user evaluations and expert reviews a number of requirements were produced that an audio tactile system should conform to in order to be viable as a distance learning tool. These requirements led to the design, implementation and evaluation of a prototype system. Further details can be found in [7][8][9][10].

In relation to independent usability, the evaluations showed that users could accurately identify diagrams when a generic method of tactile identification, which did not require the user to posses any previous knowledge, was used. This is in contrast to using a Braille method of identification which is only usable to those experienced in reading Braille. Additionally, it became apparent that when exploring a diagram users were unsure what areas of the diagram to press and in what order.

Given these factors, the ability for a producer to define a suggested path for exploration of a tactile diagram and the ability to add a unique identifier for diagram identification are important elements in any audio tactile production environment.

3.2 Audio Tactile Production

Additional insights in relation to the production process emerged during the creation of sample audio tactile content by various European partners. The graphical images were produced in Italy and the layer content was produced in Austria. The final tactiles were also assembled in Italy, however, this could conceivably have taken place in another institution. The distribution of responsibilities revealed the existence of multiple roles in the tactile production process; tactile diagram producers, content producers and audio tactile assemblers. These multiple roles should be capable of operating independently but also making their content available for others to use.

The issue of reusability became a factor, especially for the purpose of localisation. Audio tactiles needed to be produced in multiple languages to maximise their potential as a distance learning tool. Producers were copying the same graphical image purely for the purpose of translating the layer content. Additionally, if a producer wished to use an image with different layer content, the graphical image was copied once again. The same problem can exist with using the same layer content with different graphical images. This produces a lot of unnecessary replication.

The difficulty associated with producing tactile diagrams often leads to them being avoided by teachers [11]. As such producer support is important particularly for those who are non experts in tactile production. There may be suitable tactile images or layer content that have been previously created that would be of use to a producer. The ability to search for and retrieve existing content would support the producer as they created their audio tactile.

Interoperability is another important factor to be considered. A producer should be able to create their audio tactile in the production environment of their choice and then deliver that content in multiple delivery environments. The key to this approach is the use of standardisation. Audio tactiles should conform to an agreed standard which delivery environments can support.This would ensure that a producers audio tactile could be accessed by a user in the delivery environment of their choice. A producer would not be required to create multiple copies of their audio tactile in multiple formats to suit various different delivery environments.

4   Current and Future Work

It is the authors belief that e-learning for the blind should utilise modern techniques and approaches that have become commonplace in mainstream e-learning in recent years. The problems of reusability and interoperability have been solved to a great extent by the emergence of learning objects, learning object repositories and packaging and delivery standards. Repositories such as MERLOT [12], Ariadne [13] and the NDLR [14] store large amounts of learning objects that course producers can reuse. Authoring environments such as RELOAD [15], allow for producers to combine learning objects from repositories into coherent lessons and courses. Packaging and delivery standards such as IMS Content Packaging [16] and SCORM [17] allow content to be exported in a format that is interoperable amongst compliant delivery environments. This research applies a similar approach to the production and delivery of audio tactile diagrams.

The key to the approach is to separate an audio tactile diagram into its component parts, namely it's visual component and content components. These components are then stored independently of one another in repositories and are thus independently reusable. Not only is content separated from other content, but it is also separated from the interface that displays it and the mode of interaction used to access it.

4.1 Web Services

The suggested approach is called the Audio Tactile Construction and Delivery Framework (ATCDF). It consists of a number of web services which expose repositories to the production environments that wish to use them [18].

The *Visual Object Service* is responsible for the storage and retrieval of SVG [5] tactile image files referred to as visual objects. Layer contents are arranged into content objects and the *Content Object Service* is responsible for their storage and retrieval. A content object contains a title and a number of fragments. The fragments of information are played back to a user when they interact with the audio tactile diagram. The *Assembly Service* is used to maintain assembly files. Assembly files contain a list of instructions for combining independent visual object and content objects into a coherent audio tactile diagram. Finally, the *Identifier Service* generates unique identifiers for use in the content object, visual object and assembly repositories. These identifiers ensure that content can be uniquely identified for retrieval and usage. An architecture diagram of the ATCDF can be seen in Figure 1.

Standards are used throughout the framework. Each web service uses SOAP [19], XML-RPC [20] and HTTP for communication. This means that any programming language compatible with those technologies can be used to write interfaces that communicate with the services. All of the content is stored using XML [21], SVG for visual objects and a subset of DTBook [22] for content objects. The use of web services and XML ensures the scalability of the framework as additional services and functionality can be continuously added.

4.2 DAISY

For the purpose of delivery, audio tactile diagrams are exported using the DAISY 3 standard [23].When an audio tactile is exported for delivery, the relevant SVG image is retrieved from its visual object repository and the relevant content objects are retrieved from their content object repository. The content objects are combined into a single DTBook XML file, an NCX file is generated, the necessary SMIL files are created and the OPF package file is produced. All of these files are brought together to make a text only DAISY 3 book. The framework can be expanded to support audio only or text and audio DAISY 3 books in the future but is restricted to text only for the purposes of the prototype. When the DAISY package is opened in a DAISY player it behaves like a standard DAISY book. The title of the diagram appears at the top of the interface, the SVG image is displayed beneath it and the content objects are displayed as headings and

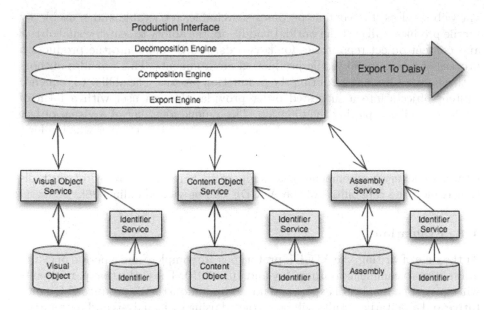

Fig. 1. ATCDF Architecture Diagram

paragraphs beneath that. This of course is not suitable for tactile interaction. For this purpose the XML must be rendered in an alternative manner. For the purposes of the prototype a custom DAISY player has been created but the functionality could be implemented as an alternative view in standard DAISY players in the future.

This research therefore produces *DAISY Based Audio Tactiles*. When rendered, the SVG image is the only component displayed on screen. When a user presses on a region of the diagram the relevant section of the DTBook XML is played using text to speech. This functionality is facilitated by the NCX file and is similar to selecting an item from the index in a standard DAISY player. In order to guide a user around the diagram the spine section of the package file is used to define the default navigational sequence. The DAISY content has not changed in any way, and no modifications have been made to the specification, it has just been rendered differently to how a standard DAISY player would render it. Anyone wishing to deliver DAISY based audio tactile diagrams need only render the DAISY content in the manner suggested by this research. This allows for a user to choose the delivery environment they prefer without the need for diagram producers to create their content in multiple formats. Additionally, other modes of interaction are possible, such as the pen based audio tactile interface developed by Joshua Miele and Steven Landau [24][25].

4.3   Solutions

Solutions for the issues raised in Section 3 are embedded into this approach. By storing audio tactile components in independent repositories and exposing them via web services, the content becomes searchable, retrievable and reusable by tactile producers all over the world. In addition, the ability to search visual object and content object repositories for keywords, can be built into the production process of future audio tactile production environments. This provides authors with a support framework during the production process. The ability to sequence content objects into a suggested order provides the end user with a form of guidance whilst exploring the diagram. The unique identifier of a visual object component can be represented on the printed diagram in a manner which allows for the end user to identify the specific diagram that we wish to use. Finally, the use of DAISY as a standard for audio tactile delivery can provide interoperability between delivery environments that support it. Screencasts of prototype tools that exploit the capabilities of the ATCDF can be viewed online [26].

4.4   Evaluation

At the time of writing, the ATCDF prototypes are complete and a period of evaluation is set to commence during May and June 2010. The evaluation participants will consist of a number of expert and non expert audio tactile producers. Quantitative and qualitative results will be retrieved using task analysis and user survey usability methods. The results will be assessed using effectiveness, efficiency and user satisfaction usability metrics. Preliminary results from the period of evaluation will be discussed during the ICCHP conference presentation.

5   Conclusion

This research contributes to the area of audio tactile diagrams, specifically suggesting a new approach for their production and delivery. The work harnesses mainstream techniques in the area of learning technology and applies them in the domain of audio tactile diagrams. The effect of such an approach would be the emergence of numerous repositories around the world containing suitable images and content that can be used for the production of audio tactile diagrams. It also suggests the use of the DAISY standard as a backend for audio tactile delivery in the future. This would allow for interoperability between audio tactile delivery environments, provide a user with more choice and reduce the burden on the audio tactile producer. Finally, the approach would allow for multiple forms of interaction to take place using the same content, providing a multimodal learning experience for the user with limited effort on the part of the producer.

References

1. T3,
   http://www.touchgraphics.com/catalog/
   product_info.php?cPath=1&products_id=33
2. IVEO, http://www.viewplus.com/products/touch-audio-learning/IVEO/

3. Landau, S., Gourgey, K.: A new approach to interactive audio/tactile computing: The talking tactile tablet. California State University Northridge, Center On Disabilities Technology And Persons With Disabilities Conference (2004)
4. Gardner, J.A., Bulatov, V.: Scientific diagrams made easy with iveo. In: Miesenberger, K., Klaus, J., Zagler, W.L., Karshmer, A.I. (eds.) ICCHP 2006. LNCS, vol. 4061, pp. 1243–1250. Springer, Heidelberg (2006)
5. SVG, http://www.w3.org/TR/SVG/
6. AHVITED, http://www.ahvited.org
7. McMullen, D.: Multimodal access to visually intensive material at a distance. In: Miesenberger, K., Klaus, J., Zagler, W.L., Karshmer, A.I. (eds.) ICCHP 2008. LNCS, vol. 5105. Springer, Heidelberg (2008)
8. Fitzpatrick, D., McMullen, D.: Distance learning of graphically intensive material for visually impaired students. In: Miesenberger, K., Klaus, J., Zagler, W.L., Karshmer, A.I. (eds.) ICCHP 2008. LNCS, vol. 5105, pp. 219–225. Springer, Heidelberg (2008)
9. McMullen, D., Fitzpatrick, D.: Tactile diagrams at a distance: A multimodal e-learning prototype. In: Carthy, J.M., Pitt, I., Kirakowski, J. (eds.) Irish Human-computer Interaction Conference, University Of Limerick, pp. 101–105 (2008)
10. McMullen, D., Fitzpatrick, D.: Autonomous access to graphics for visually impaired learners. In: EdTech (2009)
11. Sheppard, L., Aldrich, F.K.: Tactile graphics in school education: perspectives from teachers. British Journal of Visual Impairment 19, 93–97 (2001)
12. MERLOT, http://www.merlot.org/merlot/index.htm
13. ARIADNE, http://www.ariadne-eu.org/
14. NDLR, http://www.ndlr.ie/
15. RELOAD, http://www.reload.ac.uk/
16. IMSCP, http://www.imsglobal.org/content/packaging/
17. SCORM, http://www.adlnet.gov/Technologies/scorm/default.aspx
18. McMullen, D., Fitzpatrick, D.: Service based approach to the construction and delivery of audio tactile diagrams. In: Center On Disabilities Technology And Persons With Disabilities Conference, California State University, Northridge (2010)
19. SOAP, http://www.w3.org/TR/soap/
20. XML-RPC, http://www.xmlrpc.com/spec
21. XML, http://www.w3.org/XML/
22. DTBook, http://www.daisy.org/z3986/structure/SG-DAISY3/index-of-elements.html
23. DAISY, http://www.daisy.org/about_us/dtbooks.asp
24. Miele, J., Landau, S.: Audio-tactile interactive computing with the livescribe pulse pen 2. In: Center On Disabilities Technology And Persons With Disabilities Conference, California State University, Northridge (2010)
25. Miele, J.: The live scribe smartpen: A revolutionary new platform for audio/tactile graphics. In: International Cartographic Conference (2007)
26. Screencasts, http://www.computing.dcu.ie/~dmcmullen/Doctorate.html

Wiki, a New Way to Produce Accessible Documents

Alex Bernier[1], Dominique Burger[1], and Bruno Marmol[2]

[1] INSERM UMRS_968, Université Pierre et Marie Curie
9, quai Saint-Bernard
75252 Paris Cedex 5, France
alex.bernier@upmc.fr, dominique.burger@upmc.fr
[2] INRIA Grenoble-Rhone-Alpes
ZIRST - 655 Av de l'Europe - Montbonnot St Martin
F-38334 St Ismier Cedex, France
bruno.marmol@inria.fr

Abstract. Adapting complex documents to make them accessible for print disabled persons is an iterative process which involves various skills and requires the intervention of several people. Collaborative approaches are well suited, especially those based on Wikis which are now widely used to edit contents on the Web. A Wiki offers useful features to overcome some of the difficulties encountered when using word-processors. MediaWiki is a popular Wiki software which can be extended to allow users to import, edit and export contents using XML DTBook, the format designed by the DAISY Consortium for structuring text in an accessible way.

1 Introduction

In 2000, BrailleNet launched the Helene Server [1] [2] [3], a book repository on the Internet, open to centers producing adapted books in Braille or large-print. Further, a book delivery service for visually impaired readers was created, called Helene Library. In 2002, XML DTBook, defined in the NISO Z3986-2002/DAISY 3.0 specification, was adopted as a central format for structuring textual contents, for storing them and for producing various output formats on demand. Later, the server was updated to respect the Z3986-2005 DAISY 3.0 specification.

BrailleNet has contracted with more than 100 publishers providing their book source files. Beginning 2010, more than 4800 DTBook files were available on the server. To ensure the access to copyrighted files, a secured delivery mechanism based on S/MIME and digital certificates has been set up and since February 2010, DAISY contents are encrypted according to the PDTB2 (Protected Digital Talking Book) specification.

The main barrier to the development of the catalog is the transformation of source files (provided by publishers or obtained by digitization) into accessible DTBook files. This production process includes three main steps:

K. Miesenberger et al. (Eds.): ICCHP 2010, Part I, LNCS 6179, pp. 20–26, 2010.

- Optical Character Recognition (OCR), to extract the text from images colection;
- Correction and structuration of text obtained by the OCR;
- Document adaptation (like description of figures);

The first step is optional, depending of the source content type (some publishers provide Microsoft Word or XML files). The two last steps are iterative because the creation process of an accessible document is rarely completed at the first time : so, the original work needs to be corrected or the adaptation needs to be improved.

Recently, the release of DTBook export functions for popular word-processors, namely "Save as DAISY" for Microsoft Word, and "ODT2DAISY" for OpenOffice, proved to simplify the production of well structured DTBook files. Exporting a DTBook file from a Microsoft Word or OpenOffice document is now a straightforward task. However, it is still not possible to import a DTBook in those word-processors. So, to correct or improve an XML DTBook, the original document should be kept in Microsoft Word or OpenOffice format and exported again in DTBook after modification. To increase the productivity, DTBook should become the central format from initial content creation to future modifications.

In another perspective, adapting complex contents often implies various skills. In some cases, several experts may contribute to the adaptation of a book, making this task a collaborative work. Furthermore, adapting large documents requires a lot of time. Also, to improve the efficiency, it could be useful that several people work at the same time on the same document. Classical word-processors are not very convenient to work collaboratively, this is why other solutions to create and edit documents should be considered [4] [5].

In section 2, we describe the most important features of a Wiki and introduce the basics of our proposal, especially which software platform we have chosen and why we did so. In section 3, we describe how to import and edit DTBook documents in a Wiki, and in section 4, how to export documents from the Wiki to DTBook : developments and improvements made in the MediaWiki software are detailed.

2 Basics on Wiki sofwares and MediaWiki Introduction

2.1 Survey of Classical Wiki Features

Over the past few years, Wiki has become the most widely used way for a community to edit contents on the Web. A Wiki is a website that uses a software called "Wiki software" which makes available pages that can easily be modified using a simple markup language (the Wikitext) and/or a WYSIWYG (What You See Is What You Get) editor. As a Wiki is a web application, only a Web browser is required to use it. Wikitext can vary greatly among Wiki implementations, but most of the time, they are designed to be easy to use. For example, starting a line of text with an asterisk is often used to enter it in a bulleted list ; putting a text between equal signs make the text a title, etc.

A Wiki page is editable by anonymous people or identified users only, depending of the administrator wishes. The Wiki software can provide access control mechanisms allowing the administrator to restrict access on some pages to only selected users (or groups). All modifications done on the Wiki are keeped in memory thanks to a revision control system : for each page, it is possible to view an older version of it, and if required to restore a previous version. Differences between revisions of a same page are easily viewable (added or deleted text is clearly marked). To each page of the Wiki, a discussion page is linked : this feature is useful for to talk about conflicts or different points of view among contributors.

A Wiki appears to be a good framework for adapting documents and making them accessible in the DTBook format : the Wikitext language can express information regarding the structure of a document, and features like revision control system and discussion pages are well suited for a collaborative approach. Nevertheless, existing Wikis did not provide all the technical features required to support all accessibility possibilities offered by the DTBook format.

2.2 Platform Selection

We first conducted a preliminary survey of open-source existing Wiki solutions available on the Web. Among many, some of them designed for very specific applications, we made a first selection of three platforms supported by large communities.

– MediaWiki [6] which is the widely used Wiki software and highly extendable;
– MoinMoin [7] which owns XML DocBook (near of DTBook) import and export features;
– DokuWiki [8] because of its powerful access control mechanisms.

Then, a qualitative evaluation of their respective functionalities led us to adopt MediaWiki which appeared to be the most appropriate for our application. The main reasons were the following:

– It is used by several huge projects (Wikipedia, Wikisource, Wikibooks) : the program has proved its stability and robustness for many years;
– It is actively developed and supported by a dynamic community;
– The software core can be extended. Particularly, it is possible to easily improve the parser (the part of the code responsible of the Wikitext processing) and to add new tags in the input mark-up language;
– An extension is available for book proofreading. It has been developed for the Wikisource project, under the name ProofReadPage. The aim of this extension is to improve the quality of a text document, comparing it with the original source: a book can be displayed either page by page as a column of text (manually typed or automatically produced by an OCR program) beside the scanned image, or broken in its logical organisation units (parts, chapters, etc). This feature matches one important requirement of our project which is to facilitate the adaptation process of newly scanned books. For that the image of each pages of a book has to be displayed in front of the corresponding well-structured DTBook content;

– It provides some access control mechanisms (even if limited): for example, it is possible to create users groups and to give them rights to read and/or edit only specific pages of the Wiki.

3   XML DTBook Contents Importation and Edition Using MediaWiki

The platform to be developed had to make possible to correct and improve already existing DTBook documents and create new DTBook from different sources (PDF files from publishers or images collection obtained by digitization processes). To achieve this, we needed to develop some extensions to MediaWiki as to make possible to import, to edit and to export DTBook contents. This is because MediaWiki uses Wikitext input language which is much simple but less expressive than the DTBook language. So, to avoid information loss, it was necessary to extend the Wikitext to make it as "powerful" as DTBook.

3.1   Extending the Wikitext

MediaWiki uses a simple Wikitext input language. For example, it allows (with a user friendly syntax) to basically structure a document (to mark titles, references, links, italic, bold), to create tables and lists, etc. As Wikitext is less espressive than DTBook, we have created an Extended Wikitext input language, which uses the simple syntax of the original MediaWiki Wikitext when it is possible and uses tags of DTBook language when needed. Unfortunately, no formalisation of the extended Wikitext is currently available. This is because original Wikitext itself has not been clearly specified for the moment. There are projects to elebaorate a grammar description and to specify the parser behaviour, but they are not complete.

To give an idea of the expressiveness of DTBook compared to Wikitext, here is the list of DTBook tags which have no equivalent in Wikitext : dtbook, head, meta, book, frontmatter, bodymatter, rearmatter, level, level1, level2, level3, level4, level5, level6, line, linenum, author, prodnote, sidebar, note, annotation, byline, dateline, linegroup, epigraph, poem, sent, w, pagenum, noteref, annoref, doctitle, docauthor, covertitle, bridgehead.

Content importation. To import DTBook contents in the Wiki, we use an XSLT converter to transform a DTBook file into Extended Wikitext and a tool to store the result into the Wiki.

To import newly digitized books, we use features provided by the Proofread-Page extension of MediaWiki and OCR software to transform images in text. A possible method is the following:

– Scan a book with an imaging software (there are free ones available like Sane);
– Use image processing software (like Unpaper) to improve the appearance of the images (remove margin, perform rotations, etc) and to get one image by page if needed;

- Create a PDF or DjVu file containing all the images;
- Upload the file on the Wiki.

Once the file has been uploaded, a robot is used to perform an OCR: for each page, it runs the OCR program and feeds the Wiki with the text. Then text is editable, users can correct and structure the book using the original image displayed beside. Wikisource provides such a robot which uses Tesseract, a free OCR software. Tesseract gives good results but using (non-free) Finereader or Omnipage softwares could sometimes be a better choice with complex contents. Based on the Wikisource OCR robot, we have created a new robot to interface MediaWiki and the ABBYY FineReader OCR program. FineReader can produce pure text but also HTML. Thus, it is possible to keep simple structure information of a document. Our robot is able to simplify the HTML code produced by FineReader to keep only useful information (italic, bold, table or list structure, etc), and to remove non significant or useless HTML tags.

3.2 Edition

The edition in the Wiki is done using the extended Wikitext input language described above, whose principle is very similar to the original Mediawiki Wikitext. Documentation and tutorials for introducing to DTBook can be implemented in the wiki. For instance, MediaWiki toolbars can provide contextual assistance on tag names as to make the DTBook edition process easier.

4 Content Rendering and XML DTBook Export

4.1 The Rendering of Extended Wikitext

A Wiki is viewable by a Web browser. In MediaWiki, this is achieved using XHTML language. This means that after a text has been edited, it should be converted into XHTML. The transformation from Wikitext into XHTML is done by a parser. The MediaWiki parser is flexible enough to be extended: the new tags in the Wikitext can be translated in XHTML. This is a part of our project: write some code to improve ther parser for rendering the extended Wikitext in XHTML.

4.2 The Exportation into DTBook

After contents have been corrected, improved and properly structured in the Wiki, they have to be converted back into DTBook. There is two ways to do this : either to convert the XHTML rendered by MediaWiki into DTBook, or to convert the extended Wikitext source. We have examined the first solution which might be supported by the fact there is an XHTML to DTBook converter in the DAISY Pipeline. Eventually this approach was not chosen because basically, MediaWiki does not clearly distinguish appearance and semantic : this means that part of the information related to content structure present in the Wikitext source is not translated in the XHTML output. Alternatively converting extended Wikitext into DTBook allows to avoid this problem. This can be achieved simply using a MediaWiki extension called Wiki2Xml which converts a page of the Wiki to XML. To get XML, this extension uses the MediaWiki API and particularly some parser related functions. Even if the Wikitext to DTBook converter is not directly integrated in MediaWiki, it uses parts of code which are maintained by the MediaWiki team. For example, we don't have to parse Wikitext from zero : Wiki2Xml uses parser function to pre-process the source (cleaning, template inclusion, etc). This provides an XML output, very similar to the Wikitext input but better structured, which contains all information needed to create a DTBook. The final conversion from XML generated by Wiki2Xml into DTBook can be performed with an XSLT style sheet.

5   Conclusion

The result of our project is a collaborative Wiki platform that to be used by authorized proofreaders and accessibility specialists. Content edition and structuration are performed using the Extended Wikitext language. The work on PDF or scanned books is facilitated by features of the ProofreadPage extension : for each page of a book, the original image is displayed beside the OCR recognized text, so, an user has the ability to refer permanently to the original source.

France has adopted a new legislation on copyright exception in 2006, which consequence is a platform for delivering files provided by publishers to accredited organizations. This platform will be run by the French national library. Thus it is expected an important increase in demands for adapted books and a difficult problem for the accredited organizations to be able to process these demands. The Wiki platform we developed should help solve this problem.

Programs developed for this project will be made available according an open-source model. If possible, they will be integrated in already existing softwares (MediaWiki and its extensions) and will be made available on the Internet for free. Future developpments will be focused on complex documents adaptation, especially including figures and mathematical contents.

Acknowledgement

This research is supported by the Agence Nationale de la Recherche - Lpod Project ANR 2008 CORD 012 06 and by the Ministre de l'Education Nationale - Schene project (convention 080006307). We are grateful to the French Ministry of Culture and Communication, to the company Alcatel-Lucent, and to Association BrailleNet for their support and cooperation.

References

1. http://www.serveur-helene.org/
2. Guillon, B., Monteiro, J.-L., Checoury, C., Archambault, D., Burger, D.: Towards an Integrated Publishing Chain for Accessible Multimodal Documents. In: Miesenberger, K., Klaus, J., Zagler, W.L., Burger, D. (eds.) ICCHP 2004. LNCS, vol. 3118, pp. 514–521. Springer, Heidelberg (2004)
3. Guillon, B., Desbuquois, C., Burger, D.: A model for Accessible Information Networks Findings of the EUAIN Project. In: Miesenberger, K., Klaus, J., Zagler, W.L., Karshmer, A.I. (eds.) ICCHP 2006. LNCS, vol. 4061, pp. 85–91. Springer, Heidelberg (2006)
4. Desbuquois, C., Burger, D.: Lessons from the Hlne Digital Library. In: 2nd European eAccessibility Forum, Accessible e-books: an opportunity for the disabled, Cit des sciences et de l'industrie - Paris - France, January 28 (2008)
5. Lilian, G.M., Dominique, B.: Adapting diagrams for DAISY books. In: Daisy International Technical Conference 2009, Leipzig, Germany (September 24-25, 2009)
6. http://www.mediawiki.org/
7. http://moinmo.in/
8. http://www.dokuwiki.org/

Guided Generation and Evaluation of Accessible Scalable Vector Graphics

Bernhard Dürnegger, Christina Feilmayr, and Wolfram Wöß

Institute of Application Oriented Knowledge Processing (FAW),
Johannes Kepler University Linz, Altenberger Straße 69, 4040 Linz, Austria
{christina.feilmayr,wolfram.woess}@jku.at

Abstract. Web content, such as text, graphics, audio and video, should be available and accessible for everybody, but especially for disabled and elderly people. Graphics (like figures, diagrams, maps, charts and images), above all graphics with a high explanatory and content value, still may constitute massive barriers for specific user groups. Using Scalable Vector Graphics (SVG), an open standard published by the World Wide Web Consortium (W3C), provides new possibilities for the accessibility of web sites. SVG is based on XML and consequently gains important advantages like search and index functions. Moreover, SVG files can be processed by tactile displays or screen readers. To support the authoring process of graphics in order to make them accessible guidelines are developed, which empower the authors to detect and evaluate potential barriers in their own SVGs. An additional software-based evaluation tool conducts the authors in fulfilling the accessibility guidelines and simplifies the process of making SVG documents usable and valuable for as many people as possible.

Keywords: Graphics Accessibility, Scalable Vector Graphic (SVG), Accessibility Guidelines, Software-Supported Evaluation.

1 Introduction

The web provides many opportunities for elderly/disabled people. Nevertheless, there are low efforts regarding the improvement of graphics accessibility. One major cause of the lack of attention to graphic accessibility is the fact that the majority of graphics used today are pixel-based and therefore somewhat limited in terms of accessibility improvement.

A large number of initiatives, organizations and legislative bodies engage themselves in enabling accessibility of electronic communication and making various media accessible. In national and international specifications and regulations, the area of accessibility of pixel- and vector-based graphics is mentioned aside [3][4][5].

The W3C has specified a set of guidelines that form a foundation on which further developments should follow. The *Web Content Accessibility Guidelines* (WCAG) [8] explain how to make web content accessible to people with disabilities. Therefore, these guidelines provide a list of checkpoints categorized by topic and priority. Nevertheless, providing an alternative text for graphics as its proposed in the WCAG

K. Miesenberger et al. (Eds.): ICCHP 2010, Part I, LNCS 6179, pp. 27–34, 2010.

is not always satisfactory for people with visual impairments. Physically disabled users often have problems with the non-scalability of images, resulting in loosing image quality. Therefore, the specification of Scalable Vector Graphics (SVG) [6] can be exploited to grant accessible graphics and tackle these shortcomings.

SVG, an XML-based two-dimensional graphics standard recommended by the W3C, can provide support in making graphics accessible for everyone. Opposed to pixel-based graphics, SVG is predominant in the area of two-dimensional graphics that makes an integration and interaction possible and consequently enables multimedia applications. Unlike pixel-based graphics SVG graphics can be dynamically changed in response to the needs of elderly/disabled people. Therefore the basic SVG information is generated once and can be adapted dynamically corresponding to specific demands [1]. Another important benefit of the text-based graphic format is that SVG is more accessible than other graphics formats in the sense that people with disabilities, e.g., with visual impairment, need some special equipment like a text-to-speech or text-to-braille converter. This feature enables text search and an easier editing of an image's content. In addition, a SVG graphic can be resized or altered without degrading the image quality. SVG's advantages result in a wide area of applications and can be expanded to dynamical generation of graphs and charts resulting from database queries, geographical maps, complex image maps, interactive images and animated graphics.

So far, there exist no commonly used accessibility guidelines for developing accessible graphics. Only some related work has been done in the field of developing guidelines for SVG. Recent publications concerning access to SVG for visually impaired people focused on specialized areas, especially extracting meta information as well as visualization of tactile maps. Research on exploring SVG for visually impaired users in general is becoming more common. Currently, WCAG covers topics like images, multimedia, frames etc. but does not mention the ability of SVG to describe graphics in detail. In 2000 the W3C has published an informal document about "Accessibility Features of SVG" [7]. Nevertheless, this document only lists the accessible features of SVG but does not provide guidelines, which elements are compulsory and which are recommended to define. Overall, a subset of the WCAG has to be defined in order to explain how to make SVG graphics more accessible to a broad community. Many of the WCAG are adaptable for describing graphics and their elements and for that reason build a basic foundation for web developers.

The contribution of this research work is twofold.

Firstly, guidelines for graphics are developed that are characterized by high information content. Technical, or explanatory graphics and graphical teaching material can be characterized as graphics that offer information content and provide information. In the area of graphic's accessibility this application area is consequently the most important one. The accessibility guidelines give a theoretical support for authors of scalable vector-based graphics by detecting potential barriers and suggesting instructions for avoiding barriers. The guidelines consider different aspects of SVG (like textual content, structural design, formatting, relative vs. absolute units, contrast, color schema).

Secondly, a tool for the software-based evaluation of SVG images is implemented. The web-based evaluation tool aims on facilitating compliance with the guidelines and is integrated in the existing project *Access2Graphics*[1] [2]. In the *Access2Graphics* project, SVG is used to dynamically generate graphics that are adapted to the user's individual requirements in order to make them accessible for each user. Consequently, guidelines with high priority would present checkpoints, which have to be fulfilled to be able to create user-dependent output with the *Access2Graphics* application.

2   Accessibility Guidelines for Scalable Vector Graphics

The World Wide Web Consortium and its SVG Working Group are responsible for the design and the development of the standard for scalable vector-based graphics, which is primarily applied in the application area of the World Wide Web.

In the course of this research work 15 guidelines and their appending checkpoints are worked out. The following section lists all accessibility guidelines, describes each of them in brief and explains the benefit of the individual guideline.

Guideline 1: Provide an alternative text for graphical information, which effects short and long descriptions that summarize the overall image content. This can be achieved by adding a SVG <title> element and a SVG <desc> element to groups of graphical elements that require description. Providing well-written alternative text aids people with different types of impairments. Short and long descriptions summarize the overall image content and are required for any image. Consequently, alternative text eases people who have difficulties in understanding complex concepts.

Guideline 2: Keep alternative text short and concise that means that information should be possible to read within a reasonable amount of time. It is important to keep in mind that accessibility tools and devices generally provide a rather slow way of information access. Avoiding certain phrases (e.g., *"the image shows..."*) and a complex sentence structure are also important in order to produce well-written alternative text. Using a simple wording enables access to image information to people with cognitive limitations.

Guideline 3: Separate content from presentation using style sheets or SVG presentation attributes. To achieve the best separation of presentation and content, external or internal style sheets must be used and avoid the SVG style attribute where possible and use the corresponding SVG presentation attributes instead. Probably the most important benefit is the ability to provide different ways of rendering graphical content and thereby supporting specific user needs. For example, one style sheet contains the default rendering information of a SVG document, while another provides rendering information with very high contrast to aid visually impaired users.

Guideline 4: Structure your SVG documents and provide a meaningful structure for your SVG documents instead of placing all elements on the same layer. Use the SVG <g> element to group graphical components together and provide text equivalents for these groups. Structured graphics makes it easier for all users, regardless of their abilities, to understand the information presented in a picture. The SVG element structure should resemble the structure of the core visual components that make up the picture (procedure of the *Painter's algorithm*).

---

[1] http://a2g.faw.uni-linz.ac.at/

Guideline 5: To support users in getting an idea of the information conveyed in the picture, the order of SVG elements and alternative text is important. Providing a meaningful structure in a way that enables linearization means that authors of SVG documents must order elements and build blocks of the SVG document that accordingly improves accessibility. A hierarchy with more than one element group on the same markup level requires ordering of these element groups. Assuming the element groups are not overlapping and their order is therefore not relevant for painting, they should be ordered in a sequence making sense when accessed in a linear way.

Guideline 6: Reusing markup within a SVG document avoids redundancy in graphical information. Defining named graphical building blocks with the SVG <defs> element and using the SVG <use> and <image> element enables reuse of graphical information. The SVG <image> element is suitable for including entire images into a SVG document and it helps to improve the structure and clarity of the including SVG document. The SVG <use> element can reference almost any SVG element that has a unique id attribute assigned. Besides avoiding redundancy in the structure, it is also important to avoid redundancy in presentation. Thus, it is recommended that the presentational information is stored as an internal or external style sheet inside the SVG <style> element.

Guideline 7: Use relative ("em", "ex", "%") rather than absolute ("pt", "pc", "cm", "mm", "in") units in the SVG documents and style sheets. Specifying units for SVG properties that accept a length value avoids rendering problems when mixing SVG presentational attributes with CSS styling. Using relative units supports graceful scaling and other geometric transformations of the graphical content. Scaling of graphical content is very important because it is required by a wide variety of assistive technologies used by people with different types of impairments. For example, interactive elements need to be scaled for elderly people and people with motor disabilities. Screen magnifiers used by people with low vision also rely on scaling of graphical content.

Guideline 8: It is a basic requirement that XML documents must be well-formed and valid defined by the SVG standard. Furthermore, all elements, attributes and properties must be used in the way intended by the SVG standard (see SVG 1.1. document type definition). Most of XML processors check SVG documents for both well-formedness and validity, there are also some standalone tools for that task are existing (e.g., the W3C validation service).

Guideline 9: Colors should upgrade the information in SVG documents, but colors itself should not communicate information. People with limited vision or different deficiencies are unable to perceive color in the way intended by the image's author, or are unable to perceive color at all. Therefore, it is important that the content of a SVG document, text as well as graphics, are understandable when viewed without colors. In many cases small adaptations are sufficient to make color-coded information accessible. Text simply needs to be transformed in a color-neutral way and for graphical elements a texture added to color can help making information accessible.

Guideline 10: Avoid inappropriate color combinations known to be problematic for people with color deficiencies. In addition, color-coded information that is indistinguishable for people with color deficiencies should be avoided. It strongly depends on the specific person what shades of color are found hard to be differentiated. In general, combinations of reds and greens for *protanopia*, *protanomaly*, *deuteranopia*, *deuteranomaly* and combinations of blues and greens for *tritanopia* are known to be problematic.

Guideline 11: Ensure enough contrast between the elements of an image in order to make them perceptible, distinguishable and consequently the image accessible. Especially elderly people, people with low vision and people affected by color-blindness have difficulties resolving the contents of an image when the contrast of an image is too low, The WCAG 2.0 [0] guidelines provide a founded definition of contrast that helps to evaluate the colors of an image. The contrast is defined as the ratio of the relative luminance L1 of the first color and the relative luminance L2 of the second color. The relative luminance is computed as L = (0.2126 * R) + (0.7152 * G) + (0.0722 * B) where R, G and B are values of the sRGB color space. Their contrast C is computed as C = (L1 + 0.05) / (L2 + 0.05) where L1 is the higher and L2 is the lower luminance value. The value of contrast C ranges from 1 to 21, the higher the number, the stronger the contrast.

Guideline 12: The size and proportions of important and interactive (e.g., clickable or selectable) graphical elements are of importance for people with impaired vision, motor impairments and elderly people. In general, the more important a part of an image is, the larger it should be. When interactive elements are included in an image, they must be of a size efficiently operable by the indented user. The size and the proportions of graphical elements must be adapted to meet the people's requirements. Furthermore, if using interactive elements in an image, the slower input speed and the less accuracy of alternative input devices must be taken in account.

Guideline 13: In general, providing pixel-based images, like *.bmp, *.jpg, *.png or *.gif should be avoided. Only in some special cases (e.g., a photograph for technical graphics) the SVG <image> element should be used to include a pixel-based image into a SVG document. If it is necessary to include pixel-based images, alternative descriptions with direct SVG <title> and <desc> child elements are essential.

Guideline 14: Interactive elements of a SVG document must be operable in a device-independent way in order to make them accessible for people with impairments. Device-independent events supported by SVG (and the Document Object Model Version 2) are focusin, focusout and activate. To make interactive content accessible, these events must be used instead of or in addition to device-dependent events (see SVG Standard 1.1. [6]). To emulate keyboard input with e.g., mouth sticks, head wands, simple switches, eye-tracking or voice recognition, interactive elements should not rely only on mouse input.

Guideline 15: In the context of SVG documents, animation can constitute flickering and flashing effects with problematic frequencies (4Hz to 59Hz), which can cause photo epileptic seizures. Especially animations with periodically moving or switching image content can cause health problems. The size of a flashing or blinking area is of importance as well. A large area will more likely cause harmful effects than an area with small dimensions.

3 Software-Based Support for Guideline Evaluation

The accessibility guidelines support authors in generating accessible scalable vector-based graphics in a theoretical way. However, a software-based evaluation applies the theoretical guidelines and enables authors to test their graphics against accessibility in a web-based graphical user interface. The graphical user interface is designed as simple as possible and focuses on the essential functionalities.

The implementation of the evaluation tool bases on Java and various open source libraries. Java Server Pages (JSP) is used for the implementation of the front end and the Apache Batik SVG Toolkit 1.7 for facilitating the processing of scalable vector-based graphics. Some core functionalities of the SVG toolkit are the presentation of SVG documents in a Java program, the transformation of SVG into other graphic formats and the representation of SVG documents in Java classes.

The architecture of the web application is according to the architectural model-view-controller-pattern and follows a reference software architecture for Java and JSP based web applications.

The following example-chart (see Figure 1) about a fictive study of a correlation of apple color and worm infestation demonstrates some core features of the software-based accessibility evaluation. The example chart is designed to give an overview, how the evaluation tool points out warnings and errors, if an author did not adhere the accessibility guidelines.

During the process of image generation some checkpoints of the accessibility guidelines are disregarded, which the evaluation tool should indicate, namely in terms of warnings and errors.

The web-based evaluation tool shows several warnings because of missing alternative descriptions in various groups and the non well-expressed description of the SVG document (e.g., phrases like <title>Image of analysis... </title>). In addition, color pairs have a contrast value fewer than 5, indicating an insufficient contrast between the blue and the green bar. Furthermore, the SVG document contains element with device-dependent interaction but no corresponding device-independent interaction is found. An error, for example, is the missing <desc> element for the main document, which contains the textual description of the graphics. Another error is that one <title> element contains too many words, considering that the suggested number of words is 15. Above all, absolute units are used in the attribute height ("cm"), but the attribute requires a relative unit (like height="50px") instead of the absolute one.

All in all seven checkpoints of the accessibility guidelines are fulfilled and are listed in the section "*passes*". The verification of the document's well-formedness and validity did not fail, as well the SVG 1.1 grammar was accurately considered. The author of the SVG document is requested to provide a <title> element, comprising a short description of the image's content, which, as mentioned above, is not formulated very well. Moreover, every <g> element contains a non-empty <title> child element and therewith each element complies with the guideline. In addition, the author of the SVG document does not include external pixel-based graphics, which considerably enhances the accessibility of the example-chart.

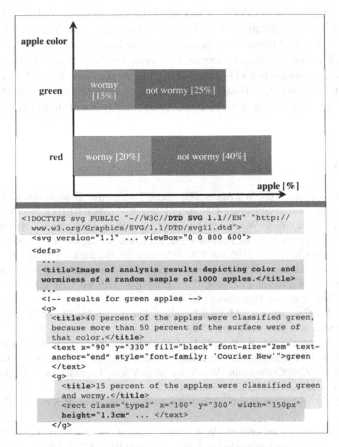

```
<!DOCTYPE svg PUBLIC "-//W3C//DTD SVG 1.1//EN" "http://
www.w3.org/Graphics/SVG/1.1/DTD/svg11.dtd">
  <svg version="1.1" ... viewBox="0 0 800 600">
  <defs>
    ...
    <title>Image of analysis results depicting color and
    worminess of a random sample of 1000 apples.</title>
    ...
    <!-- results for green apples -->
    <g>
      <title>40 percent of the apples were classified green,
      because more than 50 percent of the surface were of
      that color.</title>
      <text x="90" y="330" fill="black" font-size="2em" text-
      anchor="end" style="font-family: 'Courier New'">green
      </text>
      <g>
        <title>15 percent of the apples were classified green
        and wormy.</title>
        <rect class="type2" x="100" y="300" width="150px"
        height="1.3cm" ... </text>
      </g>
    </g>
```

Fig. 1. SVG example-chart and XML-code of the SVG file

4 Conclusion

It is a fact that pixel-based graphics provided without an alternative text are useless for blind people and bar charts that have similar colors for different bars are difficult to be identified by people with color deficiencies. To overcome such problems a SVG guideline catalogue was developed, which offers users of web applications accessible graphics with improved structural and textual description quality. Despite that the main focus of developing accessibility guidelines was on graphics with high information content, the wording of the individual guideline became a great challenge. It is important that the phrasing of the guidelines is not too abstract and therefore leaves much room for interpretation or gets too strict that result in necessary restrictions.

In contrast to pixel-based graphics, which several disabled people find difficult to work with, SVG graphics are very beneficial and offer various possibilities in accommodating graphics for many kinds of disabilities. To enhance the application of scalable vector-based graphics and its acceptance, (software-) support in the development process of SVGs is essential. In this work a tool was implemented, which enables the evaluation of SVG documents and eases the understanding of the information provided through the accessibility guidelines.

Opposed to the Microsoft Internet Explorer, Firefox, a web browser out of the Mozilla project, supports SVG images and partially implements the SVG Standard 1.1 in its actual version 3.0. Finally, SVG, as an open standard for XML-based two-dimensional graphics, can achieve a sustained improvement in the field of accessible graphics.

References

1. Altmanninger, K., Wöß, W.: Access2Graphics: Barrier-free Graphics in Web Applications. International Journal on Human-Computer Interaction (eMinds) 1(2), 59–73 (2006)
2. Altmanninger, K., Wöß, W.: Accessible Graphics in Web Applications: Dynamic Generation, Analysis and Verification. In: Miesenberger, K., Klaus, J., Zagler, W.L., Karshmer, A.I. (eds.) ICCHP 2008. LNCS, vol. 5105, pp. 378–385. Springer, Heidelberg (2008)
3. Bulatov, V., Gardner, J.A.: Directly Accessible Mainstream Graphical Information. In: Miesenberger, K., Klaus, J., Zagler, W.L., Burger, D. (eds.) ICCHP 2004. LNCS, vol. 3118, pp. 739–744. Springer, Heidelberg (2004)
4. Bulatov, V., Gardner, J.A.: Making Graphics Accessible. In: Proceedings of the 3rd SVG Open Conference, Tokyo, Japan (2004)
5. Campin, B., McCurdy, W., Brunet, L., Siekierska, E.: SVG Maps for People with Visual Impairment. In: Proceedings of the 2nd SVG Open Conference, Vancouver, Canada (2003)
6. World Wide Web Consortium (W3C). Scalable Vector Graphics (SVG) 1.1 Specification. W3C Recommendation (January 14, 2003)
7. World Wide Web Consortium (W3C). Accessibility Features of SVG. W3C Note (August 7, 2000)
8. World WideWeb Consortium (W3C).Web Content Accessibility Guidelines (WCAG). W3C WCAG 1.0 Recommendation 5 May 1999 and W3C WCAG 2.0 Working Draft (April 27, 2006)
9. Web Accessibility Initiative, WAI (2006), http://www.w3.org/WAI/

Improving the Re-digitisation Process by Using Software with Automatic Metadata Detection

Reinhard Ruemer[1], Klaus Miesenberger[1], Franz Kummer[2], and Claus Gravenhorst[2]

[1] Institute Integriert Studieren, Johannes Kepler University of Linz, Altenberger Strasse 69, 4040, Linz, Austria
{reinhard.ruemer,klaus.miesenberger}@jku.at
[2] CCS Content Conversion Specialists GmbH, Weidestrasse 134, 22083, Hamburg, Germany
{f.kummer,c.gravenhorst}@content-conversion.com

Abstract. The provision of electronic documents for print-disabled persons is a key service of many institutions like libraries for the blind, educational facilities and other service providers for people with disabilities. Generally speaking all these institutions have defined a common internal workflow for providing these documents. A large amount of work falls on the task of restructuring the text and adding structural metadata for navigation. In this paper we describe the use of the commercial product docWORKS[e] by German company CCS and the challenges and benefits in terms of time and output quality we encountered by using this tool.

Keywords: documents processing, OCR, service provision, digitisation, conversion, workflow, metadata, print-disabled persons, accessible publishing, ebooks.

1 Introduction

The invention of the mechanical book press in the 15th century revolutionised the book production process in terms of both quality and quantity. This started something that we can call a media revolution. From then on it was possible to produce identical copies of a work in a noticeably shorter amount of time. Another effect was the availability of the work to the common people. From now on everybody who could read had the opportunity to consume information. Today the amount of produced books exceeds our imagination by far.

Nevertheless in the last century we witnessed another media revolution – the invention of the computer and the internet. It lead to people being able to find and consume even more information in a shorter amount of time.

Later the development of Assistive Technologies was the key enabler to offer access to information on an almost equal level for people with disabilities. There have also been various improvements in legislature to grant the equal access to information for the disabled.

Now that the legal framework permits the adaptation and reproduction of copyrighted work for people with disabilities, a foundation on how to define,

K. Miesenberger et al. (Eds.): ICCHP 2010, Part I, LNCS 6179, pp. 35–42, 2010.

implement and fulfil this task in an effective and efficient way is needed. In this paper we will describe our R&D work to improve the creation process of accessible versions of books. We will also corroborate the research work with practical data. The goal is to define a process that is as general as possible but nevertheless can be used and adapted for different types of input and output media.

2 State of the Art and Necessary Steps Beyond

For the last 19 years the institute Integriert Studieren has performed extensive research work in the field of information processing, archiving and accessibility in publishing environments [1], [2], [3], [4], [5], [6]. Although considerable progress has been achieved in the publishing field, the production of accessible versions is still not a common thing. That is why different service organisations specialised in the field of accessible document creation produce the disability-friendly versions. In the beginning these organisations produced mainly Braille printed versions of books. Later, when Assistive Technologies were introduced and became affordable for consumers also, these organisations started to widen their range to include text versions of books. In addition, audio versions - produced by recording the human voice while a person reads the book out loud – were also being made. In the last few years, as a result of the increase in computing power of desktop systems there were also strong developments in the area of synthetic speech and automatic generation of audio books. DAISY [7] has become the mostly used format for audio books.

By looking at the book publishing process of different publishing houses in Austria [5], [8] we saw that the publishing process is a very diverse process and a lot of steps (e.g. layouting, typesetting, etc.) are done by external contractors. Each of them has his own tools and methods of doing the work. And although the Desktop Publishing Tools (DTP) do provide the functionalities and methods for the creation of structured content with XML in the background [9], they are rarely used by publishers especially those in small and medium size publishing houses and in the educational sector.

As a result the most efficient way to obtain a digital version of a book is still to re-digitise an existing one, starting with the creation of electronic versions of the title. The basic production process for accessible textbooks has not distinctly changed over the last years. It can be described as sequence of the following steps:

1. (Re)Digitisation [optional]
2. Optical Character Recognition (OCR)
3. Structuring
4. Export

The software tools used to support the process have increased the output quality. For example OCR-tools produce a higher recognition rate and fewer text errors. The most important and simultaneously also the most time consuming work in this process is the structuring process of the information. This means re-editing the text in a way that metadata such as headings, page numbers etc. are marked in the text. This enables a disabled reader to navigate and recognise the structure of the text.

The required export must be in machine readable file format and must contain:

- the text (i.e. the logical content of the document)
- information about bibliographic metadata (such as tile, author, publishing date etc.),
- structural information (i.e. which content belongs to which structural element like contribution, section, article, chapter, subchapter, illustration&caption, table&caption etc.) together with a
- description of the respective structural element (which can be the OCRed headline, the OCRed caption or a description by manual input).

The most common files that are currently produced for the visually impaired readers are DOC files for use with Microsoft Word or any other writer application but also fully tagged PDF files and file formats that combine text and audio, like the DAISY format.

Currently, different software tools are being used in different stages of the process. Improving the structuring part of the digitisation workflow would be a massive boost to the whole production process in rendering accessible information. Additionally it should also be looked at the benefits of having one single tool that can cover the whole process instead of having a patchwork of many different tools.

3 Methodology for Improving the Production Process

As mentioned above one challenge is to improve the structuring and metadata recognition stage in the accessible information creation process. For this we used a commercial software tool called docWORKS[e] by German company CCS. An overview on the technology was also published in [10]. The basic version of this software was first released in 1996 and had been significantly improved in cooperation with 12 international libraries in the METAe Project [4] funded by the European Commission through the 5th Framework Research Program.

In cooperation we evaluated commonly, how docWORKS technology can support the accessible information creation process. Specific questions to be answered were:

- Which steps of the current workflow can the commercial conversion tool cover?
- Does the software's integrated workflow help to make the workflow faster and safer?
- Is the generated metadata sufficient to cover the needs of readers with disabilities?
- Are the exported documents accessible and usable for readers with disabilities?

To achieve results that are as representative as possible, we used many different types of literature as input, such as novels, theses, schoolbooks, study literature and also cultural heritage material. The results of the evaluation process are described in the next section.

4 R&D Work and Results

CCS's technology docWORKS[e] offers various automated document analysis steps within one single application. These steps are described below.

4.1 Recognising the Physical Structure of the Document

Pages are automatically classified into cover, title, table-of-contents or blank pages. Then pages are grouped to front, main and back matter. Additionally, page numbers are detected for labelling the pages, both physically (page sequence) and logically (according to printed pages number in several page sequences). All page types, front/main/back grouping and page sequences can be corrected within the user interface, if required. Customised page types can be created to serve custom needs.

4.2 Creation of Layout Metadata of Each Page

docWORKS[e] recognises the layout of each page and classifies certain zones automatically according to their type. Among others, these include text blocks, illustrations, formula, tables, captions, running titles, authors, advertisements and footnotes. The user interface allows fast manual verification (based on colour indications) and correction (using keyboard shortcuts) of the results. New zone types can be defined by the user to serve special requirements.

4.3 Running OCR on Each of the Layout Elements

Based on these zones OCR is applied to recognise the printed text. docWORKS[e] uses ABBYY Finereader as its standard OCR engine. Both Antiqua and Gothic (Fraktur) fonts can be recognised. Additional algorithms are applied, e.g. to detect the font type in case documents show a mix of Antiqua and Gothic or to detect hyphenated words for making them available as complete words. Manual OCR correction can be applied on the entire text or on certain zones (e.g. headlines) only.

4.4 Detection of Structural Information of the Document

The detected layout elements are automatically grouped into logical units (chapters, subchapters, contributions, articles, sections etc). Theses units are labelled with the OCR result of the according headline or caption. The user interface allows manual OCR correction, editing chapter/article grouping, linking of caption to tables/illustrations and levelling of chapter/subchapter.

4.5 Integration of Existing Bibliographic Metadata

Via the Z39.50 interface, docWORKS[e] can communicate with the library catalogue to import existing bibliographic metadata. This data can be edited in the user interface based on MODS [11] or Dublin Core metadata sets. Based on the layout recognition, OCR result on Author zones can be added automatically to the metadata set.

4.6   Human Interaction for Verifying Results of Automated Analysis

It is common knowledge that a conversion software tool can never deliver 100% correct data without manual interaction. Thus, the idea of docWORKS[e] is not only to offer a high degree of automation but also to allow efficient manual interaction for verifying or editing the analysis results. A docWORKS[e] system is designed to have an optional manual step for quality assurance after the automated recognition steps described above. These manual steps are carried out within the user interface of the software. An example can be viewed in the following screenshot.

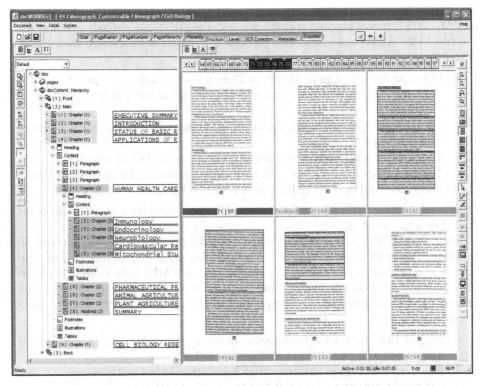

Fig. 1. Screenshot of docWORKS[e]: Verifying e.g. the logical structure of the document to enable visually impaired to navigate within the Digital Original that is exported thereafter

The amount of manual interaction varies depending on

- scanning quality, original document quality and quality of the digital image: better quality will result in better analysis results regarding layout analysis, and OCR result and thus less need for manual correction;
- document type: sophisticated layouts with ornamented letters, text within graphics and illustrations may need to be corrected manually in terms of layout recognition and OCR result;
- page number recognition, headline recognition hardly require any manual verification;

- building the logical structure runs very well but should always be checked in order to get near 100% correctness. Handy tools are provided within the docWORKS[e] interface to correct grouping of elements to logical units and hierarchy level.

While it is possible to convert documents using automation alone, quality of results and depth of analysis increase with the amount of manual work that is applied.

4.7 Description of Output

All data which is harvested in the conversion process described above will be part of the output files. Generic output format of docWORKS[e] is XML files in METS [12] and ALTO [13] format together with the images. The METS file not only contains file pointers to the ALTO and image files but also incorporate the harvested metadata as described below:

- Bibliographic metadata in MODS or Dublin Core format of the printed and the electronic version of the document and of all logical and physical elements of the document.
- Administrative metadata like technical information on each scanned image in MIX format [14].
- The physical structure with all page number and page class information.
- The logical structure with the article or chapter structure, linking of captions to illustrations and tables together with their labels based on corrected OCR result.

OCR result, word coordinates and position of illustrations/tables are saved within the ALTO files for each page.

The set of METS/ALTO/images is the so-called Digital Original and contains all the above mentioned information. It can be used for ingest into commercial or non-commercial presentations systems. docWORKS[e] uses METS/ALTO/image export also to create predefined and customised derivative files as a post-conversion process. The most important derivative files that are created automatically within docWORKS[e] are:

- Tagged PDF files with bookmarks, illustrations, hidden text, which allows navigation on chapter/article headlines and full text search.
- RTF files with tagged headlines, linking of illustrations and captions. All text that does not belong to the full text (e.g. page numbers, running titles etc.) is filtered out, so that the file can be used for further editing or further transformation into DOC, DAISY or other formats like EPUB.

The conversion software docWORKS[e] not only helps to speed up the conversion process but also allows a digitisation project to be managed and controlled. Using the integrated workflow of docWORKS[e] ensures data integrity and high quality output.

5   Impact on the Field

The use of semi-automatic metadata recognition in the production process provides a solid base for higher quality output. As a result of the testing phase we can see that there is potential for timesaving in the production process. Due to the short testing period and the relatively short time available for exploring the functions of docWORKS[e] we cannot give detailed figures here. It must also be said that the potential of time savings may vary for the different types of documents. The potential for timesaving in producing novels or similar, very flatly structured books is greater in docWORKS[e], than in complex structured documents (i.e. biology books, accounting books) for which the verify task in docWORKS[e] is probably the same or maybe slightly less time consuming than in the current production process. The basis for this assertion is that the person operating docWORKS[e] has received extensive training and is familiar with the functions and structuring concepts in docWORKS[e].

The capacities in terms of workforce, that become available can then either be used for improving special types of content (e.g. mathematics, graphics, etc.) or can be returned to the user by decreasing production costs. For our field of application, which is the support of students with disabilities by providing them with accessible digital learning material, the evaluation showed that there is potential to increase the quality and quantity of the produced material. Since the literature we re-digitise is of very complex structure in many cases, the process and software evaluated in this co-operation might be even higher benefit when applied on less structured literature like novels or fiction.

6 Conclusion and Future Work

From past project co-operations with publishers we have learned that it is almost impossible to create accessible documents directly in-house at the publishing company. This is because of the high number of actors and the multi-facetted publishing process itself. So the re-digitisation of a work is still the most common and fastest way to make published works accessible to users with disabilities. If we can support this re-digitisation process with comprehensive tools and implement workflows that avoid media breaks we can deliver high quality documents in an affordable time and under affordable costs. For this we need intelligent tools that are capable of recognising structure and metadata. The co-operation with CCS showed that such tools exist and are capable of supporting the information creation process.

In order to cover the needs of institutions like the institute Integriert Studieren, CCS has developed a self-installing one-workstation version of its technology called docWORKS[e]. Based on the results and experiences achieved in the evaluation phase at the institute Integriert Studieren, CCS will also further develop its software in order to improve the conversion and re-digitisation processes with visually impaired people in mind.

References

1. Project ETAB - electronic newspapers for the blind, 1993-1994,
   http://fodok.jku.at/fodok/forschungsprojekt.xsql?FP_ID=608
2. Project Dieper (Digitised European Periodicals) (1999),
   http://fodok.jku.at/fodok/forschungsprojekt.xsql?FP_ID=1524

3. Project ALO - Austrian Literature Online (1999-2002),
   `http://fodok.jku.at/fodok/forschungsprojekt.xsql?FP_ID=579`
4. Project META-E (2000-2003),
   `http://fodok.jku.at/fodok/forschungsprojekt.xsql?FP_ID=577`
5. Project Schulbuch barrierefrei (accessible school books) - Cooperation between Publishers and Service Providers in Austria (2004-2005),
   `http://fodok.jku.at/fodok/forschungsprojekt.xsql?FP_ID=1538`
6. Project EUAIN - The European Accessible Information Network (2004-2007),
   `http://fodok.jku.at/fodok/forschungsprojekt.xsql?FP_ID=1526`
7. Specifications for the Digital Talking Book (DAISY), `http://www.niso.org/workrooms/daisy/Z39-86-2005.html` (February 01, 2010)
8. Miesenberger, K., Ruemer, R.: Schulbuch Barrierefrei (Accessible School Books) - Cooperation Between Publisher and Service Provider in Austria. In: Miesenberger, K., Klaus, J., Zagler, W.L., Karshmer, A.I. (eds.) ICCHP 2006. LNCS, vol. 4061, p. 32. Springer, Heidelberg (2006)
9. Ruemer, R., Miesenberger, K.: Using XML for Publishing on Demand in Different Output Formats. In: Second International Conference on Automated Production of Cross Media Content for Multi-Channel Distribution, AXMEDIS 2006, pp. 153–156 (2006)
10. Gravenhorst, C.: Making the Past a Thing of the Future: Automated Workflow for the Conversion of Printed Items into Fully Structured Digital Objects Based on Common Open Metadata Standards. In: Miesenberger, K., Klaus, J., Zagler, W.L., Karshmer, A.I. (eds.) ICCHP 2006. LNCS, vol. 4061, p. 92. Springer, Heidelberg (2006)
11. Metadata Object Description Schema (MODS),
    `http://www.loc.gov/standards/mods/`
12. Metadata Encoding And Transmission Standard (METS),
    `http://www.loc.gov/standards/mets/`
13. Analyzed Layout and Text Object (ALTO) XML Schema,
    `http://www.loc.gov/standards/alto/`
14. NISO Metadata for Images in XML Schema (MIX),
    `http://www.loc.gov/standards/mix/`

New Production and Delivery System for Pupils with Disabilities in Austria as Chance for Higher Quality Output

Reinhard Ruemer and Klaus Miesenberger

Institute Integriert Studieren, Johannes Kepler Universität,
Altenberger Strasse 69, 4040, Linz, Austria
{reinhard.ruemer,klaus.miesenberger}@jku.at

Abstract. The educational sector is a very diverse field when it comes to the type of content that is being used in the teaching of school pupils. To make these documents accessible and usable needs much more work than just to create a structured document that is readable and navigable for blind and visually impaired pupils. Often, exercise types especially in the first few grades at school very much rely on visual activities for example colour matching, naming of things etc. To make these types of exercises accessible additional work needs to be done. In the last years we have improved the production process of schoolbooks inasmuch as we were able to provide a solid basic accessibility now on which special education teachers can now work on the adaptation of specific exercise types like the above mentioned.

Keywords: documents processing, OCR, service provision, workflow, metadata, print disabled persons, accessible publishing, ebooks.

1 Introduction

For more than 15 years now the Arbeitsgemeinschaft zur Erstellung der Lehr und Lernmittel für sehgeschädigte Schüler (= "Working Group for the Creation of Teaching- and Learning Materials for Visually Impaired Students", short: ALS) [1] is the central organisation in Austria that provides all the study and learning materials for pupils with disabilities and chronicle diseases. The ALS always is in close co-operation with the institute Integriert Studieren. Many of the outcomes from the project and research work at the institute flows directly into the day-to-day production work at the ALS.

This paper will describe on the one hand the improvements that have been made in the production and delivery process of the school literature, but give also and outlook on the needs and future work in this very special and diverse field of education. The idea is to create a technical environment that acts as enabler for pedagogues to concentrate on the adaptation of specific types of exercises and sharing of knowledge on how to adapt them for pupils with disabilities or chronicle diseases.

K. Miesenberger et al. (Eds.): ICCHP 2010, Part I, LNCS 6179, pp. 43–46, 2010.

2 State of the Art

The current state of the Art in providing study literature for people with disabilities covers output formats such as plain text files, Braille output, structured .doc files or .pdf files. In most cases the produced output is a text-only document with a transcription of the illustrations from the original document. The production process for the documents can be described in the following four steps:

1. **Digitalization [optional]:** Since the practical work and also past projects have shown it is the best way to start the production process of accessible versions of books at the stage where the print book is finished. And since many publishers do not give away digital files we must re-digitise the work by scanning the book in a regular document scanner.
2. **Optical Character Recognition (OCR):** The next step is to analyse the structure of the document (identify tables, illustrations and text) and to apply the OCR. The result of this stage is a file that contains the text and other non-textual elements of the original document.
3. **Structuring:** Metadata from the original document is now added to create a structured file. This means tagging headlines, lists, page numbers etc. This has to be done to ensure that it is possible to navigate through the document afterwards.
4. **Export:** The structured document is exported to the target delivery format. This can be Braille print, pdf, (X)HTML or just as .doc or .odt file for reading in MS Word or OO Writer.

In the last years screen reader technology and also synthetic speech technology has improved dramatically. This is why new ways of delivery have to be found such as producing audio books and also to increase the quality of the books to be able to target a greater group of pupils not only the blind and visually impaired. In the next section we describe how we targeted this goal.

3 Methodology for Improving the Quality

In [2] we defined structural elements for electronic versions of books. The usage of these metadata guarantees that in the export stage of the process the documents can be transformed smoothly and without loss of information into the various output formats.

The defined small set of structural elements proofed to be sufficient for the needs and field of application, which is a very diverse one. We produce teaching and learning material for grammar school as well as law or language books for university students.

In a further step, we explicitly defined a clear structured and well-documented workflow and used state of the art software tools in each step of the process.

The transforming methods realign itself on standards in software, metadata and the used file formats. It is based on state of the art XML formats such as [3] and open source software like [4]. This guarantees standard compliance, comparability and exchangeability with other services and tools.

4   R & D Work and Results

One result of the applied research we did is that we have now a clearly structured production process for digital accessible school learning materials as shown in Fig. 1 below.

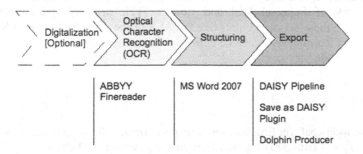

Fig. 1. Workflow and Tools

The scanned images are Analysed and read in ABBYY Finereader. After an automatic detection of the three basic types (Text, Table and Image) a manual validation and correction of the automatic process is necessary to ensure high quality output in this stage. This minimizes also the efforts in the following steps. The structuring is done in MS Word using the metadata tags we defined earlier (Headings, Images, List, Paragraphs, Footnotes, etc.). The working document is saved as a .docx file, which is a open XML standard [5]. This document is also the source format for all the export transformations in the next stage. Akin to the ideas of [6] in the Export stage we can produce output formats. [4] and [7] are open source software and work basically with XML transformation in the background, while [8] is a commercial product, that installs as a plug-in in MS Word.

The output formats we can now deliver are .pdf, .doc, docx, .odt, Braille print, adopted large print and Full Audio Daisy books with synthetic generated speech.

The electronic versions of the books are delivered through our new download portal [9]. It grants access to currently over 55 000 documents available for research tasks and also for downloading. It is a closed system, where only people who register themselves beforehand can have access.

5   Impact to the Field

The described process for the production and delivery of school literature is beyond the general current state of the art. This new types of school literature can be used for a greater group of users e.g. pupils with chronicle diseases or pupils with specific learning difficulties. Furthermore the high basic quality of the documents sets also a better ground for the adaptation work done by pedagogues in schools for the blinds or other special schools.

6 Conclusion and Planned Activities

The next logical steps after the successful introduction of this new production and delivery system is to focus on the specifics of the different exercise types and how to make the accessible. Another area that we will set the focus on is the one of access to certain teaching subjects like mathematics and chemistry. Here we can see a strong tie with the work of Federsel [10] and Cooper [11]. In a co-operation between pedagogues and these service centres like the ALS or the institute Integriert Studieren new alternative learning types can be defined that can substitute the inaccessible ones in the original book.

References

1. Arbeitsgemeinschaft zur Erstellung der Lehr und Lernmittel für sehgeschädigte Schüler, http://www.integriert-studieren.jku.at/als/ (February 01, 2010)
2. Miesenberger, K., Ruemer, R.: Schulbuch Barrierefrei (Accessible School Books) - Co-operation Between Publisher and Service Provider in Austria. In: Miesenberger, K., Klaus, J., Zagler, W.L., Karshmer, A.I. (eds.) ICCHP 2006. LNCS, vol. 4061, p. 32. Springer, Heidelberg (2006)
3. Specifications for the Digital Talking Book, http://www.niso.org/workrooms/daisy/Z39-86-2005.html (February 01, 2010)
4. The DAISY Pipeline, http://daisymfc.sourceforge.net/ (February 01, 2010)
5. Standard ECMA-376, Office Open XML File Formats, http://www.ecma-international.org/publications/standards/Ecma-376.htm (March 10, 2010)
6. Guillon, B., Monteiro, J.-L., Checoury, C., Archambault, D., Burger, D.: Towards an Integrated Publishing Chain for Accessible Multimodal Documents. In: Miesenberger, K., Klaus, J., Zagler, W.L., Burger, D. (eds.) ICCHP 2004. LNCS, vol. 3118, p. 514. Springer, Heidelberg (2004)
7. Save As DAISY - Microsoft Word Add-In, http://www.daisy.org/project/save-as-daisy-microsoft (March 10, 2010)
8. EasyProducer - Digital talking book creation tool, http://www.yourdolphin.com/productdetail.asp?id=10 (March 10, 2010)
9. ADL - Accessible Digital Learningmaterial, http://literatur.integriert-studieren.jku.at (February 01, 2010)
10. Stephan, F., Miesenberger, K.: Chemical Workbench for Blind People – Accessing the Structure of Chemical Formula. In: Miesenberger, K., Klaus, J., Zagler, W.L., Karshmer, A.I. (eds.) ICCHP 2008. LNCS, vol. 5105, p. 953. Springer, Heidelberg (2008)
11. Cooper, M., Lowe, T., Taylor, M.: Access to Mathematics in Web Resources for People with a Visual Impairment. In: Miesenberger, K., Klaus, J., Zagler, W.L., Karshmer, A.I. (eds.) ICCHP 2008. LNCS, vol. 5105, p. 926. Springer, Heidelberg (2008)

A Flexible Software Architecture Concept for the Creation of Accessible PDF Documents

Alireza Darvishy, Hans-Peter Hutter, Alexander Horvath, and Martin Dorigo

ZHAW Zurich University of Applied Sciences
InIT Institute of applied Information Technology
P.O. Box 805
CH-8401 Winterthur, Switzerland
`alireza.darvishy@zhaw.ch`

Abstract. This paper presents a flexible software architecture concept that allows the automatic generation of fully accessible PDF documents originating from various authoring tools such as Adobe InDesign [1] or Microsoft Word [2]. The architecture can be extended to include any authoring tools capable of creating PDF documents. For each authoring tool, a software accessibility plug-in must be implemented which analyzes the logical structure of the document and creates an XML representation of it. This XML file is used in combination with an untagged non-accessible PDF to create an accessible PDF version of the document. The implemented accessibility plug-in prototype allows authors of documents to check for accessibility issues while creating their documents and add the additional semantic information needed to generate a fully accessible PDF document.

Keywords: Document accessibility, automatic generation of accessible PDF, screen reader [3], visual impairment, accessibility, tagged PDF, software architecture.

1 Introduction

There are thousands of PDF documents available on the internet, but most of them are not accessible for visually impaired people using screen readers [3]. In many cases authors use authoring tools such as Adobe Indesign [1], Microsoft Word [2] and others to create these PDF documents. But all too often the resulting PDFs are not tagged correctly and have to be manually post-processed in order to become accessible PDFs. This is inefficient, very time-consuming, and tedious. In addition, a separate solution is needed for each authoring tool because there is no software solution that can be used with different authoring tools.

The following list outlines typical issues that arise when creating a PDF document with an authoring tool such as Microsoft Word [2]:

- Table layouts: If tables are used for layout purposes only and not to present tabular data, the author of the Word document is not alerted to the fact that the information should be formatted with style sheets rather than in table layouts.
- Table headers: Word only allows for the creation of column headers – the Word author has no option to define row headers.

K. Miesenberger et al. (Eds.): ICCHP 2010, Part I, LNCS 6179, pp. 47–52, 2010.

- Form fields: The specified entry fields in Word are not carried over into the PDF.
- The Word author is not alerted if no alternative text is entered for a picture.
- The Word author is not alerted if the document is not structured with headings, or if standard style sheets are not used in Word for structuring purposes.
- The Word author cannot indicate the correct reading order.
- The author is not alerted if there is insufficient contrast between text and background.

Although newer versions of Microsoft Word [5] provide facilities to overcome some of the above-mentioned issues, this solution can only be used with MS Word [2] but not with other authoring tools. This paper introduces a new flexible software architecture approach that enables accessible PDF documents to be created from a variety of authoring tools.

2 Our Approach

The diagram in Fig. 1 shows the structure of the suggested architecture for MS Word [2].

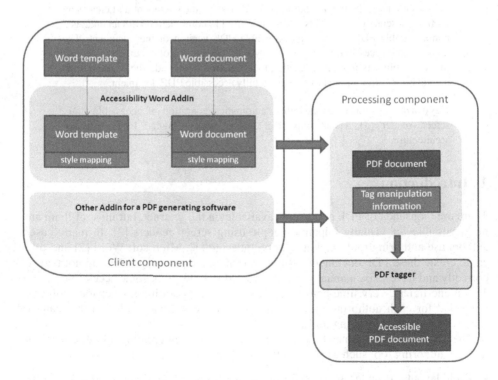

Fig. 1. Proposed software architecture for the generation of accessible PDFs

The architecture illustrated above consists of two components which can be implemented together on the authoring tool side or separately as client and server components:

2.1 Client Component

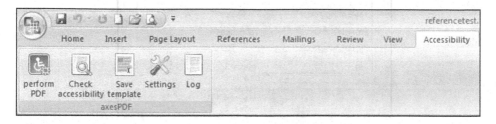

Fig. 2. Word Ribbon of Accessibility Add-in

This client component (authoring tool plug-in, see Fig. 2) executes the following steps:

- Accessibility Repair Tool (Fig. 3): Checks for accessibility problems associated with defined contents like headers, pictures, tables etc. and enables the author to correct them simply and easily.

PDF Tag Abdeckung		
Struktur Tag PDF	**axesAddin**	**PAW**
Headings / Überschriften	Ja	Teilweise
Alternativtext Bilder	Ja	Ja
Alternativtext Links	Ja	Nein
Tabellenüberschriften	Ja	Nein
Zitate / Blockquote	Ja	Nein
Saubere Dokumentensyntax	Ja	Nein
Listen	Ja	Ja

Fig. 3. Repair tool for table header issues

- Mapping (Fig. 4): Mapping of style sheets defined in an authoring tool (e.g. MS Word) to PDF tags. These mapping settings are then stored in the source document (in this case a Word document). The illustration shows, for example, that the "TableHeaderRow" style maps to the "Table header" tag in the PDF.

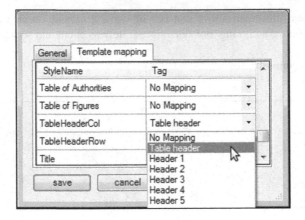

Fig. 4. Word style mapping to PDF tags

Based on the steps described above, an untagged PDF document and an XML document are generated. The XML document contains the structural elements (e.g. tables, form fields etc.) and their position in the Word document. This information is then used to tag the PDF document in the <Processing Component>.

2.2 Processing Component

This component uses the structural elements from the XML document and their positions to set the right tags in the PDF document (see Fig. 5).

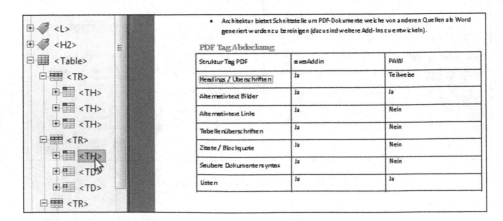

Fig. 5. PDF table structure tags

3 Use Cases

The following scenarios are planned for the use of the implemented software:

3.1 Use Case 1: Publishers

In large companies web publishers, among others, are responsible for generating templates. By using the client component described above web publishers can generate templates that are fully accessible. These can then be locked so that end users cannot subsequently modify them. This means that corporate identity and accessibility standards can be implemented without any need for end users to concern themselves specifically with the accessibility aspects.

3.2 Use Case 2: End Users

For small and medium-sized enterprises the implemented software can help end users to identify and resolve accessibility problems.

4 Existing Solutions

Tools that enable the production of tagged PDFs can be placed in the following categories:

1. Accessibility user support: Tools which in principle enable the production of tagged PDFs but which offer authors little or no help in identifying and dealing with accessibility issues when producing the source documents. These include MS Word [2], Open Office Writer [6] and Adobe Acrobat Professional [7].
2. Integrated pdf tagging component: Tools that have an integrated component for producing tagged PDFs and therefore do not require the installation of any add-ins.
3. Direct production of tagged PDFs: These tools come from Adobe inc. and require a license.

For almost all categories it is essential that the author be familiar with the accessibility requirements and knows how to put these into practice in the tool in question. One exception is:

- NetCentric PDF Accessibility Wizard for MS Office [4] Accessibility problems are highlighted with the support of a software assistant. The author of the Word document has the option of correcting the issues highlighted. The PDF tags are saved locally through the allocation of styles to the structured information and are therefore not incorporated into the document itself. The software is not language-sensitive, so for example the headings are recognized in a German document even if they are defined in English (e.g. Heading 1). This wizard is only available for MS Office.

5 Conclusion

This paper presents a new concept for a software architecture that enables the automatic generation of fully accessible PDF documents. The suggested software architecture enables a reusable infrastructure that can be used with any authoring tool to create accessible PDF documents. The implemented software prototype for MS Word [2] using an accessible PDF Word add-in is designed to resolve the issues mentioned in the introduction section of this paper. On the one hand the existing Word document is reviewed and assistance is offered to eliminate problems during the creation process. On the other hand, weak points that cannot be eliminated within Word [2] itself are analyzed and then eliminated using the external PDF tagger following export to PDF. The add-in can also be used to save documents as templates, whereby the structural information assigned to the user-defined styles is saved directly in the Word [2] file itself. Locked templates generated in this way can guarantee to a great extent the accessibility of documents created using these templates.

References

1. Adobe InDesign, http://www.adobe.com/products/indesign/
2. Microsoft Office Word, http://office.microsoft.com/word/
3. Freedom Scientific JAWS for Windows Screen Reading Software,
   http://www.freedomscientific.com/products/fs/
   jaws-product-page.asp
4. NetCentric PDF Accessibility Wizard for MS Office,
   http://www.net-centric.com/products/PAW.aspx
5. Microsoft Office (2010), http://us1.office2010beta.microsoft.com
6. Open Office Writer, http://www.openoffice.org
7. Adobe Acrobat Professional, http://www.adobe.com/products/acrobat

DAISY Kindergarten Books and Rocket Science Journals

John A. Gardner[1], Carolyn K Gardner[1], Vladimir Bulatov[1], Blake Jones[1],
Elizabeth Jones[1], Robert A. Kelly[2], Masakazu Suzuki[3], and Katsuhito Yamaguchi[4]

[1] ViewPlus Technologies, Inc, Corvallis, OR 97333 USA
john.gardner@viewplus.com, carolyn.gardner@viewplus.com,
vladimir.bulatov@viewplus.com, blake.jones@viewplus.com
elizabeth.jones@viewplus.com
[2] American Physical Society, Ridge, NY 11961 USA
rakelly@aps.org
[3] Kyushu University, Fukuoka 812-8521, Japan
suzuki@math.kyushu-u.ac.jp
[4] Nihon University, Junior College Funabashi Campus, Chiba 274-8501, Japan
eugene@mbg.nifty.com

Abstract. ViewPlus is creating universally-usable DAISY math and science
supplementary curricula for United States kindergarten and first grade children.
These books are rich in interactive, fully accessible graphics and may be read
with modern DAISY software readers. Graphics are accessed by audio/touch
using the ViewPlus IVEO technology. ViewPlus is also collaborating with the
American Physical Society (APS) to permit APS journals to be published in this
text+graphics DAISY format. APS is the leading publisher of professional
physics journals in the world. Examples of a DAISY first grade science book
and an APS journal article will be demonstrated at the conference.

Keywords: DAISY, IVEO, math/science, children, professional, graphics.

1 Introduction

DAISY (Digital accessible Information SYstem http://www.daisy.org) is an
international organization of non-profit libraries and agencies for people who are
blind or have other severe visual disabilities. DAISY has developed the industry
standard for creating synchronized text and voice presentation of written materials.
This format allows users to see as well as hear and easily navigate these materials.
The current DAISY XML format allows authors to include content such as graphics
and math. There are several DAISY reader software packages available that can
access this content. Both the GH Braille and the Dolphin EasyReader DAISY Readers
allow the inclusion of graphics. Other graphics-capable DAISY readers are under
development by other companies.

DAISY graphics are in Scalable Vector Graphics (SVG) format, an XML format
which allows the user to resize images as much as needed without loss of sharpness.
They are authored and displayed using IVEO Creator, software developed and
marketed by ViewPlus. The IVEO Viewer, which displays SVG images, is a free

K. Miesenberger et al. (Eds.): ICCHP 2010, Part I, LNCS 6179, pp. 53–56, 2010.
© Springer-Verlag Berlin Heidelberg 2010

application that can be downloaded from the ViewPlus web site and is bundled with software DAISY readers.

Math is also necessary for science and math literature. Math is accessible in DAISY books if authored using the MathML language. ViewPlus and DAISY are presently collaborating to define authoring guidelines, to define DAISY SVG attributes for improved access, and to expand SVG with additional namespaces to increase its capabilities for both accessibility and mainstream usefulness.

The IVEO Hands-On-Learning System supports more advanced SVG capabilities including linking to internal and external information, playing audio files, and using Javascript to create highly flexible SVG applications. ViewPlus is currently using Javascript in developing supporting computer software to add feedback to the graphics pages in its DAISY book curricula. It is using additional DAISY namespaces to permit inclusion of quantitative data in physics figures. ViewPlus and the Infty group are collaborating to improve recognition of math expressions and to include MathML for all math expressions found in graphics.

2 ViewPlus Math and Science DAISY Books for Small Children

Math and science are difficult subjects for many children, and they are particularly difficult for those with visual or learning disabilities. Mathematics and science, especially in the early years, are very visual subjects. In mathematics, young students are counting, comparing, and representing numbers. They are joining and separating sets, describing shapes and space, and comparing measurable traits of objects or sets. For example, arranging two-digit numbers in columns to add or subtract is an extremely visual construct. Additionally, viewing addition as combining groups or subtraction as take-away involves a visual aspect in picturing objects to be added or taken away.

In science, young children are learning about the world around them including plants and animals, the earth, movement, the human body, and basic forces. Much of this learning is through observation and exploring what they see. For example, sighted students know what the moon is, how it looks, and can see that it seems to change over time. These are ideas that a visually impaired child can be told but it is hard to make it more than an abstract concept for them because sight is the only sense we can use to learn about the moon. So, students with visual disabilities are at a disadvantage in both mathematics and science learning from the beginning.

ViewPlus is developing a range of accessible DAISY math and science supplementary curricula to address the issues that many students, in particular visually impaired students, face. These curricula meet United States national and state mathematics and science standards (1, 4). Additionally, these curricula allow students to access information in a variety of ways. Using IVEO technology developed and marketed by ViewPlus, these books will enable students to simultaneously see, hear and touch the math and science they are studying. Thus, allowing children to learn in the ways that work best for them. They can access information through touch, sound, sight or any combination of these three learning modalities. The current curricula are at the kindergarten and first grade level, developed for students approximately five to seven years of age. It is widely believed that by making these books universally accessible, they are almost automatically better for all students than those that are not useful to children with print disabilities.

3 Publishing American Physical Society Journals in DAISY Form

The American Physical Society (APS) has committed to being the first major publisher to publish its scientific journals in DAISY XML format. APS converted its publishing methodology years ago to an XML (eX-tensible Markup Language) work flow in order to permit straightforward re-purposing of its content. After APS and ViewPlus collaborated on a research project in 2008(5) to demonstrate the feasibility of repurposing APS XML to DAISY XML, APS realized that DAISY XML could be far more useful to everybody than APS' present paper and PDF publications. In 2009 APS, ViewPlus, and several other agencies and companies joined to form the Enhanced Reading Group that would develop software and infrastructure to enable APS and other publishers to create rich, highly-accessible DAISY XML content(6). This is not charity for the blind. APS will publish DAISY XML articles because DAISY XML provides much more value for money to all subscribers.

No human labor is required to transform APS text and math into DAISY XML. A computer can do it automatically. A straightforward XSLT (eXtensible Style Language Transform) transforms APS XML to DAISY format. During this transformation, a utility made by Design Science, Inc. automatically adds an image of the math and a text description. The images and descriptive text are required in DAISY XML files for use by playback devices that are not fully MathML-aware.

The major unavoidable difficulty for APS in creating DAISY XML articles is the necessity of converting PostScript figures to highly accessible SVG. The present printing technology requires that paper printing still be done from the PostScript files, so the SVG files must be made solely for the DAISY XML files. Fortunately, several composition vendor members of the Enhanced Reading Group have already developed prototype conversion methodologies using some of their current graphics conversion software, to save as SVG versions at very little additional labor cost. These SVG images can easily be added to a folder containing all other electronic information for a given article. In the end, a single computer application can process this folder to convert the APS XML to DAISY, insert appropriate links for the SVG, and process the SVG files, to assure that they are as rich and accessible as possible. The DAISY XML article that is created by this computerized procedure should require negligible additional human labor beyond what is presently required for creating and publishing APS articles. Very low cost is critical.

APS plans to distribute DAISY XML as an additional option to their present procedure for making PDF files available to APS journal subscribers. In addition to the choice of downloading a PDF or opening it in a PDF reader, the future subscriber can opt to download a DAISY XML article or read it in a DAISY Reader. An on-line DAISY Reader is under development so that any APS subscriber can use any web browser, including mobile phones, to read articles. Blind readers can use a screen reader and a browser that supports MathML and SVG accessibility. Presently, only Internet Explorer with the Design Science MathPlayer plug-in and the ViewPlus IVEO plug-in is capable of providing full access for blind readers. Blind users can also opt to download the APS DAISY XML file, which will not be subject to any digital rights software control, and read it in any modern scientific DAISY Reader.

Initial publications, processed as described above, will use presentation MathML as presently created in the composition process. Consequently, these publications will not have math content that is as rich in content or accessibility as it could be. Improved authoring methods should increase the accessibility and usefulness of MathML.

Initial images will be accessible only if audio access to the visible text and math is sufficient. There will be no titles or descriptions for figures, because these cannot be inserted by a computer. No quantitative data will be present, because there is no practical means of introducing it. Nonetheless many figures in physics articles are reasonably accessible without these additions.

Future authoring applications that can save as DAISY SVG would be an excellent way to improve the richness and accessibility of figures. Generally these authoring applications could include all the data, the titles of data sets, titles of fitting lines, etc. Such figures would be highly desirable for all readers and can be extremely accessible. ViewPlus is presently creating software that could save such rich information from several applications including GIS and x-y data plots software.

Acknowledgements

DAISY book development and the Enhanced Reading Group project have been supported in part by a Phase II SBIR grant from the National Eye Institute of the US National Institutes of Health.

References

1. Center for Science, Mathematics, and Engineering Education. National Science Education Standards. National Academy Press, Washington (1996)
2. Ginn, P.: Meta-analysis of the modality effect. Learning and Instruction 15(4), 313–331 (2005)
3. Mayer, R.: Multimedia learning: Are we asking the right question? Educational Psychologist 32(1), 1–19 (1997)
4. National Council of Teachers of Mathematics. Principles and Standards for School Mathematics. Author, Reston (2000)
5. Kasdorf, B.: ViewPlus Makes Images Accessible to the Sight-Impaired (Including Computers). Society for Scholarly Publishing web news (July 2008),
   http://www.viewplus.com/about/news/#n2066p (Retrieved January 2009)
6. Gardner, J., Bulatov, V., Kelly, R.: Making Journals Accessible to the Visually-Impaired – The Future is Near. Learned Publishing 22(4), 314–319 (2009)

Exploiting the Daisy Format for Automated, Single-Source Braille Publishing

Lars Ballieu Christensen

Synscenter Refsnæs and Sensus ApS,
Torvet 3-5, 2.tv.,
DK-3400 Hillerød, Denmark
lbc@robobraille.org

Abstract. This paper presents the background and status of the projects and discusses opportunities and challenges of the AutoBraille/NorBraille approach of using Daisy talking books as the foundation for creating well-formatted, multi-volume Braille books ready for embossing. Whereas the current R&D projects are limited to relatively simple document structures, preliminary research suggests that it will be possible to automatically process even complicated math and science titles.

Keywords: Braille transcription, Daisy, DTB, RoboBraille, single-source publishing, accessibility, visual impairment.

1 Introduction

In an effort to increase availability and quality of Braille material, enable customised Braille productions and reducing the overall cost of producing Braille, Sensus and the National Danish Centre for Visual Impairment for Children and Youth (Synscenter Refsnæs) have worked with the national libraries for the blind in Denmark and Norway to enable fully automated Braille production based on well-structured Daisy books [7]. Using Daisy Talking Books (DTBs) as input, the output are well-formatted, multi-volume Grade 1 and Grade 2 Braille books ready for embossing. Thus far this has resulted in two projects: The AutoBraille project with Danish Library for People with Reading Deficiencies (2008-) and the NorBraille with the Norwegian Library for the Blind (2009-). A similar project will commence in Iceland in 2010 in collaboration with the Icelandic Institute for blind, visually impaired and deaf-blind individuals with the aim of producing books in Icelandic Braille. To a large extend, the work has been inspired by previous work on automated Braille translation, see for example [1], [2], 3], [4] and [5].

The rationale behind the projects is simple: while significant efforts are being invested in scanning, proofing, tagging and validating documents for production of Daisy Talking Books, the resulting source files are rarely used for other purposes. However, documents that have been tagged for DTB production may well contain all the information required for producing material in other alternative formats including Braille, large print and customized formats, making the Daisy format an ideal master format for single-source publishing. In addition to enabling automating production

K. Miesenberger et al. (Eds.): ICCHP 2010, Part I, LNCS 6179, pp. 57–61, 2010.

workflows, it is anticipated that the reuse of master files for multiple purposes will eventually reduce the cost of individual productions. The concept of single-source publishing is illustrated in Figure 1 below:

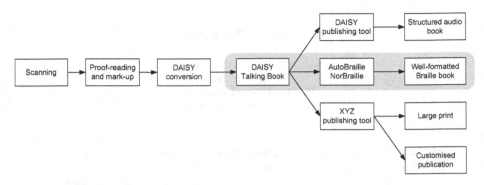

Fig. 1. The concept of single-source publishing to produce material in a variety of alternative formats including Daisy Talking Books, Braille, Large print and customized formats.

The paper presents the background and status of these two projects and discusses opportunities and challenges of the AutoBraille/NorBraille approach, including limitations in terms of the complexity of documents: Whereas the current R&D projects are limited to relatively simple document structures (e.g., TOCs, headings, notes, lists, images, poems), preliminary research suggests that it will soon be possible to automatically process even complicated math and science titles using a combination of 8-dot Braille, LaTeX/MathML, Daisy mark-up, automated Braille translation and AutoBraille/NorBraille.

2   Braille Codes and Formatting Guidelines

Although Braille codes are well-documented and have been used extensively to automatically transform documents into Braille, the formatting specifications are less stringent. In Denmark, no formal layout specification for Braille material appeared to exist; rather, different formatting regimes were implemented at each of the four main production centres. In Norway, a formal layout specification exists but implementation varies across production centres [8] and [9]. Hence, the initial part of each project was to define the how each Daisy tag should be treated in a Braille context.

In general terms, formatting requirements were divided into two overall categories for processing by AutoBraille/NorBraille. The first category covered structural elements from the Daisy specification that are mainly used for formatting and reference purposes, and included major structural elements, block elements, tables and lists. The second category covered inline elements as well as attributes and classes on other elements that directly impacts how the Braille is constructed. These included tags for emphasis, acronyms, abbreviations, anchors, and changes to the natural languages and page numbering scheme. The first category of tags was implemented in the AutoBraille/NorBraille formatting component, while tags and attributes of the latter were implemented in the SB4 contraction engine. SB4 also forms the foundation for Braille translation in the RoboBraille service, and supports translation between ordinary text and contracted/uncontracted Braille in multiple languages [1], [2] and [3].

Braille readers usually make up a rather conservative group who insists on adhering to standard Braille specifications; however, when the first results of AutoBraille were presented to a representative group of Braille readers, it was decided to implement two different levels of formatting regimes: a rigid regime that formats according to the formal specifications, and a loose regime that formats according to user preferences.

3 NorBraille Implementation

Though implemented using different technologies, the AutoBraille and NorBraille share many characteristics. For reasons of simplicity, only the NorBraille project is discussed in dept in this paper. The figure 2 below illustrates the architecture and main components of NorBraille.

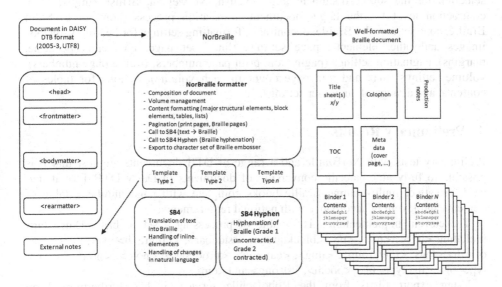

Fig. 2. The NorBraille architecture

As can be seen from Figure 2, a Daisy document (DTB, 2005-3 in UTF8) is passed to NorBraille along with a set of external notes. In effect, the external notes are generated from the list of options in a settings file, and used to generate the production notes presented in the final document.

The solution is comprised by three main components:

1. The NorBraille formatter composes the document based on options in a settings file. As such, the formatter creates the title page (from meta data), the document colophon (from meta data), the production notes (from options settings), table of contents (from structural elements and page numbers), cover

page as well as the actual contents of the document. The formatter furthermore divides the documents into one or more binders depending options settings. Also subject to options settings, the formatter paginates the document with print and Braille page numbers. It processes and formats all major structural elements (e.g. headers), block elements, tables and headers. Finally, the formatter is managing calls to the underlying SB4 Braille translation and Hyphenation engines.

2. The SB4 Braille Translation engine translates text to and from Braille according to the specified language, contraction level and process definition. Furthermore, it handles inline elements and changes in the natural language flow according to language-specific definitions.

3. The SB4 Braille Hyphenation engine hyphenates contracted and uncontracted according to language-specific hyphenation rules.

The overall process is managed by a set of parameters defined in a settings file. Hence, a settings file is in effect a document template that specifies how a particular document should be contracted. Available parameters include natural language selection for the source document (e.g., Danish, Norwegian, British English, …), contraction level for the target document, translation process (contract to 8-dot Braille, contract to 6-dot Braille, decontract), formatting settings for headings, blocks, images and other elements, page settings (lines per page, characters per line, margins), pagination settings (pagination, print page numbers, Braille page numbers), volume settings (max and min page count in each volume), options for tables of contents, and a range of embosser settings.

4   Preliminary Results

Preliminary tests with NorBraille and a range of DTB documents suggest that it is possible to fully automate the conversion of documents in Daisy DTB format into well-formatted, multi-volume Braille books complete with page numbers, table of contents and layout in accordance with national requirements.

The current implementation is capable of processing a set of basic Daisy tags including <h1>…<h6>, <p>, <blockquote>, <sidebar>, <epigraph>, various classes of <div> tags, <imggroup>, <img>, <caption>, <prodnote>, <note>, <noteref>, <list type=ol>, <list type=ul>, <poem>, <strong> and <em>.

Using export filters from the RoboBraille service, it has furthermore been demonstrated that the resulting digital Braille documents can exported from the internal OctoBraille character set of the SB4 Braille translation engine [4] to be embossed on a variety of Braille embossers, including embossers from Index and Braillo.

In terms of speed, processing of book-size documents, including contraction to the selected contraction level, composition, pagination and layout formatting is completed in 20-30 seconds on a standard computer.

5   Future Potential

Preliminary results suggest that it will be possible to automate the production of well-formatted Braille documents from source documents in DTB format including a most tag types found in the Daisy specification. Based on the current results of the NorBraille implementation, two additional phases have been proposed, each aimed at exploring the possibilities of extending support for documents containing more complex structures and content. Phase 2, schedules to commence in 2010, is aimed at exploring how it may be possible to process tables with of varying complexity, as well as adding support for preview/post editing capabilities. Furthermore, export capabilities will be extended to support the Portable Embosser Format, PEF [6].

Building on the experiences from the first two phases, phase 3 due to commence in 2011, is planned to explore how documents containing math and other scientific notation may be automatically converted into Braille using LaTeX or MathML in combination with DTB. The phase will furthermore how support for technical drawings and other complicated illustrations may be supported.

6 Conclusions

The current AutoBraille/NorBraille projects have documented that it is possible to produce well-formed, multi-volume Braille documents using the DTB format as the source. Preliminary results furthermore suggest that it will be possible to automate the processing of documents with more complex structures (e.g., tables) and content (e.g., math and scientific notation), thus automating the production of Braille editions of textbooks in a variety of different subjects.

Ultimately, it is suggested that the AutoBraille/NorBraille approach has the potential of significantly increasing availability and quality of Braille material while reducing the cost through reuse.

References

1. Christensen, L.B.: Multilingual Two-Way Braille Translation. In: Klaus, J., et al. (eds.) Interdisciplinary Aspects on Computers Helping People with Special Needs, Österreichische Computer Gesellschaft/R. Oldenbourg Wien München (1996)
2. Christensen, L.B.: RoboBraille – Automated Braille Translation by Means of an Email Robot. In: Miesenberger, K., Klaus, J., Zagler, W.L., Karshmer, A.I. (eds.) ICCHP 2006. LNCS, vol. 4061, pp. 1102–1109. Springer, Heidelberg (2006)
3. Christensen, L.B.: RoboBraille – Braille Unlimited. The Educator. ICEVI 2009 XXI(2), 32–37 (2009)
4. Christensen, L.B., Thougaard, S.: The OctoBraille character set. Web document, http://www.sensus.dk/sb4/OctoBraille1252.pdf
5. Christensen, L.B., Thougaard, S.: Report on pilot test. Deliverable 4.2 in eTEN RoboBraille Market Validation (2007) (available from the authors)
6. Håkansson, J.: PEF 1.0 - Portable Embosser Format, Public draft. Daisy Consortium (2009), http://www.daisy.org/projects/braille/braille_workarea/pef/pef-specification.html
7. Specifications for the Digital Talking Book, ANSI/NISO Z39.86-2005. National Information Standards Organization (2005), http://www.daisy.org/z3986/2005/Z3986-2005.html
8. Håndbok i litterær punktskrift, Offentlig utvalg for blindeskrift, OUB (2008)
9. Norsk Punktskrift Del 4, Standard for utforming av bøker i punktskrift, Huseby Kompetesesenter (1995)

Rapid Listening of DAISY Digital Talking Books by Speech-Rate Conversion Technology for People with Visual Impairments

Naoyuki Tazawa[1], Shinichi Totihara[3], Yukio Iwahana[1], Atsushi Imai[1],
Nobumasa Seiyama[1], and Toru Takagi[2]

[1] NHK Engineering Services, INC.
1-10-11, Kinuta Setagaya-ku, Tokyo, 157-8540, Japan
{tazawa,iwahana,imai,seiyama}@nes.or.jp
[2] NHK(Japan Broadcasting Corp.) Science & Technology Research Laboratories,
1-10-11, Kinuta Setagaya-ku, Tokyo, 157-8540, Japan
takagi.t-fo@nhk.or.jp
[3] Keio Research Institute at SFC
5322 Endo, Fujisawa 252-8520, Japan
torihara@sfc.keio.ac.jp

Abstract. We have performed studies and evaluation experiments of more acceptable rapid speech, aimed at implementation in applications such as installation in commercial devices designed for visually impaired persons. Although our method's playback time is same as the conventional High-speed playback technology, listener might feel playing in slower speeds and listen words clearer. Our proposal technology makes it possible to adaptive speech rate control in utterance position and pitch/power in the speech information, instead of changing the speed of the utterance uniformly. We performed an experiment in Japanese and American subject with visual impairments respectively to compare the conventional high-speed playback technology and that of our adaptive high-speed playback technology in terms of "Listenability". The reaction to our proposal method from subjects with visual impairments has been very positive underscoring its potential as an effective tool for listening to high-speed speech.

Keywords: DAISY, digital talking books, Visual impairment, Rapid listening, Assistive Technology.

1 Introduction

In this work we explored a listener-friendly scheme for playing back recorded speech at faster rates than normal tailored specifically for people with visual impairments, based on NHK's speech-rate conversion technology. In contrast to the widely used conventional method that plays back accelerated speech at the same uniform faster rate from beginning to end, in our approach the playback rate is varied adaptively depending on the point within the spoken phrase and fluctuations in the pitch and power of the speaker. With the goal of developing a robust speech data playback

K. Miesenberger et al. (Eds.): ICCHP 2010, Part I, LNCS 6179, pp. 62–68, 2010.
© Springer-Verlag Berlin Heidelberg 2010

system for the market that is tailored for blind and partially sighted users, we investigated an algorithm that moves us closer to practical implementation of such a device, and we conducted a series of side-by-side evaluations to compare the listening experience of our method versus the conventional method.

The response from visually impaired persons were very positive, thus confirming the excellent potential of the proposed scheme for implementing a useful assistive tool for listening to recorded speech at faster than normal rates. This paper provides a summary overview of this work.

This adaptive speech-rate conversion approach should also work with English and other languages besides Japanese. Later in the paper we describe a preliminary assessment trial of our method optimized for English on a group of English speaking test subjects with visual impairments.

2 Overview

People with visual impairments obtain much of their information from speech. Most commonly, information is obtained from talking books prepared from novels, magazines, and other printed materials; and from text information on the web read out using a screen reader. However, many have complained that given the sequential nature of speech, it is sometimes harder to grasp the overall content from speech compared to print material. For this reason, many people speed up the normal playback of talking books and screen readers to jump ahead, and many have indicated that they would like to listen at even faster speeds if possible [1][2][3]. This led us to survey vision impaired users of these kinds of playback devices to see if there was any demand for a more advanced text-to-speech system, and to investigate the shortcomings and issues associated with the most widely used playback system, the DAISY (Digital Accessible Information SYstem) talking-book player. In addition to the DAISY player there are a number of other high-speed speech playback systems on the market, but none has given much thought to the listenability factor so they are all very hard to listen to at playback speeds of 2 times the normal rate and beyond. It was this situation that led us to the present challenge of developing an even faster speech playback scheme, or that offers a more pleasurable listening experience at the same playback speeds at the conventional method.

3 Listenability Algorithm

We incorporated NHK's speech-rate conversion technology into our algorithm [4][5][7]. In contrast to the prevailing method in which the speech rate is uniformly altered from beginning to end, NHK's technology varies the playback rate adaptively depending on the point within the spoken phrase and fluctuations in the pitch and power of the speaker. As illustrated in Figure 1, the phrase starts out at a low speech rate but then becomes faster in the latter half of the phrase. In addition, segments in the speech where the pitch and power of the speaker's voice are acoustically higher are extracted and slowed down, while segments where the pitch and power are lower are speeded up.

This combination of techniques should have the effect of making the recorded speech sound less hurried even when it is speeded up. Primary objectives of this work

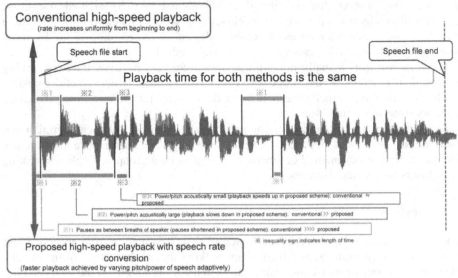

Rather than a uniform rate of increase from beginning to end of the speech file, speed processing varies the pitch and power of the speech adaptively.
Portions needed to understand (power and pitch are high) are prolonged and slowly absorbed, so important information is not greatly impaired at playback and content is easily grasped when played back at high speed. This also alleviates listening fatigue.
Places where power and pitch are low such as pauses between breaths of the speaker are shortened, so there is no delay in the playback time.

Fig. 1. Comparison of the proposed speech-rate conversion method and the conventional method

is to see if this sense of leisureliness translates into better listenability, and to determine if this adaptive approach can meet the needs of those visually impaired users who have been calling for faster playback rates. One might assume that, because speech starts out at a low speech rate and high pitch and power segments are slowed down, the proposed scheme take longer than the conventional method, but such is not the case. By shortening the pauses between phrases or when the speaker takes a breath, the playback time of the two schemes is the same.

In applying the algorithm that was developed for Japanese directly to English speech, we ran into a number of problems. Because of the different accents of the two languages, it was found that a short interval at the beginning of some words is necessary to hear the words correctly and when that little interval is missing, it becomes difficult to understand the meaning of those words. We are now reexamining the distribution of pitch and power detected when performing the speech-rate conversion to optimize the scheme for the unique attributes of English pronunciation.

4   Performance Evaluation

4.1   Perception of Slowness and Listenability(Japanese)

We conducted a study to compare the *perception of slowness* and listenability of the conventional fast playback scheme used on DAISY talking-book players and our proposed adaptive speech-rate conversion method using 19 subjects (ranging in age from 20s to 60s) with visual impairments. In other words, we did a side-by-side comparison and independently evaluated the perception of slowness and the listenability of identical spoken phrases converted using the conventional method and our proposed method.

We prepared five different types of samples covering a good range of situations where the high-speed speech might actually be used including: two samples prepared for DAISY talking-book players, a news broadcast, and a radio program. Five different speech-rate conversion playback rates were tested ranging from 1 to 3 times the normal rate. We observed similar responses for the five different types of content, so we aggregated the results in Figure 2. First in terms of listenability, the conventional scheme scored better up to speeds of 1.5 times the normal rate, but the proposed method performed better at 2 times the normal speed and higher. Turning to perception of slowness, the subjects preferred the sample converted using the proposed method at every conversion rate, thus demonstrating the effectiveness of the proposed method for enabling listeners to comprehend the faster playback speech.

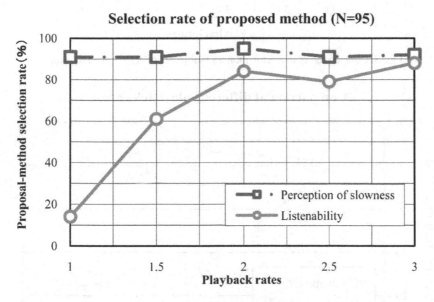

Fig. 2. Comparison of perception of slowness and listenability for the two methods

4.2 Listening Comprehension Results(Japanese)

We conducted a listening comprehension test in which 34 subjects answered questions based on speech samples that were processed using the conventional method and the proposed method at conversion rates ranging from 2 to 5 times the normal rate, and the results are shown in Figure 3. As one can see, the percentage of correct responses was about 50% for both the conventional and proposed methods at 2 times the normal rate, but the percentage of correct responses fell precipitously to less than 10% using the conventional method at 5 times the normal rate. By contrast, the percentage of correct responses for our proposed method fell slightly but still

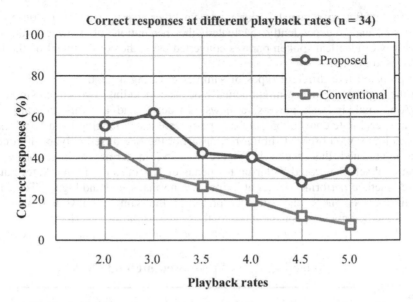

Fig. 3. Comparison of correct responses (subjects not accustomed to rapid

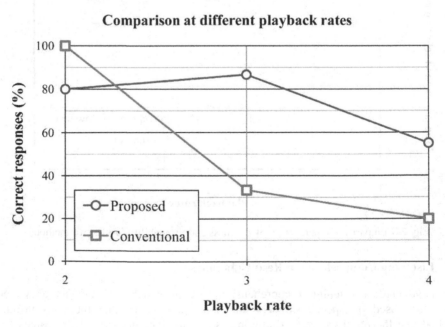

Fig. 4. Comparison of correct responses (subjects accustomed to rapid playback)

achieved 40% correct responses at 5 times the normal rate. The proposed method thus shows enormous potential as a high-speed playback scheme that enhances listenability while accelerating speech up to 5 times the normal rate with no great loss in comprehension. We also administered the same listening comprehension test to a select group of 5 subjects who are accustomed to listening to accelerated speech, and the results are presented in Figure 4. As one can see, using the proposed speech-rate conversion scheme, the percentage of correct responses was 100% at 2 times the normal rate and over 50% at 4 times the normal rate.

4.3 Assessment of Spoken English Content(English)

After adjusting our algorithm for English, we compared our proposed method with the conventional method using 11 visually impaired English-speaking subjects at the Blind Community Center of San Diego. We prepared 24 different samples including an except from a CNN news story, TOEIC listening test questions, and English DAISY talking-book content, which we played at three different speed increments ranging from 2 to 4 times the normal speaking rate, and we asked the subjects to tell us if one version was easier to understand than the other, or to not respond if they could not differentiate the two. Here we define speech speed rates in terms of number of syllables per second using the DAISY talking-book standard playback rate of about 5 syllables per second (*i.e.*, 1 time the normal speech rate), such that a playback speed of 10 syllables per second would be 2 times the normal rate, and so on.

Figure 5 shows the acceptance rates for the two playback schemes. One can see that at playback rates ranging from 2 to 3 times the normal speech rate, more than 70% of the subjects evaluated the proposed scheme highly. At 4 times the normal speech rate, the acceptance rate for the proposed scheme fell to 40% while the non responses increased, but this was still a marked improvement over the conventional scheme. These findings are encouraging and demonstrate that our proposed method significantly enhances the listenability of English when played back at faster than normal rates of speed.

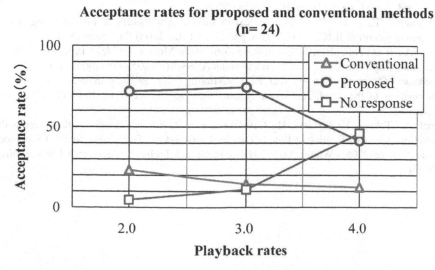

Fig. 5. English acceptance rates for the proposed scheme versus the conventional scheme at different playback rates

5 Conclusions

In this work we established that our proposed adaptive speech rate conversion method provides a greater sense of unhurried speech than the conventional DAISY talking-book approach at the same rates of accelerated playback. And in terms of listenability, we demonstrated that the proposed method is a valuable assistive tool for listening to recorded speech at rates 2 times the normal speed and faster. While previous studies as recently as 2005 set their sites on playback speeds up to 3 times the normal rate [6], we have shattered this record and shown that even faster playback rates are feasible with reasonable comprehension. Good listenability at faster playback not only alleviates fatigue when listening to recorded speech for long periods, it also promises to open new horizons for value-added applications. To the extent that this adaptive speech-rate conversion method helps people—visually impaired and normal sighted people alike— understand and enjoy listening to recorded speech, we can expect it will see widespread adoption in applications for a wide cross-section of people.

References

1. Watanabe, T.: A Study on Voice Settings of Screen Readers for Visually-Impaired PC Users. IEICE Transactions on Information and Systems, D-I J88-D-I (8), 1257–1260 (2005) (in Japanese)
2. Torihara, S.: An Oblique Listening Method for the Blind and Visually impaired. In: The Sixteenth Annual Conference on Technology and Persons with Disabilities, CSUN 2001. California State University, Northridge (March 2001)
3. Torihara, S., Nakamura, M., Ueda, N., Wada, T., Ishizaki, S.: English "Oblique" Listening System – Rapid Listening System for the Blind and Visually Impaired, and Its Evaluation. In: Miesenberger, K., Klaus, J., Zagler, W.L., Karshmer, A.I. (eds.) ICCHP 2006. LNCS, vol. 4061, pp. 53–60. Springer, Heidelberg (2006)
4. Nishimoto, T., et al.: Evaluation of text-to-speech synthesizers at fast speaking rates. Technical Report of IEICE, WIT2005-5, pp. 23–28 (May 2005) (in Japanese)
5. Imai, A., et al.: An Adaptive Speech-Rate Conversion Method for News Programs without Accumulating Time Delay. IEICE Transactions A J83-A(8), 935–945 (2000) (in Japanese)
6. Asakawa, C., et al.: The optimal and maximum listening rates in presenting speech information to the blind. Journal of Human Interface Society 7(1), 105–111 (2005) (in Japanese)
7. Imai, A., Takagi, T., Takeishi, H.: Development of Radio and Television Receivers with Functions to Assist Hearing of Elderly People. In: Broadcast Technology No.35, Combined Issue Autumn 2008 - Winter 2009 (NHK Science and Technology Research Laboratories) (2009)

E-Books and Audiobooks: What about Their Accessibility?

Jan Engelen

Katholieke Universiteit Leuven, ESAT-SCDocarch
Kasteelpark Arenberg 10 box 2442, B-3001 Leuven (Belgium)
jan.engelen@esat.kuleuven.be

Abstract. Widespread distribution of electronic book readers, commonly called "e-readers" seems to have taken off seriously over the last year. Although the first e-readers popped up almost twenty years ago, last year's market appearance of a completely reworked Amazon Kindle 2, a new series of Sony PRS readers and several Bookeen & Cybook devices made e-books quite popular. All of them can store thousands of books, are extremely light weight and very mince. Many of them however present problems for persons with low vision or blindness. We will discuss briefly the situation and possible solutions.

1 Introduction

One of the major, recent e-book reader improvements is linked to the display technology: so called *e-ink* pages [1] are using battery power only during a text change; in between their power consumption is almost nil. Battery life for these devices now routinely extends to one or two weeks. E-ink screens however do not produce light: one needs ambient lighting on the screen to see the text. The International Digital Publishing Forum (IDPF) provides impressive statistics on the booming US e-book industry [2].

E-books (as opposed to e-book readers) have yet to gain global distribution. Amazon provides a huge amount of e-books, but only in their own (Kindle) format and up to now only in English. Publishers in other languages often prefer the more open ePub format (e.g. BE & NL).

Furthermore, not all authors have endorsed the concept of electronic publishing. J.K Rowling, author of the Harry Potter series, has stated that there will be no e-versions of her books...[3]

E-books can easily be obtained from many internet book stores. Two bottlenecks do remain however: their price (often still at almost the same level as printed copies...) and a copyright protection mechanism that hinders changing the electronic format of a book (consequently, when a person buys another brand of e-reader, previously bought e-books become unusable).

E-books and audiobooks have been discussed by the author at previous occasions [4]. This contribution focuses on recent developments only.

K. Miesenberger et al. (Eds.): ICCHP 2010, Part I, LNCS 6179, pp. 69–73, 2010.

2 E-Book Formats

Current e-books are made to several different standards with their own advantages and disadvantages, which will briefly be described below.

Besides popular formats such as HTML, RTF and PDF that can be read by all e-book readers, following major e-book standards are commonly used[5]:

- Amazon Kindle has his own format, loosely based on an older French Mobi-pocket format
- Sony and many other e-book readers use the ePub format (Open standard for e-books)
- the Cybooks use an Adobe protected PDF format

Except for public domain books, an encryption feature (DRM, Digital rights management) is used on all e-books.

3 E-Book Distribution

Evidently most e-books simply can be downloaded from the internet.

As a few years ago, internet was not yet routinely available when travelling (and therefore buying books on the move was not possible), Amazon decided to distribute the Kindle books through Whispernet which is based on mobile network technology (3G, EDGE...). The cost of the data connection is covered by Amazon (and constitutes part of the e-book price). Up till last year it was impossible to download Kindle books within Europe as Amazon's Whispernet was not available. Since then agreements with EU mobile providers have been made.

4 Using E-Book Readers as Audiobook or Talking Book Devices

Starting with the Kindle-2[6] in 2009, a text-to-speech module has been incorporated in an e-reader device. This feature permitted to listen to the text and was very much appreciated by print impaired persons (persons with low vision, blindness, dyslexia or a severe motor handicap). Unfortunately this possibility was turned off soon after by Amazon unless the author had explicitly agreed with it or if public domain books (= mainly elder books) are read. In practice many authors and publishers opted out and the ban on text-to-speech output was almost general.

This lead to several US cases in court (e.g. National Federation of the Blind *vs* the Arizona State University).This university had planned to provide university course material in Kindle DX format only which was seen by NFB as a discriminatory measure.

On January 10, 2010 a settlement was reached in which ASU promised to provide course material in accessible formats in parallel with the Kindle format[7].

Another bottleneck is situated in commanding the e-reader itself. Up to now no auditory feedback was produced when pressing buttons or choosing commands on the device. But in the summer of 2010 a new Kindle should become available in which the speech output can be used for accessing the menu functions and an extra large font will be added so that the device is more usable for persons with low vision[8]. However nothing apparently will change for the text-to-speech blocking for most books…

5 Audiobooks/Talking Books

The distinction between commercial audiobooks and specially developed talking books for reading impaired users has been discussed extensively in our ICCHP 2008 paper.

The major conclusions were:

- Specialised audiobooks are produced within state supported production centres (directly or indirectly, e.g. when libraries get state funding to buy the audiobooks from the production centres).

   Commercial audiobooks constitute one of the more recent channels for literature distribution
- Specialised audiobooks use the Daisy format (cf. below), the commercial ones often are just a collection of mp3 files (with or without DRM) or use specialised formats with DRM protection built-in (e.g. Audible.com and its *.aa format).

It is clear that a system that would permit to turn any e-book into an audiobook[9] would be highly appreciated by print impaired users.

6 Daisy Format E-Books (and Audio-Books)

For use within the community of print impaired persons an e-book/audiobook standard has been developed almost 15 years ago. The Daisy format not only links the text to the audio version of the same book but permits also an extensive tree-like navigation through the document. This results in easy jumping to parts of the book, including up to the sixth level down in a table of contents. Furthermore Daisy permits to produce several kinds of e-books such as text-only, audio-only, text & audio, text & images etc[10].

Daisy is promoted by the Daisy consortium and some of their standards are nowadays recognised by international bodies[11].

Daisy books technically consist of a collection of computer files that can be stored on a cd (very popular as it can be read with a portable cd player) but also on any other computer medium including SD-cards (popular for pocket size readers) and simply via the internet.

Despite a decennium of efforts, the Daisy standard is still not in use outside the field of print impaired users. To make it more popular several open-source software solutions have been developed. So is it possible to produce a Daisy talking book directly from within Microsoft Word[12].

Within the European Aegis project three add-ons for OpenOffice.org (file extension: *.odt) have been developed at K.U.Leuven[13]:

- an odt to Daisy convertor (xml output)
- an odt to Daisy talking book convertor
- an odt to Braille convertor – still under development

The Daisy consortium currently focuses its efforts on:

- the DAISY Online Delivery Protocol: this is basically a definition of SOAP messages permitting easy web based content provision [14].
- Daisy version 4.0: this standard will permit an easier transfer of e-books and talking books to the popular ePub format for e-books (mentioned above)
- copyright protection for Daisy books.
  Up to now such protection was deemed unnecessary as special equipment or software was needed to read a Daisy book.

7 Social Networks and Accessible Documents and E-Books

The current popularity of social networks and widely distributed high speed internet connections makes it possible to try out new ideas for accessible document production. One of them is "Collaborative Barrier Freedom" or "Access Commons", a system in which volunteers will turn inaccessible web pages, documents and e-books into accessible ones. The system is in place for web pages but for e-books additional copyright hurdles have still to be taken [15].

8 Conclusions

It can be stated that the market of e-books and e-readers finally has taken off. Although the phenomenon in general terms still remains a by-product of standard and traditional book publishing, new applications e.g. for print impaired persons seem to be growing. But a tough copyright hurdle is still to be taken before e-books routinely also will become audio- or talking books.

Remark

This ICCHP contribution is a reworked and updated version of my previous presentations to both ICCHP 2008 and ELPUB [16].

Acknowledgements

The author would like to acknowledge the help of the Aegis and Kamelego projects in preparing this contribution. Furthermore the support of the Kath. Univ. Leuven is highly appreciated.

References

1. Wikipedia entry for e-ink, http://en.wikipedia.org/wiki/E_Ink
2. The trend figures and numbers collected by the International Digital Publishing Forum can be found at, http://www.idpf.org/doc_library/industrystats.htm

3. This statement is based on fear for piracy. Ironically enough all Harry Potter books have been turned (illegally) into e-books within hours of the release of the printed version, `http://www.bradsreader.com/2009/01/` `jk-rowling-harry-potter-ebooks-and-the-definition-of-irony/`
4. Engelen, J.: Marketing Issues related to Commercial and Specialised Audiobooks, including Digital Daily Newspapers. In: Mornati, S., Hedlund, T. (eds.) ELPUB 2009, Milano, Italy, June 10-12, pp. 621–624 (2009), ISBN 978-88-6134-326-6; Engelen, J.: A Rapidly Growing Electronic Publishing Trend: Audiobooks for Leisure and Education. In: Chan, L., Mornati, S. (eds.) Electronic Publishing Conference - ELPUB 2008, Toronto, June 26-27 (2008), ISBN 978-0-7727-6315-0; Engelen, J.: Modern Digital Libraries, the Case of the Audio-book Boom. In: Miesenberger, K., Klaus, J., Zagler, W.L., Karshmer, A.I. (eds.) ICCHP 2008. LNCS, vol. 5105, pp. 284–290. Springer, Heidelberg (2008)
5. Wikipedia entry for e-book formats, `http://en.wikipedia.org/wiki/Comparison_of_e-book_formats`
6. Amazon Kindles are described at, `http://en.wikipedia.org/wiki/Amazon_Kindle`
7. Details about the court case Amazon vs ASU can be found in following press message, `http://www.prnewswire.com/news-releases/` `blindness-organizations-and-arizona-state-university-` `resolve-litigation-over-kindle-81131122.html`
8. SQUIDOO publishing platform, lens on the Kindle, `http://www.squidoo.com/kindle-for-the-blind`
9. Although the quality of synthetic speech is still far away from human produced speech
10. Daisy consortium website, technology references at, `http://www.daisy.org/daisy-technology`
11. Daisy 3.0 is in fact an ANSI standard, ANSI/NISO Z39.86 Specifications for the Digital Talking Book
12. Beraud, P.: Produire des documents accessibles avec Microsoft Office 2010 Web Applications, une application "Web 2.0" accessible". Presented at the 4th European eAccessibility Forum: eAccessibility of Public Services in Europe (12-4-2010), `http://inova.snv.jussieu.fr/evenements/colloques/colloques/` `62_Programme_en.html`
13. Daisy consortium website, information on save as daisy, `http://www.daisy.org/project/save-as-daisy-openoffice.org`
14. Daisy consortium website, the Daisy online technology is referenced at, `http://www.daisy.org/projects/daisy-online-delivery/` `drafts/20100402/do-spec-20100402.html`
15. Weber, G.: Aufbereitung von E-books ohne Barrieren. In: Proceedings of the Daisy 2009 conference (Leipzig), Published by Th. Kahlisch, German Central Library for the Blind, pp. 247–250 (March 2010)
16. Details about the annual Electronic Publishing conferences can be found at, `http://www.elpub.net`

E-Books and Inclusion: Dream Come True or Nightmare Unending?

Alistair McNaught, Shirley Evans, and Simon Ball

JISC TechDis Service, Higher Education Academy Building,
Innovation Way, York YO10 5BR, U.K.
{alistair,simon}@techdis.ac.uk,
shirley.evans@virgin.net

Abstract. Nine e-book delivery platforms were tested for various aspects of accessibility. The results of this testing are discussed in terms of the roles and responsibilities in creating an accessible e-book delivery platform. The e-Book Access Bridge Model is introduced as a potential means of explaining to publishers the importance of ensuring every step in the process is barrier-free.

Keywords: accessibility, usability, e-books, inclusion, platforms, publishing.

1 Introduction

Books in digital formats offer numerous benefits to all users, but they offer disproportionate benefits to readers with disabilities. Globally, there has been a strong move towards the EPUB standard which offers a range of accessibility benefits [1]. EPUB is supported by the Association of American Publishers, a wide range of European publishers and is reported [2] as being adopted 'in principle' by China and Taiwan. For the foreseeable future, textbooks are likely to be available in either PDF (where print is the target destination) or EPUB (where online libraries are the target). PDF is a mature technology with reasonably accessible text content, EPUB is potentially highly accessible: consequently the basic text content of most textbooks is capable of manipulation in many ways. However, e-books are often delivered via platforms which are not as accessible as these formats could provide. To isolate the individual accessibility problems that currently occur in a range of e-book platforms, JISC TechDis [3] tested them with a range of disabled users.

This research, conducted in partnership with JISC Collections [4] and the Publishers Licensing Society [5], is of fundamental importance because the e-book industry is at a pivotal point. If good practice in inclusive design can be locked into industry norms at an early stage, the book famine experienced by so many disabled people will end. At present 'less than 5% of all published works are produced in accessible formats which the... reading disabled can read- furthermore, 95% of those accessible formats are actually produced by someone other than the original publisher' [6]. The UK Right to Read Alliance campaigns for 'same book, the same day, same price' and e-books make that dream plausible.

K. Miesenberger et al. (Eds.): ICCHP 2010, Part I, LNCS 6179, pp. 74–77, 2010.

2 Research

Access to the text content of an e-book is surprisingly multi-layered for an average user. The authors have developed the e-Book Access Bridge model (Fig.1) to illustrate key issues. To get from raw digital content to constructed knowledge, a student has to negotiate up to eight separate systems. The user with specific access requirements depends on every stage being accessible to his or her assistive technology. In conducting the research, the focus was placed at the point where the supplier's responsibilities begin - logging on to the e-book platform.

For each of nine platforms studied, an objective questionnaire based on typical user scenarios was constructed, for example logging onto the platform, searching for a book and reading pages, navigating within the book, etc. Expert assistive technology users were asked to objectively measure the number of actions required for each user scenario on each platform and to comment on the ease or difficulty of the task.

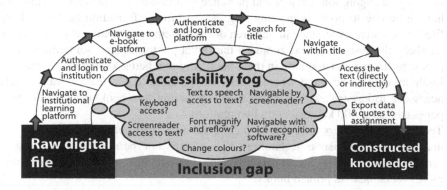

Fig. 1. e-Book access for disabled users: The e-Book Access Bridge Model

The tasks were user-oriented rather than technology-oriented. Testers looked for

- Personalisation options – font size, colour, and style.
- Accessibility information – plain English advice for disabled users.
- Assistive technology compatibility when performing key tasks.

The focus was on ease of use, not technical standards - how easy were the tasks for disabled users engaging in learning-oriented tasks. A key tenet of the Holistic Approach to Accessibility [7] is that whilst standards have an important role to play, they do not necessarily guarantee an accessible user experience. An interesting area of current research [8] is the extent to which accessibility standards formally feature in the design of e-book platforms. Whether or not implementation of standards increases or decreases the significance assigned to user testing is a key area for future research.

2.1 Method

The ultimate aim of this research was to understand the accessibility landscape of e-book platforms in order to help reshape that landscape. It was therefore vital that publishers/aggregators were actively and willingly engaged as partners, yet it is a risk to open up your system to expert scrutiny, especially if the results may not be flattering. To address these sensitivities, confidential reports were provided for participating publishers and anonymised versions provided for the researchers. A total of nine platforms were tested in four areas: voice recognition, keyboard only access, screenreader access and low vision. Data was collected both quantitatively (number of actions required to complete a task) and qualitatively (free text comments about the process). Participating publishers were invited to observe the testing of their platform.

2.2 Results

Analysis of the data indicated three types of barriers:

- Perceptual barriers were those where the users were unable to find a feature that was both present and accessible to their technology, examples included text zooming, changing font colours and presence of accessibility statements. This may have been due to poor signposting (e.g. accessibility information buried in Help files) or negative experience in one area of the system conditioning expectations in another - the absence of text zoom on the initial platform pages sometimes led to problems finding text zooming in the e-book despite it being a separate interface.
- Usability barriers occurred where access was possible (e.g. a feature was entirely accessible to keystrokes) but impractical – browsing to a book and reading three pages took over 100 keystrokes on two platforms.
- Technological barriers were due to incompatibilities between the e-book platform and the user's assistive technology – e.g. text not being readable by their screenreader. However, for assistive technology users most e-book platforms were more accessible than printed books.

3   Discussion: What Is Accessibility and Who Is Responsible?

The good news from the research was that a minimal level of access was afforded to most of the e-book platforms. From a technology point of view the screenreader user was able to access books to some extent on seven of the nine platforms trialled. However the usefulness of the access could be compromised unnecessarily. On one platform access required clicking a button that was not visible to the screenreader software. On others, a search returned a list of non unique links (e.g. 'Go to book') which meant the user had to listen to all the text in every description instead of skimming by hyperlink descriptions. A surprising result was how badly the keyboard-only user fared. Many functions were accessible but unusable due to the number of keystrokes needed. In this respect screenreader users were better served by some platforms. Three example results are shown in Table 1: the task was browsing to a book and reading three pages.

However the relative merits of each platform for this task did not necessarily carry through to other tasks; platform y scored best for keyboard access above but was wholly inaccessible to keyboard-only users in another task. A further consideration is 'improvability'; keyboard access to platforms w and x could be rapidly improved with

Table 1. Number of 'actions' needed to browse to a book and read three pages

Navigation by:	Platform w	Platform x	Platform y	Platform z
Keyboard-only	125	170	3	11
Mouse-only	7	5	9	3
Screenreader	9	18	Not possible	9
Voice-input	6	7	Not possible	6

judicious 'skip links' that could be added easily whereas platform y may need an entire rebuild to incorporate screenreader access. With slim profit margins, publishers might ask how much each will cost and whether they are required in law. Under UK legislation the organisation procuring a platform is providing a service [9] and they must procure the most accessible option. There is also a positive influence in the community of new users who are disabled not by impairment but by technology - the growing cohort of smartphone users who expect to access Internet services in an efficient way from their device. Designing an interface for mobile use requires the consideration of issues very similar to those involved in accessibility [10][11].

For many years, disability campaigners have had an uneasy relationship with the publishing industry. e-Books offer a unique opportunity to deliver the dream of accessible mainstream texts, while the experiences of disabled users have enormous value for publishers wanting to exploit the mobile market. This research has shown that both may benefit greatly from mutual engagement in e-book platform design.

References

1. Smith, M.: Difference a Year Makes - EPUB - Adoption of a Digital Standard. IDPF -2009 BookNet Canada Tech Forum (2009), http://bit.ly/WpcsF
2. Nystedt, D.: China and Taiwan agree to promote EPUB e-book standard. The Industry Standard (12. 02. 2009), http://bit.ly/bog1Sy
3. JISC TechDis, http://www.techdis.ac.uk
4. JISC Collections, http://www.jisc-collections.ac.uk
5. Publishers Licensing Society, http://www.pls.org.uk
6. Friend, C.: Programme Development Advisor, Sightsavers International (personal comm.)
7. Kelly, B., Phipps, L., Howell, C.: Implementing A Holistic Approach To E-Learning Accessibility (2005), http://bit.ly/cgJKh0
8. Whitehouse, G., et al.: Still destined to be under-read? Access to books for visually impaired students in UK higher education. Publishing Research Quarterly 25(3), 170–180 (2009)
9. JISC TechDis (2008a), Obtaining textbooks in alternative format, http://bit.ly/aoKQwF
10. McKiernan, G.: Iowa City Public Library Goes Mobile. Mobile Libraries Blog. 13.12.2009 (2008), http://bit.ly/9xo8rq
11. JISC TechDis (2008b), Upwardly Mobile, http://www.techdis.ac.uk/upwardlymobile

Collaboratively Generated Content
on the
Audio-Tactile Map

Armin B. Wagner

Vienna University of Technology
Institute for Design & Assessment of Technology
Human Interaction Group
Favoritenstraße 9-11, 1040 Vienna, Austria

Abstract. The objective of the present study was to investigate the usage of audio-tactile maps in an educational context with visually impaired users, to pinpoint problem areas and to enhance or re-design a suitable system correspondingly. The gained insights led to the design of a modular e-learning tool, based on playful exploration, expression and participation. This is accomplished by harnessing recent advancements in collaborative content generation and geo-localized data available online.

Keywords: visual impairment, e-learning, collaboration, tactile map.

1 Introduction

Access to geographical information plays a crucial role in the education of visually impaired children. Since the 18th century tactile maps are used to foster knowledge and mobility of their users. Technological advancements, such as thermoform and microcapsule paper, simplified the construction while facilitating time-efficient reproduction considerably. However, tactile maps come with substantially different design constraints compared to their graphical counterparts. Most notably graphical maps can present multiple layers of information at once, often including rotated or even intersected textual descriptions distinguished by colour and typographic choices. For visually impaired use, braille labels are restricted in this manner and considerably demand much more space on the map. Exploring a tactile map cluttered with abbreviations and symbols poses a difficult challenge to a trained user, even more to a student struggling with the principles of cartographic abstraction themselves. A possible solution to this problem is the speech and audio enhanced tactile map. Corresponding research has led to computer based systems which return auditory information if the user presses on or points at specific locations on a tactile map.

The objective of the present study was to investigate the usage of audio-tactile maps and explore new possibilities in an educational context, namely the Federal Institute for the Blind in Vienna/Austria.

K. Miesenberger et al. (Eds.): ICCHP 2010, Part I, LNCS 6179, pp. 78–80, 2010.

2   A Participatory Approach

2.1   Method

The study was model-driven and based on participatory design practices. The involved methods included passive observations during class sessions, and open ended interviews and group workshops held together with mobility trainers, visually impaired teachers and students at the age of 14-17 years. An already existing prototype of a low cost audio-tactile map [1], which was already known and used by several teachers and students, was used as a first reference model during early discussions. In the following meetings mock ups and new prototypes were designed, presented and discussed.

2.2   Results

Participating teachers stressed the importance of portability, durability, usability, adaptability, affordability, long-time support as well as compatibility to learning materials already in use.

But most notably the creation of audio-tactile maps demanded additional work and expertise from the teacher. The preparation of content takes considerable time which isn't necessarily paid and may be needed for other important activities at the school. In general the benefits of investing time into the system seemed to be unclear. After all, auditory information can be provided without the aid of a computer. The system seemed to mimic the role of the teacher in an oversimplistic way, while degrading her to a mere editor of static data. Interviewed students on the other hand showed a general interest in technological gadgetry. Text based services like SMS and the usage of the WWW are an integral part of their daily life. Shifting the design focus, which attributed the teacher to the sole producer of content, to more collaborative strategies, seemed a promising strategy. The new system should give students the chance to act as active contributors instead of relatively passive consumers of pre-fabricated content.

Starting from a familiar and safe environment, the school building itself, students of the Federal Institute for the Blind were given the task to collect audio recordings of their surroundings. Afterwards tactile maps made out of micro-capsule paper were used to link the recorded sounds with positions on the map. This exercise combines body movement with acoustic and tactile perception and helps blind students to better understand the relation between their surrounding space and the principles of cartographic abstraction. Furthermore, the produced audio-tactile maps can later assist new students getting acquainted with the building and the people working inside.

The next step widened the mapped area and increased the number of content contributors. Recent developments have shown how geo-localized data provided by online audio archives and micro-blogging platforms can be integrated into geographical maps. The abundance and popularity of such web services pose an opportunity to enrich tactile maps and offer a space for expression and participation reaching far beyond the borders of the classroom, task-driven learning practices and the static information provided by conventional tactile maps.

Furthermore the system bridges the gap between assistive technologies and inaccessible Web 2.0 services.

3 Implementation

Taking the necessity of durability and adaptability of teaching aids into account the developed system is based on a modular framework as well as open code and interfaces. Early prototypes used IR-led blob tracking and EMR pens as input devices. To take the rapid advancements in tracking technology into consideration, the tangible input device is interchangeable by supporting the TUIO protocol [2].

The rapidly evolving services available online demand a separate module, which manages the retrieval of geo-localized information using web services. The current prototype supports the audioboo-API [3] and is able to collect and share site- and context-specific audio recordings online.

The third module processes all incoming data and manages the auditory display, thus easing further development in terms of user-map interaction.

The forth module is dedicated to the identification of the tactile map and relies in its current implementation on RFID technology. Upcoming advancements in haptic feedback technology may render the use of a tagged microcapsule paper obsolete. Till then this approach is a practical solution based on existing infrastructures and working practices at school.

4 Ongoing Work

In general the modular design fosters the incremental improvement of the system. Planned activities include the refinement and open sourcing of the developed e-learning tool, the integration of a open low-cost capacitive sensor matrix and a durable and portable casing for the whole device.

Further work may include the collaboration with related organizations abroad to stimulate synergetic effects regarding pedagogical valuable content generation.

Acknowledgements

This study was funded by the Sparkling Science program, led by the Austrian Federal Ministry of Science and Research. The author also thanks all the involved students and teachers as well as the Institute "Integrated Study" for their support.

References

1. Seisenbacher, G., Mayer, P., Panek, P., Zagler, W.L.: 3D-Finger – System for Auditory Support of Haptic Exploration in the Education of Blind and Visually Impaired Students – Idea and Feasibility Study. In: Assistive Technology: From Virtuality to Reality, pp. 73–77. IOS Press, Amsterdam (2005)
2. Kaltenbrunner, M., Bovermann, T., Bencina, R., Costanza, E.: TUIO – A Protocol for Table Based Tangible User Interfaces. In: Gibet, S., Courty, N., Kamp, J.-F. (eds.) GW 2005. LNCS (LNAI), vol. 3881. Springer, Heidelberg (2006)
3. audioboo-api, http://code.google.com/p/audioboo-api

Generating Braille from OpenOffice.org

Bert Frees, Christophe Strobbe, and Jan Engelen

Katholieke Universiteit Leuven,
Kasteelpark Arenberg 10,
B-3001 Heverlee-Leuven, Belgium
{bert.frees,christophe.strobbe,jan.engelen}@esat.kuleuven.be

Abstract. Odt2Braille is an open-source extension to OpenOffice.org with the goal to generate Braille from an office suite. It is powered by liblouisxml, a library intended to provide complete Braille transcription services for XML documents. Odt2Braille will enable authors to print their document to an embosser or to export a Braille file. The output is well-formatted and highly customizable. The work is part of the European R&D project ÆGIS.

Keywords: Braille, OpenOffice.org, extension, odt, liblouis, accessibility, ÆGIS.

1 Introduction

The most common ways of creating Braille documents are presented in figure 1. Specialized Braille software can be used to create Braille documents by directly entering Braille characters. For large documents like books, this conventional and straightforward method can be tedious and time-consuming. Therefore, most Braille editors provide automatic translation services. This way, a transcriber can enter regular text and must only be concerned about layout. As the document should have a simple and clear layout, it is generally not suited to be ink-printed though.

The state of the art in Braille production is a multi-stage process. First a document is created in a word processor, or an existing document is scanned, converted with optical character recognition (OCR) and tagged. Then Braille software is used to translate *and* reformat the document into an accessible version. (Alternatively, documents can be converted to DAISY[1] format first, and transcribed by Braille software afterwards.) This approach has a clear advantage. The original document can preserve its rich layout and can be ink-printed, while the Braille edition is automatically formatted under Braille specifications, and can be independently printed on an embosser. However, any changes the author makes to the original means that the derivative edition must be re-created. Furthermore, any translation or layout issues arising from poor choices made in the original cannot simply be fixed in the derivative edition, or they will be lost with the next source update.

The work described in this paper tackles this problem by merging these multiple stages into one single Braille authoring environment. The result is

K. Miesenberger et al. (Eds.): ICCHP 2010, Part I, LNCS 6179, pp. 81–88, 2010.

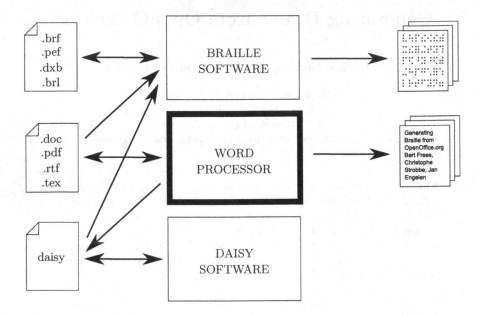

Fig. 1. Most common ways of creating Braille documents

Odt2Braille. It will be available as a free extension to OpenOffice.org (OOo)[2]. It is part of the ÆGIS[3] project, an integrated project funded under the European Commission's Seventh Framework Programme. ÆGIS aims at embedding open source based accessibility support into every aspect of ICT. ÆGIS does this by providing embedded and built-in accessibility solutions (to improve end-user experience), developers tools (to facilitate development of accessible software) as well as document creation tools (to support document authors in creating accessible information).

2   Related Work

There are a number of interesting projects related to Odt2Braille that deserve attention.

- The *RoboBraille*[4] service is a centralised, e-mail based Braille translation agent capable of translating to and from contracted Braille and to synthetic speech, including any pre-or postprocessing steps required to convert between document types, formats and character sets. The service can be used by sending a document to the appropriate e-mail account (for example, `britspeech@robobraille.org` for synthetic speech in British English), and the service returns the converted file via e-mail. The service is offered free of charge to all non-commercial users.
- *AutoBraille*[5] and *NorBraille* are the result of collaborations between Sensus ApS[6], Synscenter Refsnæs[7] and the national libraries for the blind in Denmark and Norway. A similar project will commence in Iceland this year. The

purpose of both projects is to automate the production of well-formatted, multi-volume Braille books, based on well-structured DAISY Talking Books. The Braille formatter processes the document based on options in a settings file and manages calls to the underlying RoboBraille/SB4 Braille translation and hyphenation engines.

- Another interesting project is *Dots*, an open-source Braille transcriber program for the GNOME desktop. It is basically a graphical user interface for liblouisxml[8]. It provides easy conversion from rich document formats to clean embosser ready literal Braille. Dots is in early stage of development and not as feature rich as commercial Braille editors. With Dots one can import Microsoft Word files, customize the output, preview the output in both ASCII and dot notation, and save the output to an embosser-ready file.
- A product very similar to Odt2Braille is *Braille Maker*[9]. Braille Maker is a long established Braille translation package, first released in 1988. It provides a user-friendly and quick way to produce high quality Braille direct from a word processing package such as Microsoft Word. In its most basic mode of operation, Braille Maker is accessed from the file Menu in Word. The document is then translated into Braille and the user is given the option to either print the file to any Braille embosser, or to edit the Braille. Most commonly used European languages are supported and mathematics Braille can be produced. Unfortunately, Braille Maker is not free.
- Finally, it is also worth mentioning *Odt2Daisy*[10], another free extension for OpenOffice.org. It is part of ÆGIS as well and is closely related to Odt2Braille. It enables users to export DAISY 3 XML and Full DAISY (XML and audio) from OOo Writer. It is cross-platform and relies on the operating system's text-to-speech engines to generate audio. With Odt2Daisy and Odt2Braille embedded, OpenOffice.org will become the ultimate free office suite for authoring accessible and high-standard documents.

3   Solution

Odt2Braille is an open-source Braille transcription extension to OpenOffice.org. OpenOffice.org is the leading free and open-source office suite for word processing, spreadsheets, presentations, graphics, math and databases. It is available in more than 80 languages and works on all common computer platforms (Windows, Mac OS X , Linux and Solaris).

By embedding Odt2Braille, OpenOffice.org becomes a complete Braille authoring environment, a central place where source material can be entered and maintained and Braille can be produced. The main objectives are to make the Braille transcription process as *seamless*, as *flexible* and as *predictable* as possible. The underlying thought is to drop the need of editing Braille material after conversion. This bypasses any potential synchronization problems.

The Braille transcription, i.e. translation and reformatting, is fully automated and configurable, and well-documented. The amount of required user interaction is kept to a minimum, while still providing enough freedom to customize the

Braille output. Also, users are being prompted to address structure problems at the source that would possibly lead to unwanted and unexpected artifacts at the Braille output. The main features of Odt2Braille are summarized in figure 2.

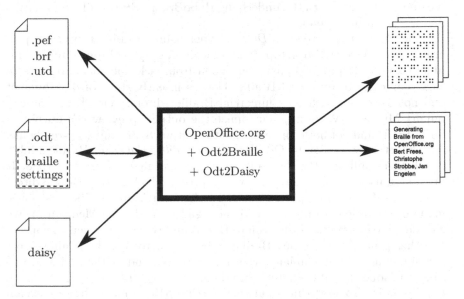

Fig. 2. Main features of Odt2Braille

Odt2Braille provides two ways of producing Braille. As a first option, the Braille document can be printed on a variety of Braille embossers. The list of supported devices is limited but growing. Currently embossers from Interpoint[11], Index[12] and Braillo[13] can be used. The second option is to export a Braille file which can be read by other Braille software. This option is necessary when the transcriber may want to edit the Braille document afterall. Also, there exist many situations in which the Braille transcriber is not responsible for the actual Braille production. The following is a list of Braille files currently supported.

- *Braille Formatted* files (filename extension .brf) are the most common non-proprietary Braille files. They are plain text files with hard returns and hard page ejects. The Braille characters are encoded in ASCII computer Braille. They can be imported by most Braille editors, including *Duxbury DBT*[14], *MegaDots*, *Braille2000*[15], *WinBraille*[16], *MicroBraille*, *Pokadot*[17], ...
- The *Portable Embosser Format* (PEF)[18] is an upcoming document type for representing Braille pages in digital form, accurately and unambiguously. It's a digital Braille hardcopy - the PDF of Braille. It can be used for Braille embossing and archiving anywhere in the world. PEF uses markup (XML) rather than control characters to define structure, and uses Unicode Braille patterns rather than ASCII characters, because Unicode is locale-independent. PEF can also contain meta-data. Scripts in the *DAISY Pipeline*[19] allow you to emboss a PEF file, convert a PEF file to other formats or prepare a PEF file for easy distribution.

- Instead of embossing directly, one can also print the document to an embosser-specific file for later use.
- Finally, other Braille formats including UTD (*Universal Tactile Document*), BRL (*MicroBraille* file), DXB (*Duxbury* file), may be supported in the future.

For ease of use, all transcription-related user preferences are stored as meta-data in the source document file. As a result, the OOo file can even be used as a digital representation of Braille, e.g. for archiving or distributing purposes.

In this project, great importance was attached to compliance with formal Braille specifications (e.g. BANA, BAUK, UEB, but also non-english specifications). Formatting is strictly done according to these standards. However, if it turns out that many users prefer their own rules to formal ones, more flexibility will be provided through user preferences.

4   Odt2Braille in Detail

Figure 3 below illustrates the architecture and main components of Odt2Braille. As can be seen from the diagram, the architecture is composed of a configuration module that collects user preferences, and sends these as parameters to the three document processing modules.

- The *configuration* module takes care of the user interface. The Odt2Braille output can be customized extensively through user preferences. Available parameters include: main language and contraction level, inclusion of preliminary pages (such as a title page, a list of special symbols, transciber's note pages, a table of content, ...), inclusion of transription information and/or

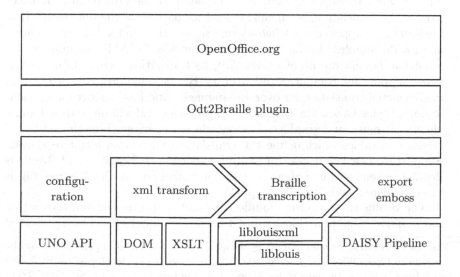

Fig. 3. Architecture and main components of Odt2Braille

volume information, page settings (page dimensions, margins, print page numbers, Braille page numbers) and export settings (file format/embosser type, character set, alignment options, recto or recto-verso, . . .). For convenience, settings from previous sessions are automatically loaded in advance and new settings are saved afterwards.

This module makes use of OpenOffice.org's *UNO API*. UNO is a language independent application programming interface which allows developers to use OpenOffice.org as service provider in other applications, extend it with new functionality or simply customize and control OpenOffice.org.

– The *XML transform* module prepares the document for actual Braille transcription. The OOo source file is an *OpenDocument Text* file (ODT), one of the formats defined by the OpenDocument[1] specification. An ODT file is a zip of files and folders, among which the most relevant are XML files that contain document content (content.xml), document style definitions (styles.xml) and document meta-data (meta.xml). This set of highly interconnected XML files is simply to complicated for the main transcription module alone to handle.

The XML transform module basically performs some DOM manipulations and XSL transformations. The module deals with volume management (dividing the document into one or more binders), pagination and numbering of listitems and headings. The transformation also involves shifting elements, cleaning up or removing elements, adding typeface and language tags, adding transcriber's notes, replacing images by alternative descriptions and adding captions to tables, textboxes and images. Finally, the module is responsible for creating notesections and constructing a preliminary section containing a title page, a list of special symbols, a transcriber's notes page and a table of content. The result is a set of clean and simplified, DAISY-like XML files, ready for Braille transcription.

– The *Braille transcription* module is the heart of the architecture. It takes care of the translation, hyphenation and formatting of the document. It is basically a wrapper around *liblouisxml*[8], an open-source library intended to provide complete Braille transcription services for XML documents. Liblouisxml is built on top of *liblouis*[20], its translation engine. Liblouis features support for computer and literary Braille, supports contracted and uncontracted translation for over 40 languages, and has support for hyphenation. Liblouis handles mathematical expressions and will ultimately handle chemistry, music and graphics. The translation is driven through text based translation tables which define the translation rules in an intuitive syntax. Support for new languages can easily be added. The formatting of Braille is defined in semantic mappings that define how a specific XML input tag is to be rendered in the Braille output.

The Braille transcription module is capable of processing and formatting most major structural (block) and text-level (inline) elements. Supported

---

[1] The *OpenDocument Format* (ODF) is an open-source format used principally by the office suite OpenOffice.org. The specification was originally developed by SUN Microsystems, but the standard is developed and maintained by the OASIS ODF Technical Committee.

structural elements include paragraphs, headings, tables, lists, textboxes, notes, captions, pagenumbers, bibliographies, tables of content ... Supported text-level elements include hyperlinks, special typefaced text, text in foreign language, references to notes or bibliography entries, ... Odt2Braille tries to cover the whole ODF specification. However, it is clear that the current implementation can only handle a certain subset of all elements. More features will be covered in the future.

– The last module is responsible for exporting or embossing the final Braille document. First, the document is formed in the universal and unambiguous PEF format. Subsequently, the document can be converted to any other format, either generic or embosser-specific. For this purpose, Odt2Braille uses the *pef2text* transformer from the DAISY Pipeline. The DAISY Pipeline is a cross-platform, open source transformation utility, supporting conversion to and from a wide variety of file formats. Currently, the list of supported embossers and export formats is limited, the expansion of this list is a major concern for the future.

5   Future Work and Conclusions

At the time of writing, all mentioned features are only available in OOo Writer, the word processing component of OpenOffice.org. Odt2Braille is planning to provide the same functionalities for OOo Calc (spreadsheets) and OOo Impress (presentations). Developers will keep putting effort in expanding the set of supported ODF elements. Ideally, Odt2Braille should be able to handle complicated tables, mathematical expressions and tactile graphics in the end, in order that scientific material can be processed as well, but this is no priority. An absolute necessity however is to make Odt2Braille compatible with a more representative set of embossers. It is also very likely that other Braille formats such as UTD (Universal Tactile Document) will be added to the list of export formats soon. Finally, as indicated above, real-life tests will have to determine whether users prefer there own formatting rules to formal ones and whether they need more decision-making. Yet compliance with Braille standards will remain an important point of interest.

Acknowledgements. This work was funded by the EC FP7 project ÆGIS - Open Accessibility Everywhere: Groundwork, Infrastructure, Standards, Grant Agreement No. 224348.

References

1. National Information Standards Organization. The ANSI/NISO Z39.86-2005 specifications for the Digital Talking Book (2005),
   http://www.daisy.org/z3986/2005/Z3986-2005.html
2. OpenOffice.org - The Free and Open Productivity Suite,
   http://www.openoffice.org

3. ÆGIS - Open Accessibility Everywhere, http://www.aegis-project.eu
4. Christensen, L.B.: RoboBraille - Automated Braille Translation by Means of an E-Mail Robot. In: Miesenberger, K., Klaus, J., Zagler, W.L., Karshmer, A.I. (eds.) ICCHP 2006. LNCS, vol. 4061, pp. 1102–1109. Springer, Heidelberg (2006)
5. AutoBraille, a project with The Danish National Library for the Blind, http://www.punktskrift.dk
6. Sensus - Accessibility Consultants, http://www.sensus.dk/sensus/frontpage39.aspx
7. Synscenter Refsnæs, http://www.synref.dk
8. Liblouisxml, a braille transcription software for xml documents, http://code.google.com/p/liblouisxml
9. Braille Maker, http://www.braillemaker.com
10. odt2daisy - OpenDocument to DAISY Talking Book, http://odt2daisy.sourceforge.net
11. Interpoint NV, http://www.interpoint.be
12. Index Braille, http://www.indexbraille.com
13. Braillo Norway AS, http://www.braillo.com
14. Duxbury systems, http://www.duxburysystems.com
15. Braille 2000 (2000), http://www.braille2000.com
16. WinBraille 5 - Braille editor, http://www.indexbraille.com/Products/Software/WinBraille-5---Braille-editor.aspx
17. Braille with Pokadot, http://www.braille-pokadot.com
18. Håkansson, J.: PEF 1.0 - portable embosser format, public draft (2009), http://www.daisy.org/projects/braille/braille_workarea/pef/pef-specification.html
19. DAISY Pipeline, http://www.daisy.org/projects/pipeline
20. Liblouis, a braille translation and back-translation library, http://code.google.com/p/liblouis

Sonification of ASCII Circuit Diagrams

Angela Constantinescu and Karin Müller

Karlsruhe Institute of Technology (KIT)
Study Center for the Visually Impaired Students (SZS)
Engesserstr. 4, D-76131 Karlsruhe, Germany
{angela.constantinescu,karin.e.mueller}@kit.edu

Abstract. Graphics and diagrams can be made available to blind users mainly in two ways: via speech descriptions or tactile printing. However, both approaches require help from a sighted, well instructed third party. We propose here a fast and inexpensive alternative to making graphics accessible to blind people, using sound and a corpus of ASCII graphics. The goal is to outline the challenges in sonifying ASCII diagrams in such a way that the semantics of the graphics is successfully brought to their users. Additionally, the users should have the possibility to perform the sonifications themselves. The concept is exemplified using circuit diagrams.

Keywords: Sonification, ASCII graphics, accessibility, blind.

1 Introduction

The Study Center for the Visually Impaired Students (SZS) at the Karlsruhe Institute of Technology used ASCII art in the past to convert diagrams found in lecture notes or course books into a form accessible to blind students. These diagrams could then be read with a Braille display or printed in tactile form with an embosser. However, the Braille terminal can only display one row of up to 80 characters at a time, while the characters are translated into Braille, thus changing their initial form. All this makes the interpretation of an ASCII diagram difficult. Preparation and printing in tactile form, on the other hand, requires training, time and an expensive tactile printer.

2 State of the Art and Proposed Solution

Most work in the area of making diagrams accessible to blind people concentrates on using tactile or speech feedback, such as [1] or [2]. Of those works that focus on sound output, some make complex analyses and interpretations, require assistance to convert the diagrams ([3]) or use additional hardware ([4]).

This study proposes an alternative solution to making ASCII diagrams accessible to blind users, by means of sonification (representation of data through sound). This method is at the same time fast, inexpensive and can be performed by the blind users themselves.

Two applications were written in the Java programming language to perform sonifications. The first one produces what we called the "sequential sonification" and the

K. Miesenberger et al. (Eds.): ICCHP 2010, Part I, LNCS 6179, pp. 89–91, 2010.

second one an "exploratory sonification". In both cases, a midi sound is produced for each type of character used in the diagram. In the sequential mode, the circuit is sonified starting at the upper left corner line by line, one character at a time, and then saved into a midi track that the user can listen to at any time. In the exploratory mode the user controls, using keys on the keyboard, in which direction the sonification proceeds. In this way, the user may 'explore' the circuit and discover elements (such as resistors, gates, batteries, etc).

3 Discussion

The following observations that arise from the research refer both to the technical aspects of the sonification (preparation of the diagram, translation of text to sound), as well as to the way in which the blind users work with and perceive the system:

Graphics and text. The first issue that arises when sonifying a circuit diagram is the existence of text within the graphics, such as the values of resistors, batteries, etc. A solution to the problem of automatically disambiguating between text and graphics is proposed by Müller et al. [5]. However, the information must still be brought back together in a meaningful way to the user. One solution is to put the text into a legend and establish a convention for numbering the values, which either depends on the order in which the elements are sonified, for a sequential sonification, or is based on the topology of the entire diagram, for the exploratory mode. Alternatively, the text could be spoken out in the context of the diagram.

Intuitive text-to-sound mappings. Ideally, the sound describes not just the character it represents, but rather its meaning, as accurately as possible. For instance, a small 'o' stands for a 'crossroad' point in the diagram, and could be sonified by a more complex sound that suggests spreading in several directions. A slash '/' could be sonified by a high-pitched sound or a short raising sequence. White spaces can be sonified by very low volume, middle-pitched sounds, or even no sounds at all.

The required learning phase. When using the sonification strategies mentioned above that the user must first learn how individual circuit elements (such as batteries) sound like, then discover them in the sonification and finally put the picture together. With the sequential approach there is the further problem that the user must first remember entire lines in the diagram and then 'assemble' the picture in his head, which makes the identification of the circuit elements very difficult. Thus, it might be feasible to identify the elements in the diagram and sonify them individually. Sounds would then not be associated to characters anymore, but to batteries, capacitors, etc. This approach should lower the learning time as well as the playing time of a circuit.

Overview of completed tasks. When using the exploratory approach it is difficult for the user to tell how much of the diagram has been covered already, and what it is still to be discovered, and where. A solution is to have the program speak up to the user, upon request (button click), how much of the diagram has been visited [3], in percentage and excluding the white spaces, and the direction in which one should move to get to the closest area not yet covered.

Environment awareness. There are situations when the user does not know in which direction/s he may continue, based on the character at the current position. This is thus information that should be contained in the sonification. A 'crossroad', for instance, could be followed by (or even sonified as) a sequence of short sounds that describe the directions in which the user may go on.

Play order. The order in which the circuit is sonified may help the user to put the entire picture together more easily. For instance, when a sighted person analyzes a circuit, many times they would read it by 'loops', in no case line by line. So sonifying the circuit based on the existing loops in it might make sense, at least for the sequential mode. One must be careful though that the connection between loops is also made obvious to the user.

Fun. This aspect also plays a role in the acceptance of an application. If the sonification sounds annoying to the user, it is less likely that the method will be used often. Thus, music principles should be applied in order to make the sonification sound more melodic. If possible, it should be made to sound like a music piece, where different sound characteristics like instruments, tempo, pan, volume or pitch are variable and relate to characteristics of the circuit diagram.

4 Conclusion and Future Work

The sonification approaches described above try to bring some light into the complexity of making graphical representations accessible to blind users. ASCII diagrams have the advantage that they can be drawn by blind users themselves, just as sonifying them should succeed without any external help.

The sequential sonification has the advantage that it can be done automatically and in bulk (many at a time). Additionally, it can be played while the user is away from the computer, or even on an mp3 player or mobile phone, but it has the disadvantage of being more difficult to interpret. The exploratory approach, on the other hand, allows the user to „discover" elements in the diagram (such as resistors, capacitors), go back and forth or follow loops in the circuit and may be more intuitive, at the cost of requiring the user's full attention.

Both approaches have the disadvantage that they require a previous learning phase: the user must be able to associate sounds with characters and to make a mental mapping of the diagram.

The next steps in this research would be to use the results thus obtained and build on them, by establishing more concrete guidelines for successfully sonifying circuit diagrams. Furthermore, the results should be extended to other ASCII graphics used in academia, such as flow charts, trees, tables, and others.

References

1. Kawai, Y., Ohnishi, N., Sugie, N.: A support system for the blind to recognize a diagram. Systems and Computers in Japan 21(7), 75–85
2. Blenkhorn, P., Evans, G.: Using speech and touch to enable blind people to access schematic diagrams. Journal of Network and Computer Applications 21, 17–29
3. Bennett, D.J.: Effects of navigation and position on task when presenting diagrams. In: Hegarty, M., Meyer, B., Narayanan, N.H. (eds.) Diagrams 2002. LNCS (LNAI), vol. 2317, p. 161. Springer, Heidelberg (2002)
4. Kennel, A.R.: Audiograf: a diagram-reader for the blind. In: Proceedings of the 2nd Annual ACM Conference on AT, pp. 51–56. ACM, New York
5. Mueller, K., Constantinescu, A.: Improving the accessibility of ASCII graphics for the blind students. In: Proceedings of the 12th ICC 2010 Conference, Vienna, Austria (to appear, 2010)

Accessing Google Docs via Screen Reader

Maria Claudia Buzzi[1], Marina Buzzi[1], Barbara Leporini[2],
Giulio Mori[1], and Victor M.R. Penichet[3]

[1] CNR-IIT, via Moruzzi 1, 56124 Pisa, Italy
[2] CNR-ISTI, via Moruzzi 1, 56124, Pisa, Italy
[3] Computer Systems Department, University of Castilla-La Mancha, Albacete, Spain
{Claudia.Buzzi,Marina.Buzzi,Giulio.Mori}@iit.cnr.it,
Barbara.Leporini@isti.cnr.it, victor.penichet@uclm.es

Abstract. Groupware systems allow remote collaboration via computer in a simple, economic and efficient way. However, to be universally valuable, groupware systems must be accessible and usable for all, including the differently-abled. In this paper we discuss the results of testing the accessibility and usability of Google Docs (http://docs.google.com) when using a screen reader and a voice synthesizer, and suggest some basic guidelines for designing effective, efficient and satisfactory User Interfaces (UIs).

Keywords: Accessibility, usability, groupware, screen reader, blind.

1 Introduction

In the early 1990s groupware systems transformed the way people worked together toward a common goal, allowing them to collaborate remotely via computer in a simple, economic and efficient way. In a few years these collaborative tools spread from organizations to the Internet. This opened up extraordinary opportunities for creating new world-wide collaboration tools, of which Wikipedia is one of the best known.

Collaborative tools range from classic email, blogs, chats, calendars and wikis to groupware systems such as eGroupware (http://www.egroupware.org/) or Google Docs (http://docs.google.com/). All these systems enable cooperation and increase productivity; however to be universally valuable, groupware systems must be accessible and usable for all, including the differently-abled. Accessibility is a pre-requisite for users to reach on-line application content, while usability offers simple, efficient and satisfying navigation and interaction. In order to evaluate whether a certain service/product is usable for those with special needs, it is first necessary to ensure that it is accessible.

Various accessibility and usability guidelines have been proposed in the literature to provide design criteria for developing Web contents. One of the more authoritative sources is the World Wide Web Consortium (W3C, Web Accessibility Initiative group), which defines accessibility guidelines for Web content, authoring tools and user agent design. The W3C Web Content Accessibility Guidelines (WCAG) are general principles for making Web content more accessible and usable for people with disabilities [19]. The latest version of the WCAG (2.0) is organized in four

K. Miesenberger et al. (Eds.): ICCHP 2010, Part I, LNCS 6179, pp. 92–99, 2010.

categories, relying on the clear perception of content information (*content perceivable*), complete interaction with an interface in its functionalities (*interface elements operable*), comprehension of meaning (*content understandable*), and maximizing the interface's compatibility with new assistive technologies and devices (*content robustness*) [19]. Accessibility is closely related to usability; an interface should permit the user to achieve her/his target goal (*effectiveness*) in the best (*efficient*) and in a fully satisfactory way [5]. Important properties for website usability concern navigability as well as interaction. An interface should fulfill peoples' needs (*utility*), be easy to use in a gradual learning process for users who visit the site repeatedly (*learnability and memorability*) and limit user errors (*few easily recoverable errors*) [10].

In this paper we analyze the accessibility of Google Documents via screen reader and suggest some basic design guidelines. Section 2 briefly illustrates issues regarding interaction via screen reader and Section 3 presents some related works. Section 4 describes exploring Google Docs via screen reader, highlighting potential problems, and finally Section 5 introduces a discussion and future work.

2 Interacting via Screen Reader

Blind people perceive page content aurally and sequentially when accessing the Web by screen reader and voice synthesizer. Furthermore, blind users navigate mainly via keyboard. This kind of interaction with pages and user interface (UI) leads to several problems in perceiving content. Specifically, screen reader interaction causes:

- Content serialization. Content is announced sequentially, as it appears in the HTML code. This process is time-consuming and annoying when parts of the interface (such as the menu and navigation bar) are repeated on every page. As a consequence, blind users often quit a screen reading at the beginning, preferring to navigate by Tab key from link to link, or explore content row by row via arrow keys.
- Mixing content and structure. With Web content, the screen reader announces the most important interface elements such as links, images, and window objects as they appear in the code. For the blind user, these elements are important for figuring out the page structure, but require additional cognitive effort to interpret it. For instance, if a table's content is organized in columns, the screen reader (which reads by rows) announces the page content out of order; consequently, the information is confusing or misleading for the user.

This can lead to problems with user perception, such as lack of context, lack of interface overview (if the content is not organized in logical sections), difficulty understanding UI elements or working with form control elements (if not appropriately organized for interaction via keyboard), etc. This is discussed in greater detail in [8]. Thus, when designing for blind users it is essential to consider the three main interacting subsystems of the Human Processor Model: the perceptual, motor and cognitive systems [2]. The cognitive aspect of an interaction is extremely important, since many learning techniques are relevant for people with normal vision but not for the visually-impaired. Thus, alternative ways to deliver content should be provided. Furthermore, a blind person may develop a different mental model of both the interaction and the learning process, so it is crucial to provide a simple overview of the system as well as content.

3 Related Works

Web 2.0 applications brought a new dimension to the Web, moving from simple text and images created by single programmers, to multimedia and dynamic content increasingly built by users in collaborative environments. In the same way, the complexity of interface layout also increased. Since groupware environments vary greatly as to functions, interfaces, cooperation schemes and more, it is difficult to generalize very specific findings, whereas it is easier to compare homogenous classes of groupware applications. Regarding usability of on-line contents available in the World Wide Web, Takagi et al. suggest spending more time on the practical aspects of usability rather than focusing on the syntactic checking of Web pages, since some aspects are difficult to evaluate automatically, such as ease of understanding page structure and interface navigability [15].

Cooperative environments are particularly useful in the educational field, where knowledge is cooperatively assembled. Khan et al. carried out a usability study on ThinkFree, a collaborative writing system, in an educational environment, with four novice and four experienced users. Specifically, authors compared ThinkFree to Google Docs by means of a user test with Think Aloud protocol, a post-test questionnaire to collect user feedback and interviews to validate gathered results. Although the effectiveness of ThinkFree for the proposed tasks was shown, efficiency and availability of resources were more limited than in Google Docs.

To identify groupware accessibility issues and analyze proposed solutions, Schoeberlein et al. [13] revised recent literature highlighting the need for future research. Authors observed that most articles address the needs of a specific category of differently-abled persons. In particular, the needs of visually impaired persons are analyzed, due to the object difficulties these persons' experience when interacting with a complex layout via screen reader [7], [16], [17], [1].

Groupware should be usable for all, while the blind user is often required to have considerable computer skill. For simplifying access to a popular groupware system (i.e. Lotus Notes), Takagi et al. developed a self-talking client for allowing the blind to access groupware main functions efficiently and easily, masking the user from the complexity of the original visual interface [16]. Recently Kobayashi developed a client application (Voice Browser for Groupware systems, VoBG) for enabling visually impaired persons who are inexperienced with computer technology, to interact with a groupware system that is very popular in Japan (Garoon 2). The VoBG browser intercepts Web pages generated by the groupware server, parses their HTML code and simplifies on-fly their content and structure in a more understandable format for the target users [7].

Baker et al. adapted Nielsen's heuristic evaluation methodology to groupware; by means of a usability inspection conducted by expert and novice evaluators, they showed that this methodology can also be effectively applied by novice inspectors, at low cost [1]. Ramakrishnan et al. [12] investigate usability assessment in "information management systems", groupware environments characterized by mostly user asynchronous usage, integrating and adapting Nielsen's usability heuristics.

Awareness, one of the main properties of a groupware system, is also one of the accessibility principles: a user would be able to perceive when portions of UI reload and by means of the screen reader, to know the associated event occurring (e.g. a new person joining the chat, a new message arriving on the board, a new user working on the document, and so on). To attempt to fill this gap, the WAI group is working on the Accessible Rich Internet Applications specification (WAI-ARIA) to make dynamic web content and applications (developed with Ajax, (X)HTML, JavaScript) more accessible to people with disabilities [18]. Using WAI-ARIA web designers can define roles to add semantic information to interface objects, mark regions of the page so users can move rapidly around the page via keyboard, define live regions, etc. [18].

Thiessen showed an example of using WAI-ARIA to design and implement a chat, highlighting some limitations of live regions [17]. However this problem is common with emerging standards, since browsers and assistive technologies need to conform to the new specifications, and this takes some time before reaching stable implementations.

4 Exploring Google Docs via Screen Reader

4.1 Methodology

In this first phase of our research we decided to examine interaction via screen reader with Google Docs in order to evaluate the real opportunities for blind people to write a document collaboratively. In this paper we consider accessibility issues, since accessing the tool and its main functions is a pre-requisite to considering other usability issues. With this in mind, we examined the Google Docs log-in, the Main (after the log-in access) and Document Editing (to create/modify an item of 'document' type) pages. The pages were analyzed by the authors, who performed a usability and accessibility inspection.

The pages were navigated using the screen reader JAWS for Windows Ver. 10.0 (http://www.freedomscientific.com), commonly used in Italy [8], and both the MS Internet Explorer (IE) version 8.0 and Mozilla Firefox version 3.0.5 browsers. One author has been totally blind since childhood and uses the JAWS screen reader every day; thus she is very familiar with JAWS functions and is able to use advanced commands. The different experiences of the authors when using JAWS allowed us to simulate both novice and proficient users (using advanced screen reader commands).

Testing Google Docs via screen reader was organized in three steps: (a) sighted user interaction with monitor power off (to simulate the experience of the blind or novice screen reader users) and power on (to confirm what was perceived in the first step) (b) blind user interaction (carried out by the blind author of this paper), (c) open discussion of personal experiences to verify and refine the collected data.

4.2 Results

Results showed that several main functions are practically inaccessible via keyboard, so interaction with Google Docs can be very frustrating for blind users. Main accessibility and usability issues encountered can be summarized as follows:

1. Orientation on the interface is difficult (not *efficient* or *satisfactory*): the main functions for an editing tool, such as creating or accessing a document, are announced after many elements (see Fig. 1, parts 1 and 2).

2. Accessing basic functions is very difficult (not *perceivable* and *operable*): some control elements cannot be accessed by the blind because they are not standard (X)HTML, so they are not correctly perceived by the screen reader; thus some tasks are impossible to complete (*not effective*). For example 'Offline' and 'Show search options' links (in the home page) are built programmatically and 'div' elements are used for visual rendering, but the focus via keyboard is not provided. Similarly, when accessing a Document, important menus (file, edit, view, insert, format, etc.) are impossible to access.

   Furthermore, style properties (font type or size, etc.) are not accessible (not focusable via Tab key) since it is not possible to reach the formatting toolbar, while bold, italic or underlined functions can be used only through shortcuts, for the same reason. Unfortunately Google Documents shortcuts are different from those of MS Word; consequently, additional cognitive effort is required of the blind JAWS user (who is familiar with the Windows environment). Moreover, most editing functions do not have associated access keys.

3. Control elements are unclear (*not understandable*): buttons, links, etc. have labels which do not provide clear explanations about their usage and meaning.

4. Working with the documents is nearly impossible via keyboard (*not robust*): the IE browser does not allow selecting a document by checkbox (see Fig. 1, part 4), preventing the activation of related functions (e.g. delete, rename, mark as unviewed, revisions, etc.). The Firefox browser does not have this problem.

5. There are other differences in the behavior of the two browsers. Navigating via Tab key in the main page with Firefox, the 'Create new' pull-down menu does not receive the focus and is not announced; the tree view in part 3 of Fig. 1 is announced saying it must be explored via arrow keys, but arrows do not work. With IE the 'Create new' element is announced without specifying the type (pull-down menu) and the tree view is not announced via Tab key, but with arrows the user may access its single elements. Also toolbar visual buttons ('Delete' and 'Rename') and visual pull-down menu in part 4 of Fig. 1 ('Share', 'Folders', 'More actions', 'Last Modified') are not accessible using IE, while they are accessible with Firefox, with unpredictable blocking behavior after exit (using ESC key) from 'Folders' pull-down menu.

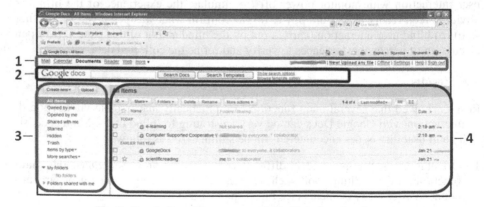

Fig. 1. Google Docs Home page, divided into functional areas

6. Tables used for layout purposes or for arranging the list of available documents have no summary attribute. In the main page of Google Docs IE announce a table without a summary, while Firefox does not announce it at all. A brief, functional and descriptive content could be assigned to the summary attributes in order to facilitate navigation through special commands like the letter "t" to quickly reach the next table, or to make the table content more understandable when reading sequentially via arrow keys. Furthermore, the 'EARLIER THIS MONTH' and 'OLDER' labels are not announced in both the browsers (when documents are ordered by date).

7. Dialogue windows are not accessible at all (Fig. 2).

Fig. 2. An inaccessible dialogue window showing an informative message

4.3 Discussion

Groupware systems can be a great opportunity for people with mobility difficulties, such as blind users, in order to collaborate at a distance. However, if not appropriately designed, electronic barriers can prevent access to or enjoyment of all benefits of available resources. As reported in the previous section, several accessibility issues negatively affect potential use by the blind.

To have a perception "equivalent" to that of a sighted person, a blind user should know: a) where it is located on the interface, b) its status and c) what (s)he can do from that point. These three aspects are key factors in truly improving the overall efficiency of the interface. Feedback is not only important for user interaction with the system, but also to monitor the status of other users in the collaborative environment.

The W3C WAI-ARIA suite [18] resolves many of these issues. Indeed, WAI-ARIA adds semantics to interface objects (roles, states, properties) improving the interface control via screen reader. For instance, Web designers can define page regions, permitting the blind user to orientate him/herself in the UI (list of regions) and move rapidly from one section to another. WAI-ARIA allows marking sections specifying standard XHTML landmarks (main, navigation, search, banner, etc.) or defining regions, if they do not appropriately reflect the aim of the section. Especially, these customized regions can provide the user with a useful page overview. For example, the Google Docs home page could be organized into four main areas, representing different function groups: (1) applications and settings (2) search (3) file management and (4) documents and properties (Fig. 1). Regarding awareness of what is happening in the UI, the definition of WAI-ARIA live regions enables the screen reader to intercept dynamic changes in the page (which does not reload the whole page, but only a portion, typical of Ajax applications) and informs the user.

Furthermore, to arrange a well-structured interface, a good approach would be to limit its complexity by dividing all commands or tools into functional groups, and providing the user with only those necessary for the current interaction, according to the user context based on the system focus.

Another facility provided by a well-designed interface is that the screen reader automatically enters Editing mode (e.g., when the focus is on a text edit widget) or Exploration mode (e.g., the focus is on a text-box or a link). In this way, for a blind user the learning process becomes more automatic and natural.

5 Conclusions and Future Work

In this paper we highlighted the main accessibility and usability issues that arise when interacting via screen reader with Google Docs. We analyzed the Google Docs home page and document editing to verify the accessibility and usability for blind people. Our analysis revealed issues that have a dramatic negative impact on the user interface and on user efficiency when carrying out basic tasks such as selecting and updating a document. We also formulated basic suggestions for improving the interaction and making user experience more satisfactory, allowing anyone to benefit from this collaborative tool, regardless of his/her ability.

In conclusion, we believe that design guidelines could have general applications, and that applying the WAI-ARIA suite would enhance usability via screen reader in any groupware environment. In the future we plan to evaluate how some WAI-ARIA properties applied to the Google Docs interface and its main functions can improve not only accessibility but also usability when interacting via screen reader.

References

1. Baker, K., Greenberg, S.: Empirical Development of a Heuristic Evaluation Methodology for Shared Workspace Groupware (2002)
2. Card, S.K., Moran, T.P., Newell, A.: The Psychology of Human-computer Interaction, pp. 29–97. Lawrence Erlbaum Associates, London (1983)
3. Davoli, P., Monari, M., Severinson Eklundh, K.: Peer activities on Web-learning platforms—Impact on collaborative writing and usability issues. In: Education and Information Technologies, September 2009, vol. 14(3), pp. 229–254. Springer, Netherlands (2008), doi:10.1007/s10639-008-9080-x
4. Huang, E.M., Mynatt, E.D., Russell, D.M., Sue, A.E.: Secrets to success and fatal flaws: The design of large-display groupware. IEEE Computer Graphics 26(1), 37–45 (2006)
5. ISO 9241-11. Ergonomic requirements for office work with visual display terminals (VDTs) - Part 11: Guidance on usability (1998)
6. Khan, M.A., Israr, N., Hassan, S.: Usability Evaluation of Web Office Applications in Collaborative Writing. In: 2010 International Conference on Intelligent Systems, Modelling and Simulation, Liverpool, United Kingdom, January 27 - 29, pp. 147–151 (2010)

7. Kobayashi, M.: Voice Browser for Groupware Systems: VoBG - A Simple Groupware Client for Visually Impaired Students. In: Miesenberger, K., Klaus, J., Zagler, W.L., Karshmer, A.I. (eds.) ICCHP 2008. LNCS, vol. 5105, pp. 777–780. Springer, Heidelberg (2008)
8. Leporini, B., Andronico, P., Buzzi, M., Castillo, C.: Evaluating a modified Google user interface via screen reader. Universal Access in the Information Society (7/1-2) (2008)
9. Leporini, B., Paternò, F.: Applying web usability criteria for vision-impaired users: does it really improve task performance? International Journal of Human-Computer Interaction (IJHCI) 24(1), 17–47 (2008)
10. Nielsen, J.: Usability engineering. Morgan Kaufmann, San Diego (1993)
11. Petrie, H., Hamilton, F., King N · Tension, what tension? Website accessibility and visual design. In: 2004 International Cross-Disciplinary Workshop on Web Accessibility (W4A), pp. 13–18 (2004)
12. Ramakrishnan, R., Goldschmidt, B., Leibl, R., Holschuh, J.: Heuristics for usability assessment for groupware tools in an information management setting (2004)
13. Schoeberlein, J.G., Yuanqiong, W.: Groupware Accessibility for Persons with Disabilities. In: Stephanidis, C. (ed.) UAHCI 2009. LNCS, vol. 5616, pp. 404–413. Springer, Heidelberg (2009)
14. Schoeberlein, J.G., Yuanqiong, W.: Evaluating Groupware Accessibility. In: Stephanidis, C. (ed.) UAHCI 2009. LNCS, vol. 5616, pp. 414–423. Springer, Heidelberg (2009)
15. Takagi, H., Asakawa, C., Fukuda, K., Maeda, J.: Accessibility designer: visualizing usability for the blind. In: 6th International ACM SIGACCESS Conference on Computers and Accessibility, pp. 177–184 (2004)
16. Takagi, H., Asakawa, C., Itoh, T.: Non-Visual Groupware Client: Notes Reader. In: Proceedings of Center on Disability Technology and Persons with Disabilities Conference. California State University (2000)
17. Thiessen, P., Chen, C.: Ajax Live Regions: Chat as a Case Example. In: Proceedings of the 2007 International World Wide Web Conference, W4A (2007)
18. W3C. WAI-ARIA Best Practices. W3C Working Draft 4 (February 2008), http://www.w3.org/TR/wai-aria-practices/
19. W3C. Web Content Accessibility Guidelines 2.0, http://www.w3.org/TR/WCAG20/ (December 5, 2008)

Making Digital Maps Accessible Using Vibrations

Bernhard Schmitz and Thomas Ertl

Institute for Visualization and Interactive Systems, Universität Stuttgart
Universitätsstr. 38, 70569 Stuttgart, Germany
{Bernhard.Schmitz,Thomas.Ertl}@vis.uni-stuttgart.de

Abstract. In order to allow blind and deafblind people to use and explore electronically available maps, we have developed a system that displays maps in a tactile way using a standard rumble gamepad. The system is intended for both on-site and off-site use and therefore includes mechanisms for getting overviews of larger regions as well as for the exploration of small areas.

Keywords: Haptic Maps, Vibrating Maps, Blind Users.

1 Introduction

Maps form an integral part of navigation, especially in unknown areas. They give information about an area even before visiting it and provide guidance once in the area. However, blind people cannot access maps as easily as sighted people. Therefore we have developed a system that is capable of conveying maps using only a standard rumble gamepad and a text-to-speech engine or a Braille display. In this paper we first introduce some related work in the field of maps for blind users. After that, we introduce our system by first explaining the basic mode of operation and then detailing some more advanced techniques that we introduced for better interaction. Before we get to the conclusion, the results of a preliminary user study are presened.

2 Related Work

Maps for blind people can be distinguished by the sense that is used to convey the desired information, normally hearing or touch, whereas maps for deafblind people must rely solely on touch.

Auditory Maps. Heuten et al. play different sounds corresponding to different locations on the map, where the connection between the location and the sound can either be natural (e.g. a water sound for a lake) or artificially created [3,2]. These sounds are then played in a 3D environment in which the user can locate their source. The approach by Cohen et al. was not primarily developed with the intention to display maps, however it can be used to do so [1]. It was developed to

K. Miesenberger et al. (Eds.): ICCHP 2010, Part I, LNCS 6179, pp. 100–107, 2010.

convey graphs to blind users by representing edges and vertices by sound. Zhao et al. use auditory maps to present the geographic distribution of statistical data (e.g. number of inhabitants) but do not concentrate on exploring standard city maps [6].

Tactile Maps. In the HyperBraille project it was shown that maps can be produced on a tactile graphics display [5]. The TANIA system uses a tactile-acoustical map that consists of a touchscreen augmented with tactile strips indicating the points of the compass [4]. The user can explore the map by tapping anywhere on the screen and having the name of the object announced by a text-to-speech engine or displayed on a Braille device.

3   Standard Map Interaction

3.1   The Virtual Observer

A sighted person observing any standard map can get an immediate two-dimensional overview of the general layout. But when acoustic or tactile maps are used, this immediate overview is not as easy to get. Even if tactile maps are layed out two-dimensionally and the user employs several fingers, the overview is limited. Therefore most approaches to digital maps for blind users employ a cursor or "virtual observer" that can be moved across the (virtual) map. Feedback is only given about the area under the cursor or immediately surrounding it. Accordingly, only one point (or its immediate surroundings) can be observed at any given point in time. Getting an idea of a larger area therefore necessarily involves moving the cursor. This is equivalent to a single finger moving across a real tactile map.

Our Approach to the Virtual Observer. In our approach the user can move the virtual observer across the map using the gamepad's controls. A vibration is emanated from the gamepad whenever the virtual observer is on or near a street. This conveys a basic idea of the layout of the streets. The user can then inquire about the name of the current street with a press of a button. The name is output by a text-to-speech engine or a Braille device. However, due to hardware limitations, there are some additional tweaks that need to be introduced before the tactile map is usable.

3.2   Moving the Virtual Observer

The virtual observer has to be moved by the user. Moving it with an analog stick of the gamepad is an obvious choice. However, there are two fundamentally different ways of implementing this movement.

Scrolling Movement. The intuitive implementation is to allow the user to move the virtual observer freely across the map. This is akin to scrolling. As we use an analog stick, the speed of the movement can be made adjustable by linking it to the inclination of the stick. This implementation has the disadvantage of not having a fixed mapping of the stick position to a map position, which can make the examination of an area rather unintuitive.

Fixed Area Movement. The other possible implementation is to directly map a stick position to a map position. In this implementation, the center position of the stick is fixed to a position on the map. Moving the stick results in a movement in a fixed area around that position. As an example, pushing the stick slightly up will result in the virtual observer going to a position slightly to the north of the center position. Pushing it all the way down will result the virtual observer going to a position further to the south. The obvious disadvantage of this implementation is that it limits the area of observation. However, as each position of the stick is directly mapped to a position on the map the examination of a certain area is much easier than using scrolling movement. Another advantage of fixed area movement is that the center position can be fixed to the current position of the user if used in a navigation system. This allows a quick and easy exploration of the area immediately surrounding the user.

Combination of Scrolling and Fixed Area Movement. As both implementations have their pros and cons, we have included both versions in our prototype, mapping one to each of both analog sticks. We call the one that allows free movement the scrolling stick and the one that allows for the detailed examination of a certain area the observer stick. This enables the user to scroll quickly across the map and then examine a certain area in detail.

3.3   Vibration

As vibration is our choice for announcing a street, the different possibilities of implementing vibrations need to be discussed.

Vibrating Near a Street. It might seem obvious, that vibration should occur when the virtual observer is on or near a street. However, as our test implementation showed, this mode of operation has serious drawbacks. Because of the latency inherent to the hardware it is possible to cross streets without any feedback from the device. The resulting effect is similar to streets appearing and disappearing at random. This seriously hampers the ability to build a mental map of a certain area.

Vibrating when Crossing a Street. The solution to the problem mentioned above is easy: Check whether a street has been crossed and in that case emanate a short vibration regardless of the current position of the stick. The disadvantage of this solution is that it slightly reduces the connection between stick position and map position in the fixed area movement implementation of the virtual observer, because a vibration might occur when no street is beneath the virtual observer. However, we have found this to be a minor inconvenience when compared to the disappearing streets problem mentioned above.

3.4   Street Announcement

The virtual observer combined with the vibration gives the user an idea of the general layout of the streets. However, the names of the street are not conveyed by the vibration and need to be announced by a text-to-speech engine or a Braille device. We chose to announce a street name upon user request by pressing a button. Again, there are different ways of implementing this.

Announcing Nearest Street. The intuitive implementation of street announcement always outputs the name of the street that is currently closest to the virtual observer. This works best together with the "Vibrating Near a Street" implementation. However, the user will make a connection between the vibration and the street name, which does not always reference the same street in this implementation.

Announcing Last Crossed Street. This problem can be overcome by announcing the street that was last crossed by the virtual observer. This street is not necessarily the one closest to the current position of the stick. However, this allows the user to build a direct connection between the vibration and the announced street name, improving the mental map built by the user.

3.5 Zooming

Exploring a map does not only involve scrolling around but also zooming. Zooming out has different effects on scrolling and fixed area movement.

Zooming Effects on Scrolling. When zoomed out, the scroller stick will scroll over a larger area in the same time and with the same inclination of the stick.

Zooming Effects on Fixed Area Movement. The observer stick will cover a large area when zoomed out. This has a negative effect on the facility of inspection of the area, as more and more streets are accumulated in the area covered by the stick.

Reduced Details on Zooming Out. Therefore we display fewer details when zooming out. We display all streets when zoomed in and remove residential roads when zooming out. Upon zooming out even more, all roads are removed and only towns or suburbs are displayed, with their borders activating the vibration. This loss of details is equivalent to the reduced details in small scale maps as compared to large scale maps. Zooming with reduced detail allows the user to both gain an overview and get more detailed information about certain areas.

4 Advanced Map Features

The techniques presented so far can convey an idea of the layout of a map; however there remain several problems which need to be overcome.

4.1 Intelligent Zoom

First, there is the problem of cluttering the output with too many streets. Often there are still more roads than can be reasonably handled with a small analog stick on many zoom levels, even if roads are masked when zooming out. A minimal movement of the stick will result in the virtual observer crossing several streets, making a clear distinction between these hard if not impossible. However, on certain zoom levels there is an appropriate number of streets within reach of the observer stick. Therefore, presenting the user only with those views that deliver a satisfying result is a reasonable solution to the problem of "street cluttering".

Implementation of Intelligent Zoom. Unfortunately there are no fixed zoom levels that will always yield satisfying results. The optimal zoom levels depend on the density of the streets in the observed region. We therefore developed an intelligent zoom, that will always zoom to a level that displays a reasonable number of streets, main streets or suburbs.

4.2   Single Street Observation Mode

The methods described above are well suited for getting an overview of the general layout of streets in an area, and for finding out which streets lie next to each other. However, a user inspecting a map will often also be interested in the exact layout of a specific street. This can become problematic when streets are bent or winding. Following the street with the observer stick becomes hard or impossible, especially when it is connected to many side streets. For this reason, we have developed the "Single Street Observation Mode".

Implementation of Single Street Observation Mode. When the user presses a button, all but the last crossed street are removed from the display. Upon the button press the name of the street is announced so that the user is aware which street he is currently observing. At the same time, the vibration mode is switched to "Vibrating Near a Street" (see 3.3). The street can be displayed wider, i.e. the distance to the street necessary for vibration is increased. As it is now the only street being displayed, this cannot lead to problems related to overlapping streets but leads to an easier observation of the street.

5   Evaluation

As a way of evaluating our concept and implementation, we have conducted a preliminary user study with four participants. All participants are sighted but could not see any output on the screen. Two of the four participants had never used a gamepad with analog sticks before, one participant had used one once several years before, and one was a regular user of such a gamepad. We have designed two tasks with the goal of testing the intelligent zoom and Single Street Observation Mode.

The first task was to name the southern parallel street of a given street. We gave a rough location description for these streets wich consisted of the suburb and a triangle of major streets in which they are located. At the beginning of the task, the virtual observer was located in another suburb.

The second task was to roughly draw the course of a certain street (which has one notable turn). For this task the virtual observer was already located on that street.

5.1 Results for Intelligent Zoom

Table 1 shows the time that was needed by each participant to finish the task and whether the result was correct. Participants 1 and 3 (using Intelligent Zoom) were able to complete the task correctly in about 11 minutes each. Of those without fixed zoom participant 2 canceled the task after 20 minutes without a result; participant 4 was able to complete the task in 8:32 minutes. Thus, we have no clear conclusion about the effects of Intelligent Zoom. We suspect that participant 4 profited from his regular use of a gamepad with two analog sticks and would have been even faster with Intelligent Zoom.

Table 1. Results of Task 1 (Intelligent Zoom)

Mode	Intelligent Zoom		Fixed Zoom	
Participant	1	3	2	4
Gamepad Use	Never	Once	Never	Regularly
Time (min:sec)	11:06	10:55	20:00+	8:32
Correct Answer	Yes	Yes	No	Yes

5.2 Results for Single Street Observation

The results for Single Street Observation are shown in table 2. Participants 1 and 2 (both using Single Street Observation) were able to complete the task, taking 4:10 and 9:10 minutes. Of those with no Single Street Observation, participant 3 stopped after 5:41 minutes without a correct result and declared the task to be "very difficult". Participant 4 took 10:43 minutes for the correct result. Again it has to be kept in mind that participant 4 was the only proficient dual analog stick user. Participant 4 suggested a mode similar to Single Street Observation for this task on his own. With these results we feel confident to assert that the Single Street Observation mode is indeed an improvement that makes it possible to inspect the layout of a street.

Table 2. Results of Task 2 (Single Street Observation)

Mode	Single Street Observation		No Single Street Observation	
Participant	1	2	3	4
Gamepad Use	Never	Never	Once	Regularly
Time (min:sec)	4:10	9:10	5:41	10:43
Correct Answer	Yes	Yes	No	Yes

5.3   General Results

Our preliminary user study has shown that it is possible to inspect maps using a standard rumble gamepad with our implementation. Furthermore, both the results and our observations during the study seem to suggest that routine in using analog thumbsticks are an important factor regarding the efficiency of the system's use. One user suggested a bookmark function that would allow the user to save the current location of the virtual observer and quickly jump back to that location.

6   Future Work

Currently, our system is based on maps downloaded from OpenStreetMap and is not fully accessible in all components. Its current state was sufficient for our testing purposes, however, it should be fully accessible and interact directly with OpenStreetMap in order to be useful for blind users. Further improvements could be made to the basic functionality with different vibration patterns for the distinction of streets, main streets, crossings and other relevant entities. Regarding the hardware, we want to keep using cheap and easily available products for the end-user market, however the performance of a force feedback joystick in comparison to a rumble gamepad should be examined.

Spatial conceptualization skills of blind people vary greatly, depending on whether they were blind from birth, when they have lost their vision and how these skills were taught during their childhood. Therefore, the results of our preliminary study can not be transfered directly to the realm of blind users. Accordingly, the effects of these factors on the use of our system should be evaluated in a further study.

Acknowledgements

This project is funded by the Deutsche Forschungsgemeinschaft within the Collaborative Research Center 627 "Spatial World Models for Mobile Context-Aware Applications". We would like to thank Dr. Andreas Hub for his valuable input and all participants in our study for their time and effort.

References

1. Cohen, R.F., Haven, V., Lanzoni, J.A., Meacham, A., Skaff, J., Wissell, M.: Using an audio interface to assist users who are visually impaired with steering tasks. In: Assets 2006: Proceedings of the 8th International ACM SIGACCESS Conference on Computers and Accessibility, pp. 119–124. ACM, New York (2006)
2. Heuten, W., Henze, N., Boll, S.: Interactive exploration of city maps with auditory torches. In: CHI 2007: CHI 2007 Extended Abstracts on Human Factors in Computing Systems, pp. 1959–1964. ACM, New York (2007)

3. Heuten, W., Wichmann, D., Boll, S.: Interactive 3d sonification for the exploration of city maps. In: NordiCHI 2006: Proceedings of the 4th Nordic Conference on Human-Computer Interaction, pp. 155–164. ACM, New York (2006)
4. Hub, A., Kombrink, S., Bosse, K., Ertl, T.: TANIA – a tactile-acoustical navigation and information assistant for the 2007 CSUN conference. In: Proceedings of the California State University, Northridge Center on Disabilities' 22nd Annual International Technology and Persons with Disabilities Conference (CSUN 2007), Los Angeles, CA, USA (March 2007)
5. Rotard, M., Taras, C., Ertl, T.: Tactile web browsing for blind people. Multimedia Tools and Applications 37(1), 53–69 (2008)
6. Zhao, H., Smith, B.K., Norman, K., Plaisant, C., Shneiderman, B.: Interactive sonification of choropleth maps. IEEE Multimedia 12(2), 26–35 (2005)

Non-visual Navigation of Spreadsheet Tables

Iyad Abu Doush[1] and Enrico Pontelli[2]

[1] Dept. Computer Science, Yarmouk University,
idoush@cs.nmsu.edu
[2] Dept. Computer Science, New Mexico State University,
epontell@cs.nmsu.edu

Abstract. This paper presents a new system for non-visual navigation of tables located within a spreadsheet. The purpose is to provide a novel hierarchical non-visual navigation of tabular structures. The hierarchical view of the spreadsheet content, along with the user ability to select the desired table within a complex spreadsheet, provides greater flexibility than what offered by current assistive technologies. The proposed system allows the user to select a table and choose between different navigation strategies. The proposed approach introduces the solution in two stages: (i) table detection and recognition and (ii) non-visual navigation of the selected table. The system is provided as a plug-in for MS Excel^{TM}.

1 Introduction

Surveys (e.g., [1]) show that one of every three working adults who are blind deals regularly with spreadsheets and databases. As such, it is of vital importance to provide these individuals with accessible solutions in the use of these tools—without such solutions, individuals with visual disabilities will be prevented from effectively entering the workplace and access advanced educational opportunities. In particular, accessibility of spreadsheets is a particular complex problem—a spreadsheet combines a number of features that have individually been recognized as challenging for individuals with visual disabilities (e.g., tabular structures [8] and mathematical formulae [9]). The common medium used for accessing such information by individuals who are blind or visually impaired is synthetic speech, Braille displays, and printed Braille.

Fig. 1 shows an example of a worksheet in MS Excel^{TM}. The worksheet includes different components—a table (on the right) and a chart (underneath). Traditional screen readers are unable to identify the components within a spreadsheet (e.g., a collection of cells that together constitute a table) and navigate them in a semantically meaningful manner. Another problem is if the user wants to navigate the table. In this case, the user needs to skip several rows to reach the table in the worksheet. If the current worksheet contains several tables, the navigation using the screen reader becomes frustrating, especially if the user wants to navigate the tables individually.

Tables are an important medium for presenting information; they provide a spatial visualization of data and highlight relations between its components [7].

K. Miesenberger et al. (Eds.): ICCHP 2010, Part I, LNCS 6179, pp. 108–115, 2010.

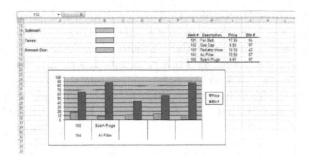

Fig. 1. A Spreadsheet in Microsoft Excel™

Several researchers (e.g., [11,10,8]) have proposed accessible solutions for non-visual navigation of tables. Most of the research has been proposed in the context of tables in Web pages. According to [10], the main problems encountered by visually impaired users when accessing tables using a screen reader are:

- The user faces difficulties in keeping track of context during navigation (e.g., position in the table). In the case of tables in a spreadsheet this is even more difficult because tables are not explicitly recognized as a separate objects and the user is unaware of his position according to the table boundaries.
- Screen readers tend to provide excessive aural feedback while moving within a table (e.g., read all cells).
- Screen readers are unaware of the abstract structure of a table. To get a better idea about the table data, a user needs to know the role of this piece of information in the context of the table, the size of the table, etc.

This paper introduces a system that provides a hierarchical view of the table structure. The user can directly access different functional components of the table (e.g., table title, table headers). The information about the tabular data is rendered using synthesis speech. The system starts by detecting tables within a worksheet created in MS Excel™. After identifying the tables, the user can select one table and navigate it. The user can request automated positioning in specific points of the table (e.g., minimum value in a specific row/column).

The results from a pilot study show that users can quickly (in less than 18 seconds) answer different questions about the content of a table. The study also compares accessibility of a table using our system and a Braille presentation. The findings from this study show that the time needed to answer similar questions about the table take less time in the proposed system (i.e., using speech) than in the Braille printed version.

2 Background

The literature has offered several solutions concerning the problem of recognizing tables and allowing non-visual table navigation. Due to lack of space, we will here discuss only some relevant proposals, without any pretense of completeness.

Table Detection and Recognition: The problem of recognizing tables is articulated in two sub-problems: *detecting a table* and *recognizing its functional components* [3]. Table detection is the problem of determining the occurrences of a table model in a document [3]. Table recognition is the problem of analyzing a table to determine its different elements according to the table model (e.g., title and header) [3]. To solve the problem of table detection and recognition it is important to analyze both the language and layout of a table. Some researchers (e.g., [12,4]) rely on identifying separators (e.g., lines, spaces, ruling lines) to identify the components of a table. The use of clustering to detect table components has been suggested by other researchers (e.g., [12,5,8]).

Non-Visual Navigation of Tables: Scanning tabular data to develop an overview and a mental model of a table is easy for sighted people. On the other hand, this is a harder task for visually impaired users. [2] indicates that identifying specific information inside a table is one of the most difficult tasks for visually impaired users.

Sonification has been suggested as a viable mechanism to provide an aural overview of tabular data (e.g., [10,6]). Non-speech sounds with different tones are used for table navigation—e.g., using higher pitch sounds to denote larger table values. Other approaches for non-visual table navigation rely on navigation plans that are either pre-constructed by the table author or constructed on-the-fly by the system (based on the results of table recognition) [8,10].

3   Methodology

In this work we propose a system for detecting and navigating tables in Excel™ spreadsheets. Spreadsheets are used to organize diverse information in a tabular format. A worksheet in a spreadsheet may contain multiple tables (along with other components, e.g., graphs), and there is no mechanism to explicitly identify a collection of cells of a worksheet as a table. For example, ideally we would like to consider the group of cells on the top right of Fig. 1 as a single table.

The attributes of each cell in a worksheet—e.g., color, font style, presence of borders, cell type—and its relation with the surrounding cells can be used to detect different functional component of the table. The boundaries of a table are based on the density of information within close-distance cells.

Once a table has been detected, we wish to offer to the user navigation strategies that are bounded to a specific table. The navigation should prevent the user from accessing cells that do not belong to the table, and the navigation should provide the user with strategies and reading modalities that account for the specific task the user is trying to accomplish. Let us elaborate on how these two issues are handled in the proposed system.

Table Detection and Recognition: A table in a spreadsheet contains three types of cells: *header* cells, *data* cells, and *title* cells. An *header cell* is a cell that contains a value that describes the contents of a table column or row. A *data cell* is a cell that contains a value or a data item—i.e., it is a component of the "body" of the table. A *title cell* is a cell that contains a description of the contents (or purpose) of the table.

Many attributes about the layout structure used within a worksheet, the formatting of its cells, and the values inside the cells can be used to detect and recognize occurrences of tables in the worksheet. We have developed an algorithm which recognizes tables and its functional components through a two-stage process. First, the non-empty cells in a worksheet are scanned and classified into one of the three categories (header, data or title). The classification process is based on assigning values to the different formatting attributes and computing overall *attribute-weights* for each cell with respect to the three categories; the weight-category that receives the highest value will determine the classification of the cell. The weight of each category is also dependent on the weight assigned to the neighboring cells. The computation of the weights takes into account:

- Similar formatting (e.g., border and color) for the cells in a worksheet—this is often an indicator of cells belonging to a similar table functional component (i.e., headings, columns, row, or title).
- Presence of separators (e.g., empty rows, different cells formatting, use of different kinds of borders, different cell value types)—this changes often denote the transition from a functional component to a different one.

Second, based on the weights and on the classification, it is possible to conduct a clustering process which leads to assembling the functional components of the table, organized as title, headers, and data body.

Non-Visual Navigation of Tables: Once the process of table detection and recognition has been completed, the proposed system allows the user to proceed with the process of non-visual navigation. The system informs the user of how many tables the current worksheet includes and their titles (using speech). It provides the user with a hierarchical view in which all the tables inside the current worksheet can be browsed by using the tables titles and each table can be selected for navigation. Observe that the hierarchical view is necessary as the detection algorithm can also recognize multi-tables (i.e., tables within tables).

Table 1   Table 2

Fig. 2. Table Selection and Circular Navigation

Once a table is selected for navigation, the focus of the system is on such table; in particular, the user is limited to navigating and browsing the section of the worksheet included in that table, and he/she is prevented from slipping outside the boundaries of the table (and, for example, entering by mistake a different table or some unrelated cells of the worksheet).

The system provides two navigation modes that the user can select from: *(i)* *row navigation* and *(ii)* *column navigation*. In *row navigation* mode, the user can freely move in the four directions within the table (using the cursor keys) and listen to a speech description of the content of each encountered cell; each time the end of a dimension is reached, the user is given the option of automatically moving to the beginning of the next dimension (e.g., next row or next column). In the *column navigation* mode, the user can select a column to navigate by listening to the various column headers in the selected table; once a column is selected, its content is sequentially read to the user. This type of navigation is helpful if the user is interested in browsing a specific category in the table (e.g., browse only the students grades in math). The user can switch between the two navigation modes at any time without losing the navigation context.

In both navigation modes (row and column), a circular navigation is applied (see Fig. 2) in which when the user reaches an edge cell (i.e., last cell or first cell) and moves to the next cell (or previous cell in the case of the first cell), then the user will be taken to the next cell in the edge.

Within each navigation mode, the system allows the user to select alternative cell-reading modalities; these determine how the content of each encountered cell is presented to the user. The reading modes available for the user are: *cell value* (only the actual value of the cell is presented), *contextual cell value* (the cell value is presented along with its coordinates), *cell value with formula presence* (the cell value is presented along with a description of the formula used for computing it), and *cell category and value* (the cell value is presented along with the category of the cell, described by its headers).

Providing the user with a quick method to access specific information in a table reduces the time required for certain navigation tasks. The system allows the user to access standard properties of a table, including the minimum or the maximum value in a column containing numerical data.

Fig. 3. An Outline of the Non-Visual Table Navigation System

Implementation: The system has been implemented using Visual Basic for Applications (VBA). An overview of the different stages of the system implementation is illustrated in Fig. 3.

4   Results and Evaluation

Data Set: In order to test the system with tables from different domains, we collected a diverse set of Excel^TM worksheets from different online repositories (e.g., tax statistics). The selected worksheets contain tables with different lay-outs. The benchmark set includes 21 worksheets with 55 tables. The sample data set has 1, 737 rows and 426 columns.

The proposed algorithms are capable of correctly identifying all the tables in the worksheets (100% detection rate) and 98% of the functional components of each table. The tables for which our algorithm encounters difficulties have an unusual use of numbers both in the header cells as well as in the table body—thus, the algorithm fails to correctly classify header cells as such.

Evaluation of the Non-Visual Navigation of Tables: The table navigation component of the system has been evaluated in two user studies. The first study has been performed with 8 sighted subjects (5 females and 3 males), recruited from an introductory psychology class at NMSU. The age range of the subjects is from 18 to 24. All the participants had familiarity with Microsoft Excel™. The second study has been conducted with 5 blind students (4 males and 1 female) from the New Mexico School for the Blind and Visually Impaired (NMSBVI). The age range of the subjects is between 15 and 28. In the second study, the students' class levels range from 8th grade to 12th grade and all of them have high cognitive abilities. Only 40% of them had previous experience with Excel™.

While in the first study we focused on the ability to conduct table navigation tasks, in the second study we also performed a comparison of table navigation using our system with table navigation using printed Braille. In this second collection of experiments, we represented the tables using 2nd grade Braille.

Table Navigation Using the System: In both user studies, the participants have been asked to perform three navigation tasks: browse one table from a list of tables, browse one table containing values computed using formulae, and detect specific information about one table. One additional task has been tested only in the first study, which required navigating a multi-level table. The features that we investigated during the study are: the time needed to answer questions about the table, the time required to find summary information about the table, the time required to find a formula for a specific table category, the accurate identification of the formula, the user accuracy when answering questions about the table, and how accurate and effective are the audio cues.

In the first study, we exposed the students to a worksheet that contains 4 tables from different domains (movie store, grocery store, and school grades) and ask them to detect and work on three specific tables. The navigation has been performed with the computer screen turned off.

The results show that selecting a table from 4 different tables by listening to the table titles took an average time of 24 seconds. In the task of browsing one table (which has 7 rows and 7 columns), it took the user an average time of 42 seconds, with 88% accuracy, to answer the question *"what movie title has the maximum price?"*. All the participants correctly answered the question *"how many copies are there of the movie title X?"*, with an average time of 57 seconds. All the students agreed on the simplicity of non-visual table navigation. Most of the students (88%) agreed that finding the maximum value was easy.

In the second task, the students used a table (14 rows and 5 columns) with formula-calculated cells. The average time to answer *"what is the retail price for the item X?"* was 49 seconds with 75% accuracy. When using the system to locate the minimum value in each column, it took 30 seconds on average to answer the question *"which item has the lowest profit?"* with 75% accuracy.

The second study has been conducted using 2 tables in a worksheet that contains 3 tables from different domains (movie store, grocery store, and school grades). The findings from this study show that the average time to select a specific table from 3 tables and start the navigation was about 35 seconds.

The first task performed was browsing one table (7 rows and 3 columns). All the students identified correctly the table title in an average time of 5 seconds. Answering questions about the table (e.g., *"what is the rating for the movie X?"*, *"What movie title has the minimum price?"*) took an average time of 16 seconds, with 100% accuracy. When searching the table to see if a movie title exist, it took the students an average time of 6 seconds, again with 100% accuracy.

The second task performed was browsing a table (4 rows and 7 columns) with formula-calculated cells. All the students answered correctly the question *"What is the retail price for the item X?"*, with an average time of 36 seconds. The average time when answering the question *"which item has the lowest profit?"* was 50 seconds with 100% accuracy. 80% of the students agreed that the system was usable, but they indicated the desire of having more training time.

Comparison Between Braille and the System: In order to compare the system with a common medium used to present tables to individuals with visual impairment, we asked the same group of students to browse the same tables using our system and using Braille versions printed on tactile paper. All the participants are familiar with reading Braille and they have been using it for reading for more than three years.

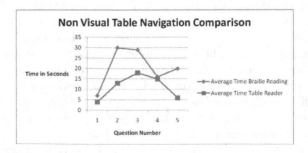

Fig. 4. Comparison Between Table Navigation Using the Proposed System and Braille

Compared to the table presented in Braille, all the participants indicated a strong preference to the audio navigation system, claiming it to be easier to follow. In comparison, the participants complained about the difficulty of keeping track of their position on the table when browsing the Braille version. This emerged, for example, when asking questions like *"what is the name of the movie in row 5 of the table?"*, which was answered in 30 seconds with 100% accuracy using the audio navigation, and in 18 seconds but with an accuracy of only 20% using Braille. Many students indicated that the proposed system is better than the Braille table because *"it explains everything to you and there is no need to search for the information"*.

The results between navigating the table using speech and using Braille (Figure 4) show a faster navigation average time using speech (for a table with 7 rows and 3 columns). Larger tables would further increase the gap due to the need of reducing the scale of the table on the Braille paper or spread the table across multiple pages (with further difficulties of maintaining context while reading).

5   Conclusion and Future Work

In this paper we described a system for detecting and recognizing tables in spreadsheet worksheets and for providing non-visual navigation strategies to access such tables without any visual aid. The tool has been integrated in Microsoft Excel™ and evaluated using different groups of students, with excellent results (especially if compared to Braille representations of the tables).

We are currently expanding the work to add a query-answering mechanism, which allows users to filter the spreadsheet data according to user-defined search criteria, further reducing the amount of overhead during navigation.

References

1. Douglas, G., et al.: The role of the who icf as a framework to interpret barriers and to inclusion. British Journal of Visual Impairment 25(1), 32–50 (2007)
2. Gunderson, J., Mendelson, R.: Usability of world wide web browsers by persons with visual impairments. In: RESNA (1997)
3. Hu, J., et al.: Evaluating the performance of table processing algorithms. Int. J. on Document Analysis and Recognition 4(3), 140–153 (2002)
4. Itonori, K.: Table structure recognition based on textblock arrangement and ruled line position. In: Int. Conf. Document Analysis and Recognition, pp. 765–768 (1993)
5. Kieninger, T.: Table structure recognition based on robust block segmentation. In: Proc. Document Recognition V. SPIE, pp. 22–32 (1998)
6. Kildal, J., Brewster, S.: Providing a size-independent overview of non-visual tables. In: Int. Conf. on Auditory Display, pp. 8–15 (2006)
7. Pinto, D., et al.: Table extraction using conditional random fields. In: Annual National Conf. on Digital Government Research, pp. 1–4 (2003)
8. Pontelli, E., et al.: A system for automatic structure discovery and reasoning-based navigation of the web. Interacting with Computers 16(3) (2004)
9. Pontelli, E., et al.: Mathematics Accessibility: a Survey. In: Handbook of Universal Access. CRC Press, Boca Raton (2009)
10. Ramloll, R., et al.: Using non-speech sounds to improve access to 2D tabular numerical information for visually impaired users. In: Procs. BCS IHM-HCI (2001)
11. Shamilian, J., Baird, H., Wood, T.: A retargetable table reader. In: Int. Conf. on Document Analysis and Recognition, pp. 158–163 (1997)
12. Zuyev, K.: Table image segmentation. In: Int. Conf. on Document Analysis and Recognition, pp. 705–708 (1997)

New Testing Method for the Dyslexic and the Newly Blind with a Digital Audio Player and Document Structure Diagrams

Mamoru Fujiyoshi[1], Akio Fujiyoshi[2], and Toshiaki Aomatsu[3]

[1] National Center for University Entrance Examinations
2-19-23 Komaba, Meguro, Tokyo, 153-8501 Japan
fujiyosi@rd.dnc.ac.jp
[2] Department of Computer and Information Sciences, Ibaraki University
4-12-1 Nakanarusawa, Hitachi, Ibaraki, 316-8511 Japan
fujiyosi@mx.ibaraki.ac.jp
[3] National School for the Blind of Tsukuba University
1-2 Namiki, Tsukuba, Ibaraki, 305-8564 Japan
aomatsu@nsfb.tsukuba.ac.jp

Abstract. A new testing method with a digital audio player and document structure diagrams is developed for the dyslexic and the newly blind, who have difficulties with reading in braille or print. Since documents in the National Center Test for University Admissions are very long and have very complicated document structure, ordinary auditory testing media such as human reader or audio cassette are not appropriate. The new testing method can be administrated only with a digital audio player with 2-dimensional code reader and sheets of paper on which document structure diagrams and corresponding invisible 2-dimensional codes are printed.

Keywords: university admissions, testing method, the newly blind, the dyslexic, auditory testing media.

1 Introduction

It is almost impossible for the dyslexic and the newly blind, who have difficulties with reading in braille or print, to take the National Center Test for University Admissions. The National Center Test is the joint achievement test for admissions into all national and local public universities as well as many private universities in Japan. Every year, about 550,000 students take the National Center Test. As for test-takers with disabilities, special arrangements regarding testing media such as large-print-format test and braille-format test have been administered [6]. However, auditory testing media have not been available yet. Moreover, it is considered to be difficult to take the National Center Test with ordinary types of auditory testing media because the documents are very long and the document structure very complicated. This study introduces a new testing method for the dyslexic and the newly blind with a new auditory testing medium.

K. Miesenberger et al. (Eds.): ICCHP 2010, Part I, LNCS 6179, pp. 116–123, 2010.

In most advanced countries, auditory testing media such as human readers [4], audio cassettes [2,8,9] or computers with a screen reader [1] are available for test-takers with disabilities. The simplest method is to recruit readers and have them read out a test booklet to a test-taker directly, but it is not easy to find enough well-trained readers for each test-taker. And for fairness and security reason, it might be necessary to supervise such readers by another person. Audio cassettes make it easy for test-takers to listen to the test sequentially, but it is inconvenient to go directly to a particular section of the test unless rewinding and fast-forwarding can be done easily. Computers are also inappropriate for tests written in Japanese even with an advanced screen reader because of the ambiguity of reading Kanji in Japanese sentences. A screen reader often fails to convert Japanese sentences into correct Japanese speech.

For auditory testing media for the National Center Test, the utilization of DAISY (Digital Audio Accessible Information System) and Tablet PC has been studied [5]. DAISY [3] is a world standard audio system for people with visual disabilities, taking the place of audio cassettes. DAISY offers speech sound in CD quality, and test-takers can listen to the document from any point, such as from an underlined or blank part, without delay. They can also use the talk-speed-control function, by which the speech sound can be adjusted from 1/2 to 3 times normal speed. However, DAISY is not convenient enough for tests which have complicated document structure. Tablet PC has been identified as appropriate testing media [5]. However, there are difficulties in administration because prevention of machine trouble cannot be ensured.

A new testing method with a digital audio player and document structure diagrams is developed. In Fig. 1, an image of administration of the new testing method is shown. Tests can be administrated only with a digital audio player with 2-dimensional code reader and sheets of paper on which document structure diagrams and corresponding invisible 2-dimensional code have been printed. For the dyslexic, the document structure diagrams are printed with ordinary characters, while, for the newly blind, they are printed with braille characters.

2   New Testing Method

A new testing method that can be administrated only with a digital audio player and sheets of document structure diagrams is developed. The introduction of invisible 2-dimensional codes and a digital audio player with 2-dimensional code reader enable us to develop the method.

2.1   Document Structure Diagrams

Document structure diagrams are sheets of paper on which the document structure of each problem is illustrated. The document structure and corresponding invisible 2-dimensional codes are printed on white paper by an LED printer (OKI Data Corporation). For the newly blind, the braille document structure is also embossed overlappingly by a braille printer (ESA721; JTR Corporation).

Fig. 1. An image of administration of the new testing method

現代社会K 第4問				
(1)	文	a	b	
(2)	文			
(3)	文	c	文	
(4)	文			
(5)	文	文	d	文	e
(6)	文	f		
(7)	文	g	文	
(8)	文	文		

問1	20	①	②	③	④			
問2	21	①	②	③	④			
問3	22	①	②	③	④			
問4	23	①	②	③	④			
問5	24	①	②	③	④			
問6	25	①	②	③	④			
問7	文	A	B	文	C			
26	①	②	③	④	⑤	⑥	⑦	⑧

Fig. 2. An example of the document structure diagram printed on a paper

Fig. 2 is an example of a document structure diagram. Each document structure diagram of a problem can be arranged within a sheet of paper.

On the same paper of a document structure diagram, invisible 2-dimensional codes can be printed overlappingly. For an evaluation experiment, we employ 'GridOnput', an invisible 2-dimensional code system developed by Gridmark Solutions Co.,Ltd. Fig. 3 is an image of dot pattern of GridOnput. Dots are arranged at intervals of about 0.25mm. The size of a code is about 2mm square.

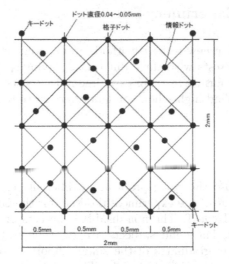

Fig. 3. An image of dot pattern of GridOnput

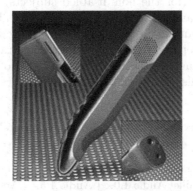

Fig. 4. Speaking Pen (Gridmark Solutions Co.,Ltd.)

2.2 Digital Audio Player with 2-Dimensional Code Reader

As a reading device for the new testing method, we employ 'Speaking Pen' developed by Gridmark Solutions Co.,Ltd. Fig. 4 is a picture of Speaking Pen. Speaking Pen has a 2-dimensional code reader at its top. When a 2-dimensional code is scanned with Speaking Pen, the corresponding digital sound will be reproduced. We can listen to the sound through a headphone or built-in speaker. The sound volume can be adjusted with its buttons mounted at the front side. The sound data is stored in an SD memory card. 1G byte is enough to store all sound data of 1-year amount of the National Center Test.

3   Evaluation Experiment

In order to evaluate the new testing method, an experiment was conducted by comparing new audio tests with three different speaking speeds and a normal-print-format or braille-format test. For experimental subjects, non-disabled high-school students and blind high-school students were recruited.

3.1   Method

The experimental design was a repeated 4x4 Graeco-Latin square method because we could not use the same problem in different testing media for the same person. The image of the experimental design for the Graeco-Latin square method is shown on Table 1. The non-disabled subjects are 20 students from ordinary high schools. The blind subjects are 16 students from a high school for the blind (some are graduates of the same school), who are familiar with both braille and audio learning materials. There were 4 subject groups, i.e., the subjects were evenly divided into 4 subgroups. There were 4 testing media: normal-print-format test (for the non-disabled subjects) or braille-format test (for the blind subjects), audio test of normal ($1.0\times$) speaking speed, audio test of $1.5\times$ speaking speed, and audio test of $2.0\times$ speaking speed.

Four problems were prepared from tests in 'Contemporary Social Studies' previously used in the National Center Test. The allotment of number of characters and number of braille cells are shown on Table 2.

Table 1. Image of the experimental design for the Graeco-Latin square method

	Subect Groups			
	Group 1	Group 2	Group 3	Group 4
1st	Print/Braille Problem 1	Audio 1.0× Problem 3	Audio 1.5× Problem 4	Audio 2.0× Problem 2
2nd	Audio 1.0× Problem 2	Print/Braille Problem 4	Audio 2.0× Problem 3	Audio 1.5× Problem 1
3rd	Audio 1.5× Problem 3	Audio 2.0× Problem 1	Print/Braille Problem 2	Audio 1.0× Problem 4
4th	Audio 2.0× Problem 4	Audio 1.5× Problem 2	Audio 1.0× Problem 1	Print/Braille Problem 3

Table 2. Allotment of number of characters and number of braille cells

	Characters	Braille
Problem 1	2,255	4,866
Problem 2	2,000	4,543
Problem 3	1,796	3,996
Problem 4	2,410	5,247
Total	8,461	26,190

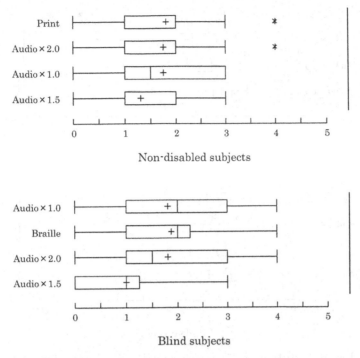

Fig. 5. Distributions of score (marks)

The test procedure is administered without time limits. The behavior of blind subjects was observed by test monitors, and the answer-process time of blind subjects was recorded by the monitors using stop watches.

3.2 Result

The distributions of score of the four testing media were almost same for both non-disabled subjects and blind subjects. In Fig. 5, the box-and-whiskers plots of distribution of score of the four testing media are shown. The vertical lines in the middle of the boxes indicate the median, and the '+' symbols in the boxes are the mean. The vertical lines on the right side of the plots are the results of Scheffe's grouping among the four testing media. For both non-disabled subjects and blind subjects, there were no significant differences among the four testing media.

As a result of Mann-Whitney test on the distributions of score, there were no significant differences between non-disabled subjects and blind subjects for each testing media.

There were some significant differences concerning answering speed in Scheffe's grouping test. In Fig. 6, the box-and-whiskers plots of distributions of answering speed of the four testing media are shown. The vertical lines on the right side of the plots are the results of Scheffe's grouping among the four testing media. For non-disabled subjects, the answering speed of normal-print-format test is significantly faster than audio tests of all speaking speed, and the answering speed

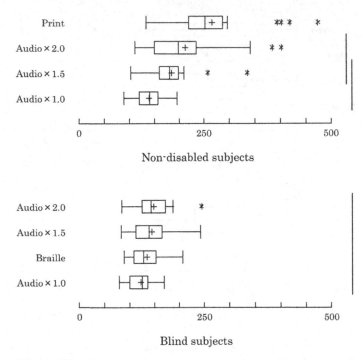

Fig. 6. Distributions of answering speed (characters/minuites)

of audio tests of 2.0× is significantly faster than audio test of normal speaking speed. For blind subjects, there were no significant differences among the four testing media.

As a result of Mann-Whitney test on the distributions of answering speed, the answering speeds of non-disabled subjects are significantly faster than blind subjects except audio test of normal speaking speed.

We found that the answering speed becomes 29% faster for non-disabled subjects and 10% faster for blind subjects if audio test of 1.5× speaking speed is used comparing to normal speaking speed. If audio test of 2.0× speaking speed is used, the answering speed becomes 41% faster for non-disabled subjects and 13% faster for blind subjects.

4   Conclusion

The new testing method enables the dyslexic and the newly blind to take the National Center Test for University Admissions since the administration of the new testing method is easy, and test-takers can handle problems with complicated document structure. We can administrate tests only with a digital audio player with 2-dimensional code reader and sheets of paper on which document structure diagrams and corresponding invisible 2-dimensional code have been printed. The use of testing materials is considerably easy. After brief training, test-takers can start reading problems at any point of their preference. Studies about auditory explanation of figures [7] might be applied to this testing method. If we print 2-dimensional codes on figures, we can set problems with figures.

As a result of evaluation experiment, the new audio tests are almost equivalent to normal-print-format and braille-format tests in score. Since we can estimate fair extension ratios of testing time for students with disabilities [6], the new audio tests can be fairly administered.

Acknowledgement

This work was partially supported by Grant-in-Aid for Scientific Research (B) (20300282) of Japan Society for the Promotion of Science (JSPS).

References

1. Allan, M.J., Bulla, N., Goodman, S.A.: Test access: guidelines for computer administered testing. American Printing House for the Blind, Kentucky (2003)
2. Allman, C.B.: Test access: making tests accessible for students with visual impairments: A guide for test publishers, test developers, and state assessment personnel, 2nd edn. American Printing House for the Blind, Kentucky (2004)
3. DAISY Consortium: DAISY 2.02 Specification (2001), http://www.daisy.org/publications/specifications/daisy/_202.html
4. Educational Testing Service: Resources for test takers with disabilities: Guidelines for a Test Reader (2006), http://www.ets.org/disability/index.html
5. Fujiyoshi, M., Fujiyoshi, A.: A new audio testing system for the newly blind and the learning disabled to take the national center test for university admissions. In: Miesenberger, K., Klaus, J., Zagler, W.L., Karshmer, A.I. (eds.) ICCHP 2006. LNCS, vol. 4061, pp. 801–808. Springer, Heidelberg (2006)
6. Fujiyoshi, M., Fujiyoshi, A.: Estimating testing time extension ratios for students with disabilities from item cumulative curves. In: New Developments in Psychometrics, Proceedings of the International Meeting of the Psychometric Society IMPS 2001, pp. 265–272 (2003)
7. Landau, S., Bourquin, G., Van Schaack, A., Miele, J.: Demonstration of a universally accessible audio-haptic transit map built on a digital pen-based platform. In: Pirhonen, A., Brewster, S. (eds.) HAID 2008. LNCS, vol. 5270, pp. 23–24. Springer, Heidelberg (2008)
8. Ragosta, M., Wendler, C.: Eligibility issues and comparable time limits for disabled and nondisabled SAT examinees. ETS Research Report, RR-92-35, 1–33 (1992)
9. Willingham, W.W., Ragosta, M., Bennett, R.E., Braun, H., Rock, D.A., Powers, D.E.: Testing handicapped people. Allyn and Bacon, Boston (1988)

Annotating and Describing Pictures – Applications in E-Learning and Accessibility of Graphics

Ivan Kopeček and Radek Ošlejšek

Faculty of Informatics, Masaryk University
Botanicka 68a, 602 00 Brno, Czech Republic
{kopecek,oslejsek}@fi.muni.cz

Abstract. The paper describes the ontology based approach to the annotation of graphical objects in relation to the accessibility of graphics. Some applications in e-leaning are also discussed. The problem concerning the optimality of graphical ontologies in relation with the annotation process is addressed and an optimality measure enabling algorithmic solution of this problem is proposed. Finally, an approach to generating picture description is presented.

Keywords: Accessibility of graphics; picture annotation; e-learning; ontology.

1 Introduction

For visually impaired Internet users, accessibility of graphics is the matter of primary importance. Up to now, some papers concerning accessing a graphical content by means of annotation and semantic data in various contexts have been published, see e.g. [1,2,3]. The ontology-based annotation of photos is discussed in [4]. Some works analyze to what extent the sound information can be used to investigate graphical objects, see e.g. [5,6,7,8].

The dialogue-based annotation and inspection of vector and raster images is supported by the *GATE (Graphics Accessible To Everyone)* project [9]. The communication is based on *What-Where Language – WWL*. Each sentence of WWL has the form of "WHAT is WHERE" or "WHERE is WHAT". It enables the user to ask simple questions about the objects in the scene and their position. The following fragment of a dialogue demonstrates how the annotated picture in Fig. 1 (left) can be inspected by WWL (*U = User, S = System*):

U: What is on the left?
S: On the left there is a small elephant.
U: Where is the elephant?
S: There are two elephants. One is on the left, another on the right.
U: What is in the foreground?
S: In the foreground there is a big gray stone.

K. Miesenberger et al. (Eds.): ICCHP 2010, Part I, LNCS 6179, pp. 124–130, 2010.

Fig. 1. Annotated photography with explicitly marked out significant objects (left) and the Christmas card generated by means of dialogue (right)

The GATE system also offers basic services for generating pictures by means of a dialogue. The user can ask for object from database and place it in desired position of target picture using the *Recursive Navigation Grid – RNG* [10,11]. The Christmas card in Fig. 2 (right) has been generated by the blind user through the following dialogue:

U: Put a comet in the sector 9.
S: Object comet has been added into the location upper right.
U: Put a snowman into the bottom left corner.
S: Object snowman has been added into the location bottom left.
U: Write the text "Merry Christmas and Happy New Year" into the horizontal center, color yellow.
S: Text Merry Christmas and Happy New Year has been added into the location horizontal center.
U: Write the text "PF 2010" into the bottom right corner, color blue.
S: Text PF 2010 has been added into the location right down.
U: Generate.
S: Please choose a style of background from combo-box and wait a while until generation ends.

2   Graphical Ontology

Ontology, as described by the *Ontology Web Language – OWL* [12], for instance, represents a formalism which structures the knowledge, prevents chaos in terminology and keeps the semantics consistent. Ontology-driven annotation guides users to create structured and semantically correct picture description. However, ontology does not restrict abstraction used to describe the real world, as shown in Fig. 2 (left). To maximally exploit ontologies in the context of pictures, the abstraction should cover only the aspects of graphical objects that are visually recognizable and thus valuable for the image recognition and description. *Graphical ontology* [13] restricts the generic ontology by prescribing important global visual characteristics and constraints and thus guides the users to create proper abstraction. It consists of four classifications covering different visual aspects of annotated pictures.

- *Picture classification* covers the properties which are related to the whole annotated picture, e.g. genre (photography, sketch, graph, painting, ...), central focus (i.e. dominant objects in the picture), etc. These peaces of information are useful mainly in the first stage of dialogue when the user is supplied with a brief description of the picture and the dialogue system selects a suitable dialogue strategy.
- *Topological classification* categorizes objects by their compactness and topology. *Compact objects* are those having significant shape, e.g. tree, human being, etc., as opposed to non-compact objects, e.g. sky, fog, smoke, etc. *Clusters* represent collections of objects of the same type, e.g. forest, crowd, etc., while *conglomerates* represent collections of variable objects, e.g. computer consisting of case, monitor and printer. These characteristics are useful for pictures navigation, image recognition and information filtering (cluster of many trees in the picture can be identified as a forest, for instance).
- *Geometric classification* handles geometric aspects of depicted objects, e.g. unusual size (abnormally big, high, narrow, ...), significant shape (oval, angular, crooked, ...), orientation in space (front-view, rear-view, ...), etc. These characteristics are to be used to describe significant geometry divergence from the obvious state in terms of natural language. For example, elephant is obviously a big animal and thus this fact need not to be included in the annotation until a concrete elephant in a picture looks abnormally big.
- *Color classification* covers aspects related to illumination and colors. Significant changes in colors and contrast often affect atmosphere of the picture and may cause misunderstanding of the scene. Color classification aims to avoid this problem be defining several characteristics, e.g. dominant color (ravens are usually black), light direction· (dark silhouettes due to a back light), ambient light (red shades of the picture due to the sunset), etc.

3   E-Learning

The knowledge-driven annotation supported by ontologies seems to be very valuable for e-learning. Specialized ontology can contain a lot of additional information, which is not directly present in the picture, e.g. detailed description of objects in many languages, links to other relevant objects and terms in the ontology, etc.

For example, let us consider Fig. 2 (right) showing the chemical structure of the antioxidant reservatrol. Knowing nothing about chemistry, we stand no chance of being able to annotate the picture reasonably until there is a knowledge database associated with the chemical ontology. Moreover, the sub-objects, e.g. benzene nucleus or hydroxyl group, can be linked to their definitions in the ontology, which enables the students to recall them when "viewing" the picture. The students can ask the question "What is benzene nucleus" and they obtain the correct answer.

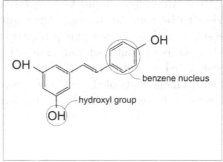

Fig. 2. Object abstraction [14] (left) and antioxidant reservatrol (right)

4   Enhancing the Efficiency of the Annotation

The structure of graphical ontology substantially influences the time in which the annotator annotates a graphical object. Moreover, some attributes of the graphical objects can be determined automatically (color, shape, special sub-objects that can be detected by the current graphical methods, etc.). To make the annotator's task easier, the structure of the graphical ontology should be optimized. This can be done by giving preferences to substantial attributes contributing to efficient ontology structure and the attributes that can be determined automatically.

4.1   Graphical Ontology Construction and Optimization

Unfortunately, graphical ontologies mostly cannot directly incorporate existing special ontologies. For example, consider an ontology of living objects based on the biological taxonomy. The living objects are divided into so called "Kingdoms": animals, plants, protists (single-celled creatures), Fungi (mushrooms, mold, etc.) and Monera (consisting of three types of bacteria). Kingdom is divided into Phyla. A well known example of phylum is Chordata, containing animals having backbone. The next category is Class. For example, the phylum Chordata is divided into Birds, Reptiles, Amphibians, Mammals, etc. Each class is divided into one or more Orders. Mammals consists of Rodentia (mice, rats), Primates, Insectivora (shrews, moles), Carnivora (dogs, cats, weasels), Perissodactyla (horses, zebras), Artiodactyla (cows), Proboscidea (elephants), etc. Next categories are Families, Genus and Species, where the specification goes into more and more detail.

It is clear, that this ontology would be for our purposes not usable, because only specialist would be able to characterize living objects using this classification. On the other hand, our goal is not to precisely characterize the object, but just to get a satisfactory description. Therefore, it is reasonable to restrict ourselves to well known types of living objects like dog, cat, blackbird, cow, etc., and instead of using exact biological denotations to give the user an understandable description.

What attributes should be utilized to create an ontology and what is a criterion to be used to measure optimality of a given ontology? To answer this question, we have to put this problem formally.

Let M be a finite set and S a subset of M. Let us assume that we have constructed a rooted tree R which nodes are elements of M and leaves are exactly all elements of the set S. R represents our ontology, the set S represents objects in the ontology, nodes that are not leaves represent attributes and edges represent the values of the attributes.

Rooted trees (see e. g. [15]) are denoted by ordered pairs $R = (V, A)$ of nodes and edges. A root is denoted by r. We denote the set of all successors of a node x by $q(x)$. Further, we denote by $L(R)$ the set of all leaves of R.

The search algorithm, classifying the annotated object within the ontology, is performed in the following way.

1. We start at the root r of the tree.
2. In each node s we proceed to the node, which is a successor of s and the edge connecting it with the node s is the value of the attribute that characterizes the classified object.
3. We finish when the actual node is a leaf.

Let $R = (V, A)$ be a finite rooted tree, $x, y \in V$, and suppose that there exists an $(n + 1)$-tuple $(x_0, x_1, \ldots, x_n)$ such that $(x_{i-1}, x_i) \in A, x_0 = x, x_n = y$. The set $\{x_0, x_1, \ldots, x_n\}$ will be denoted $P(x, y)$ and we use notation $y < x$.

Let $R = (V, A)$ be a rooted tree, $x, y \in V$, $card(V) > 1$ and $y < x$. We put

$$w(x, y) = \sum_{z \in P(x,y) - \{y\}} card(q(z))$$

and

$$W(R) = \sum_{z \in L(R)} w(r, z)$$

($card(M)$ denotes the number of elements of the set M).

The value $w(r, z)$ is the number of decisions to be taken by the user to classify the annotated object provided that the classification of the object is the leaf of the rooted tree denoted by z. It is reasonable to take it as a measure that approximately expresses the time needed to annotate this object. Consequently, the value $W(R)$ can be taken as a measure of optimality for the whole rooted tree R. (When divided by $card(L(R))$, it can be understood as a mean time needed to annotate an arbitrary object within the ontology R.)

Having adopted $W(R)$ as an optimality measure for the ontology R, we are able to optimize the ontology structure. When constructing the graphical ontology, we cope the problem of how to optimally (with respect to the optimality measure $W(R)$) choose the ontology attributes from a set of possible attributes and how to construct an optimal rooted tree. It can be shown, that this problem is NP-complete. Therefore, when the number of possible attributes is large, we might face a problem with exponential algorithmic complexity and some approximative algorithms have to be applied.

5   Generating Picture Description

Brief description of a picture in natural language gives to the visually impaired user a basic and important summary about the picture. In the GATE project, it is coupled with other ways of investigating the picture. Nevertheless, even as a "standalone" piece of information, description of a picture can be assigned to graphical objects, making them more accessible.

The annotation of a picture gives a convenient base for the algorithms used for generating a picture description. The simplest and straightforward way to generate a picture description from the values of the attributes that annotate a picture is a frame based approach.

Within this approach, the values of the attributes enable the system to fill slots in a template in order to create natural language sentences describing the substantial pieces of information about the described picture. The templates are divided into groups corresponding to the basic types of graphical objects (photographs, sketches, graphs, etc.) and are applied if the types of the slots agree with the types of a convenient subset of the attributes of the annotated picture. For instance, the sentence "The picture shows a landscape with a chalet in the foreground and woods in the background" is generated from the template "The picture shows SLOT1 with SLOT2 in the foreground and SLOT3 in the background", where the slots are filled with the attributes taken from the picture annotation. The template may be taken from the group of the templates assigned to the graphical type "photography".

Although the basic idea is straightforward and simple, there are some problems that are to be solved. The first problem is how to create the set of the templates corresponding to a database of pictures? To what extent can it be done automatically? Another key problem is related to the necessity to decide what pieces of information in the generated description will be explicit. For instance, in the simple example mentioned before, we apparently need not add that the woods in the background are green, because it is a "default value". If, however, the woods are red (in Autumn), this piece of information has a greater weight and should possibly be mentioned, depending on how brief we are trying to be. This can be either determined by the user when the description is generated on the fly or decided in relation to other aspects of the relevant context. In the paper, we present more detailed discussion of the topic and provide some basic algorithms and illustrative examples.

6   Conclusions and Future Work

The presented approach to annotating and describing pictures seems to be promising and suitable for web applications, e-learning applications and electronic textbooks. Knowledge-driven annotation and description will enhance the possibility of fully automatic annotation and description. In the future work we plan to concentrate on this topic. The GATE project is being developed in collaboration with Support Centre for Students with Special Needs of Masaryk University. The Center participates in testing system modules and provides feedback for the methods being developed. Further testing and making the system as comfortable for the blind users as possible represent another important goal of the future work.

Acknowledgments. The authors are grateful to the students and staff of the Support Centre for Students with Special Needs of Masaryk University for their advice, support and collaboration. This work has been supported by the Czech Science Foundation, Czech Republic, under Contract No. GA 201/07/0881 and the MSMT under the research program LC-06008.

References

1. Bulatov, V., Gardner, J.: Making graphics accessible. In: 3rd Annual Conference on Scalable Vector Graphics, Tokyo (September 2004)
2. Fredj, Z.B., Duce, D.: Grassml: Accessible smart schematic diagrams for all. In: Theory and Practice of Computer Graphics, June 2003, pp. 49–55. IEEE Computer Society, Los Alamitos (2003)
3. Mathis, R.M.: Constraint scalable vector graphics, accessibility and the semantic web. In: SoutheastCon Proceedings, pp. 588–593. IEEE Computer Society, Los Alamitos (2005)
4. Schreiber, G., Dubbeldam, B., Wielemaker, J., Wielinga, B.: Ontology-based photo annotation. IEEE Intelligent Systems (2001)
5. Daunys, G., Lauruska, V.: Maps sonification system using digitiser for visually impaired children. In: Miesenberger, K., Klaus, J., Zagler, W.L., Karshmer, A.I. (eds.) ICCHP 2006. LNCS, vol. 4061, pp. 12–15. Springer, Heidelberg (2006)
6. Franklin, K.M., Roberts, J.C.: Pie chart sonification. In: Proceedings of Information Visualization (IV 2003), London, UK, July 2003, pp. 4–9. IEEE Computer Society Press, Los Alamitos (2003)
7. Kopeček, I., Ošlejšek, R.: Hybrid approach to sonification of color images. In: The 2008 Int. Conf. on Convergence and Hybrid Information Technologies, pp. 722–727. IEEE Computer Society, Los Alamitos (2008)
8. Matta, S., Rudolph, H., Kumar, D.K.: Auditory eyes: Representing visual information in sound and tactile cues. In: 13th European Signal Processing Conference, Antalya (2005)
9. Kopeček, I., Ošlejšek, R.: GATE to accessibility of computer graphics. In: Miesenberger, K., Klaus, J., Zagler, W.L., Karshmer, A.I. (eds.) ICCHP 2008. LNCS, vol. 5105, pp. 295–302. Springer, Heidelberg (2008)
10. Kopeček, I., Ošlejšek, R.: The blind and creating computer graphics. In: Proceedings of the Second IASTED Int. Conf. on Computational Intelligence, pp. 343–348. ACTA Press, Zurich (2006)
11. Kamel, H.M., Landay, J.A.: Sketching images eyes-free: a grid-based dynamic drawing tool for the blind. In: Proceedings of the fifth international ACM conference on Assistive technologies, pp. 33–40. ACM Press, New York (2002)
12. Lacy, L.W.: Owl: Representing Information Using the Web Ontology Language. Trafford Publishing (January 2005)
13. Ošlejšek, R.: Annotation of pictures by means of graphical ontologies. In: Proc. Int. Conf. on Internet Computing, ICOMP 2009, pp. 296–300. CSREA Press (2009)
14. Booch, G., Maksimchuk, R.A., Engel, M.W., Young, B.J., Conallen, J., Houston, K.A.: Object-Oriented Analysis and Design with Applications. Addison-Wesley Professional, Reading (2007)
15. Mayeda, W.: Graph Theory. Wiley, New York (1972)

New Concepts of PC Interaction for Blind Users Based on Braille Displays with ATC Technology (Active Tactile Control)

Siegfried Kipke

Handy Tech GmbH, Brunnenstraße 10, 72160 Horb, Germany
info@handytech.de

Abstract. Braille presented as a combination of raised dots is a very important way of accessing information for blind computer users offering crucial advantages compared to speech output. The ATC (Active Tactile Control) technology allows new PC interactions based on detecting the tactile reading position in real-time on a Braille display. Reading position sensitive assistant functions and context depended controls, like task overview and Braille frames, are introduced.

1 Braille Displays Used for PC Interaction by Blind Users

Braille presented as a combination of tactile raised dots is a very important way of accessing information for blind computer users. Compared to speech output systems, Braille showing as a combination of raised dots on a so-called Braille display offers a lot of advantages. Braille shows structured information and allows blind users a self determined reading. Braille is an excellent literacy tool and at the same time is a discreet way for presenting information.

By detecting the reading position with Active Tactile Control (ATC), new interaction for blind users with computer systems are now possible to improve their productivity.

2 State of the Art Braille Displays

Braille displays present tactile information as a combination of raised dots using 2 by 4 dots matrix on each Braille cell. Often a row of 40 or 80 Braille cells is used for Braille output. Beside Braille output, a Braille display offers a set of control elements like command keys, cursor routing keys and navigation keys.

3 ATC (Active Tactile Control) Technology

The ATC (Active Tactile Control) technology allows detecting the tactile reading position on a Braille display in real-time. 20 times a second the reading position is calculated by analyzing the force applied to each tactile pin of a Braille display. In the case of a Modular Evolution 88 there are 704 Pins to be monitored.

K. Miesenberger et al. (Eds.): ICCHP 2010, Part I, LNCS 6179, pp. 131–134, 2010.

The detection of the reading position makes it possible to improve the efficiency of a blind user to interact with a computer.

The most commonly used assistance function of ATC is the automatic scrolling: When reaching the end of the line, the next section of the text will be displayed on the Braille display. Especially when reading a lot of text on a Braille display, this function becomes really appreciated. Without ATC it is necessary to navigate a text manually by pressing the navigation keys.

To be able to assist in different reading situations, ATC distinguishes between four different reading behaviours and different function can be assigned for each

— Reading – the normal reading moving from left to right
— Speed reading – if reading above a certain defined speed
— Resting – when reading longer than a specific time
— Backwards – when reading backwards on a Braille display

3.1 Logging the Reading Behaviour (Log File)

Since the reading position is detected by ATC, it is also possible to save the changes of the reading position in a log file. As part of the universal driver of Handy Tech, supporting different screen readers, log files can be created monitoring the reading position. All changes on the Braille display as well as the time sequence of the tactile reading positions are recorded in a Log file. This Log file enables the teacher in detail to analyze the student's reading behaviour and isolate certain areas for improvements.

The ATC-LogAnalyser was created as an analyzing tool for log file providing teachers with information about the tactile reading flow like:

— How many words per minute, how many characters per minute have been read
— Changes of the reading speed within a session
— How often the student has to read backwards
— How many characters and how many words have not been read by the student
— The reading flow during the whole session
— Reading speed for different characters and character combinations.

4   Research and Methodical Approach

The first implementation of assistant function was mainly focused to support the process of learning Braille. Meanwhile new approaches have been developed to investigate how the use of ATC could improve the productivity of Braille readers in the work environment. An international group of experts, mainly Braille display users, have defined the areas of where ATC can be turned into an effective tool for PC interaction. Three areas of PC interactions where prioritized:

4.1   Providing Background Information for the Tactile Reading Position

Braille characters presented on the Braille display have a constant size and a constant height of the dots presenting the tactile information. This does not allow displaying properties of the information like the font size and text attributes simultaneously to the actual textual information. With the knowledge of the tactile reading position, detected by ATC, it is now possible to provide the Braille reader additional information of the context of their reading position.

There are two general approaches of how to present this background information. The first option is to show additional information as modification of the tactile presentation or secondly have the context information like changes of text attributions announced by a speech output.

4.2 Manipulation the Tactile Content by the Detected Reading Position

Similar to the idea of using cursor routing bottoms at the Braille output to be able to place the cursor at the corresponding position it is possible to use the ATC technology to directly interact with the content shown on the Braille display. So, without the need to reach for the PC keyboard, a blind user can directly control the feedback to the PC by reading the tactile presentation of information on the Braille display. One simple example is tracking or placing the mouse pointer along with the reading position.

Another implementation of a PC interaction control by the reading position is that after activation, e.g. by tapping twice on a selected position on the Braille display, the section of text covered by the position read will be marked.

4.3 Simultaneous Access to Several Active Windows or Sub Windows

4.3.1 Task Overview and Direct Access on the Braille Display

Only the active task running on a computer is presented to the blind computer user on a Braille display from computer access programs, called screen reader. When using a multi tasking operating systems, such as Microsoft Windows, the blind user also wants quick access to the different task running.

ATC is able to provide quick access to different tasks. Implemented as a script for the screen reader Window-Eyes, the different task running are presented by a self explaining letter e.g. o for Outlook, w for MS Word and so on. If e.g. 5 tasks are running, 5 letters representing them are shown on the Braille display in the order they were started. This task indication is followed by a blank Braille cell. So at a Braille display with 88 Braille cells six of them will be occupied by the task representation. The remaining Braille cells of the Braille display are acting like a 82 character Braille display.

The active task is presented in addition to the letter with the Braille dots 7 and 8. by touching the different letters, ATC enables the system to announce the different tasks. By clicking on a task with cursor routing, the task presented will be shown in the foreground. By activating cursor routing on the active task, all tasks will be minimized.

4.3.2 Reading Position Sensitive Controls Using Braille Framing

The ATC Technology allows blind users for the first time the direct control of several applications presented as windows parallel on the screen. Applications or sub windows of applications are displayed on dedicated sections on the Braille display in so-called Braille frames.

Depending on the tactile reading position on the Braille display the focus will position on the corresponding frame. The current frame is the frame with the current reading position detected by ATC.

A good example to use this Braille framing technology is the Windows Explorer. Here the two frames are the directory tree and the file list. When the tactile reading position is at the directory tree frame, the controls of the Braille display can be used to scroll in the folder list. When reading in the file list frame, the controls are for scrolling in the list of files.

Frames can also be used to show additional information depending on the reading position. When for example a spelling mistake is detected at the reading position, a frame could appear showing the correction selection of the spell checker dialog. By selecting the correction, the frame will vanish from the Braille display. Then, the Braille display is showing the whole content of the original text field.

Using this Braille framing technology, a blind computer user can benefit from presentation of multiple applications or frames shown as windows on a screen.

The Modular Evolution from Handy Tech is the world's first sensitive Braille display using the ATC-Technology. Designed for the work environment, the Modular Evolution is available with 88 or 64 Braille cells.

5 Conclusion and Next Steps

ATC opens up new methods of interaction with a PC for blind users. This technology step in the field of computer access for blind user is comparable with the introduction of touch screens for sighted users. This new interaction helps to increase the efficiency of blind computer users.

After the complete implementation of the described new methods the next area for implementing ATC is the presentation on the Braille display. It will be investigated how displaying Braille can be modified to improve the tactile reading flow of blind users. It is also planned to improve the flexibility of ATC used for teaching Braille remotely.

Inclusive E-Services for All: Identifying Accessibility Requirements for Upcoming Interaction Technologies

Alejandro Rodriguez-Ascaso[1], Erik Zetterström[2], Martin Böcker[3],
Helge Hüttenrauch[4], Michael Pluke[5], and Matthias Schneider[3]

[1] aDeNu research group / UNED, Spain
arascaso@dia.uned.es
[2] Omnitor AB, Sweden
erik.zetterstrom@omnitor.se
[3] Böcker & Schneider GbR, Germany
boecker@humanfactors.de, msch@usability-labs.de
[4] Royal Institute of Technology (KTH), Sweden
hehu@csc.kth.se
[5] Castle Consulting Ltd., England
mike.pluke@castle-consult.com

Abstract. Information and Communication Technologies (ICT) have the potential of facilitating the lives of citizens. However, experience consistently shows that user-interface innovations for consumer products are being researched and developed without taking into account the needs of people with disabilities. This situation is not helped by the fact that product and service developers can be unaware of the requirements of customers with impairments and therefore lack the insight into appropriate design solutions that may not be very demanding in terms of R&D and production costs. ETSI, the European Telecommunications Standards Institute, has established a Specialist Task Force (STF) 377 on "Inclusive eServices for all: Optimizing the accessibility and use of upcoming user interaction technology". The aim of this working group is to systematically evaluate ongoing and forthcoming interaction technologies to sketch a 10-year roadmap of foreseen technological enablers.

Keywords: Design for All, Accessibility, User Interaction, HCI and Non Classical Interfaces, Technology Roadmap, Standardisation, ETSI.

1 Introduction

Experience consistently shows that user-interface innovations for electronic products and services are being researched, developed, and introduced without taking into account the needs of people with disability. In the case of the IT research sector, it generally lacks of limited awareness about functional diversity of ICT users.

Design for all in ICT should not be conceived as an effort to advance a single solution for everybody, but as a user-centred approach to providing environments designed in such a way that they cater for the broadest possible range of human needs, requirements and preferences, see [1]. For most user-interface design tasks, a number

K. Miesenberger et al. (Eds.): ICCHP 2010, Part I, LNCS 6179, pp. 135–138, 2010.

of different solutions exist that differ in terms of their suitability for different user groups. User-interface design should include the selection and combination of various user-interface modalities with the goal of supporting the most diverse user community possible.

As the ICT industry has not typically offered designed-for-all innovative products and services, ETSI, the European Telecommunications Standards Institute, has established Special Task Force (STF) 377 on "Inclusive eServices for all: Optimizing the accessibility and use of upcoming user interaction technology" in order to help industry to easily do so in the future. This project is funded by the Commission of the European Communities (EC) and the European Free Trade Area (EFTA).

The aim of the task force is to systematically evaluate ongoing and forthcoming interaction technologies in order to sketch a 10-year roadmap of foreseen technological enablers. Main aspects of the accessibility of such interaction technologies will be specifically addressed, in order to allow stakeholders in different stages of the research and development lifecycle (researchers, designers, developers, etc.) to spot potential difficulties to be experienced by elderly or disabled users and to learn about solutions that rectify those shortcomings. At the time of writing, first results are available. However, any comments and contributions can still be considered for inclusion in the final deliverable.

2   Method and First Results

Throughout this work, the focus is on the user, the usage context and the interaction components of the eService. In the course of the project the following tasks are being performed. Particular attention will be paid to the task dealing with Design for All provision for new interaction technologies.

Step 1: Analysis of forthcoming services. The analysis of existing and forthcoming services leads to the selection, definition, and categorization of the services covered by the ETSI Guide. Those include services such as eHealth, eGovernment, eLearning, eCommerce, travel, and leisure, as these and other services are likely to affect older and disabled citizens and consumers.

Step 2: Analysis of service interaction profiles for each service category. The services within the scope of the ETSI Guide (result of task 1) have been analysed in terms of their likely service components (atomic functional components of eservices such as identification, exchange of synchronous and asynchronous messages, voice conversation, information browsing, etc.). This is done by defining the service components a service can be expected to employ. The list of service components has been adapted from ITU related work [5]. The service components are then mapped onto user interaction styles such as gesture recognition, virtual reality, touch input, key input, and voice input. At this stage, any eService can generally be broken down into relevant user interaction styles. At the next step, forthcoming user interaction technologies need to be identified that are likely going to be employed for those forms of user interaction.

Step 3: Analysis of forthcoming interaction technologies (technology roadmaps). Roadmaps of forthcoming user interface technologies are being developed by employing established R&D procedures. During this step relevant interaction technologies for the services defined in step 2 will be identified. For each user-interaction technology, a number of characteristics are being collected in the form of a database. Among the data collected are:

- A description of the technology, related technologies, and expected mass-market deployment.
- User requirements in terms of accessibility required for making use of the technology.
- Benefits for all users and potential benefits for users with disabilities.
- Solutions for overcoming the exclusion of disabled users, implementation requirements for the solution, and harmonization issues.

Step 4: Matching of service interaction profiles and interaction technologies roadmap. In the fourth step, the services interaction profiles identified in step 2 are being mapped onto the interaction technologies identified in step 3. The resulting relation between services and their possible interaction technologies can be used to identify solutions for design-for-all provisions required.

Step 5: Design-for-All provisions for new interaction technologies. The outcome of this step will be the definition of provisions that have to be made prior to or at the introduction of each new technology in order to enable the support of emerging services for users with disability. Previous standards have produced an excellent basis on accessibility requirements of ICT users. Hence, standards on requirements and guidance about accessibility to ICT, such as [2], [3] and [4], will be used as the methodological framework when analysing accessibility of new interaction technologies and styles. However, emerging interaction techniques may pose interaction challenges that still remain unaddressed by generic standards. One of the reasons behind may be that certain modalities (e.g. haptic/tactile) that have an increasing importance in user interfaces have been traditionally used more as a complement to other modalities (e.g. visual and auditory) than as main interaction channels. Therefore, attention will be paid to on-going standardisation activities which are specific to such modalities (e.g. [6]). Furthermore, a scientific review on accessibility aspects of emerging interaction paradigms such as gesture recognition or virtual reality has been done.

As an example of our work in a particular interaction technology, a preliminary list of accessibility requirements based on [3] (section 5.1.2), [7], [8] and [9] has been identified for the need to perceive visual information when interacting with eServices using Visual Augmented Reality:

- Renderings should disambiguate information about distance or position (eliminate depth ambiguity). This can be achieved by using the appropriate clues (e.g., motion parallax, size-constancy/scaling, transparency, occlusion, binocular clues, etc.).
- Users should be able to select perceptual cues. Specific perceptual cues (e.g., motion parallax, binocular clues, or size-constancy/scaling) should be selected if displays are operating in an environment of a limited range of depths/distances, or according to user accessibility needs.
- Information should be displayed in order to be accommodated to human visual sensitivity. To achieve this, unneeded AR motion (e.g., the slowly moving self-organization of rendered AR tags) should be removed.

- To perceive foreground visual information in the presence of background. Changing backgrounds are inherent to augmented reality. Robust mechanisms should ensure that foreground visual information is perceivable to users.
- Text should be readable with reduced visual acuity. To achieve this, ensure that the algorithms for text presentations are robust to ensure that text is readable with reduced visual acuity.
- Visual information should also be available in auditory and tactile form.
- Rendering should be configurable in a way that all the information generated is perceived by users who see with only one eye.

3 Discussion

ETSI STF 377 will publish an ETSI Guide (EG) that will allow designers and implementers of novel user-interface technologies or eServices to assess at a very early stage whether a proposed product or service potentially excludes elderly and/or disabled users and to learn about corrective solutions ideally to be applied as part of the mainstream design process prior to the market introduction of the device or service. In addition, interaction technology areas needing human-factors standardization work will be identified.

Acknowledgments. The ETSI Specialist Task Force 377 "Inclusive eServices for all: Optimizing the accessibility and use of upcoming user interaction technology" is co-funded by EC/EFTA.

References

1. Stephanidis, C., Salvendy, G., et al.: Toward an Information Society for All: An International R&D Agenda. International Journal of Human-Computer Interaction 10(2), 107–134 (1998)
2. ETSI EG 202 116: Human Factors (HF); Guidelines for ICT products and services; Design for All (2002)
3. ISO TR 29138-1:2009 Information technology — Accessibility considerations for people with disabilities — Part 1: User needs summary
4. ISO/TR 22411:2008 Ergonomics data and guidelines for the application of ISO/IEC Guide 71 to products and services to address the needs of older persons and persons with disabilities
5. ITU-T. NGN FG. Proceedings. Part II. ITU (2005),
   http://www.itu.int/ITU-T/ngn/files/NGN_FG-book_II.pdf
6. ISO/FDIS 9241-920 Ergonomics of human-system interaction — Part 920: Guidance on tactile and haptic interaction
7. Furmanski, C., Azuma, R., Daily, M.: Augmented-reality visualizations guided by cognition: Perceptual heuristics for combining visible and obscured information. In: Proceedings of the International Symposium on Mixed and Augmented Reality, ISMAR 2002 (2002)
8. Gabbard, J.L., Swan, J.E., Hix, D., Kim, S.-J., Fitch, G.: Active Text Drawing Styles for Outdoor Aug-mented Reality: A User-Based Study and Design Implications. In: Proceedings of the Virtual Reality Conference, VR 2007 (2007)
9. Zhou, Z., Cheok, A.D., Yang, X., Qiu, Y.: An experimental study on the role of 3D sound in augmented reality environment. Interacting with Computers 16(6), 1043–1068 (2004)

HAIL: Hierarchical Adaptive Interface Layout

John Magee and Margrit Betke

Computer Science Department, Boston University
111 Cummington St, Boston, MA 02215 USA
{mageejo,betke}@cs.bu.edu

Abstract. We present a framework to adapt software to the needs of individuals with severe motion disabilities who use mouse substitution interfaces. Typically, users are required to adapt to the interfaces that they wish to use. We propose interfaces that change and adapt to the user and their individual abilities. The Hierarchical Adaptive Interface Layout (HAIL) model is a set of specifications for the design of user interface applications that adapt to the user. In HAIL applications, all of the interactive components take place on configurable toolbars along the edge of the screen. We show two HAIL-based applications: a general purpose web browser and a Twitter client.

Keywords: Adaptive User Interfaces, Video-Based Interfaces, Camera Mouse, Web Browsers, Social Networking.

1 Introduction

Severe paralysis can have several causes. Degenerative neurological diseases such as Amyotrophic Lateral Sclerosis (ALS) and Multiple Sclerosis (MS) can result in progressive impairments. Brain and spinal cord injuries due to cerebral palsy, brain-stem stroke, or trauma can cause paralysis and impairments that remain static or may improve with therapy over time. It is important that the assistive technology that individuals with these movement impairments use can adapt to changes of the individuals' conditions. We present a framework for adapting software applications that individuals use with mouse substitution interfaces. We tested our work with the Camera Mouse[1], a video-based interface that detects and converts head movements into mouse pointer movements.

The Camera Mouse has emerged as a popular assistive technology used by individuals with severe motion impairments. Connor et al. [1] conducted experiments with several individuals using the Camera Mouse. We here address some of the observations from these experiments: individuals with disabilities have widely ranging abilities, and their abilities may change over time. We propose interfaces that change and adapt with the users and their individual abilities. Our target audience generally has difficulty with precise control of a mouse pointer. This makes tasks such as clicking on small buttons or web links difficult. With the

---

[1] Available as a free download at http://www.cameramouse.org

K. Miesenberger et al. (Eds.): ICCHP 2010, Part I, LNCS 6179, pp. 139–146, 2010.
© Springer-Verlag Berlin Heidelberg 2010

Camera Mouse, a click command is issued when the mouse pointer has dwelled over the button or link for a certain amount of time.

A great amount of effort has been devoted to making the web accessible to blind or vision-impaired computer users. Individuals with motion-impairments generally have few options. Previous efforts to create accessible web browsers involved zoom-able interfaces, designing larger buttons on standard web browsers, adding confirmation boxes before following a link (e.g., [2]), dynamically changing the layout [3], or growing the size of links. Other work on adaptive interfaces present interfaces that are too complex for some of our users (e.g., [4]).

We propose the Hierarchical Adaptive Interface Layout (HAIL) model, which is a set of specifications for the design of user interface applications that adapt to the user, rather than requiring the user to adapt to the interface. We present two applications designed to the HAIL model specification: a general purpose web browser and a Twitter client. These were chosen to compare the number of user inputs needed to complete certain tasks. For the purposes of this paper, the applications are not fully featured, rather they were made to serve as a proof of concept for HAIL interface applications. After conducting experiments and receiving user feedback, we plan to expand the applications by adding features such as text input via on-screen keyboards or bookmarking.

Although we designed these interfaces for users of the Camera Mouse, users of other mouse substitution devices, such as mouth joysticks, may also benefit from applications that are based on the HAIL model.

2   Hierarchical Adaptive Interface Layout Model

The hierarchical concept of the HAIL model means that each increasing level of the interface is slightly more complex than the previous level. There are two important specifications for HAIL applications. First, all of the interactive components take place on toolbars along the edge of the screen. The center of the screen is by default reserved for display only and can be used as a rest area for the mouse pointer. This helps avoid the "Midas touch" problem of unintentionally selecting every item the mouse happens to stop near, and gives users a large area in the center where they do not have to worry about the mouse position. Second, each level of the HAIL model specifies minimum button dimensions as a percentage of screen size (Table 1). This assures that a user comfortable with a certain level in one application would be able to use other applications with the same setting.

We built upon experiences in designing user interface programs that offer configurable complexity and difficulty. In particular, Magee et al. [5] designed the game BlockEscape to evaluate user interactions by allowing settings such as changing the speed of the game, or varying the number of objects that must be navigated around. Adjustment of the settings resulted in a game that was easier or harder for the user to interact with. Following this approach, the HAIL model offers a range of interface layouts from easy-to-use and uncomplicated at one end, to having more features and being more complex at the other end. The

Table 1. Minimum button size as a percentage of screen width. Intermediate levels can be used to add or subtract buttons.

HAIL Level	Button Size as a Percentage of Screen Width
1	14%
2–4	12%
5–7	8%
8–10	4%

intent is that individuals using mouse substitution interfaces should be able to set their user interface at the level of complexity that is right for them. Users who are adept at clicking on small buttons will be able to use the more complex interface with more buttons and thus be able to accomplish tasks faster. Users who have difficulties selecting small buttons will be able to choose interfaces with increasingly large buttons (and as a result, fewer buttons on the screen). Although tasks may take longer with the simpler interface, they can now be accomplished without requiring the mouse-pointer accuracy of the more complex interface. HAIL model levels are shown graphically on a sliding scale in Fig. 1.

Fig. 1. Graphical depiction of HAIL levels. Low levels on the left, high levels on the right, intermediate steps in the middle.

Traditional pointer-based interfaces allow movement of the pointer in any direction, allowing the user to select any interface element on the screen directly. HAIL interface applications instead highlight the currently selected interface element. Buttons on the toolbars navigate between those interface elements, and provide a mechanism for activating the currently selected element or executing an event on the selected element. Navigation between interface elements is more akin to keyboard arrow keys – Up, Down, Left, Right – than a mouse pointer. Due to this, HAIL applications work best with information and interfaces that can be organized into linear lists or grids.

3   The HAILbrowser

The HAILbrowser is an implementation of a web browser following the HAIL model specifications. Since the HAIL model is a generalization, this implementation is an application to test the model presented. There are several good reasons for choosing a web browser as a testing platform for the HAIL model. The web browser could be called the most important piece of software for today's computer users. It has become the ubiquitous application not only for accessing information, but also as a gateway for communication applications like email and social networking.

Specialized web browsers like the Zac Browser (Zone for Autistic Children) [6] have made the web an accessible tool for people with autism. The goal of the HAILbrowser is to open up the web to users of accessibility technology like the Camera Mouse. We have previously used standard web browsers with the Camera Mouse and found that only the most adept Camera Mouse users can successfully navigate the world wide web with these browsers. The standard web browser assumes that users have pinpoint accuracy with their mouse pointer to select links. This is often an unrealistic assumption for users with movement impairments. Even Camera Mouse users without disabilities may have trouble keeping the mouse pointer hovering over small hyperlinks in order to select them. The HAILbrowser offers a different mechanism to select hyperlinks. It displays toolbars to allow individuals to navigate through links on a page and select one of the links to follow (Fig. 2). At the high end of the layout hierarchy, the HAIL framework yields a browser with smaller toolbars and more buttons; at the low end of the hierarchy, the HAIL framework yields a browser with larger toolbars and fewer buttons.

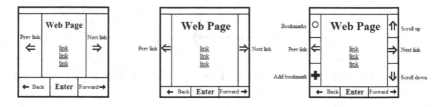

Fig. 2. Layout of three layers of the HAILbrowser

The web pages can have links and interactive elements arranged arbitrarily, which can make the task of navigating to a specific link difficult and time consuming for Camera Mouse users. The lower complexity levels of the HAILbrowser therefore display the mobile web version of web pages by default (Fig. 3). These pages are designed for display on small electronic devices like mobile phones that have small screens. The layout of the web pages is thus simplified, less cluttered, and often easier to navigate. These pages often present navigation links in a linear list format, which is easier to navigate by iteratively selecting subsequent links. The obvious trade-off of this format is that the page may display less information than the non-mobile counterpart. The mobile web default is configurable by the users.

At the least-complex level of the HAIL hierarchy, the browser incorporates a set of basic features for browsing the Internet, as described in Table 2. At a more advanced level of the HAIL hierarchy, the browser incorporates a set of additional features that are convenient for browsing such as bookmarking and jumping links (Table 2).

Fig. 3. HAILbrowser screen shots

Table 2. HAILbrowser required and optional features

Basic Features	Advanced Features
Select Next/Previous Link	Bookmarks
Follow Selected Link	Text Entry / Keyboard
Back/Forward	Jump 10 Links
Page Up/Down	Smart navigation (not implemented yet)

4   HAILtwitter

HAILtwitter is a second application designed to be a proof of concept. HAILtwitter uses the application "Twitter." Twitter is a social networking and microblogging service that can be accessed through web browsers, portable electronic devices, or custom client programs that communicate with Twitter servers over the Internet. As of April 2010, it has over 100 million registered users. Users make accounts and designate a list of other users they wish to receive updates from. Messages posted to the site are limited to 140 characters in length. Users can choose to view messages only from others that they follow, or can search for messages containing a word or phrase, choose from a list of trending topics, or can see all messages from a specific user. The small message size and the information organization in list form makes Twitter an ideal application for users with disabilities. Navigating up and down a linear list of information is an interaction style that is well-suited for a HAIL application.

Two screen shots of the HAILtwitter application are shown in Fig. 4. Each message occupies a row in the list of messages, along with the sender's profile picture, the sender's name, and the time that the message was posted. The toolbar buttons are used to navigate up and down the list of messages to select one to interact with. Once a message is selected, the user can choose to interact with it in a number of ways. The user can "retweet" the message – essentially rebroadcast it to their friends. Other options are to see all messages from the sender of

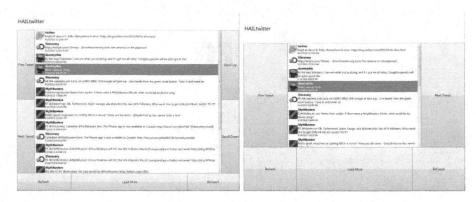

Fig. 4. HAILtwitter screen shots

the current message, or to add or remove the sender from the user's following list. Users can also refresh the page to see newer messages, or load another group of older messages from the current set of messages they are viewing.

We developed the HAILtwitter application with a limited feature set that nonetheless gives the user quick access to social networking and communication. With the addition of an on-screen keyboard, this application can also allow two-way social interaction for some users. Many users use Twitter to post web addresses, links to other Twitter users, or links to pictures. Adding the ability to follow these various kinds of links can provide a richer interactive environment for users (see Table 3).

Table 3. HAILtwitter required and optional features

Basic Features	Advanced Features
Get more / Refresh	View other timelines
Page Up/Down	Text Entry / Keyboard
Select Next/Previous Msg	Trending topics
Retweet (forward msg)	Follow/Unfollow friends

5   Discussion

Preliminary testing of the applications with able-bodied Camera Mouse users was positive. Users observed that it was much easier to select the buttons in our interface compared to standard-sized links in traditional web browsers.

We found that buttons on the edge of the screen were easier to select than interface elements in the middle of the screen. The reason was that once the mouse pointer reached the edge of the screen, for example, the bottom, selection of buttons placed along the bottom mostly involved control of horizontal movements. The control of the vertical pointer movement did not require as precise pointing abilities from the user, because the user could simply push the mouse pointer downwards, and this would result in the pointer remaining at the edge of the screen. A similar situation exists with corners: the user only needs to move towards the corner and the edges of the screen "catch" the pointer and direct it onto the corner button.

Our experimentation with buttons at the corner of the screen brought our attention to a problem that Camera Mouse users sometimes encounter – unintended simulated mouse clicks that wreak havoc with the users' interaction experience. The top-right corner of an application window typically contains a button with which a user can close the application. Similarly, another corner may be dedicated to menu buttons. The bottom edge of the computer screen may contain a task bar. We have observed that Camera Mouse users of traditional applications sometimes unintentionally hover over these buttons and thus issue unintended selection commands that close their applications or switch to other applications. To avoid these scenarios, we therefore designed our HAIL applications to utilize the full screen.

6   Current and Future Work

We are currently testing the prototype implementations of our HAILbrowser and HAILtwitter applications. Feedback from the first round of testing will be incorporated into our software. We will make the software available as a free download so that Camera Mouse users will be able to try it out and provide additional feedback.

To become a successful end-user application, the software must include features beyond what we implemented initially as a proof of concept. Integration with an on-screen keyboard or other text-entry methods is one focus. Text-to-speech abilities would also be useful for some users.

The HAILtwitter application would benefit from incorporating all of the features available on the Twitter website, such as trending topics and lists. For the web browser application, the browser could exploit navigation advancements of semantic understanding of web content used by screen reader navigation. Our browser could leverage the work presented by Takagi et al. [7], using collaborative web accessibility information to aid in navigating the content of a web page. Other approaches navigate by groups of links [3] or via a tree structure [8]. In these approaches, the user would navigate between sections of a web page before navigating through individual links.

We are moving the development of our web browser and Twitter applications to a common HAIL framework with a plug-in architecture. Similar to how a smartphone device provides a basic interface for a variety of smaller "apps," the HAIL framework would allow HAIL applications to share the same user interface program. A similar approach is proposed by Andrews et al. [9], where a common user interface framework interprets interface elements defined within metadata. Users will be able to switch between applications and have the framework remember their preferred settings. This will ease the development of future applications that would benefit from the HAIL model. It would also allow links in one application to open in another application. An email client, news-feed aggregator, Facebook interface, and media player application are currently planned.

Acknowledgments. The authors gratefully acknowledge NSF funding (HCC grant IIS-0713229).

References

1. Connor, C., Yu, E., Magee, J., Cansizoglu, E., Epstein, S., Betke, M.: Movement and recovery analysis of a mouse-replacement interface for users with severe disabilities. In: HCI International 2009, San Diego, CA (July 2009)
2. Larson, H., Gips, J.: A web browser for people with quadriplegia. In: Stephanidis, C. (ed.) Universal Access in HCI: Inclusive Design in the Information Society, pp. 226–230. Lawrence Erlbaum Associates, Mahwah (2003)
3. Waber, B., Magee, J., Betke, M.: Web mediators for accessible browsing. In: 9th International ERCIM Workshop "User Interfaces For All" UI4ALL, Königswinter, Germany (September 2006)
4. Gajos, K.Z., Wobbrock, J.O., Weld, D.S.: Improving the performance of motor-impaired users with automatically-generated, ability-based interfaces. In: SIGCHI Conf. on Human Factors in Computing Systems (CHI 2008), pp. 1257–1266 (2008)
5. Magee, J.J., Betke, M., Gips, J., Scott, M.R., Waber, B.N.: A human-computer interface using symmetry between eyes to detect gaze direction. IEEE Transactions on Systems Man and Cybernetics: Part A 38, 1261–1271 (2008)
6. Zac browser Zone for Autistic Children, http://www.zacbrowser.com/
7. Takagi, H., Kawanaka, S., Kobayashi, M., Sato, D., Asakawa, C.: Collaborative web accessibility improvement: challenges and possibilities. In: Proceedings of the 11th International ACM SIGACCESS Conference on Computers and Accessibility (Assets 2009), pp. 195–202 (2009)
8. Walshe, E., McMullin, B.: Browsing web based documents through an alternative tree interface: The webtree browser. In: Miesenberger, K., Klaus, J., Zagler, W.L., Karshmer, A.I. (eds.) ICCHP 2006. LNCS, vol. 4061, pp. 106–113. Springer, Heidelberg (2006)
9. Andrews, J.H., Hussain, F.: Johar: a framework for developing accessible applications. In: Proceedings of the 11th International ACM SIGACCESS Conference on Computers and Accessibility (Assets 2009), pp. 243–244 (2009)

Customizable Software Interface for Monitoring Applications

Manuel Merino, Isabel Gómez, Octavio Rivera, and Alberto J. Molina

Electronic Technology Department, University of Seville,
Avd. Reina Mercedes s/n,
41012, Seville, Spain
{Manmermon,Octavio}@dte.us.es {igomez,almolina}@us.es
http://matrix.dte.us.es/grupoimyt/

Abstract. In this paper we propose an application based on virtual keyboard and automatic scanning to communicate with a PC and the others people. The aim users are the people with disabilities. A high degree of customization is possible in the software. So the user can selected the color of buttons, position of system on screen, the kind of scanning, timer, the interface of communication, etc. Five people without disabilities tested our system. The results of the tests show the application reduce the fatigue of user and increased the text entry rate.

Keywords: interface, prediction system, control system, disability.

1 Introduction

Communication is a fundamental quality for human beings. People use different ways of Communication in their diary life. Communication skills are necessary in order to get a social integration. Nevertheless degenerative diseases, accidents, psychological disorders and others reason can make difficult the human communication. So, according to the Eurostat [1], the total population in Europe was 362 million in 1996 which 14.8% of the population between 6 and 64 years old have physical, psychological or sensorial disabilities. Therefore, assistive and adapted systems have to be developed. The aim of these ones is to help users in their diary tasks, letting them to live in a more comfortable way.

The development of a general purpose system is a complex task because every people have different skills and preferences. These systems have a degree of flexibility and customizable. However the limitations of these systems are heightened when people have severe disabilities.

Nowadays there are several tools and devices that allow disabled people to use specific applications. This paper describes a system located among three research main areas: Human-Computer Interface (HCI), Augmentative and Alternative Communication (AAC) y Assistive Technology (AT). A user can interact with this system using keyboard-handled software applications. An appropriate device which is adapted to user needs is only required to interact with it. The developed system can be

K. Miesenberger et al. (Eds.): ICCHP 2010, Part I, LNCS 6179, pp. 147–153, 2010.

handled with several kinds of input devices which increases the number of potential users. In our tests are performed using electromyography signal (EMG).

2 Related Work

Development of interfaces adapted to the user physical skills is necessary because the users can have different diseases. In most cases, some residual user movements are required to interact with these interfaces, like adapted switches or eye-tracker. Electric biosignals are used in some of these ones, such as electrooculography [2] or electromyography [2]. There exists another kind of interfaces that a user movement is not required to interact with it, like one is used in Brain Computer Interaction (BCI) [3]. This one is based on detecting some electric biosignals (electroencephalogram).

In addition to these input interfaces, an application to make possible the interaction between user and computer/PDA is necessary. Text entry is one of the most common features of this kind of applications. The main aim must be to reduce the numbers of user actions when users have some physical disabilities. To get this goal, prediction systems are used, like character prediction, word prediction or sentence prediction. Examples of this kind of applications are shown in [4, 5]. Both applications are virtual keyboards (VKs). First one [4] is a commercial application based on Windows Operative System. Different kinds of extended VKs can be selected but reduced VKs are not implemented. It uses an automatic scanning method and word prediction. On the other hand, the position of keys in the VK is not suitable to scan through column-rows or serial method. Prediction list length is setting to six words so it is not customizable. Configuration options (such as the color or size of buttons, position or size of application, etc.) cannot be changed by a handicapped.

Second one [5] is a fluctuating VK that uses a manual scanning method and character prediction. When a character is selected, the buttons around of this are changed based on the character prediction system. This property provokes the user fatigue is increased.

Dasher [6] is a different text input method using a character prediction. This one is based on a mouse pointer tracking system to select the wished character from a shown set. This is a text input system that allows a high rate character/minute. The selected text can be used by a voice synthesizer, but is not possible to send to another application. Also the operative system cannot be handled by this application.

3 Methodology

3.1 Software Description

The proposed application is an automatic scanning based VK using a prediction system. It runs on Windows XP and was implemented using Java 1.5. The prediction system requires a dictionary which is a database that was implemented using SQLite. Special features were implemented using C# 2.0.

Our software works like a daemon, it means that it is always visible in foreground and never catches the focus (fig. 1). Different input events can be generated by user to interact with the system. When an input event is received, it is processed by the Application Handler, and a set action is done depending on the state of the system. Computer applications can be handled by keyboard [7] and this software uses this fact. So, the selected action is send to Operative System like a real keystroke on a conventional keyboard, letting user to open/close computer applications, to send/receive e-mails, to browse the Internet, to enter texts, etc.

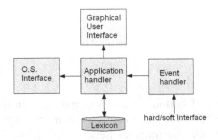

Fig. 1. Functional description

The Graphical User Interface (GUI) is composed of five different automatic scanning based VKs: a numeric VK (from 0 to 9), a punctuation mark VK, a command VK (including alt, shift, ctrl, enter, tab, f1, f2, etc., buttons), and an advanced command VK (this one can be customized setting on each button a sequence of commands, for example alt + f4, or alt + c), an application VK (is equivalent to start menu of Windows XP – fig. 3), and a letter VK (can be a reduced VK or an extend VK – fig. 2). Two alternatives have been implemented: a row-column scanning method or a serial scanning method.

OK	e	o	r	c	b
a	s	i	t	a	f
n	l	u	v	h	ñ
d	p	q	l	x	w
m	v	z	k	<-	0-9
Com	Paleta	Puntaci...	App	Exit	Apagar

OK	abc	def	ghi
lkl	mnñ	opq	rst
uvw	xvz	<-	0-9
Com	Paleta	Puntaci...	App
Exit	Apagar		

Fig. 2. GUI – Extend/reduced letter VK

7.Zip >>	Accesorios >>	Asistencia remota	ATI Catalyst Control Center >>
ATI HYDRAVISION >>	Atmel AVR Tools >>	CodeGear RAD Studio 2009 >>	Desktop Sidebar >>
Eset >>	EssentialPIM >>	g.tec >>	Gimp >>
Roxio >>	SPT >>	VisiBroker >>	WinAVR-20080610 >>
Windows Live >>	Windows Movie Maker	ZeallSoft >>	Txt
0-9	Com	Exit	Apagar

Fig. 3. GUI – Application VK

On the other hand, a personal VK can be defined by the user. This VK is based on an xml file and its structure is:

```
<teclado teclasPorFila="number of buttons in a row">
  <boton tipoBoton="button type" texto="text">
    <letra orden = "position"> letter </letra>
    ...
    <letra orden = "position"> letter </letra>
  </boton>
  <boton ...>
  ...
  </boton>
  ...
</teclado>
```

The maximum number of buttons in a row is indicated in the property *teclasPor-Fila* in *<teclado ...>...</teclado>*. The labels *<boton...>...</boton>* have two properties. One is *tipoBoton* that discriminates between letter, number, punctuation mark and command keys. The other property is *texto* that is used to descriptor text in the key. The last label is *<letra...>letter</letra>* where the *orden* indicates the position of the letter, number, command or punctuation mark.

Three text entry methods have been incorporated. One of them consists on a conventional text entry method. Characters of the wished word are entered one by one in this method. Other ones are word prediction systems. A study of different prediction systems is presented in [8, 9], in which we can check word prediction systems are the most commonly used. First of these ones is called NT and is only available when an ambiguous VK (more than one character per key) is used. NT is a modification of NT predictor system. When a key of VK is selected a new prediction list is made. In the new list, the words of the previous one whose characters match with those typed orderly so far are remained. Second one is called K-Word. In this method, first characters of the wished word have to be selected before a prediction is made. After that, K-Word predictor builds a list of suggestion using a k-gram algorithm with selected characters.

The user-application communication is realized by the user control interface. It has to be able to adapt dynamically to the user context. This dynamic adaptability and costumer of application are contained in the concept of plasticity [10]. Thus our application has been development to enable that the user personalizes the appearance of GUI, so the user can choose the color of scanned and no-scanned buttons, the color of button's text, the size of buttons, the position of application in the screen, the scanned time, selected/no-select special VK, configure special VK, select and configure prediction system, select the type of scanned system, etc. A configure application allows to personalize the properties described before. The options of the configure application are automatic scanning to allow to person with disability can personalize the software. When an option is chosen a VK is shown which allows the user selects the new value of the actual option.

Otherwise, two log files are generated by the application. These files can be used in research tasks. The user events are registered by one of them. The prediction words are stored by the other log file. This saves the selected prediction word and its different lists of prediction, the time, the number of automatic reset of system and the number interaction by rows, columns and letters. The files allow study the advantages of a kind of VK and/or a prediction system.

3.2 User Control Interface

Three kinds of communication ports were designed: parallel/serial port and TCP/IP. In the future usb port will be added. These ports allow a lot different types of interface. At least an event has to be generated by the interface. Two different events are allowed. One is the selection event to select current option (mandatory) and the other is the change event to advance to next option (optional). These events are evaluated in [11, 12]. Events are distinguished based on time. The parallel port was tested by a stick switch based on the select event. The serial port was used by a button switch based on selection and change events and a microphone based on selection event. The TCP/IP was tested by EMG interface. In addition the system could be handled by control and/or shift button of conventional keyboard.

Any interface that generates input events based on user actions can be used to interact with this software. At the moment, it has been tested using different switches and an electromyography based device. The last one uses three electrodes placed on the user's arm. Hence, a movement of his/her hand can be detected and an adequate event can be generated. The signal processing procedure splits the electromyography signal on non-overlapping windows that are 100 samples width. An absolute value operation is applied on each window and the result is integrated. The signal is interpreted as a selection when obtained value is above a set threshold.

3.3 Procedure

Some trials focused on text input system have been done. Five users without disabilities between 25 and 35 years old participated in these trials. They had not used the application before. Results using conventional text entry, K-Word and NT prediction system are compared between each in order to obtain time savings. Also penalization time due to user errors is calculated. Maximum prediction list length is set to 14 words. The list of suggestions in K-Word predictor is displayed when user has selected three first characters of the wished word. The main objective of these trials is to entry text without mistakes. The application implements a functionality that let user to fix errors. Some tests with handicapped people must be done in the future.

4 Work and Results

The trial results were stored in two log files. Time measurements included increments due to penalization sources. These sources were: wrong character selections (in this case, time was required to set them); wrong word selections from prediction list; selections using more than one user input (users was not able to choose the desired row, column, letter or word); reset of system due to time out, etc. Besides time measurements, information about different types of mistakes can be found in the aforementioned log files.

Trial results are shown in tables 1 and 2. The table 2 shows the gain using the predictor systems. The K-Word predictor gain about text entry conventional is 27.58%, which means a time saving of 192.537 seconds. So, the gain using NT predictor is 52.02% about text entry conventional, which is 353.04 seconds. On the other hand, NT predictor is 34.36% faster than K-Word.

Table 1. Times in text entry systems

User	KWord	NT	Conventional
1	475.05	318.79	572.68
2	501.21	356.38	580.48
3	357.15	238.14	522.87
4	512.76	335.20	868.18
5	501.02	296.15	765.65

Table 2. Gains of text entry systems

User	KWord vs. Conventional (%)	NT vs. KWord(%)	NT vs. Conventional (%)
1	17.05	33.06	44.33
2	13.66	29.90	38.61
3	31.70	33.32	54.46
4	40.94	34.63	61.39
5	34.56	40.89	61.32

5   Conclusion and Planned Lines of Research

It has been presented an application that is easy to use and it does not require any training. The operative system can be handled, and text can be written. It must be mentioned that users must have knowledge in handling computer using control keys of a standard keyboard. So, it is not operating system dependent, because it is based on Java.

All its possibilities are included in graphical interface that is shown permanently on the computer screen. The design of this application is flexible in respect of main keyboard displayed on screen and the used input signal. It is possible to change among several configurations of keyboard during execution time. Also, three different prediction systems have been implemented. Furthermore, the inputs which handle the software come from several devices (parallel port, serial port or TCP/IP).

On the other hand, the application is a research tool. Two log files are made. They both store information about a using session. Therefore, different kinds of results can be extracted, such as penalize due to wrong character selections, wrong word selections from prediction list, selections using more than one user input (users was not able to choose the desired row, column, letter or word), reset of system due to time out, etc.

Acknowledgements

This project has been carried out within the framework of a research program: (p08-TIC-3631) – Multimodal Wireless interface funded by the Regional Government of Andalusia.

References

1. Eurostat. Health Statistics. Luxembrourg: Office for Official Publications of the European communities (2002) ISBN: 92-894-3730-8,
   http://epp.eurostat.ec.europa.eu (Retrieved on December 2009)
2. Dhillon, H.S., Singla, R., Rekhi, N.S., Rameshwar, J.: EOG and EMG Based Virtual Keyboard: A Brain-Computer Interface. In: 2nd IEEE International Conference on Computer Science and Information Technology, ICCSIT 2009 (2009)
3. Nam, C.S., Jeon, Y., Li, Y., Kim, Y.-J., Yoon, H.-Y.: Usability of the P300 Speller: Towards a More Sustainable Brain-Computer Interface. International Journal on Human-Computer Interaction 1(5) (2009)
4. Wivik on-screen keyboard software, http://www.wivik.com/ (Retrieve on December 2009)
5. Merlin, B., Raynal, M.: Increasing Software Keyboard Key by Recycling Needless Ones. In: Assistive Technology from Adapted Equipment to Inclusive Environments - AAATE 2009, vol. 25, pp. 139–143 (2009) ISBN: 978-1-60750-042-1
6. Ward, D.J., Blackwell, A.F., MacKay, D.J.C.: Dasher - a Data Entry Interface Using Continuous Gestures and Language Models. In: UIST 2000 (2000),
   http://www.inference.phy.cam.ac.uk/dasher
   (Retrieve on December 2009)
7. Gómez González, I.M., Molina Cantero, A.J., Romero, O.R.: Multi Purpose Interface for Handling General Computer Applications. In: 9th European Conference for the Advancement of Assistive Technology in Europe (AAATE 2007), San Sebastián, España, pp. 7–8 (2007)
8. Garay-Vitoria, N., Abascal, J.: Text prediction: a survey. Univ. Access Inf. Soc. 4, 188–203 (2006)
9. Rivera, O., Molina, A.J., Gómez, I., Sánchez, G.: Evaluation of Unambiguous Virtual Keyboards with Character Prediction. In: Conference of the Association for the Advance of Assistive Technology in Europe (AAATE 2009), Florence, Italy, vol. 25, pp. 144–149 (2009) ISBN: 978-1-60750-042-1
10. Sendín, M., López Juan, M.: Contributions of Dochtomic View of plasticity to seamlessly embed accessibility and adaptivity support in user interfaces. In: Advances in Engineering Software, pp. 1261–1270 (2009)
11. Rivera, O., Molina, A.J., Gómez, I., Merino, M.: A Study of Two-inputs Scanning Methods to Enhance the Communication Rate. In: Conference of the Association for the Advance of Assistive Technology in Europe (AAATE 2009), Florence, Italy, vol. 25, pp. 132–137 (2009) ISBN: 978-1-60750-042-1
12. Rivera, O., Molina, A.J., Gómez, I.: Two-Input Based Procedures Using a Single Device. In: Conference of the Association for the Advance of Assistive Technology in Europe (AAATE 2009), Florence, Italy, vol. 25, p. 881 (2009) ISBN: 978-1-60750-042-1

Towards to Real–Time System with Optimization Based Approach for EOG and Blinking Signals Separation for Human Computer Interaction

Robert Krupiński and Przemysław Mazurek

West–Pomeranian University of Technology, Szczecin, Department of Signal
Processing and Multimedia Engineering,
26–Kwietnia 10 Str, 71126 Szczecin, Poland
{robert.krupinski,przemyslaw.mazurek}@zut.edu.pl
http://www.rkrupinski.zut.edu.pl, http://www.media.zut.edu.pl

Abstract. Electrooculography (EOG) systems could be used for Human Computer Interaction but measurements with minimal number of electrodes and appropriate signals processing algorithms for the separation of EOG and blinking signals are required. Median filter with a carefully selected mask size could be used for the initialization of the evolution–based algorithm, which is used for the estimation and separation of EOG and blinking signals.

Keywords: Biomeasurements, Biosignals, Electrooculography.

1 Introduction

EOG systems are well known occulography methods used for the medical purposes from many years. Such systems are used for Human–Computer–Interaction [5]. This method was successfully used for numerous devices and applications: the human-computer interfaces (e.g. virtual keyboard [8,17], the wheelchair control [2], the wearable computers [4]), the motion–capture systems (the direct animation of eyes of computer generated character based on the real measurements of actor's eye–movement [3,15]), the optimization of web–services, the optimization of advertisement [16], the video compression driven by eye–interest [9].

EOG systems are based on biomeasurement of retina–cornea voltage using a set of electrodes connected to the skin surface. For the fixed electrodes the result of eyes movements is the amplitude modulation of this voltage source and could be used for the estimation of the eyes orientation. The simplest systems are based on the 3/4 electrode configuration (two differential channels and a reference electrode) (Fig. 1).

Blinking signal is additive to EOG and is the effect of eyelid movement. For typical blinking an EOG signal is disturbed by these pulses so blinking signal removal is necessary. Both signals should be separated for HCI applications, what gives the ability of using blinking as an additional degree–of–freedom in

K. Miesenberger et al. (Eds.): ICCHP 2010, Part I, LNCS 6179, pp. 154–161, 2010.

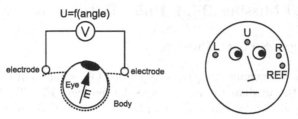

Fig. 1. EOG measurement model for single channel; Electrodes placement in the 3/4 configuration

such systems. There are proposed numerous separation algorithms and the most valuable are median filters because they give the possibility of the real–time processing of measured signals at very low computation cost. The median filters are unsuitable if blinks are near the neighborhoods of saccades [6] (the rapid changes of the eye orientation, observed in the signal as a step shape).

2 Evolution–Based Technique for EOG and Blinking Signals Separation

Alternative approach uses an optimization method for the separation of EOG and blinking by iterative operations. In [11] the model of EOG and blinking signal was proposed, which is based on the set of well–defined parameters like positions of saccades, the EOG signal levels between two saccades, the blink pulses positions and amplitude. By using this model, the optimization algorithm gives the possibility of finding parameters, so the signal separation and estimation are combined together [12]. As an optimization algorithm the combination of the non–gradient search using the random generator (due to discreet and unknown number of saccades and blinking pulses) and the gradient descent (for local optimization as an optimization speed–up) is used. The non–gradient search method is the kind of mutation from the evolutionary programming point–of–view with the random generation of parameters values. The optimization operation is additionally driven by a random generator so during a single iteration a few randomly selected operations are used for the new proposed set of parameters. The next iteration incorporates these values if the parameters set is better, otherwise the previous set is restored. Overall process could be infinite–time what is not suitable for HCI with a real–time requirements.

For the real–time system a processing time is limited and the most promising method for optimization improvement is the reduction of amount of local minima. It can be realized by the proper initialization (non–random) of the model parameters around a global minima. It is possible by: the estimation of pulse position by using a median filter [1,7,10,11,14], the saccades positions and EOG signal levels between saccades. The blinks could be detected by the subtraction of measured signal and the output of median filter.

3   False and Missing Blink Pulse Detections

3.1   Pulses from Smooth Pursuit

Smooth pursuit movements are the sources of EOG signal slopes [5] and they are filtered by the median filters in a specific manner (Fig. 2). The hills and valleys are clipped so false blinking could be generated. The valley based errors could be filtered by the assumption of only positive blink pulses appearance. A typical error for this case is a low level pulse, which is longer in comparison to the typical blinking what could be applied for the detection and removal.

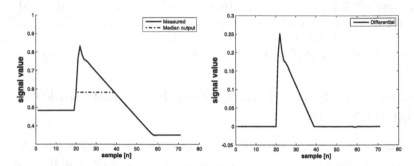

Fig. 2. Pulse from smooth pursuit

3.2   False Pulses from Early or Delayed Saccades

This effect is related to the mask size of the median filter. A large mask shifts the saccades position and after the substraction of the estimated and original signals a false pulse occurs (Fig. 3). The positive pulses could be detected as a blinking and negative are ignored by the pulse detection algorithm.

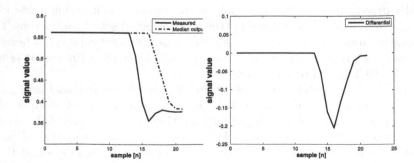

Fig. 3. False pulses from early or delayed saccades

3.3   Removal of Blink Pulses in Saccade Neighborhood

A blink pulse before the raising edge of EOG signal or after the falling edge of EOG could be removed (Fig. 4). In this situation amplitude of pulse could be below detection threshold. An additional false negative pulse occurs that could be ignored by the pulse detection algorithm.

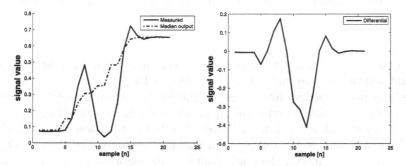

Fig. 4. Removal of blink pulses in saccade neighborhood

3.4   Lost Pulses for Burst Blinking

The burst of blinking pulses could be interpreted as an EOG constant level. This is the result of false detection of blinking pulses. The blinking pulses are processed in an initialization step before the EOG initialization and it is effect of wrong mask size. In Fig. 5 are shown results for mask size equal to the 11 and first two pulses are about three time reduced.

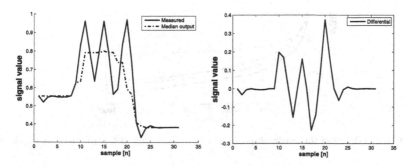

Fig. 5. Lost pulses for burst blinking

4   Median Filter Mask and It Influence on Evolution–Based Algorithm

The evolution based technique needs a lot of interaction for the successful estimation of blinking and EOG signals. The computation time and the number of interactions depends on the number of possible parameters and a signal length. For the real–time processing this length should be minimized for delay reduction. There are two methods related to this processing scheme of continuous signals.

The first one is based on the overlapping windows so the current results are based on the previous results (form the previous usage) and the current update. This method could reduce the number of iteration and the processing time.

The second method is based on the non–overlapping window, which is useful for the performance tests. The final result for this method is independent from the previous calculations and it is assumed in this paper. Such a method is not recommended for the real–time applications, because if the signal length is high (due to the large windows of median filter) the number of parameters is also high and additional delay related to acquisition is large.

The influence of median filter mask on the blink pulse detection (availability with a specific tolerance) and a time position error is considered in numerous papers [11], but such algorithms are used directly for detection. The evolution–based algorithm uses such a result for an initialization only, and there is a question about the influence on the final results of this algorithm. Such an assumption gives much better results of evolution–based algorithm in comparison to the alone median filtering [13]. Even if situation presented on Fig. 2, 3, 4, and 5 occurs after a some iterations are corrected.

Processing speed for initialization using different median masks and random initialization is presented in Fig. 6.

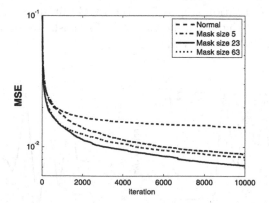

Fig. 6. Error reduction for evolution–based algorithm and different median mask sizes

Such results are obtained for 100 test with random generated signal for each mask size. Similar MSE value could be obtained a hundreds faster or more in comparison to the random initialization. Median filter based initialization is much better in comparison to the random initialization of estimated blinking and EOG signals. Optimal mask size for particular sampling frequency could obtained from Fig. 7 and Fig. 8.

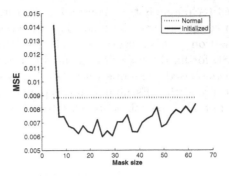

Fig. 7. MSE value dependent on mask size

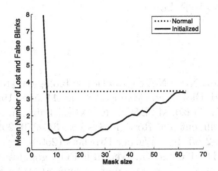

Fig. 8. Mean number of lost and false blinks depending on mask size

Obtained mean from all test of MSE value after 10000 iterations is shown in Fig. 7. The mask size selection is simple due to low sensitivity and the mask size should be larger then 7. A large mask sizes increases MSE value and very large e.g. 45 or more should be not used.

The MSE value is ideal for performance analysis and another techniques should be used like lost and false blinks metric. Fixed number of blink pulses (eight) is used in EOG generator and optimal selection of mask size are 13 and 15. There are high ratio of lost and false blinks for optimal masks because EOG generator support a very high range of EOG and blinking phenomenons that are not typical for regular HCI systems.

5   Conclusions

The blink pulses could be detected by using median filtering, but it efficiency depends on the EOG signal shape and a median filter mask. These cases were shortly introduced, because they appear from a non–linear filtering. These errors are very important for the reliability of the EOG based HCI systems and they can not be simply fixed by median filtering.

The evolution–based technique is time consuming algorithm but gives much better performance in comparison to the much simpler algorithms like median filtering. Correct estimation of mask sizes reduce significantly a number of iterations or improves MSE for fixed number of assumed iterations.

The iterative evolution–based technique with iterative processing is the most promising for real–time processing. Estimated in this paper a range of median filter mask sizes used for initialization will be used for iterative evolution algorithm.

Acknowledgement

This work is supported by the UE EFRR ZPORR project Z/2.32/I/1.3.1/267/05 "Szczecin University of Technology – Research and Education Center of Modern Multimedia Technologies" (Poland).

References

1. Bankman, I.N., Thakor, N.V.: Noise reduction in biological step signals: application to saccadic EOG. Med. Biol. Eng. Comput. 28(6), 544–549 (1990) (PMID: 2287177)
2. Barea, R., Boquete, L., Mazo, M., López, E.: Wheelchair Guidance Strategies Using EOG. Journal of Intelligent and Robotic Systems 34, 279–299 (2002)
3. E.O.G Beowulf DVD 2'nd disc. Warner Brothers (2008)
4. Bulling, A., Roggen, D., Tröster, G.: Wearable EOG goggles: Seamless sensing and context–awareness in everyday environments. Journal of Ambient Intelligence and Smart Environments (JAISE) 1(2), 157–171 (2009), doi:10.3233/AIS–2009–0020
5. Duchowski, A.: Eye Tracking Methodology: Theory and Practice. Springer, Heidelberg (2007)
6. Gu, E., Lee, S.P., Badler, J.B., Badler, N.I.: Eye Movements, Saccades, and Multiparty Conversations. In: Deng, Z., Neumann, U. (eds.) Data–Driven 3D Facial Animation, pp. 79–97. Springer, Heidelberg (2008)
7. Juhola, M.: Median filtering is appropriate to signals of saccadic eye movements. Computers in Biology and Medicine 21, 43–49 (1991)
8. Hori, J., Sakano, K., Miyakawa, M., Saitoh, Y.: Eye Movement Communication Control System Based on EOG and Voluntary Eye Blink. In: Miesenberger, K., Klaus, J., Zagler, W.L., Karshmer, A.I. (eds.) ICCHP 2006. LNCS, vol. 4061, pp. 950–953. Springer, Heidelberg (2006) doi:10.1007/11788713–138
9. Khan, J.I., Komogortsev, O.: Perceptual video compression with combined scene analysis and eye–gaze tracking. In: Duchowski, A.T., Vertegaal, R. (eds.) ETRA 2004 – Proceedings of the Eye Tracking Research and Application Symposium, San Antonio, Texas, USA, March 22–24, p. 57 (2004)
10. Krupiński, R., Mazurek, P.: Estimation of Eye Blinking using Biopotentials Measurements for Computer Animation Applications. In: Bolc, L., Kulikowski, J.L., Wociechowski, K. (eds.) ICCVG 2008. LNCS, vol. 5337, pp. 302–310. Springer, Heidelberg (2008), doi:10.1007/978–3–642–02345–3–30
11. Krupiński, R., Mazurek, P.: Median Filters Optimization for Electrooculography and Blinking Signal Separation using Synthetic Model. In: 14th IEEE/IFAC International Conference on Methods and Models in Automation and Robotics MMAR 2009, Miedzyzdroje (2009)

12. Krupiński, R., Mazurek, P.: Optimization–based Technique for Separation and Detection of Saccadic Movements and Eye–blinking in Electrooculography Biosignals. In: Software Tools and Algorithms for Biological Systems, Advances in Experimental Medicine and Biology. Springer, Heidelberg (in print, 2010)
13. Krupiński, R., Mazurek, P.: Convergence Improving in Optimization-Based Estimation of Electrooculography and Blinking Signals. In: 2nd International Conference Information Technologies in Biomedicine ITiB 2010 (in print, 2010)
14. Martinez, M., Soria, E., Magdalena, R., Serrano, A.J., Martin, J.D., Vila, J.: Comparative study of several Fir Median Hybrid Filters for blink noise removal in Electrooculograms. WSEAS Transactions on Signal Processing 4, 53–59 (2008)
15. Sony Pictures Entertainment, Sony Corporation, Sagar, M., Remington, Oh Oja tem and method for tracking facial muscle and eye motion for computer graphics animation, Patent US., International Publication Number WO/2006/039497 A2 (13.04. 2006)
16. Poole, A., Ball, L.J.: Eye Tracking in Human–Computer Interaction and Usability Research: Current Status and Future Prospects. In: Ghaoui, C. (ed.) Encyclopedia of Human Computer Interaction, pp. 211–219. Idea Group, USA (2005)
17. Usakli, A.B., Gurkan, S., Aloise, F., Vecchiato, G., Babiloni, F.: On the Use of Electrooculogram for Efficient Human Computer Interfaces. Computational Intelligence and Neuroscience 2010, 5 pages (2010), doi:10.1155/2010/135629

Towards Accessible Interactions with Pervasive Interfaces, Based on Human Capabilities

Matthew Tylee Atkinson[1], Yunqiu Li[1], Colin H.C. Machin[1], and David Sloan[2]

[1] Department of Computer Science, Loughborough University, LE11 3TU, UK
{M.T.Atkinson,K.Y.Li,C.H.C.Machin}@lboro.ac.uk
[2] School of Computing, University of Dundee, DD1 4HN, UK
dsloan@computing.dundee.ac.uk

Abstract. We draw on the literature, established standards and practices, contemporary funded projects and ongoing proof-of-concept work to argue for accessibility advocates to capitalise on the current paradigm shift towards ubiquitous, distributed and collaborative information systems. We discuss the contemporary interaction trends and accessibility challenges that give rise to our proposal; describe and provide an argument for capability-based development over the current, more device-focused, approach and document ongoing proof-of-concept and funded development work in this area.

1   Introduction

One perennial barrier to improving the accessibility of ICTs is that of providing incentive for developers and content creators to make their work accessible. By social means, this may be partly addressed by recognising that accessibility barriers affect a range of people [1], including older users [2]. A further major challenge is that there is a growing requirement for accessibility to be appropriately managed in applications that involve collaborative and/or social interaction, including situations where an application may be used in company, for example older people's use of e-mail [3].

One cause of the classic barrier to accessibility provision is the perceived expense of its incorporation into development practices. Due to the present trends towards web-based and progressively more ubiquitous applications, however, these practices, are currently in flux, presenting an ideal opportunity for our field to develop techniques that can ease the development process for heterogeneous applications, whilst also mainstreaming accessibility techniques. This paper proposes our vision of such a technique, which is based on the notions of (a) adaptivity as a means to mainstream accessibility and (b) human capabilities as the primary, portable, measure of adaptation requirements.

Our contributions are: (1) a discussion of the disconnect between the trend towards ubiquity and the current methods of providing accessibility, leading to the need for portable adaptive accessibility being identified; (2) the overview of and justification for our proposed solution to the technical challenge and

K. Miesenberger et al. (Eds.): ICCHP 2010, Part I, LNCS 6179, pp. 162–169, 2010.

(3) a description of how our techniques are being developed and tested as part of the Sus-IT[1] project.

Adaptive systems raise serious matters of privacy, user interruption, security and ethics (e.g. do we have a responsibility to alert the user to suspected medical problems?) These are key matters and are being considered in parallel to the technical work described here [4].

2   Complementary and Closely-Related Work

The need for improved accessibility is inherently a social one and social factors are key to the successful provision of accessibility—however, the scope of this paper is the technical aspects of the development process.[2] It is important to keep in mind that adopting practices such as User-Centred Design or Design for All can motivate developers to improve accessibility and provide useful data on how this might be achieved. However these practices improve the design, not technical development processes—the latter being the focus here.

Some key complementary technical outputs include the growing array of highly-focussed accessibility adaptations being developed by researchers in the area. Examples include models of motor difficulties and compensation techniques (from key-debouncing to models of performance [5,6]) and sensory impairments, such as Jefferson's techniques for compensating for colour deficit [7]. The focussed nature of these projects—each addressing only one specific problem— makes them highly suitable candidates for becoming accessibility adaptations, as will be elaborated upon later.

Related work includes that of Gajos, who developed techniques to render a GUI corresponding to an abstract interface specification in which the concrete interfaces may be rendered on desktops, portables, PDAs and mobile telephones. These techniques were extended to support users with some kinds of vision or motor impairments—including combinations of the two [8].

IBM's Web Adaptation Technology (WAT) [2] is able to make changes to system accessibility settings based on both detected problems (such as tremors whilst typing) and at the request of the user. The way accessibility settings are presented and applied is interesting, for two reasons: (1) the many accessibility-related settings buried deep within the operating system are brought into the WAT in-browser interface so that users can easily find and change them; (2) the settings are applied not just to web content but the application as well—i.e. a text size increase will affect the browser's menus too. This is almost certainly what the user would wish for, going a long way to addressing the issues of user awareness of ATs (for one specific application), but the literature yields very few examples of this sort of approach.

---

[1] http://sus-it.lboro.ac.uk/

[2] Most workpackages in the Sus-IT project are focussed on social aspects, providing requirements, input data and validation for technical processes and artefacts developed as part of the project.

The ÆGIS project [9] is a current research effort that seeks to better deploy ATs on desktop and mobile systems. This project is focussed on providing an open framework and standards for deployment of ATs, which will provide a foundation for future work. The Sus-IT project seeks to develop reasoning processes that could run on top of such a framework, to direct deployment of the correct ATs for a given user at a given time, thus at least partially addressing users' lack of awareness of available ATs.

The tripartite ISO 24751, based on work from the IMS AccessForAll project, covers accessibility profiling of a learner and of an electronic learning object and describes how these might be used together in a learning management system to deliver appropriately-adapted resources for an individual. While it provides a useful reference in terms of accessibility profiling, its scope does not extend to methods of initial data population, nor of maintenance of accurate user profile information over time. Additionally, the adaptations it considers are couched in very machine-oriented terms (e.g. font enlargement, cursor size or double-click speed), which would not necessarily be portable to new device types.

3   Adaptivity as a Means to Mainstream Accessibility

Individuals' fluctuating capabilities can lead to a lack of awareness of accessibility needs and the appropriate solution for them [4]—so a system that can help close this gap by matching a person with appropriate accessibility accommodations at a given time can provide a valuable extension to existing accessibility support. While employing inclusive design practices is important, since perceptions of an interface and the situations in which applications are used are variable, no single interface can satisfy the needs of all users at all times.

Adopting standards can increase the likelihood that a given accessibility adaptation will be able to render any given content in a manner accessible to a given user, because standard methods for adaptation may be used (such as the DOM [2]). It is of key importance, however, to note that adopting such baseline standards is *just the beginning*—doing so provides a common platform for adaptations to build upon but is not the final step in ensuring accessibility, due to the dynamic diversity of users, devices and environments.

For example, it is far from always possible to anticipate the context in which information or applications may be accessed. Often, users would benefit from slight changes (adaptations) to the manner in which information is rendered, based on their capabilities and preferences, device and environment (which may change suddenly, e.g. in terms of light/noise levels, or familiarity), mandating a reactive adaptation to be executed (such as contrast changes, or redirection of output to other modalities).

In order to minimise unintended side-effects, adaptations would have to be focussed on solving one particular accessibility problem, be aware of specific users' characteristics *and* be applicable in a very localised fashion (e.g. be able to read aloud the content of long documents to a user with vision fatigue, but not the containing application or browser's menus or toolbar, if this is the user's preference). This makes some traditional ATs unsuitable in their current form (often applicable to an entire output modality, rather than specific applications or parts thereof), and the adaptations developed through research, introduced above, seem more ideal. Infrastructure to allow adaptations to be targeted at specific parts of applications (akin to Gajos' and others' abstract UI systems described above) would be required to support this. In addition, the reasoning system would have to recognise that combinations of adaptations could produce "interference" and that the effects of this may vary for each user [10].

4   Capability-Based Adaptive Accessibility

In order to reason about users, devices and adaptations, reliable methods and metrics are required to match users to devices—i.e. to relate device input and output functionality to the human capability requirements for providing or perceiving that input or output. Examples include optimising content displayed on the screen of a PDA for an outdoor environment when a substantial change in light level is detected (or switching to audio output, if necessary). Such metrics are also required for matching users to accessibility adaptations, including some degree of temporal flexibility, due to users' changing needs over time. The diversification in terms of device form-factors and platforms mandates a portable solution (or already-learnt user capabilities and preferences may not be transferable to new devices, applications or content). Currently the problems of reliable discovery and monitoring of user capabilities, as well as the interactions of potentially-conflicting accessibility adaptations, present formidable challenges.

However, there is a body of work that provides a basis for such reasoning. There exists an internationally-recognised standard for classifying human capabilities: WHO's ICF [11]. Existing work by Billi uses the ICF to assist with modelling human-computer interaction scenarios [12]. The approach taken by Billi is to extend the existing classification in two ways: (1) Extending the human skills classification via an appendix to include more fine-grained details such as the user's performance in clicking, dragging and moving the mouse, and (2) adding a device functionality appendix, in a similar vein to the extra human capabilities, which categorises device functions such as screen resolution, colour depth, whether joystick input is supported and whether voice input is supported.

It is argued that, although this approach could help improve modelling of interaction with—and therefore hopefully the accessibility of—*current* devices, it is not the correct approach for the medium- and long-term. This is because it is device-dependent. A more sustainable approach would be to express the additional classifications in terms of *human* functionality, as (a) human capability classifications change incredibly slowly over time[3] and (b) expressing the capability requirements of device functions in terms of human capabilities allows the same classification to support new devices as they are developed. Consider the mouse scroll wheel as an example: this may eventually be phased-out in favour of

---

[3] For the purposes of this work, the gamut of capabilities of the human species may be considered static.

multi-touch control surfaces. When this happens, the information "user can use the mouse scroll wheel" becomes irrelevant. It would be better to express that the user has a certain level of sustainable, repeatable bending in their finger(s), as this information can be used for reasoning independently of device class.

Expressing as much data as possible in terms of human capability requirements has another benefit: it allows any "interference" relationship between adaptations to be exposed within the reasoning process. For example, the use of larger text may have a positive effect on visual acuity, but—through enlarging the volume of information when rendered visually—it may impose a requirement for scrolling, which may burden the user's motor capabilities. Each adaptation could be thought of as an overlay, or delta, to the user's overall capabilities data structure (which would be similar to that prescribed by the ICF, though not necessarily fully-populated). Further, when two or more users are collaborating, the reasoning technique can consider the combination of each user's requirements in the same way, effectively simply tightening the constraints on the process.

The promise of capability-based reasoning is to unify the process by which: (a) users can be matched to devices; (b) the rendering of information can be tailored for each user-device pair and (c) the application of accessibility adaptations can be orchestrated. However there are significant challenges to overcome. Using human capabilities as the basis for this reasoning requires a means to: (1) accurately assess and subsequently monitor user capabilities, as well as (2) the effects of the environment on a user and (3) the interference caused by the application of multiple adaptations.

The following sections provide a technical overview of our proposed capability-based reasoning process, particularly regarding how such a system can be made sufficiently passive (so as to avoid distracting users) and self-regulating, through the provision of metrics to enable performance and reliability to be assessed. A description of the user-visible adaptivity components is given in other work [4].

5   The User as the Expert

Our system seeks to map minor-to-moderate impairments brought about by capability change on the part of the user, environment or device to the appropriate accessibility adaptations. We begin with the basic assumption that the user's actions can enable us to learn a great deal about their capabilities and preferred adaptations. Further, we acknowledge that: (a) in many cases it may not be possible to directly measure individual capabilities and (b) users may employ undetectable means to address accessibility problems (e.g. reading glasses).

Some basic features of our model follow. A user has a set of capabilities (as in classifications such as ICF). A computer system's purpose is to transmit information to and receive information from the user in various modalities. Four are self-explanatory: audio, vision, motor and cognition. Our system also considers two further channels: time (as devices may impose constraints and users may have impairments that alter the time needed or available for certain interactions) and volume of information (because impairments and situations can alter the amount of information a user may be capable of perceiving or processing). There is a 1:n relationship between a modality and the capabilities that operate over it (i.e. both visual acuity and colour perception are visual capabilities).

If, at any time, the requirements of the system, device and environment outweigh the level of capability afforded by the user, then an adaptation must be made. Figure 1 demonstrates such a situation and two alternative courses of action. According to the adaptations available, multiple courses of action may be available; a decision-tree algorithm similar to those used by Gajos could be used to select the most appropriate, based on a statistical model of the user's preferred actions in similar situations (e.g. when web-browsing vs. when watching DVDs). As suggested by the figure, a typical system contains many points that can be monitored for such activity, thus providing us with a passive way to monitor for capability change.

The notion of change is of key importance here: the system could not always poses an accurate picture of the user's capabilities in detail. Instead it should attempt to use monitoring techniques to gauge the *change* in capabilities over time. It is also important to recognise that some of the most profound adaptations (such as putting on reading glasses) will be undetectable to the system—and that the fact that an adaptation is made does not indicate that the user's capability was outweigh by the requirements at the time. However, the information continuously gathered will still be of use in formulating a list of possible useful adaptations, from which the user can select after requesting

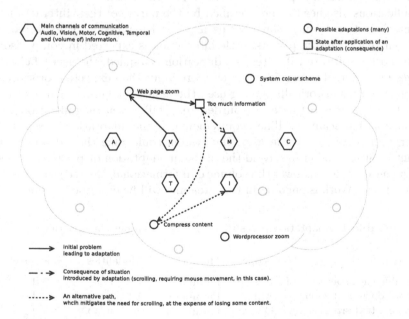

Fig. 1. Cloud representing the entire system, with particular adaptation hooks pointed out. The user has activated one of these and this has had consequences which could be dealt with in one of two ways.

help. Our system seeks to raise awareness of and augment the processes by which users may receive help, not to replace existing support methods.

Sometimes it may be necessary to interrupt the user to perform a more direct assessment of capability in order to calibrate the system. The approach we are currently trialling is to trade some rigour in the testing with making the tests into engaging "mini-games" for the user. We only require a moderate indication of capability (such as double-click speed or reading text size) but certainly do not wish to alienate users. It may also be necessary to present a choice of adaptations in a given situation when the computer cannot determine a "clear winner." Finally, the user's feedback after an adaptation has been applied—namely acceptance, rejection or a request for further help—would be taken into consideration in much the same way as it is in systems such as those discussed elsewhere [4].

6   Classifications

The reasoning process must be capable of mapping capability information into the appropriate adaptations (expressed as in ISO 24751). To assist with this mapping, a small number of classifications are being developed. Adaptations are classified on several dimensions; a brief example is given Table 1. Some potential side-effects (in terms of channels that may become restricted when an adaptation is applied) are given (which, in turn, may require supplementary adaptations to be made to counteract the side-effects—monitoring of users' actions can indicate which course of action is preferred in different situations).

Applications also need to be classified by the nature of their interaction and presentation styles, which can give us a general expression of expected user behaviour (e.g. in media players, little interaction is expected in comparison to web authoring software). If, after an adaptation is applied, the user's behaviour changes unexpectedly—providing much more input than expected, or switching to keyboard after historically having used the mouse—we may surmise that the adaptation has caused this extra burden (e.g. full-screen magnification would introduce a significant scrolling requirement). If the adaptation is rejected or further help is sought by the user, the system could take the side-effects into account in future and either avoid the problem adaptation or perhaps suggest a supplementary one (e.g. lower the volume of information presented) to counteract its side-effects. Work is ongoing in this area and will be described in due course.

Table 1. Adaptation types (brief excerpt from our classification)

Action	I/O	Scope	Method	Modalities	Side-effects
Double-click speed	I	Device	Parameter	M	T
Word document zoom	O	App.	Parameter	V(Acuity)	I
System text size	O	OS/App.	Parameter	V(Acuity)	I
Screen mag.	O	Device	Filter	V(Acuity,Colour)	I

7 Conclusion and Further Work

We have presented part of our vision for mainstreaming accessibility through adaptations and the adoption of human capabilities as a benchmark for doing this. Work on the temporal aspects of the reasoning system is ongoing. Our reasoning process is being integrated into a pilot system, to be tested shortly. Longitudinal data gathering with users for approximately one year will be carried out towards the end of the project—the collected data on adaptation usage and prediction accuracy will be an additional output. This work was funded under the UK's New Dynamics of Ageing cross council research programme

References

1. Keates, S., Clarkson, P.J.: Countering design exclusion: bridging the gap between usability and accessibility. Universal Access in the Information Society 2, 215–225 (2003)
2. Richards, J.T., Hanson, V.L.: Web accessibility: a broader view. In: WWW 2004: Proceedings of the 13th international conference on World Wide Web, pp. 72–79. ACM, New York (2004)
3. Sayago, S., Blat, J.: Telling the story of older people e-mailing: An ethnographical study. International Journal of Human-Computer Studies 68(1-2), 105–120 (2010)
4. Sloan, D., Atkinson, M.T., Machin, C.H.C., Li, Y.: The potential of adaptive interfaces as an accessibility aid for older web users. In: W4A (July 2010) (in press)
5. Hurst, A., Hudson, S.E., Mankoff, J., Trewin, S.: Automatically detecting pointing performance. In: Proceedings of the ACM International Conference on Intelligent User Interfaces (IUI), January 2008, pp. 11–19 (2008)
6. Biswas, P., Sezgin, T.M., Robinson, P.: Perception model for people with visual impairments. In: Sebillo, M., Vitiello, G., Schaefer, G. (eds.) VISUAL 2008. LNCS, vol. 5188, pp. 279–290. Springer, Heidelberg (2008)
7. Jefferson, L., Harvey, R.: An interface to support color blind computer users. In: CHI 2007: Proceedings of the SIGCHI conference on Human factors in computing systems, pp. 1535–1538. ACM, New York (2007)
8. Gajos, K.Z., Wobbrock, J.O., Weld, D.S.: Automatically generating user interfaces adapted to users' motor and vision capabilities. In: UIST 2007: Proceedings of the 20th annual ACM symposium on User interface software and technology, pp. 231–240. ACM, New York (2007)
9. Korn, P., Bekiaris, E., Gemou, M.: Towards open access accessibility everywhere: The ægis concept. In: Stephanidis, C. (ed.) UACHI 2009. LNCS, vol. 5614, pp. 535–543. Springer, Heidelberg (2009)
10. Kurniawan, S.H., King, A., Evans, D.G., Blenkhorn, P.L.: Personalising web page presentation for older people. Interact. Comput. 18(3), 457–477 (2006)
11. World Health Organization: International classification of functioning, disability and health (ICF) (2001), http://www.who.int/classifications/icf/
12. Billi, M., Burzagli, L., Emiliani, P., Gabbanini, F., Graziani, P.: A classification, based on ICF, for modelling human computer interaction, for modelling human computer interaction. In: Miesenberger, K., Klaus, J., Zagler, W.L., Karshmer, A.I. (eds.) ICCHP 2006. LNCS, vol. 4061, pp. 407–414. Springer, Heidelberg (2006)

Accelerometer & Spatial Audio Technology: Making Touch-Screen Mobile Devices Accessible

Flaithri Neff [1], Tracey J. Mehigan[2], and Ian Pitt[2]

[1] Dep't Electrical & Electronic Engineering, Limerick Institute of Technology, Ireland
[2] Dep't Computer Science, University College Cork, Ireland
Flaithri.Neff@lit.ie, {t.mehigan,i.pitt}@cs.ucc.ie

Abstract. As mobile-phone design moves toward a touch-screen form factor, the visually disabled are faced with new accessibility challenges. The mainstream interaction model for touch-screen devices relies on the user having the ability to *see* spatially arranged visual icons, and to interface with these icons via a smooth glass screen. An inherent challenge for blind users with this type of interface is its lack of tactile feedback. In this paper we explore the concept of using a combination of spatial audio and accelerometer technology to enable blind users to effectively operate a touch-screen device. We discuss the challenges involved in representing icons using sound and we introduce a design framework that is helping us tease out some of these issues. We also outline a set of proposed user-studies that will test the effectiveness of our design using a Nokia N97. The results of these studies will be presented at ICCHP 2010.

Keywords: Spatial Audio, Accelerometers, Vision Impaired, Mobile Devices.

1 Introduction

Mobile phones are now a ubiquitous and necessary technology for social and business activities. Therefore, it is essential that these devices be accessible to all members of society, including the visually disabled. The current design trend increasingly favors the touch-screen form factor. This introduces some serious challenges for the blind user since the design approach requires accurate visual knowledge of the location of functional icons onscreen. Due to the lack of tactile feedback in comparison to the projecting button design, the blind user is stripped of one of the most important sensory mechanisms for interacting with mobile devices. As the majority of manufacturers move away from older hardware designs and introduce more touch-screen models, the choice of handset for blind users will become extremely limited. Additionally, as the buttoned keypad form factor becomes less common, it is likely to become a specialist product, much like Braille devices, and the cost may rise. Therefore, an alternative means of navigating touch-screen devices without the need for vision and touch is required so that blind users are at the same level as sighted users in terms of technology and trend. We propose the use of two facilities that are being increasingly incorporated into mobile device hardware and software specifications – spatial audio and accelerometer functionality. Although they are commonly used separately and for

K. Miesenberger et al. (Eds.): ICCHP 2010, Part I, LNCS 6179, pp. 170–177, 2010.

very different applications, we believe that these two technologies when combined will allow the blind user to interact with a touch-screen device.

1.1 Primary Challenges and Proposed Solution

There are two primary challenges that we face when attempting to make touch screen devices accessible. The first is to present icon information to the blind user in an effective way. This means is that the blind user should be able to precisely locate each icon and clearly interpret what it represents. The second challenge is to find a mechanism that will allow the blind user to easily and quickly navigate the target icons and interact with them effectively.

As a potential solution to the first challenge, we propose an interface that is built on the use of spatialized, non-speech sound. Using non-speech sound at this stage of the interface design has a number of benefits over speech, such as offering a more concise and rapid overview [1][2][3][4]. Furthermore, non-speech sound is easier to texturally vary than speech, which helps to maintain icon autonomy and avoid perceptual interference [5][6].

In addition to using non-speech sound, the implementation of sound spatialization is of further benefit when presenting simultaneous sonic events because it is an effective means of accentuating auditory segregation between discrete sonic events [7]. This helps to avoid auditory scene clutter that tends to plague non-spatial auditory presentation [8][9]. Similar approaches are being employed for interfaces that involve the monitoring of several discrete, yet simultaneous, events such as air-traffic control, pilot cockpit applications and auditory graph presentation [10][11][12]. In terms of the presentation of non-speech sonic icons on a mobile device, spatialization may help the user to more easily identify each independent icon in space, and subsequently clearly interpret its meaning while other sonic icons remain constantly present.

In relation to the second challenge, which is to find an effective mechanism to allow the user to navigate the spatialized sonic icon environment, we propose combining the spatialized audio with accelerometer technology. Obviously, in their current capacity, touch-screen devices cannot exhibit the same level of tactile feedback as projected buttons on a keypad. In order to interact with an icon on a touch-screen device, the user needs to know the precise location of that icon. Touching the screen at an incorrect point, even if it is only slightly off target, will result in the wrong icon being chosen or no reaction from the device. We propose the use of accelerometers to allow blind users to 'roll' toward their icon target. The implementation of gesture movements will allow the user to interact with the sonic icon once the target has been reached, thus removing any reliance on interfacing with the device using its touch-screen facilities. Using this approach means that existing hardware can be sold to both sighted and blind individuals, and only some form of software system setting is required to customize the same device depending on whether you have a visual disability or not.

2 Spatial Sound on Mobile Devices & Accelerometer Technology

For a number of years, several 3D audio solutions have existed for mobile devices. However, the actual practical implementation of spatial audio in the industry has been surprisingly slow and piecemeal. Although major manufacturers have been heavily involved from a research and development point of view, only a select number of devices have the inbuilt capability to perform spatial audio tasks. Currently, only the higher-end models support the use of spatial sound, and even that remains unpredictable at best. Most of the implemented spatial audio examples are concentrated in the entertainment arena and rely on third-party APIs hooking into a supporting OS.

One of the most established APIs that allows for the implementation of spatial audio on some mobile devices is JSR-234, or the Advanced Multimedia Supplements (AMMS). Initiated by Nokia and developed under the Java Community Process [13], it is an optional add-on to MMAPI (JSR-135 - Mobile Media API). This API is targeted at J2ME/CLDC mobile devices, but even if the device supports MMAPI, it may not necessarily support AMMS. Only a small number of devices, such as the Nokia N97, currently fully implement the specification.

Another spatial sound API implementation is the open source OpenSL ES standard developed by the Khronos Group [14]. Target devices include PDAs, basic mobile phones, smart phones, and mobile digital music players [15]. Based on the C-language, and similar in approach as AMMS is to MMAPI, it significantly extends the capabilities of OpenMAX AL for mobile devices.

An accelerometer is a sensor device that measures the acceleration and speed of motion of an object across the x, y and z axes. This is achieved by measuring non-gravitational accelerations caused by movement and vibration of an accelerometer device. To date, these devices have been used mainly in engineering to measure vibration, as well as in the health and fitness industry to determine inertial movement for the measurement of a runner's speed and distance, or the progress of a patient's stroke rehabilitation [16]. In recent years we have seen the emergence of the accelerometer in mobile technology. Research has also been conducted for Text Entry / Dialling [17], Browsing [18], Scrolling [19], Media Control and Zooming & Scaling [20]. Accelerometers are now shipping as standard in high-end Symbian 60 / 80 series mobile devices such as the Nokia N97 and the iPhone, and are expected to be included in one third of devices by the end of 2010.

3   Designing the Interface

The auditory interface implemented in our system continues to be updated based on a comprehensive perceptual model we have developed (see Fig. 1). The model incorporates findings from contemporary research relating to auditory cognition and perception [7][21][22][23][24]. According to our model, the auditory scene presented to the user is processed by the human perceptual system in several stages. The effectiveness of how the user interacts with the device's interface (auditory scene) is highly dependent on the user's experience and on the primitive sonic structures present in the scene itself.

Within our model structure, the initial stage involves primitive perceptual organization of acoustic structures and sonic events within the auditory scene [7]. The result is the segregation of some sonic elements and the amalgamation of others into individual auditory streams. In our model, this initial process is followed with a sensory

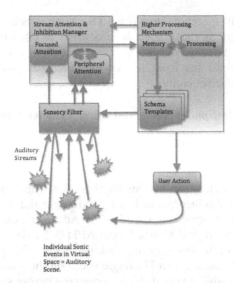

Fig. 1. A summary of the auditory user interface model. Rules are applied to every stage. In a complex auditory scene, a primitive perceptual process segregates sound events into separate auditory streams. Some streams are blocked by the sensory filter and others are allowed pass to the attention mechanisms. From there, only select streams are given privilege to be processed by higher processing mechanisms. The user's actions/reactions to these events influences the structure of the original scene, and the cycle begins again.

filter stage that allows some auditory streams to pass and blocks others from continuing to the next stage of perceptual processing. The sensory filter is strongly influenced by user-experience, which itself is built up over time in human memory and encapsulated as schema templates [24]. If an appropriate schema is selected from memory for the current auditory scene, then only the most important auditory streams will continue their journey onto the next stage of our model. Following the sensory filter stage, attention and inhibition procedures further define and qualify the importance of certain auditory streams. Those streams deemed important enough are allowed to progress to the final stage, which involves prioritized processing by what is termed "Higher Processing Mechanisms" in our model.

Therefore, according to our model, the acoustic structure of sonic icons (be they auditory icons[1], earcons[2], spearcons[3] etc.) plays a pivotal role in how effective an auditory interface is at maintaining the clear relay of information to the end-user. A sonic icon should consist of acoustic properties that conform to human auditory perception traits along each stage in the model so that the user can clearly identify the icon's location and meaning without interfering with other primary tasks, such as

---

[1] Auditory Icons are "everyday sounds designed to convey information about events by analogy to everyday sound-producing events." [27]

[2] Earcons are "abstract, synthetic tones in structured combinations to create auditory messages." [28]

[3] Spearcon are compressed "spoken phrase (created either by a TTS generator or by recorded voice) without modifying the perceived pitch of the sound." [29]

listening to concurrent speech content if a TTS engine is being utilized. This can be achieved through ensuring that a sonic icon consists of pitch or temporal properties that are well outside the range of other icons or speech, or that its location is spaced significantly apart from other icons so that the perceptual system can immediately identify it as being a distinct entity.

3.1 Implementing the Spatial Audio and Accelerometer Interface

Due to the ongoing refinement of the auditory user interface model, two types of interfaces have been so far generated, with several other concepts also in development. The system was developed using J2ME (Java 2 Micro Edition) through the NetBeans IDE incorporating the 3.0 Development Kit. The Nokia N97 SDK (S60 & Symbian OS 9.4) was also incorporated into the IDE. Spatial sound and audio content was facilitated by the incorporating the JSR 234 Advanced Multimedia Supplements API, which extends the original Mobile Media API (JSR 134).

The user-interface of the first implementation provides a simplistic graphic display based on a 3x4 grid formation in a 3D single-room setting - see Fig. 2a. The display comprises an enclosed single virtual room, containing twelve sonic icon sprites, each representing a particular sound source. The virtual room is contained within an overall grid. A Listener Sprite is also included in the display. The purpose of the Listener Sprite is to highlight the position of the subject within the environment. The subject can move, using the navigation arrow keys, around the virtual room to access the Sonic Icon Sprites.

A second user-interface has also been implemented. This incorporates very similar features as the first interface, but with the distinction of separating the sonic icons into pairs (2x6 grid) - see Fig. 2b. This is achieved by implementing virtual partitions within the room to block out the sound of other pairs. Again, user studies are underway to determine what type of sonic icon performs best for this particular design.

The types of sonic icons being tested in our system is based on previous research by Dingler et al. [25], where non-speech sound was examined for its effectiveness in relaying interface menu items in a non-spatial context. All sonic content (including speech) will not be based on any known existing Nokia phone menu icon. This is to ensure that users already familiar with Nokia menu icons (or any phone menu palette)

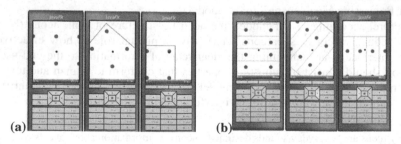

Fig. 2. (a) The first interface implementation running on the emulator device screen. The Listener Sprite (black dot) navigates around the single virtual room towards a Sonic Icon Sprite in the corner (red circle). (b) The second interface implementation. The Listener Sprite navigates from one partition of the virtual room containing a pair of Sonic Icons to another partition.

will not bias the study. We will use the same sound-set as utilized by Dingler et al. [25], categorized as follows: a) Speech, b) Earcon, c) Auditory Icon, d) Spearcon, e) Parallel Hybrid, and f) Simple Hybrid. We will then be able to compare our results (spatial context) with those of Dingler et al. (non-spatial context) [25].

We will also be testing the capabilities of accelerometers to replace arrow key functions, allowing the blind users to 'roll' toward their target and employ gesture movements to interact with sonic icons. As the subject turns the device left or right the display direction rotates to facilitate movement by the Listener Sprite in that direction (see Fig. 2a and 2b). By moving the device up and down, the subject can navigate forward or backward as required for interaction. By using the test initially utilizing the navigation keys as a control, we can assess the performance of using the accelerometer approach. To incorporate the accelerometer device sensor facility JSR-256, Mobile Sensors API will be included in the development of the system.

These tests are currently ongoing and it is expected that results will be available for presentation at the upcoming ICCHP conference 2010.

4 Study Methodology

39 subjects will take part in the study. This is to ensure the closest comparison possible to the study performed by Dingler et al [25] where 39 subjects were also used. Each subject will be sighted and have normal binaural hearing abilities. They will be constrained from seeing onscreen action by being blindfolded during the tasks. The blindfold will be such as to not obstruct the pinnae of the subject, as headphones will need to be properly seated into position. After the completion of the tasks, a short questionnaire will be completed by the subject, which will contain subjective questioning.

The sonic content has been kindly supplied by Walker and Lindsay [26]. All files are 16bit, 44.1 kHz, mono WAV files. The sonic content comprises of environmental objects and abstractions, and do not correlate with any mobile phone menu icon (such as 'Settings', 'Messages', etc.). The following is a list of the environmental objects and abstractions that will be used in the study: Bench, Bus-stop, Bush, Emergency Phone, Fountain, Garbage Can, Parking Meter, Pedestrian Light, Public Phone, Road Works, Stairs Down, and Tree.

Subjects will receive a brief training session whereby earcons, auditory icons, spearcons and speech will be associated with the elements listed above. They will also be allowed three test trials of each scenario in the actual virtual spatial environment.

The user-study environment will consist of 12 elements from the above list relayed spatially in one of the following sonic formats: Earcons; Auditory Icons; Parallel Hybrids; Simple Hybrids; Spearcons; Text-to-Speech. These will be spatially rendered as a MIDlet using JSR-234 (J2ME) and implemented on a Nokia N97 device.

5 Future Work

In future implementations, we aim to extend this work to include encircled spatialization (azimuth) of six types of sonic icon: a) Speech b) Earcon c) Auditory Icon d) Spearcon e) Parallel Hybrid f) Simple Hybrid. Again, the objective will be to determine the best sonic icon for relaying short, comprehensive, menu-orientated information cues within a spatial context. It is also intended to include a facility for the measurement of inertial movement facilitating the tracking of a subject's hand and body position, for example the direction in which they are turned when operating the system. This could potentially have benefits for the vision impaired for increased efficiency in operating such systems in virtual environments.

Acknowledgments. Funding for this research provided by the Irish Research Council for Science, Engineering and Technology in collaboration with the Digital Hub.

References

1. Brewster, S., Leplâtre, G., Crease, M.: Using Non-Speech Sounds in Mobile Computing Devices. Glasgow Interactive Systems Group, Dept. Computing Science, University of Glasgow (1998)
2. Stevens, R.D., Wright, P.C., Edwards, A.D.N., Brewster, S.A.: An Audio Glance at Syntactic Structure Based on Spoken Form. In: Proc. of ICCHP 1996, Linz, pp. 627–635 (1996)
3. Brewster, S., Wright, P.C., Edwards, A.D.N.: A detailed investigation into the effectiveness of earcons. In: Kramer, G., Smith, S. (eds.) Proc. International Conference on Auditory Display, USA (1994)
4. Stevens, R.D., Brewster, S.A., Wright, P.C., Edwards, A.D.N.: Design and Evaluation of an Auditory Glance at Algebra for Blind Readers. In: Kramer, G., Smith, S. (eds.) Proc. International Conference on Auditory Display, USA (1994)
5. Brown, G.J., Cooke, M.: Perceptual grouping of musical sounds: A computational model. Journal of New Music Research 23(2), 107–132 (1994)
6. Kashino, K., Nakadai, K., Kinoshita, T., Tanaka, H.: Organization of Hierarchical Perceptual Sounds: Music Scene Analysis with Autonomous Processing Modules and a Quantitative Information Integration Mechanism. In: Proc. International Joint Conf. on Artificial Intelligence, pp. 158–164 (1995)
7. Bregman, A.: Auditory Scene Analysis: The Perceptual Organization of Sound. MIT Press, USA (1994)
8. Neff, F., Pitt, I., Keheo, A.: A Consideration of Perceptual Interaction in an Auditory Prolific Mobile Device, Spatial Audio for Mobile Devices. In: 9th International Conference on Human Interaction with Mobile Devices and Services, Mobile HCI 2007, Singapore (2007)
9. Neff, F., Kehoe, A., Pitt, I.J.: User Modeling to Support the Development of an Auditory Help System. In: Matoušek, V., Mautner, P. (eds.) TSD 2007. LNCS (LNAI), vol. 4629, pp. 390–397. Springer, Heidelberg (2007)
10. Begault, D.R.: Virtual Acoustics, Aeronautics and Communications. Presented at the 101st Convention, Los Angeles, California, November 8-11; Journal of the Audio Engineering Society (1996)
11. Cabrera, D., Ferguson, S., Laing, G.: Development of Auditory Alerts for Air Traffic Control Consoles. In: 119th Convention, NY, USA, October 7-10; Journal of the Audio Engineering Society (2005)
12. Brown, L., Brewster, S., Ramloll, R., Burton, M., Riedel, B.: Design Guidelines for Audio Presentation of Graphs and Tables. In: Proceedings of International Conference on Auditory Display, Boston, MA, USA, July 6-9 (2003)

13. JSR-234 Expert Group: Advanced Multimedia Supplements API for JavaTM2 Micro Edition. Nokia Corporation 2004-2005 (May 17, 2005)
14. The Khronos Group, http://www.khronos.org/opensles/
15. The Khronos Group: OpenSL ES Specification, Version 1.0. The Khronos Group Inc. (2007-2009) (March 16, 2009)
16. Zheng, H., Black, N., Harris, N.: Position-Sensing Technologies for Movement Analysis in Stroke Rehabilitation. Medical and Biological Engineering and Computing 43(4), 413–420 (2005)
17. Wigdor, D., Balakrishnan, R.: TiltText: Using Tilt for Text Input to Mobile Phones. In: Proceedings UIST 2003, Vancouver, BC, Canada, pp. 81–90 (2003)
18. Cho, S., Murray-smith, R., Choi, C., Sung, Y., Lee, K., Kim, Y.: Dynamics of Tilt Based Browsing. In: Proceedings of CHI 2007, San Jose, USA (2007)
19. Darnauer, J., Garrity, S., Kim, T.: Orientation-based Interaction for Mobile Devices (June 10, 2007),
   http://hci.stanford.edu/~srk/cs377a-mobile/project/final/darnauer-garrity-kim.pdf
20. Eslambolchilar, P., Murray-Smith, R.: Tilt-based automatic zooming and scaling in mobile devices-a state-space implementation. In: Brewster, S., Dunlop, M.D. (eds.) Mobile HCI 2004. LNCS, vol. 3160, pp. 120–131. Springer, Heidelberg (2004)
21. Wrigley, S.N., Brown, G.J.: A model of auditory attention. Technical Report CS-00- 07, Speech and Hearing Research Group, University of Sheffield (2000)
22. Jones, D.M., Macken, W.J.: Irrelevant Tones Produce an Irrelevant Speech Effect: Implications for Phonological Coding in Working Memory. Journal of Experimental Psychology: Learning, Memory, and Cognition 19(2), 369–381 (1993)
23. Jones, D.M., Madden, C., Miles, C.: Privileged access by irrelevant speech to short-term memory: The role of changing state. Quarterly Journal of Experimental Psychology 44A, 645–669 (1992)
24. Baddeley, A.: Your Memory: A User's Guide, 2nd edn., Prion, UK, June 1 (1996)
25. Dingler, T., Lindsay, J., Walker, B.: Learnability of Sound Cues for Environmental Features: Auditory Icons, Earcons, Spearcons, and Speech. In: Proceedings of the 14th International Conference on Auditory Display, Paris, France, June 24-27 (2008)
26. Walker, B., Lindsay, J.: The Georgia Tech Sonification Lab, School of Psychology and the School of Interactive Computing. Georgia Institute of Technology, USA
27. Buxton, W., Gaver, W., Bly, S.: Auditory Interfaces: The Use of Non-Speech Audio at the Interface (1994) (Unpublished)
28. Brewster, S.: Nonspeech Auditory Output. In: Sears, A., Jacko, J. (eds.) Human-Computer Interaction: Fundamentals, Evolving Technologies and Emerging Applications. Taylor & Francis Group, LLC CRC Press, USA (2009)
29. Walker, B.N., Kogan, A.: Spearcon performance and preference for auditory menus on a mobile phone. In: Stephanidis, C. (ed.) UAHCI, Part II, HCII 2009. LNCS, vol. 5615, pp. 445–454. Springer, Berlin (2009)

An Open Source / Freeware Assistive Technology Software Inventory

Alexandros Pino[1], Georgios Kouroupetroglou[2], Hernisa Kacorri[1],
Anna Sarantidou[2], and Dimitris Spiliotopoulos[2]

[1] National and Kapodistrian University of Athens, Accessibility Unit,
Panepistimiopolis, Ilissia, 15784, Athens, Greece
[2] National and Kapodistrian University of Athens,
Dep. of Informatics and Telecommunications,
Panepistimiopolis, Ilissia, 15784, Athens, Greece
{pino,koupe,c.katsori,ea05538,dspiliot}@di.uoa.gr

Abstract. Assistive Technology (AT) software market is expensive, and related products are hard to find, especially for non-English speaking users. Open Source and free AT software partially solve the cost problem, and online inventories facilitate the search for the appropriate product. Even so, users don't have all the information gathered and systematically organized in one place. Furthermore, free software often needs to be tested and reviewed by computer and AT experts in order to detect and point out reliability, installation, and compatibility issues. We propose a methodology for creating web-based free AT software inventories, which will make the search and selection of such products straightforward. The methodology is based on the systematic organization and consistency of the information available for each product, and its effective presentation; the goal for the users is to be able to quickly find, compare and understand the functionality and features of each product. We have applied this methodology to create the Open Source / Freeware AT software inventory http://access.uoa.gr/fs.

Keywords: Open Source, Assistive technology, Accessibility.

1 Introduction

One of the main problems that Assistive Technology (AT) software users face is the high cost of such products [1]. Even when cost is not an issue, the potential AT user comes across a second obstacle: the dispersion of the locations that these products can be found; information for each product is available on its own website, with no easy way to overview all available software in one place. Online free AT software inventories or lists try to address these challenges. Other problems that arise when a specific product is about to be selected include compatibility issues and the limited number of languages that it usually supports; in many cases the software is not compatible with the user's computer or operating system [2]. Moreover, for non-English speaking users, finding an AT software that "speaks" their own language is often a difficult task. Furthermore, there is no reassurance that a free AT application is tested by a

K. Miesenberger et al. (Eds.): ICCHP 2010, Part I, LNCS 6179, pp. 178–185, 2010.

specialist team in terms of usability and stability [3]. Free software usually does not have warranty, support or extensive documentation available, so testing it is an important issue. Finally, in existing inventories there is no consistent way of presenting AT applications with the same level of information detail and covering all important features. In order to facilitate disabled users to find, select, and afford AT, we propose a methodology for creating a well-structured, easy to use and understandable online inventory of tested, free of charge AT software products.

Free of charge software can be found in various forms: Open Source software, freeware, shareware, and trial versions of commercial software [4], [5]. Open Source[1] software means that the source code, as well as the compiled form of the application is freely redistributed [6]. Freeware[2] is computer software that is made available free of charge, but is copyrighted by its developer, who retains the rights to control its distribution, modify it and sell it in the future. It is typically distributed without its source code, thus preventing modification by its users. Shareware[3] is software that is distributed freely or on a trial basis with the understanding that the user may need or want to pay for it later. Some software developers offer a shareware version of their application with a built-in expiration date, after which the user can no longer get access to the program. Other shareware (sometimes called liteware) is offered with certain capabilities disabled as an enticement to buy the complete version of the product. Trial versions of commercial software is similar to shareware or liteware, with the difference that shareware can sometimes be used for an unlimited period of time free of charge, while trial versions will certainly expire and need to be purchased eventually.

2 Related Work

Several lists of free AT software can be found on the Internet: The Open Source Assistive Technology Software (OATSoft[4]) website currently (April 2010) lists 162 Open Source projects [7]. A brief description for each project is given as well as the possibility to download the software and/or source code from an external developer's site. There are three ways to search the OATSoft inventory, namely based on the needs that the software meets (options include: Text Input, Communication, Using the Mouse, Viewing the Screen, Accessing the Web, Symbols, Alternative Access, Learning and Education, General Tools, and Other Need), by type of software (options include: On Screen Keyboards, Symbol Libraries, Text to Speech, Computer Automation, Switch Input Software, Alternative and Augmentative Communication, Environmental Control, Educational and Learning, General Tools, and Other Function), or by simply listing the whole inventory. OATSoft website also includes a rating system (scale 1-Average to 5-Brilliant) for each product and the possibility to add comments on each product's page. Project:Possibility[5] website provides a smaller inventory of Open Source AT projects that currently lists 16 applications. Projects are divided into six sections, namely Educational, Intelligent Input, Mobile, Music, Video Game, and

---

[1] http://www.opensource.org/docs/definition.php
[2] http://www.linfo.org/freeware.html
[3] http://searchenterpriselinux.techtarget.com/sDefinition/0,,sid39_gci212977,00.html
[4] http://www.oatsoft.org/
[5] www.projectpossibility.org/

Web. Raising the Floor[6] website lists 13 Open Source projects divided into three sections: a) for individuals with blindness, low-vision or reading difficulties, b) for individuals looking for assistance with reading skills, and c) for web content developers. Other websites listing a number of Open Source, freeware, and shareware AT applications, and offering the corresponding files for download, include Emptech[7] (134 applications), and Adaptech[8] (124 applications).

All of the inventories mentioned above list AT software applications without taking into account or commenting on features like usability, stability, and functionality. This would require testing of each application by AT specialists, and the inclusion of results/comments about, for example, the installation process, the settings options, and the actual language support of each individual AT application [8]. The existing aforementioned websites do not include such data.

Among the most important characteristics of our proposed methodology for building an AT inventory that set this work apart from what already exists in the Internet is that all the included applications have been already installed and tested by experts (authors of the AT software inventory). That means that there is a high degree of reassurance for the users that all software included in the list works as intended [9]. This is quite helpful especially for novice or non expert users that don't have the time, capability or knowledge to test or evaluate the software themselves. Especially for users from countries with not common or widespread languages, like Greek, testing each piece of software for local language support is quite important.

3 Methodology

The proposed methodology consists of seven steps described in the next sections. Each section contains details of our implementation as a proof of concept for good practice.

3.1 Searching and Locating Free AT Software Available on the Internet

Resources explored include all the inventories mentioned in section 2, as well as links found in user forums and additional AT vendors' websites for individual applications. A total number of 224 individual applications were found. Among these, 46 of the applications, although they were characterized as AT software in an inventory, they were actually general purpose software or irrelevant to any disability, so they were excluded from our list (for example office automation, web browsing or gaming software without any special accessibility options or features).

3.2 Installing the Application

All applications were installed on computers with the Operating Systems they supported. A total number of 19 applications failed to successfully complete the installation process; in most of them, either installation files were missing or purchase was needed in contrast of what their description stated.

---

[6] http://raisingthefloor.net/
[7] http://www.emptech.info/categories_list.php
[8] http://adaptech.dawsoncollege.qc.ca/fandi_e.php

3.3 Testing the Application

Subsequent to installation, all the applications were launched and tested, in order to investigate whether they realize the functionality their documentation or description depicted. Program stability was also tested for 3 hours of operation for each application. Different settings and layouts were tested where applicable. A total of 14 applications failed to run smoothly, exhibiting stops and crashes at run-time, so they were excluded. As our inventory has to address a disabled community speaking a less common language, all software that would be unusable by Greek users was excluded, for example, text to speech software that does not "speak" Greek, or screen readers that do not recognize Greek fonts. 63 applications were evaluated as unusable for Greek users specifically. At the end of all filtering and testing, 82 free AT software applications were selected to populate our inventory. Table 1 summarizes the number of applications processed in the first three steps.

Table 1. AT software located, tested, and selected during the application of our methodology

	number	percentage
Total applications located	224	100%
Non-AT applications (excluded)	46	21%
Applications failed to install (excluded)	19	8%
Applications failed to run (excluded)	14	6%
Applications not supporting Greek language (excluded)	63	28%
Applications finally selected for our inventory	82	37%

3.4 Documenting

After the successful testing of each free AT software, the application was documented and the following fields of information were filled:

- *Application name*: The name of the free AT application.
- *Developer*: The company's or individual developer's/author's name, with a link to the corresponding website where available.
- *Version*: The version number of the application along with the characterization "open source" or "freeware" or "shareware".
- *Related category(ies)*: All applications were classified in one or more of the following categories: Voice recognition, Screen reader, Daisy, Calculator, Mouse pointers, Click helper, Virtual keyboard, Camera mouse, Alternative communication, Text to speech, Screen magnifier, Braille translator, Web browser, Mouse emulator, Contrast adjustment, Keyboard shortcuts, Voice mail, Clock, Video call. Categories can be added when free software of a new category appears.
- *Related disability(ies)*: All applications were also classified according to one or more disabilities: Speech, Hearing, Motor, Blindness, Low Vision. Additional disabilities can be added.
- *Description*: A description of the functionality of each application. The most important features of the AT application are listed in this field. Special or unique features that set each application apart from its competitors are stressed out.

- *System requirements*: The Operating Systems on which the free application runs were listed, and machine requirements like free hard disk space, RAM memory, screen resolution, etc.
- *Installation notes*: The software installation procedure is explained in this field, starting with which file the user has to run first, and focusing on tricky steps of the installation procedure when such steps exist (for example, if further prerequisites are required for the program to run, how to set it up on a browser in the case it is a browser add-on, how to unzip the installation files when needed, etc.).
- *Settings*: An important aspect of the documentation that is not present in any other online inventory. The main settings of the AT software are analyzed and hints are given to the potential users about the best way to setup the program according to their needs. Language settings were included, as well as comments on what effect each available option has to the operation of the software. This way, users can always know whether the application has the adaptation features they're searching for without having to download and install all available software and explore the settings menus by themselves, often making several "trial and error" circles.
- *Internal download link:* All software is gathered in our inventory's file server, offering a local link for fast download for the potential users. This way we avoid the possibility of unavailable files due to remote server downtimes, disappeared websites, or discontinued projects.
- *External download link*: The original external download link is also given.
- *Screenshot(s)*: A typical screenshot image of the running application.
- *Comments*: The text in this field is written by the members of our research team who tested the software, and includes opinions like how easy is to use the application, tips about its operation, etc.
- *Help*: Information about the existence of a help system built-in the application, availability of user manual, and in some cases tutorials (built-in or online).
- *Language*: Supported languages in the applications menus, help files, user manuals, text-to-speech, Unicode support, with emphasis to local language.
- *License*: The type of the user license of each application is given when available.
- *Product home page*: A link to the original product home page is given here.
- *Additional links*: Additional links include web pages with reviews of the product, previous versions, current issues or bugs, future plans of the developers, etc.
- *Related software*: This field provides links to other software in our database that is similar to the current software, or to dependent software (for example, a web browser will be linked to a browser add-on's page).
- *File size*: The size of the file that the user has to download in order to install or run the application.

3.5 Usable Online Inventory Design

The new web-based inventory for Open Source, freeware and non-expiring shareware AT software was designed having usability and ease of use in mind. There are three ways to search for a free AT application: a) by disability - selecting one of the *related disabilities* mentioned above, b) by application category - selecting one of the *related categories*, and c) selecting to view all available applications in an alphabetical order.

This 3-way navigation menu is available at all web pages of the inventory. Each individual application is described in its own web page that contains all information listed in the *Documenting* step, as well as user rating results, user comments, and statistics showing numbers of visitors and downloads. Thus, each AT software application's web page is enriched with user evaluation data (1 to 5 star rating by users) as well as comments, tips and tricks, or complaints that users make on the comments section. Illustrative disability category icons are always next to each application's name in order to depict related disabilities.

3.6 Accessible Website Development

The website http://access.uoa.gr/fs was built according to W3C Web Content Accessibility Guidelines 1.0[9], and a Level Triple-A Conformance was achieved. The CSS level 2.1 Conformance was reached (based on the W3C CSS Validation Service), as well as the HTML 4.01 Transitional compatibility (based on W3C's Markup Validation Service) [10].

3.7 Update and Maintenance

Our research team members are often checking for new versions of all free AT software of the inventory. Every time a new version is available, the old one is replaced and all documentation information is updated, while old versions history is kept. The date and time of the last modification that was done to an application's information fields is noted, and a "*recent changes*" section informs visitors about all additions, deletions and modifications made. We have also subscribed to several mailing lists, RSS feeds and user forums, as additional sources of information for new releases, as well as newly created AT applications that need to be tested and added. Finally, user and visitor contributions like comments on individual applications' pages, problem reports, and e-mails are often very useful, as they recommend new software to be added, or make comments on usability issues for the already included applications, as well as their own experience on using free AT software.

4 Discussion

Table 2 summarizes the information given explicitly for each product (in terms of fields described in 3.4), and the most important features of the corresponding inventory websites. It is made clear that the inventory we propose provides systematically (in individual fields and not in a general description text) all necessary information and details needed for each AT software application it contains.

The free AT software inventory http://access.uoa.gr/fs has been online for six months at the time that this paper was written. This work has been disseminated through the press, special interest mailing lists and announcements to all disability organizations and associations. The first reactions and feedback of the Greek disabled community and related professionals are positive. The website statistics show 94,528 hits and 1,886

---

[9] http://www.w3.org/TR/WCAG10/

Table 2. Overview of the information fields given for each product, and the most important website features for *A: OATSoft, B: Project:Possibility, C: Raising the Floor, D: EmpTech, E: Adapttech*, and *F: http://access.uoa.gr/fs*.

A	B	C	D	E	F	Information fields
						Product details
	•		•		•	Additional links
•	•	•	•	•	•	Application name
•					•	Comments
•	•	•	•		•	Description
		•	•	•	•	Developer
•	•			•	•	External download link
•	•	•			•	Help
	•		•	•	•	Installation file size
					•	Installation notes
					•	Internal download link
				•	•	Language
	•				•	License
•		•	•		•	Product home page
•		•	•		•	Related category(ies)
					•	Related disability(ies)
•		•			•	Related software
•	•		•		•	Screenshot(s)
					•	Settings
	•		•	•	•	System requirements
	•				•	Version
						Website features
•		•			•	Accessibility
•					•	Add comment
				•	•	Last updated
•	•	•	•		•	News (product related)
•		•			•	Rate product
•					•	Recent changes
					•	Report a problem
•	•	•	•	•	•	Search
					•	Statistics

downloads by 13,440 unique visitors. 78% of the visitors were from Greece and the rest accessed the web site from abroad. We have also received more than 150 user messages (comments on products, product rating entries, and e-mails).

5 Future Work

Future plans include the addition of a user forum about AT software, as well as a "most popular applications" section, according to downloads statistics that are collected. The inventory will be continuously updated and new software will be added; we are especially looking forward to the free AT software contributions by the ongoing AEGIS [11] and Accessible[10] European projects.

---

[10] http://www.accessible-eu.org/

Acknowledgments. The work described in this paper has been funded by the Special Account for Research Grants of the National and Kapodistrian University of Athens.

References

1. Vanderheiden, G.C.: Redefining Assistive Technology, Accessibility and Disability Based on Recent Technical Advances. J. Technology in Human Services 25, 147–158 (2007)
2. Emiliani, P.L.: Assistive Technology (AT) Versus Mainstream Technology (MST): The Research Perspective. Technology and Disability 18, 19–29 (2006)
3. Law, C.M., Yi, J.S., Choi, Y.S., Jacko, J.A.: Are Disability Access Guidelines Designed for Designers?: Do They Need to Be? In: 18th Australia Conference on Computer-Human Interaction: Design: Activities, Artifacts and Environments, pp. 357–360. ACM Press, New York (2006)
4. Chopra, S., Dexter, S.: Decoding Liberation: A Philosophical Investigation of Free Software. Routledge, New York (2007)
5. Morelli, R., Tucker, A., Danner, N., De Lanerolle, T.R., Ellis, H.J., Izmirli, O., Krizanc, D., Parker, G.: Revitalizing Computing Education Through Free and Open Source Software for Humanity. Communications of the ACM 52, 67–75 (2009)
6. Richle, D.: The Economic Motivation of Open Source Software: Stakeholder Perspectives. IEEE Computer 40, 25–32 (2007)
7. Judge, S., Lysley, A., Walsh, J., Judson, A., Druce, S.: OATS - Open source assistive technology software - a way forward. In: 12th Biennial Conference of the International Society for Augmentative and Alternative Communication, ISAAC (2006)
8. Savidis, A., Stephanidis, C.: Inclusive Development: Software Engineering Requirements for Universally Accessible Interactions. Interacting with Computers 18, 71–116 (2006)
9. Crowston, K., Howison, J., Annabi, H.: Information Systems Success in Free and Open Source Software Development: Theory and Measures. Softw. Process Improve. Pract. 11, 123–148 (2006)
10. Votis, K., Lopes, R., Tzovaras, D., Carriço, L., Likothanassis, S.: A Semantic Accessibility Assessment Environment for Design and Development for the Web. In: Stephanidis, C. (ed.) HCI 2009. LNCS, vol. 5616, pp. 803–813. Springer, Heidelberg (2009)
11. Korn, P., Bekiaris, E., Gemou, M.: Towards Open Access Accessibility Everywhere: the AEGIS Concept. In: Stephanidis, C. (ed.) HCI 2009. LNCS, vol. 5614, pp. 535–543. Springer, Heidelberg (2009)

Designing and Developing Accessible Java Swing Applications

Theofanis Oikonomou[1], Konstantinos Votis[1,2], Dimitrios Tzovaras[1], and Peter Korn[3]

[1] Informatics and Telematics Institute, Centre for Research and Technology Hellas,
6th km Charilaou-Thermi Road, P.O. Box 60361, Thessaloniki, GR-57001 Greece
{thoikon,kvotis,tzovaras}@iti.gr
[2] Pattern Recognition Laboratory, Computer Engineering and Informatics,
University of Patras, Rio Patras
botis@ceid.upatras.gr
[3] Sun Microsystems, Inc.,
17 Network Circle, MPK17-101, Menlo Park, CA 94025, USA
Peter.Korn@Sun.com

Abstract. Existing development tools provide little out-of-the-box assistance in order to design and develop accessible ICT Java solutions for impaired users. Two new approximation simulation tools are presented in an attempt to achieve accessibility design and development of Java Swing applications.

1 Introduction

Information and Communication Technology (ICT) applications and systems are not fully accessible today. This is because accessibility does not happen on its own. Many developers and designers are not fully equipped with evidence and knowledge related to the accessibility of their products or services [1]. Existing development tools and packaged solutions give little out-of-the-box assistance or make it impossible to design and develop accessible ICT Java solutions for impaired users. It is important that the design and development of accessible ICT solutions can be supported in an automated fashion, as much as possible. Thus, developers and designers need tools that provide guidance to them in how to apply the accessibility principles.

This work presents two approximation simulation tools that can be used as plugins to the Netbeans Integrated Development Environment (IDE) [4] to achieve accessibility design and development of Java Swing applications.

2 Related Work

In order to verify and simulate the accessibility of a Java Swing application an appropriate approximation and simulation tool should be introduced as most of the existing tools support only web applications. Java Accessibility Utilities [2] contain a set of tools which can assist developers and designers in developing accessible Java applications. Thus, each user can use these tools to ensure that relevant accessibility information is available on components. Furthermore, the Java Accessibility Helper [3] is a

K. Miesenberger et al. (Eds.): ICCHP 2010, Part I, LNCS 6179, pp. 186–188, 2010.

graphical tool that helps software developers and test engineers examine main accessibility issues of Java applications. This tool can be used to evaluate any AWT- or Swing-based application and creates accessibility reports based on test sets. Moreover, a Netbeans plugin called a11y [5] supports Java developers without any special knowledge on accessibility constraints to develop accessible Swing Graphical User Interfaces (GUI). Finally, a tool for simulating various vision impairments in developing Java Swing applications was presented in [6], aiding the designer/developer throughout the phases of the whole development process.

3 Developing Accessible Applications

An extension of the tool proposed by authors in [6] is being introduced in this paper. Two new plugins for the Netbeans IDE, namely "DIAS Preview plugin" and "DIAS Run plugin", were implemented. Color blindness, Parkinson's disease and various low vision impairments such as loss of central and peripheral vision, blurred vision, extreme light sensitivity and night blindness are approximately simulated.

The "Preview plugin" provides a visual design preview feature that allows developers and designers to realize how their implemented forms are being displayed. The plugin panel consists of two different window boxes that present the previewed and the simulated forms in addition to the impairment selector and the severity controls panels. Any action that happens in the previewed form box is being propagated to the simulated one. Also the developer/designer can be supported by the tool through the presentation of all the detected and possible accessibility errors and warnings of the simulated GUI form. Moreover, appropriate description of the potential problems as well as specific guidelines and recommendations on how to solve the detected problems (**Fig. 1**) can be presented. Thus the system user can select and fix any of the identified errors through an appropriate editor which is also responsible for handling the user's action.

The "DIAS Run plugin" gives the developers/designers the ability to execute and run in real time their Java Swing applications and verify if the included functionalities and components contain any accessibility constraint. The plugin automatically simulates the focused by the user component. Moreover the plugin panel consists of the simulated version of the actually running application as well as the impairment chooser and the severity controls panels. Another interesting feature is that the plugin inherits the Look and Feel (L&F) that was set to the application by the developer. Also, the plugin respects the system preferences regarding the display of high contrast

Type	Rule	Recommendation / Description	Component
🔴	Background Color	No red/green color combination for Background/Foreground should be used. Users with pr...	jTextArea1
⚠	Background Color	No red/green color combination for Background/Foreground should be used. Users with pr...	jRadioButt...
🔴	Preferred Size	The Width/Height should be increased so that users with Parkinson's disease will not have ...	jLabel1
⚠	Foreground Color *(Double click/Enter to fix)*	No red/green color combination for Background/Foreground should be used. Users with pr...	jTextArea1
⚠	Foreground Color	No red/green color combination for Background/Foreground should be used. Users with pr...	jRadioButt...
⚠	Preferred Size	The Width/Height should be increased so that users with Parkinson's disease will not have ...	jDesktopPa...

Fig. 1. "DIAS preview plugin" error/warning list

accessibility options and the mouse pointers. Finally, the "Run plugin" gives useful information on any Java GUI component with possible accessibility problems. Red rectangles are drawn on top of the simulated version of the running application, indicating the boundaries of the problematic GUI components found in the application. The designer/developer can get more details about a specific GUI component by clicking inside these red rectangles. Then, an information window will appear containing some information regarding the GUI component and why there is a problem with it as well as recommendations on how to fix it.

4   Conclusion and Future Work

In this work two Netbeans IDE plugins for simulating various impairments of Java Swing applications are presented. They can be used in order to assist designers/developers to introduce accessibility constraints at all stages of the designing and development process of Java Swing applications. Thus, the system users can overcome possible accessibility barriers and improve the overall quality of their applications in order to support the design for all methods. Various impairments as well as different severity levels for each impairment can be approximately simulated. Moreover, useful information, recommendations and appropriate guidance in order to fix the detected accessibility problems are being provided for specific categories of impairments such as color blindness and Parkinson's. Ongoing work is currently being done in several fronts of the presented plugins in (1) improving the simulation outcome in order to support more impairments, (2) enhancing the information and recommendations provided about problematic components and (3) improve the simulation process with the introduction of specific personas for the further support of system users' knowledge.

Acknowledgments. This work was partially funded by the EC FP7 project ACCESSIBLE - Accessibility Assessment Simulation Environment for New Applications Design and Development [7], Grant Agreement No. 224145.

References

1. Harper, S., Khan, G., Stevens, R.: Design Checks for Java Accessibility. In: Accessible Design in the Digital World, UK (2005), http://www.simonharper.info/publications/Harper2005zr.pdf (accessed January 25, 2010)
2. Java Accessibility Utilities, http://java.sun.com/javase/technologies/accessibility/docs/jaccess-1.3/doc/index.html (accessed January 25, 2010)
3. Java Accessibility Helper, http://java.sun.com/developer/earlyAccess/jaccesshelper/docs/index.html (accessed January 25, 2010)
4. Netbeans IDE, http://www.netbeans.org (accessed January 25, 2010)
5. Netbeans a11y plugin, http://a11y.netbeans.org/ (accessed January 25, 2010)
6. Oikonomou, T., Votis, K., Tzovaras, D., Korn, P.: An Open Source Tool for Simulating a Variety of Vision Impairments in Developing Swing Applications. In: Stephanidis, C. (ed.) HCII 2009, San Diego, USA. LNCS, vol. 5614, pp. 135–144. Springer, Heidelberg (2009)
7. ACCESSIBLE project, http://www.accessible-project.eu (accessed January 25, 2010)

Effects of Visual Stimuli on a Communication Assistive Method Using Sympathetic Skin Response

Fumihiko Masuda and Chikamune Wada

Graduate School of Life Science and Systems Engineering,
Kyushu Institute of Technology,
2-4, Hibikino, Wakamatsu-ku, Kitakyushu-city, Fukuoka-ken, Japan
masuda-fumihiko@edu.life.kyutech.ac.jp, wada@life.kyutech.ac.jp

Abstract. We propose a communication assistive method that uses sympathetic skin response (SSR) as the input indicator for a device that will assist the disabled. To develop this method, we investigated the influence of optimal display conditions. SSR evokes visual stimuli. Therefore, we first clarified the optimal combination of background and character colors. The results show that the perception of conspicuousness increased as the contrast ratio increased. Then we investigated the change in the SSR appearance ratio in the conspicuous display condition; the result showed that the contrast had no influence on the SSR appearance ratio. In the future, we will conduct experiments on more subjects and further clarify the influence of visual stimuli.

Keywords: sympathetic skin response, disabled, communication assistive method, visual stimuli, contrast.

1 Introduction

Recently, a number of input support devices have been developed for the disabled. However, the residual motor function of a disabled person is necessary to operate most of them. If a disabled person has a progressive disease such as amyotrophic lateral sclerosis, it is necessary to modify the input support device according to the person's residual motor functions. Whenever the input device is modified, the disabled person has to relearn how to use it. To overcome this problem, it is necessary to develop a device that would not depend on residual motor function.

One possible way to deal with this would be to use the sympathetic skin response (SSR), which can be obtained non-invasively and is independent of residual motor function. SSR is a biomedical signal that reflects the activity of the sympathetic nervous system and can be affected by cognitive thinking and decision-making [1]. We hypothesized that SSR could be used as a switch for an input support device. However, we expected the SSR appearance ratio to change and reflect the activation of the sympathetic nervous system if the environmental condition changed.

K. Miesenberger et al. (Eds.): ICCHP 2010, Part I, LNCS 6179, pp. 189–192, 2010.

It is known that SSR is triggered by visual stimuli [2]. Therefore, it may be elicited by a change in color, regardless of the original intention. By investigating the relationship between SSR and color, it is possible to clarify whether a color-dependent condition exists under which SSR appears readily.

2 Method

The subjects were three able-bodied males in the age group 22 to 27 years without any visual abnormality. The subjects understood the experiment and provided prior consent for inclusion in the study. The experiment was performed in a darkroom to remove the influence of outside light. The room was maintained quiet with temperature at 24–26°C. Fig. 1 shows the experimental conditions. The subjects sat comfortably in chairs, and put their faces on a chin rest so as to maintain a constant viewing distance. A display was placed on the desk 50 cm in front of the subject.

The background consisted of achromatic colors in three patterns. The character color used achromatic and chromatic colors in twenty-one patterns. Sixty-three (3 × 21) patterns to be displayed were prepared by combining background and character colors. The subjects were asked to evaluate the ease with which they could see each pattern. We determined the color combinations that were easy to see from these evaluations, and chose six patterns of color combinations that were easy to see. We performed the task of character selection with SSR using the selected color combinations. The subjects were asked to imagine selecting a pre-determined kana (the target kana), which was displayed at 2.5-second intervals. The other character was assumed to be the non-target kana.

Three Ag/AgCl electrodes were used to detect the SSR. The detection electrode was placed on the palm of the hand, and the reference and ground electrodes were placed on the back of the hand. An LEG-1000 polygraph equipment (Nihon Kohden) was used for recording at a sampling frequency of 200 Hz.

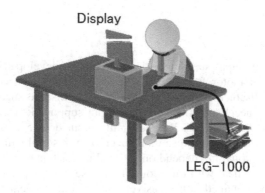

Fig. 1. Experimental set-up. The subject's face was placed on a chin rest to maintain a constant viewing distance. A display was placed on the desk 50 cm in front of the subject.

The contrast ratio between background and character colors was calculated according to the following equation. C indicates contrast ratio, Lmax indicates higher luminance, and Lmin indicates lower luminance, in background and character colors.

$$C = \frac{L_{\max} - L_{\min}}{L_{\max} + L_{\min}} \tag{1}$$

3 Results and Discussion

3.1 Combining Background and Character Colors

Fig. 2 shows the relationship between contrast ratio and conspicuousness. From the results, the subject perceived the character as more conspicuous as the contrast ratio increased. The change in the contrast influenced sensitivity [3]. Therefore, we investigated conditions of high contrast ratio in the character selection task using SSR.

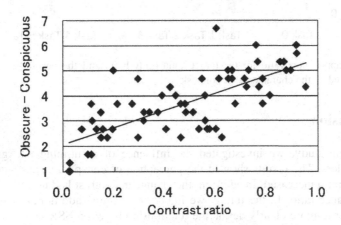

Fig. 2. Relationship between contrast ratio and conspicuousness. The horizontal axis indicates the contrast ratio. The vertical axis indicates the conspicuousness on a scale from obscure (1) to conspicuous (7). The solid line indicates the fit to the data ($R^2 = 0.52$).

3.2 Character Selection Task

Fig. 3 shows the SSR appearance ratio for the target and non-target kana, calculated by dividing the total number of times SSR signals were detected by the total number of times the kana were displayed. Task 0 indicates our previous results. Tasks 1–3 indicate the color condition in which the contrast is high and easy to see. Task 4–6 indicate the color condition in which contrast is low and easy to see.

For both the target and non-target kana, the SSR appearance ratio was not different in any of the tasks, compared to that in Task 0.

The change in the contrast did influence sensitivity [3]. Accordingly, we believe that if the contrast ratio is high, the SSR appearance ratio would be high. However, the change was not seen in the SSR appearance ratio in this experiment. From the results, we found that the change in contrast has no influence on the SSR appearance ratio.

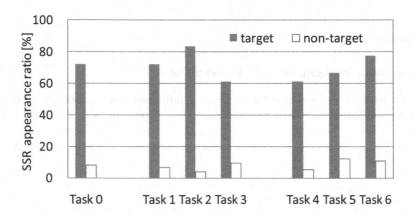

Fig. 3. SSR appearance ratio for the target kana (gray bars) and the non-target kana (white bars), calculated by the character selection task

4 Conclusion

In the present study, we investigated the influence of combining background and character colors. The results showed the perception of conspicuousness increased as the contrast ratio increased. In addition, the change in contrast had no influence on the SSR appearance ratio. In the future, we intend to examine additional display conditions in order to more clearly define the relationship between SSR and visual stimuli, and to evaluate the use of SSR as a communication support method.

References

1. Friedrich, E.V.C., McFarland, D.J., Neuper, C., Vaughan, T.M., Brunner, P., Wolpaw, J.R.: A scanning protocol for a sensorimotor rhythm-based brain-computer interface. Biological Psychology 80, 169–175 (2009)
2. Yamashiro, D., Aihara, M., Ono, C., Kanemura, H., Aoyagi, K., Go, Y., Iwadare, Y., Nakazawa, S.: Sympathetic Skin Response and Emotional Changes of Visual Stimuli. No To Hattatsu 36(5), 372–377 (2004) (in Japanese)
3. Yoshihiro, K., Uchikawa, Y., Takaki, M., Fukai, S.: The influence of contrast in letters on our emotion. J. of Kyushu Univ. of Health Welfare 6, 273–276 (2005)

Computerized Assessing the Mouse Proficiency through Multiple Indicators

Ming-Chung Chen[1], Yun-Lung Lin[2], and Chien-Chuan Ko[3]

[1] Department of Special Education, National Chiayi University
No.300 Syuefu Rd., Chiayi, 600 Taiwan, R.O.C.
mtchen@mail.ncyu.edu.tw
[2] Department of Information & Computer Education, National Taiwan Normal University
162, Sec. 1 Hoping East Rd., Taipei, Taiwan
harrison@ice.ntnu.edu.tw
[3] Department of Computer Science and Information Engineering, National Chiayi University
300 Syuefu Rd., Chiayi, Taiwan
kocc@mail.ncyu.edu.tw

Abstract. This study presents a computerized assessment tool which provides multiple parameters for evaluating a subject's pointing and selecting proficiency. The Mi-CAT system could provide effect parameters, quality parameters, and visual information that serve as the multiple indicators for clinical professionals to decide whether a pointing device or a setting is proper for a client. Besides introducing the Mi-CAT system, this study also explore the effectiveness of applying Mi-CAT in identifying a proper pointing device for a 7-year-old girl. The results reported that the multiple indicators generated from Mi-CAT system would pinpoint a better device or setting for this girl.

Keywords: mouse proficiency, people with disabilities.

1 Introduction

In order to effectively interact with computer, more flexible and effective access methods are essential to people with severe physical disabilities. Recently, various technologies, software and hardware have been developed to meet the client's needs [1]. For example, commercialized devices, consisting of trackball, joystick, touch panel, or touch screen, were available for poor hand control capabilities [2]. For the clinical professional to make decision scientifically, the proper procedure for selecting devices or setting are required. But, how to select a proper device or adapted computer interface is a major problem a clinical professional usually meet. Lucking scientific data result in making decision hard. The clinical professionals need some software to collect scientific data for them.

Using software to evaluate the performance of pointing and clicking is a useful method to collect the objective evidences for decision making [3]. The software could

K. Miesenberger et al. (Eds.): ICCHP 2010, Part I, LNCS 6179, pp. 193–199, 2010.

generate testing tasks, automatically record the participant's response, and provide the results of the performance [3], [4], [5], [6]. The results of the performance could serve as the internal evidence for making decision. However, what kind of results should be used to represent the performance?

Traditionally, accuracy and movement time are the most popular parameters adopted in the past studies [7], [8]. Currently some parameters were proposed as quality indicators to detect the difficulties or characteristics of pointing-and-selecting performance [8]. For example, target re-entry (TRE), task axis crossing (TAC), movement direction change (MDC), orthogonal direction change (ODC), movement variability (MV), movement error (ME), movement offset (MO), missed click (CL), movement units (MU), and ratio of path length to task axis length (PL/TA) were adopted.

The abovementioned parameters, of course, could discriminate the difference between individuals with different abilities [9], [10], or between different pointing devices [11]. But those information failed to show what happened during the task-completing process in different settings. In contrast, visualized information could provide concrete image for discussion between the professionals and the clients or their carriers [3].

As mentioned above, the effect of performance, quality of cursor movement and visualized information are essential parameters for the professionals to understand the client's performance of pointing and selecting holistically and comprehensively. However, no study has been made to develop an evaluation tool that provides such essential information. No study applies these parameters to select the proper device or setting for a client neither. Therefore this study aimed to develop an integrated assessment system that could provide effect parameters, quality parameters, and visualized information.

2   Mi-CAT System

A Computerized Assessment Tool (CAT) developed and used by the previous studies [3], [9] was modified for this study. The architecture of this multiple indicators computerized assessment tool (Mi-CAT) is shown in figure 1. As the figure indicated, Mi-CAT consisted of four major modules, evaluation program, cursor detection module, video capturing module, and analysis program. The evaluation program shows the task on the screen according to what the evaluator set in advance. The cursor detection module records the coordinates of cursor every deci-second and the activation the clicking. Meanwhile the synchronized video capturing module (SVC module) takes a picture every deci-second synchronized with cursor detection module once an evaluation of task started. The analysis program comprises three kinds of indicators represented the performance of pointing and selecting task. First, the effect indicators comprised accuracy, numbers of missing click, reaction time, movement time, and adjusting time. They reflected how accurate and fast a participant could complete the tasks. Second, the quality indicators represented the efficiency and micromovments [7], [8], [9]. Rate of PL/TA was the parameter for efficiency. Micromovemenets consisted of numbers of target reentry (TRE), movement units (MU), movement variety (MV), and N of target entry at the first click (TEF). Third, the visualized parameters used to redisplay the process of completing a task. It comprised animating the trajectory of cursor, speed variation, acceleration variation, and the movement of the participant's control site. The definitions of these parameters are described below:

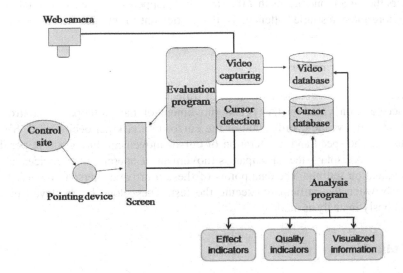

Fig. 1. Framework of Mi-CAT system. This shows the four major program modules in the system.

2.1 Effect Indictors

Accuracy is the percentage of correct responses. Correct response is achieved when the mouse is clicked when the cursor is in the target area. Missed click (CL) occurs when the click is activated out of the target [8]. N of CL represents numbers of click the participant produces before completing the click inside the target. Reaction time (RT) is defined as the time from the target display to the beginning of cursor movement. Movement time (MT) is defined as the time from the beginning of cursor movement to the cursor reach the edge of a target. Adjusting time (AT) is defined as the time it takes for the participant to achieve accuracy once he enters cursor in the target area. Summing up RT, MT, and AT could gain the total time spent in completing a task.

2.2 Quality Indicators

Rate of PL/TA, defined as the actual length of the trajectory of the cursor movement, divides the distance of the task [9]. TRE represents the numbers of cursor reentry the target before correct clicks. MV displays the extent to which the sample cursor points lie in a straight line along an axis parallel to the task axis [9]. MU occurs at the phase where the cursor accelerates and decelerates [12]. TEF indicates the number of cursor enters the target before the participant first clicking. Higher of Rate of PL/TA, TRE, MU, and MV signify worse mouse cursor control. N of TEF could present the error clicking type recorded in a task. Zero refers to the first click activated before the cursor enters the target, one means that the first click happened after cursor overshot, and two or more indicates failed attempts of the participant to retarget the cursor into the target.

2.3 Visualized Parameters

Visualized parameters comprise the clips of trajectory of cursor (TC), speed variation (SV), acceleration variation (AV), and movement of the participant's control site (MCS). TC redraws the coordination of the cursor in a task per deci-second. SV and AV illustrate the speed and acceleration of cursor movement during a task per deci-second. MCS redisplays the participant's movement of operating the devices as well as the evaluation setting. The data points of these four parameters are recorded synchronously when the participant execute the test. They cloud be displayed in clips synchronously in analysis module.

3 Application

3.1 Participants

Mary, a 7-year-old participant, was diagnosed with quadriplegia cerebral palsy, mild intellectual disability and serious communication disorder. She was referred for computer access assessment because of her poor mouse proficiency and oral expression. She operated the standard mouse with very low efficiency due to her poor stability and hand fine motor control. She was used to sitting in a wheelchair with supportive position system to keep her body position stable. No hearing or visual impairment was reported. Her parents' consent was obtained prior to the study.

3.2 Apparatus and Evaluation Tasks

A physical therapist (PT) and a speech therapist (ST) visited the participants' school together to assess the participant's capabilities of motor control, speech and communication, and mouse operating. Two settings, mouse on desk and mouse on lap tray, and a joystick were explored according to the results of control assessment.

Mi-CAT was executed on an ASUS laptop with AMD Turion ZM 82 processor equipped with 16 inches LCD monitor. The subtest of "targeting and clicking" was used. Each time Mi-CAT system displayed a task only. The system would not display the next task until the client click the target correctly. Mi-CAT system recorded the responses (e.g., time spent, coordination of cursor per deci-second and that of the first clicks) automatically without feedback. A middle size optical mouse was used at the beginning since the participants could hold and move the mouse.

The evaluation tasks began with short distance (170 pixels) and middle size target (diameter=51 pixels), then the long distance (510 pixels) and middle size (51) if the participant could complete the task. Otherwise, enlarged target or adjusted setting would be provided for the participant. Each kind of task consisted of 8 directions (0°, 45°, 90°, 135°, 180°, 225°, 270°, and 315°).

3.3 Results

The performance results were reported in table 1. The accuracy of operating joystick was much better than that of using mouse both on table and on lap tray, especially when the size of target was bigger. The mean of missed click (CL) also illustrated that joystick performed best, and then, the mouse on the lap tray. The RT of joystick was longest. Bigger RT meant that joystick required longer time for Mary to start the cursor.

In addition, operating joysticks also created the lowest rate of PL/TA, about half the rate by mouse-on-the-tray and one fourth the rate by mouse-on-the-table. The vast amount of MU disclosed that these differences might be due to unstable speed of cursor moving, accelerating and decelerating in a short while. However, it needs confirmation by looking at the visualized information.

Table 1. The performance in nine parameters across three conditions for Mary

Parameter	Table		Lap tray				Joystick			
	170*51		170*51		510*51		170*51		510*68	
	Mean	SD	Mean	SD	Mean	SD	Mean	SD	Mean	SD
Accuracy	0.00		0.25		0.13		0.50		1.00	
CL	2.38	1.69	1.13	0.99	1.88	1.64	0.75	0.96	0	0
RT	0.50	0.53	0.28	0.33	0.10	0.21	2.28	0.96	3.53	2.74
MT	3.65	2.86	5.61	3.92	10.44	6.25	5.74	4.53	29.34	7.12
AT	14.40	18.90	5.10	6.82	10.50	8.40	12.48	5.48	5.83	3.33
PL/TA	8.28	12.81	4.42	4.42	4.00	1.86	2.16	1.17	2.39	0.23
MU	28.63	20.76	16.25	12.08	31.00	16.31	28.50	17.14	83.50	14.84
MV	45.50	60.80	32.03	23.16	79.37	39.52	7.73	10.71	51.58	18.24
TRE	3.25	3.20	1.13	1.64	2.50	1.93	1.25	0.50	0.50	0.58

Visualized parameters comprise the clips of trajectory of cursor (TC), speed variation (SV), and movement of the participant's control site (MCS). The MCS in Fig. 2 showed that Mary could pose normally only when using the joystick (see Fig. 2d). The condition of speed variation in Fig. 2c and Fig. 2d both showed a major movement that should be performed by a user without control problems.

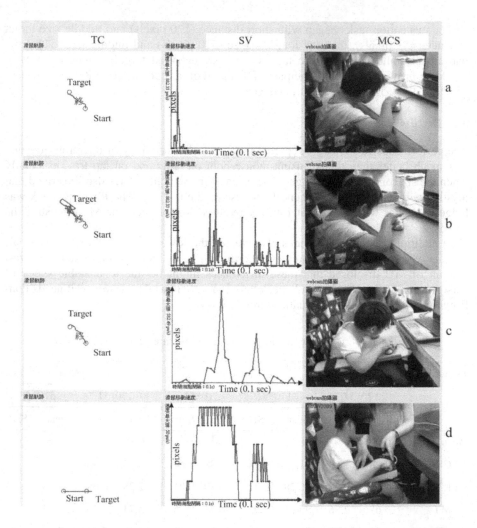

Fig. 2. The snapshots of the visualized analysis of three tasks in same distance and size for Mary (a & b), (c), (d). TC presented the trajectory of cursor moving during the task. SV displayed the speed variation of the cursor movement. MCS showed the participant's gesture and motor movement. The data points in TC, SV, and MCS display synchronously.

According to the results of the multiple indicators, joystick performed very high accuracy both in short and long distance tests. However, joystick generated longer reaction time (RT) and movement time (MT). The visualized information demonstrated that joystick could induce normal posture and allow smoother curser-movement in short distance tests. Therefore, the professionals concluded that joystick would be appropriate for Mary. Meanwhile, Mary also demonstrated a preference to use joystick. However, she needed additional training because she was not familiar with operating the joystick.

4 Discussion and Conclusion

The Mi-CAT system could provide rich and complementary information regarding the choice of proper pointing device or setting. The joystick was identified as the perfect device for Mary when the focus was on performance accuracy and gesture position. However, the MT and MU generated from the long distance tasks revealed the essential information that she usually moved the joystick unstably. This crucial information would allow professionals to set up training program for the client.

Acknowledgment

The authors would like to thank the National Science Council of the Republic of China for financially supporting this research under Contract No. NSC 95-2524-S-415-001-.

References

1. Cook, A.M., Polgar, J.M.: Cook and Hussey's assistive technology: Principles and practice, 3rd edn. Mosby, Baltimore (2007)
2. Brodwin, M.G., Cardose, E., Star, T.: Computer assistive technology for people who have disabilities: Computer adaptations and modifications. Journal of rehabilitation 23(3), 28–33 (2004)
3. Chen, M.C., Chu, C.N., Wu, T.F., Yeh, C.C.: Computerized assessment approach for evaluating computer interaction performance. In: Miesenberger, K., Klaus, J., Zagler, W.L., Karshmer, A.I. (eds.) ICCHP 2006. LNCS, vol. 4061, pp. 450–456. Springer, Heidelberg (2006)
4. Kirkpatrick, A.: ISO2d: Data preparation software for 2-dimensional Fitts' Law experiments (1998),
   http://www.cs.uoregon.edu/research/hci/research/winfitts.html
5. Koester, H.H., LoPresti, E.F., Simpson, R.C.: Measurement validity for compass assessment software. Paper presented at RESNA 2006 Annual Conference, Arlington, VA (2006)
6. Lane, A., Ziviani, J.: Enabling computer access: Introduction to the test of mouse proficiency. Occupational Therapy Journal of Research 22, 111–118 (2002)
7. Hwang, F., Keates, S., Langdon, P., Clarkson, J.: Mouse movements of motion-impaired users: A submovement analysis. In: Proceedings of the 6th international ACM SIGACCESS Conference on Computers and Accessibility, pp. 102–109 (2004)
8. Keates, S., Hwang, F., Langdon, P., Clarkson, P.J., Robinson, P.: The use of cursor measures for motion-impaired computer users. Universal Access in the Information Society 2, 18–29 (2002)
9. Lin, Y.L., Chen, M.C., Chang, U.T., Yeh, C.C., Meng, L.F.: The performance of mouse pointing and selecting for pupils with and without intellectual disabilities. Research in Developmental Disabilities 30, 1188–1195 (2009)
10. Wobbrok, J.O., Gajos, K.Z.: A comparison of area pointing and goal crossing for people with and without motor impairments. In: Proceedings of the 9th international ACM SIGACCESS Conference on Computers and Accessibility, pp. 3–10 (2007)
11. Anson, D., Lawler, G., Kissinger, A., Timko, M., Tuminski, J., Drew, B.: Efficacy of three head-point devices for a mouse emulation task. Assistive Technology 14, 140–150 (2002)
12. Meng, L.F., Chen, M.C., Chu, C.N., Wu, T.F., Lu, C.P., Yeh, C.C., Yang, C., Lo, C.Y.: The directional effects on cursor dragging kinematics. International Journal of Computer Science and Network Security 7, 1–6 (2007)

PUIR: Parallel User Interface Rendering

Kris Van Hees and Jan Engelen

Katholieke Universiteit Leuven
Department of Electrical Engineering
ESAT - SCD - DocArch
Kasteelpark Arenberg 10
B-3001 Heverlee, Belgium
kris@alchar.org, jan@docarch.be

Abstract. While providing non-visual access to graphical user interfaces has been the topic of research for over 20 years, blind users still face many obstacles when using computer systems. The higher degree of flexibility for both developers and users poses additional challenges. Existing solutions are largely based on either graphical toolkit hooks, queries to the application and environment, scripting, or model-driven user interface development or runtime adaptation. Parallel user interface rendering (PUIR) is a novel approach based on past and current research into accessibility, promoting the use of abstract user interface descriptions. PUIR provides the mechanism to render a user interface simultaneously in multiple forms (e.g. visual and non-visual).

1 Introduction

Over the past few years, our world has become more and more infused with devices that feature graphical user interfaces (GUIs), ranging from home appliances with LCD displays to mobile phones with touch screens and voice control. The emergence of GUIs poses a complication for blind users due to the implied visual interaction model. Even in the more specific field of general purpose computer systems at home and in the work place, non-visual access often still poses a problem, especially in Unix-based environments where mixing graphical visualisation toolkits is very common. While popularity keeps growing for this group of systems, advances in accessibility technology in support of blind users remain quite limited.

Currently available solutions use a combination of toolkit extensions, scripting, and complex heuristics to obtain sufficient information to make non-visual renderings possible [1,2]. Alternative approaches use model-driven user interface (UI) composition at development time, or runtime adaptation [3,4]. Leveraging the adoption of UI development using abstract user interface (AUI) definitions [5,6], it is possible to build a solid base for providing non-visual access as an integral component of the UI environment [7,8]. Rather than trying to interpret a visual presentation in a non-visual context, the renderings are presented in parallel from the same abstract UI description. This also ensures that information

K. Miesenberger et al. (Eds.): ICCHP 2010, Part I, LNCS 6179, pp. 200–207, 2010.

on semantic relationships between UI elements is available across all presentations, eliminating problems such as trying to guess what "label" belongs to an input field in the UI.

The Parallel User Interface Rendering (PUIR) technique expands upon UI development by means of AUIs by providing a framework in which multiple rendering agents can provide presentations of the UI in parallel [9]. The application can remain completely unaware of the specific renderings that are presented to the user.

While PUIR is rendering-independent, simultaneous rendering in visual and non-visual modalitities has been selected as the proof-of-concept. This choice is in line with the overall scope of the research that led to the PUIR design, and builds on extensive past research on challenges that blind users face when operating a computer system.

The remainder of this paper first presents related work on GUI accessibility and UI abstraction. The third section provides a description of the PUIR framework. This is followed by more in-depth implementation details, and the conclusion, offering a description of future work.

2   Related Work

Accessibility of GUIs for blind users has been the topic of research for many years. Mynatt and Weber discussed two early approaches [10], introducing four core design issues that are common to non-visual access to GUIs. Expanding on this work, Gunzenhäuser and Weber phrased a fifth issue, along with providing a more general description of common approaches towards GUI accessibility [11].

Savidis and Stephanidis researched alternative interaction metaphors for non-visual user interfaces [12], which formed the basis for the HAWK toolkit [13]. It provides interaction objects and techniques that have been designed specifically for non-visual access. The AVANTI project [4] uses this toolkit in its context-based runtime user interface adaptation mechanism. Gajos and Weld also propose a UI adaptation mechanism [3], approaching the problem of different user and environment models as a search for the most optimal UI representation given specific device characteristics and a user interaction model.

The Visualisation and Interactive Systems Group of the University of Stuttgart describes a system for black-box UIs [14], introducing the concept of replacing a user interface by interposing libraries. It shows the power of capturing UI information at the application-toolkit crossover rather than obtaining similar information inside the toolkit implementation, even though the described system of non-invasive adaptation still depends on programmatic UI construction.

The use of AUIs in UI development lies at the core of the UsiXML [5] project at the Belgian Laboratory of Computer-Human Interaction (BCHI) at the Université Catholique de Louvain. Earlier work on application UIs and Word Wide Web forms provides important insights into the obstacles that blind users face when dealing with user interaction model, as reported by Barnicle [15], Pontelli et al [16], and Theofanos/Redish [17].

The concept of parallel user interface rendering as a way to provide non-visual access to GUIs emerged from doctoral research into the use of abstract UI definitions as basis for accessibility technologies [7,8,9]. Stefan Kost's GiTK project [6] also builds on the value of UI abstraction to provide dynamically generated user interfaces. His work briefly touches on the topic of multiple interfaces, offering some ideas for future work in this area.

3   Parallel UI Rendering

The PUIR framework is shown schematically in Fig. 1. It provides for multiple simultaneous runtime interpretations of a given abstract UI description. Rather than constructing the UI by means of function calls into a specific widget toolkit, application developers define the UI in an abstract form, often by means of design tools. The result is an AUI description in a standardised form (e.g. UsiXML [5], GIML [6], ...). This description is interpreted by the AUI engine.

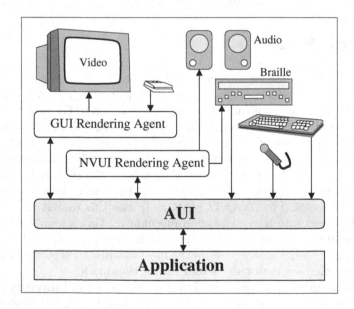

Fig. 1. Schematic overview of PUIR

The presentation of the UI is delegated to one or more rendering agents, each providing its own interpretation of the UI in one or more modalities. This technique does require the AUI to be able to represent both data and a description of how to present that data, as suggested by Trewin [18]. It also promotes the AUI handling to active component status in order to support rendering-independent semantics for the UI. This also requires the AUI engine to not depend on any implementation details of the rendering agents.

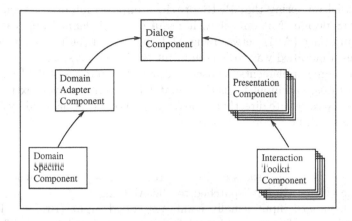

Fig. 2. ARCH model adapted for PUIR

Various models for user interface management systems (UIMS) have been suggested in past research. One model with a reasonably high degree of modularisation is the ARCH model [19]. The PUIR framework maps well onto this model, if we account for the novel features that parallel rendering introduces as shown in Fig. 2. The following five components are identified:

- **Domain Specific Component:** This component is provided by the application itself. The PUIR framework does not cover this component, other than providing a mechanism for the application to interact with the UI and to retrieve information from the UI.
- **Domain Adaptor Component:** The abstract UI description covers this component. It defines the UI from the perspective of the application, and it serves as the source for the AUI engine. The UI element descriptions can contain rendering agent specific annotations that control cosmetic aspects of the element. These annotations are ignored by the AUI engine.
- **Dialog Component:** This function is provided by the AUI engine, an active component in the PUIR framework. It implements the interaction semantics of UI elements, it encapsulates the UI data elements, it provides synchronised event processing for all semantic UI events, and it implements UI focus management.
- **Presentation Component:** Rendering agents serve as presentation components. The ARCH model does not address the possibility of multiple instances of a specific component. Within the PUIR framework, the collection of implemented rendering agents constitutes the presentation component of the ARCH model.
- **Interaction Toolkit Component:** Each rendering agent utilises a toolkit that provides functionality to present the UI elements in one or more output modalities. In terms of the ARCH model, every instance of the *Presentation Component* is associated with an *Interaction Toolkit Component*.

The parallel rendering that PUIR provides imposes important requirements on the UIMS design. Not only does it require a well defined application programming interface (API) between the AUI engine and the rendering engine, it also requires a modified way to handle input device processing.

The AUI engine implements the user interaction semantics of the UI elements, their interactions, and input focus (i.e. what UI element receives textual input). Some input devices relate directly to one or more modalities handled by a specific rendering agent while others are more independent:

- Mouse operations are inherently graphical in nature, operating in the two dimensional graphical space in which the UI is rendered. Positional information needs to be processed by the rendering agent, and where needed semantic events will be dispatched to the AUI engine.
- Braille keyboard input usually combines coded input (Braille cells) with a limited form of cursor addressable input (positional input). The coded input gets translated into textual input, and can then be handled as regular keyboard input.
- Keyboard input is not directly related to any specific rendering agent. It gets interpreted in terms of focus on a specific UI element.

4   Implementation

A proof-of-concept implementation of the PUIR framework has been implemented in Java, as a generic UI toolkit. It provides 25 UI elements that are commonly used for applications, such as buttons, text input fields, labels, editable combox-boxes, mutually exclusive toggle lists, ... The rest of this section describes important implementation details.

4.1   The AUI Engine

The AUI engine interprets an abstract UI description provided in an XML file, and constructs the user interface. The application can operate on its UI by making direct calls to elements at the AUI level. In return, the AUI engine dispatches events to the application to provide notification of various state changes. The AUI engine also implements focus management.

Interactions between the AUI engine and rendering agents are also handled through event dispatching, whereas direct calls from rendering agent objects to AUI engine objects are used to query specific information. This design supports the requirement that the AUI engine has no knowledge about the implementation details of the rendering agents.

4.2   Rendering Agents

The PUIR framework requires that rendering agents implement a specific API. The experimental implementation provides for in-process rendering agents and remote rendering agents. Events dispatched by the AUI engine are sent to all rendering agents for processing, to ensure consistency between the presentations.

In-Process Rendering Agents. The proof-of-concept implementation provides a Java Swing based in-process rendering agent. Due to the design of widgets in the Swing toolkit, the rendering agent turned out to be quite complex. The PUIR framework requires user interaction semantics to be handled in the AUI engine, whereas Java Swing widgets implement semantics within the toolkit. Various aspects of widget functionality have been bypassed to ensure that any and all interaction with the UI elements is triggered by events dispatched from the AUI engine.

The swing rendering agent provides a graphical presentation of the UI, and implements an interaction model for mouse operations. While most mouse events are ignored because they have no semantic significance, select events are translated into their PUIR equivalents and dispatched to the AUI engine.

Remote Rendering Agents. A speech output presentation of the UI is provided as a remote rendering agent, communicating with applications by means of a message bus. Regardless of the number of remote rendering agents, only a single stub is instantiated within the application. The message bus handles multiplexing between applications and remote rendering agents. The custom communication protocol provides for mutual discovery, event passing, and request/response dialogues.

The actual rendering agent operates on a proxy of the actual UI, providing both transparency and caching.

4.3 User Input

The proof-of-concept implementation supports three input modalities:

- Keyboard input: this is processed directly at the AUI engine level. While this is a simplification of the design, it does not actually impact the expected functionality.
- Mouse input: as described above, mouse input is processed by the in-process graphical rendering agent. Relevant events are presented to the AUI engine for processing.
- Braille keyboard input: Braille input (albeit in coded form) is transcribed into equivalent keyboard input, and presented to the AUI engine as if it were entered on a regular keyboard. Positional input by means of cell selections keys is translated into its equivalent semantic PUIR event, and presented to the AUI engine.

Regardless of the delivery path, input is processed by the AUI engine, and any results are broadcast to rendering agents (and often the application) by means of events.

5 Testing

The design and implementation of the PUIR framework has been tested throughout its entire development cycle, both in terms of functionality and correctness.

Basic unit testing was conducted by comparing the functionality of UI test cases implemented both using the PUIR framework and as Java Swing applications. This testing has proven to be extremely important in view of the complexity of interfacing with existing user interface toolkits (such as Java Swing), and in terms of verifying the accuracy of the chosen abstractions.

The project is currently entering the stage of real user testing, to assess the effectiveness of the PUIR framework in providing blind users access to applications with graphical user interfaces, and to assess whether it successfully promotes effective collaboration between users.

6   Conclusion

Parallel user interface rendering is proving to be a very powerful technique in support of the Design-for-All principle. It builds on a solid base of research and development of abstract user interfaces, and provides a framework where alternative renderings of the UI operate at the same level as the native rendering rather than being a derivate. The coherence between the renderings supports close collaboration between users because they can communicate about interacting with an application based on a substantially similar mental model of the user interface.

The PUIR framework can contribute to the field of accessibility well beyond the immediate goal of providing non-visual access to GUIs. The generic approach behind the PUIR design lends itself well to developing alternative rendering agents in support of other disability groups. Because rendering agents need not necessarily execute local to applications, accessible remote access is possible as well. The PUIR framework may also benefit automated application testing, by providing a means to interact with the application programmatically without any dependency on a specific UI rendering. functional access to GUI applications.

Acknowledgements

The research presented in this paper is part of the author's doctoral work at the Katholieke Universiteit Leuven, Belgium, under supervision by Jan Engelen (ESAT-SCD-Research Group on Document Architectures).

References

1. Weber, G., Mager, R.: Non-visual user interfaces for X Windows. In: ICCHP 1996: Interdisciplinary aspects on computers helping people with special needs, pp. 459–468 (1996)
2. Haneman, B., Mulcahy, M.: The GNOME accessibility architecture in detail. Presented at the CSUN Conference on Technology and Disabilities (2002)
3. Gajos, K., Weld, D.S.: SUPPLE: automatically generating user interfaces. In: IUI 2004: Proceedings of the 9th international conference on Intelligent user interfaces, pp. 93–100. ACM Press, New York (2004)

4. Stephanidis, C., Savidis, A.: Universal access in the information society: Methods, tools and interaction technologies. Universal Access in the Information Society 1(1), 40–55 (2001)
5. Limbourg, Q., Vanderdonckt, J., Michotte, B., Bouillon, L., Florins, M.: UsiXML: A user interface description language supporting multiple levels of independence. In: Lauff, M. (ed.) Proceedings of Workshop on Device Independent Web Engineering, DIWE 2004 (2004)
6. Kost, S.: Dynamically generated multi-modal application interfaces. PhD thesis, Technische Universität Dresden, Dresden, Germany (2006)
7. Van Hees, K., Engelen, J.: Abstract UIs as a long-term solution for non-visual access to GUIs. In: Proceedings of the 3rd International Conference on Universal Access in Human-Computer Interaction (2005)
8. Van Hees, K., Engelen, J.: Abstracting the graphical user interface for non-visual access. In: Pruski, A., Knops, H. (eds.) Assistive technology from virtually to reality, 8th European conference for the Advancement of Assistive Technology in Europe, pp. 239–245. IOS Press, Amsterdam (2005)
9. Van Hees, K., Engelen, J.: Non–visual access to GUIs: Leveraging abstract user interfaces. In: Miesenberger, K., Klaus, J., Zagler, W.L., Karshmer, A.I. (eds.) ICCHP 2006. LNCS, vol. 4061, pp. 1063–1070. Springer, Heidelberg (2006)
10. Mynatt, E.D., Weber, G.: Nonvisual presentation of graphical user interfaces: contrasting two approaches. In: CHI 1994: Proceedings of the SIGCHI conference on Human factors in computing systems, pp. 166–172. ACM Press, New York (1994)
11. Gunzenhäuser, R., Weber, G.: Graphical user interfaces for blind people. In: 13th World Computer Congress, pp. 450–457 (1994)
12. Savidis, A., Stephanidis, C.: Building non-visual interaction through the development of the rooms metaphor. In: CHI 1995: Conference companion on Human factors in computing systems, pp. 244–245. ACM Press, New York (1995)
13. Savidis, A., Stergiou, A., Stephanidis, C.: Generic containers for metaphor fusion in non-visual interaction: the HAWK interface toolkit. In: Proceedings of the Interfaces 1997 Conference, pp. 194–196 (1997)
14. Rose, D., Stegmaier, S., Reina, G., Weiskopf, D., Ertl, T.: Non-invasive adaptation of black-box user interfaces. In: AUIC 2003: Proceedings of the Fourth Australasian user interface conference on User interfaces 2003, pp. 19–24. Australian Computer Society, Inc. (2003)
15. Barnicle, K.: Usability testing with screen reading technology in a Windows environment. In: CUU 2000: Proceedings on the 2000 conference on Universal Usability, pp. 102–109. ACM Press, New York (2000)
16. Pontelli, E., Gillan, D., Xiong, W., Saad, E., Gupta, G., Karshmer, A.I.: Navigation of HTML tables, frames, and XML fragments. In: Assets 2002: Proceedings of the fifth international ACM conference on Assistive technologies, pp. 25–32. ACM Press, New York (2002)
17. Theofanos, M.F., Redish, J.G.: Bridging the gap: between accessibility and usability. Interactions 10(6), 36–51 (2003)
18. Trewin, S., Zimmermann, G., Vanderheiden, G.: Abstract user interface representations: how well do they support universal access? In: CUU 2003: Proceedings of the 2003 conference on Universal usability, pp. 77–84. ACM Press, New York (2003)
19. Bass, L., Faneuf, R., Little, R., Mayer, N., Pellegrino, B., Reed, S., Seacord, R., Sheppard, S., Szczur, M.R.: A metamodel for the runtime architecture of an interactive system: the UIMS tool developers workshop. SIGCHI Bull. 24(1), 32–37 (1992)

Transient Cooperation in Social Applications for Accessibility Mapping

Harald Holone[1] and Jo Herstad[2]

[1] Østfold University College, Norway
[2] University of Oslo, Norway

Abstract. Collecting, disseminating and maintaining accessibility information about the physical world is a daunting task. Through the *OurWay* concept, end users are involved to provide feedback on suggested routes in a route planning system, thereby solving both their own navigational tasks at hand, and helping other users by leaving behind traces of their activity. We define and explore *Transient Cooperation*, the type of cooperation we have observed in a prototype evaluation of the concept. This exploration is undertaken in the light of established research on accessibility, cooperation and social software. We also suggest implications this type of cooperation can have for for accessibility mapping.

1 Introduction

Accessibility is a wide term, which applies in different ways to a wide variety of resources, be it information and communication technologies or physical access in public areas. In this paper we're concerned with sharing of location-based accessibility information in the physical world. We pay special attention to the forms of cooperation that take place when sharing such information. Accessibility information is frequently shared between users, either directly through friends or contacts, or indirectly through formalized initiatives undertaken by organizations. Collecting, verifying and distributing accessibility information is a formidable task.

Through OurWay we have introduced a concept in which end users play a central role in creating and maintaining accessibility information. The OurWay concept is described in more detail in the Research Setting section. Involving the end users makes sense both from a resource perspective and maintenance perspective. After all, these are real *citizen sensors* [6] experiencing the urban accessibility issues on the street level, day by day.

In this paper, our main research questions are: 1) *What characteristic features do we find in the collaboration taking place in OurWay as a social application* and 2) *What implications can this have for accessibility mapping?* The paper is organized as follows: First we review relevant work, then we describe the OurWay concept and prototype, and present a summary of OurWay as a social application. In the discussion we take on the main research question about cooperation in accessibility mapping. Finally we conclude the paper with implications for social applications in accessibility mapping.

K. Miesenberger et al. (Eds.): ICCHP 2010, Part I, LNCS 6179, pp. 208–215, 2010.

2 Related Work

2.1 Accessibility

Accessibility has different meanings in different situations. For instance, in results from the AUNT-SUE project [5], social aspects like *fear of crime* are mentioned as important factors when users assess the overall accessibility of an area. Similarly, the AMELIA project [15] identify surrounding factors such as places to rest and public toilets as important in the overall accessibility picture. Völkel et al. [17] describes requirements for accessibility annotation of geographic data, with the aim to collect detailed information for different needs and preferences.

Existing literature on accessibility focuses mostly on the interaction between a single user and a computer system, with some notable exceptions, e.g. [20] and [8]. Hedvall [8] argues that the accessibility field is lagging behind the HCI field, focusing mostly on regulations and predictability.

2.2 Cooperation

Human Computer Interaction is about making the computer usable and accessible. A shift of focus within HCI came with the emergence of CSCW. Whereas traditional HCI has focused on human-computer interaction, CSCW concerns how computers facilitate human-to-human communication. Groupware and CSCW represent a paradigm shift in computer use. Human-Human interaction, rather than human-machine interaction is the primary focus; the computer facilitates human communication rather than acting as a purely computational device [2].

Hedvall [8] compares the evolution of the accessibility field with three waves of HCI, and concludes that the accessibility field has much to learn from the focus on individuals found in the third wave of HCI. He, as we, does not argue that the efforts with regards to rules and regulations to ensure universal access is misplaced, however there is a need to extend the accessibility field and take the perspective of the individual user, the situatedness in use of technology into serious consideration when designing tools and technology.

The term Social Navigation of Information Space was coined by Dourish and Chalmers in 1994 [4] to to discuss information sharing on the Internet (as opposed to collaboration in work environments, which had so far been the main focus of CSCW). Social Navigation takes an information centric approach, whereby information left behind by users from their activities form *places* where people interact. Sharing of information then, is not necessarily a result of participation in a Community of Practice, rather it is a *by-product of use*, which might well be without any thought for other users.

By regarding the traces of activity as an opportunity for a shared information space [12], it becomes paramount to allow users to negotiate the the interpretation of this information. In other words, it is not sufficient to collect and share the information; alternative communication channels must be available for the users to make sense of the traces.

Initiatives to make user activity and information validity in Wikipedia more visible include WikiDashboard [14] and WikiTrust [1]. Both of these efforts are working to make Wikipedia more socially transparent, by visualizing author credibility and article revision history. Part of the Wikipedia guidelines dictates that care must be taken to reflect a balanced view on every topic. The Wikipedia concept of a Neutral Point of View is being challenged, for instance by van der Velden [16], who argues for multiple points of view and ways of representing knowledge, and what she and others call *Cognitive Justice*. Coming from the work by social scientists to understand learning processes, the term *Communities of Practice* (CoP) refers to ways in which apprentices learn from taking part in a communities that share a common goal [19].

2.3 Social Software

Jonathan Grudin, although not using the term social software, puts forward four characteristics he considers key in these kinds of technologies [7]: ... they 1) can be extremely lightweight, 2) make information and activity highly visible, 3) provide individual and group benefits, and 4) are grassroots, self-organizing phenomena. Grudin refers to studies of using project blogs and wikis as well as the use of hash tags for coordinating and maintaining project-related content and activities. We use Grudin's characteristics for discussing OurWay as a social application.

3   Research Setting and Methodology

3.1 Methodology

The research approach from the IS tradition adopted for this paper is the interpretive approach to a case study [18,11]. Interpretive research aims at producing an understanding of the context of the information system, and the process whereby the information system influences and is influenced by the context [18]. The use activity is always in a particular context or situation, and not seen as an abstract activity detached from specific users and specific technologies within an interpretive case study.

Interviews and direct observation has been conducted in order to understand the use of the OurWay prototype. The main basis for the current analysis is eight in-depth interviews conducted with users, following nine sessions (consisting of six navigational tasks each) with observation of the activity of use. The observational data includes video, audio and field notes. The interviews and observations have been transcribed, analyzed and interpreted. In addition, data has been recorded and analyzed by investigating the logs from the use activities.

3.2 Previous Work with OurWay

OurWay is a collaborative route planner, where users are providing feedback on accessibility through their interaction with the system. Users are equipped with mobile phones running a client application, which connects to a central route planning and feedback server over a mobile Internet connection. The client displays a map of the area, and allows the user to ask for a route between two locations, which is then displayed on the map. The user can at any time provide feedback to the central server about the part of the route being traversed. To keep the threshold for contribution low, we have used only three levels of feedback: *good*, *uncomfortable*, and *inaccessible*. The submitted ratings are attached to route segments, and are used as weights by the route planning server when calculating new routes.

Viewing OurWay as a social navigation tool, several design limitations become obvious, especially with regards to awareness of other users, their actions and identities. This gives us an incentive to attempt to re-frame OurWay as a social application, and re-assess some of the design choices made in the current prototype.

3.3   Accessibility Mapping as a Social Application

Using Grudin's four characteristics, we now summarize our discussion of accessibility mapping with social applications [10].

3.4   Lightweight

From the end user's perspective, OurWay can be considered extremely lightweight. The feedback mechanism is a vast simplification of the typically form based inquiry taking place in traditional accessibility mapping. It also contrasts with the requirements suggested by Völkel et al. [17]. We do not propose that the OurWay concept should replace such detailed approaches, rather that the information generated by users can *augment* existing information. One obvious challenge is the use of mobile phones for people with special needs. Although mobile phones are ubiquitous among all user groups, the necessary HCI challenges related to use in the field must be considered carefully. One key argument for using an open, lightweight infrastructure for a social accessibility mapping application is that the opportunities for adaption to different needs and requirements are moved away from the core of the system and towards the end user.

Information and activity made visible. A tool which provides accessible routes must adhere to high standards when it comes to dependable information and social transparency. There is little doubt that allowing the user to see the ratings and context which is used to calculate the routes is important. Some suggestions can be found in the WikiTrust and WikiDashboard projects mentioned earlier, where exposing the source and history of information is a key point. Perhaps the main drawback of the current OurWay prototype is that it only indirectly provides this information, through the *resulting* route suggested to the user. In other words, there are no clues provided as to who provided the annotations that led to the suggested route, or what context they were captured in.

Individual and group benefits. Some individual benefits of a social software system for accessibility mapping are obvious, such as the opportunity to provide feedback on suggested routes and get immediate reward in the form of an alternative route from the system. The benefits for the group(s) are, as we have shown through the work with OurWay, more accessible routes over time. Another benefit for the group as a whole, is that this way of collecting and maintaining accessibility information is a potential resolution to the resource challenge mentioned in the introduction of this paper. Further, by utilizing existing social software infrastructures, the social awareness of mobility challenges and special needs can be raised, also outside of the group of core users.

Self-organizing grassroots phenomena. There is obvious value in the networks, agendas and political power represented by established interest organizations. At the same time, parts of what make social applications work is the ability for users to rapidly form groups and processes, often to influence the organizations or establishments they are taking part in. There should be a mutual interest from institutions, individual users and user groups to make use of social software tools, however the suitable balance of initiative and power remains to be established. See for instance Borchorst et al. [3], where they look at the application of Web 2.0 technology in the interaction between citizens and municipalities in Denmark.

4   Discussion

4.1   Accessibility and Cooperation

The accessibility of technology, information and other people are prerequisites for cooperation. Cooperation provides the opportunity for sharing experiences in the world, in our case information about accessibility in the urban landscape. It is important to remember that not all parties are approaching this cooperation on the same terms [20], the individual needs and preferences combined with the situation at hand provides a context within which the artifacts and meaning of information is negotiated. This is what Hedvall describes as *activity-tied and experienced accessibility* [8].

Keeping in mind the heterogeneity of users, it becomes obvious that providing access to systems for cooperation demands a multitude of ways for interaction. This demand can be covered in part by designing for *all*, however the result must not be a least common denominator of technology, rather it should be taking the individuals seriously and allow for appropriation close to the end user.

Even when we take the individuals into consideration, it is important to remember that users are not static. They change over time, and can and will negotiate the situation depending on contextual information, such as available assistance, tools, and weather conditions. We can use the Wikipedia concept of a *Neutral Point of View* (NPOV) as a contrast to this insight. Both Wikipedia and OurWay captures facts about the world around us, however it would be meaningless to attempt to agree on a neutral point of view regarding physical access. The same argument has been made against Wikipedia's NPOV, see for example van der Velden [16] about Cognitive Justice.

4.2 Transient Cooperation

In all the simplicity of the OurWay concept, an important question arises: *What constitutes a group of users?* In the groupware and CSCW fields, groups of users are mostly regarded as organized groups in a work setting. The 'W' in CSCW is work, which reflects the origin of the term. We choose to interpret cooperative work as *any activity that provides input to a process*, which makes it possible to describe OurWay as a CSCW system. However, the groups of people interacting with the system are not necessarily organized, and the way they interact with the system would rarely be regarded as 'work' by the users. Further, any group consists of individuals with their own preferences, needs, practices and tools.

In Communities of Practice we also find that the organizational setting is dominating the discussion. Our view is that organization is not a prerequisite for cooperation, rather that cooperation can, through discussion and negotiation, lead to organization. Through the work of individuals, value can be provided to groups of varying sizes, where the number of shared needs and preferences diminishes as the groups grow in size. At the larger end of the scale, we find interest organizations who lobby and work with political processes and regulations. These are very important, however it should not be the only focus in accessibility work, since the results tend to play a conservative role [8].

Transient Cooperation [9] is not carrying the organizational connotations of CSCW or Communities of Practice, rather it suggests a way to look at cooperation as any activity that involves multiple users of an information space [12]. As users coordinate, it is perhaps more fruitful to talk about loyalty towards peers than group membership in the traditional sense. It becomes clear with the insight from CSCW [12] and accessibility [8] that there is a need for additional forms of communication channels to allow for negotiation of the situation at hand. It is also important to remember that the system is part of the world, the world is not captured in its entirety within the system. Negotiation of the situation happens with the system as a tool or medium, and involves communication outside of the system as well.

Transient Cooperation is not suggested as a naïve idea about automatic capture of activity traces that can be applied through information sharing alone. Rather, it attempts to capture the ephemeral nature of interaction between individual users through the use of an information system which does not require a long-time commitment or shared goal by the users. This form of ad hoc cooperation becomes important in activity-tied accessibility, and involves negotiation of the situation at hand.

4.3 Implications for Accessibility Mapping

It should be clear from our discussion so far that we argue strongly for the individual's role in the field of accessibility in general, and in the process of collecting, sharing and interpreting information about physical accessibility specifically. We agree with Hedvall in his view that the accessibility field has much to learn from decades of work in HCI and CSCW. This is especially true with recent cross-domain research into social applications in the age of Web 2.0. OurWay is an example of a concept that is inspired by successes on the social web to involve the end users and take individuals seriously.

The *Transient Cooperation* we observe in OurWay gives further insight into how these systems can be designed. We see that the cooperative effort by individuals provides value to others even when the primary use of the system is for personal navigational tasks. Also, even though the idea of "the others" is presented to users, they soon focus purely on their own activity, disregarding the potential benefits (or other consequences) for other users. In light of the CSCW literature, it becomes obvious that there is a need to provide good support for visualization of user activity, as well as communication channels for negotiation.

Experienced accessibility is the "real" accessibility, a sum of the accommodation of the physical environment and the situation in which the individual acts. Design of new solutions for accessibility mapping requires attention to this, by enabling flexibility and interpretation, both in information capture and interpretation. Creating social applications for accessibility mapping requires balancing the role of the organizations and the individuals. The individual perspective, the experienced accessibility, can only be negotiated and described by the individual or small groups. Other issues, such as regulatory work and political processes are better handled by the organizations. However, one must not disregard the collective power of individuals [13]. Using ideas from social applications in accessibility mapping seems to be a promising way to put focus on the individual.

5   Conclusion

We have reviewed literature from accessibility, cooperation and social software. Further, we have presented a re-iteration of the OurWay concept as a social application, to frame a discussion of accessibility mapping as a topic for social applications. By discussing accessibility and cooperation and defining the concept of *Transient Cooperation* we have suggested implications for the design of new systems for accessibility mapping. Truly putting focus on the individual in this context is inspired by successful social applications in other domains. Balancing the power of the individuals and established organizations has its challenges, however both ends of the scale has much to gain from the insights provided by decades of research in HCI and CSCW.

References

1. Adler, B., Benterou, J., Chatterjee, K., De Alfaro, L., Pye, I., Raman, V.: Assigning trust to wikipedia content. In: WikiSym 4th Intl. Symposium on Wikis (2008)
2. Baecker, R.: Readings in groupware and computer-supported cooperative work: Assisting human-human collaboration. Morgan Kaufmann, San Francisco (1993)

3. Borchorst, N.G., Bødker, S., Zander, P.-O.: The boundaries of participatory citizenship. In: ECSCW 2009: Proceedings of the 11th European Conference on Computer Supported Cooperative Work, Vienna, Austria, September 7-11, p. 1. Springer, Heidelberg (2009)
4. Dourish, P., Chalmers, M.: Running Out of Space: Models of Information Navigation. Short paper presented at HCI 1994 (1994)
5. Evans, G.: Accessibility, Urban Design and the Whole Journey Environment. Built Environment 35(3), 366–385 (2009)
6. Goodchild, M.: Citizens as sensors: the world of volunteered geography. GeoJournal 69(4), 211–221 (2007)
7. Grudin, J.: Enterprise knowledge management and emerging technologies. In: Hawaii International Conference on System Sciences, vol. 39, p. 57 (2006) (Citeseer)
8. Hedvall, P.: Towards the Era of Mixed Reality: Accessibility Meets Three Waves of HCI. In: HCI and Usability for e-Inclusion, pp. 264–278 (2009)
9. Holone, H.: Retrospective Altruism and Transient Cooperation in Accessibility Mapping. In: Travel Health Informatics and Telehealth, EFMI Special Topic Conference, Antalya, Turkey. European Federation of Medical Informatics (2009)
10. Holone, H., Herstad, J.: Social software for accessibility mapping: challenges and opportunities. In: Unitech 2010, Oslo, Norway. Tapir Forlag (2010)
11. Klein, H., Myers, M.: A Set of Principles for Conducting and Evaluating Interpretive Field Studies in Information Systems. MIS Quarterly 23(1), 67–93 (1999)
12. Schmidt, K., Bannon, L.: Taking CSCW seriously. Computer Supported Cooperative Work (CSCW) 1(1), 7–40 (1992)
13. Shirky, C.: Here Comes Everybody: The power of organizing without organizations. Penguin Press, New York (2008)
14. Suh, B., Chi, E., Kittur, A., Pendleton, B.: Lifting the veil: improving accountability and social transparency in Wikipedia with wikidashboard (2008)
15. Titheridge, H., Mackett, R., Achuthan, K.: From footway design to the street environment: removing the barriers to walking (2009)
16. van der Velden, M.: Design for a common world: On ethical agency and cognitive justice. Ethics and Information Technology 11(1), 37–47 (2009)
17. Völkel, T., Kühn, R., Weber, G.: Mobility impaired pedestrians are not cars: Requirements for the annotation of geographical data. In: Miesenberger, K., Klaus, J., Zagler, W.L., Karshmer, A.I. (eds.) ICCHP 2008. LNCS, vol. 5105, pp. 1085–1092. Springer, Heidelberg (2008)
18. Walsham, G.: Interpreting information systems in organizations. John Wiley & Sons, Inc., New York (1993)
19. Wenger, E.: Communities of Practice: learning, meaning, and identity. Cambridge University Press, Cambridge (1999)
20. Winberg, F.: Supporting cross-modal collaboration: Adding a social dimension to accessibility. In: McGookin, D., Brewster, S. (eds.) HAID 2006. LNCS, vol. 4129, pp. 102–110. Springer, Heidelberg (2006)

A Social Approach to Accessible Social Networking Using the CAT Model

Jennifer George[1], Gilbert Cockton[2], and Thomas Greenough[2]

[1] SAE Institute, 297 Kingsland Road, London E8 4DD, United Kingdom
Tel.: +94 207 923 9159
jennifer.george@sae.edu
[2] School of Design, Northumbria University, City Campus East,
Newcastle upon Tyne NE1 8ST, United Kingdom
Tel.: +94 191 243 7861
{gilbert.cockton,thomas.greenough}@northumbria.ac.uk

Abstract. The social model of disability looks beyond medical and technical solution moving towards social approach. This paper applies the label and table attributes of the CAT models to understand the social setting of the child with the disability together with the care circle. It goes on to understand their social needs and identifies accessibility challenges in communication between members of the care circle. Evaluation is carried out in both a computer and Internet based environment and a traditional communication environment. Finally brief guidelines are drawn upon which an accessible social network based design solution could be built for the reduction of disability of children with motor impairment.

Keywords: Social model, CAT Model, Accessibility, Social Networking, Social Inclusion.

1 Introduction

The demand for social inclusion in services provided to the general public continues to grow. This not only applies to public places involving physical components, but also to virtual and online environments. This has been further emphasised by the amendment to Disability policies and legislation across the world in order to remove discrimination against disabled individuals.

1.1 Social Models of Disability

The Union of the Physically Impaired Against Segregation [1] developed the first social model that was modified by the Disabled Peoples International (DPI) [2]. This model defines the concept of impairment as "the functional limitation caused by physical, sensory, or mental impairments" and disability as "the loss or reduction of opportunities to take part in the normal life of the community on an equal level with others due to physical, environmental, or social barriers" [3]. Thus disability is not

K. Miesenberger et al. (Eds.): ICCHP 2010, Part I, LNCS 6179, pp. 216–223, 2010.

wholly a consequence of an individual's functional limitations, but is also due to the extent to which social environments limit the ability of impaired individuals to participate in everyday activities.

1.2 Rationale for Social Models

Increased opportunities will follow from bridging the gap through Assistive Technology (AT) and their associated human support systems. This requires communication "between the disabled end-user community, social services, the clinical rehabilitation services, and the professional engineering disciplines involved in the development, provision, assessment, and ongoing support for assistive technology" [3].

2 The CAT Model

Hersch and Johnson [3] have reviewed a range of models for accessibility: the HAAT model [4], MPT model [5], and the ICF [6] disability model. They concluded that their approaches to disability have remained predominantly medical, even when they have attempted to involve personal and environmental factors. Although the ICF defines disability as a condition defined by the environment and personal factors, the emphasis remains on the individual's health and physical condition. In order to support the need, the Comprehensive Assistive Technology (CAT) has been developed to rebalance the medical and social. The CAT model's top level of its hierarchy comprises of: Person Context, Activities and Assistive Technology (Fig.1).

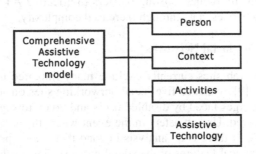

Fig. 1. CAT Model level 1

Social components from the three reviewed models have influenced the CAT model [3], offering a range of benefits, including:

- Identifying gaps in provision of assistive technology and develop systems where to meet need;
- Analysing existing systems to modify in order to improve existing devices;
- Developing design specifications for new devices;
- Providing support for design for all, providing a structure for design approaches.

The CAT model is represented using Tree diagrams, which provide visual support for design discussions; Labelled attributes support compact and tabular representations that can be commented. Alternatively, the CAT model can provided an initial specification of a model for specific case study, or can function as a checklist. Hersch and Johnson [7] have applied their CAT model within four independent case studies, involving real world usage environments and social settings. The first study demonstrated how CAT 'Person' and 'Context' attributes could be used to identify the target audience and the 'Activities' attribute could be used to identify accessibility challenges. The second study illustrated how a specific assistive device could be analysed using the CAT model. The third study showed how a potential communication solution could be designed by analysing the disabled individual. The fourth supported evaluation and choice of assistive technology for a specific individual. Further, the authors are conducting research that focuses on providing design support for a chosen user group.

This paper reports how the CAT model has been used to identify accessibility challenges and a potential solution within a research programme focused on the use of social networking. The aim is to support improved selection and use of assistive technologies for individuals with severe motor impairment, with a particular focus on young children, their families, and their wider *care circles* spanning neighbours, relatives, and community and professional groups.

This research is applying the CAT model within a wider framework of worth-centred design and evaluation approaches [8] to the development of a virtual social environment where the *care circle* for a disabled individual can co-ordinate and support everyday tasks. The aim of the research is to ascertain whether such a social network would actually reduce existing barriers to effective AT selection and usage, without creating new ones, e.g., through increased complexity.

2.1 Accessibility of Social Networks

Social networking web sites currently exclude many impaired users from social activities. AbilityNet [9] evaluated five social networking sites on accessibility and have described the challenges faced by disabled users and go on to suggest how they could technically be resolved. Unfortunately in the event where the user is unable to register on the social network, there is no analysis beyond that. The report focused on users' disabilities and technical features of the social network. The evaluation is particularly interesting as the subject of study is social in nature and covers every type of activity in the CAT model. This has been followed up by a further study by AbilityNet [10] concentrating on four key factors, which are seen by users as preventing users from engaging with social networks: Time on and complexity of tasks; Abrupt or regular interface changes; Text-based help "It would be nice to have videos or photos... text is hard to read sometimes"; A reduction in "perceived communication independence and privacy".

The CAT model is being applied to identify barriers that arise from common features of social networks for a defined set of activities. Analysis will be carried out separately for each user group and then combined to guide a design solution.

The research explores the limitations of accessibility based on technical and physical solutions and investigates how virtual environments could be made more accessible and effective by considering social and environmental factors. The aim is to use the CAT model to identify current barriers to activities, and to explore how social networks can be designed to overcome these barriers by enabling an impaired individual's care circle, rather than by simply modifying existing ATs. There is a specific focus on care circles of young children with cerebral palsy, but the developed social network support will generalise beyond this group.

2.2 Identifying Accessibility Barriers of Care Circles

With a view to understanding the barriers those members of the care circle face in real life, the CAT model level 1 is applied to the functionality and needs of care circle. This step follows the first case study of Hersch and Johnson [7] where the person and context components of the model have been defined using the labelled attribute representation to provide information about the end-user group and their context.

Our primary focus is the child with motor impairment. A child's capability and needs are assessed by medical practitioners and assessment centers with support from family members, school teachers, teaching assistants, speech and occupational therapists whenever possible. This could be for the initial assessment to choose suitable assistive devices or regular challenges they face as the child learns new skills and works towards being independent. The Person and Context sections of the CAT model attempts to understand the functionality and the needs of the child and the care circle.

Person (P): *P.1 Characteristics*: *P.1.1 Personal information*: Children up to the age of initial tertiary education, both genders, diverse fitness, lifestyle and educational needs; *P.1.2 Impairment:* Could have sensory, or motor impairment; Motor impairment here means that, with support, the person is able communicate. ; *P.1.3 Skills*: Basic motor skills, though coordination is reduced, able to follow instructions given verbally, or using audio-visuals; *P.1.4 Preferences*: communicate with all involved in their regular decision-making, active life, doing things themselves with technology if necessary, but without personal assistance.

P.2 Social aspects: *P.2.1 Community support*: Most children have support from family members, medical and educational practitioners. Some also have support from friends and/or local community/organisations; *P.2.2 Education and employment*: Actively involved in either vocational or academic education.

P.3 Attitudes: *P.3.1 Attitudes to assistive technology*: Willing to use assistive technology as long as it is fun, entertaining and helps them communicate with care circle members and provides them with more independence. Slightly older children are also concerned with its appearance; *P.3.2 General attitudes*: independence is important, but compared to older individuals children seek gradual independence.

Context (C): *C.1 Cultural and social context:* *C.1.1 Wider social and cultural issues*: All children speak English with some who understand a second language but there are members of the care circle for example, grandparents who do not speak

English; *C.1.2 User's social and cultural context*: Diverse multicultural society but adapt to local cultures.

C.2 National context: *C.2.1 Infrastructure*: Modern infrastructure, newer technologies, Assistive Technology is used and computer and internet access is available to most; *C.2.2 Legislation*: Disability discrimination legislation and accessible web content guidance in place with increasing enforcement; *C.2.3 Assistive technology context*: A wide range of assistive technology is available and there is some financial and other support to obtain them. Facilities for repair and maintenance are also available. There are challenges in identifying and using the most appropriate device with most devices ending up in the cupboard unused.

C.3 Local settings: *C.3.1 Location and environment*: Classroom, school environment, home and other regular social settings; *C.3.2 Physical variables*: Moderate temperatures, sometimes noisy and/or crowded environments.

Table 1. Activities (plain text indicates no accessibility barrier, *italic* indicates *mild* barriers; ***bold italic*** indicates ***moderate*** barriers, and **bold** indicates **severe** barriers

Accessibility barriers for care circle members for communication			
	Category of Activity	Accessibility status for communication of care circle	
		Without internet	With internet
Activities: Mobility Impaired Group	Communication and Access to information	All information only locally available	Information locally and remotely available
		Access to information locally available or personal copies	Access to digital copies available on demand
		Telecommunications	Email, chats, forum, groups
		Low tech devices	*High tech devices*
		Observations, visual, audio, text	Observations, visual, audio, text
		Travel time and cost	Minimum travel time and cost
	Mobility	***Travel to meetings***	Access needed to internet
		Fine motor skills i.e. writing	***Accessible input/output***
		Synchronous discussion	Synchronous and asynchronous discussion
	Cognitive activities	**Analysing, assessing and evaluating information**	Analysing, assessing and evaluating information
		Logical, creative and imaginative thinking	Logical, creative and imaginative thinking
		Planning and organising	Planning and organising
		Decision making	Decision making
		Categorising	Categorising
		Calculating	Calculating
		Experiencing and expressing emotions	Experiencing and expressing emotions

Table 1. (*continued*)

Activities: Mobility Impaired Group	Daily living	Personal care and hygiene	***Personal care and hygiene***
		One-one support	Peer and expert support
		Environmental control	Virtual environmental control
	Education and employment	Learning and teaching	e-learning and teaching
		Individual and group based activities	Emails, chats, forums and conferences
		Curriculum and therapy	Curriculum and *therapy*
		Indoor and outdoor activities	Social gaming activities
		Extra curricular activities	Extra curricular activities
		Occupational therapy	***Occupational therapy***
	Recreational activities	Home, school and other clubs	Different online groups
		Individual and team based	Online gaming
		Holidays and visits: museums, galleries, heritage sites	Web browsing
		Indoor and outdoor sports	***Indoor and outdoor sports***
		Art and handcrafts	***Art and handcrafts***
		Social events	Online social events

Table 1 shows the outcome of the checklist approach to identify potential barriers to communication between care circle members both with and without the use of the computers and Internet, indicating potential reductions in accessibility barriers.

It shows the accessibility challenges of children with motor impairment and their care circle members. Taking into consideration that a virtual or online solution is suggested, the potential impact is shown in the right column, with some details of potential web-based solutions. However there are residual challenges that could only be met with further assistive devices.

2.3 Improving Accessibility of and through Social Networking Web Sites

The third case study of Hersch and Johnson [7] is being applied to indentify a potential design solution to meet the needs of the care circle.

Activity (A) - Assessment for choice of appropriate assistive devices
Assistive Technology - *AT*
AT.1 Activity specification - *AT.1.1 Task specification:*
Involvement of all possible members of care circle, who would potentially be communicating with the child using the assistive device; *AT.1.2 User requirements* Convenient and user friendly interface with access to a single platform; entire care circle should be able to participate at the discretion of the parent or official guardian of the child; should not demand additional time or cost in travel; should be able to obtain continuous support from the distributor and decision maker.

AT.2 Design issues - *AT.2.1 Design approach*: Design for the child and members of the care circle an accessible interface where they could log in, discuss and make decisions securely. The interface should be inclusive of many types of disability on web-based interfaces.

Architecture: Web-based social network where a few people have the rights to approve members of the care circle to be involved with the child. This network could be accessed remotely either by a personal computer or a mobile phone-based device. *Device realisation:* the child's profile, calendar with events, chats, videos, technical support for the assistive devices, and any other up-to-date discussions could be shared according to the privileges assigned by the parent or guardian. *Options:* The interface should be compatible with still images, audio, video and text information.

AT.2.2 Technology selection

Input: The user should be able to access and interact with the information by keyboard, mouse, touch, stylus or any other assistive device that the would otherwise use to interact with the personal computer or smart phone.

Output: The display should be compatible with most computer resolutions and mobile phones; if necessary, individual applications should be made for mobile phones.

Programming: Could use any language that does not work against web accessibility guidelines [11].

AT.3 System technology issues

AT.3.1 System interfaces

Standard accessible web components should be used to reduce the need for specialized plug-ins.

AT.3.2 Technical performance

The system needs to be secure as sensitive information relating to a person under the age of eighteen would be included; there will also be an application of Data Protection and Privacy related legislation due the nature of information concerned.

AT.4 End-user issues

AT.4.1 Ease and attractiveness of use

The system needs to be informative, robust, usable and provide options in choice of variety of themes to include users with visual impairments; design themes for personal preference could also be provided;

AT.4.2 Mode of use

Whenever possible there should be an option of online and off-line modes.

AT.4 3 Training requirements

Information should be arranged with the best possible information architecture to reduce training; suitable help should be provided.

AT.4.4 Documentation

There should be an archive feature for all information and an option to print any information for those who may require a hard copy; this option should be bound by a data protection agreement.

The above has illustrated how the CAT model can be used by researchers other than its authors to structure the initial user research and design for a social network that could reduce the challenges facing care circles, thereby enhancing the capabilities of the child. This application of the CAT model will be continuously iterated and continuously evaluated as the system is being developed. It will thus extend into a more comprehensive design specification.

3 Conclusion

The CAT model (and the WHO ICF on which it is based) relates activity limitations to personal and environmental factors that cannot be overcome solely through the design of assistive technologies. Instead, it is the understanding and use of assistive technologies by and with care circles that can make impacts that technology alone cannot. This research applies the CAT model to identifying challenges for care circles and thereafter identifying potential design solutions to meet the needs of the identified challenges. A social network has been chosen to improve the capabilities of care circles to support and improve the selection and use of assistive technologies by individuals with physical and/or mental impairments.

References

1. UPIAS, Fundamental principles of disability. UPIAS (Union of the Physically Impaired Against Segregation), London (1976)
2. Barnes, C.: Disabled People in Britain and discrimination: a case for anti-discrimination legislation. Hurst & Co., London (1994)
3. Hersh, M.A., Johnson, M.A.: On Modelling Assistive Technology Systems Part I: Modelling Framework. Technology and Disability 20(3), 193–215 (2008a)
4. Cook, A.M., Hussey, S.M.: Assistive technology: principles and practice, 2nd edn. Mosby Inc., St. Louis (2002)
5. Scherer, M.J., Craddock, G.: Matching person and technology (MPT) assessment process. Technology and Disability 14, 125–13 (2002)
6. World Health Organization, International Classification of Functioning, Disability and Health (ICF), Geneva (2010),
   http://www.who.int/classifications/icf/en/ (accessed January 30, 2010)
7. Hersh, M.A., Johnson, M.A.: On Modelling Assistive Technology Systems Part 2: Applications of the Comprehensive Assistive Technology Model. Technology and Disability 20(4), 251–270 (2008b)
8. George, J., Cockton, G.: Towards Comprehensive ICF Compatible Sociodigital Approaches to Choice and Use of Assistive Technology for Young Children. In: Dias, M.S., Hadjileontiadis, L., Barroso, J. (eds.) Proc. DSAI 2009, pp. 87–94 (2009) ISBN 978-972-669-913-2
9. AbilityNet, State of the eNations Report (2008),
   http://www.abilitynet.org.uk/enation85 (accessed December 2, 2009)
10. AbilityNet, Makayla Lewis on Social Networking for people with Cerebal Palsy (2009),
    http://www.abilitynet.org.uk/accessibility2/2009/09/17/makayla-lewis-on-social-networking-for-people-with-cerebal-palsy/ (accessed January 29, 2010)
11. World Wide Web Consortium, Web Accessibility Initiative (2009),
    http://www.w3.org/WAI/ (accessed March 30, 2010)

Entertainment Software Accessibility: Introduction to the Special Thematic Session

Dominique Archambault

Université Pierre et Marie Curie, INOVA/UFR 919
4 place Jussieu, 75252 Paris cedex 5, France

This year will see the fifth edition of this Special Thematic Session. In ten years we have seen the growing awareness of game accessibility in our community of people who aim at helping other people with digital devices, and in the same time in the community of games designers. But this is not enough. Indeed in the real market there is about no accessible game in the blockbusters. For readers interested in this topic, more information can be found in [3], an extensive State-of-the-Art paper about Computer Games and Visually Impaired People.

Games are important in the early development of children. Computer games can provide a lot of benefits to children with special needs. Actually they are the ones who need technology the more dramatically. There are at least two reasons to that. First computer allow a high adaptability to the actual user. One of the greatest feature is the very high level of rewarding effect. One can set up a system which will detect the slightest action from the user and turn it into lots of visual and/or audio effects. Phil Ellis showed a very nice example in [5] : music was created by children with very heavy handicap using to motion detectors. For children who need help with very structured framework, the game can be a good tool which always reacts in a predictable way. The second reason is that this group of people can benefit a lot of technological aids and becoming familiar with them at an early stage is a very important training for their future.

Then we see 2 big categories of accessible games: specific games dedicated to children with special needs, providing some special features well adapted to educate or entertain these children, and accessible mainstream games, which can be used directly or with a specific interface. The first category seems more simple. Here we want games which fulfil a very specific need. In the first session of this STS, in 2002, Anita Hildén was pointing an important idea: *"...focus on opportunities and possibilities for young disabled children instead of disabilities"* [7]. We have seen several examples in past sessions, for instance [12,1,10,11].

The second category is very important too. [B] reminds us the The Convention on the Rights of the Child recognising the right of the child to rest, leisure, play and participate in cultural life and the arts (see the full citation in the paper). In addition *serious games* are taking more and more importance in various parts of the society (simulation, training, etc), and game-like interfaces as well [8]. In this session [A] will discuss interfaces issues about serious games for students with intellectual disability.

Various studies about accessibility have been reported, like for instance [9,4]. Showing the growing awareness of this issue in the community of games

K. Miesenberger et al. (Eds.): ICCHP 2010, Part I, LNCS 6179, pp. 224–226, 2010.

developers, the IGDA[1] have published a *Game Accessibility White Paper*. In this session [B] shows a pilot study about a game for PlayStation and, based on a case study, [C] proposes an interesting discussion about why accessibility is not taken into account and new ways, to maybe bringing accessibility to the mainstream. [D] proposes also an interesting study about improving efficiency of captioning videos for deaf and hard of hearing people.

To achieve accessibility of mainstream games there is a tremendous need of various research on alternative ways of performing game interaction, like for instance [6]. [E] proposes a new interface for board games, dedicated to visually impaired people.

All these researches are very interesting and create a lot of opportunities for designing games that are accessible for people with special needs, but the next break-through, necessary to achieve real accessibility of mainstream games, and also to improve the design of specific games, is a standard interface that would be implemented by mainstream games developers to allow specific interfaces to command these games [2]. This is a vast research topic but funding is still missing. Let's hope that the near future will at least give us opportunities to carry on projects in this direction.

References to Entertainment Software Accessibility Session

A. Sik Lányi, C., Brown, D., Standen, P., Lewis, J., Butkute, V.: User interface evaluation of serious games for students with intellectual disability
B. Elena, L., Bulgheroni, M., Serenella, B.: Making mainstreaming videogames more accessible: a pilot study applied to Buzz!TM Junior Monster Bluster for PlayStation
C. Ossmann, R., Miesenberger, K.: Accessibility of a Social Network Game
D. Vy, Q., Fels, D.: Using Names and Location for Speaker Identification in Captioning
E. Nagasaka D., Kaneda, N., Itoh, K., Otani, M., Shimizu, M., Sugimoto, M., Hashimoto, M., Kayama, M.: A real-time network board game system using tactile and auditory senses for the visually impaired

References

1. Archambault, D.: The TiM Project: Overview of Results. In: Miesenberger, K., Klaus, J., Zagler, W.L., Burger, D. (eds.) ICCHP 2004. LNCS, vol. 3118, pp. 248–256. Springer, Heidelberg (2004)
2. Archambault, D., Gaudy, T., Miesenberger, K., Natkin, S., Ossmann, R.: Towards generalised accessibility of computer games. In: Pan, Z., Zhang, X., El Rhalibi, A., Woo, W., Li, Y. (eds.) Edutainment 2008. LNCS, vol. 5093, pp. 518–527. Springer, Heidelberg (2008)

---

[1] International Game Developers Association.

3. Archambault, D., Ossmann, R., Gaudy, T., Miesenberger, K.: Computer games and visually impaired people. Upgrade VIII(2), 11 pages (2007), digital journal of CEPIS. A monograph in spanish was published in Novática, http://www.upgrade-cepis.org/issues/2007/2/upgrade-vol-VIII-2.html
4. Atkinson, M.T., Gucukoglu, S., Machin, C.H.C., Lawrence, A.E.: Making the mainstream accessible: What's in a game? In: Miesenberger, K., Klaus, J., Zagler, W.L., Karshmer, A.I. (eds.) ICCHP 2006. LNCS, vol. 4061, pp. 380–387. Springer, Heidelberg (2006)
5. Ellis, P.: The Sound of Movement. I3 Magazine. European Network for Intelligent Information Interfaces 4 (March 1999)
6. Evreinova, T., Evreinov, G.E., Raisamo, R.: Non-visual gameplay: Making board games easy and fun. In: Miesenberger, K., Klaus, J., Zagler, W.L., Karshmer, A.I. (eds.) ICCHP 2008. LNCS, vol. 5105, pp. 561–568. Springer, Heidelberg (2008)
7. Hildén, A., Svensson, H.: Can All Young Disabled Children Play at the Computer. In: Miesenberger, K., Klaus, J., Zagler, W.L. (eds.) ICCHP 2002. LNCS, vol. 2398, p. 191. Springer, Heidelberg (2002)
8. Ossmann, R., Archambault, D., Miesenberger, K.: Accessibility issues in game-like interfaces. In: Miesenberger, K., Klaus, J., Zagler, W.L., Karshmer, A.I. (eds.) ICCHP 2008. LNCS, vol. 5105, pp. 601–604. Springer, Heidelberg (2008)
9. Ossmann, R., Miesenberger, K.: Guidelines for the development of accessible computer games. In: Miesenberger, K., Klaus, J., Zagler, W.L., Karshmer, A.I. (eds.) ICCHP 2006. LNCS, vol. 4061, pp. 403–406. Springer, Heidelberg (2006)
10. Sepchat, A., Monmarché, N., Slimane, M., Archambault, D.: Semi automatic generator of tactile video games for visually impaired children. In: Miesenberger, K., Klaus, J., Zagler, W.L., Karshmer, A.I. (eds.) ICCHP 2006. LNCS, vol. 4061, pp. 372–379. Springer, Heidelberg (2006)
11. Tollefsen, M., Flyen, A.: Internet and accessible entertainment. In: Miesenberger, K., Klaus, J., Zagler, W.L., Karshmer, A.I. (eds.) ICCHP 2006. LNCS, vol. 4061, pp. 396–402. Springer, Heidelberg (2006)
12. Velleman, E., van Tol, R., Huiberts, S., Verwey, H.: 3d shooting games, multimodal games, sound games and more working examples of the future of games for the blind. In: Miesenberger, K., Klaus, J., Zagler, W.L., Burger, D. (eds.) ICCHP 2004. LNCS, vol. 3118, pp. 257–263. Springer, Heidelberg (2004)

User Interface Evaluation of Serious Games for Students with Intellectual Disability

Cecilia Sik Lanyi[1], David J. Brown[2], Penny Standen[3], Jacqueline Lewis[4],
and Vilma Butkute[5]

[1] University of Pannonia, Egyetem u. 10., H-8200 Veszprem, Hungary
lanyi@almos.uni-pannon.hu
[2] School of Science and Technology, Nottingham Trent University, Clifton Campus,
Clifton Lane, Nottingham NG11 8NS, UK
david.brown@ntu.ac.uk
[3] Division of Rehabilitation and Ageing, School of Community Health Sciences,
University of Nottingham. B Floor, Medical School, QMC. Clifton Boulevard,
Nottingham NG7 2UH, UK
p.standen@nottingham.ac.uk
[4] Greenhat Interactive Ltd, 6 Church Street, Kidderminster , DY10 8AD, UK
jacqui.lewis@virgin.net
[5] Vilnius University, The Faculty of Philosophy, Education department,
Universiteto str. 9/1, Vilnius, Lithuania
vilma.butkute@imotec.lt

Abstract. We have designed and evaluated around 10 serious games under the EU Leonardo Transfer of Innovation Project: Game On Extra Time (GOET) project http://goet-project.eu/. The project supports people with learning disabilities and additional sensory impairments in getting and keeping a job by helping them to learn, via games-based learning; skills that will help them in their working day. These games help students to learn how to prepare themselves for work, dealing with everyday situations at work, including money management, travelling independently etc. This paper is concerned with the potential of serious games as effective and engaging learning resources for people with intellectual disabilities. In this paper we will address questions related to the design and evaluation of such games, and our design solutions to suit the individual learning needs of our target audiences.

Keywords: intellectual disability, serious games, user interface testing.

1 Introduction

We have designed and evaluated around 10 serious games under the EU Leonardo Transfer of Innovation Project: Game On Extra Time (GOET) project. The project supports people with learning disabilities and additional sensory impairments in

K. Miesenberger et al. (Eds.): ICCHP 2010, Part I, LNCS 6179, pp. 227–234, 2010.

getting and keeping a job by helping them to learn, via games-based learning; skills that will help them in their working day. These games help students to learn how to prepare themselves for work, dealing with everyday situations at work, including money management, travelling independently etc. In this paper we will address questions related to the design and evaluation of such games, and our design solutions to suit the individual learning needs of our target audiences. It is necessary to design the user interfaces for maximum accessibility and usability. In this way we will minimise the additional cognitive load placed on the user while navigating within the software. In order to achieve these goals we have followed published design guidelines, and placed emphasis on using graphics, animations, interactivity, choice and auditory output to promote user engagement and provide alternatives to text. In this paper we will address the pilot testing of the user interface of these serious games.

These games which are tested in all partner countries (UK, Lithuania and Hungary) include [1]:

- 3D Work Tour: simulating the first days at work in a games 'mod' created using the Half Life 2 engine
- Cheese factory: teaching the students using fractions and percentages based on the popular Tetris Game.
- Memobile: trains the student in the important things to do in preparing to leave the house and throughout their working day using mobile phone technology programmed using Flash.
- My Appearance: covering everyday routines such as personal hygiene and getting ready for work-tasks from getting up until leaving home using a Flash game.
- VR supermarket: helps to teach students about money management skills within a store environment developed using Flash.

2   Description of the Tested Serious Games

In this section the main design requirements of the tested games: "3d Work Tour", "Cheese factory", "Memobile", "My Appearance", and VR supermarket" game are described.

2.1 3D Work Tour

3D Work Tour: simulates the first days at a workplace in a games 'mod' created using the Half Life 2 engine. After selecting the language there are two possibilities: subtitles and video tour with BSL (British Sign Language) for hearing impaired users. The user interface is very simple and very clearly organised. The VR environment and avatars are realistic and look similar to the work-based environments and people in the real world (Fig 1 and Fig 2).

Fig. 1. Using subtitles and sound files   **Fig. 2.** Using BSL

2.2 Cheese Factory

Cheese factory: teaches the students using fractions and percentages based on the popular Tetris Game. The user interface of this game is simple too. The instructions are clear, the colours are appropriate, and they are in harmony with the overall interface. The users' results are shown on the right side of the game and the next piece of the cheese is also shown. These features support the user in their ongoing learning tasks (Fig 3 and Fig 4).

 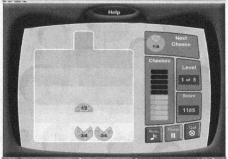

Fig. 3. Options of the game   **Fig. 4.** Showing the process of the game

2.3 Memobile

The Memobile game trains the student in the important things to do in preparing to leave the house and throughout their working day using mobile phone technology programmed using Flash.

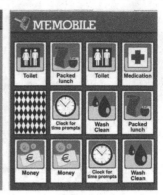

Fig. 5. Main menu of the "Memobile" game

Fig. 6. A and B. Solving one task in the game

2.4 My Appearance

My Appearance: teaches the students' everyday "morning" tasks from getting up until leaving home using a Flash game. The graphic interface of the game is clear and understandable, and cartoon-like. It simulates the sequencing of morning tasks in preparation for leaving for work, and the structure of the game is very consistent. For example after getting up, after having a shower, getting dressed (Fig. 7) and eating breakfast (Fig 8), the user's avatar is ready to leave for work and its appearance improves (Fig 9).

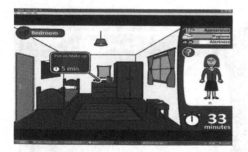

Fig. 7. After having a shower and getting dressed

Fig. 8. Eating breakfast

Fig. 9. Ready for leaving home

Fig. 10. Showing the results graphically

At the end of the game the user receives feedback on his/her performance using sound, subtitles or BSL. If the student forgets to wash his/her hands or forgets to have a morning drink , the game doesn't interfere – it lets the student make mistakes and learn from doing so by reflecting on the game responses to their actions (Fig 10).

2.5 VR Supermarket

VR supermarket game helps to teach students about money management skills within a store environment developed using Flash. The player enters the virtual supermarket (Fig 11), and is given a virtual wallet, shopping list (Fig 12) and shopping cart.

The goods on a given shelf are displayed with their names, prices and images attached to them. To place an item to the shopping cart, the player only has to click on the given item (Fig 13).

Fig. 11. VR supermarket

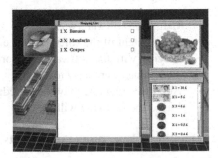
Fig. 12. Shopping list

Before paying, the bar code scanner registers the price of each item in the shopping cart one by one. During this both the cashier and the cash register will give feedback to the student (Fig 14). To pay for the items the student has to place a sufficient sum of money onto the drop panel by clicking the separate banknotes and coins in the wallet and then hitting the pay button. After payment the cashier gives change if necessary, and the "go home" button appears to finish the task. If the student has a insufficient amount of money or has forgotten something, the "back" button leads the user back into the store. Clicking on the "help" button reveals a small panel on which the paid amount of money is shown.

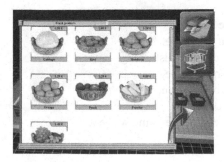
Fig. 13. Goods on a shelf

Fig. 14. At the cash register

3 Evaluation of the User Interface

We have developed a 5 point Likert Scale close-ended questionnaire for testing the user interface of the newly developed serious games.

Likert Scales: Likert scales are scales on which the participants register their agreement or disagreement with the statement. "_Strongly Disagree, _ Disagree, _Neither Agree nor Disagree, _ Agree, _Strongly Agree" on a five-point scale.

This questionnaire contains 29 questions arranged in 4 themes:

3.1 To What Degree Are the Games Enjoyable? (6 Questions)

How engaging are the games?

- Using the software was tiring.
- The content of the software was engaging.
- Playing with the software was boring.
- The games were easy to play.
- Activities in game play were predictable.
- I used the software willingly.

3.2 Questions Concerning the Usability of the Software (4 Questions)

Questions regarding the usability of the software:

- The software displays realistic situations.
- The presented situations were relevant and important.
- Are you satisfied with the quantity and diversity of the questions used?
- Using the software was easy.

3.3 Questions Concerning the Software's Manageability: (9 Questions)

Questions regarding the software's manageability:

- There is sufficient opportunity to correct or revisit responses given in the game
- The content areas between levels are distinct.
- It was easy to follow the activities in the game.
- The noises or music used in the games were disturbing.
- The speech used was clear and understandable.
- Failures were typically results of disorientation.
- Starting the software was an easy process.
- Closing the software/Quitting at the end of the game was easy.
- Quitting during the game was easy.

3.4 Questions Concerning the Graphics (10 Questions)

Questions regarding the graphics:

- The software's look is realistic.
- The software's look is likeable.
- The software's look was appropriate to its aim.
- The pictures used were easy to recognize.
- The illustrations and backgrounds used were helpful.
- The connection between the pictures and the actions rendered to them were unambiguous.
- Failures were typically results of not being able to recognise pictures.
- Failures were typically results of not understanding instructions.
- The software was rich in (visual and audio) stimuli.
- The screens of the software were detailed.

After every question there is a "If you wish comment, why you have selected the given answer" open ended question to supplement the response given. At the end of the test there is a "30th question" - a half page for further notes, comments and remarks.

3.5 Further Testing

In a mixed methods approach the questionnaires are complemented by two further tools suitable for testing accessibility and usability early on in the implementation process. The first is an Expert Review Tool using usability heuristics (guidelines for good design) selected by the multivariate design team (project steering group) against which the games will be assessed in group project meetings (two passes of the software). The second is an Observational Checklist for use by the evaluation researcher to record data in categories including accessibility, usability, engagement, unsolicited comments, and help required (actions and verbal prompts) whilst users are trialling the serious games.

3.6 Design Principles

We tested the following serious games: 3D Work Tour, Cheese factory, Memobile, My Appearance and VR Supermarket software. Based on the evaluation results we iterated our own design guidelines for serious games for use by people with intellectual and additional sensory impairments which can currently be summarised as [1], [2]:

- Ensure presentation at appropriate speed
- Allow users to go back
- Allow User Control
- Make any text plain text
- Never convey information by colour alone
- Ensure sufficient contrast
- Help users navigate

- Make clear Maintain organisation
- Use unique and informative text descriptions for any hyperlinks (never click here!)
- Use accessibility features
- Design simply in simple layouts
- Use fallbacks
- Make systems consistent and error free
- Aim for compatibility with assistive technologies
- Allow keyboard access
- Do not include elements that are known to cause seizures

4 Conclusion

In this paper we have discussed the design and evaluation of five serious games' and their user interfaces. These serious games were developed for students with intellectual disability to help them in activities of daily living, their working life and specifically in managing a budget. We have demonstrated the test process of the user interface design of the serious games and our solutions for any identified problems for students with intellectual disability. The detailed pedagogical tests will run until July 2010.

Acknowledgments. This project has been funded with support from the EU's Transfer of Innovation Leonardo da Vinci Lifelong Learning Programme, Game on Extra Time, GOET Grant Agreement number: UK/08/LLP-LdV/TOI/163_181 for.

References

1.   Sik Lanyi, C., Brown, D.J.: Design of serious games for students with intellectual disability. In: India HCI 2010, Interaction Design for International Development 2010, Bombay, India, March 20-24, pp. 151–160 (2010)
2.   Brown, D.J., Standen, P., Evett, L., Battersby, S., Shopland, N.: Designing Serious Games for People with Dual Diagnosis: Learning Disabilities and Sensory Impairments. In: Zemliansky, P., Wilcox, D. (eds.) Press in Educational Gaming. IGI Global

Making Mainstreaming Videogames More Accessible: A Pilot Study Applied to Buzz!™ Junior Monster Rumble for PlayStation

Elena Laudanna[1], Maria Bulgheroni[2], Francesca Caprino[1], and Serenella Besio[1]

[1] Università della Valle d'Aosta, strada Cappuccini 2A, 11100 AOSTA, Italy
{e.laudanna,f.caprino,s.besio}@univda.it
[2] AB ACUS Via Domodossola, 7 - 20145 Milano, Italy
mariabulgheroni@ab-acus.com

Abstract. In this article the authors analyse the critical factors concerning accessibility of the videogame *Buzz!™ Junior Monster Rumble* for the Playstation console. The objective of the study is to propose a series of modifications that, on the one hand, do not change the graphic and playability features of the game and, on the other, expand the target of users to include children with cognitive and/or motor disabilities. If this method turns out to be feasible and applicable it could also be extended to more complex games in terms of functions and required skills, contributing to a more inclusive approach within the research and study of videogame accessibility. The reasons for choosing this particular game are an essential precondition for a comprehensive study.

Keywords: Mainstream videogames, ICF-CY, accessibility.

1 Introduction

Article 31 of the Convention on the Rights of the Child [1] clearly states: "States Parties recognize the right of the child to rest and leisure, to engage in play and recreational activities appropriate to the age of the child and to participate freely in cultural life and the arts." Playing is a right not only of every child but also of every person and it is a basic factor to enhance the quality of life. Play is also the essential means through which persons develop: through play, we learn, explore the social and physical environment, and build fruitful social relationships.

Today, videogames have the biggest share of the games universe and are becoming an increasingly mainstream and "socially acceptable" form of leisure. Playing videogames has become a cross-generational phenomenon, and game makers are searching for new customers. Because they are increasingly targeting the family as a whole, videogames must be accessible to everyone: this means children, teenagers, adults and the elderly, all of whom have different abilities and skills.

A Universal Design approach that aims at developing more accessible videogames could be an added value in such a global market: the focus of this pilot research study

K. Miesenberger et al. (Eds.): ICCHP 2010, Part I, LNCS 6179, pp. 235–242, 2010.

is to explore how to make mainstream videogames "playable" by a wider audience, i.e. to include people with motor and cognitive disabilities, without changing the game and using its own inherent functions in new and different ways. In reality, since many different resources are required to produce mainstream videogames (a game producer oversees the complete development process, one or more game designers are responsible for creating the story and actions, while artists and composers manage character visualization, scenes and sounds), an average videogame costs between 3 and 10 million USD and requires 12-24 months to complete. Games resulting from this complex process are therefore much more "playable", rich in graphic effects and complex as regards number and type of activities compared to "special" or "accessible" videogames developed mainly for people with disabilities. Moreover, making mainstream videogames more accessible increases the importance of the inclusive approach.

2 State of the Art

In the past "play" often has been relegated to the back shelf when setting educational objectives, such as developing mathematical or language skills. However, state-of-the-art research emphasises the important role of play in personal development since it is a crucial means for learning about oneself, the environment, and for developing social relationships. Opportunities to play, e.g. with peers or family members, increases social skills and builds confidence, and social play makes it possible to acquire skills needed to develop and maintain social relationships. In addition, from an educational perspective, play is a "natural" way to learn in an enjoyable manner. The importance of play has been proven and play is also included in the WHO's International Classification of Functioning – Children and Youth Version (2007) [2], both as an important "Activity" related to the acquisition of knowledge through objects, and as a recreational and leisure means for "Participation" in social life.

Moreover, in recent years different technologies have been studied as a means of play for children and people with disabilities in rehabilitative and educational contexts: some important examples are robots [3], immersive virtual reality [4], and gesture recognition. Mainstream products like PlayStation 2 Eye Toy [5] and Nintendo Wii [6] have also been used as low-cost alternatives to tailor-designed and expensive rehabilitation instruments. In this context, commercial videogames can be an important means for improving the quality of life and the social inclusion of children and adults with disabilities, especially owing to their widespread diffusion and availability.

Accessibility studies have now been extensively developed and some of the early attempts at creating accessible products have led to the development of educational software and multimedia ware. Further developments in the specific field of videogames have been made by the Special Interest Group (SIG) on Accessibility in Games of the International Game Developers Association that defined Guidelines for developing accessible videogames [7]. These guidelines and their subsequent developments have been applied to create or re-design accessible games [8] but the impact on the mainstream market has been negligible to this point. As already occurred with other markets and products we need to prove that creating accessible videogames based on a Design-for-All approach makes them better videogames for everyone!

3 Methodology

The purpose of this pilot study is to define a possible set of changes or improvements to be applied to an existing mainstream videogame with the following conditions: the videogame should remain the same as regards playability, graphic interface and controls ("normal" players should interact with the same game) and accessibility should be improved using existing built-in functions. While the proposed changes will not necessarily produce a game with perfect and full accessibility for everyone with various disabilities, it should nevertheless enlarge the group of possible users and make communication with Assistive Technology interfaces easier or possible. The main target user groups of our study are children with motor and/or cognitive impairments.

The videogame investigated in this study is *Buzz!^{TM} Junior Monster Rumble*. This game is designed for kids (more than 3 years old but probably less than 7-8 years old; in fact no actual reading skills are required) and is mainly proposed as a multiplayer family activity: "it's so simple that even mum and dad can play!". Like other previous titles in the series, *Buzz!^{TM} Junior Monster Rumble* consists of 25 different games that explore and "train" functions, skills and play objectives of more complex and advanced games. This series of videogames is clearly oriented to acquire new young customers thanks to the simplified hardware interface. Since it is proposed as a multiplayer activity parents will be motivated to buy it. The hardware interface consists of just five buttons: a big round illuminated red button and four rectangular buttons of different colours. This type of videogame was selected for the following reasons:

- Target players for this type of game are very small children whose motor, cognitive and play skills have not yet been fully developed. The differences between children with and without disabilities are not so marked and it is easier to play together (inclusion should be the main objective of accessibility);
- Producers use this type of game to create new costumers and increase fidelity, and they can also be used to loyalize costumers regarding the features of accessible games: children with disabilities playing now with an accessible version of Buzz!TM Junior games will then ask for accessibility to more complex games, a request which may affect the entire market;
- The small number of control buttons used and the simple activities required to play the game make it technically easier to improve game accessibility;
- The large number of simple activities included in the same game makes it possible to explore many types of games and functions;

Because of the strong motivation that videogames generate in children such games could be used as a education and rehabilitation tool to develop cognitive, motor but also social skills.

As in some previous studies related to accessibility of educational software, the authors applied an empirical analysis of the game based on their experience in assessing AT for children with disabilities and in other related research fields (e.g. robots for play).

Body functions required to play and the skills trained by single game activities have also been mapped according to ICF-CY [2], and possible improvements have then been suggested.

4 Analysis of the Games

In this first research stage only the "practice" game-mode has been considered: the child plays alone against the computer game's Artificial Intelligence (AI) that adapts the other characters' behaviours to the child's performance (usually two of the three characters perform worse than the player): in this case accessibility is related only to the possibility of playing and not to being "competitive" with peers.

The following critical factors have been identified in relation to the accessibility of the 26 activities (two different activities can be played in one of the 25 games) of *Buzz!*[TM] *Junior Monster Rumble*.

Number of controls. Eight activities require only one action button, two activities need two buttons, one activity needs three, thirteen need four and two need five: fine hand use (ICF-CY d440 – Fine hand use – Performing the coordinated actions of handling objects, picking up, manipulating and releasing them using one's hand, fingers and thumb, such as lifting coins off a table or turning a dial or knob) should be possible or at least Assistive Technology interfaces (Icf-CY e11521 – Adapted products and technology for play – Objects, materials, toys and other products adapted or specially designed to assist play, such as remote-controlled cars and modified playground equipment) should be used [9]. The greater the number of controls required, the more difficult it is to access the game for children with motor impairments. Usually we can assume that at least one single "easy" voluntary movement can be found for each child and used through AT switches and AT interfaces. Two voluntary movements are possible in some cases, but more than two might often be impossible to manage. But the number of controls may also be critical if some cognitive impairments affect hand-eye coordination functions.

Timing. Four types of timing are used. Five activities involve a maximum time, meaning that the player has to act before a fixed period of time elapses. There are "casual games"[1] or really simple "strategy games"[2] involving thinking functions, such as short-term memory, concentration, counting up and planning, but quick actions are not required (strategy is obviously related to the young age of the players!). Four activities require fast action: a short reaction time to some visual stimuli is required to play the game. For two activities a single button must be pressed in a particular rhythm. In twelve activities action must be synchronized with the games' visual stimuli: the button(s) should be pressed within some defined intervals (results do not only depend on speed). Two activities can be performed without time constraints, even if the score depends on speed. Timing of actions is linked to executive mental functions (ICF-CY b164 – Higher-level cognitive functions – Specific mental functions especially dependent on the frontal lobes of the brain, including complex goal-directed behaviours such as decision-making, abstract thinking, planning and carrying out plans, mental flexibility, and deciding which behaviours are appropriate under what circumstances; often called executive functions) and to the ability to perform complex

---

[1] Casual games usually have very simple rules or play techniques and a very low degree of strategy.
[2] Strategy videogames focus on game play that requires careful and skillful thinking and planning in order to win.

movements (ICF-CY b176 – Mental function of sequencing complex movements – Specific mental functions of sequencing and coordinating complex, purposeful movements).

Timing and Number of Controls are critical factors related both to motor impairments and cognitive impairments, while those listed below are related only to impairments of mental functions.

Attention. In every activity the player has to identify his/her own character and focus attention on it: in twenty-one activities that means that the player is interested in only one part of the screen (ICF-CY d160 – Focusing attention – Intentionally focusing on specific stimuli, such as by filtering out distracting noises). Eight of these activities also require to focus attention on fixed target(s) that change colour or appearance, while there are moving targets in eleven activities. In five activities the characters move around and interact with each other and with other elements and attention should be focused on numerous moving visual stimuli at the same time (ICF-CY b1402 – Dividing attention – Mental functions that permit focusing on two or more stimuli at the same time). A number of elements on the screen (characters and targets) and their movements can hardly be managed when attention function impairments are present.

Types of environmental interactions. In eight activities the player can have two different types of interactions with the environment that, in these particular games, mainly consists of targets and other characters: interactions with positive effect (increasing score) and interactions with negative effect (decreasing score or temporary "accident"). The player has to decide how and when to interact (ICF-CY d177 – Making decisions – Making a choice among options, implementing the choice, and evaluating the effects of the choice, such as selecting and purchasing a specific item, or deciding to undertake and undertaking one task from among several tasks that need to be done). Impairments in mental functions can limit the number of choices that can be managed by the child.

Movement direction control. Six activities require the player to control movements on the screen. In one activity two directions, up and down, are controlled and the character jumps from one level to another (right and left movements are defined by the level where the character is located); in a racing activity right and left movements are controlled while the character slides down a slope (speed can be increased for a defined time three times during each round); one activity controls direction through a 360° rotation; three activities control direction and speed of movement. Note that not more than three controls are used for defining movements. These activities are the most complex among those proposed and they require integration of many mental functions (ICF-CY b164 – Higher-level cognitive functions – Specific mental functions especially dependent on the frontal lobes of the brain, including complex goal-directed behaviours such as decision-making, abstract thinking, planning and carrying out plans, mental flexibility, and deciding which behaviours are appropriate under what circumstances; often called executive functions). They are probably the least accessible for children with cognitive impairments.

Colour recognition. Eleven activities do not require colour recognition. Seven activities use association of colours between targets on the screen and buttons on the

Buzzer, but all the colours are present and they are in the same sequence as the buttons: the relative position is enough to identify them. Finally, seven activities require the player to recognize the colour of one target on the screen, selecting the right button (ICF-CY b21021 – Colour vision – Seeing functions of differentiating and matching colours).

Two activities differ from the others as they are not an action game but can be considered more similar to very simple "strategy games" since they require careful and skilful thinking (obviously in relation to the young age of the players!!) more than quick reflexes, timing and physical challenges (hand-eye coordination and reaction-time). They involve *short-term memory* (ICF-CY b1440 – Short-term memory – Mental functions that produce a temporary, disruptable memory storage with a duration of around 30 seconds from which information is lost if not consolidated into long-term memory) and *concentration* on one moving target for a defined period of time (ICF-CY b1400 – Sustaining attention – Mental functions that produce concentration for the period of time required): severe cognitive impairments can create some play problems.

5   Results

To overcome the previously discussed critical factors a limited set of features may be created to support accessibility.

• *Reduced number of controls.* Eight activities, requiring only one control, can be accessed through assistive technology, if at least one voluntary movement can be identified for each child. Of the other games, six can also be played with a reduced number of buttons, reducing the possible overall score (i.e. "shooting" a few of the possible targets). Seven activities can be modified and made accessible with less controls through AI that could present stimuli with only two or three colours instead of four. For six activities reducing the number of controls would also require a change in the graphic interfaces. Two other activities can be performed with less controls only if the AI interfaces manage some of the functions (i.e. accelerating in the racing game or automatically falling in the jumping game). Reducing the number of controls not only improves accessibility for children with motor impairments but also decreases the difficulty of the cognitive task. This can be a considered a positive effect if the task matches the cognitive skill level of the child, but may be a negative effect if the task is not challenging enough.

• *Reduced time constraints.* Except for two activities that have no time limitations (reacting slowly only reduces the final score), all games can be made more accessible by increasing the amount of time required to do an action: increasing the maximum time available for performing the task or slowing down all the activities.

• *Reduced number of "distracting" elements.* Not every visual element is important in the "practice" game mode. In particular the presence of game characters controlled by the CPU can be a strong "disturbing" element. On the other hand this probably could be one of the least affordable adaptations since the graphic interface of the game must be modified. There may be alternative solutions: the number of characters controlled by the Artificial Intelligence could be limited to just one, while the others don't move.

- *Changing environmental interactions.* Increasing the number of possible interactions with elements with a positive effect and reducing those with a negative effect, thus making the activity easier, would raise the overall score while enhancing motivation and increasing involvement.
- *Additional stimuli.* To support cognitive functions, such as colour recognition, concentration, counting of elements and timing of actions, additional stimuli can be implemented: sound can make the child alert, spoken explanations can suggest the right choice, and clearer visual indications can support playing.

Most of the adaptations described can be implemented with existing game Artificial Intelligence. In any case the game development process and choices are often based on the use of numerous parameters through which it is possible to customise and adapt the program to create different games. The customisation and learning capabilities of the game itself can be used to tailor the game to match player abilities. It is a fact, for example, that most commercial games create a balance between "awards" and "game-over" to keep the player interested in the game. This is particularly true in our example since it addresses small children who are not yet ready to deal with frustration.

6   Conclusions and Future Activities

From these pilot activities, it is clear that an operative approach aimed at modifying existing mainstream games, rather than starting from scratch in designing new accessible games, leads to different results. If on the one hand, the accessibility level that may be obtained with this approach is unable to satisfy most of the needs of players with disabilities, on the other it is possible to enlarge the range of players of any commercial videogame to include users with motor and/or cognitive disabilities. this will generate a meaningful cultural shift towards an inclusive approach to game design, something that has already occurred in fields such as architecture, industrial design, the Internet and many others.

As already demonstrated in those other fields of applications we hope to show that a design that takes into account disability-related needs improves the final product and makes it more usable for the entire community.

An additional conclusion can be drawn: if it can be assumed that the problem of accessibility for children with motor impairments can be managed through AT hardware interfaces, most of the accessibility and usability problems are linked to cognitive impairments (attention, hand-eye coordination, high level functions, etc.) that are widespread enough to be an interesting market for developers and distributors.

Future plans are now moving in two main directions: to carry out some experimental trials with children with disabilities to determine if the identified modifications are really necessary (single cases); to contact game developers working on products similar to the one investigated here to perform a feasibility analysis on implementation of the required modifications.

References

1. United Nations, Convention on the Rights of the Child (November 20, 1989), http://www2.ohchr.org/english/law/crc.htm
2. International Classification of Functioning, Disability and Health – Children and Youth Version (2007), http://www.who.int/classifications/icf/en/
3. Besio, S., Caprino, F., Laudanna, E.: Guidelines for using robots in educational and therapy sessions for children with disabilities. Uniservice, Trento (2009)
4. Weiss, P.L., Rand, D., Katz, N., Kizony, R.: Video capture virtual reality as a flexible and effective rehabilitation tool. Journal of Neuro Engineering and Rehabilitation 1, 12 (2004), http://www.jneuroengrehab.com/content/1/1/12
5. Rand, D., Kizony, R., Weiss, P.L.: Virtual reality rehabilitation for all: Vivid GX versus Sony PlayStation II EyeToy. In: Sharkey, P., McCrindle, R., Brown, D. (eds.) 5th International Conference on Disability, Virtual Environments and Associated Technologies. University of Reading, Oxford (2004), http://www.icdvrat.reading.ac.uk/2004/papers/S03_N2_Rand_ICDVRAT2004.pdf
6. Davalli, A., Orlandini, D., Cutti, A., Gruppioni, E., Mainardi, E., Malavasi, M.: New Video Games Generations: Only Games or an Opportunity for Assistive Technology? In: Emiliani, P.L., Burzagli, L., Como, A., Gabbanini, F., Salminen, A. (eds.) Proceeding of Assistive Technology from Adapted Equipment to Inclusive Environments, AAATE 2009, pp. 665–670. IOS Press, Amsterdam (2009)
7. Special Interest Group on Accessibility of International Games Developers Association: Accessibility in Games: Motivations and Approaches (2004), http://www.igda.org/accessibility
8. Ossmann, R., Miesenberger, K., Archambault, D.: Tic Tac Toe – Mainstream Games Accessibility: Guidelines and Examples. In: Eizmendi, G., Azkoitia, J.M., Craddock, G.M. (eds.) Proceedings of Challenges for Assistive Technology, AAATE 2007, pp. 791–795. IOS Press, Amsterdam (2007)
9. Iacopetti, F., Fanucci, L., Roncella, R., Giusti, D., Scebba, A.: Game Console Controller Interface for People with Disability. In: International Conference on Complex, Intelligent and Software Intensive Systems, pp. 757–762. CISIS (2008)

Accessibility of a Social Network Game

Roland Ossmann and Klaus Miesenberger

University of Linz, Institute Integriert Studieren
Altenbergerstr. 69, 4040 Linz, Austria
{roland.ossmann,klaus.miesenberger}@jku.at

Abstract. The social network Facebook is one of the largest social communities in the internet, where people meet online to post messages and pictures, chat and play games. While Facebook is accessible, Framville, the most played online game, embedded in Facebook, is not accessible for several user groups. This work will give a short overview about state of the art in games accessibility and will give a detailed view about accessibility issues in Fameville and the used technology, Flash. Additionally, possible improvements for Farmville and positive examples of accessible Flash games will be shown.

Keywords: Games Accessibility, Flash Accessibility, Farmville Accessibility.

1 Introduction

The social network Facebook is one of the largest social communities, where people meet online to post messages and pictures, chat and play games. Accessibility of social networks is an issues and a remarkable level has been reached. [1]

Nowadays social networks introduce gaming. The most famous game in Facebook is Farmville [2]. It is the most played online game [3]. While Facebook is accessible, Farmville is not accessible to several groups of gamers with disabilities. [4] gives a good overview about the social aspects and the interaction on Facebook.

Facebook is an example how gaming impacts on inclusion and participation of people with disabilities. Gaming is not only a suspicious stand alone activity of minor importance but is more and more understood as a new and more efficient way of learning [5] but also as a new way of interaction and designing standard Human-Computer Interfaces.

This paper, following research conducted over the last years on game accessibility [6], discusses accessibility of games in social networks using the example of Farmville. It demonstrates the feasibility of game accessibility and underlines once more the importance of including gaming into the accessibility agenda.

2 State of the Art in Games Accessibility

Over the last years several groups have started to work on games accessibility (e.g. IGDA [7], AGA [8]). A comprehensive overview can be found in [9], which

K. Miesenberger et al. (Eds.): ICCHP 2010, Part I, LNCS 6179, pp. 243–246, 2010.

demonstrates the availability of guidelines, examples of accessible games and game scenes of general importance towards first approaches towards development frameworks like AGA. This first body of knowledge is by far not completed and also the awareness for game accessibility is still lacking.

In the following we apply this body of knowledge to Farmville to a) allow participation of people with disabilities in playing this game and b) prove the concept and enhance the body of knowledge in games accessibility.

3   The User Interface of Farmville

Farmville is implemented on Adobe Flash. Flash is not accessible by itself, but also not inaccessible. It provides according accessibility support to allow the implementation of accessible applications [10]. The switch from WCAG1.0 to WCAG2.0 now also includes such non W3C techniques into accessibility considerations [11]. An accessibility framework for the authoring tools and the Flash player has been designed and integrated, but three issues has been given, why it is quite hard making Flash content accessible: First, the content is often primary based on graphics and frequently changed content. Second, there is no tool for the evaluation and third, most of the Flash content developers do not even know about the accessibility features of Flash. [12]

The developers from Zynga (www.zynga.com) have created a typical Flash game, mainly controlled by mouse, with some minor keyboard interaction. The main tasks are planting and harvesting farm products.

The game field is divided in the planting areas, which are adjusted along an imagine raster. A toolbox offers several tools, including a multi tool, a plow tool and a market. It is a board game with no real time interaction, the only time component is to harvest the fruits before they wither. Figure 1 shows a screenshot of Farmville.

4   Accessibility Issues of Farmville

The game has been tested against the game accessibility guidelines [13]; these are the main issues: The game comes with an easy to understand tutorial. Also, the difficulty of the game is no issue, friends can help you gaining more points. A real issue are the input modalities of the game. The only supported input device is the mouse, only a very limited keyboard interaction (only some fields can be selected, the tab order is like a randomise-algorithm) is possible. During "rush hour" the game reacts very slowly, so it is often not clear if an input was recognised be the system, no feedback is given.

The game provides an in-game zoom function, but only on a very limited way. In combination with the browser zoom functionality, many control icons become unreachable. Also colour and contrast can not be changed. The graphical objects did not provide any meta data, they are just invisible for screenreaders.

Fig. 1. Screenshot of Farmville

Sounds are only used to improve the gameplay and making it more fun, no important information it transported by sounds. Furthermore, the music and the sounds can be switched off. Summarising, the game is not playable for persons using a screenreader, having problems with low contrast or size or can not use the mouse.

5 Possible Solutions

In the work of [9] the possibility of making a board game accessible has been shown. The methods presented there can also be used for Farmville. The guidelines for games accessibility are available, an accessible framework for the development environment (Flash) is available but the game developers do not use them. The main improvements for this game have to be a fully supported keyboard control on the input side and several improvements on the output side. All graphic objects have to provide meta information for assistive technologies, the size of the objects, the details and the colours have to be adjustable. The gamefield bases on rectangles, a keyboard based navigation will be possible and useful. The structure for the menus might also need some rework to make the navigation within them more useable.

A request about future consideration of accessibility issues at Zynga was answered, but the answer did not take the question or any future plans about accessibility into consideration.

6 Conclusion

It seems that accessibility issues in games has not reached the mainstream marked yet, so the question is, if more support (with guidelines, tools, frameworks, etc.) is enough or, if further information, "advertisement" and support for the game developers and companies is needed. Especially in the internet, where accessibility has already a fundamental basis (e.g. [11]), more sensitisation in the area of games is needed.

On the other hand, some companies are specialised on Flash accessibility, showing that accessible Flash games are possible. A good example is [14].

References

1. Ingber, J.: A New Way to Find Old Friends: A Review of the Accessibility of Facebook (2009), http://www.afb.org/afbpress/pub.asp?DocID=aw100204 (accessed 29.03.2010)
2. Farmville, http://www.farmville.com
3. Farmville, N.M.: Social Gaming, and Addiction (2009), http://www.gamasutra.com/blogs/MarkNewheiser/20091204/3733/Farmville_Social_Gaming_and_Addiction.php (accessed 29.03.2010)
4. Valentina, R.: Facebook Applications and playful mood: the construction of Facebook as a "third place". In: MindTrek 2008 (2008)
5. Prensky, M.: Digital game-based learning. ACM Computers in Entertainment 1(1) (2003)
6. Archambault, et al.: Towards generalised accessibility of computer games. In: Edutainment 2008 (2008)
7. International Game Developers Association. Accessibility in games: Motivations and approaches (2004), http://www.igda.org/accessibility/IGDA_Accessibility_WhitePaper.pdf (accessed 29.03.2010)
8. Ossmann, R., Archambault, D., Miesenberger, K.: Accessibility issues in game-like interfaces. In: Miesenberger, K., Klaus, J., Zagler, W.L., Karshmer, A.I. (eds.) ICCHP 2008. LNCS, vol. 5105, pp. 601–604. Springer, Heidelberg (2008)
9. Ossmann, R., Miesenberger, K., Archambault, D.: A computer game designed for all. In: Miesenberger, K., Klaus, J., Zagler, W.L., Karshmer, A.I. (eds.) ICCHP 2008. LNCS, vol. 5105, pp. 585–592. Springer, Heidelberg (2008)
10. Flash Accessibility, http://www.adobe.com/accessibility/
11. Web Content Accessibility Guidelines, http://www.w3.org/TR/WCAG20/
12. Sato, et al.: Automatic accessibility transcoding for flash content. In: Assets 2007 (2007)
13. Ossmann, R., Miesenberger, K.: Guidelines for the development of accessible computer games. In: Miesenberger, K., Klaus, J., Zagler, W.L., Karshmer, A.I. (eds.) ICCHP 2006. LNCS, vol. 4061, pp. 403–406. Springer, Heidelberg (2006)
14. New System Informatics (2009), http://www.n-syst.com/ourshowcase.php#acc (accessed 29.03.2010)

Using Placement and Name for Speaker Identification in Captioning

Quoc V. Vy and Deborah I. Fels

Ryerson University, 350 Victoria Street, Toronto, Ontario M5B 2K3, Canada
{qvy,dfels}@ryerson.ca

Abstract. The current method for speaker identification in closed captioning on television is ineffective and difficult in situations with multiple speakers, off-screen speakers, or narration. An enhanced captioning system that uses graphical elements (e.g., avatar and colour), speaker names and caption placement techniques for speaker identification was developed. A comparison between this system and conventional closed captions was carried out deaf and hard-of-hearing participants. Results indicate that viewers are distracted when the caption follows the character on-screen regardless of whether this should assist in identifying who is speaking. Using the speaker's name for speaker identification is useful for viewers who are hard of hearing but not for deaf viewers. There was no significant difference in understanding, distraction, or preference for the avatar with the coloured border component.

Keywords: speaker identification, captioning, subtitles, universal design.

1 Introduction

Film and television represent a significant method of cultural distribution in western society. The ability to access film and television is important for participation in the cultural development of one's society. Captioning is the main method used by deaf (DF) or hard-of-hearing (HOH) individuals to access this content. Captioning is a text transcription of dialogue and other sounds using text descriptions and symbols [2]. The most popular form of captioning is on television, called *closed captioning* (CC) in North America or *subtitles (for the hard of hearing)* in Europe. The font is usually mono-spaced with either mixed-case or uppercase lettering. The colour is usually white text on a black background, but as found in subtitles, different colours combinations may also be used.

The practice of using text and symbols for captioning has essentially remained the same since they first appeared in the early 1970s on television. Despite advancements in technology, captioning for digital television included only a few minor improvements such the ability to use different fonts, sizes, and colours or transparency for background. In fact, some of these features are actually discouraged in North American standards due to a stated lack of research to develop proper guidance for their use for CC [1]. However, colour has been used for subtitles in Europe to indicate NSI such as different speakers, sound effects, and emphasise [4].

K. Miesenberger et al. (Eds.): ICCHP 2010, Part I, LNCS 6179, pp. 247–254, 2010.
© Springer-Verlag Berlin Heidelberg 2010

Beside dialogue, *non-speech information* (NSI) such as music, sound effects, who is speaking, and speech prosody, is also crucial for presenting a coherent and entertaining experience. However, due to the limited time or space on-screen, a considerable amount of NSI is often excluded from captioning. When possible, text descriptions surrounded in brackets or symbols are used to represent some of these NSI. However, text description and symbols for NSI is often ambiguous or ineffective, leading to confusion or misinterpretation for the viewer. For example, a name is sometimes used for speaker identification (e.g., `>>ANNE: Good evening everyone`), but this assumes and requires viewers to be able to recall and associate that name with a particular character. However, this may still be difficult or confusing for viewers when there are multiple characters in groups or off-screen speakers. For subtitles, different colours are used for each speaker, but this can also be ambiguous in these same situations and requires viewer to somehow learn and remember which colour is associated with which character.

In this paper, results of a user study are presented, which compares an *enhanced captioning* (EC) system (see Figure 1) with conventional *closed captioning* (CC).

Fig. 1. Example of Enhanced Captioning (EC) system

2   Background

Among the few studies to address issues with NSI, [3] indicated that users wanted to use explicit descriptions to indicate speakers, onomatopoeia words (e.g., BOOM, CLICK, ZAP), mood of music, and emotion of speakers. A study conducted by [6] found that use of colour improved speaker identification, but placement of the captions had no effect on understanding. According to proximity theory [7], captions placed near a speaker should have some pre-attentive benefit. However, moving captions around the screen in order to be near to the speaker requires the viewer to search for the caption before reading it. If captions are in the same predictable location at all times, there is no need to engage the extra cognitive activities required for this searching. King [6] also suggested further studies using combinations of colour, placement, and names of the characters for speaker identification was needed.

An enhanced captioning (EC) system has been developed to explore new concepts for speaker identification [9]. With the EC system, an "avatar" is used to represent the speaker. The avatar consists of the name and image of the character, and a coloured border that matches the character's clothing. The EC system also visually indicates the flow of the dialogue between speakers in a two-column format. The location, size and order of the avatar are customizable and can be moved and the components can be toggled on/off independently by the user (see Figure 2). This system is designed for use on rich media platforms and portable devices, and is not limited by current captioning technology for television.

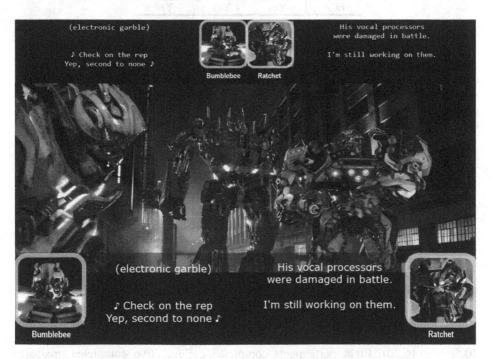

Fig. 2. Possible configurations of components for EC system

3 Method

A mixed factorial design was used with four captioning styles and four different video clips as within-subjects factors and hearing status as the between-subjects factor. The independent variables were participant's preferences, distraction levels and understanding of the components of the EC system. Participants watched 16 short video clips, which consisted of four different captioning styles (see Table 1) and four different video clips (see Table 2). The captioning styles consisted of combinations of the speaker identification components: EC1 used the speaker's name, EC2 used the avatar with a coloured border, and EC3 that used the speaker's name and the avatar with the coloured border. CC was used as a control condition and was the original captions that appeared with the content on DVD [8]. The viewing order of captioning styles and video was randomly presented to minimize any learning or ordering effects that may exist between the independent variables.

Table 1. Captioning Styles and Components

Style	Dialogue	Name	Avatar
CC	Yes	Sometimes	N/A
EC1	Yes	Yes	
EC2	Yes		Yes
EC3	Yes	Yes	Yes

Participants were asked to complete a pre-study questionnaire that consisted of demographic questions (e.g., gender, age, hearing status, and education) and experience questions regarding television and captioning. After viewing each video clip, participants were then asked to complete a trial questionnaire, consisting of three 5-point Likert scale questions regarding the understanding, distractibility and preference of the components used in each of the captioning styles.

Table 2. Properties of Video Clips

Video	Setting	Duration	Speakers	Speech Rate
A	Narration	1m 13s	1	104 WPM
B	Aircraft Cargo	51s	4	173 WPM
C	Dealership	1m 36s	3	184 WPM
D	Transformers	1m 24s	7	124 WPM

Study Participants. Nineteen participants (12 female and 7 male) recruited from various Deaf culture events and listings carried out the user study over a span of two months. Twelve participants were DF (nine females, three males) and seven were HOH (three females, four males). Their age ranged from 18 and 75 years old (μ = 40.5, σ = 16.20). Eight participants completed college, five completed graduate school, three completed university, and the remaining three completed high school. Participants watched an average of 9.5 hours of television per week (σ = 5.00). Sixteen participants always used captioning for watching television, while the remaining three participants never used captioning.

4 Results

A Repeated Measures ANOVA was carried out to determine differences in the ratings for preference, distraction and comprehension using within-subjects variables: captioning_style, video, and between-subjects factor: hearing_status.

The 5-point Likert-scales were reduced to 3-point Likert-scales due to the low number of participants ($N = 19$), which is a permissible and standard data compression technique [5]. For the 3-point Likert-scale of all dependent variables, ratings of 1 are positive (e.g., liked, not distracting, helpful), ratings of 2 are neutral or no opinion, and ratings of 3 are negative (e.g., disliked, distracting, not helpful).

Preference of Speaker's Name. There was a significant difference for preference of speaker's name between Video, $F(3, 15) = 3.25$, $p < 0.05$. Paired t-tests between the videos showed only one significance between Videos A and C, $p < 0.10$. Overall, the DF group disliked having the speaker's name visible more than the HOH group (see Table 3). The exception is with Video A, where HOH participants disliked having the name most. The DF group disliked having the name visible most for Video D.

Table 3. Descriptives for Preference of Speaker's Name

Style	Video	HOH Mean	SD	N	Deaf Mean	SD	N
EC1	A	2.86	0.38	7	2.64	0.81	11
	B	2.14	1.07	7	2.58	0.79	12
	C	2.00	1.10	6	2.20	1.03	10
	D	2.33	1.03	6	2.73	0.65	11
EC3	A	2.71	0.76	7	2.60	0.70	10
	B	2.17	0.98	6	2.64	0.67	11
	C	2.60	0.89	5	2.55	0.82	11
	D	2.33	1.03	6	2.70	0.67	10

Understanding of Speaker's Name. There was a significant difference for understanding of speaker's name between Video * Hearing, $F(3, 15) = 3.07$, $p < 0.05$. Paired t-tests between the videos showed significance between Videos A and B, $p < 0.05$. Overall, the HOH group rated the name of speakers more helpful than the DF group (see Table 4). HOH participants found the name the least helpful in Video A and the most helpful in Video B. DF participants found the name the least helpful for all videos other than Video C.

Table 4. Descriptives for Understanding of Speaker's Name

Style	Video	HOH Mean	SD	N	Deaf Mean	SD	N
EC1	A	2.86	0.38	7	2.55	0.82	11
	B	2.14	1.07	7	2.67	0.78	12
	C	2.33	1.03	6	2.30	0.95	10
	D	2.33	1.03	6	2.73	0.65	11
EC3	A	2.86	0.38	7	2.80	0.63	10
	B	2.17	0.98	6	2.82	0.60	11
	C	2.60	0.89	5	2.55	0.82	11
	D	2.50	0.84	6	2.80	0.42	10

Distraction of Speaker's Name. There were two significant differences for distraction: Video $F(3, 14) = 3.65$, $p < 0.05$, and Video * Hearing, $F(3, 14) = 5.31$, $p < 0.05$. Paired t-tests between the videos showed significance between Videos A and D, $p < 0.05$. Overall, the HOH group rated the speaker's name as more distracting than the DF group (see Table 5). The HOH group found that having the speaker's name was least distracting for Video A for both caption styles while the DF group found that the name was least distracting for Video C.

Table 5. Descriptives for Distraction of Speaker's Name

Style	Video	HOH			Deaf		
		Mean	SD	N	Mean	SD	N
EC1	A	1.14	0.38	7	1.82	0.98	11
	B	1.86	1.07	7	1.67	0.98	12
	C	2.00	1.10	6	1.80	1.03	10
	D	1.83	0.98	6	1.73	1.01	11
EC3	A	1.00	0.00	7	1.90	0.88	10
	B	2.17	0.98	6	1.73	0.79	11
	C	1.80	1.10	5	1.64	0.92	11
	D	1.67	1.03	6	2.30	0.95	10

There was no other significant difference for the dependent variables of the avatar with the colour border component. Further study with more subjects may be required to examine the impact of this component.

5   Discussion

Use of Speaker's Name. The HOH group preferred and found the speaker's name more helpful but also more distracting than the DF group. The use of a person's names for speaker identification, as found in most guidelines and standards for captioning [1, 4], incorrectly assumes that using text descriptions is adequate and satisfies the needs of both groups. However, deaf people typically identify others by their physical appearance or personality (e.g., body size/height, hair, job/position, etc.) rather than by their name. In contrast, a written name is a written and speech identifier, which is a more familiar convention for HOH and hearing individuals. The EC system allows for the use of graphical and text-based identifiers to adapt to the different needs and preferences of its users.

Placement of Captioning. The distraction of the speaker's name for the HOH group may have been caused by the increased attention required, especially when the captions changed location to match the on-screen location of the character. This provides some evidence that any movement increases distraction and reduces the advantage of proximity theory. In the comments from participants, there was some consensus that this movement was too distracting and that captions should be placed in a constant location. Deaf participants may have found the speaker's name less distracting because it was less important and not as useful to them, so they did not attend to it as much.

Significance of Video. There was a significant main effect of video for all of dependent variables. As shown in the paired t-tests and Tables 3 - 5, Video A had the most influence on preference, distraction, and understanding of the EC components. Video A has the slowest word per minute (WPM) rate of all of the clips as it only contained a single speaker who was off-screen, narrating. This likely made it easier for users to follow Video A and its captions, regardless of the captioning style. The remaining videos had more speakers and a faster WPM of dialogue (see Table 2). This may have increased the cognitive and perceptual workload required to keep up with these videos and resulted in the more negative ratings compared with Video A.

6   Conclusion and Future Work

In this study, HOH participants found that using the speaker's name was more helpful and preferred, but was also more distracting, than DF participants. There were some important implications for using text-based practices for captioning, as they may be less effective for deaf audiences. A graphical technique, as in this EC system, may be more useful for a deaf audience, especially for speaker identification. Future research will examine the effectiveness of these graphical techniques and components of the EC system in longitudinal studies.

It also seems that the name of the speaker and the associated dialogue moving on-screen, is difficult to follow. As a result, we recommend that captioning should remain in a consistent location on-screen. Future work will examine eye movement, fixation, duration, and user preferences data for placement of captioning, and explore user's perceptual and cognitive workload.

Acknowledgements. Funding for this research was provided by a SSHRC Community-University Research grant. Finally, we gratefully acknowledge the participants in our study who provided their time and effort for this project.

References

1. Canadian Association of Broadcasters (CAB): Closed captioning standards and protocol for Canadian English language television programming services (2008),
   http://www.cab-acr.ca/english/social/captioning/captioning.pdf
2. Canadian Radio-television and Telecommunications Commission (CRTC): A new policy with respect to closed captioning (2007),
   http://www.crtc.gc.ca/archive/ENG/Notices/2007/pb2007-54.htm
3. Harkins, J.E., Korres, E., Virvan, B., Singer, B.: Caption Features for Indicating Non-Speech Information: Guidelines for the Captioning Industry. Gallaudet Research Institute (1996)
4. ICT: ITC Guidance on Standards for Subtitling. Independent Television Commission, London (1999)
5. Jacoby, J., Mattel, M.S.: Three-Point Likert Scales Are Good Enough. Journal of Marketing Research (JMR) 11(8), 495–500 (1971)

6. King, C., Lasasso, C., Short, D.: Digital Captioning: Effects of Color-Coding and Placement in Synchronized Text-Audio Presentations. In: ED-MEDIA, vol. 94, pp. 329–334 (1994)
7. Quinlan, P.T., Wilton, R.N.: Grouping by proximity or similarity? Competition between the Gestalt principles in vision. Perception 27(4), 417–30 (1998)
8. Spielberg, S.(Producer), Bay, M.(Director): Transformers [Motion Picture]. DreamWorks, United States of America (2007)
9. Vy, Q.V., Fels, D.I.: Using Avatars for Improving Speaker Identification in Captioning. In: Gross, T., Gulliksen, J., Kotzé, P., Oestreicher, L., Palanque, P., Prates, R.O., Winckler, M. (eds.) INTERACT 2009. LNCS, vol. 5727, pp. 916–919. Springer, Heidelberg (2009)

A Real-Time Network Board Game System Using Tactile and Auditory Senses for the Visually Impaired

Daisuke Nagasaka[1], Naoki Kaneda[2], Kazunori Itoh[2],
Makoto Otani[2], Michio Shimizu[3], Masahiko Sugimoto[1,4],
Masami Hashimoto[2], and Mizue Kayama[2]

[1] Graduate School of Science and Technology, Shinshu University
4-17-1 Wakasato, Nagano-shi, Nagano 380-8553 Japan
t09a542@shinshu-u.ac.jp
[2] Faculty of Engineering, Shinshu University
4-17-1 Wakasato, Nagano-shi, Nagano 380-8553 Japan
t055021@shinshu-u.ac.jp,
{itoh,otani,hasimoto,kayama}@cs.shinshu-u.ac.jp
[3] Nagano Prefectural College
8-49-7 Miwa. Nagano-shi, Nagano 380-8525 Japan
michio@nagano-kentan.ac.jp
[4] Takushoku University Hokkaido Junior College
4558 Memu, Fukagawa-shi, Hokkaido 074-8585 Japan
sugimoto@takushoku-hc.ac.jp

Abstract. In this paper, we introduce an interactive board game system using tactile and auditory senses for the visually impaired. Reversi was implemented because it has relatively simple rules. We performed experiments to evaluate the system with visually impaired and sighted persons. Results show that the visually impaired could play Reversi smoothly using the interactive system.

Keywords: visually impaired person, Reversi, tactile guide, speech guide, auditory display, vibrating stimulus.

1 Introduction

Recently, in order to improve the quality of life for people with visual impairment, various communication systems using a personal computer (PC), such as network board games, have been studied [1-3]. Board games are fun not only for sighted people but also for the visually impaired, and some board games can be played using a PC [4]. However, although computer board games enable us to play against people at a distance through the Internet, we cannot recognize the board and piece positions by touching.

To solve this problem, we developed a computer board game system which can provide tactile information and auditory information to players. In this work, Reversi [5] is

K. Miesenberger et al. (Eds.): ICCHP 2010, Part I, LNCS 6179, pp. 255–262, 2010.

implemented using the system we have developed [6]. Reversi is also known as Othello. We implemented Reversi because it has relatively simple rules compared with other games such as Go and Checkers, and lots of people play it.

This paper describes improvements to our system's auditory interfaces and an interactive system to play Reversi through the Internet for the visually impaired. In addition, experimental results show that the visually impaired can play Reversi using our interactive system.

2   Components of the Board Game System

When we play Reversi, first of all, we need to grasp the arrangement of pieces on the board. Then, we put a piece at an available board position. Such information is called *positional information* in this work. Furthermore, while playing Reversi, a player has to handle some information: piece colors, available positions, start and end of the game, and whether the player won or lost the game. Such information is called *semantic information* in this work. In this system, *positional information* is provided using an auditory display and a speech guide (AquesTalk[7]), while *semantic information* is provided using vibrating stimuli and the speech guide. Input devices for the *positional information* are a tactile guide and an input interface attached to a finger.

Figure 1 shows a block diagram of the interactive board game system. This system consists of five input/output devices. The system employs a client-server model for data communication, which facilitates expansion of the system. The tactile guide for Reversi is shown in Fig. 2.

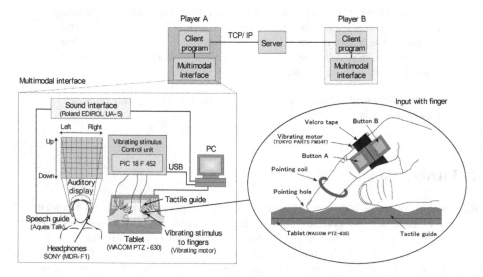

Fig. 1. Block diagram of the board game system

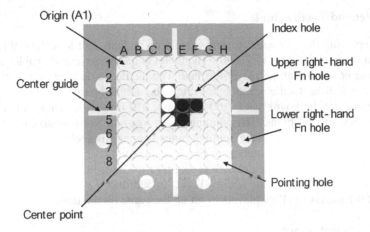

Fig. 2. Layout of tactile guide for Reversi

Reversi using the system proceeds as follows:

(a) *Player A* selects a black or white piece to start the game by pushing *button B* with his/her index finger pointing at the upper-right or lower-right function hole (*Fn* hole) of the tactile guide, respectively.

(b) The speech guide informs both players of each player's turn, namely, which player goes first.

(c) Using vibrating stimuli, the speech guide, and the auditory display, *Player A* searches for available positions and, subsequently, puts his/her piece on the board. *Semantic information* such as available positions and piece colors are provided by the speech guide and the vibrating stimuli. Three vibration motors (coin type coreless vibration motor; FM34F, Tokyo Parts) are installed on the index finger of the right hand and the ring and index finger of the left hand. The corresponding information is also provided by the speech guide and the auditory display. *Player A* can determine the position of the index finger of his/her right hand by pushing *button A*. Also, *Player A* puts his/her piece by pushing *button B*. Then, the board position at which *Player A* put his/her piece is transmitted to *Player B*'s PC.

(d) The speech guide informs *Player B* of the board position where *Player A* put his/her piece. Then, the system automatically changes all the white pieces lying on a straight line between the new black piece and any anchoring black pieces into black pieces.

(e) The speech guide informs both players that *Player A*'s turn is over. Then, *Player B* operates in the same manner as *Player A*.

(f) Players take alternate turns. If one player cannot make a valid move, the speech guide informs the player that the turn passes back to the other player. If neither player can move, the speech guide informs the players that the game is over and which player is the winner.

The five input/output devices are explained below.

2.1 Tablet and Tactile Guide

To enable playing the computer Reversi game with realistic tactile feeling, this system employs a tablet (WACOM PTZ-630). The tablet is inexpensive and enables us to get the absolute position that the player touched. The tactile guide is placed on the tablet to produce a similar tactile sense as touching the actual board. The tactile guide is made from an acrylic board that is 160-mm long, 210-mm wide, 4-mm thick and has pointing holes and *Fn* holes. The pointing holes form an 8 x 8 matrix to imitate an actual board. The diameter of the pointing holes is approximately 1 cm to fit the size of a finger. The letters and numbers in Fig. 2 respectively represent the row and column addresses of the pointing holes. The origin of the coordinate system is located at the top-left pointing hole whose address is A1. In addition, *Fn* holes are also provided outside of the matrix to allow players to set up the game on the tablet.

2.2 Finger Input Interface

An illustration of the instruments which are attached to a finger is shown Fig. 1. The pointing coil is used to input *positional information* to the system by using electromagnetic induction. The pointing coil is attached to the first joint of the index finger like a ring. Moreover, *buttons A* and *B* are attached respectively at the middle of the second and third joint, which correspond to left and right buttons of a mouse. With the pointing coil, the tablet detects the state of the buttons and the index finger position. The buttons can also be used to determine commands. As stated above, if *button A* is pushed, the board position of the index finger and *semantic information* are output through headphones (SONY MDR-F1). Also, if *button B* is pushed, *positional information* is conveyed to the system.

2.3 Vibrating Stimulus

We use a small vibration motor so that input movement is not disturbed. To provide information about piece color and available positions, vibration motors are attached to the right index finger, the left index and ring finger. The motor at the right index finger vibrates when the player's right index finger points at available positions. Similarly, two motors at the left ring and index fingers vibrate when the player's right index finger points at positions on which black or white pieces already exist. The motors vibrate for 70-ms at a frequency of 200-Hz.

2.4 Speech Guide

Game mode announcements, position coordinates, and choice of various commands are output through the headphones using synthesized speech. The female voice of AquesTalk is chosen as the synthesized speech for its availability and clear voice. If *button A* is pushed, the board position of the index finger is announced. Furthermore, the speech guide also provides *semantic information* to the players as well as information about the game progress such as the start or end of the game and the game result.

2.5 Auditory Display

The conveyed *positional information* is used by the auditory display which provides auditory *positional information* to the players through a set of headphones. 3D sounds are presented to the players so that they can recognize *positional information* projected on a vertical plane in a 3D auditory space, as demonstrated in Fig. 1. Table 1 illustrates the relation between sound image positions and pointing holes on the tactile guide. In the next chapter, we explain the way to make white noise convoluted with HRTFs (Head Related Transfer Functions) [8].

Table 1. The direction of sound images vs. pointing holes on the tactile guide

			Horizontal angle [degree]							
			Left							Right
			−60	−43	−26	−9	9	26	43	60
Vertical angle [degree]	Up	60	A1	B1	C1	D1	E1	F1	G1	H1
		43	A2	B2	C2	D2	E2	F2	G2	H2
		26	A3	B3	C3	D3	E3	F3	G3	H3
		9	A4	B4	C4	D4	E4	F4	G4	H4
		−9	A5	B5	C5	D5	E5	F5	G5	H5
		−26	A6	B6	C6	D6	E6	F6	G6	H6
		−43	A7	B7	C7	D7	E7	F7	G7	H7
	Down	−60	A8	B8	C8	D8	E8	F8	G8	H8

3 Auditory Display Improvements

In the previous system we had developed, the auditory display (*auditory display A*) was implemented using median plane HRTFs obtained by measurements and ITD (Interaural Time Difference) and ILD (Interaural Level Difference) adjustments. However, *auditory display A* has a problem that the player cannot grasp the positions near the center of the board easily. To solve this problem, we developed a new auditory display (*auditory display B*). In *auditory display B*, 64 spatialized audio signals are produced by convolving a source signal with HRTFs for 64 source positions at a distance of 50-cm from the listener, which were obtained by measurements using a dummy head (KOKEN SAMURAI). We conducted an experiment to compare both auditory displays.

3.1 Method

Three sighted persons whose ages are between 20 and 30 years participated in the experiment. Subjects wore an eye mask to simulate blindness. Subjects moved their finger toward the target position from the top right Fn hole as a start position and subsequently pushed *button B*. The time they spent was recorded and their movement was observed. 20 coordinates were chosen evenly from the 64 points. 5 trials were performed for *auditory displays A* and *B*.

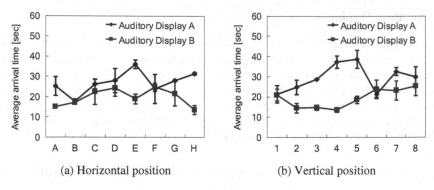

(a) Horizontal position   (b) Vertical position

Fig. 3. Comparison of the average arrival time

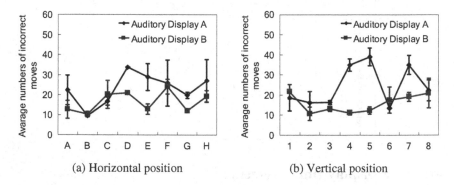

(a) Horizontal position   (b) Vertical position

Fig. 4. Comparison of the average wrong times

3.2 Result

Results are shown in Figs. 3 (a) and (b) and Figs. 4 (a) and (b). Average results and standard deviations among subjects are shown because no marked difference was observed among subjects. Figs. 3 (a) and (b) show the average arrival time in seconds at each column and row of the board position. Figs. 4 (a) and (b) show the average number of incorrect moves at each column and row of the board position.

Figures 3 (a) and (b) reveal that the average arrival time is generally smaller with *auditory display B* than *auditory display A*; with *auditory display A*, the average arrival time is larger when the target position is closer to the center of the board. Moreover, Figs. 4 (a) and (b) demonstrate that the average number of incorrect moves is larger with *auditory display A* than *auditory display B*. Additionally, with *auditory display A*, the average arrival time and the average number of incorrect moves vary prominently among different target positions.

The above results reveal that using *auditory display B*, subjects can reach target positions faster and more accurately with a smaller variation in performance among various target positions. Therefore, we use *auditory display B* in our system.

4 Evaluation of the System's Effectiveness

An experiment was performed to evaluate the system's effectiveness, namely, if the visually impaired can play Reversi smoothly using the system.

4.1 Method

Four subjects participated in the experiment. Two subjects were visually impaired persons who had previously played Reversi for the blind (*Blind 1* and 2), and the other two subjects were sighted persons with an eye mask (*Sighted 1* and 2). *Blind 1* and 2 played the game against each other, and so did *Sighted 1* and 2. The conditions are as follows: 1) using our system (*Proposed*) and 2) using Reversi for the blind (*Conventional*). Moreover, two sighted persons played Reversi in the following way: 3) using our system without an eye mask (*Visual*). For each play, the time to put a piece was measured, and the behavior of subjects was observed.

4.2 Result

Figures 5 (a) and (b) show the results of the first player and the second player in each case. The abscissa and ordinate represent the number of moves and the elapsed time, respectively. The results demonstrate that all the subjects could play Reversi by using this system. Figure 5 (a) reveal that the visually impaired can play Reversi in a time close to that by a sighted person without an eye mask. Moreover, both Figs. 5 (a) and (b) indicate that the sighted persons took longer to put a piece in the latter half of the game. The visually impaired were able to find available positions quickly, thereby indicating that they played the game smoothly. On the other hand, it was difficult for sighted persons to find available positions. In the first half of the game, the visually impaired could play the game smoothly when using Reversi for the blind. However, in the latter half of the game, the visually impaired could play the game more smoothly using our system. The visually impaired were able to find available positions easily by using the vibrating stimuli and the speech guide. Therefore, the vibrating stimuli and the speech guide are useful interfaces to play the game.

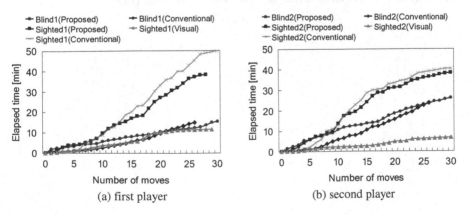

Fig. 5. Relation between number of moves and elapsed time

Consequently, it can be concluded that the visually impaired can play Reversi by using this system. The subjects reported various sentiments and problems about the system such as "It is very fun.", "I feel frustrated at having lost.", and "It is hard to understand the change in the board after putting a piece."

5 Conclusion

We developed an interactive system to play Reversi through the Internet for the visually impaired. Experimental results show that the visually impaired can play Reversi by using the system. In future work, to simplify the system, we will use a touch panel. Moreover, we plan to apply this system to other board games such as Mini-Go and Checkers.

References

1. Kaczmirek, L., Wolff, K.G.: Survey Design for Visually Impaired and Blind People. In: Proc. UAHCI 2007, Part I, Held as Part of HCII 2007, pp. 374–381 (2007)
2. Bruder, I., Jaworek, G.: Blind and Visually Impaired People, Human-Computer Interaction and Access to Graphics. In: Miesenberger, K., Klaus, J., Zagler, W.L., Karshmer, A.I. (eds.) ICCHP 2008. LNCS, vol. 5105, pp. 767–769. Springer, Heidelberg (2008)
3. Yatani, K.: Towards Designing User Interface on Mobile Touch-screen Devices for People with Visual Impairment. In: Proc. UIST 2009, pp. 37–40 (2009)
4. http://www.afb.org/Section.asp?SectionID=40&TopicID=219&DocumentID=2241 (accessed 2010/03/30)
5. http://en.wikipedia.org/wiki/Reversi (accessed 2010/03/30)
6. Hamaguchi, Y., Nagasaka, D., Tamesue, T., Itoh, K., Shimizu, M., Sugimoto, M., Hashimoto, M., Kayama, M.: A Multimodal Board Game System Interface Using Finger Input for Visually Impaired Computer Users. In: Proc. UAHCI 2009 Part II, held as part of HCII 2009, pp. 68–77 (2009)
7. http://www.a-quest.com/products/aquestalk.html (accessed 2010/03/30) (in Japanese)
8. Blauert, J.: Spatial Hearing. revised edn. MIT Press, Cambridge (1997)

Realizing Accessible Tourism by Matching Stakeholders: Introduction to the Special Thematic Session

Kerstin Matausch[1] and Franz Pühretmair[2]

[1] University of Linz, Institute Integriert Studieren, Altenbergerstr. 69, 4040 Linz, Austria
kerstin.matausch@jku.at
[2] Competence network information technology to support the integration of people with disabilities (KI-I), Hafenstraße 47-51, 4020 Linz, Austria
franz puehretmair@ki-i.at

Abstract. The following paper discusses the necessity for a tourism for all which is realized along the whole tourism service chain and the need to match various stakeholders. It points out that policy- and management-driven activities are advantageous and that the achievement of ambitious goals has to be realized by single steps.

Keywords: accessible tourism, tourism for all, stakeholder interests.

1 Introduction

The tourism industry is a complex system which compasses of independent providers aiming to serve the consumer. A variety of stakeholders are involved, often with conflicting needs, wants and interests in the tourism industry [2]. The potential players involved in the provision of accessible tourism products range from specialised operators that serve that exclusively serve this market to mainstream providers that are often not yet concerned with accessibility. The following categories stand exemplary for involved stakeholders. They have a strong impact on the arrangement and provision of accessible tourism offers, services and information:

- Customers with our without disabilities
- Tourism providers (i.e. venue owners, harbourer, service personnel, etc.)
- Tourism intermediaries and vendors
- Organizations and single persons creating the physical environment (i.e. architects, construction and sanitary firms)
- Marketing industry
- Transportation providers
- Sport, culture and leisure time providers

Basically, a match of all stakeholder interests is necessary for a successful realization of tourism for all. In addition to this Neumann [1] presents in a study which deals with economic impulses of accessible tourism the accessibility aspect along the whole tourism service-chain as a necessity to gain best possible economic effects.

K. Miesenberger et al. (Eds.): ICCHP 2010, Part I, LNCS 6179, pp. 263–265, 2010.

2 Aspects of Success for the Development of Accessible Tourism

Single regional projects such as «Fränkisches Seenland» [6] and «Barrierefreie Modellregion im Verband Naturpark Thüringer Wald» [7] in Germany and Tourism for All UK [3] are demonstrating that an adjustment of stakeholder interests is possible and advantageous for the customers and in an economic and ethic way for themselves. They still are facing the external environment and the transportation aspect to and from the tourism destination but reveal an internal stakeholder match which is exemplary for other projects.

What is necessary to realize such an internal match? How is best practice characterized? Existing research is lacking of scientific-based results concerning how to best match stakeholder needs. Practice shows the necessity to assign on legal, social and economic experiences. To achieve success, it is not just a question of legal frameworks. It is, more than anything, a matter of public attitudes and customer service and statisfaction.

Neumann [5] lists seven aspects of success. They describe affairs which are necessary to realize accessible tourism along the service chain by matching stakeholders:

1. Commitment of decision makers: Strong support by the local regional tourism management and political commitment are required. They have the «penetration power» to reach ambitious aims but are also dependent on single persons and organizations which have to commit themselves to accessibility.
2. Coordination and continuity: A coordinating person or organization is needed. Persons in charge of the projects have to belief in the success of the project in order to continuously extend activities and the partnership.
3. Networking and participation: A successful network needs several members from the tourism and non-tourism sector. Networking among local players as well as with external stakeholders is crucial. They are positioned along the tourism service chain and integrate people with disabilities in the planning and decision making to design and offer valuable, accurate and reliable services and information.
4. Strategic planning: Basically accessible tourism can be implemented by single actions but is more successful when planned strategically such as the region «Barrierefreie Modellregion im Verband Naturpark Thüringer Wald» [7] is demonstrating. They intend an above-average provision of accessible tourism offers aiming to gain a healthy margin with respect to other tourism-generating regions. Strategic planning compass of accessibility as an integral part of all planning and public relation.
5. Qualification and knowledge transfer: Service providers and employees have to be sensitized and qualified. Referring to the aspect of networking a knowledge transfer and personal coaching i.e. regarding practical experiences between partners is crucial.
6. Development of infrastructure and offer: Tourism along the whole service-chain needs the development of a mostly comprehensive accessibility and thus consideration of infrastructure and an adaptability according to specific needs. Additional stakeholders such as cultural, sport and outdoor activity providers should be involved.

7. Communication and distribution: The success of above mentioned criteria is dependent on according target group oriented marketing and communication channels. Often tourism providers that offer accessible products and services fail to communicate this fact, failing to inform people with accessibility requirements and therefore missing a huge market opportunity. A definition of goals, target groups and communication strategy is needed.

A journey of a thousand miles has to start with a single step, single persons have to make the first move. The tourism industry can count itself lucky for more and more steps are done, and sensitivity and knowledge is growing. This Special Thematic Session will introduce some examples which can support a fully accessible tourism chain in the future.

3   The Special Thematic Session: Accessible Tourism

This Special Thematic Session will be characterized by reports on single projects which are carried out in order to support single aspects of accessible tourism. The project Route4you is dealing with accessible route-planning. The project concentrates on the implementation of a user-specific web-based route planning considering predominantly the needs of blind and visually impaired people as well as wheelchair users. It is thus contributing a crucial aspect for the mobility aspect which is often unconsidered in the area of tourism for all.

The second paper concentrates on another transportation-related aspect which plays a crucial role for an improved accessibility. It concerns user feed-back during the development of public transport information systems. It points out the necessity and advantages of user involvement.

The third paper discusses from a more general view the accessibility of events and gives advice on various aspects which are crucial in order to realize accessible events.

References

1. Neumann, P.: Ökonomische Impulse eines barrierefreien Tourismus für alle (2003),
   http://www.bmwi.de/BMWi/Navigation/Service/
   publikationen,did=28398.html
2. OSSATE, Accessibility Market and Stakeholder Analysis (2005),
   http://www.accessibletourism.org/?i=enat.en.reports.426
3. Tourism for All UK, http://www.tourismforall.org.uk/
4. Bundes-Behindertengleichstellungsgesetz,
   http://www.ris.bka.gv.at/Dokumente/BgblAuth/BGBLA_2005_I_82/
   BGBLA_2005_I_82.html
5. Neumann, P.: Barrierefreier Tourismus für Alle in Deutschland – Erfolgsfaktoren und Maßnahmen zur Qualitätssteigerung (2008),
   http://www.bmwi.de/BMWi/Navigation/Service/
   publikationen,did=269772.html
6. Fränkisches Seenland, http://www.seenland-barrierefrei.de/
7. Barrierefreie Modellregion im Verband Naturpark Thüringer Wald,
   http://www.naturpark-thueringer-wald.de/

Planning of Inclusive and Accessible Events

Kerstin Matausch and Klaus Miesenberger

University of Linz, Institute Integriert Studieren, Altenbergerstr. 69, 4040 Linz, Austria
{kerstin.matausch,klaus.miesenberger}@jku.at

Abstract. This paper presents a "Handbook for Accessible Events" providing structured advice to prepare and run events which are accessible and inviting to a divers set of participants including in particular those with disabilities. This handbook has been created with the goal to be adaptable to different kind and scales of events and, besides general accessibility requirements, to specifically address selected target groups. The "Handbook for Accessible Events" is available on an open source basis to support as many as possible event organizers but in particular also to invite to contribute out of own experiences and expertise to brush up the tool.

Keywords: accessibility, inclusion, events, accessible events.

1 Introduction

Events are usually characterized by their periodic or even unique nature. This temporal confinement and the density of parallel activities tends to neglect accessibility issues which are often only of importance for only a few participants. Although, in general, the understanding of the importance of accessibility increases, this specialty of events might lead to accessibility problems if not planned accordingly and if the knowledge needed is not integrated. Typical barriers, therefore, frequently complicate the visit of events by people with disabilities, but also older adults and parents with children. The exclusion of single groups and the withholding of social interaction that events as platforms usually provide have to be seen as weaknesses. A consideration of accessibility matters affords improvements for everyone. A fully accessible event, however, can only then be realized when the whole service-chain has been considered and designed in an accessible way [5].

Accessibility as an issue for events is often limited to special events addressing people with disabilities in particular. Reasons seem to be a lack of awareness and knowledge in the public for the purpose and impact of events designed to all. The aim of organizing an accessible event should be to enable all participants, and in particular participants with disabilities, to take part in all aspects of the event, including networking, formal and informal social components, respectful treatment and maintenance of the participants' dignity at all times. Event accessibility should be therewith recognized as an integral part of event organization, rather than an add-on at a later stage.

K. Miesenberger et al. (Eds.): ICCHP 2010, Part I, LNCS 6179, pp. 266–272, 2010.
© Springer-Verlag Berlin Heidelberg 2010

Another constraint regarding the realization of accessible and inclusive events has to be identified with regard to organization committees. First, during the planning and organization many individuals interact, each of them being responsible for single sub areas. An in-house coordination is necessary. Secondly, different disabilities ask for different accessibility specifications but many organization committees are lacking of according knowledge. Event organizers are thus facing a challenge. Clearing the hurdle, however, will without question lead to improvements regarding the presentation of an event as well as concerning its image.

Following this accessibility should be considered from the very beginning and become an integral part of the whole workflow in planning and running an event. The "Handbook for Accessible Events" intends giving access to a profound body of knowledge allowing an according planning and running of events.

2 State of the Art

In general a number of guidelines for the planning of accessible events do exist but they differ from the underlying one. Whereas some are more oriented towards small or medium-sized events [9], others give general proposals what one should consider without giving detailed information how to realize and implement the mentioned issues [3, 6]. So, the user has to gather useful information from different providers.

In former times many accentuated physical disabilities and reduced accessibility references concerning further target groups. This changed during the last years. More guides for the planning of accessible events nowadays consider a wider scale of accessibility [2, 6], but hardly anyone refers to the needs of people with special learning difficulties. Tiresias [10] indeed points out that people with specific learning difficulties are facing problems in understanding but hardly proposes how to improve accessibility for this target growing group. The number of people asking for Easy-to-Read service is mounting because of increasing illiteracy even in highly developed western countries [8].

The "Handbook for Accessible Events" [4] intends to provide a comprehensive guide for the planning and realization of accessible events. First, it addresses accessibility of a variety of events including big scientific conferences, exhibitions or symposia, it compass of accessibility background information and checklists and third consider a wide target group of people with specific needs.

3 The Handbook for Accessible Events

3.1 Background and Acknowledgement

The "Handbook for Accessible Events" has been started in the framework of the EU funded project CWST (Conferences, Workshops, Seminars and Tutorials to support eInclusion) [1]. In the frame of this project a lot of experiences and know how has been gained concerning accessible event organization by supporting the organization of 25 events. As a result and sustainable output of the project, besides the events themselves, event organization software and other tools, the handbook has been started.

3.2 How to Use the Handbook

Although, the handbook originated from a more academic and research context, the information provided is relevant to other types of events, either small-, medium- or large-sized. The focus is on events which involve some combination of speakers, presentations, discussion, interaction and networking. Due to a categorization the handbook, however, is modular and can be adapted to one's own needs. An event profile offered may help the user to classify the own event and to define which modules of the handbook one should at least use for own preparations.

The handbook covers the whole organization process of events including i.e. the venue choice, accommodating participants, public relation, the program, registration, social events, catering, transportation, presentations, interactive sessions, and proceedings or other publications. The single topics cover a description of the activity areas, a checklist which summarizes what the handbook user should consider during the preparation of this topic. It offers detailed descriptions of tasks as well as according examples which enable a deeper understanding of tasks. Many topics interrelate, so references between the modules are given which may help to consider all necessary tasks which accord to one topic.

The handbook give suggestions for the following target groups: visually impaired people, blind people, people with mobility impairment, wheelchair users, people who are hard of hearing, deaf people, and people with specific learning difficulties. Information for an accessible design of events related to one or more of these target groups is additionally highlighted by pictograms at the right hand side of the textual information.

3.3 Guidelines on How to Make an Event Accessible

It is advisable to event organizing committee to encourage the participation of people with disabilities. So, the "Handbook for Accessible Events" [4] foresees the participation of people with disabilities as an integral part during the whole preparation. This allows the provision of an event which is accessible to non-disabled and disabled participants at a wide scale. Thus, the handbook gives advices with respect to the following topics:

1. **Announcements:** The handbook gives proposals what to consider during the creation of accessible print, electronic, film and audio documents as well as accessible web applications including a conference management tool and a reviewing tool.
2. **Program building** is of crucial importance and includes a number of accessibility aspects to be remembered. It comprises i.e. the definition of topics, a (first) call for papers or contributions, the submission of contributions, their review, an announcement of presentations and presenters as well as the specification of the schedule.
3. The section on **"finance, registration, payment"** is concerned by accessibility features in such a degree as a drawing up a budget has to consider accessibility (i.e. assistive technologies, speech-to-text reporters, sign language interpretation). Moreover an online registration and payment possibility has to follow W3C WAI standards. A payment opportunity on-site asks for a registration desk which can be reached accessibly and which is accessible itself (i.e. registration documents in accessible format, induction loop)

4. A **help desk** will provide information and assistance to participants including the availability of specific needs assistants.

5. **Transport:** This module is about transport possibilities to the venue and during the event. When visiting the venue the organizers should investigate transport to the venue and their accessibility. The handbook proposes which accessibility information and how it should be published. Moreover, the user finds a checklist for assessing public and private transport to the venue. If the organizers find that it will be very difficult for many participants with specific needs to reach the venue, particularly if they use public transport or require accessible taxis, the organizers should think very seriously about changing venue to one that is easier to reach. The provision of special transportation during the event may help people with mobility Impairment to reach the venue and receptions.

6. **Sign-posting** should be taken seriously and provided at various levels. Visual, tactile, verbal, audio and audio-tactile location maps and sign-posting at the event venue are meaningful in order to address as many participants as possible. Additional notes about sign-posting make sense for people with specific learning difficulties. The handbook gives advice what the sign-posting should contain (i.e. tactile maps: simplified arrangement of rooms, entitling of rooms, different textures for the indication of different features), how the sign-posting should be structured and presented.

Please note to use large print and sans-serif font for your labelling. Remind colours and contrasts. Partially sighted persons need clearly arranged signs; large, serif-less as well as high contrasting print. However, care has to be taken in the choice of colour to maintain high colour contrast with the background and avoid excessive use of colour. This can cause confusion to all participants and is likely to be particularly difficult for some groups of disabled people.

All signage should be displayed in consistent locations, to make it easier to find. Signage should not be obstructed by anything.

Signage should be at eye level or below, since it is more difficult to read sign if you have to peer up at them. Following this signs should be fixed at a height between 85 and 120 cm so that also wheelchair users or people of restricted growth may easily read them.

Visual signage should be well lit, but lighting should be diffuse and avoid glare. Although illuminated signs can be helpful for some groups of disabled participants, they should be avoided, as they can be difficult to look at for other groups of people with disabilities.

In general, information should be provided using clear everyday language which is of especially necessary for people with special learning difficulties.

Fig. 1. Screenshot Sign-Posting [4]

7. The **accommodation** should be checked concerning its accessibility for different groups of guests with specific needs. The handbook offers site accessibility checklists categorized to various disabilities. Moreover, additional information packages for event participants at the accommodation are advisable. They will help them to get all necessary information in advance. The handbook proposes which kind of information the package should contain.

8. **Catering** at the event asks of course for adequate food and drinks. The choice should be done with respect to restrictions deriving from i.e. food allergies, special diets, vegetarian and vegan. Catering has additionally to remember a location which can be reached in an accessible way, accompanying technology and further supporting equipment which enables all audience to listen to speeches or lectures. The handbook transfers knowledge concerning the accessible execution of small breaks in-between as well as receptions at large events.

9. **Conference / Event venue:** During the event organization one has to consider the type of delegates that are to be expected at the event (i.e. conference, meeting, and seminar). The choice of the venue has to be decided accordingly. A conference addressing disability issues, for example, is likely to attract more delegates with disabilities than a conference on a subject unconnected with disabilities. The handbook provides suggestions and checklists for different cases which may organizers help to do accessibility checks for the arrival of venues and the location. The handbook user is informed how to sensitize the staff on-site, how to be prepared for disability assistance dogs as well as for evacuations in case of emergency.

10. A further module is related to **presentation technology** which suggests along with the provision of electronic and non-electronic presentation technology, the provision of an audio system and a check of its interaction with an induction loop.

11. The chapter "**presentation**" familiarizes with alternative accessible formats and additionally refers to the presenters themselves. This needs an investigation who of the presenters has specific needs and which needs are these. The module additionally advices to brief presenters concerning accessible presentations (i.e. slides, abbreviations, the speech itself, and the use of assistive and accompanying technology).

12. Besides already described measures which enable the preparation of an event accessible to a large extent, one should also prepare for the described tasks below which allow the offer of a mostly 'custom made' **specific needs service**.

For an individualized service one should provide a questionnaire asking for single specific needs of participants and a description of services one will offer at the event. The handbook provides as a service to its users samples of specific needs questionnaires. It additionally provides advices for the assignment of specific needs assistants as well as which materials the organization committee should keep ready for participants with disabilities (i.e. route descriptions, maps and the event program in alternative document formats). Finally it describes the necessity of sign language interpretation and speech-to-text translation and what to consider when preparing these offerings.

4   Using the Handbook – An Example

A team of highly motivated people tends to realize a training program and like to execute it in an accessible way as they plan to involve as many people as possible. They use the "Handbook for Accessible Events" as a base for their planning. A first look into the section "Event Profile" of the guide shows that they will not need the whole handbook as they are not planning for a large event. So, they exclude several activity areas such as a section on their website referring to finance, registration and payment, a registration and info desk on-site, and a conference-related program building. They won't need a large catering service but decide to use the proposed principles for the planning of accessible breaks (chapter 9.2). They know that they will not offer any special transport but consider an accessible transportation opportunity to the venue (chapter 6.3). Moreover, they recognize their benefits deriving from the detailed information and checklists for the choice of the venue and rooms, accessible announcements and the advices for the usage of presentation technology and a structuring of presentations. As proposed at the beginning of the handbook they arrange the according task sections to their own individualized guide which meets their needs.

While reading up on the new topic they benefit from the pictured pictograms on the right-hand side of the text passages allowing an easier identification which tasks are meant for which category of disability. Afterwards they collect all checklists from the activity sections, perhaps even like to expand the proposed list and are now ready to start their preparations.

5 Impact

The "Handbook for Accessible Events" [4] provides a mostly comprehensive guide for the planning and realization of accessible events. As it is modularized, adaptable to the size of the event and compass of detailed background information as well as checklists for a wider target group of specific needs, the guide addresses accessibility of a variety of events and disabilities. Due to the usage of pictograms, it helps to categorize accessibility tasks to different beneficiaries.

Moreover, the handbook provides a comprehensive guide including the planning from the very beginning till the actual event execution including many practical examples. These lessons learned during past disability and accessibility related research and practice will help event organizers to better understand the matter.

The handbook should also be seen as an incentive to include accessibility into according educational programs. As the handbook can additionally be downloaded for free [4], we hope to motivate more organizing committees either of events addressing disability issues or even beyond this to prepare and realize accessible events which include as many people as possible.

6 Future Plans

It is intended to further elaborate the check lists in the handbook. It is also planned to implement a checklist tool which allows to select the checkpoints relevant for an own event and which provides the user a personalized check list. Social network facilities should allow further improvements and specialization.

As outlined the handbook is seen as a basis for ongoing co-operation to provide better support for accessible event organization. There are still further specific needs such as allergies or chronic illnesses which should be remembered. Moreover, the technical surrounding is developing and so does the knowledge concerning a best possible serving of needs and demands of people with disabilities. It is thus planned to further update the handbook and to keep it a vivid document.

References

1. CWST: Conferences, Workshops, Seminars and Tutorials to support eInclusion, project homepage, http://cwst.icchp.org
2. Elliot, T., Phipps, L., Harrison, S.: Accessible Events – A good practice guide for staff organizing events in Higher Education, http://new.techdis.ac.uk/resources/files/accessibleevents.pdf
3. Hall, D.: Accessible Event Planning, http://www.queensu.ca/equity/ Accessible%20Event%20Planning%20Checklist.pdf
4. Handbook for Accessible Events, http://cwst.icchp.org/node/63
5. Heiserholt, M.: Events für Alle – Qualitätsstufen für barrierefreie Veranstaltungen, http://www.thueringen.de/imperia/md/content/bb/ seiten_1_50.pdf
6. Kalamidas, O., Götzinger, K.: Barrierefreie Events, http://www.diversityworks.at/newsletter/ checkliste_barrierefreie_events_nl.pdf
7. National Educational Association of Disabled Students, Making Extra-Curricular Activities Inclusive, http://www.neads.ca/en/about/projects/inclusion/guide/ inclusion_reference_guide.pdf
8. Petz, A., Tronbacke, B.: People with Specific Learning Difficulties: Easy to Read and HCI. In: Miesenberger, K., Karshmer, A., Zagler, W., Klaus, J. (eds.) ICCHP 2008. LNCS, vol. 5105, pp. 690–692. Springer, Heidelberg (2008)
9. Planning an accessible meeting, http://www.mcss.gov.on.ca/en/accesson/tools/ planning_meeting.aspx
10. tiresias.org, Accessible Events, http://www.tiresias.org/research/guidelines/ accessible_events.htm

User Feed-Back in the Development of an
Information System for Public Transport

Christian Bühler[1], Helmut Heck[1], Christian Radek[1], Rainer Wallbruch[1],
Josef Becker[2], and Claudia Bohner-Degrell[3]

[1] Forschungsinstitut Technologie und Behinderung, Grundschötteler Str. 40,
58300 Wetter, Germany
baim@ftb-net.de
[2] Rhein-Main-Verkehrsverbund GmbH (RMV), Postfach 14 27,
65704 Hofheim a. Ts., Germany
baim@rmv.de
[3] Rhein-Main-Verkehrsverbund Servicegesellschaft mbH, Am Hauptbahnhof 6,
60329 Frankfurt am Main, Germany
baim@rms-consult.de

Abstract. Within the German projects BAIM and BAIM *plus*, information services for people with reduced mobility have been developed. These accessible and adaptable services provide information on public transport. The challenge was to provide sufficient information so that accessible, barrier free journeys can be planned in advance and undertaken in real life. These services are available on the internet and on telephones (mobile phones) prior to and while travelling. User evaluation of these developed and implemented services lead to notable suggestions for further development activities.

Keywords: accessible public transport, people with reduced mobility, user involvement, information services, barrier-free travelling.

1 Introduction

When people with reduced mobility (e.g. due to a disability, luggage, frailness) want to use public transport they face the problem of finding barrier-free travelling chains (including vehicles, buildings, footpaths, ramps, assistive infrastructure) that correspond to their special needs [1].

Some systems have been developed to provide users with information regarding the accessibility of the public transport facilities [2, 3].

The German research project BAIM *plus*, based on the results of the preceeding project BAIM, focuses on the development of innovative information services including the use of real time data, enhanced travel planning applications, electronic travel companions, and spoken dialog based systems. While early project stages focused on user requirements analysis [4], and the needs and requirements of public transport providers [5], in the recent project phase users were involved in the practical test of the system in the field. Several services with different access paths have been developed

K. Miesenberger et al. (Eds.): ICCHP 2010, Part I, LNCS 6179, pp. 273–279, 2010.

and were evaluated: services available via internet and services available via a spoken dialogue based system.

The developed services include a journey planner for barrier-free journeys according to a preselected specified requirements profile. Query results yield not only information about possible travel connections but also detailed information regarding paths and rides, and information about vehicles and stations.

2   The BAIM *plus* Travel Information Services

The services developed in BAIM *plus* cover information about schedules, vehicles and stations. In the query interface of the journey planner shown in figure 1, different user profiles (e.g. no limitation, wheelchair user, restricted in walking) can be chosen in order to get customized suggestions for barrier-free tavel connections as well as information about the accessibility of facilities to be used during the journey.

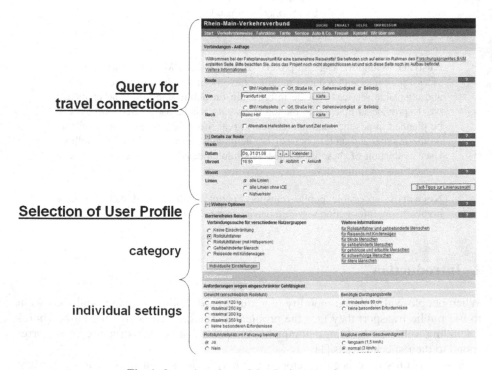

Fig. 1. Query interface of the the journey planner

The journey planner takes realtime data of facilities into account. This means for instance, if a wheelchair user searches for the best connection from station A to station B and normally would be required to change lines at station C and the required elevator at station C is currently out of order, other wheelchair-accessible connections would be listed in the schedule (figure 2).

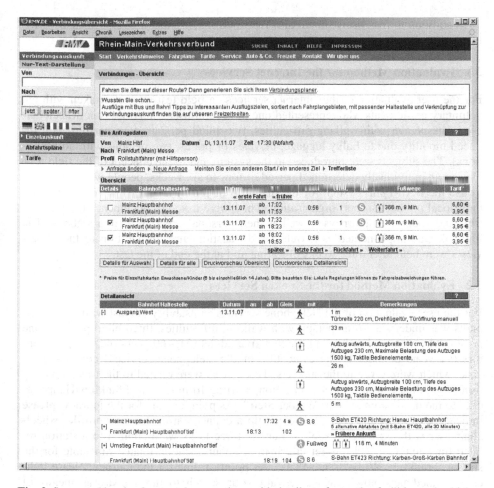

Fig. 2. Suggested barrier-free travel connections with details on foot paths, facilities and vehicles

Different situations need different access paths: For the planning of a journey the information system is available via the standard web pages of the public transport service provider RMV; for information during the journey the system is available via mobile devices. Additionally, the most important information is available also via a spoken dialogue based telephone system (either for planning or while travelling), which covers the special needs of travellers with low vision and elderly users as well. While the developed "internet services" are already available to the public, the "telephone services" are currently available as a prototype version.

3 User Evaluation

The user evaluation of the "internet services" aimed at proving the full functionality of the services in practice while the user evaluation on the "spoken services" rather was focused on aspects for further improvement of the prototype version.

In addition to that, users should also report on inconsistent data (for instance if the information obtained contradicted users' experiences).

3.1 Evaluation Method for the Internet Services

For the user evaluation of the "internet services" a field test was undertaken with ten voluntary participants who represented one of several user categories (one wheelchair user, one person with walking difficulties, two blind persons, four persons with reduced mobility due to bulky luggage, bicycles or prams, two persons with no limitations). The subjects were introduced to the system and to the concept of the field test. During an individually determined period of four to six weeks, people were instructed to use the BAIM *plus* system for the planning of journeys and while travelling with their local public transport organisation. They were asked to document their planned trips and undertaken journeys as well as their personal experiences in a logbook. The logbook was implemented as a web based questionnaire. In addition to this, interviews were held after three weeks of testing and at the end of the test.

3.2 Evaluation Method for the Spoken Services

For the user evaluation of the "telephone services" a usability lab test with 14 participants was undertaken (one person with walking difficulties, three blind persons, one person who was hard of hearing, three active adults (51 - 60 years old), and six seniors (61 years or older)). The evaluation of the "telephone services" comprised six tasks which were given to the subjects. Three tasks were related to the travel connection (e.g. "Please search for a connection, starting from station 'Frankfurt Hauptwache' to the destination station 'Weißer Stein'. As point of time for the journey, please indicate 'tomorrow at 4 pm'. Please call up a connection for the user profile 'wheelchair user with assisting person'."). Further three tasks were applied to a station related timetable (e.g. "Please get information about a station related timetable for the station 'Frankfurt, Willy-Brandt-Platz'. As point of time for the journey, please indicate 'immediately now'. Please restrain your search to the subway as means of travel."). Subjects were asked to complete these tasks while their statements and activities were recorded.

In addition to the evaluation by users, the "telephone services" were also evaluated by usability experts.

4 Results

4.1 Internet Services

The test persons identified "data problems" in 9 out of 59 trips (15,3 %). The wheelchair user reported a technical problem with the profile for wheelchair users.

There were some remarks with regard to the appearance of the web site of the travel planner. Comments made by the test subjects included that essential information such as the state of operation of elevators and escalators (i.e. realtime data) should be more prominently visible, the web site of the travel planner should be optimized to provide more clarity, and while the information regarding the lengths of footpaths was welcomed, the description of those received some criticism.

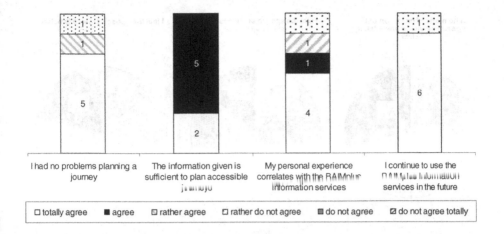

Fig. 3. Experiences of the test persons with the internet services

The test candidates were asked to rate satisfaction and helpfulness for each planned and/or undertaken journey. The marks given for satisfaction and helpfulness correlated with encountered problems. Journeys without reported problems were rated as 'very helpful' / 'very satisfied' or 'quite helpful' / 'quite satisfied'. Journeys with problems were rated more negatively.

As shown in figure 3, six out of seven users who participated in the final interview at the end of the field test will continue to use these services in the future.

4.2 Spoken Services

Test users of the "spoken services" identified several weaknesses of the prototype dialogue system. For instance, right at the start the system would enquire whether the users wanted to use the travel planner or the time table. The question was phrased in such a way that users using the system for the first time would say 'yes' after the system said 'travel planner'. However, the setup was as such that the system expected the user to say either 'travel planer' or 'time table'. As the voice recognition operates at the time of speaking, the answer 'yes' by the user caused an error.

More experienced users knew that and could use the system much more efficiently as they would just started talking as soon as a question was spoken by the system. It took a bit of getting use to this as it is considered impolite to speak up while spoken to. Politeness was also an issue which was mentioned by the users. In general the system was considered to be too polite.

Other issues which were identified by the test subjects and usability experts included shorter instructions, shortcuts to leave the system, a help command to get assistance, more use of synonyms and colloquial expressions in order to enhance the performance of the voice recognition unit etc.

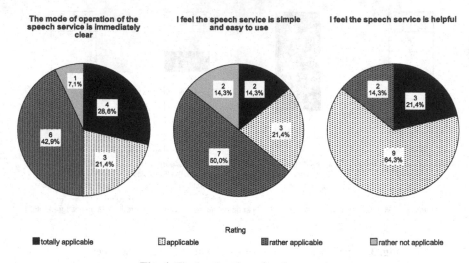

The mode of operation of the speech service is immediately clear

I feel the speech service is simple and easy to use

I feel the speech service is helpful

Rating

■ totally applicable   ⊞ applicable   ▦ rather applicable   ☐ rather not applicable

Fig. 4. Final estimation of spoken services

The most interesting result of the analysis of user comments and activities was that blind persons had the least problems with the "spoken services". All test candidates had a positive view of the system. Two third of the test persons said that the mode of operation was immediately clear to them, that it was easy to use and very helpful.

5 Discussion

Active user involvement was an important success factor in BAIM *plus* and the pre-ceeding BAIM research project. Users were involved at various stages of develop-ment of the information services. The methodologies employed included field testing and laboratory set ups of operational systems, prototype systems and mock-ups. The key issue was not assessment using large numbers of participants but the time con-suming yet rewarding individual qualitative investigation. Combined with assess-ments carried out by usability experts, this approach led to fruitful input in the ongo-ing development process of the novel information services.

The importance and potential of user involvement in the process of development of information services was underlined.

Field testing of the internet services and laboratory evaluation of the spoken dialog based services provide valuable input for further improvements of the services being developed. However, the evaluation of the usefulness of certain system functionalities appeared to be biased by improper functionality of that feature in some cases. This means that usefulness was valued higher in case of features without faults in contrast to features which were faulty.

Acknowledgement

BAIM *plus* is a research project co-funded by the German Federal Ministry for Econ-omy and Technology following a decision of the German Federal Parliament (refer-ence: 19 P 8002 B).

The project consortium consists of two public transport associations: Rhein-Main-Verkehrsverbund RMV (coordinator) and Verkehrsverbund Berlin-Brandenburg VBB; their traffic and information technology provider: IVU Traffic Technologies AG; the information service provider HaCon Ingenieurgesellschaft mbH; the service provider of spoken dialog based systems SemanticEdge GmbH; the rehabilitation centre Evangelische Stiftung Volmarstein with its Research Institute for Technology and Disability (FTB).

References

1. Bühler, C., Wallbruch, R., Becker, J., Heck, H., Sischka, D.: Users' Information Needs in Accessible Public Transport. In: Challenges for Assistive Technology, AAATE 2007, pp. 831–835. IOS Press, Amsterdam (2007)
2. Sustrate, V., von Grumbkow, P., Heck, H., Becker, J., Pilz, A., Franzen, J., Dirks, S.: Implementation and Evaluation of Information Services on Public Transport for People with Reduced Mobility. In: 2nd Int. ASK-IT Conference, Nuremburg, June 26-27 (2008), http://www.ask-it.org
3. Pühretmair, F., Wöß, W.: A Flexible Concept to Establish Accessible Information in Tourism Web-Pages. In: Miesenberger, K., Klaus, J., Zagler, W.L., Karshmer, A.I. (eds.) ICCHP 2008. LNCS, vol. 5105, pp. 981–988. Springer, Heidelberg (2008)
4. Bühler, C., Heck, H., Becker, J.: How to Inform People with Reduced Mobility about Public Transport. In: Miesenberger, K., Klaus, J., Zagler, W.L., Karshmer, A.I. (eds.) ICCHP 2008. LNCS, vol. 5105, pp. 973–980. Springer, Heidelberg (2008)
5. Bühler, C., Heck, H., Becker, J., Radek, C., Wallbruch, R.: Information Services on Public Transport for People with Reduced Mobility – a Survey among Public Transport Providers. In: Assistive Technology from Adapted Equipment to Inclusive Environments, AAATE 2009, pp. 231–235. IOS Press, Amsterdam (2009)

User-Specific Web-Based Route Planning

Bettina Pressl[1], Christoph Mader[2], and Manfred Wieser[1]

[1] Institute of Navigation and Satellite Geodesy
Graz University of Technology, Austria
`pressl@tugraz.at, wieser@geomatics.tu-graz.ac.at`
[2] Solvion information managment
Graz, Austria
`christoph.mader@solvion.net`

Abstract. A web-application for route planning should allow users with special requirements like blind or visually impaired people, and wheelchair users to increase their mobility in urban areas. Especially when visiting an unknown city as a tourist, detailed information is needed. Based on a developed digital map for these special user groups, route planning of barrier-free routes with additional information and pre-trip training will be provided. Moreover, public transport is essential for these user groups. Individual user profiles enable the definition of preferences for every single user which will influence route planning and visualization. The upcoming challenges in data modeling and route planning by using time schedules of public transport and multi-criteria optimization are discussed in this article.

1 Introduction

The research project *Route4you* at the *Institute of Navigation and Satellite Geodesy of the Graz University of Technology* is funded by the program *ways2go* of the *Austrian Federal Ministry of Transportation, Innovation, and Technology*. A close cooperation with the *Beauftragte für Behindertenfragen der Stadt Graz* permits the involvement of specific user groups into the project. In addition, the *Graz AG* is responsible for including the public transport, and *Solvion information management* supports the software development.

This project deals with the development of a prototype for an web-based route planning service for people with disabilities who have special requirements on their mobility. The system is based on the fact that people with different types of disabilities have contrasting demands on a planned route, e.g., blind people have other requirements on a barrier-free route than wheelchair users. While for the latter, routes must not contain stairs, for blind people obstacles on the pavement (e.g., traffic signs) are dangerous. Moreover, blind people need much more information about the surrounding like buildings or infrastructure when visiting unfamiliar cities [1]. To realize the planning of a barrier-free route for different user requirements, each user should be able to define their own individual user profile to specify the criteria for an optimal route from an arbitrary starting

K. Miesenberger et al. (Eds.): ICCHP 2010, Part I, LNCS 6179, pp. 280–287, 2010.

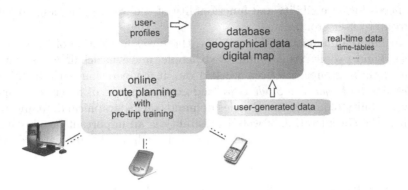

Fig. 1. Overview

point to the desired destination. In the existing case of pedestrian users, footpaths as well as public transport is included. This leads to a multi-modal and multi-criteria time-constrained shortest path problem [2]. Such optimization can not be solved with a conventional shortest path algorithm. An extended search algorithm has to be implemented.

Some electronic timetable information systems are already existing. Well known systems are for example HAFAS (http://www.hacon.de/hafas/) especially for railways and EFA (http://www.mentzdv.de) for local traffic in smaller regions. In contrast to these systems, this project concentrates on information for people with disabilities and allows user-specific route planning, weightings, and selection functions.

This work will focus on the definition of user profiles for blind and visually impaired people as well as wheelchair users, and the development of an adequate route planning algorithm taking care of restrictions and time tables. The definition of user profiles allows the expansion of the system to a wide range of other groups of users and applications - like parents with a buggy or safe ways to school for children. The basis of the system consists of a network based on different data sources, created network data, and a specialized route planning algorithm. The data sources include existing and self-created network data on various levels of detail, as well as time schedules of public transport and comprehensive information (e.g., points of interest). The algorithm enables route planning for pedestrians considering user profiles and time schedules of public transport. A pre-trip training provides blind people an application to learn difficult routes by heart, to prepare for routes and obstacles in unknown areas, and to compare alternative routes. A system overview is shown in Figure 1.

2   Requirements

The user requirements are divided into two different groups. On the one hand, there are requirements regarding constraints to be considered in the calculation of routes and infrastructural information needed for orientation. On the other hand, needs for accessibility and functionality of the web-application vary from user group to user group.

Regarding requirements of accessibility, there was a selection of three groups of users: blind people, visually impaired people, and wheelchair users. The selection of these groups has been worked out in cooperation with *Beauftragte für Behindertenfragen der Stadt Graz* and covers a range of functional aspects and accessibility requirements. Besides demands on geographical data and route planning, the consideration of web accessibility is an important fact in the development of web interfaces for people with disabilities. People with cognitive or visual disabilities are reliant on textual information which could be readily output to a screen reader and a braille display.

To involve potential users in evaluating necessary geographical data and system functions, we did two studies which were sent out to organizations of people with disabilities as well as lots of private individuals. The first step was an extensive questionnaire about preferred information needed before traveling to an unknown city. The detailed questions have concerned the following five topics:

- Which obstacles at the sidewalk are worth to be mentioned?
- Which additional functions besides route planning shall be provided?
- What is the optimal structure for describing guidance information?
- What is important for the use of public transport?
- What are the requirements on the accessibility of the user interface?

The second task was sorting the outcome of recommended information and obstacles from the previous questionnaire by priority, divided by user groups. Table 1 and 2 show the first five most important information.

From hundreds of contacted people over thirty replied the first part. For the next step only these people were asked again to sort the objects. Unfortunately, the response was not very high. For this reason, the groups of blind and visually impaired people were combined in the analysis, since their answers had nearly the same distribution. Within the application, not only the first five objects were included but also as most as possible from the whole priority list. The output of the whole questionnaire were lists of preferred content of geographical data and obstacles, as well as favored user functions, necessary landmarks which are essential for orientation, and examples of guidance instructions.

Table 1. Top five obstacle aspects defined by user groups

blind and visually impaired	wheelchair users
bus and train stops with exit at the lane	stairs and steps
construction sites	material of path surface
crossings without traffic lights	missing sidewalk ramps
material of path surface	cordons and gates
squares and parks	rails at street

Table 2. Top five additional information defined by user groups

blind and visually impaired	wheelchair users
acoustic traffic lights	disabled parking
medical care	wheelchair accessible toilets
tactile paving	wheelchair accessible hotels
shopping facilities	sights
barrier-free toilets	museum

3   User Profiles

The results from the study of user requirements revealed an appropriate profile for each selected type of disability. Unregistered users can select one of these standard profiles for calculation of the optimal route. For providing individual settings, users have to register to receive their login data. This creates a personal profile based on the selected standard profile and allows the user to configure visualization, route planning, and geographical data.

4   Geographical Data

Existing route planning systems, available on the Internet, are mainly focused on vehicle navigation. The necessities of pedestrians and even more of impaired people are commonly neglected. Especially, navigable information for people with disabilities like pavements, tactile paving, or acoustic traffic lights is missing [3].

The missing data can be divided into three categories:

1. data is not geographically referenced
2. data is not routable
3. data is not available

Category 1 is related to points of interest, obstacles, and additional information which has already been acquired but is only available as textual information without georeferencing. Our research revealed that in the city of Graz information on acoustic traffic lights is available as a text-based list of crossings, referenced by street names. Another example is the register of restaurants usable for wheel-chair users which contains various parameters like door-width and existence of ramps. To make this kind of data accessible for routing, their coordinates have to be determined and added to the underlying database as points of interest. A more complex task is the integration of obstacles like stairways and additional information like tactile paving. For these instances, it is not sufficient to map point coordinates, it is necessary to match them to the edges in the path network and include them as attributes of corresponding edges.

Whereas in route planning for vehicle navigation the public transportation system is normally not included, it plays an important role for pedestrian route planning. Typical for data of category 2 is that it can not be used in algorithms

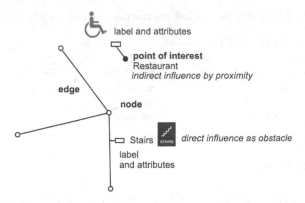

Fig. 2. Network overview

without previous conversion. In the example of public transport, data is often available as time schedules containing stops and departure times. A first step integration is the transformation of schedules to navigable networks by generating a time-dependent node-edge structure from time tables. A second step is the connection of different networks by defining transfer nodes which do not only generate a multi-modal network but also reflect waiting times and additional distances.

Category 3 focuses on special data for pedestrians and people with disabilities which are not required in any system and therefore are not yet recorded. Existing networks are road-based and do not contain pavements as edges [4]. For peoples with disabilities, it is important to know on which side of the road obstacles occur and how to cross streets exactly. This leads to the necessity of a network consisting of center lines of pavements and crossings which are not a single junction point of roads. Another difficulty is special information needed by people with disabilities like material of path surface and ramps, for example. Such detailed information has to be acquired and included in the path network. For generating a huge data base, the combination of different data sources is indispensable as well as the acquisition of new data. To enhance the existing data, the application allows registered users to add Points of Interest to the data base.

5   Route Planning

As explained in former sections, the goal is to find the most efficient path from an origin to a destination including constraints, user preferences, and time constraints based on time schedules. In applications containing time tables, the criterion of efficiency is defined as the duration of the route combined with the number of transfers. For people with disabilities differences in the definition of the "'best"' route appear. Some might prefer a short travel time putting up with some transfers but others may choose a longer travel time with less transfers, or the ability to stay at a station for transfer instead of changing the station.

These preferences are added in the user profile and influence the data model as well as the route planning algorithm.

A network is defined as a graph consisting of a set of nodes and interconnecting edges [5]. In case that edges contain information about their length (cost) and direction, the graph is referred to as weighted directed graph. Finding the shortest path in a weighted directed graph is a well discussed problem where a multitude of algorithms exist. An algorithm often used for solving single-criterion shortest path problems is Dijkstra's algorithm due to its efficiency, effectiveness, and extensibility to variants of shortest path problems.

One extension to a weighted directed graph are time schedules which have to be added to the network to reflect departure and arrival times of public transport. In other words, the departure from a node can take place only at these predefined departure times. This means, the total time in the optimization does not only consist of traveling time but also includes waiting times [2]. Using public transport also means traveling with different kinds of vehicles in combination with a path network. This leads to a multi-modal network which can be seen as a number of independent networks. These networks are connected by transfer nodes [6]. The network also includes foot-edges for walking between stations and the computation of the route from the starting point to the entrance station as well as from the last station to the final destination. Multi-modal networks do not only increase the size of complexity but demand new optimization criteria [7]:

- Minimum total time:
  the calculation of the earliest arrival time to meet time restrictions.
- Minimum number of transfers:
  people with disabilities prefer a single mean of transportation over multiple changes even if the travel time is longer.
- Minimum walking distance:
  people with physical disabilities might prefer less walking distance to a station or between stations than a quicker route on means of transport.

In a system for people with disabilities not only the fastest but a barrier-free route is calculated based on user preferences. This imposes additional constraints to the optimization which have to be reflected in the underlying data model (e.g., stairs, missing sidewalk ramps or inclination and cross-fall of sidewalk).

The user preferences affect the data model as mentioned. As shown in Figure 2, user preferences correspond to labels and attributes assigned to geographical items and have an effect on the weight of the underlying edges. Two different kinds of influences can be distinguished. On the one hand, labels and attributes assigned to edges directly influence the weight of the edge. This allows regarding obstacles or preferred paths. On the other hand, indirect influence on the weight is given by the proximity of points of interest decorated by selected attributes and labels.

There are different ways of modeling a network with time schedules. In this work a time-expanded approach introduced in [8] and [9] was chosen. This model consists of copies of nodes for every time event. Combining different optimization criteria at the same time leads to a multi-criteria search. To solve this, the search algorithm has to be extended which is done by an modified Dijkstra's algorithm [2]. The main difference in the algorithm is the use of cost vectors for edges instead of one cost-value for each edge as in the single-criterion case. These cost vectors also lead to label vectors for nodes in the search algorithm. Nodes are selected by a selection function, e.g., the lexicographical minimum in our first approach. The lexicographical minimum is defined by $(a, b) < (a', b')$ if $(a < a')$ or $(a = a'$ and $b < b')$ in a bi-criteria case [8]. In our work this selection function will be adapted to the user preferences and will be extended to more optimization criteria. The solution of multi-criteria search are Pareto-optimal paths. These different solutions are called *Pareto optima*, introduced by the Italian economist and sociologist *Vilfredo Pareto* (1848-1923): A path is Pareto optimal if one of its cost components cannot be reduced without increasing at least one of the others [10]. In general, more than one solution is available at each node before selecting the "'best"' one, using the selection function.

6   Pre-trip Training

Before the journey, a training adapted to the requirements of blind people, not only for route planning but also with respect to the user interface, is performed. Detailed information for disabled people allows preparing for routes, especially in unknown areas like on holiday [11]. The pre-trip training allows listening step by step to the guidance instructions. Another feature is to navigate forward and backward in the guidance list to go through the route virtually. Moreover, different solutions for one route can be compared to each other (longer route but less transfers, short route but more transfers) and can be chosen individually. For taking the guidance instructions along at the journey itself, text files and sound files of the instructions are provided for download.

7   Web Accessibility

For completion, the web accessibility should be mentioned, although this paper is focused on the functionality. Web accessibility deals with the development of websites usable by people of all abilities and disabilities. To make a website accessible for individuals living with a disability, specific guidelines have to be satisfied. Blind people and visually impaired people depend on textual information. As one example, this requires a text equivalent for every non-text element. Detailed guidelines defined in [12] are well-known guidelines on how to create accessible websites [13] and are considered in the application.

8   Conclusion

Within the project *Route4you* a prototype for a web-based route planner for people with disabilities is under development. As one difference to standard route planners, users can customize information in their individual user profile.

Special data is included in the data base and path network to provide an optimal solution for the user groups at a defined test area of Graz. The implementation of time tables combined with criteria concerning people with disabilities leads to a multi-criteria search problem which has more complexity than single-criterion problems, since the solution is ambiguous.

References

1. Bühler, C., Heck, H., Becker, J.: How to inform people with reduced mobility about public transport. In: Miesenberger, K., Klaus, J., Zagler, W.L., Karshmer, A.I. (eds.) ICCHP 2008. LNCS, vol. 5105, pp. 973–980. Springer, Heidelberg (2008)
2. Chen, Y.L., Tang, K.: Minimum time paths in a network with mixed time constraints. Comput. Oper. Res. 25, 793–805 (1998)
3. Pressl, B.: Navigationssystem für blinde Personen. VDM Verlag Dr. Müller, Saarbrücken (2008)
4. Völkel, T., Weber, G.: A New Approach for Pedestrian Navigation for Mobility Impaired Users Based on Multimodal Annotation of Geographical Data. In: Stephanidis, C. (ed.) UAHCI 2007 (Part II). LNCS, vol. 4555, pp. 575–584. Springer, Heidelberg (2007)
5. Hofmann-Wellenhof, B., Legat, K., Wieser, M.: Navigation – principles of positioning and guidance. Springer, Wien (2003)
6. Disser, Y., Müller-Hannemann, M., Schnee, M.: Multi-criteria Shortest Path in Time-Dependent Train Networks. In: McGeoch, C.C. (ed.) WEA 2008. LNCS, vol. 5038, pp. 347–361. Springer, Heidelberg (2008)
7. Wu, Q., Hartley, J.: Accommodating user preferences in the optimization of public transport travel. International Journal of Simulation Systems, Science & Technology 5, 12–25 (2004)
8. Schulz, F.: Timetable Information and Shortest Paths. PhD thesis, University of Karlsruhe (2005)
9. Müller-Hannemann, M., Schulz, F., Wagner, D., Zaroliagis, C.: Timetable Information: Models and Algorithms. In: Geraets, F., Kroon, L.G., Schoebel, A., Wagner, D., Zaroliagis, C.D. (eds.) Railway Optimization 2004. LNCS, vol. 4359, pp. 67–90. Springer, Heidelberg (2007)
10. Hallam, C., Harrison, K.J., Ward, J.A.: A multiobjective optimal path algorithm. Digital Signal Processing 11, 133–143 (2001)
11. Mayerhofer, B., Pressl, B., Wieser, M.: ODILIA - A Mobility Concept for the Visually Impaired. In: Miesenberger, K., Klaus, J., Zagler, W.L., Karshmer, A.I. (eds.) ICCHP 2008. LNCS, vol. 5105, pp. 1109–1116. Springer, Heidelberg (2008)
12. W3C. Web content accessibility guidelines 1.0 (1999)
13. Hardt, A., Schrepp, M.: Making Business Software Usable for Handicapped Employees. In: Miesenberger, K., Klaus, J., Zagler, W.L., Karshmer, A.I. (eds.) ICCHP 2008. LNCS, vol. 5105, pp. 502–509. Springer, Heidelberg (2008)

Results of a Workshop Series on Ambient Assisted Living

Martin M. Morandell and Erwin Fugger

AIT Austrian Institute of Technology GmbH,
Health & Environment Department, Biomedical Systems
Viktor Kaplan-Strasse 2/1, A-2700 Wiener Neustadt, Austria
{martin.morandell,erwin.fugger}@ait.ac.at

Abstract. Within a series of four workshops selected topics of the research field Ambient Assisted Living are discussed with the relevant stakeholders. The aim is to bring experts with different points of view together. Thus, new ideas for projects should be generated, experiences exchanged and barriers and possible attempts to overcome them identified. Furthermore the workshop series aims to make the possibilities of Ambient Assisted Living more transparent.

Keywords: Ambient Assisted Living, ICT, Workshops.

1 Introduction

At the AIT Austrian Institute of Technology, a workshop series on Ambient Assisted Living (AAL) is organized, focusing on ICT-based solutions for the encouragement of successful aging in the living environment of choice. Even though AAL is a very popular research topic, in Austria hardly any solutions or services can be found on the market and no strategies to finance a broader application exist.

1.1 Aim of the Workshop Series

As a main objective, the combined views of many different stakeholders are intended to create new knowledge on the different topics discussed. Bringing those stakeholders together will foster the collaboration within the AAL community. Thus the workshop series aims to motivate user-organizations, scientists, companies, assurances and other stakeholders to collaborate closer in further AAL projects.

1.2 Organization of the Project

The project consists of a series of four workshops and a panel discussion. Each workshop puts the focus on a selected AAL-topic. For each workshop a certain set of stakeholders (end-users, care givers, public authorities, insurances, etc.) are invited to allow many points of view. The workshops are held within one year.

K. Miesenberger et al. (Eds.): ICCHP 2010, Part I, LNCS 6179, pp. 288–291, 2010.

2   Workshops and Their Results So Far

In the following, the single workshops and their preliminary results are described.

2.1   Togetherness But Loneliness – ICT for the Social Interaction of Elderly Persons

In the beginning of the workshop a impulse-speech was given about *loneliness*, what it is, its possible psychological and physiological effects and how ICT and AAL technologies can have effects on the loneliness. It was followed by presentations on existing technologies:

- A video-telephony system for elderly people developed by CEIT RALTEC[1].
- The website Seniorkom[2] and how elderly people use it to find new friends.
- Facebook[3], its possible application fields and why it could be of interest also for elderly people.

These presentations served as input for the the group work where solutions for the following scenarios had to be found:

Scenario A - Networking in a public housing area: Three elderly persons living in a public housing area have different abilities, needs and hobbies that would partly complement each other. Which kind of ICT can be used to connect these people and which side activities are needed for a wider use of new technologies?

Scenario B - Contact within the family: Grandma lives 500 km away from her daughter and her grandchild. Even though she has attended a computer course two years ago, she does not use the PC. What is needed that the grandma can get in closer contact with her family.

The solutions elaborated put the focus mostly on organizational and social aspects, as needed ICT exists, but elderly people hardly know about it. Advice centers are needed to inform users about challenges and risks. Accompanying measures are needed, i.e. for creating a hardware installation & maintenance support and training courses. As a crucial factor for the usage, factors that can motivate the users have to be identified, and barries minimized. Especially huge platforms with an elusive amount of functions were seen as unsuitable for elderly people.

2.2   ICT Based Home Care: Autonomy through ICT – A Risk or a Chance?

The workshop was organized following the "World Cafe Method"[4], thus moderators remained at their original table while participants changed tables subsequently. The moderators' task was to present a certain topic with a number of

---

[1] http://www.ceit.at/ceit-raltec
[2] http://www.seniorkom.at
[3] http://www.facebook.com
[4] http://www.theworldcafe.com/principles.htm

referring questions. Participants discussed on this topic and results were gathered by the moderators. After finalization of a turn the moderator presented the results of the preceding group to the new group, serving as input for discussion. Organized within three groups, workshop participants discussed three specific topics:

- What are possible enablers for the use of ICT in home-care?
- In which areas of home-care is the use of ICT conceivable?
- Identify existing and missing ICT for the use in home-care within (the flat / closer surrounding / city / global)

Outcomes were that: The user has to see an obvious benefit why the ICT is used. ICT should only be used to assist personal care, but not replace it. For the acceptance of ICT in homecare, it is important that the technology works in the background and is available automatically when needed.

For the way of human-computer-interaction, well elaborated concepts and easy adaptation strategies to user needs are crucial. For a widespread use of ICT in homecare innovative and creative business models have to be developed integrating the different stakeholders. A step by step approach is needed to apply the ICT in everyday's homecare.

For a successful exploitation of ICT in homecare, best practice cases are required and user organizations as well as home-care nurses have to be integrated as peer groups. In addition accounting possibilities for telecare have to be elaborated.

2.3   Science Theater: When Grandma Is Chatting with Her Granddaughter

This workshop took place in a senior-citizens home. The aim was to identify enablers for getting elderly people closer to ICT. In order to start the discussion process, a theater group (kernzone100) performed three sketches, about a grandma, her granddaughter Luiserl and a friend of the grandma called Maria.

Sketch A: Luiserl visits her grandmother. Showing her the new iPod and telling her about a new project in school where pupils teach senior citizens how to use computers and the internet. Even though the grandma has some doubts, she accepts to take part in this project.

Sketch B: Some months later, the grandma is already surfing the internet on her own. Maria is visiting her, not really interested in this topic. The grandma shows her a dating platform for the generation 50+. Looking at some profiles, also Maria gets more interested, and they decide to register to contact one of the users, until they get to a point, where they have doubts about filling in personal data into a online-form.

Sketch C: The grandmother is looking at photos of her family on facebook. Initially she is very cheerful about what she sees, but then she finds photos of Luiserl at a party showing her granddaughter in an unpleasant way.

After each sketch, the participants of the workshops were asked for their statements and for own experiences and positions respectively. There was a lively discussion during the workshop when the older persons came out with valuable information concerning their use of a PC and/or internet as well as on acceptance of these technologies. Summarizing it could be stated that the "digital divide" in many cases is not supported by disinterest or refusal of older persons. Frequently it is the mode of implementation and the way of teaching or advising older people which is decisive for the proper use and acceptance of ICTs.

One of the inhabitants started to use the internet during her stay at the residence to allow more frequent contact with her daughters. She mentioned that it was worth starting to use the internet event at a later point in her life; ones will is decisive in spite of adverse conditions.

Other inhabitants mentioned the idea of personal advice and training by younger persons, e.g. pupils. Learning in groups or using internet for contacting family members or friends were indicated as highly valuable.

The discussion showed that some keywords like "iPod" or "Laptop" were hard to interpret by older users of ICT. Another critical point in relation to internet use was the question if one should reveal personal data (e.g. date of birth, full name). It was seen as critical that personal contact to internet partners does usually not exist.

3   Outlook

The workshop series will continue with the 4th workshop, where especially decision makers from politics, (home) care institutions, interest groups of elderly people, economy and research & development will try to find solutions to overcome identified barriers that "AAL becomes a benefit for ALL". The project will be ended by a panel discussion on "When and how does AAL become a benefit for ALL?"

The workshop series shows, that the lack of general knowledge in the different applications fields of AAL is definitely one of the major reasons why there is hardly any user driven demand. Beside developing AAL technologies along with social services, also information campaigns for different target groups have to be elaborated.

Acknowledgments

The project "Workshop series Ambient Assisted Living 2009/2010" is funded by the Austrian Research Promotion Agency (FFG) within the benefit program.

Challenges for Norwegian PC-Users
with Parkinson's Disease – A Survey

Miriam Eileen Nes Begnum

MediaLT, Jerikoveien 22, 1067 Oslo, Norway
`miriam@medialt.no`

Abstract. This paper presents the results from a Norwegian survey on the computer use of people with Parkinson's disease (PD), conducted through the PIKT project in the summer of 2008. The study shows that nearly 80 % of the user population has significant and severe PD related challenges using a computer. Frequent problem areas include inertia, muscle stiffness, using a computer mouse, tremor and issues related to keyboard and ergonomics. Assistance in optimizing computer use is severely lacking, non-systematic and coincidental, and the employment rate among the respondents is about half of the national average. This paper describes the main findings from this study. It highlights main challenges for the user group in question, confirms national findings on gender, computer illiteracy and usage aspects, paints a picture of the current situation for PC-users with Parkinson's disease in Norway and discusses the implications of the findings.

Keywords: Computer adaptation, Parkinson's disease.

1 Introduction

Parkinson's disease (PD) is a progressive, degenerative and chronic illness. Today, one in 500 people are afflicted with PD. Moreover, the disease is projected to double in the next 25 years [1]. Typical symptoms include tremor, muscle stiffness and pain, reduced and slowed motor skills, reduced balance, difficulties coordinate and resulting clumsiness, dementia-related symptoms, weakened voice, visual disturbances and lack of energy.

Norwegian studies from the mid 90s reveal that somewhere between 15-20% with the PD diagnose are of working age [2, 3]. However, only about 10 % of the PD population receives any training or follow-ups regarding their progressive illness, even though their situation is continuously deteriorating - often over a period of ten to twenty years. Further, 70 % wished such support could be provided [4].

In spite of general PD ailments, people with PD want to continue living as normally as possible. However, half of Tandberg et.al.'s [2] sample needed public assistance and as many as 80% have to depend on family members to manage their everyday life [4]. These numbers support the need to reinforce people with PD, and increase the opportunities for independent living. In today's modern societies, this includes continuous use of technology. Digital inclusion is important in this context.

K. Miesenberger et al. (Eds.): ICCHP 2010, Part I, LNCS 6179, pp. 292–299, 2010.

For disabled people, technology may be of great value - compensating for the disability and enabling social participation and employment. Focus group interviews assessed use of PC as of especially high priority for people with Parkinson [5]. Computers are used for many purposes, and in particular the maintenance of social contact networks is notably appreciated by PC-users with PD - who often struggle with isolation, loneliness and depression [4].

Overall, little is known on the specific needs and troubles of people with PD in relation to computer usage. This paper investigates the main challenges for PC users with PD, and how computer interaction may be improved for this user group. A survey on the use of PC among the Norwegian PD population is presented, as well as findings from user tests of device alternatives and adaptations

2 Background

Usually, the disease course of Parkinson starts when one is 55-60 years of age. However, about 10% of those who receive a PD diagnosis are between 30 and 55 years. There are about 4-4.5 million people with PD worldwide [6]. More than 1.6 million of these reside in Europe, more than 1 million in the USA and about 100 000 in Canada - all examples of countries where use of PC is considered a part of everyday life.

3 Survey Methodology

Around 6-8000 Norwegians have PD. About 1/3 of these (more than 2600) are members of the nationwide Norwegian Parkinson Foundation (NPF). Through collaboration with NPF, their members were used as population for the survey. All members with PD born after 1938 (below 70 years old) were included in the survey selection. The size of the selection was 794 individuals.

Many people with PD lose their ability to handwrite either fully or partially. Thus, an online survey response could be beneficial. However, the number of people within the population not able to use a computer, not having access to a computer or being computer illiterate was unknown - questions the survey was designed to help clarify. To avoid receiving responses from sub-populations, the decision was made to provide both online and paper based form filling. The survey was sent out on paper along with a return envelope, but with the alternative for online response encouraged on the front introduction page. The choice of format ensured maximum accessibility to respond. Electronic responses were handled through the online form filling system Questback. The Questback form was developed alongside the paper form, so that item design could be made as equal as possible in the two formats. Items have neutral language, and avoid hypothetical, ambiguous or biased formulations.

Both formats had an equivalent 4 weeks response period. Electronic and paper based responses were merged for a common SPSS data analysis. Data was analyzed using frequency distributions, and Chi-squared (two-sided) and Phi/Cramer's V is used to look for significances and associations - since the variables are nominal.

4 Survey Results

The survey had 294 respondents (37 %). About 54 % of the respondents were male. Respondents seem randomly distributed within the selection. As an example, the age distribution of the respondents fit very well with the age distribution in the selection (1 % below 44 years; 3 versus 4 % were of ages 45-49; 9 vs. 7.5 % were 50-54; 19 vs. 18.5 % were 55-59; 31 vs. 31.5 were 60-64; 33 vs. 37.5 above 65 years).

4.1 Importance of Computer Usage in Everyday Life

The survey shows that computers are used frequently by PD users - 75 % use computers on a daily (55 %) or weekly (20 %) basis. Overall, 79 % of the sample considers the computer use an important or highly important part of their everyday life, of which 63 % feel PC-use is highly important.

Nearly all respondents in the younger age categories (age below 54 years) use a PC daily or at least several times per week. This coincides with national data on the general use of computers within different age groups in the total Norwegian population [7, 8].

When looking at the importance ratings for work-related PC-use only, 76 % rate computer use highly important, and an additional 12 % rate it important.

4.2 Tipping-Age for Computer Illiteracy Confirmed

Since 80 % of the respondents are in the age group 55-69 years, according to national data about 20 % should never or seldom use a computer. This holds true for the PD-selection. A weak indication (Phi: 0.4) of a relation between age and non-use of PC was detected; most of the 18 % that report not to use a computer are older than 65 years. This tendency was expected, as national data show the same critical age tipping point in relation to PC-use and access. For respondents that do use a computer, age seem irrelevant to type and frequency of use.

The survey results also fit with the national data from Statistics Norway, which show no gender differences in frequency of use or access to a computer among people under the age of 65 years. 82 % of the women use a PC, and 82 % of the men. Only above the 65 years age limit are women found to fall behind on computer usage.

4.3 Challenges Related to Computer Use

77 % of the respondents describe significant, severe and highly severe troubles using the computer due to PD. Around 50 % report to have at least one problem area that is highly severe or severe. The reported troubles in relation to computer usage span from pain related issues to use to device related troubles. Type and degree of problem areas vary - some users report mild PD symptoms while other have several serious issues related to the use of a PC.

Table 1 shows the most common problem areas, and the percentage of respondents that describe these as significant, severe and highly severe. Inertia and muscle stiffness are the major PD challenges when using a computer. The use of a computer mouse is the main device related problem reported.

Table 1. Common Challenges Related to Computer Use

Problem area	Percentage experiencing significant to highly severe difficulties
Inertia	53 %
Muscle stiffness	46 %
Tremor	30 %
Using a standard computer mouse	42 %
Using a standard keyboard	27 %

There are no correlations between type of PD-related problem (inertia, balance issues, muscle stiffness, tremor) and the equipment related trouble ratings, nor connections between device related problems and workability. In addition, employment does not seem to influence PC-use: being employed correlates only with daily use of a computer at work – and does not influence private computer use. An interesting finding is that significant PD-caused troubles using the computer have no influence on frequency of computer use.

4.4 Availability of Assistance

The study further shows that very few respondents have received any assistance or support related to the use of computer technology, for using or adapting the computer or computer peripherals. In addition, any assistance received is random, non-systematic and coincidental. Even through random, and often provided from family and friends, the aid received is largely rated positively.

Table 2 show the number (and percentage) of respondents receiving assistance, who provided this support, and how the aid is rated.

Table 2. Computer Usage: Assistance and Adaptations Received

	Number	Percent	Not useful	Little useful	Quite useful	Useful	Very useful	No rating
Norwegian Labor and Welfare Administration	15	6 %	-	6.5 %	20 %	27 %	40 %	6.5 %
Norwegian Parkinson Foundation	3	1 %	-	-	-	33 %	67 %	-
Municipality	7	3 %	-	-	14 %	57 %	29 %	-
Personal Assistant	12	5 %	-	-	-	25 %	42 %	33 %
Family	14	6 %	7 %	-	7 %	7 %	72 %	7 %
Friends	7	3 %	-	-	-	29 %	14 %	57 %
OT/Physiotherapist	8	3 %	-	-	12.5 %	-	12.5 %	75 %
Other	5	2 %	-	-	-	-	20 %	80 %
Sum	*54*	*22 %*	-	-	-	-	-	-

4.5 High Unemployment Rate

Although almost 80 % of the respondents are of working age, only around 30 % of these are working. Unemployment rates within the sample are almost doubled relative to the national average [9], when checking against the age of the selection as well as equating full-time and partial employment (including partial sick leave and/or disability pension). More than half of the respondents receive partial or full disability pension.

4.6 Lacking Experience with Alternative Peripherals

Despite high troubles reported, few respondents have any acquaintance with alternative PC peripherals. This is particularly the case for keyboard and mouse solutions. Respondents are asked to rate the mouse and keyboard peripherals used, but the lack of experience makes it difficult to reliably assess and generalize how well the different non-standard alternatives work for the user group and make any statements on which equipment may help solve specific PC-related problem areas. The share of non response on items asking for experience is large (9 to 22 %)[1] – these respondents are assumed not to have experience with alternative equipment.

In relation to alternative computer mice, the typical respondent has tried the touchpad as well as a standard mouse. Less than a third (28.5 %) of the selection has tested a more non-standard mouse peripheral. Most frequently, this is either a joystick mouse (10 %) and/or a left hand mouse (10 %). The mouse peripheral that receive the highest assessment is the trackball mouse. Only 5 people out of the 294 have tried the trackball, illustrating the lacking acquaintance. Two of these are very pleased with the mouse, two are pleased and one person is partially pleased.

When it comes to ergonomic and screen solutions on the other hand, the proportions of respondents claiming to have serious difficulties related to computer use and those that have tried a non-standard alternative fit well. 29 % reported significant ergonomic troubles and 35.5 % have tried at least one alternative ergonomic solution. The alternatives are mainly vertically raiseable tables, ergonomic chairs and arm supports. All ergonomic solutions used are overall rated positively. About 10 % of the respondents report significant or serious troubles related to using the standard screen, compared to 32 % who have tested an alternative screen solution: 28 % have tried a larger screen and 15 % enlarged text on screen.

5 Discussion

The survey shows that people with PD use computers at the same terms and frequencies as the rest of the Norwegian population, despite a high degree of significant troubles. Nearly 80 % of the sample can be described as consisting of frequent computer users, whose computer use is a vital and important part of their everyday life. At the same time, these users experience serious interaction challenges.

Virtually none of the respondents report having received qualified aid. In fact, few have received any computer usage assistance at all, and the aid given can be described as coincidental, random and overall unskilled. Only 9 % have received aid from the

---

[1] Between 1 and 5 % replies "I do not know" on these items.

public sector[2]. Since 75 % use computers on a weekly or daily basis and regards this as an important part of their everyday life and in addition 77 % report significant, serious or very serious troubles using the computer, it seems there is a significant gap between the proportion that is likely to need assistance and those that currently receive adequate support. It is regarded as purposeful to systematize the aid provided to the user group, in order to ensure all receive necessary assistance.

Ergonomic issues arise when using keyboard and computer mouse peripherals, often linked to muscle stiffness and inertia, and also to pain and fatigue. Significant, severe or highly severe muscle stiffness is reported to be experienced by around half of the user population, and so is inertia. These are therefore the most common and serious general PD problem areas reported in relation to PC use. This is an interesting aspect, as many tends to think of tremor and shaking hands as the main issue for PC users with PD. Tremor affects arm/hand control and coordination, and is reported as a significant, severe or highly severe problem by about 30 % of the user population.

The experienced interaction issues challenges the use of standard keyboard and mouse solutions: 27 % reported significant or serious troubles using a standard keyboard, and 42 % had significant or serious difficulties when using a traditional computer mouse. However, there is a lack of acquaintance with alternative peripherals. Respondents have little knowledge of potential solutions to their device-related challenges. As an example, only 6 % of the sample has tried either a roller mouse, trackball or Mousetrapper – however these receive the highest alternative mice assessments: all of the respondents positively assess the mentioned solutions.

Since few respondents had alternative peripheral experiences, the survey generated less information about suitable adaptations for the user group and specific population subgroups. A complementary study testing alternative peripherals, focused on keyboard and mice solutions, were thus executed post the survey [10].

Aid provided seems to focus on ergonomics. Equipment designed to reduce ergonomic troubles, such as strain and fatigue, seem quite well known in the population. To the degree that ergonomic solutions can provide help for the user group, they are considered useful and beneficial. What type of aid is needed by the user group should however be investigated, as the assumption is made that they do not receive help adapting the core issues of their PC-related challenges: solving device-related and technical issues. In general, it seems PC-users with PD do not receive proper support and computer accommodation, but instead patiently struggle with mouse and keyboard solutions, not knowing possible alternatives. Alternative mouse and keyboard peripherals and adjustments should therefore receive more focus when informing the user group of possible beneficial adaptations. To accomplish this, measures might need to be taken to ensure a proper level of technical competence and knowledge with the aid provides.

The study further shows a doubled unemployment rate within the sample relative to the national average. In Norway, about 84 % of the population between 40-54 years of age is employed, dropping to a 66 % for ages 55-60 and 19 % of those between 67-74 years [9]. When controlling for respondent age, the sample should have had an employment rate of 58 % if adhering to the national average. Instead, the employment rate is a mere 30 %, including many partially employed workers, as well as workers

---

[2] Norwegian Labor and Welfare Administration or Municipality.

on disability pensions or sick leave. The social and economical costs of unemployment are high, both for the individual and for the society. It is therefore attractive to explore possible reason for the low employment rate.

Many with PD face the challenge of prioritizing their limited energy between friends, family and work. Work adaptation becomes an important incentive to inspire them to continue working. The findings raise interesting questions related to the potential of IT to sustain or discontinue workability among employees with PD in technology-centered positions, including:

1. Is IT and PC-use currently contributing to expelling persons with PD from employment?
2. If so, could systematic assistance in work place adaptation benefit the short-term or long-term workability?
3. Furthermore, what are the ongoing demands (as the illness progresses and changes) for training and assistance?

PD and IT is an important subject regardless of effect on workability, because of the social importance and the sense of coping appropriate use can provide in life. The hypothesis made is that technology has the potential to ease the everyday life of people with PD if adapted; compensating for reduced motor skills within the user group, such as handwriting. The share of computer users with PD could therefore be expected to be higher than in corresponding age groups in the general population.

Cognitive aspects of PD received little attention in this project. Research [11] shows these are mainly apathy and memory impairment (reduced short-term memory, attention and concentration). The changes in the brain affect everyday-life: insomnia and day-time sleepiness, lack of motivation, interest and determination, difficulties getting started with tasks etc. This may increase feelings of stress – particularly if in a demanding work situation with frequent deadlines or a high work pace.

Lastly, it is worth noticing that the PD symptom variation and their resemblance to common issues among elderly makes such a systematized adaption arrangement relevant for large portions of the general population - and even more so in the future due to the expected increasingly aged as well as computer literate demography.

6 Conclusion

The study proves the high importance of computer usage in everyday life among the vast majority of the population, and also confirms the national tipping age for computer illiteracy. It describes the main challenges of the user group in relation to computer use, and raise questions related to the low degree of employment within the sample - only half of the national average in comparable groups. Findings suggests PC-users with PD struggle without receiving necessary support to deal with their illness in relation to computer use, have little experience with suitable adaptations and lack knowledge of how to solve problems related to the use of standard keyboard/mouse peripherals. The gap between received and needed computer use adaptation and assistance is considered significant. Continued use of computers is important for the ability to continue working, and to maintain social relations. Therefore, the study suggest there is a need to install systematized support or workplace accommodation for this user group, increasing and improving assistance, in order to ensure all receive necessary assistance related to the adaptation of computer usage. It is considered highly interesting to investigate any resulting effect on community participation and employment within the user group.

Acknowledgements

The author would like to thank the PIKT project group for valuable comments and contributions, and in particular the Norwegian Parkinson Foundation and Oslo University College for contributing to the facilitation of the study.

References

1. Dorsey, E.R., Constantinescu, R., Thompson, J.P., Biglan, K.M., Holloway, R.G., Kieburtz, K., Marshall, F.J., Ravina, B.M., Schifitto, G., Siderowf, A., Tanner, C.M.: Projected number of people with Parkinson disease in the most populous nations, 2005 through 2030. Neurology 2007 68(5), 384–386, Epub (2006)
2. Tandberg, E., Larsen, J.P., Nessler, E.G., Riise, T., Aarli, J.A.: The epistemology of Parkinson's disease in the County of Rogaland, Norway. Movement Disorders 10(5), 541–549 (1995)
3. Larsen, J.P.: Parkinsonprosjektet i Stavanger. Nevrologisk avdeling, Sentralsykehuset i Rogaland (1993)
4. Arntzen, E.: Rehabilitering av personer med Parkinsons sykdom. The Norwegian Parkinson Foundation, Cited from St.meld.34 (1996)
5. Tollefsen, M., Nes, M.E.: En sekretær ville løst alle problemer! MediaLT (2006)
6. Parkinson's Disease Society, http://www.parkinsons.org.uk/
7. Lorentzen, K.: Kjønns- og aldersforskjeller ved bruk av IKT, Digital verden uten eldre kvinner. SSB Statistics, Norway (2008),
   http://www.ssb.no/ssp/utg/200802/08/
8. SSB Statistics Norway: IKT i husholdningene, 2. kvartal (2008),
   http://www.ssb.no/ikthus/
9. SSB Statistics Norway: Register-based employment statistics (4th quarter, 2008),
   http://www.ssb.no/english/subjects/06/01/regsys_en/
10. Begnum, M.E.N.: Improving Computer Interaction for People with Parkinson's Disease. In: UniTech 2010, Tapir (2010) (Yet to be published)
11. Aarsland, D., Pedersen, K.F., Ehrt, U., Bronnick, K., Gjerstad, M.D., Larsen, J.P.: Neuropsychiatric and cognitive symptoms in Parkinson disease. Tidsskr Nor Laegeforen 128(18), 2072–2076 (2008)

Usability and Usefulness of GPS Based Localization Technology Used in Dementia Care

Øystein Dale

Norsk Regnesentral, P.O. Box 114 Blindern, 0314 Oslo, Norway
oystein.dale@nr.no

Abstract. Dementia is a chronic brain disease affecting cognitive functioning. People with dementia have a higher risk of getting lost. In recent years GPS based technology has been utilised to locate lost persons with dementia. We interviewed six families using such technology focusing on perceived usability, user-friendliness and usefulness. The informants also completed the QUEST 2.0 questionnaire which measures satisfaction with assistive technology. By and large the informants found the equipment easy to use, and it was viewed by all as being very useful. There were a number of usability issues which adversely affected usage, e.g. system stability, secure fastening, size, user interface issues and varying GPS-reception. The QUEST 2.0 results corresponded with the findings in the interviews. Further usability studies, as well as R&D to address issues such as security and privacy protection and use in the public health sector are needed.

Keywords: Dementia, localization, assistive technology; GPS, usability.

1 Introduction

Dementia is a collective term for several chronic brain diseases that leads to a general reduction in cognitive functioning [1]. Worldwide the prevalence of dementia is estimated at 35.6 million persons, and the projected prevalence for the year 2050 is 115.4 million [2]. Due to a diminished ability to orientate to their surroundings persons with dementia are at greater risk of getting lost outdoors [3]. This may lead to an increased risk of harm [3][4][5], and it may cause worry and stress for carers [6].

A number of localization and tracking devices that can assist with locating missing persons with dementia are available. A common combination is the use of Global Positioning System (GPS) and Global System for Mobile communications (GSM) based radio devices built into a small portable unit. See Figure 1 for example. The person with dementia carries this on his or her person when ambulating outdoors. A localisation is done with a mobile phone or a computer with Internet access. The location can be given as a set of map coordinates, an address, a link to or a point on a map, or a combination of the above. See Figure 2 for an example. This paper details the findings of a project in which six families who use such technology were interviewed.

K. Miesenberger et al. (Eds.): ICCHP 2010, Part I, LNCS 6179, pp. 300–307, 2010.

The focus was on the perceived usability and usefulness of the localization equipment. The project was commissioned and partially funded by the Norwegian Labour and Welfare Administration, Department of Assistive Technology.

Fig. 1. Example of localization unit. (Source: OnSat AS. Used with permission).

Fig. 2. Example of SMS alert with link to map from GPS/GSM-unit. (Source: Author).

2   Related Work

There are a number of reports focusing on the use of localization and tracking device set ups in dementia care [3][4][7][8][9][10]. Often the focus is on attitudinal, ethical and privacy issues pertaining to the use of such technology [4][7][8]. Although, these issues are of great importance to the potential adoption and use of such technology, it is also important to shed light on people's practical experiences with such devices [11]. Are they easy to use? Is the accuracy adequate? How useful is the equipment, and does it live up to the user's expectations? What kind of technical difficulties do the users experience? These are but some of the questions which may be of interest to dementia sufferers and their families, health personnel and the health authorities, procurers, bureaucrats, vendors, researchers and other stakeholders and interested parties.

Some works examine the usefulness and usability aspects of localization and tracking devices. [12] state in a review article that the adoption of such devices is "proven to result in enhanced feelings of safety and less fear and anxiety". [10] report that GPS/GSM based technology can localise persons within 5 metres accuracy, and that the locating is done swiftly. The study also reports problems with compliance and usability and practical issues such as the devices being perceived by some as difficult to use and should be simplified [10].

[7] identified in a literature review the following practical problems with the use of tracking and tagging devices: Cost; need for training and support; technical problems; size of equipment; battery issues and increased demand on carers. [9] also point out that potential problematic issues may be too large size and anaesthetic appearance of such devices, as well as malfunction, inaccuracy, battery life and absence of desired features. [11] tried out GPS/GSM-devices with two families. Relevant usability issues which arose were: remembering to bring the device, remember to charge the equipment and inaccuracy of location provided [11].

The literature consulted shows that there is a lack of knowledge in terms of the users' practical experiences. There is especially a deficiency in the knowledge pertaining to perceived usability and usefulness of GPS/GSM based localization devices used in dementia care.

3 Aim and Goals

The main aim of the study was to explore and document how private citizens experience the usability and user friendliness of GPS/GSM based localization devices used to locate persons with dementia. The research problems guiding the activities in the project were:

- To what extent are the localizations devices perceived as usable and user friendly?
- What are the interface challenges the users experience with the localization aids?
- Which other factors influence the user experience?
- What utility value or benefit has the localization aids had on the care of the person with dementia?

4 Method

Seven family members were interviewed about their experience with GPS/GSM based assistive technology (AT) used for localization purposes. The material consisted of six spouses and a son (N=7). In total this comprised six families caring for five persons with dementia and one person with acquired brain injury with dementia-like symptoms. One lived in a nursing home, while the remaining five lived out in the community. See Table 1 for further description of the informants. A comprehensive interview guide was devised for the semi-structured interviews. In addition the informants completed a Norwegian translation of the Quebec User Evaluation of Satisfaction with assistive Technology 2.0 (QUEST 2.0) questionnaire [13]. Due to the low number of informants no statistical analysis was conducted of the QUEST 2.0 data beyond basic summaries. Interviews of the persons with dementia was planned, but deemed inappropriate in all instances due to the advanced state of the illness. Each individual family made this call. All interviews were digitally recorded and transcribed, and subsequently analysed by the author.

Table 1. Description of the informants

Attribute:	Interviewees N=7 :	Person with dementia N=6[*] :
Age (years)	Span 33-72; mean 57.3; median 59	Span 60-78; mean 65; median 64
Gender	Female 4; male 3	Female 2; male 4
ICT skills**	Poor 2; Fair 2; Good 3	Not applicable (N/A)
Relation to person with dementia	Spouse 6; Son 1	N/A
Duration of condition (years)	N/A	Span 4-10; mean 7.3; median 8
Time used equipment (years)	Span 0.25-5, mean 1.2; median 1.4	
Living arrangements	N/A	At home 5; nursing home 1***
Still using equipment	Yes: 5; No 1	

* One did not have dementia, but an acquired brain injury with dementia like symptoms.
** Self appraised skills in information and communication technology.
*** Some of the other persons with dementia were also occasionally in residential care.

5 Results

The informants reported that it was a major problem for them that their family member with dementia got lost repeatedly. This resulted in a lot of worry and time spent searching, and several adverse episodes had occurred involving the dementia sufferers. The main reason for obtaining the localization equipment was that there had been a worsening in the condition, and the person with dementia was increasingly getting lost. The families interviewed had used the localization equipment between three months and five years (mean 1.2/median 1.4). Between them they used five different types/models. All were GPS/GSM based and had similar functionality (See Table 2 for overview of models). All families used the equipment in conjunction with a mobile phone, and three of them also used a computer with Internet access to conduct searches. Five of the families still use the equipment, while one family has stopped due to a worsening of the illness.

There is great variation in how the equipment is used. In two families the different tasks are split between several family members when conducting a search, e.g. one person conducts the localisation and another goes out and does the physical searching whilst maintaining communication with the former. The persons with dementia are all passive users of the equipment, i.e. they only carry it on their person. Some of the persons with dementia were responsible for donning the equipment, but by and large this was done by their spouses.

All informants only use the most basic localization functions, i.e. conducting a basic search establishing the location of the device and person being located at one point in time, and repeating if necessary. The use of more advanced functionality like geofence, continuous tracking, user invoked alarm, and two way communication or one way audio surveillance was not utilised. One family reported that two way communication had been used in the early stages of the illness.

Table 2. Overview of types of equipment used by informants

Type/model:	Distributor/manufacturer	Web:	#:
Vandrofon	Cognita AS (Norway)	http://www.cognita.no	1
Benefon Seraph	Tele Scan AS (N)	http://www.telescan.no**	1
Safetracker	OnSat AS (N)	http://www.on-sat.no	2
Micro-tracker SL1*	Safelink (Denmark)	http://www.safelink.dk	1
GlobalSat TR-101*	Globalsat (Taiwan)	http://www.globalsat.com.tw	1

* Both these products have been discontinued and superseded by new models.
** Norwegian distributor.

The study showed that the informants by and large find their localization solutions easy to use, and that the equipment is very useful when locating their family members when required. All informants report that they have had good use of the equipment. The frequency of how often they have to perform localisations varies depending on the activity level of the person with dementia and their ability to orientate to their surroundings. Some families use it occasionally, and others need to locate and search for their family member with dementia frequently. They report an increased feeling of security and freedom, and using the equipment has had a positive impact on their overall situation. All families would recommend this type of equipment to others in a similar situation.

Some difficulties when using the devices are reported, but most of the informants report that the equipment works as it is supposed to for the majority of the time. Some of the difficulties encountered are related to system stability, secure fastening of the device to the person with dementia, impractical size of the device, not adequate detail of the localization maps, some user interface issues, in addition to general weaknesses with GPS-technology, i.e. does not function indoors.

Two of the families used the equipment in collaboration with health staff when the persons with dementia were in residential care. There are a number of particular challenges encountered when using the equipment together with staff in the health service. Some of the issues raised were covering costs, training of staff, routines for charging and maintenance, roles in physical searching et al. One family and the nursing staff had set in place a system which included staff training, documentation, routines for usage and follow up, as well as rosters which ensured that an especially trained staff member always was present. Despite all this, the next-of-kin was contacted on several occasions having to conduct localisations as the staff were unable to use the equipment on their own.

Most of the interviewees state that although they have received a minimum of amount of training in use, this has been adequate. Many of the informants are satisfied with the support provided by the distributing vendors. One of the families had to be totally self reliant on training, set up and support as this was not available for the product they had chosen.

It is an unambiguous wish from the informants that there is a need for a publicly run service in Norway which can inform, assist and guide potential buyers of localization AT. Currently it is somewhat arbitrary what sort of equipment is being obtained, and this can affect whether or not one ends up with suitable equipment matching needs and prerequisites for use. Further the informants state that such equipment should be funded by the public.

There is agreement between the findings from the interviews and the self-administered questionnaire QUEST 2.0 in which the respondents rate their satisfaction with the AT. The questionnaire consists of a total of 12 questions – eight of which relate to the device itself and four which cover respondent satisfaction with related services [13]. In addition the respondents are to select the three most important areas to them from a list of 12 aspects relating to the AT equipment and auxiliary services. The scale for each question is from one to five, with one indicating "Not satisfied at all" and a score of five indicating "Very satisfied" [13].

The overall mean score for all informants was 4.33 (median 4.42) which translates into the "Quite satisfied" and "Very satisfied" range. This can be broken down into a mean score for satisfaction with the equipment itself 4.36 (median 4.5), and a slightly lower mean score for satisfaction with the auxiliary services 4.17 (median 4.5). See Table 3 for further details. The most important areas listed by the informants were Safety/security (mentioned 7 times), Ease of use (5 mentions) and fulfilment of needs which was listed four times.

In terms of individual questions in QUEST 2.0 relating particularly to usability and usefulness, it is noteworthy that for the question relating to ease of use, five respondents answered "Very satisfied" which is the highest rating and one answered "Quite Satisfied". On the question pertaining to fulfilment of needs and effectiveness, all answered "Quite satisfied" (3 respondents) or "Very satisfied" (4 respondents). It can thus be interpreted that the informants find the equipment easy to use, and that it fulfils their needs.

Table 3. QUEST 2.0 responses. Scale: 1 "Not satisfied at all" to 5 "Very satisfied"

Informant:	Score for assistive technology, Q1-8.	Score for related services, Q8-12:	Total score:	Omitted or invalid responses:
1	4,25	5	4,5	0
2	4,88	4,75	4,84	0
3	4,13	3,67	4	1
4	4,75	-*	4,67	3
5	4,5	4,25	4,42	0
6	3,5	5	4,1	2
7	4,5	2,33	3,78	3
TOTAL	4,36	4,17	4,33	9

* Too many omitted responses. Informant reported that the questions related to auxiliary services not were relevant as no services were received.

6 Contributions to the Field

This study – although modest in size - sheds light on the practical usage of GPS/GSM-based localization equipment when used out in the community with people with dementia. It complements prior studies by focusing on the perceived usability and user-friendliness of the technology, as well as its usefulness. These issues have not been adequately addressed in previous research endeavours. The fact that the equipment is viewed as very useful by the informants in the care of their dementia suffering spouses or parent, suggest that the uptake and implementation of localization technology in dementia care is a worthwhile undertaking.

The findings indicate that the users find the equipment relatively easy to use. This is interesting given that we are dealing with quite sophisticated and advanced technology. It may be that the characteristics of the interviewees are not representative of the average person caring for dementia patients. The informants can be described as being: Relatively young, quite familiar with ICT and highly motivated. This may have given the results a somewhat more positive and favourable slant than what one can expect with average carers. The fact that several of the informants received assistance from their children who were very skilled at ICT when obtaining and using the equipment, is also likely to have had a bearing on this. Further, the interviewees only used the most basic functionality of the equipment. One would expect additional challenges with use of more advanced functionality. As such, further studies with larger samples would be useful to examine usability and user friendliness more broadly.

None of the informants reported to have any disabilities which affected use of the equipment. As most carers of dementia patients are elderly one would expect that a number of them will have sensory, cognitive and/or physical impairments affecting usage. No accessibility assessments were done on the equipment used. This should be a priority in future work to gauge how suited the set ups are for operation of carers who have specific disabilities such as vision impairment, reduced hearing, dexterity problems etc.

Given the nature of and context of usage it is essential that such equipment is reliable and as accurate as possible at all times. The findings indicate that the equipment used for localization purposes are largely stable and reliable for the majority of the time, but that there are some usability and technical issues which occasionally adversely affects the use of the equipment. This is also reflected in other studies, and should be pursued and addressed further [7][9][10].

An important aspect concerning accuracy, stability and reliability is the type of technology used. As GPS (by and large) does not work indoors and its accuracy is adversely affected by physical objects and poor weather conditions, it is important to look at technologies which can supplement GPS to ensure accurate and reliable localization at all times. The use of wireless networks, A-GPS, RFID, altimeters, digital compasses, accelerometers et al. can be utilised for this purpose. None of the set ups in this study utilised such technology. Future enquiries and product development should examine and incorporate such relatively new technological advances.

Such new technologies are increasingly added to mainstream technology such as smartphones and tablet computers exemplified through the iPhone and the iPad from Apple Computers. There are also a number of existing services which allow for localisation available for such devices. The suitability of such mainstream devices with tailor-made software used in the localization of persons with dementia is yet another line of enquiry worth pursuing.

7   Conclusion and Planned Activities

In conclusion one can say that GPS/GSM-based localization equipment can successfully be used to locate persons with dementia who go missing. The informants found the equipment very useful. The devices are viewed by the informants as relatively easy to use despite some usability and technical issues. The equipment is perceived as stable and reliable most of the time. Further R&D on the use of localization technology is urgently needed. Security and privacy protection, the potential of new technologies, use in the public health sector and additional usability studies are but some of the areas requiring further scientific scrutiny. It is also important to find innovative ways of involving the persons with dementia in R&D-activities. Funding for a follow up project involving usability, privacy protection and data security is currently being sought.

Acknowledgements

The author would especially like to thank the informants who shared their stories. Many thanks to Lise Fjeldvik and Sidsel Bjørneby for their input, and Rehab-Nor for permission to use QUEST 2.0.

References

1. Brækhus, A., et al.: Hva er demens?, 4th edn. UUS (2009)
2. Alzheimer's Disease International. World Alzheimer Report - Executive Summary (2009)
3. McShane, R., et al.: The feasibility of electronic tracking devices in dementia: a telephone survey and case series. Int. J. Geriatr. Psyc. 13(8), 556–563 (1998)
4. Landau, R., et al.: Attitudes of Family and Professional Care-Givers towards the Use of GPS for Tracking Patients with Dementia: An Exploratory Study. British Journal of Social Work 39(4), 670–692 (2009)
5. Kibayashi, K., Shojo, H.: Accidental fatal hypothermia in elderly people with Alzheimer's disease. Med. Sci. Law. 43(2), 127–131 (2003)
6. Hermans, D.G., Htay, U.H., McShane, R.: Non-pharmacological interventions for wandering of people with dementia in the domestic setting. Coch Database Syst. Rev. (1) (January 24, 2007)
7. Robinson, L., et al.: Balancing rights and risks: Conflicting perspectives in the management of wandering in dementia. Health, Risk & Society 9(4), 389–406 (2007)
8. Robinson, L., et al.: Effectiveness and acceptability of non-pharmacological interventions to reduce wandering in dementia: a systematic review. Int. J. Geriatr. Psyc. 22(1), 9–22 (2007)
9. Faucounau, V., et al.: Electronic tracking system and wandering in Alzheimer's disease: a case study. Ann. Phys. Rehabil. Med. 52(7-8), 579–587 (2009)
10. Miskelly, F.: Electronic tracking of patients with dementia and wandering using mobile phone technology. Age and Ageing 34, 497–499 (2005)
11. Bjørneby, S.: Å føle seg trygg med demens. Nasjonalforeningen for folkehelsen (2006)
12. Lauriks, S., et al.: Review of ICT-based services for identified unmet needs in people with dementia. Ageing Research Review 6(3), 223–246 (2007)
13. Demers, L., Weiss-Lambrou, R., Ska, B.: The Quebec User Evaluation of Satisfaction with Assistive Technology (QUEST 2.0): An overview and recent progress. Technology and Disability 14(3), 101–105 (2002)

Development of Universal Communication Aid for Emergency Using Motion Pictogram

Mari Kakuta[1], Kaoru Nakazono[2], Yuji Nagashima[3], and Naotsune Hosono[4]

[1] International Christian University
g099003@yamata.icu.ac.jp
[2] NTT Network Innovation Laboratories
[3] Kogakuin University
[4] Oki Consulting Solutions

Abstract. VUTE is a communication aid technology that aims to take away the communication barrier for people with hard of hearing related to old age, deaf people and people traveling abroad. VUTE uses motion pictograms and can be used without prior training. We created a prototype of VUTE (VUTE 2009), a system that can be used in emergency situations. This paper describes the design concept, overview and evaluation of VUTE 2009.

1 Introduction

People with hard of hearing related to old age, deaf people and people traveling abroad experience similar communication barrier. They cannot freely communicate in the spoken communication. Especially during emergency situations such as natural disaster, accidents and sudden illness, it is crucial that people have access to minimal communication such as calling for help. To achieve the above goals, we are currently designing a communication aid technology, VUTE (Visualized Universal Talking Environment) that does not rely on a specific language and can be used without prior training. As a preliminary stage for our project, we created a prototype of VUTE (VUTE 2009), a system that can be used to call an ambulance and or fire engine for emergency situations such as sudden illness and fire[1]. This paper describes the design concept, the overview and the evaluation of VUTE 2009.

2 Characteristics of VUTE

VUTE can be activated on a mobile information device and through interactions with the user by pictograms only it can gain the necessary information for rescue appropriate for each situation. After gaining necessary information, the information are organized so that it can create a sentence. In VUTE 2009 the sentences can be outputted as English and Japanese. For Japanese, voice synthesizing software can output spoken Japanese. By the above procedures, one can ask someone near them to call for rescue after telling them about the situation and/or call for rescue using e-mails.

K. Miesenberger et al. (Eds.): ICCHP 2010, Part I, LNCS 6179, pp. 308–311, 2010.

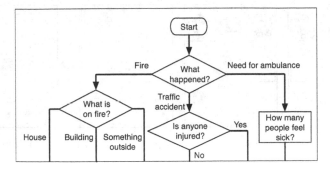

Fig. 1. Example from the flow-chart

VUTE has the following characteristics.

i) Nonuse of written language

In pictograms such as AAC, written languages are often used for supplementary information. Written information can increase the understanding of those who can understand some of the written language and can be very convenient. Yet for those who do not understand that language it has no meaning whatsoever. We strongly believe that using written language is an exclusive method and to aim for universal communication we do not use any written language in VUTE.

ii) Use of Expressions from Sign Language

Sign languages are not universal and are languages that vary like the spoken languages depending on the region/country that they are used and vocabulary, word order and grammar differs. Yet when Deaf people with different sign languages communicate for several hours, they can make minimum communication even though they may be signing with each other for the first time. Supalla and Webb state that there may be aspects in sign languages that enable minimal communication for the Deaf in international settings[2]. From this we believe the expressions used by the Deaf can be applied to VUTE.

iii) Use of Motion Pictograms

Most of AAC are paper-based so they frequently use still pictograms. On the other hand, VUTE can show motion pictograms since it can be used on a mobile information device. By using motion pictograms we can understand the movement immediately. This can enhance understanding of verbs and functional words that were difficult to express on still image pictograms.

3   Design and Development of VUTE 2009

With the aid from a local fire station in Japan, we analyzed the flow of conversation during rescue calls. We analyzed the typical interactions by focusing on factors such as what kind of information from the caller are necessary for the center and what kind of procedures are efficient. As a result, it was found that the repeated interactions where the gcenter asks the caller questions and the caller answersh can gain necessary information for rescue. Only up to 10 question and answer interactions were enough to gain necessary information.

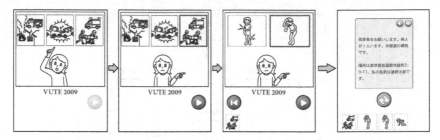

Fig. 2. Screen captures of conversation process with VUTE 2009

To systemize the emergency conversations, we made a flow chart of the conversation procedures and made it compact and simple to decrease the number of interactions. Also the questions asked by the center are all changed into alternative questions. In VUTE 2009, the user clicks the appropriate pictograms to answer to alternative questions. Therefore it is important that the user understands that gthey are selecting from several choicesh and choose the appropriate response (the user will most probably be using VUTE for the first time in an emergency situation).

For the users to understand that they have to answer an alternative question, VUTE 2009 uses an agent character in the center of the display that gestures gwhich one is the appropriate choice?h. The agent guides the users to choose the response in a natural manner. We designed VUTE 2009 taking into considerations the above factors. This program is made using Flash Application and can be accessed on the internet. People can access the site from their computers and can experience VUTE 2009.

4   Evaluation of VUTE 2009

To evaluate whether VUTE can achieve its goals as a minimum emergency conversation, subjects from different backgrounds were asked to use three types of navigational system: VUTE 2009, Japanese navigational system and English navigational system. This was a simulation providing the subjects with imaginary settings of emergency. Subjects were 13 hearing Japanese, 8 Deaf Japanese and 5 hearing foreigners. The navigational systems used in the evaluation were Japanese and English version of the pictograms used in VUTE and they were made for comparison and evaluation of VUTE. The 6 stories of imaginary situation were written in Japanese and English. The stories were printed out on A4 paper and before asking for the evaluation, the stories were handed to the subjects and they had to understand the stories. The printed material used for the imaginary stories will be presented on Figure2. At the end of each evaluation, the time spent by the subject for each evaluation were recorded and the subjects graded their comprehension of the pictograms, Japanese sentences and English sentences on a five point scale. Each subjects read 6 types of imaginary stories. 3 types of simulation (pictograms, Japanese and English) were randomly organized so that 6 types of evaluation were possible.

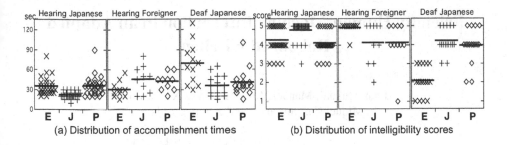

Fig. 3. Results of the evaluation

5   Results and Discussion

When using VUTE, all subjects were able to respond to the final question without hesitation and were able to select the appropriate response most of the time. Figure 3 is a scatter graph showing the distribution of the time spent on each evaluation depending on the different groups of subjects. The average of each group are shown on the horizontal line. The distribution of the understanding of VUTE is also shown on the graph.

For hearing Japanese and foreigners when using motion pictograms, they understood equally as their foreign languages and time spent were almost the same. For the Deaf, when comparing Japanese and motion pictograms, time and understanding were the same and for foreign language navigation they used the most time and their understanding were low. In this evaluation, it was found that for emergency conversations, communication aid using no written language can achieve its goals. VUTE2009 can be accessed on the Internet and can be used freely. For future research more subjects will be asked to evaluate the program for further analysis. In the future we are planning to expand the conversation situations (e.g. during a trip).

Acknowledgement

This research is granted by the Strategic Information and Communications R&D Promotion Programme (SCOPE) of Ministry of Internal Affairs and Communications, Japan.

References

1. Nakazono, K., Kakuta, M., Nagashima, Y., Hosono, N.: Universal communication aid for disabled people using motion pictograms. In: HCI International 2009 - Posters, pp. 951–955. Springer, Heidelberg (2009)
2. Supalla, T., Webb, R.: The Grammar of International Sign: A new Look at Pidgin Languages. In: Language and Gesture, Space, pp. 333–352 (1995)

Friendly Human-Machine Interaction in an Adapted Robotized Kitchen

Joan Aranda[1], Manuel Vinagre[1], Enric X. Martín[2],
Miquel Casamitjana[2], and Alicia Casals[1]

[1] Institute for Bioengineering of Catalonia (IBEC), UPC
[2] Universitat Politecnica de Catalunya, UPC-BarcelonaTECH

Abstract. The concept and design of a friendly human-machine interaction system for an adapted robotized kitchen is presented. The kitchen is conceived in a modular way in order to be adaptable to a great diversity in level and type of assistance needs. An interaction manager has been developed which assist the user to control the system actions dynamically according to the given orders and the present state of the environment. Real time enhanced perception of the scenario is achieved by means of a 3D computer vision system. The main goal of the present project is to provide this kitchen with the necessary intelligent behavior to be able to actuate efficiently by interpreting the users' will.

1 Introduction

In this work, the concept and design of an adapted robotized kitchen is described. This kitchen is conceived in a modular way in order to be adaptable to a great diversity in level and type of assistance needs. The goal of this project is to make a gradual transformation, in accordance to the user's needs, from a conventional kitchen into an adapted one. The kitchen conception puts special emphasis on the way its computer controlled modular elements can fit with these needs and at the same time, minimize the impact that technology produces in domestic environments, which can turn out to be very invasive [1][2][3].

The main interest of the present research work lies on achieving an intelligence level of such robotized environment that allows its users to interact with all the modular elements in the simplest and natural way. For this reason, the kitchen control system has to achieve the necessary intelligent behavior to be able to actuate efficiently by interpreting the users' will and perceiving the environment information that provide the state conditions of the robot and modular elements.

2 Structure of the Adapted Kitchen

Considering the premise of adaptation to the concrete needs in every situation, the project starts from several modular elements that can be incorporated in function of both, the concrete user's needs and the physical dimensions of the kitchen.

K. Miesenberger et al. (Eds.): ICCHP 2010, Part I, LNCS 6179, pp. 312–319, 2010.

The whole kitchen composition is based on the design and integration of elements in four different lines:

- External worktop and cupboards with normal appearance, but motorized, aimed at approaching the objects to the user.
- Adaptation of the manual components, as faucets or electrical stoves, by providing them with actuators which are controlled by a computer.
- One or more robotic arms which can be integrated in the kitchen when the user's level of disability requires this additional aid. A Cartesian crane structure has been selected, which is fitted to the user's kitchen free ceiling. The robot physical volume is minimized due to its three-to-one telescopic linear axis.
- An interface that enables any user to control all the modular elements in the environment from a unique control system. The interface should be able to integrate control components of many different types. The selected interface device depends in each case on the user's remaining physical capabilities. The interface is endowed with a projector that visualizes either commands or functioning states, in a very clear and intuitive way.

The current kitchen prototype has been designed as a composition of such modular elements, having a sample of each of them and their adaptations, when necessary, to evaluate the functionality of the parts as well as the whole system. Fig. 1 a) shows the initial idea of the kitchen structure where the basic modular elements are at the robot reach [4]. Fig. 1 b) shows the experimental prototype.

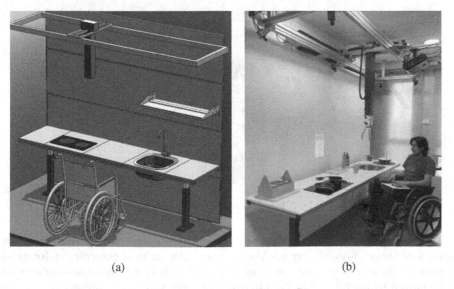

(a)   (b)

Fig. 1. a) Outline of the robotized kitchen; b) Current prototype

3 Interaction System Description

The modular conception of the kitchen has also been applied to the user-system interfaces, considering modularity in the sense of being able to adapt the interaction mechanisms to the actuation abilities and perception of the user. Actuation abilities determine the type of device that the user can manage to issue orders to the system, and its election will depend in a great extend on his or her capacity and remaining motor abilities. The perception possibilities are related to the visualization of the state of the different modules from the kitchen and phases of the tasks in course. They are also related to the visualization of the different orders given by the user.

Figure 2 shows the framework used to link the different modules of our system. A centralized synchronization of the tasks is proposed by means of an Interaction Manager Module. This manager assists the user to control the system actions dynamically according to the given orders and the present state of the environment.

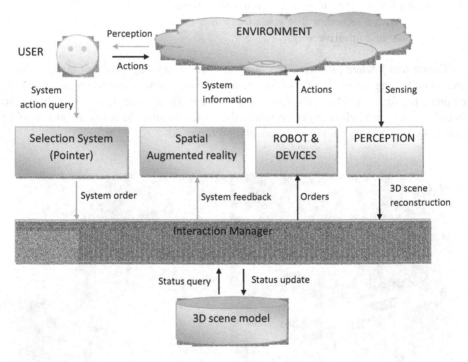

Fig. 2. Interaction System Framework

Input information can be direct orders given by the user through different input devices as mouse, joystick, eye tracking, etc, and also indirect perceptive information acquired from user actions on scene, as putting objects in defined input-output areas, to be moved by the robot. The need to adapt the high variety of available devices has forced us to specify the design in such a way that it allows connecting any of them efficiently. A flexible adaptation of input devices permits join different input data to manage the actuation system in a multimodal interface.

The state of the kitchen can be displayed in different forms. The most common option is the use of a monitor showing different menus with icons or even real time images of kitchen obtained with cameras [5].

In this paper we present a new way of visualizing the state of the system based on the use of Spatial Augmented Reality (SAR) of the actual scene. In this case a projector illuminates the objects in the kitchen with lights of different colors, in a perceptible way to the user. This allows the user to select the element or object to be used by pointing it, for example, with a joystick and pressing to right or left button, like in a carrousel. Even in case of great difficulties, it is also possible the use of eye tracking system [6][7] or other devices.

The projector shows information about the selected object over flat surfaces, like walls or cooking top, allowing the user to choose the action on the selected item, with few movements. The menus are context sensitive, presenting only possible actions for the selected item in the present moment. Moreover, when possible, this information is displayed near the object in order to avoid disturbing the user's attention from the task going on, as shown in figure 3. For users with visual impairment, a voice synthesizer can be used to present the information.

Fig. 3. a) Selected item (a glass) and its possible options. b) Resulting action.

The system that visualizes the state of the kitchen must allow the execution of the requested tasks fast and effectively. It is necessary to reduce as much as possible the number of options available so as to improve operation speed. This can be achieved with a good distribution of the different functionalities in different menus in an adaptive and collaborative way.

To enhance the usability of this operating environment, where some daily routines and repetitive actions can appear, the system controller has been provided with learning and prediction capabilities [8]. The system is able to record all the sequences performed with the objects, the place where they are taken, its order, etc, using this information to recognize routine actions and in parallel, to predict which one will be the most probable. Finally, when the operation context is perfectly checked, some commands can be only confirmation orders of the usual tasks. This progressive simplification of the interface and routinely behavior increases user comfort and system's acceptance.

4   Assisted User's Control by Means of Computer Vision

Controlling a robotic environment, especially for non professional or technical users is a difficult task. These difficulties increase when dealing with disabled, either physical or cognitive, so a classical top-down control scheme (like in industrial applications) cannot be applied. A robotized system, in such an unstructured domestic environment, must offer some extra performances, such as enhanced perception, in order to warranty safety for both, user and appliances. The control system should also be able to react properly to orders that, because of user impairments, require a higher interpretation level, and of course, the control system must allow the user to rectify or modify the execution of a command at any time.

The implemented visual system accomplishes two main tasks: the 3D location of objects in the scene and their identification (when required), and the interpretation of user commands.

4.1   Object Location and Recognition

A rig of cameras provides visual information from the operation scene. As objects are seen from several points of view, it is possible to triangulate their position and to obtain some object's volumetric information with a *Shape from Silhouette* algorithm [9]. For recognized objects, their exact shape is known and the 3D scene model data base is updated with new location. For those objects that are not recognized, an approximated convex hull of the object is generated and it is included in the data base as an obstacle. Figure 4 shows a real scene and the result of its visual 3D reconstruction where can be seen the voxels belonging to objects.

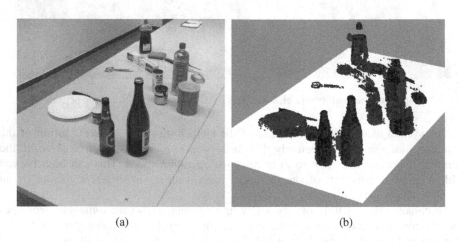

(a)   (b)

Fig. 4. a) Real scene. b) Voxels 3D reconstruction.

The visual system, in combination with the 3D model data base, is not only used to avoid obstacles but also to enrich the interface with the user. This 3D location helps the user to select an object within the pointed area. It also guides the robot towards the object according to the direction the user is pointing to, acting like a magnet.

The real time 3D reconstruction module is always checking the scenario in order to confirm the final positions of objects which position or orientation have been modified and also, and more important, to detect such changes when they are not produced by the robot. The possibility of the user to directly move objects in his/her kitchen is without any doubt the most challenging goal of this module. All this situations are preceded by a high image difference not related to the robot or other devices movement. In the present system three cases have been considered: the appearance of a new object/obstacle on the cooking top, its removal and its movement.

Sometimes, it is necessary to identify the object in order to guarantee the suitability of the commands received from the user or to resolve ambiguities. The object recognition system applied is based on a database with several IF-THEN rules or filters. For each object, the information about its volume and other physical, geometric and color features, is recorded. The system also maintains a record of the last known position for every object in the scene, so this information is used to make a first selection of the objects that are probably pointed by the user. Figure 5 shows the filter sequence for object recognition.

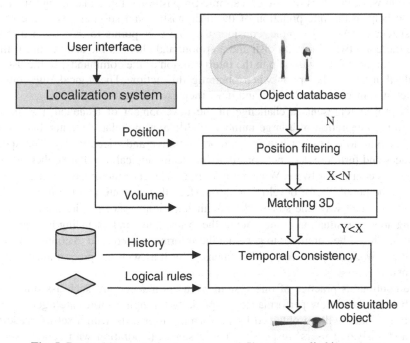

Fig. 5. Recognition system schema: several filters are applied in sequence

4.2 Command Interpretation

The system must be able to interpret the user's wishes and generate precise commands to the robotized elements taking into account the previous orders, user behavior and environment state. User intentions must be translated into explicit robot coordinate system points and trajectories. What is a simple gesture for the user will be processed by the system and referred to the scene to generate a sequence of commands.

The developed computer vision system is able to detect and track people in the scene. Furthermore it must be able to extract the user's posture and to analyze user's gestures and use them as inputs to the system [10]. All this information is available to the system interface, giving more flexibility to the system and making the adaptation of the interface to the user requirements possible.

5   Conclusions and Perspectives

The proposed adapted kitchen is now under study and an experimental prototype is being developed, aiming at advancing towards personal autonomy at home to deal with daily life activities. The system has an object database, is able to calculate object's volumes and positions, has a record of user routines and preferences and has other environment information like time, date or even temperature.

Present work involves the use of a simple propositional logic managing this data in order to help in the interpretation of the user wishes and solving possible errors or inconsistencies. As an example, consider that the user points to any given direction where there are two objects, a dish and a spoon, and chooses the action "put it into a cup". The logical filter will help in the interpretation of the commands, so the user can be only thinking in the spoon when planning this action. The logical filter must be completely transparent to the user and must increase the system usability.

This project represents a challenge in the development of technical aids in what refers to the integration of a large number of different modular elements that the user should be able to control at will in a simple, intuitive and friendly way. The specific appliances and furniture does not constitute any technological novelty, neither the robot itself nor its control hardware. What really implies a level of intelligence and ergonomic design is the possibility of developing an interface that can interpret the users' wills in the most efficient way: the so-called "human intention" concept. The convergence of learning about the situation or the state of the system, and understanding human desires or orders, allows the controller to generate the information required to control the robot, so as it can work cooperatively with humans as well as with the programmed modular elements.

The continuous practice of this system by users that require such assistance, will contribute to shape new performances, especially through a more intelligent control. A usability index will be obtained by performing user tests with a set of predefined tasks and analyzing users' response. The present collaboration with centers such as the Institute Guttmann, or the Center for Independent Life (CVI), both foundations located in Barcelona, with the robotics groups at IBEC and CREB-UPC, offers an excellent frame to learn from the prototype, advancing towards an aiding system more and more powerful.

References

1. Casals, A.: Technical aids for the disabled. Monografias de Tecnología 4. Societat Catalana de Tecnologia, Institut d'Estudis Catalans (1998)
2. http://www.pressalitcare.com
3. http://www.akw-medicare.co.uk
4. Casals, A., Merchan, R., Portell, E., Cufí, X., Contijoc, J.: CAPDI: A robotitzed kitchen for the disabled and ederly people. In: AAATE: association for Assistive Technology Conference, Dusseldorf (1999)
5. Casals, A., Cufí, X., Freixenet, J., Martíy, J., Muñoz, X.: Friendly interface for Objects Recognition in a Robotized Kitchen. In: IEEE Int Conference on robòtics and Automation (2000)
6. Aranda, J., Climent, J., Grau, A.: Human-Computer interface based on computer vision. In: Proceedings ICCHP 1998, Viena (1998) ISBN: 3-85403-118-1
7. Kim, E.Y., Park, S.H.: Computer Interface Using Eye Tracking for Handicapped. In: Corchado, E., Yin, H., Botti, V., Fyfe, C. (eds.) IDEAL 2006. LNCS, vol. 4224, pp. 562–569. Springer, Heidelberg (2006)
8. Sheth, B., Maes, P.: Evolving Agents for Personalized Information Filtering. In: Proceedings of the Ninth Conference on Artificial Intelligence for Applications 1993, Orlando, Florida. IEEE Computer Society Press, Los Alamitos (1993)
9. Martin, E., Aranda, J., Martinez, A.B.: Refining 3D recovering by carving through view interpolation and stereovision. In: Perales, F.J., Campilho, A.C., Pérez, N., Sanfeliu, A. (eds.) IbPRIA 2003. LNCS, vol. 2652. Springer, Heidelberg (2003)
10. Amat, J., Frigola, M., Casals, A.: Human Robot Interaction from Visual Perception. In: IEEE/RSJ International Conference on Intelligent Robots and Systems (2004)

Audio Classification Techniques in Home Environments for Elderly/Dependant People

Héctor Lozano[1], Inmaculada Hernáez[2], Artzai Picón[1],
Javier Camarena[1], and Eva Navas[2]

[1] Robotiker-Tecnalia, Health and Quality of Life Unit, Parque Tecnológico, Edificio 202.
E-48170 Zamudio (Bizkaia), Spain
{hlozano,jcamarena,apicon}@robotiker.es
[2] University of the Basque Country, Department of Electronics and Telecommunications,
E-48013 Bilbao (Bizkaia), Spain
{inma.hernaez,eva.navas}@ehu.es

Abstract. The study of techniques and algorithms for "non-speech" sounds analysis and processing can be foreseen as a technological progress bringing important benefits to disadvantaged groups. This article focuses on finding solutions which allow the detection and classification of household sounds with two clearly defined objectives: 1) Helping people with hearing impairment to overcome daily situations which they have to deal with, such as warnings/alarms, door bells or telephones ringing, alarm clocks, etc. 2) To collect information from the environment which may be used to track the behavior pattern of an individual.

Keywords: Sound Classification, Signal Processing, Assistive Technology.

1 Introduction

People with hearing impairments might have problems in different situations in daily life, therefore affecting their quality of life and independence. At home, events such as the doorbell, a ringing telephone or the crying of a baby come up everyday which prove the problems caused by the lack of hearing.

Household sounds recognition allows not only to warn about environmental events but also compile information about what is happening at any given moment at home. Fridge door opening, microwave bell or the sound of moving crockery may indicate that the person is about to prepare meal. This knowledge can be used to train and develop behavior modeling systems, aimed at elderly people, and helping to prevent possible physical and cognitive deterioration based on the evolution of these user patterns.

The methodology used to obtain the acoustic parameters of the signal is generally based on windowing the signal with a fixed length window, and elaborating an array of features for each windowed frame to train or test the classifier. This process does not give temporal information about each characteristics vector which trains the model [1].

K. Miesenberger et al. (Eds.): ICCHP 2010, Part I, LNCS 6179, pp. 320–323, 2010.

This paper presents the results of a study carried out to analyze the behavior of multi-resolution techniques at the feature extraction stage in order to bring a higher level of accuracy and reliability to the classification of impulsive sounds. The results are compared with a previous research [2].

2 Sound Event Detection and Classification Systems

Although in recent past decades sound recognition has been focused mainly on speech recognition, more recently significant advances have been made as far as "non-speech" sound detection and identification is concerned [3] [4]. In spite of the many differences that can be found between the two sub-areas, the general stages which define the general procedures are the same. These stages can be analyzed in three distinct modules [5]: sound detection, feature extraction and sound classification. These modules are responsible for receiving and processing the sound with the aim of notifying the user of the appropriate option every time. This article will focus on the second and third modules "Feature Extraction" and "Sound Classification".

2.1 Feature Extraction

Sound Database. In order to test and validate the sound recognition system the commercial database "Sound Scene Database in Real Acoustical Environment" [6] have been used.

The experiments were performed using eleven different types of sound (100 audio files per type): pans, cups, bottles, china, sprays, phones, clocks, rattles (kara), door locks, shavers and dryers. The selection was made on the grounds that these sounds are commonly found in the home.

Selection of Acoustic Parameters. The selection of the acoustic parameters was based on previous studies [5], where the most used characteristics are the MFCCs (Mel Frequency Cepstrum Coefficients), very common in the speech recognition field) as well as the ZCR (Zero Crossing Rate), Centroid and Roll-Off Point (very common in the field of recognition of instruments and environmental sounds).

For each window, 13 mel-cepstral coefficients, zero crossing rate, Spectral Centroid and Roll-Off Point were calculated, providing a 16-parameter vector when no multi-resolution was used.

Multi-resolution Analysis. Current techniques in signal analysis generally use a fixed-length window to extract a signal segment that will be analyzed to obtain the array of features that will be used to train and test the classifier. The multi-resolution analysis technique here proposed uses multiple windows of different sizes to describe each selected sample point of the signal. This process implies obtaining a higher number of parameters, thus worsening the performance of the classifier. This is compensated by performing a heuristic selection of the parameters to reduce the size of the features array. This multi-sized analysis provides the classifier with temporal information about the sound and its evolution over time and allows for a higher knowledge of its nature.

2.2 Sound Classification

There are several probabilistic classification techniques, but they are not all appropriate for recognising sounds that are not related to speech. The chosen classifier, GMM [7], is a simple model which can be described as a Hidden Markov Model (HMM) of a single state.

3 Experiments Performed

A study has been carried out in order to evaluate the use of multiple windows. For the evaluation of this approach, 60% of the audio files have been used to train the models, leaving aside the remaining 40% for the testing phase.

The window sizes chosen have been of 20 milliseconds for the characteristics extraction with single window and 20, 40 and 80 for the multi-resolution. A 10 millisecond frame rate has been used both for training and testing.

In a first experiment the two methods have been evaluated using all the above parameters. In a second experiment a heuristic search has been performed to reduce the number of parameters, looking for the optimum subset of them.

4 Results and Discussion

The results obtained are presented in Table 1 using three measures for the success rate: the reliability ratio by type of sound (RRS), the accuracy ratio by type of sound (ARS) and the accuracy ratio by sample point (ARSP) defined in equation 1.

$$RRS = \frac{\sum_{i=1}^{N} \frac{C_i}{SPC_i}}{N}; \quad ARS = \frac{\sum_{i=1}^{N} \frac{C_i}{TSP_i}}{N}; \quad ARSP = \frac{C}{TSP}. \tag{1}$$

where C_i is the well classified sample points of type i, SPC_i is the sample points classified as type i, TSP_i is the total sample points of type i and N is the number of class sounds.

Table 1. Comparison of the results of the different techniques

	Single Window (All features)	Single Window (Heuristic)	Multiple Window (All features)	Multiple Window (Heuristic)
RRS	76.22%	77.02%	74.58%	84.92%
ARS	73.27%	76.70%	69.14%	81.42%
ARSP	85.95%	91.90%	86.74%	92.44%

5 Conclusions and Future Lines

This work demonstrates how multi-resolution analysis obtains notable improvements regarding the use of single windows. Using all the parameters, the reliability and accuracy ratios are unfavorable owing to the high number of parameters being generated. However, looking for the optimum reduced set of parameters, the improvement of this technique is demonstrated (nearly 8% of the reliability ratio by sounds and nearly 5% of the accuracy ratio by sounds).

For future works, we are considering the use of adaptive windows, as well as the use of parameters with temporal information such as the first and second derivatives. On the other hand, larger and/or different databases should be tried. Moreover, as future work, it is necessary to develop an event detector integrated with the classification part, and being able of starting the system up in real environments.

References

1. Clavel, C., Ehrette, T., Richard, G.: Events Detection for an Audio-Based Surveillance System. In: IEEE International Conference on Multimedia and Expo. ICME, pp. 1306–1309 (2005)
2. Lozano, H., Hernáez, I., Navas, E., et al.: "Non-Speech" Sounds Classification for People with Hearing Disabilities. In: IX European Conference for the Advancement of Assistive Technology in Europe, AAATE, pp. 276–280 (2007)
3. Cowling, M.: Non-Speech Environmental Sound Classification System for Autonomous Surveillance. Phd Thesis. Faculty of Engineering and Information Technology, Griffith University (2004)
4. Temko, A.: Acoustic Event Detection and Classification. Phd Thesis. Universitat Politècnica de Catalunya (2007)
5. Istrate, D., Vacher, M., Serignat, J.F., Castelli, E.: Multichannel Smart Sound Sensor for Perceptive Spaces. In: Complex Systems, Intelligence and Modern Technology Applications, CSIMTA, pp. 691–696 (2004)
6. RWCP Sound Scene Database in Real Acoustical Environments: Voice Activity Detection in Noisy Environments (1998),
   http://tosa.mri.co.jp/sounddb/nospeech/research/indexe.htm
7. Atrey, K., Maddage, C., Kankanhalli, S.: Audio Based Event Detection for Multimedia Surveillance. In: IEEE International Conference on Acoustic Speech and Signal Processing, ICCASP, pp. 813–816 (2006)

Autonomamente: Using Goal Attainment Scales to Evaluate the Impact of a Multimodal Domotic System to Support Autonomous Life of People with Cognitive Impairment

Thimoty Barbieri, Piero Fraternali, Antonio Bianchi, and Clarissa Tacchella

Politecnico di Milano – Polo Regionale di Como, Via Anzani 42,
22100 Como, Italy
{thimoty.barbieri,piero.fraternali}@polimi.it

Abstract. The Autonomamente project developed a highly customizable application based on multimodal communication (speech, icons, text) to support autonomous living of persons with cognitive disabilities in special apartments fitted with domotic sensors. Its functionalities are designed to support everyday social activities of the users: using the telephone in a simple way, schedule appointments, keep track of time and organize personal finances and savings. This paper aims to explain the evaluation performed using the Goal Attainment Scale Method, whereby each person agrees with his/her trainer upon at least one specific goal related to the application in order to improve his/her results.

Keywords: Ambient Assisted Living, Assessment and Profiling, Augmented and Alternative Communication (AAC), Cognitive Disability.

1 Introduction

The Autonomamente[1] project addresses the theme of supporting participation and autonomous living of persons with cognitive disabilities within apartments provided with some domotic facilities and with some degree of local and remote control by health care centers. A multimodal interface has been designed to provide personalized access to the following functions: 1) control the state of the apartment, and react to alarm conditions appropriately; 2) manage communication functions, like phone calling, e-mail composition and reading; 3) manage a simplified schedule of appointments, to organize one's day in an assisted yet autonomous way; 4) keep track of domestic finances, managing daily expenses and savings, with the collaboration of the tutor from the health care center. The software is built around the concept of full customization and dynamic adaptation to the specific user's need, by means of a configuration tool. The aim of this paper is to give a quick overview about the assistive technology used and, mainly, to point out the outcomes reached after one year of training with the users, while additional improvements were added to the system, especially in relation to the communication and money modules.

---

[1] Autonomamente means both "Autonomously," and "Autonomous Mind", in Italian.

K. Miesenberger et al. (Eds.): ICCHP 2010, Part I, LNCS 6179, pp. 324–331, 2010.
© Springer-Verlag Berlin Heidelberg 2010

To evaluate the satisfaction of the users, the Goal Attainment Scale Method (GAS) has been adopted, whereby each person agrees with his/her trainer upon at least one specific goal related to the application in order to improve his/her results. Every four month of training, users and observers reviewed each scale to understand to what extent the agreed goals were reached, and determined the actions needed to improve results and user's satisfaction.

2 State of the Art

The term "smart home" entered the general vocabulary in the 1990s and, within the disability community, refers to the use of electronic assistive technology ("EAT"), including electronic aids to daily living ("EADL"), assistive technology for cognition ("ATC"), and other tools that provide support to people in the home setting. EADL systems are widely used by people with mobility impairment and may be utilized to simplify home tasks for people with cognitive impairment as well [7]. A smart home is a residence equipped with technology that enhances safety of patients at home and, sometimes, can monitor their health conditions. Therefore, the devices and sensors chosen to be installed and maintained in the residences need to address functional limitations, as well as social and health care needs [9]. Several pilot projects have introduces smart home technologies both in the US and in Europe, among which some examples are: the SmartBo project in Sweden [8] that utilizes solutions for elderly with mobility impairments and/or cognitive disabilities; PROSAFE [9] that aims at identifying abnormal behavior of monitored patients; Smart house in Tokushima, Japan [11] that emphasis on eliminating barriers within the residence and maintaining secured lifelines in case of a natural disaster and the Georgia Tech Aware Home Project, developed in the US [10] that features two identical independent living spaces to allow for controlled experiments with technology.

About one year ago, preliminary data about the usage of the Autonomamente interface were collected using two different surveys: the first one, based on the ICF protocol [5] was used to assess the level of disability of each user; the second one, instead, was used to collect data after each training session. The evaluation methodology, however, did little to measure the improvement in the autonomous living capability of the users. The need arouse to understand if the software was continuing to be useful to its users over a long period of time and if the new features added to the system under usage actually improved the capacities of the users.

To perform this evaluation, we have adopted the Goal Attainment Scale (GAS) technique, developed in 1968 by Kiresuk and Sherman [4], which allows each individual user to define his own specific goals, based on his/her perception of importance. Goals are described by Locke and Latham [2] as "something that a person wants to achieve" or "desired end states". In their goal-setting theory, the authors advocate that the mind automatically and subconsciously evaluates actions, objects and events to determine whether individual goals are being advanced or thwarted. The study performed by Rockwood, Joyce and Stolee [1] shows that GAS is a useful technique for evaluating specialized multidisciplinary interventions (as Autonomamente is), and is sensitive to clinically important change in patients in a cognitive rehabilitation program. The technique also proved to be useful in allowing people and their families to better understand the possible outcome of care, and their role in achieving such outcomes. The setting of explicit work goals has been shown to affect work performance, mainly because when people hold goals that they value highly, they are more likely to pursue them with greater energy and persistence [3]. This last sentence is even more important considering the main focus of the Autonomamente project, which is to empower people to better participating to the social context and reaching their own declination of autonomous living.

3   Assistive Technology

The three main characteristics of the software developed by the Autonomamente project are:

- *Customization*: each user can ask the caregiver to configure a number of options related to layout and some specific functionalities;

- *Multimodality*: the interface provides messages with three different means of communication: text, voice, AAC icons;

- *Concretization of abstract concepts*: time, quantities and other abstract concepts are represented through icons, images or graphic widgets.

The system provides four different modules designed to help people with cognitive disabilities to carry out some activities in their home environment through the reduction of the cognitive effort needed to understand the interfaces and interact with the computer.

1. *Communication*: guests can use the system to phone to parents and friends and send/receive "multimodal" e-mails (with mixed text, icons, and recorded speech) to a white list of contacts. To overcome problems related to phone numbers or e-mail addresses, a visual phonebook has been implemented: a simple click on the photo of a person allows the user to choose between phone call or email/sms composition, according to the specific information provided for each contact by means of the configurator application. Phone book scrolling can be both manual or automatic, to avoid paging problems (e.g., looping). E-mail composition can be personalized for each user thanks to the implementation of a system that allows the cohabitations of a number of customizable keyboards (alphabetic, iconic or mixed versions). The newest solution is represented by a series of keyboard whose buttons are used to compose entire words, part of sentences or icons and text.

2. *Agenda*: this module deals with the abstract concept of time. Each user can visualize his/her list of appointments related to a specific day, control the details of the scheduled activities and have a hint about their closeness. Different time granularities can be set at configuration time.

3. *Money*: this module is composed by two different areas, both dealing with two abstract concepts: time and quantity (of money). The first functionality is a moneybox simulation, where people can save money and, if this function is configured, control how much still need to be saved to buy a specified object. The

second functionality is related to the management of daily expenses, to control how much money are spent during a specific period of time. This part of the software can also be used as a sort of didactic application.

4. *House*: this module allows the user to check if his/her house is safe, according to a number of rules customized by the caregiver. For each apartment, it is possible to configure the meaning of "safe" according to the time of the day, the day of the week, the flatmates' profiles and, most important, the domotic devices and sensors available. The system's policy is to let users check the status of the devices but not modify it, because it is important that the actions be carried out in the real world.

4 Methodology Used

We have conducted sessions of use, collaborated and collected data with three different groups of users; the total number of persons involved in the evaluation of the prototype is 14. To accomplish the activities of setting up objectives, measuring their achievement, and processing all the data collected, we used the Goal Attainment Scale technique, as defined by Rockwood, Joyce and Stolee [1] and with the simplification presented by Kiresuk, Smith and Cardillo [6].

1. Step one - Goals setting

Within each group of users, a simple collective interview was set up, in order to have the support and reinforcement of the peers - both as motivators and to avoid to stress the concept of formality and data collection too much.

First of all, all the activities carried out in relation to the Autonomamente interface were summarized, explaining the various functionalities that can be performed with the Autonomamente software. At the end of this preliminary step, each person expressed his/her goals filling one or more guideline sheets printed before the interview. Some of them performed this activity almost autonomously, while the majority needed careful supporting. The form aimed at determining each one's objectives not through direct questions, but using a narrative approach. Each interview has been tuned to the personality and need of each participant, and the completion of the whole activity took about 6 hours for the three groups. Following the Goal Attainment Rule, for each defined goal a 5-point scale of operational outcomes was defined with each user, ranging from the least favourable one thought possible (-2) to the most favourable (+2), with a value of zero (0) assigned to the expected outcome. At the end of the measurement activity we assigned the level of goal attainment, tracking therefore a regression, a preservation, or an improvement in the ability. This issue is important, as for example, in specific situations the mere keeping of a capability can be considered an important result (avoiding therefore a regression).

2. Step two – Follow up period

The follow up period had a duration of four month, during which a biweekly training was performed with all the users.

Table 1. Sample goal attainment scaling for a middle-aged woman with cognitive disability

Goal attainment levels	Goal 1 Write an e-mail	Goal 2 Adding contacts to the phone book	Goal 3 Use the schedule
Best anticipated success with treatment (+2)	Be able to write an e-mail adding a taped message	I receive at least one message from my contacts	Add appointments to my schedule with the caregiver
More than expected success (+1)	Write an e-mail with at least ten words	I'm able to add at least two contacts	Be able to read and understand data
Expected level of treatment success (0)	Write an e-mail with at least ten words	I'm able to add at least two contact	Understand how to navigate within this module
Less than expected success with treatment (-1)	It is too difficult for me to write an e-mail	I'm able to add one contact but I don't receive messages	This module is too demanding for my skills
Most unfavorable treatment outcome thought likely (-2)	It is impossible to send the e-mail	It is impossible to add data to the system	I find this module usefulness or not interesting

3. Step three – Data analysis

The GAS score were calculated for each user using the formula[4]:

$$T = 50 + \frac{10 \sum w_i x_i}{\sqrt{(1-\rho) \sum w_i^2 + \rho \left(\sum w_i\right)^2}}. \tag{1}$$

where w_i is the weight assigned to the ith goal, x_i the numerical value (-2 to +2) of the attainment level of the ith goal and ρ is the expected overall inter-correlation among goals scores. However, for simplicity sake, we used the correlation table provided by Kiresuk and colleagues [6].

5   R & D Work and Results - Impact to the Field

Few weeks after the determination of the goals, one person expressed her unconcern about the training sessions and she preferred to leave the group of users, so in March we reexamined the tables with the thirteen remaining persons, assessing with each one the level of satisfaction about his/her personal goals.

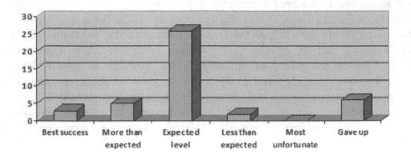

Fig. 1. Level of satisfaction after the end of the second training session

Figure 1 shows a very high prevalence of the expected level of success, meaning that all the users reached at least the minimum acceptable outcome after the training session (that can be both the development of new basic skills or the maintenance of the previous level possessed). As shown by the chart, 6 goals over 42 were abandoned/dropped by some users: this is due to a reduction of interest concerning the objective or an impossibility to train them over a specific function they were interested in, due to lack of time compared to the global number of goals.

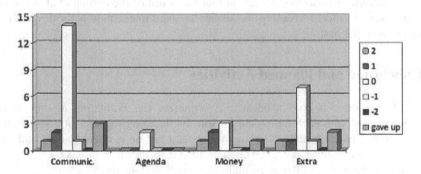

Fig. 2. Global results

Figure 2 shows the results collected among the users, classifying them across the different thematic areas of the Autonomamente interface, showing once again that the communication module is perceived as fundamental by the user. The label 'Extra' identifies all the goals that don't involve Autonomamente, but are related for instance to collateral activities done in the group, like e.g., music or painting.

The overall data are positive: every user reached at least the expected level of success for one objective (value equal to "0" in Figure 2) and only two persons experienced a less than expected result for one of their goals (value equal to "-1"). The range of scores calculated using the correlation table provided by Kiresuk and colleagues [6] goes from 69 to 46, with an average of 54,07: this means that the training sessions were quite positive, allowing the users to maintain or improve their skills, both on Autonomamente features and "Extra" activities, gaining a global better result than the one considered acceptable (represented by a score equal to 50). The goals labeled as "Extra" were considered as important as the "principal" ones because in different moments they helped the team to maintain the motivation toward the training sessions and to increase collaboration, communication and sharing of knowledge among the peers. In addition to the quantitative results determined analyzing the data, it is important to point out the great stimulus represented by the GAS approach, because it allowed users to reach some important collateral goals. Some examples are: user A. has significantly lowered his anxiety and obsession about phone calls to one specific person, allowing himself to explore communication with other interlocutors using also other communication methods (like e-mails) and enjoying his ability to teach to the peers what he had experimented. User G. finally had the possibility to write some sentences related to her preferred themes using a mixed approach including words and symbols. The buttons containing her preferred "language bricks" permit her to see "recorded" what her difficult speech conveys, and leave her the possibility to explore and compose new sentences. Last but not least, user L., one of the very first ones involved in Autonomamente, gave up her initial passive attitude toward the interaction with the information system and the whole project, developing intentional communicative actions with the peers, the project staff and other people of her network of relationships. Great satisfaction and sense of inclusion are two goals not specifically declared but already reached by him.

This approach proved to be effective not only to increase the motivation toward the training sessions, but also to stimulate autonomous use of the computer at home or at the Caregiving Center, increasing the desire to experiment new activities with less worries than in the past.

6 Conclusion and Planned Activities

The GAS method was chosen because it organizes the evaluation around specific goals determined with each individual person, by deciding together not only "what a person can do", but especially working on "what a person is interested in" and "what a person was successful in doing". The main idea is to start from goals and ask people what they really want to change in their life. GAS demonstrated several advantages over the simple protocol based on questions that we used one year ago in the first evaluation of the Autonomamente approach:

- it improves involvements and motivation of people with disabilities;
- it objectifies the discussion and the comparison of data;
- it allows to set individualized goals in a collaborative fashion;
- it allows to redefine and renegotiate goals over time;
- it doesn't expect that you should have the same effects for everyone.

Future work includes the revision of the objectives with users and caregivers, in order to update each Goal Attainment Scale, by modifying the values (where needed) or adding new objectives if requested by the users. The outcomes of this study will also help the development team to plan additional improvement to the system, based on user's requests and needs, highlighted during the evaluation.

References

1. Rockwood, K., Joyce, B., Stolee, P.: Use of goal attainment scaling in measuring clinically important change in cognitive rehabilitation patients. J. of Clinical Epidemiology 50, 581–588 (1987)
2. Locke, E.A., Latham, G.P.: A theory of Goal setting and Task Performance. Prentice Hall, Englewood Cliffs (1990)
3. Reinig, B.A., Briggs, R.O., de Vreede, G.J.: A Cross-Cultural Investigation of the Goal-Attainment-Likelihood Construct and Its Effect on Satisfaction with Technology Supported Collaboration. In: Proceedings of the 41st Annual Hawaii International Conference on System Sciences, HICSS, p. 13 (2008)
4. Kiresuk, T.J., Sherman, R.E.: Goal attainment scaling: A general method for evaluating comprehensive community mental health programs. Community Mental Health Journal 4, 443–353 (1968)
5. World Health Organization: International Classification of Functioning, Disability and Health: ICF, Geneva (2001)
6. Kiresuk, T.J., Smith, A., Cardillo, J.E.: Goal attainment scaling: applications, theory and measurement. Lawrence-Erlbaum, New Jersey (1994)
7. LoPresti, E.F., Mihailidis, A., Kirsch, N.: Technology for cognitive rehabilitation and compensation: state of the art. Neuropsychological Rehabilitation Journal 14, 3–39 (2004)
8. Elger, G., Furugren, B.: SmartBo-an ICT and computer-based demonstration home for disabled people. In: 3rd TIDE Congress: Technology for Inclusive Design and Equality Improving the Quality of Life for the European Citizen (1998)
9. Demiris, G., Rantz, M., Aud, M., Marek, K., Tyrer, H., Skubic, M., et al.: Older adults' attitudes towards and perceptions of "smart home" technologies. J. Medical Informatics and the Internet in Medicine 29, 87–94 (2004)
10. Kidd, C.D., Orr, R.J., Abword, G.D., Atkeson, C.G., Essa, I.A., Macintyre, B., Mynatt, E., Starner, T.E., Newstetter, W.: The Aware Home: A Living Laboratory for Ubiquitous Computing Research. In: Streitz, N.A., Hartkopf, V. (eds.) CoBuild 1999. LNCS, vol. 1670. Springer, Heidelberg (1999)
11. Sueda, O., Ide, M., Honma, A., Yamagushi, M.: Smart House in Tokushima. In: 5th European Conference for the Advancement of Assistive Technology (1999)

PMD: Designing a Portable Medicine Dispenser for Persons Suffering from Alzheimer's Disease

Roel de Beer[1], Roy Keijers[1], Suleman Shahid[1]
Abdullah Al Mahmud[2], and Omar Mubin[2]

[1] Department of Information and Communication Sciences, Tilburg University,
Tilburg, The Netherlands
{r.c.j.m.debeer,r.r.m.keijers,s.shahid}@uvt.nl
[2] Department of Industrial Design, Eindhoven University of Technology,
Eindhoven, The Netherlands
{a.al-mahmud,o.mubin}@tue.nl

Abstract. In this paper we present the user-centred design of a medicine dispenser for persons suffering from Alzheimer's disease. The prototype was evaluated in two phases with two caregivers and two Alzheimer's patients. Caregivers evaluated the device positively. The Alzheimer's patients faced usability problems while completing tasks due to the virtual interaction medium of the medicine dispenser. However, patients and caregivers found the concept useful for medication intake.

Keywords: User-centred design, prototype, alzheimer's disease, memory impairment, older adults, medicine dispenser.

1 Introduction

More and more people in our society are getting older and consequently due to demographic shift it becomes a crying need to help those people with technological intervention. Day by day new means of technological solutions are provided to help people with special needs to empower them and to improve the quality of lives [1]. People who suffer from the first stages of Alzheimer's disease or brain hemorrhage have difficulties in taking the right medicine on the right time [2, 4]. Taking medicine on the right time and in the right quantity requires a tool that will help them with that. The current tools available are not adequate enough to provide them with this. There are a number of devices and systems designed for helping patents in taking the right medicine at the right time such as 'Smart pill concept' [5], 'memory aid with remote communication using distributed technology' [7], and 'Daily dose' [6]. As caregivers are also middle aged people and are not expert of technology and therefore care should be given to provide support for them. So far existing solutions does not have any support for caregivers. Therefore, we propose to design a new medicine dispenser, which not only help Alzheimer's patients but also help their caregivers to prepare medicine intake for the patients.

K. Miesenberger et al. (Eds.): ICCHP 2010, Part I, LNCS 6179, pp. 332–335, 2010.

2 Design Process

We conducted a semi-structured interview with patients and caregivers. The purpose of the interview was twofold: first, the information provided in the interviews enabled us to verify the results found in the literature study. Second, the information provided by the Alzheimer's patients could be verified by the caregivers. The main findings are: 1) Patients are aware of the medicine intake of each day, but they forget when, how and what quantity, 2) Alzheimer's patients use specific functions of electronic devices which have large knobs, buttons and clear symbols.

We developed three key concepts and discussed with the patients and caregivers. During this feedback session we realized that the patients and the caregivers are interested in mobility in addition to having access to some form of customizability. They wanted to have a system, which could help them in carrying their medicine outside their home. Based on the initial round of user requirements exploration, we designed our final concept called the 'Automatic Wall Dispenser' that had two separate components to interact with each other: the 'Medmemory wall dispenser' and the 'Medmemory portable dispenser'. The dispenser can be used inside or outside the home, making sure that the medicine schedule will not be interrupted. The storage ability is for 8 to 10 different medicines, which should be sufficient to cover medication use for one patient. To help the caregiver with the input of medicine information the dispenser is equipped with a barcode scanner. Caregivers can refill the dispenser or expand the medicine use by scanning the barcode on the medicine box. When a patient does not respond to the screen for a given amount of time, the caregiver will be notified through an automated call or SMS message. The second part of the solution is the 'Portable MedMemory dispenser (PMD)'. When a patient decides to leave home, he or she can press the "I'm leaving button". The wall dispenser provides the tray with a compilation of medicines; this feature will enable the patient to leave the home for a maximum of 48 hours. The patient simply has to pull the tray out of the wall dispenser and can carry it through a string around their neck or a belt-clip. The final design is shown in Figure 1.

Fig. 1. Final design, patient's interface (left), and caregiver's interface (right)

2.1 Prototype

We first developed the low fidelity (low-fi) prototype and for this prototype we used a LCD flat screen and additional paper-made features. The prototype consists of three scenarios: 1) Patient has to take his/her medicine, 2) Patient leaves home (e.g., a day out) and 3) Back office for caregiver (maintenance). The low-fi prototype was tested with 8 graduate students. During the low-fidelity test we discovered few steps missing from our previous prototype such as at certain points the device did not give feedback to the users. We solved this by adding additional steps and tested it again. Users accomplished the task better when additional steps were made. Several problems arose during the low-fidelity testing. First of all, what to do if patients do not take his/her medication after 20/25 minutes? When adding an extra feedback element in the low-fidelity prototype users were able to follow directions more easily. Second, when a patient is leaving home, the slideshow feature does not indicate how the user must interact with the device. By making use of the in-built camera, the user will be notified of the options when standing in front of the device. Our high-fidelity prototype consists of a Flash application.

3 Evaluation

Our goal was to test the usability of the device with caregivers and Alzheimer patients. Two caregivers and two Alzheimer patients participated in our usability test. The first patient was an 80 years old female who had a medication box, which helped her taking her medication. This medication box is prepared by the caregiver (the relative). The second patient was an 81 years old female who placed her medication in a medication box. Her daughter (the second caregiver) helps her in preparing the medicines. The patient has a sight and hearing restriction. Both the patients had no experience with computers and touch-screen products. Caregiver's task: Task 1: Refill the medicines of the patient, Task 2: Remove (delete) medicines of type 'X' out of the device, Task 3: Record a personal video message, Task 4: Change your personal pin code for the access to the caregiver menu. Patient's task: Task 1: React on the alarm message and follow the instructions, Task 2: You want to leave, follow the instructions, Task 3: You arrive at home; activate the system by following the instructions on the screen.

Overall the caregivers were very positive and satisfied with the device and its usability. There were only few little difficulties. One of the difficulties the caregivers had with task 1 was the refill of the medicines. The virtual medicine box confused the caregivers because a box was displayed instead of a mouse pointer. Another problem that one caregiver dealt with, were the animations that were displayed on the device. The animations were too realistic and the caregiver scanned the animation itself instead of the scanner of the screen on the pc. One last issue was the removal of the medication because the button of the cross (delete medication) was not optimal (it requires accuracy). There was some confusion where to push the button to remove the medicine. The caregivers found it a well-designed device in order to help them with the medication preparation for patients. Both patients had some difficulties with the device and were less positive about the usability. Only task 1 went well; taking the medication was no problem via the touch screen. Task 2 (a day out) was a problem for the patients. When the mobile dispenser was taken out of the device the message 'you must be back before...' caused confusion and one patient did not press the OK button. The take out of the medication from the portable dispenser was discovered quickly but the second patient did not take the medicines out of the tray and she asked whether the dispenser closed automatically. When the alarm on the portable dispenser went off, there was some confusion on which screen the patient had to press (the one on the pc screen or the one around the neck) because she could not imagine that she was outside. For both patients task 3, arrival at home, was less successful. The patients did know that the portable dispenser should be placed back in the device, but not how it should be placed back.

4 Discussion and Conclusion

We can conclude that the idea (concept of a device for Alzheimer patients) could be a useful tool for patients' medicine intake. The working method (the analysis of the target group, and the brainstorm session) showed the restrictions for our project in relation to Alzheimer patients. During the evaluation of the high-fidelity prototype, the tasks of the caregiver were successfully accomplished (with some minor remarks). Contrary to the tasks of the caregiver, the patients had difficulties understanding and executing their tasks. Reflecting on the choice of medium, a virtual medication dispenser was not the right choice for the target group. As a consequence of this medium choice, the patient's user tests did not go well as we expected. For future testing, we are going to construct a physical device, which does not depend on patient's computer knowledge or experience and test it with Alzheimer patients and their caregivers.

References

1. Al Mahmud, A., Aliakseyeu, D., Martens, J.B.: Enabling storytelling by aphasics in an augmented home environment. In: BCS HCI 2008, vol. 2, pp. 3–6 (2008)
2. Bravo, J., Hervás, R., Gallego, R., et al.: Enabling NFC Technology to Support Activities in an Alzheimer's Day Center. In: PETRA 2008, pp. 1–5 (2008)
3. Hawky, K., Inkpen, K.M., Rockwood, K., McAllister, M., Slonim, J.: Requirements Gathering with Alzheimer's Patients and Caregivers. In: ASSETS 2005, pp. 142–149 (2005)
4. Lee, M.L., Dey, A.K.: Providing Good Memory Cues for People with Episodic Memory Impairment. In: ASSETS 2007, pp. 131–138 (2007)
5. Loh, J., Schietecat, T., Kwok, T.F., Lindeboom, L.: Technology Applied to Adress Difficulties of Alzheimer's Patients and Their Partners. Technische Universiteit Eindhoven (2004)
6. Neumann, A., Haggerty, A., Ramme, M., Riching, K.: The Daily Dose (2006), http://www.theamdd.com/ (retrieved April 2009)
7. Szymkowiak, Morrison, Gregor, et al.: A memory aid with remote communication using distributed technology. Personal and Ubiquitous Computing 9, 1–5 (2005)

Merging Web Accessibility and Usability by Patterns

Helmut Vieritz, Daniel Schilberg, and Sabina Jeschke

Center for Learning and Knowledge Management/Department of Information
Management in Mechanical Engineering, RWTH Aachen, 52068 Aachen, Germany
vieritz@zlw-ima.rwth-aachen.de

Abstract. Nowadays, usability and accessibility are two important quality aspects of user interfaces (UIs). But in research and development, both
are sometimes accounted as unity and sometimes as contradiction. Understanding Web accessibility as an essential part of usability, here an
approach is given to clarify the relationship of both. Therefore,
- a pattern approach was chosen to meet the practical requirements
  of UI designers which are often not familiar with accessibility needs,
- a collection of patterns for human-computer interaction (HCI) has
  been extended with accessibility requirements and
- finally a pattern example illustrates the cooperation of usability and
  accessibility in detail.

1 Introduction

Usability and accessibility as well are two growing factors in product design.
The use of modern technology is mostly not limited by product functionality
but UI design and usage under limiting conditions. Limits can be set by users
with special needs as people with disabilities or elderly people, technology as
cellular phones etc. or an environment with noise or bright light.

But, the relationship of accessibility and usability is still not clarified. The
usability definition most widely adopted was given by Nielsen [1] and is focused
on learnability, efficiency, memorability, few errors and users' satisfaction. The
common understanding of accessibility defines it as access to and controll of all
information for all users. Even people with impairments can perceive, understand, navigate through and interact with the (Web) application [2]. Since these
definitions are focused on different aspects of usage – general quality of usage
versus access to information – the relationship is not simply given. Accessible
applications have positive impacts for all users. Therefore, accessibility is often
seen as a part of usability [3]. Integrating usability and accessibility issues in the
software design and development process is a complex challenge. Additionally,
different (Web) technologies raise the needed knowledge and costs.

The presented research has the objective to facilitate the integretation of
accessibility requirements in practical work. Modern approaches of application
development are focused on UI design and usability since the quality of UI has

K. Miesenberger et al. (Eds.): ICCHP 2010, Part I, LNCS 6179, pp. 336–342, 2010.

a growing impact on the commercial success of products. But until now, accessibility is mostly not seen as an important commercial criterion for better product design and has not the same impact. A solution may be to see accessibility from usability point of view and to give more support for the early design process of UIs then existing recommandations as the *Web Content Accessibility Guidelines* (WCAG 2.0) [4] can do. The presented approach adapts the needs of accessibility to UI design which is focused on usability. Therefore, a pattern framework of interaction pattern has been extended with the requirements for accessible UIs.

2   Related Work

Patterns for usability and interaction design are broadly discussed in research and practice. Some frameworks already exist. Borchers [5] has developed and detailed discussed a pattern framework which is focused on an interactive music exhibition. Folmer et.al. [6] has published a framework of software architecture-relevant patterns and Graham [7] has published a pattern language for Web usability. Other pattern languages for interaction design can be found in [8,9,10]. In these frameworks, accessibility is sometimes mentioned but not integrated in detail. For example, in [6] accessibility is reduced to multimodal use. Few papers exist for Web accessibility patterns [11,12] which do not rely on usability. Abraham [13] presents a case-based reasoning (CBR) approach to improve the accessibility of interaction patterns. His approach does not clarify the relationship to accessibility standards as WCAG. In general, an overall approach to merge usability and accessibility is still missing.

3   Accessibility and Usability by Patterns

Pattern languages are a well-suited method to explain basic idea without the technological overhead. Patterns have been introduced in urban architecture by Christopher Alexander in 1977 [14]. Nowadays, they are widely known in software development and HCI as well. An *usability* or *interaction pattern language* in HCI is a collection of recommendations for the design of usable UIs. A *pattern* is a preformal construct which gives a best practice solution for a repeating problem. It is described in a defined structure such as problem, context and solution. Typical categories are:

- a name for the pattern which is memorizable and unique
- a short statement of the problem
- a description of pattern context
- a solution for the pattern which explains the problem and its solution in detail
- a graphical depiction for pattern application which underlines the pattern idea

Additionally, a *pattern framework* includes structure and relationships between patterns. Until now, attempts of stronger formalization with e.g. the *Pattern Language Markup Language* (PLML) were not successful.

Folmer et. al. [6] give an overview for common usability patterns (see fig. 1). This framework was chosen for current research of accessibility influence on software architecture (not discussed here). *Usability attributes* are precise and measurable criteria of the abstract concept. There are four common attributes: efficiency, reliability, satisfaction and learnability. Heuristics and design principles are embodied in *usability properties*. Fifteen typical architecture-relevant usability patterns are described.

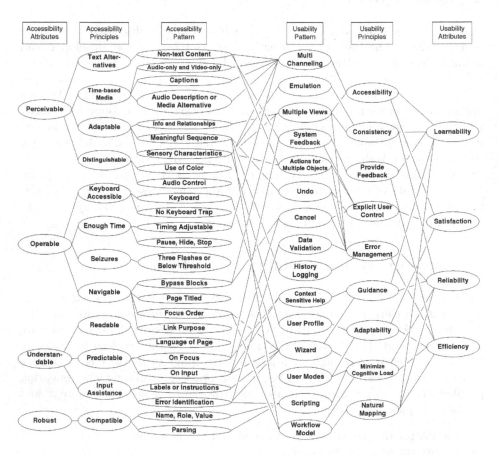

Fig. 1. A pattern collection for accessibility and usability (derived from [4,6], mappings reduced)

Using the WCAG 2.0-recommendations [4] a similar classification for accessibility patterns can be derived. The WCAG-guidelines are well-suited to form a pattern language since they are technology-independent and based on a long discussion between all interest groups. The four basic attributes are perceivable, operable, understandable and robust. The twelve different main guidelines are taken as basic principles of accessibility. Here, for better overview only the 25 level A[1] guidelines are shown. Changing by the additional guidelines for level AA and AAA is small since they only enlarge often practical and technological efforts e.g. captions for live stream additional to pre-recorded multimedia content.

After selection and classification of usability and accessibility patterns they are mapped on each other. The mapping of an accessibility pattern to an interaction pattern is sometimes caused by the same idea of solution and sometimes by the same type of pattern context. Some accessibility patterns have a context which is valid in many situations. For better overview they are included without mapping showing that they have to be integrated by all usability patterns. The relationship between both is best presented from usability point of view. The mappings show which accessibility requirements have to be respected in the context of usability patterns. The absence of contradictions underlines that accessible control of user interfaces is not counterpart of usability. The usability pattern structure is extended with categories *Relevant Accessibility Patterns*, *Main Accessibility Issues* and an additional illustration to include the requirements of accessibility in UI design. These three additional categories explain and illustrate how the proposed solution for an usable UI design can be made accessible as well.

4   A Pattern Example

The usability pattern *Wizard* is given as an illustrating example. Wizards in UI design are well-known in many situations such as shipping and payment dialogs in online shops or dialogs for the conversion of file formats. A Wizard-situation is characterized by a high level of interactivity since the user needs some information and has to make decisions. Therefore, it include access to information and UI control as well. At first, the pattern example describes the organization of a wizard and completes the description with the accessibility requirements. More pattern from the library can be found on the project Web site http:\\www.inamosys.de. Figure 2 shows the accessibility patterns which are relevant for the Wizard pattern.

4.1   Pattern *Wizard*

Problem
The user has to make several decisions to achieve a single goal. He may need additional information, previews or examples about the result of decisions.

Context
Infrequent complex tasks need to be performed by non-expert users. The task consists of several subtasks (3-10) each containing a decision. The user wants to

---

[1] WCAG have three conformance levels from A (lowest) to AAA (highest) to correspond to different needs of groups and situations.

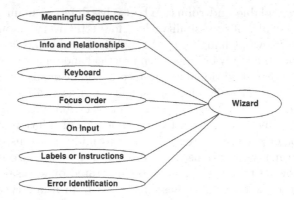

Fig. 2. Accessibility patterns for interaction pattern *Wizard* (selection from fig. 1)

complete the task but may be not familiar with or interested in the subtasks. The single steps may rely on each other and they are ordered.

Illustration

amazon.com
SIGN IN   SHIPPING & PAYMENT   GIFT-WRAP   PLACE ORDER

Enter a new shipping address.
When finished, click the "Continue" button.

Full Name:	Ernest Hemingway
Address Line1:	907 Whitehead Street
	Street address, P.O. box, company name, c/o
Address Line2:	
	Apartment, suite, unit, building, floor, etc.
City:	Key West
State/Province/Region:	Florida
ZIP/Postal Code:	33040
Country:	United States
Phone Number:	

Is this address also your billing address (the address that appears on your credit card or bank statement)?   ⦿ Yes   ◯ No (If not, we'll ask you for it in a moment.)

Continue ▸

Fig. 3. Wizard for shipping and payment on Amazons Web page

Solution
The user is taken through the entire task step by step (see fig. 3). Existing and completed steps are shown. The user is informed about the task goal from beginning on and that several decisions are to be made. Widgets are provided for

navigation through the entire task. The user can recognize that a subtask has to be fulfilled before the next is available. Revising of decisions is possible by back navigation to a previous subtask. The user is given feedback for the purpose of decisions. Explanations, previews or examples clarify the results. The final result is shown. If possible, appropriate default settings and short cuts accelerate and simplify the process for experienced users.

Relevant Accessibility Pattern
Typically, a wizard uses forms to get needed information from the user. Buttons serve to finish the single steps. To be accessible, the different input fields of the form must be labeled, accessible by keybord and the order of access must correspond with the workflow. Error identification and input help should be available and accessible as well.

Relevant accessibility patterns are (a) *Meaningful Sequence*, (b) *Keyboard*, (c) *Focus Order*, (d) *On Input*, (e) *Error Identification* and (f) *Labels or Instructions* (see fig. 4).

Solution Illustration

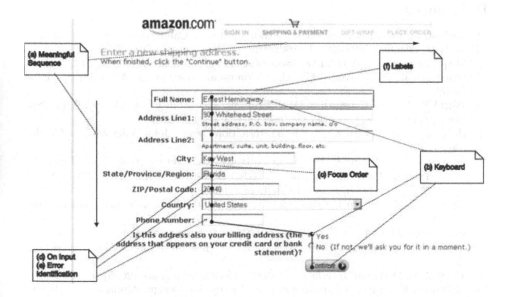

Fig. 4. Accessibility requirements for wizard

Main Accessibility Issues
Widgets are labeled and order corresponds with workflow. All functionality is available by keyboard. Name and role of interface components can be programmatically determined when scripts are used. User is advised in advance when changing the setting or focusing of user interface components does automatically cause a change of context.

5   Conclusions

The objective of the presented approach is the extention of an usability-driven UI design with the requirements of accessibility. A pattern approach was used to describe the main ideas independent from used UI platform. It gives software architects and developers an easy and quick way to understand the basic ideas of accessible user interfaces and helps them to see usability and accessibility not as a contradiction. The extension with new interaction patterns is easy.

The approach is still limited to be only a collection of pattern. Further work will be done on structure, completeness and relationships between pattern to built up a pattern framework which merges usability and accessibility in practical UI design. Furthermore, the pattern collection serves for analysis of accessibility influence on software architecture in usage-driven UI design.

Acknowledgments

We highly appreciate Deutsche Forschungsgemeinschaft (DFG) for funding the INAMOSYS project.

References

1. Nielsen, J.: Usability Engineering. Academic Press, Cambridge (1993)
2. Web Accessibility Initiative: Introduction to Web Accessibility (2005),
   http://www.w3.org/WAI/intro/accessibility.php (last visited: 03/11/2010)
3. Shneiderman, B.: Universal Usability. Communications of the ACM 43(5), 84–91 (2000)
4. World Wide Web Consortium: Web Content Accessibility Guidelines 2.0. (2008),
   http://www.w3.org/TR/WCAG20/ (last visited: 03/11/2010)
5. Borchers, J.: A Pattern Approach to Interaction Design. John Wiley & Sons, Chichester (2001)
6. Folmer, E., van Gurp, J., Bosch, J.: Software Architecture Analysis of Usability. In: Bastide, R., Palanque, P., Roth, J. (eds.) DSV-IS 2004 and EHCI 2004. LNCS, vol. 3425, pp. 38–58. Springer, Heidelberg (2005)
7. Graham, I.: A Pattern Language for Web Usability. Addison-Wesley, Amsterdam (2003)
8. van Duyne, D.K., et al.: The Design of Sites: Patterns, Principles, and Processes for Crafting a Customer-Centered Web Experience. Addison-Wesley, Amsterdam (2002)
9. Tidwell, J.: Designing Interfaces. O'Reilly Media, Sebastopol (2005)
10. Miller, F., Vandome, A., McBrewster, J.: Interaction Design. Alphascript Publishing (2009)
11. Ihmig, S.: Web-Accessibility Patterns. Master's thesis, Hamburg University (2007)
12. Vieritz, H., Jeschke, S., Pfeiffer, O.: Using Web Accessibility Patterns for Web Application Development. In: Proceedings of the 2009 ACM symposium on Applied Computing, pp. 129–135 (2009)
13. Abraham, G.: Needles in a Haystack. Improving Accessibility of Interaction Patterns (2006),
    http://idea.library.drexel.edu/bitstream/1860/1569/1/2007021001.pdf
14. Alexander, C., Ishikawa, S., Silverstein, M.: A Pattern Language. In: Towns, Buildings, Construction. Oxford University Press, New York (1977)

Towards the Convergence of Web 2.0 and Semantic Web for E-Inclusion

Laura Burzagli, Andrea Como, and Francesco Gabbanini

Institute for Applied Physics, Italian National Research Council
Via Madonna del Piano 10, 50019, Sesto Fiorentino, Firenze, Italy
{l.burzagli,a.como,f.gabbanini}@ifac.cnr.it

Abstract. The paper discusses a research approach to achieve the "wider inclusion objectives" reported in the second part of the Riga declaration. The approach is based on the convergence of two forms of intelligence on the web, given by Web 2.0 and the Semantic Web. While Web 2.0 encompasses social phenomena, often undervalued in the field of e-Inclusion (exchange and collection of large amount of information), Semantic Web is designed for interlinking and reusing structured information. The paper outlines a software architecture for the exploitation of the above concepts and gives an example of a possible application built on top of the architecture, in the domain of inclusive e-Tourism, enlightening benefits that come by the adoption of the approach, with respect to current trip planning systems.

Keywords: Web 2.0, Semantic Web, e-Inclusion, Ontology, Design for All.

1 Introduction

"e-Inclusion" means both inclusive ICT and the use of ICT to achieve wider inclusion objectives. It focuses on participation of all individuals and communities in all aspects of the information society. (Pt. 4 MINISTERIAL DECLARATION APPROVED UNANIMOUSLY ON 11 June 2006, Riga).

The definition of e-Inclusion (see Figure 1A), as given in the Riga Ministerial Declaration, consists in two different parts. The first one (Figure 1B, piece on the left) aims to ensure access to ICT to all, with particular reference to people with activity limitations. In every ICT system or service accessibility represents an essential element, without which people are excluded from some aspects of social life at private or public level.

However this definition is not limited to this concept, but includes a second one (Figure 1B, piece on the right) dealing with the opportunity to achieve wider inclusion objectives. This means that Information and Communication Technologies can go over the basic objective of accessibility and offer new and efficient solutions to support daily activities of all people.

It is noteworthy to consider that the second aspect treated by the Riga declaration constitutes itself a field of research, because research is needed to achieve "wider inclusion objectives": this requires knowledge of users, technology advancements and

K. Miesenberger et al. (Eds.): ICCHP 2010, Part I, LNCS 6179, pp. 343–350, 2010.

future Information Society developments (Figure 1C). Research activities are often limited to technological aspects: this is not sufficient, as they should also consider social phenomena which are emerging on the web, since these are completely modifying the way people communicate with each other. These aspects seem to be undervalued in the field of e-Inclusion, where focus is still mainly concentrated on access to the information. A convergence between the technological and social perspectives may give fruitful results in the domain of e-Inclusion.

An example is given by intelligence on the web, which assumes a number of forms, two of which are represented by social networks and by the Semantic Web stack (Figure 1D).

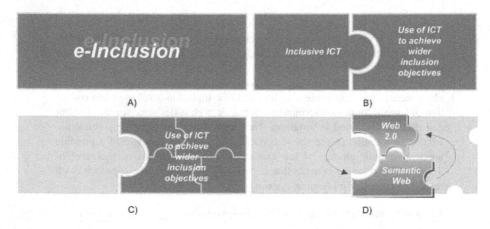

Fig. 1. Web 2.0 and Semantic Web in the e-Inclusion field

Up to now, only a few examples of applications of Web 2.0 and Semantic Web to the e-Inclusion domain exist, and, as stated above, they mostly regard the e-Accessibility field (see [1]). In order to exploit the strengths of the two aforementioned expressions of web intelligence, this paper describes the structure of a general family of systems that leverages on the synergy between Web 2.0 (to gather information) and Semantic Web (to consistently structure contents), with the aim of favoring e-Inclusion.

A feasible example of an application in the field of e-Tourism is presented to discuss possible enhancements that might come with the adoption of the approach.

2   System Architecture

In order to exploit the convergence of Web 2.0 and Semantic Web, the ICT scientific community (see [2], [3], [4]) has started to study how these forms of intelligence might come to a convergence, thus leading to merge human participation with well structured information. Among scientific literature, two main solutions appear remarkable.

The first one [5] is related to the creation of services and tools that are able to automatically analyze web pages and discover semantics, thus allowing structuring user generated content.

A different approach [6] is represented by the so-called "collective knowledge systems", in which existing semantic structures are used to organize large amounts of knowledge generated by users.

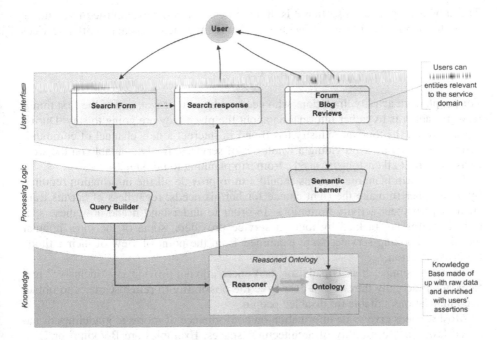

Fig. 2. System Architecture

The architecture proposed in this paper (Figure 2) seeks to combine the two solutions in order to obtain an enhanced system. The user interface layer is made up with structures to ask information to the system (translated into queries) and to read results. Moreover, it allows enriching the knowledge base with information obtained by social network tools such as Forums, Blogs or Reviewing Systems. In the processing layer, a key component in the adopted approach is represented by a "Semantic Learner", which operates as an annotation engine and an annotation-ontology mapper, capable of interpreting data that represent human intelligence (such as posts on social networking tools), using automatic learning techniques, and to insert these data in a hierarchical structure described by an ontology. As a result, the information available to the system in the Knowledge layer is continuously and automatically augmented with the system's use through the Semantic Learner, thanks to the discussions that take place between users. In this way the system is able to interact with the user in providing ever more personalized and pertinent information. These information are available for browsing and searching by an ontology driven search engine, that performs searches within a Reasoned Ontology, that is, an knowledge base that is augmented by a reasoning engine, which is able to uncover unexpected relationships and inconsistencies and to deduce (infer) conclusions from the given knowledge, thus making implicit assertions explicit.

3 An Example in the E-Tourism Domain

The approach outlined in section 2 is in the process of being exemplified by building an application in the domain of inclusive e-Tourism, which is meant to offer services regarding accommodation finding in the Florence (Italy) area.

3.1 Inclusive e-Tourism: State of the Art

For people with activity limitations who need or desire to travel, one of the first things to worry about is to gather information about the place they are going to stay. During the last years, the tourism industry has found in Internet a new channel of communication and promotion, providing a whole set of services, freely available on the web, to assist almost all customers' needs, from trip planning to booking.

Inclusive trip planning systems should aim to provide all the information required by a customer to make the right choice for her/his needs, regardless of her/his transient or permanent activity limitations. In order to understand if and how these specific concerns are tackled by tourism service providers, some of the most popular worldwide booking services were examined from the point of view of their attitude towards inclusion.

Some of them, such as Tripadvisor[1] or Venere[2], do not provide any "inclusive" features at all: actually they do not even give the possibility to refine searches to obtain accommodations suitable for disabled people.

Most services give some information on conformance of rooms to guidelines or national laws on accessibility of architectural spaces. Examples are Booking[3] or Hostelworld[4], which let customers choose rooms labeled as *accessible*, but do not offer the possibility to obtain further (and personalized) information. A more complete solution is provided by Expedia[5] which allows to filter out results of accommodation searches using an "Accessibility Options" checklist, which (although not explicitly declared) seems to be obtained as a selection of the Checklist for Readily Achievable Barrier Removal[6]. These options are meant to describe a few characteristic of an environment, such as the presence of a roll-in shower or an accessible path to the room, in order to guide the customer to choose the correct facility for her/his needs.

A similar approach was followed in research projects like the IST-2001-20656 PALIO (see [7] for a detailed description), which proposed a categorization of

---

[1] http://www.tripadvisor.com, last visited on Wednesday, April 07, 2010.
[2] http://www.venere.com, last visited on Wednesday, April 07, 2010.
[3] http://www.booking.com, last visited on Wednesday, April 07, 2010.
[4] http://www.hostelworld.com, last visited on Wednesday, April 07, 2010.
[5] http://www.expedia.com, last visited on Wednesday, April 07, 2010.
[6] The Checklist for Readily Achievable Barrier Removal constitutes compliance material in the context of the Americans with Disabilities Act. It is available at
http://www.ada.gov/checkweb.htm, last visited on Wednesday, April 07, 2010.

accommodations to be matched to users preferences and needs which were themselves categorized in a number of classes. Also the ASK-IT[7] project, in order to support accessible tourism, has developed an ontology in which categories are often used to describe entities in terms of their accessibility (eg. rooms for wheelchair users, upper limb impaired users, lower limb impaired users).

Recently, following the Web 2.0 perspective, e-Tourism services are taking advantage of possibilities given by social networking: they typically let customers write their own reviews about accommodations they have stayed in, in order to provide hints for future customers. This kind of information is potentially very important to guide choices, but it is often messy and poorly organized: retrieving really useful information from a bunch of reviews can require a lot of time. This is a context in which semantic intelligence could be of great help in exploiting these contents, representing human intelligence.

Inclusive Tourism thus represents a field of application in which the convergence between information coming from social networks and structure given by Semantic Web could enhance trip planning systems.

3.2 Inclusive Tourism: A Novel Approach

As mentioned in section 2, the basic idea of the approach described in the paper is to give a formal representation to human generated contents, by the use of ontologies and semantic web technologies.

Examination of the ontology developed within the ASK-IT project has led to adopt a rather different approach for the representation of tourism related data. Whereas the ASK-IT ontology uses categorization (see section 3.1), the ontology that is being developed in our laboratories, in line with the recent ICF classification [8] and with Design for All perspectives, drops down this kind of categorization, which appears to be a bit rigid.

For example it does not seem to be suitable to cope with preferences and requirements expressed by elderly people, which often have a mix of problems that characterize disabled people, even if in weaker forms.

The approach adopted is not based on a categorization of users (depending on their (dis)abilities) and of architectural spaces (based on them "being accessible" to some category of users). Instead, it establishes a set of relevant entities and properties that characterize indoor (and, partly, outdoor) environments (similarly to what is proposed in [9] and proposes to describe these in detail. As an example, room entrances are defined as characterized by a property named "hasWidth", that relates them to an integer value, to model the fact that they have a certain physical width.

It is left to the reasoning engine and to the ontology based search engine to match user characteristics and preferences with the characteristics of spaces. The process is exemplified in Fig. 3.

---

[7] The project "Ambient Intelligence System of Agents for Knowledge-based and Integrated Services for Mobility Impaired Users" (ASK-IT) aims to provide a service which promotes independence and mobility, by offering seamless and personalised information provision to support and promote the mobility of mobility impaired people. See http://www.ask-it.org/, last visited on May 21, 2010.

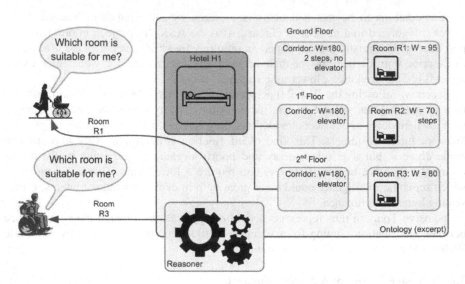

Fig. 3. Example of how the system handles requests from different users

The data on which the ontology builds are obtained according to guidelines that were set-up in the EU CARE[8] project and includes information that describes buildings and inner spaces in detail, so that it is suitable in an inclusive tourism perspective; in parallel, the guidelines issued within the project are used to set up an ontology that structures these data; for integration purposes (following the semantic web vision) the obtained ontology can be mapped with already developed ontologies that cover similar domains of interest: as an example, a partial mapping with the ontology developed within the ASK-IT project is being set up.

The approach is also in line with Design for All, because different forms of intelligence are here used to provide information to satisfy, to the greatest extent possible, preferences and needs of all people. This goal can be reached through a proper design not only of the user interface (a level on which Design for All is known to have an impact), but also of the underlying system architecture.

In this way, the final application should be capable of:

• offering completely accessible information regarding accommodation in Florence, through wizards or by entering textual queries;
• letting users discuss and comment on accommodations, so that, once interpreted by the annotation engine and the annotation-ontology mapper, their experiences constitute a collective knowledge basis that brings added value to the service.

4   What Do We Expect from the New Approach?

The approach we propose potentially gives a formal, rich and expressive description of entities and relations that characterize a domain of interest for a certain service, which

---

[8] The project "Città Accessibili delle Regioni Europee" (CARE) aimed to set up strategies for the development of accessible cities. See http://www.interreg-care.org/site/, last visited on Wednesday, April 07, 2010.

may be used in query/answer systems to provide high quality search results, thanks also to the fact that data are continuously augmented by processing user contributions.

As an example, describing indoor spaces in detail could bring noticeable advantages in the domain of inclusive e-Tourism, because more flexible and expressive searches could be allowed in search engines.

This could allow coping with situations in which traditional trip planning systems do not offer appropriate results. For instance, contacts with a major Italian travel agent revealed that rooms were classified by institutional entities as (theoretically) being accessible to motor impaired users (because they are equipped with suitable bathrooms and sufficient spaces; an example could be represented by rooms R1 and R3 in Figure 3), but were actually located on floors which could not be accessed by elevators, or were accessible only through corridors having obstacles such as steps. Current automatic booking systems as well as human agents happened to sell rooms like these to people on wheelchairs.

On the other hand, on the basis of legislations, often system classify rooms as not being accessible (for example because their bathroom entrance is less than a certain width, specified by law), while they could actually be accessed by disabled users whose characteristics are compatible with that width. This is a case where synthesis brings to over-restrict search results.

Moreover, as appears from Figure 3, it is to be noted that issues related to people with activity limitation are not handled as "accessibility features", but accessibility is taken care of within the more general view of Design for All, thus giving solutions for all people and avoiding specious classifications.

5 Conclusions

In accordance with the second part of the definition of e-Inclusion given in the Riga Declaration, the paper discusses an approach to exploit synergies between Web 2.0 and the Semantic Web and describes how this can constitute as a basis for the design of the architecture of a generic family of systems that can be adopted in different fields of applications.

While the entire system described is under development, an example of a possible application built on top of the architecture, in the domain of inclusive e-Tourism, enlightens benefits that come by the adoption of the approach. These include the availability of very flexible query/answer systems providing high quality search results, thanks also to the fact that data are continuously augmented by processing user contributions. The approach is in line with Design for All principles in that its design does not focus on disabilities and their categorizations, but it seeks to provide neutral description of spaces and users which are suitable to be searched for by ontology based search engines.

References

1. Burzagli, L., Gabbanini, F.: Intelligence on the web and e-inclusion. In: Stephanidis, C. (ed.) Universal Access in Human-Computer Interaction. LNCS, vol. 5615, pp. 641–649. Springer, Heidelberg (2009)
2. Heath, T., Motta, E.: Ease of interaction plus ease of integration: Combining Web 2.0 and the Semantic Web in a reviewing site. Web Semantics 6(1), 76–83 (2008)

3. Yesilada, Y., Harper, S.: Web 2.0 and the semantic web: hindrance or opportunity? In: W4A - international cross-disciplinary conference on web accessibility 2007 (2008); SI-GACCESS Accessibility and Computing (90), 19–31
4. Ankolekar, A., Krotzsch, M., Tran, T., Vrandecic, D.: The two cultures: Mashing up Web 2.0 and the Semantic Web. Web Semantics 6(1), 70–75 (2007)
5. Cooper, M.: Accessibility of emerging rich web technologies: web 2.0 and the semantic web. In: W4A '07: Proceedings of the 2007 international cross-disciplinary conference on Web accessibility (W4A), pp. 93–98. ACM, New York (2007)
6. Gruber, T.: Collective knowledge systems: Where the social web meets the semantic web. Journal of Web Semantics 6(1), 4–13 (2008)
7. Burzagli, L., Emiliani, P.L., Gabbanini, F.: Design for all in action: An example of analysis and implementation. Expert Systems with Applications 36(1), 985–994 (2009)
8. World Health Organization: International Classification of Functioning, Disability and Health (ICF). World Health Organization (2001)
9. Shayeganfar, F., Anjomshoaa, A., Tjoa, A.: A smart indoor navigation solution based on building information model and google android. In: Miesenberger, K., Klaus, J., Zagler, W.L., Karshmer, A.I. (eds.) ICCHP 2008. LNCS, vol. 5105, ch. 157, pp. 1050–1056. Springer, Heidelberg (2008)

Beyond a Visuocentric Way of a Visual Web Search Clustering Engine: The Sonification of WhatsOnWeb

Maria Laura Mele[1], Stefano Federici[1,2], Simone Borsci[1], and Giuseppe Liotta[3]

[1] ECoNA - Interuniversity Centre for Research on Cognitive Processing in Natural
and Artificial Systems, 'Sapienza' University of Rome, IT
[2] Department of Human and Education Sciences, University of Perugia, IT
[3] Department of Electronic and Information Engineering, University of Perugia, IT
marialaura.mele@uniroma1.it, stefano.federici@unipg.it
simone.borsci@uniroma1.it, giuseppe.liotta@diei.unipg.it

Abstract. It is widely accepted that spatial representation is processed by an amodal system. Recent studies show that blind subjects have a better motion ability than sighted people in performing spatial exploration guided only by auditory cues. The sonification method offers an effective tool able to transmit graphic information, overcoming the digital divide risen by a visuocentric modality in which contents are conveyed. We present a usability evaluation aiming at investigate the interaction differences between both blind and sighted users while surfing WhatsOnWeb, a search engine that displays the information by using graph-drawing methods on semantically clustered data. We compare the visual presentation of three different layouts with the sonificated ones, demonstrating both qualitatively and quantitatively that blind and sighted users perform with no significant differences the interaction. These results remark that the digital divide could be decreased by going beyond the visuocentric way of the commonly adopted visual content representation.

Keywords: Sonification, Information visualization, Accessibility, Usability.

1 Introduction

Many studies agree that the spatial representation of information is independent from the way in which the sensory inputs are displayed; in particular, some authors pointed out that blind subjects have a better performance in processing spatial auditory inputs than sighted people [1, 2]. Indeed, it has been highlighted that blind people show a motion ability in performing spatial exploration tasks guided by only natural acoustic cues, functionally equivalent to the visually guided way for sighted people [3].

Starting with these suggestions, an amodal system of spatial representation has been proposed, by explaining the involvement of the auditory, haptic, and kinesthetic information in the spatial mapping processing of blind people [4]. At the base of the spatial information elaboration process some different strategies lie, related to both nature of the information and different points of body references: allocentric vs egocentric. During the spatial orientation, totally or partially blind subjects show their preferences for a body-centered strategy, based on corporal references points, rather

K. Miesenberger et al. (Eds.): ICCHP 2010, Part I, LNCS 6179, pp. 351–357, 2010.

than for an allocentric strategy, often adopted in mental rotation and scanning tasks [5, 6]. Therefore, the nature of sound seems to be able to communicate the complexity of static or dynamic data representation, by keeping their inner relations unchanged [7].

In this work, we want to introduce a usability evaluation study of a sonificated version of a search clustering engine called WhatsOnWeb (WoW), an application tool based on new graph visualization algorithms, implemented at the Department of Computer Engineering (DIEI) of the University of Perugia [8]. WoW conveys the indexed dataset using graph-drawing methods on semantically clustered data [9]: the visuo-spatial data representation provides the whole information by conveying it in one single browseable page. By rebuilding the output in graphics mode, WoW's layouts provide what is conversely ordered in any Search Engines Report Page (SERP) where the query outputs are in a top-down hierarchical sequence, starting from the greatest ranking level website to the lowest in several results pages [10,11].

Unlike the operation of common search engines (e.g. Google and Yahoo), WoW does not use ranking as a hierarchical organization criterion of information, but it represents the information order even by a semantic association between data, making all the contents easily and simultaneously available and learnable. Moreover, the disappearance of browsing text - totally replaced by a gestaltic (synoptic) graphic one - allows an easy and quick use of the information by reducing accessibility barriers.

Just as Ivory, Yu, and Gronemyer [12] claimed, blind users took twice as long as sighted participants to explore search results, and three times as long to explore web pages. Those results show the gap that exists on the interaction with traditional search engines between blind people, who use screen readers to surf the Web, and sighted people. These considerations seem to suggest that accessibility is actually not enough: there is a strong necessity to implement search engines that are both accessible and usable. In this way, as Federici et al. pointed out [13], WoW overcomes the efficiency limitation of SERP search engines previously shown, since its structure overcomes the limitations of a top-down flat representation by introducing different ways to convey the spatial information.

2   What Is WhatsOnWeb

In order to redesign the WhatsOnWeb system accomplishing the accessibility and usability principles, we followed the user centered design (UCD) in accordance with the ISO 13407 "Human-centered design processes for interactive systems" [14]. First, we proceeded by decoupling the WOW algorithm and subsequently making an automatic accessibility analysis using the RAVEn Eclipse plugin provided by IBM [15], then we implemented the software code by accomplishing the Java Foundation Classes and the guidelines provided by Sun and IBM [16]. Specifically, a composite architecture was produced by allowing the vocalization function, considering both the use of screen readers and the need of an autonomous integrated synthesizer. Finally, an appropriate support to the navigation peripherals has been arranged: the navigation structure of WhatsOnWeb has been created as much independent as possible from the peripheral, considering the future aim of extending the system also to the Brain Computer Interfaces. Each graph has been organized by following different levels, using cluster nodes - i.e. the semantic sets of results- with possibility of expansion and collapse by users click - i.e. deep level of information - and leaf nodes - i.e. the sites resulted from the research - as terminal constructs.

In a recent study conducted by Di Giacomo et al. (2008) [17] on a WhatsOnWeb prototype (http://whatsonweb.diei.unipg.it:8080/wow3.2/), the effectiveness and efficiency of the four different layouts implemented -TreeMap, Layered, Radial, and Orthogonal - were compared through a navigation task and a satisfaction questionnaire. Findings showed that 56% of people judged the TreeMap as the best graphic interface layout compared to the other ones. These results were confirmed by the opinions expressed by the participants in the satisfaction questionnaires. Following the experimental data on the TreeMap model, it has been developed the actual WoW prototype by adding a new layout called Spiral TreeMap (spiral tree organization) as a new visualization layout, where the most relevant node is set at the center of the screen and the less significant data are progressively set around. This organization in the process of being tested, together with sonification, should allow a significant improvement of the layout effectiveness and efficiency.

3 Sonification of WhatsOnWeb: Design and Implementation

Sonification is the "transformation of data relations into perceived relations in an acoustic signal for the purposes of facilitating communication or interpretation" [18]. In most of the sonificated systems priority is usually given to the mapping of the sound attribution to data, but not to the interactivity with the user: in order to overcome this limit and to guarantee that the sonification represents both the interaction design and information, Zhao, Plaisant, and Shneiderman (2008) [19] provided the Action by Design Component (ADC) framework, a sonification model designed to permit an active and dynamic navigation into the interaction environment. For this reason, we chosen the ACD framework as a theoretical background for the sonification of WhatsOnWeb, in which the indexed data are organized by semantic correlations resulting in abstract information.

The sonification of WoW is combined with visual events describing both global and particular browsing information. While the global information is visualized after "search" action, the temporization technique provides to increase the intensity of each cluster. From the first to the last ranking organization result is guaranteed to the user through an overall overview of information which allows the first mental representation of the framework that users are going to browse. The complexity of the tone of each node is related with the complexity of its paraverbal information: for example, while browsing a cluster node, an harmonic chord will be executed suggesting the semantic links with the other peaks. A Low-latency (less than 100 ms) of short sounds have been used in order to grant a kind of active interaction in which sound information processing and keeping does not implicate a short term memory overload [20]. Moreover, WoW browsing is granted by the auditory reiterable feedback which provides spatial information in order to facilitate user orientation. Indeed, WoW provides to user a persistent signal which indicate his/her current position in the interface, as it happens in visual navigation. Spatial cues are uttered by a stereo-audio overview which simulates the position of selected nodes within a Cartesian coordinate plane;

the information identification and memorization is strengthened by a verbal feedback voiced by an integrated synthesizer. We implemented three different ways of sonification, by using the sound's volume, pitch, tone, blinking, and grid reference to transmit visual features in a univocal way. We tested three different sonification models. In the first one, VolumeSonification model, the Euclidean distance coding for a node compared to a significant reference is rendered through the sound volume level, whereas the panning is used to strengthen the node detection on the abscissas axis as absolute information. The second, BlinkAndPitchSonification, conveys spatial relations through an independent mapping of the two axes of the Cartesian plane (x, y) respectively with the frequency of the sound blinking together with panning, and with the note pitch. Finally, in order to optimize the graphic representation in terms of sound, the PanAndPitchSonification has been created solely considering the panning for the x axis and the pitch for the y axis.

4   Usability Evaluation of the Redesigned WoW

The experimental analysis of the reengineered and sonificated WoW software evaluated the usability of the different layouts: TreeMap, Layered Radial, and Spiral TreeMap.

Experimental Procedures. 1) The first phase investigates the usability of the sonificated WoW by an expert evaluation. Three experts, with more than five years of experience in the usability evaluation, assessed the software by the Nielsen's heuristic list [21]: a user scenario has been carried out in order to test each of the implemented layouts. In particular, the experts' tasks were to test the usability and the layout differences between the three models of sonification: PanAndPitch, PitchAndVolume, and BlinkAndPitch. The heuristic evaluation identified a small set of usability with a medium and high level of severity, suggesting us that it is necessary the redesign of the layout. Finally, all the evaluators suggested us to unify two of the sonification models - PanAndPitch and BlinkAndPitch - proposing a new model called PanAndPitchBlinking. The P&PB model conveys spatiality through the two axes of the Cartesian plane (x, y) by using the panning technique (x axis) and the note pitch (y axis) and it employs the blink effect to represent the rank order of each vertex. *2)* Following the expert analysis we fix the errors of the application and, then, we performed a usability test with two groups of participants: 4 totally blind users and 4 sighted users (mean age 28, equally distributed by sex). This phase of evaluation aims at investigate both the quality of users' interaction with the visual and sonificated WoW and the users' satisfaction. In order to achieve these evaluation goals, we used the Partial Concurrent Thinking Aloud (PCTA) [22] and the System Usability Scale (SUS) [23] questionary. Each user tested the WoW after a clear and essential description of the task and a preliminary exploration (lasting 3 min) of the layout. The experimental task, provided by a scenario, consisted in an exhaustive search of the meaning of the word "Armstrong" by using the WhatsOnWeb search engine. The keyboard navigation has been carried out by using either three typologies of layout -Radial, Layered e Spiral TreeMap- or the PanAndPitch Blinking sonification. At the end of the evaluation session, we interviewed all the subjects about their layout preferences and finally they were asked to complete the SUS survey.

Experimental Results. Problems identification during the PCTA protocols were collected and matched with the heuristic analysis of the first evaluation phase. All the subjects found 19 problems, 9 out of them are related to the visual performance and 11 to the auditory performance. The one-way ANOVA analysis, carried out by SPSS 18 on task completion times for each layout, shows no significant differences ($p > .05$) between the two groups and between the kind of layout - Layered layout (sighted M=50,25", blind M= 132,5), Spiral TreeMap layout (sighted M= 263,25", blind M= 236") - whereas significative difference was found on the Radial layout ($F_{(1,6)}=13,690$; $p<0.05$). The analysis of the SUS score shows no significant differences ($p>.01$) between the two participants' groups. Therefore, since these results highlight similar levels of efficacy, efficiency, and satisfaction between the two groups for both information presentation modalities, the sonificated modality and the visual modality performances seem to be homogeneous.

5 Conclusion

Thanks to a geometric spatial representation, WoW seems to make easier for a user the information manipulation and findability. A global homogeneity on the evaluation data shows that the use of WoW, or in general of a system that grants its accessibility, reduce the digital divide. Many accessibility and usability studies pointed out that subjects with visual disability are the main excluded from the ICTs because of the missing information concerning "not only just to text, but also to graphics, tables, and figures" that screen readers can not actually translate [24].

From the application point of view, WoW seems to be a versatile system that might be used not only for searching in the World Wide Web, but also for retrieving documents in smaller environments. Moreover, according to Anderson's theories which states that the human knowledge is organized through semantic categorizations [25], WoW, since clusterize information in semantic node, by emulating cognitive mental information processing, makes easier to all users achieve and elaborate ICT information. The indexed data representation way provided by WoW aims to optimize the effectiveness and efficiency of the interaction. Moreover, the information visualization techniques used to implement the architecture of WoW allow a remarkable reduction of the number of sensory controls necessary to perform and complete tasks. At the same time, the WoW system provides an extensible and device-independent architecture to lead the events through a two interaction states. The reduction of the number of events necessary to perform a searching task allows the user navigation through control systems and/or communication systems, such as Brain Computer Interfaces, eye-trackers, tongue controllers and speech/sound interfaces.

References

1. De Vega., M., Cocude, M., Denis, M., Rodrigo, M.J., Zimmer, H.: The interface between language and visuo-spatial representations. In: Denis, M., et al. (eds.) Imagery, Language and Visuo-spatial Thinking, pp. 109–136 (2001)

2. Avraamides, M., Loomis, J., Klatzky, R.L., Golledge, R.G.: Functional equivalence of spatial representations derived from vision and language: Evidence from allocentric judgments. Journal of Experimental Psychology: Human Learning, Memory & Cognition 30, 801–814 (2004)
3. Bryant, D.J.: A Spatial Representation System in Humans 3(16) (1992)
4. Millar, S.: Understanding and representing space: theory and evidence from studies with blind and sighted children. Oxford University Press, Oxford (1994)
5. Olivetti Belardinelli, M., Federici, S., Delogu, F., Palmiero, M.: Sonification of Spatial Information: Audio-tactile Exploration Strategies by Normal and Blind Subjects. In: Stephanidis, C. (ed.) Universal Access in HCI, Part II, HCII 2009. LNCS, vol. 5615, pp. 557–563. Springer, Heidelberg (2009)
6. Delogu, F., Palmiero, M., Federici, S., Zhao, H., Plaisant, C., Olivetti Belardinelli, M.: Non-visual exploration of geographic maps: does sonification help? Disability and Rehabilitation: Assistive Technology (accept June 07, 2009)
7. Kramer, G.: Auditory display: Sonification, audification, and auditory interfaces. In: Proceedings of the First International Conference on Auditory Display, ICAD 1992. Addison-Wesley, Reading (1994)
8. Di Giacomo, E., Didimo, W., Grilli, L., Liotta, G.: Graph Visualization Techniques for Web Meta-search Clustering Engines. IEEE Transactions on Visualization and Computer Graphics 13(2), 294–304 (2007)
9. Rugo, A., Mele, M.L., Liotta, G., Trotta, F., Di Giacomo, E., Borsci, S., Federici, S.: A Visual Sonificated Web Search Clustering Engine. Cognitive Processing 10(suppl. 2), 286–289 (2009)
10. Borsci, S., Federici, S., Mele, M.L., Stamerra, G.: Global Rank: improving a qualitative and inclusive level of web accessibility. In: 4th Biennial Disabilities study conference, CeDR, Lancaster University (2008)
11. Borsci, S., Federici, S., Stamerra, G.: Web usability evaluation with screen reader users: Implementation of the Partial Concurrent Thinking Aloud technique. Cognitive Processing (accepted October 28, 2009)
12. Ivory, M.Y., Yu, S., Gronemyer, K.: Search result exploration: a preliminary study of blind and sighted users' decision making and performance. In: Extended abstracts of CHI 2004, pp. 1453–1456. ACM, New York (2004)
13. Federici, S., Borsci, S., Mele, M.L., Stamerra, G.: Web Popularity - An illusory perception of a qualitative order in information. Universal Access in the Information Society (accept June 07, 2009)
14. International Organization for Standardization. International Standard ISO 13407:1999: Human-centred design processes for interactive systems (1999),
    http://www.iso.org/iso/iso_catalogue/catalogue_tc/
    catalogue_detail.htm?csnumber=21197
15. IBM Rule-based Accessibility Validation Environment,
    http://www-03.ibm.com/able/resources/raven.html
16. Java Foundation Classes,
    http://java.sun.com/javase/technologies/desktop/
17. Di Giacomo, E., Didimo, W., Grilli, L., Liotta, G., Palladino, P.: WhatsOnWeb+, an enhanced visual search clustering engine. In: Proceedings of the IEEE PacificVis., pp. 167–174 (2008)
18. Kramer, G., Walker, B., Bonebright, T., Cook, P., Flowers, J., Miner, N., Neuhoff, J.: Sonification Report: Status of the Field and Research Agenda, International Community for Auditory Display (1997)

19. Zhao, H., Plaisant, C., Shneiderman, B., Lazar, J.: Data Sonification for Users with Visual Impairment: A Case Study with Georeferenced Data. ACM Trans. Computer-Human Interaction 15(1), 1–28 (2008)
20. Atkinson, R.C., Shiffrin, R.M.: The control of short-term memory. Scientific American, 82–90 (August 1971)
21. Nielsen, J.: Enhancing the explanatory power of usability heuristics. In: Proc. ACM CHI 1994 Conf., Boston, MA, April 24-28, pp. 152–158 (2004)
22. Borsci, S., Federici, S., Lauriola, M.: On the Dimensionality of the System Usability Scale (SUS): A Test of Alternative Measurement Models. Cognitive Processing 10(3), 193–197 (2009)
23. Brooke, J.: SUS: a quick and dirty usability scale. In: Jordan, P.W., Thomas, B., Weerdmeester, B.A., McClelland, A.L. (eds.) Usability Evaluation in Industry (1996)
24. Jay, C., Stevens, R., Glencross, M., Chalmers, A.: How people use presentation to search for a link: expanding the understanding of accessibility on the web. In: W4A 2006 (2006)
25. Anderson, J.R.: The architecture of cognition. Harvard University Press, Cambridge (1993)

Editing Web Presentations by Means of Dialogue

Luděk Bártek

Faculty of Informatics, Masaryk University,
Botanická 68a, 602 00 Brno, Czech Republic
bar@fi.muni.cz

Abstract. The number of web pages is growing fast [1] and the ability to create and maintain their own web presentation became an important skill not only for IT professionals but for the common users as well.

This paper deals with modification of a web presentation content by means of dialogue which can allow the web presentation content maintenance to visually and motoric impaired users, to users non-familiar with the underlying technologies, etc.

Keywords: web modification, dialogue, accessibility.

1 Introduction

There exist a lot of tools supporting the editing of web pages. When using the tools like Seamonkey Suite [2], iWeb [3], Microsoft Expression Web [4], etc. the user must keep in mind the presentation structure (the position of corresponding files) and the consistence (the existence of referenced pages). The above mentioned products sometimes do not lead the user to create accessible web pages and sometimes they create web pages those are even not valid.

Another type of web authoring tools are Content Management Systems [5] like OpenCMS [6], Wiki [7], etc. Such tools allow to create presentations with a correct structure. The user is still responsible for a presentation consistence (adding links to an existing pages only) and an accessibility. The content management systems often use their own language to describe the content of the page. The language is simpler than (X)HTML[8] but the user must have an additional knowledge to be able to create a presentation.

The next disadvantage of some visually oriented authoring tools is their limited usability for people with special needs, like visually impaired users [9,10] for example.

The methods described in the paper try to avoid the disadvantages mentioned in the previous paragraphs by editing the presentations in a semantic way by means of a dialogue which can be more suitable for people referenced in the previous paragraphs [11,12].

2 Editing Web Presentations

The web-presentations may differ in many aspects. To allow editing of presentations in a more less uniform way the first step should be a unification of the presentation using an XML-based descriptor for example.

K. Miesenberger et al. (Eds.): ICCHP 2010, Part I, LNCS 6179, pp. 358–365, 2010.

To generate the descriptor from an existing web-presentation the following algorithm may be used:

1. For all pages in the presentation starting from the index page:
   (a) transform the page into the corresponding XML form (using the XSLT [13] for example) and append the resulting data into the presentation descriptor. When the XSL Transformation can not be used directly (the web page is an HTML page not an XHTML one) the system tries to transform the page into the XML (XHTML) form using some existing tool (html2xhtml [14] for example) first and the XSL Transformation is performed then.
   (b) Add the page information (title of the page and the name of the corresponding file) into the presentation menu which is part of the descriptor.

This algorithm is used only when the presentation has not been generated by WebGen [15]. In the case of WebGen-generated presentation the descriptor has been created during the process of acquiring the web presentation content.

The supported editing operations are:

1. modification of the structure of the presentation. The modification includes following particular editing operations:
   (a) adding a new page into the presentation – this task is equal to creating a new web page that is already implemented in the WebGen system [15].
   (b) Removing an existing page from the presentation.
2. Modification of a web-page – means adding, removing or changing some part of the page. To modify particular web-page the semantically specified descriptor of the page is used again.

The top-level dialogue strategy used to perform the operations consists from the two steps:

1. selection of a node (a page, a part of the page, etc.) to be modified,
2. modification of the node.

The system will use a mixed-initiative dialogue strategy in both steps. The dialogue strategy is described in more details in the sections 2.2 and 2.3.

2.1 Presentation Descriptor Structure

The presentation descriptor contains a basic information about the entire presentation including the presentation identifier and a list of elements with description of all pages included in the presentation. The element corresponding to the page contains the basic information about the page as well as information depending on the type of the page. The basic information about the page are for example its title and style sheet (means CSS [16]).

The rest of information included in the element depends on the type of the page. The system supports the following page types at the present time:

- Private page – contains the information about its owner like a name, a surname, contacts, hobbies, skills, etc. There are several subtypes like the personal, the work and the academic page type that differs in some included information like the hobbies in the private page those are not included in the work and academic page, etc.
- Blog – a page with links to the articles. The articles may be either written by a single person with multiple themes or a monothematic written by multiple authors. The articles are based on a short publication type.
- CV.
- Short publication – a publication without an internal segmentation into the sections like essays, for example. The element contains the list of paragraphs corresponding to the paragraphs of the paper. It may contain the name of the article and its author as well.
- Structured publication – a publication divided into chapters, sections, etc. like novels, articles, . . . The element contains the name of the author, the publication title, the list of sections, etc. The section elements consist from the name of the section, the content of the part (text, images, etc) and the list of subsections with their content.
- General page – describes the general (X)HTML page. The element structure corresponds to the structure of the HTML element as described in the (X)HTML specification. This type can be used when the page does not fit into the above mentioned categories. For purposes of editing the General page type is used for all pages not generated by the WebGen system.

When the presentation is generated from the descriptor then the element menu with links to all pages currently included in the presentation is added into the presentation element.

2.2   Navigation in the Presentation

To be able to modify some part of the presentation the user must specify the particular presentation part like page, part of the page (e-mail, address, photograph, paragraph, etc.) to be changed.

This task is simple when the user can exactly specify the part of the presentation to be modified.

When the user can not specify the part exactly enough the system starts traversal of the presentation tree. At every tree level the system offers to the user all available possibilities. When the number of possibilities is either five or more the options can be reorganized using the E-minimal tree [17] to minimize the length of a dialogue used to select the desired option.

The dialogue strategy used to select the requested node follows:

1. Let the user specify the node to be modified. The user can use a context information, like a node value, siblings, an ordinal number, etc. to specify the node more exactly.
2. If there is only one such node, use it.

3. If there are multiple nodes describe them to the user:
   (a) if the number of suitable nodes is less than five present them to the user and let him to select the right one,
   (b) else build a corresponding E-minimal tree and use it for a node selection.
   (c) Select the node and continue the algorithm on its child nodes.
4. If the user was unable to specify the requested node repeat the steps 1 to 3 for all tree levels until the requested node is reached.

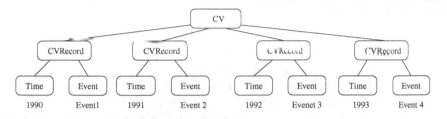

Fig. 1. Sample data used for differentiation by context

An example of the dialogue performing the selection from data on Fig. 1 using the node value follows:

System: What modification do you want to do?
User: I'd like to change the CV event time.
System: Which one? The 1990, 1991, 1992 or 1993?
User: I'd like to change the year 1990 to 1989.

The second example demonstrates the selection using the context in a single step:

System: What modification do you want to perform?
User: I'd like to remove the CV record with time 1990.

2.3 Content Editing

The second step, after selecting the part of the presentation, is its modification. The approach differs according to the type of data to be modified. The following data types are distinguished:

1. textual data - a general text, its value cannot be exactly specified by a grammar; may be even long (several sentences, paragraphs, pages, ...);
2. exactly specified values - the possible values are specified by the document type definition like the XML Schema [18], Relax NG [19], etc.

Modification of the second type of data is relatively simple. The system must only generate the corresponding dialogue and grammar. Let us have the element currency with allowed values CZK, USD, GBP, Euro for example. The dialogue that will replace the value GBP with Euro follows:

. . .

System: The present value of currency is GBP.
        Specify the new value. Possible values are
        CZK, USD, GBP, Euro.
User: Euro

The situation in the case of the textual data is more complicated. The user must perform a specification of the part of the text to be modified [20,21] prior to its modification. The text selection can be done as follows:

1. The user knows the exact sentence or part of the sentence to be modified:
   (a) The user asks the system to modify the specified text.
   (b) The system locates the part of the text.
       i. When the specified text is included only once the system selects the text and it asks for an operation to be performed.
       ii. When the text is included multiply, the system let the user specify, which occurrence has to be modified. To allow easier selection some context of the text, like the sentence containing the text or the previous and the following sentences, is included.
   (c) The system asks for an operation to be performed.
2. When the user does not know the exact text he wants to modify:
   (a) the system reads the text sentence by sentence and asks the user if the text was included.
   (b) The system asks, which part of the text, that has been read, has to be modified.

To demonstrate the approach we will use the first paragraph of this section. The user wants to change the first article *the* into the article *an* in the second sentence for example:

system: What do you want to change?
user: I would like to change the article the in the first paragraph of the section 2.3 of this paper.
system: There are multiple articles the. Specify more exactly which one. If you don't know which
        one I will read the paragraph for you.
user: I don't remember the text exactly.
        System reads paragraph sentence by
        sentence and the user stops the reading after
        the second sentence.
system: There are two occurrences of the word the in the sentence. Which one do you want to modify?
user: The first one.
system: Do you want to remove or change the word?
user: Change.
system: What is the replacement of the word?
user: An.

Task	# of successful users	mean # of dialogue turns	max. # of dialogue turns	min. # of dialogue turns
Selecting the cellular # phone	9(9)	3	5	1
Changing the home phone #	9(9)	2	6	1
Change the second occurrence of the word "a" to ","	9(9)	2	6	1
Change the word žena to paní	9(9)	1	4	1

Fig. 2. Results of the experiment

```
<contacts>
  <phones>
    <phone>
      <description> work phone </description>
      <number> +420543214321 </number>
    </phone>
    <phone>
      <description> cellular </description>
      <number> +420606606606 </number>
    </phone>
    <phone>
      <description> home phone </description>
      <number> +420234564321 </number>
    </phone>
  </phones>
</contacts>
```

Fig. 3. Data used in navigation test and test of modification of structured data

3   Experimental Results

To proof the ability of the proposed approach to allow the modification of the structured document as well as modification of a plain text an experiment has been performed. The second purpose of the experiment was to get the feedback from users that will allow us to improve the dialogue strategy.

The tests were done using the dialogue simulation between two persons either face-to-face or using instant messaging client. The principles of the dialogue strategy used in the test are described in the previous sections. The users participating in the test were from about 13 to 60 years old, males and females. The group contained the users with a good experience in processing structured data as well as users with no or minimal experience in the area. The achieved results

are shown on the Fig. 2 and the data used in the experiment on Fig. 3. To test
the plain text modifications the following text was used:
"Jedna chudá žena měla jedinou, ale tuze lenivou dceru. Její dcera celé dny
prospala a proležela v posteli a byla jí pouze na obtíž."

4   Conclusions and Future Work

The paper proposed the methods and the dialogue strategies, that allow to modify web presentations as well as a plain text. The methods has been tested on
several persons. The test has proved that the proposed method is able to collect
the information needed to perform the requested tasks as shown on the Fig. 2.

Our primary objective in the near future is to include the proposed methods
into the system for dialogue generation of web presentations and graphics WebGen that is being developed at our laboratory as well as improvement of the
used dialogue strategy according to the feedback from the users.

Acknowledgment

The author is grateful to the students and staff of the Support Center for Students with Special Needs of Masaryk University for their advice, support and
collaboration as well as to people who participated in the experiment. This
work is supported by the Grant Agency of Czech Republic under the Grant
201/07/0881.

References

1. Netcraft Ltd.: Web Survey Archives (2010),
   http://news.netcraft.com/archives/web_server_survey.html
2. Kaiser, R.: Seamonkey: Documentation & Help (2009),
   http://www.seamonkey-project.org/doc/
3. Hart-Davies, G.: iLife 2009 Portable Genius. Wiley Publishing Inc., Chichester
   (2009)
4. Cheshier, J.: Using Microsoft Expression Web 2. Que Publishing (2008)
5. Boiko, B.: Content Management Bible, 2nd edn. Wiley Publishing Inc., Chichester
   (2004)
6. Butcher, M.: Building Websites With OpenCms. Packt Publishing Ltd. (2004)
7. Barrett, D.J.: MediaWiki (Wikipedia and Beyond). O'Reilly Media Inc., Sebastopol
   (2008)
8. Pemberton, S., Austin, D., Axelsson, J., Celik, T., Dominiak, D., Elenbaas, H.,
   Epperson, B., Ishikawa, M., Matsui, S., McCarron, S., Navarro, A., Pruvemba, S.,
   Relyea, R., Schnitzenbaumer, S., Stark, P.: XHTML 1.0: The Extensible HyperText
   Markup Language, 2nd edn. (2001), http://www.w3.org/TR/xhtml1/
9. Egan, C., Johal, J., Jefferies, A.: Accessibility through usability. In: Computers
   and Advanced Technologies in Education 2000. Acta Press (2000)
10. Correani, F., Leporini, B., Paterno, F.: Automatic inspection-based support for
    obtaining usable web sites for vision-impaired. Universal Access in the Information
    Society 5(3), 82–95 (2008)

11. Dobrisek, S., Gross, J., Vesnicer, J., Pavesic, N., Mihelic, F.: Evaluation of the information-retrieval system for blind and visually-impaired people. International Journal of Speech Technology 6(3), 301–309 (2003)
12. Pieper, M., Hermsdorf, D.: BSWC for disabled teleworkers: usability evaluation and interface adaptation of an internet-based cooperation environment. Computer Networks and ISDN Systems 29, 1479–1487 (1997)
13. Lipkin, D., Marsh, J., Thompson, H., Walsh, N., Zilles, S.: XSL Transformation, XSLT (1999), http://www.w3.org/TR/xslt
14. Fisteus, J.A.: HTML to XHTML translator (2009), http://www.it.uc3m.es/jaf/html2xhtml/
15. Kopecek, I., Bartek, L.: Web pages for blind people – generating web-based presentations by means of dialogue. In: Miesenberger, K., Klaus, J., Zagler, W.L., Karshmer, A.I. (eds.) ICCHP 2006. LNCS, vol. 4061, pp. 114–119 Springer, Heidelberg (2006)
16. Lie, H.W., Bos, B.: Cascading Style Sheets: Designing for the Web, 3rd edn. Addison-Wesley Professional, Reading (2005)
17. Bártek, L., Kopeček, I.: Adapting web-based educational systems for the visually impaired. International Journal Cont. Engineering Education and Life-Long Learning 17(4/5), 358–368 (2007)
18. Gao, S., Sperberg-McQueen, C.M., Thompson, H.S.: W3C XML Schema Definition Language (XSD) 1.1 Part 1: Structures. W3C (2009), http://www.w3.org/TR/xmlschema11-1/
19. Clark, J., Makoto, M.: RELAX NG Specification. OASIS (2001), http://relaxng.org/spec-20011203.html
20. Pontelli, E., Gillan, D., Xiong, W., Saad, E., Gupta, G., Karshmer, A.I.: Navigation of html tables, frames and xml fragments. In: Proceedings of the fifth international ACM conference on Assistive technologies, Edinburgh, Scotland, pp. 25–32. ACM, New York (2002)
21. Kudrle, Z.: Generating web-based presentations by means of dialogue (in czech). Master's thesis, Faculty of Informatics, Masaryk University, Brno, Czech Republic (2007)

Fast Access to Web Pages with Finger Reading

Toshihiro Kanahori

Research and Support Center on Higher Education for the Hearing and Visually
Impaired, Tsukuba University of Technology,
4-12-7 Kasuga, Tsukuba city, Ibaraki Pref., Japan
kanahori@k.tsukuba-tech.ac.jp

Abstract. We can access to large amounts of information on the web.
Searching and getting information has become much more important.
Using assistive products, visually impaired people also can access to a
goodly portion of them, but getting information they need still takes long
time. We introduce our software *"Finger Skitter"*, which is being developed not for reading a document but for getting information with voice
navigation. This software provides 2 types of user interface to rapidly
get "what the document is written about" and "where is the information in the document". We implement a prototype of the software with
JavaScript, which uses live-regions supported in WAI-ARIA to control a
speech engine.

1 Introduction

Reading a document is a time-consuming task for visually impaired people.
Sighted people usually dip into a document once-over to get its outline. It is
hard to visually impaired people. In Braille, they must read the entire document
even to get its rough outline, or with a speech device (a screen reader, DAISY,
etc.), they also must hear all. To get a document layout is also hard. It gives
some important information to understand a document. Giving 2-dimensional
document layout with 1-dimensional information such as Braille or speech makes
understanding the document hard. Recently, a lot of Web pages have been made
accessible, but even now for visually impaired people to access to Web pages
takes much longer time than for sighted people.

In this paper, we introduce our software, *"FingerSkitter"*, which assists visually impaired people access to Web pages with touchscreen and screen reader.
This software adds navigation interface to Web pages, and reads aloud a word
or a sentence which a user is touching on a screen. Using the interface, visually
impaired people can quickly get information they need from Web pages using
fingers and ears instead of eyes with touchscreen and screen reader.

2 Outline of FingerSkitter

FingerSkitter is a bookmarklet, which is a bookmark in which a small JavaScript
program is embedded. To launch a bookmarklet, a user selects it in a bookmark
list of a Web browser like opening a bookmark.

K. Miesenberger et al. (Eds.): ICCHP 2010, Part I, LNCS 6179, pp. 366–367, 2010.

FingerSkitter provides two kinds of navigation interface. One of them is to get a rough outline of a Web page. FingerSkitter adds several buttons for that navigation on the top of the Web page after launched. When the buttons are pushed, the following information of the page is read aloud respectively:

- words in the page randomly (Skitter),
- the beginning several words of each sentence or each paragraph one after another (Intro.), which some screen readers are providing,
- all the headlincs (Headlines),
- all the alt attributes of images (Images).

Using this navigation, a user determines to read the page or not. Another is to find a sentence or a paragraph to read. A word which a user is touching on is read aloud in FingerSkitter. After some words a user is interested in are found the user makes the sentence or paragraph including the words read aloud.

To read aloud those information, FingerSkitter uses a screen reader, which supports WAI-ARIA (Web Accessibility Initiative-Accessible Rich Internet Applications)[1]. WAI-ARIA specifies how to keep rich Web pages accessible, which use JavaScript or some other interactive contents. Several screen readers are supporting WAI-ARIA now, and more will support in the future. The information for the navigation is written in a live-region. When content in a live-region is changed, it is notified to a screen reader according to its attributes. We use a live-region only to make a screen reader speak the information, because controlling a screen reader by JavaScript is hardly allowed.

3   Conclusion

This paper introduces FingerSkitter which helps visually impaired people to quickly get information they want which screen reader supporting WAI-ARIA and touchscreen. FingerSkitter provides touching and reading documents. FingerSkitter does not analyze document layout, and gives positions of components (words, sentences, paragraphs, or images) to get the layout. Using this software, users can easily get an outline of a Web page and quickly find information they need. We used live-regions of WAI-ARIA to control a screen reader. It is not smart way. We will develop the software as an extension (plug-in) for a web browser or as an individual web browser to provide more natural reading.

Acknowledgement

This research was partially supported by the Ministry of Education, Science, Sports and Culture, Grant-in-Aid for Young Scientists (B), 21700574, 2009.

Reference

1. Craig, J., Cooper, M.: Accessible Rich Internet Applications (WAI-ARIA) 1.0, W3C, http://www.w3.org/TR/wai-aria/

The Evaluations of Deletion-Based Method and Mixing-Based Method for Audio CAPTCHAs

Takuya Nishimoto[1] and Takayuki Watanabe[2]

[1] Graduate School of Information Science and Technology, The University of Tokyo
7-3-1, Hongo, Bunkyo-ku, Tokyo, 113-8656, Japan
nishi@hil.t.u-tokyo.ac.jp
[2] Department of Communication, Division of Human Science, School of Arts and
Sciences, Tokyo Woman's Christian University
2-6-1 Zenpukuzi, Suginami-ku, Tokyo, 167-8585, Japan
nabe@lab.twcu.ac.jp
http://hil.t.u-tokyo.ac.jp/ nishi/

Abstract. Audio CAPTCHA systems, which distinguish between software agents and human beings, are especially important for persons with visual disability. The popular approach is based on mixing-based methods (MBM), which use the mixed sounds of target speech and noises. We have proposed a deletion-based method (DBM) which uses the phonemic restoration effects. Our approach can control the difficulty of tasks simply by the masking ratio.

According to our design principle of CAPTCHA, the tasks should be designed so that the large difference of performance between the machines and human beings can be provided. In this paper, we show the experimental results that support the hypotheses as follows: (1) only using MBM, the degree of task difficulty can not be controlled easily, (2) using DBM, the degree of task difficulty and safeness of CAPTCHA system can be controlled easily.

Keywords: Security, Visual Impalement, Speech Recognition, CAPTCHA, Mixing-based Method, Deletion-based Method.

1 Introduction

CAPTCHAs (Completely Automated Public Turing test to tell Computers and Humans Apart) are popular security techniques on the Web that prevent automated programs from abusing online services.

A typical CAPTCHA is an image containing several distorted characters that appears at the Web forms [1]. Users are asked to type the distorted dirty characters to let the system know that they are human. Image-based CAPTCHAs are, however, preventing Web use of persons with visual disability [2]. Audio CAPTCHAs were created to solve this accessibility issue.

In this paper, we describe an attempt to create better audio CAPTCHA tasks in consideration of safety and usability. The difference of recognition performance

K. Miesenberger et al. (Eds.): ICCHP 2010, Part I, LNCS 6179, pp. 368–375, 2010.

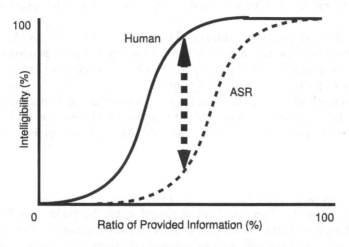

Fig. 1. Concept model of audio CAPTCHA design

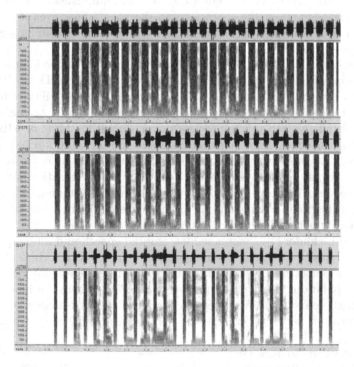

Fig. 2. Examples of audio files created with deletion-based method (D30, D50 and D70)

between human and machine can be a criterion of safeness. Mental workload of human in listening speech was also investigated from the perspective of usability.

It is important to design the audio CAPTCHAs that the audio files are difficult to be recognized automatically by machines. In other words, it is necessary that the speech recognition performance with machines should be lower than the intelligibility of human, as shown in Figure 1.

Statistical method is the mainstream in speech recognition technology. Correct answers can be estimated from the distorted speech if there are enough learning data and the human annotations for them [3]. Many improvements in speech recognition are also proposed to cope with the noise robustness. In such situation, distorted audio files for CAPTCHAs should not be created based on trial and error, but rather be created systematically.

From another point of view, audio CAPTCHAs should not increase the mental workload of the users. The workload of listening to the tasks may increase if they are difficult to listen. Workload of memorizing a number of characters is also unignorable. Human auditory sensation and language cognition should be investigated to deal with the problems.

Top-down knowledge of human acts to guess the information in an incomplete stimulus. In the case of visual sensation, we can complement an image with common knowledge about the character and the vocabulary, even if part of the character image is missing, or part of the word is hidden. Similar process exists in speech understanding.

To make use of the ability of human perception, we focused on a method of speech processing that we call "deletion-based method" or DBM. There are new ways to generate the tasks in which human can use the ability of top-down knowledge, though noises and reverberations are often added to make speech difficult to listen (we call this approach "mixing-based method" or MBM). For example, we can delete some parts of an audio file on temporal axis little by little. If every 30 msec over a period of 100 msec of the audio file is replaced with silence, it can be considered that the 30% of the information was deleted. If the ratio of remained sections go down, the degree of listening difficulty may increase. In this "temporal induction" method, the audio listening tasks can be controlled easily with "the ratio of information."

Miller and Licklider [4][5] combined interrupted speech and interrupted noise maskers, i.e., speech and noise are temporally interleaved to form a continuous signal. They reported that perceived continuity of the speech signal was increased by this manipulation. This "phonemic restoration" may help the human listening, though the effect does not affect the recognition performance of machine. In other words, it serves to enlarge the performance difference of human and machine.

Examples of audio files created with deletion-based method are shown in Figure 2. Seven digit numbers are contained in a utterance. The 30%, 50%, and 70% of the utterance is left and the gaps are filled with white noise, respectively.

2 Comparison between DBM and MBM

A comparative experiment of deletion-based method (DBM) and the mixing-based method (MBM) was performed as the Exp.1. The objective is to compare the intelligibility and mental workload of DBM with those of MBM, and to examine the effect of SNR (signal-to-noise ratio) in MBM.

The task is Japanese connected digit recognition which conforms to CENSREC-4 [6]. A set of human intelligibility test consists of 75 utterances, which include three digit, four digit and five digit numbers. The balance of the occurrence of numbers is considered and the utterances were spoken by many people including men and women. Acoustic presentation was given by the headphone at the subject's preferred reference loudness level.

The subjects were undergraduate students. They were divided into three groups (G1, G2 and G3) with different MBM task conditions. Each group consists of five persons.

The experiment consists of two parts, as shown in Table 1. At first, a set of DBN tasks with 30 % of unmasked information condition (D30) was given, followed by a set of MBM tasks with an SNR condition.

The MBM task condition consists of M0, Mm10 and Mm20, which correspond to SNR of 0dB, -10dB and -20dB, respectively. To make the disturbing signals, utterances of Japanese sentence were fragmented as short periods, shuffled and combined.

NASA-TLX [7] was used to evaluate mental workload. In this method, the trial subjects answer the amount of workload by rating the following subscales: Mental, Physical, and Temporal Demands, Frustration, Effort, and Performance. The weights of the subscales are derived for each participant by placing an order how the 6 dimensions are related to their personal definition of workload.

According to the ANOVA (analysis of variance) results as shown in Table 2, the difference of the intelligibility among the groups was marginally significant, although the conditions of DBN were same among the groups. The intelligibility of MBM also showed significant difference among the conditions of M0, Mm10 and Mm20 ($p < 0.05$). The multiple comparison test (LSD and Tukey HSD), however, indicated only the significance between M0 and Mm10.

Concerning the mental workload, the effect of the MBM task difference was investigated. To cancel the individual difference, subtraction of DBM (D30) score from MBM (M0, Mm10 and Mm20) score was performed. The results shown in Table 3 suggested that the WWL of M0 was lower than that of D30. According to the ANOVA, however, significant difference was not observed.

Table 1. The experimental setup and the average (SD) of intelligibility (%) (Exp.1). The V1 and V2 correspond to the vocabularies.

Group	# Persons	Trial 1		Trial 2	
G1	5	V1-D30	82.9 (7.0)	V2-M0	94.2 (1.8)
G2	5	V1-D30	69.1 (9.1)	V2-Mm10	80.3 (9.2)
G3	5	V1-D30	74.7 (7.6)	V2-Mm20	85.6 (3.6)

Table 2. The ANOVA results of intelligibility (%) (Exp.1)

Group	Trial 1	Trial 2
G1-G2	> *	> *
G1-G3	ns	ns
G2-G3	ns	ns

Trial 1: $F = 3.07(p < 0.10)$

Trial 2: $F = 5.82(p < 0.05)$

Table 3. The average and SD of WWL difference (%) (Exp.1)

Group	Difference	Ave. (SD)
G1	$W_{M0} - W_{D30}$	-16.2 (19.5)
G2	$W_{Mm10} - W_{D30}$	0.7 (7.9)
G3	$W_{Mm20} - W_{D30}$	1.0 (9.7)

$$F = 2.17(ns)$$

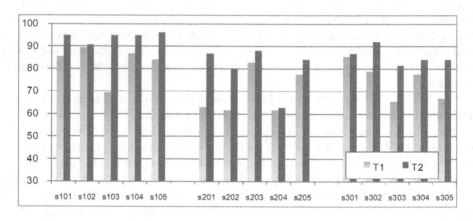

Fig. 3. Intelligibility of every trial of every subject (Exp.1)

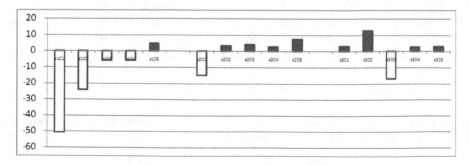

Fig. 4. Difference of workload of every subject (Exp.1)

Table 4. The experimental setup (Exp.2). The V1, V2 and V3 correspond to the vocabularies

Group	# Persons	Trial 1	Trial 2	Trial 3
G1	5	V1-D70	V2-D50	V3-D30
G2	6	V1-D30	V2-D70	V3-D50
G3	6	V1-D50	V2-D30	V3-D70

Table 5. The sentence recognition performance of Exp.2 tasks using HTK (%)

Condition	D30	D50	D70
Performance	40.5	79.0	89.4

Table 6. The human intelligibility (%) (Exp.2)

Condition	D30	D50	D70
Average (SD)	84.2 (6.5)	97.4 (2.7)	99.0 (2.0)

Table 7. The average (SD) of normalized WWL (Exp.2)

Condition	D30	D50	D70
Average (SD)	60.6 (5.5)	45.2 (7.5)	44.2 (6.9)

Table 8. The ANOVA results of intelligibility (%) and normalized WWL (Exp.2)

Group	Intelligibility	N-WWL
D30-D50	< *	> *
D30-D70	< *	> *
D50-D70	ns	ns

Intelligibility : $F = 66.95(p < 0.01)$
Normalized WWL : $F = 20.21(p < 0.01)$

The result of every subject was shown in Figure 3 and Figure 4. The hypothesis that the SNR condition of MBM gives significant difference for intelligibility or mental workload was not supported.

3   Comparison between Human and Machine with DBM

An experiment that compares the intelligibility and mental workload between the conditions of DBM was performed. The automatic speech recognition (ASR) performance was also examined. Experimental setup, shown in Table 4, is similar to that of previous section, though this experiment is to compare between the conditions in each subject. The subject was seventeen undergraduate students.

HTK (Hidden Markov Model toolkit)[1] was used for the ASR experiment. Statistical acoustic models for ASR were trained with 8440 utterances that were

---

[1] http://htk.eng.cam.ac.uk/

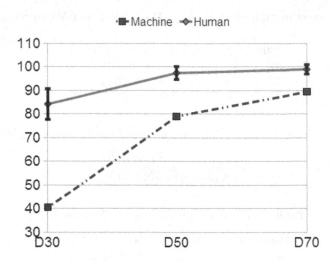

Fig. 5. The relationship between the performance of human and machine (Exp.2)

processed using DBM. This means the assumption that the correct answers for all audio files were given to break this CAPTCHA system. The evaluation of ASR was performed using 1001 utterances that were not included in training data. The trained HMM consists of 18 states with 20 mixtures of Gaussian for each number.

D30, D50 and D70 indicate the conditions that the unmasked information ratios are 30%, 50% and 70%, respectively.

The sentence recognition performance of the tasks using HTK is shown in Table 5. The average and SD of intelligibility is shown in Table 6. The average (SD) of normalized WWL is shown in Table 7.

As the result of ANOVA shown in Table 8, the human intelligibility showed significant difference among the conditions. According to the multiple comparison test (LSD), difference of intelligibility was significant between D30-D50 and between D30-D70.

Concerning mental workload, WWL scores were normalized within every subject so that their average and standard deviation become 50 and 10 respectively at first, followed by the comparison among the conditions. As the ANOVA results shown in Table 8, significant difference of normalized-WWL between the groups was observed. According to the multiple comparison test (LSD), difference of normalized-WWL was significant between D30-D50 and D30-D70.

The ASR performances were 40.5%, 79.0% and 89.4% for D30, D50 and D70, respectively. The subtraction of ASR performance from human intelligibility was 43.7 point, 18.4 point and 9.6 point for D30, D50 and D70, respectively. Although the ASR method was not optimized enough, the results supported the effectiveness of DBM (Figure 5).

4   Conclusions

Two experiments of mixing-based method (MBM) and deletion-based method (DBM) for audio CAPTCHAs were presented. Our results supported the hypothesis as follows: (1) only using MBM, the degree of task difficulty can not be controlled easily, (2) using DBM, the degree of task difficulty and safeness of CAPTCHA system can be controlled easily.

Future works include the utilization of state-of-art ASR techniques and investigations of effective combinations of MBM and DBM.

Acknowledgments

We would like to thank Kenta Nishiki, Ryo Tanemura, Jonathan Le Roux, Nobutaka Ono, Shigeki Sagayama, Chihiro Fukuoka and Hitomi Matsumura for their support and assistance in this research.

References

1. von Ahn, L., Maurer, B., McMillen, C., Abraham, D., Blum, M.: reCAPTCHA: Human-Based Character Recognition via Web Security Measures. Science 321(12), 1465 (2008)
2. Inaccessibility of CAPTCHA, Alternatives to Visual Turing Tests on the Web, W3C Working Group Note (November 23, 2005), http://www.w3.org/TR/turingtest/
3. Tam, J., Simsa, J., Hyde, S., Von Ahn, L.: Breaking Audio CAPTCHAs. In: Proceedings of NIPS (2008)
4. Miller, G.A., Licklider, J.C.R.: The intelligibility of interrupted speech. J. Acoust. Soc. Am. 22, 167–173 (1950)
5. Warren, R.M.: Auditory Perception: A New Analysis and Synthesis. Cambridge University Press, Cambridge (1999)
6. Nakayama, M., et al.: CENSREC-4: Development of Evaluation Framework for Distant-talking Speech Recognition under Reverberant Environments. In: Proc. Interspeech (September 2008)
7. Hart, S.G., Staveland, L.E.: Development of NASA-TLX (Task Load Index): Results of empirical and theoretical research. In: Hancock, P.A., Meshkati, N. (eds.) Human Mental Workload. North Holland Press, Amsterdam (1998)

Integrating Semantic Web and Folksonomies to Improve E-Learning Accessibility

Iyad Abu Doush[1] and Enrico Pontelli[2]

[1] Dept. Computer Science, Yarmouk University
idoush@cs.nmsu.edu
[2] Dept. Computer Science, New Mexico State University
epontell@cs.nmsu.edu

Abstract. The purpose of this project is to investigate ways of leveraging the collaborative and multi-user nature of modern *Learning Management Systems (LMSs)* to enhance accessibility of online courses for individuals with visual disabilities. The underlying principle of the project is the generation of semantics annotation for all components of an online course—that can be used to guide assistive devices. The semantic information can be added in a three different forms (a predefined ontology class, user tags, and annotations). This semantic information is used by assistive technologies (e.g., screen readers) to help visually impaired students when they acquire knowledge from the on-line course materials.

1 Introduction

In recent years, we have observed the fast evolution of the Internet. The introduction of sophisticated *Learning Management Systems (LMSs)*, such as *Blackboard* and *Moodle*, has widely increased the opportunities for a geographically diverse population of students to access educational programs. Recent statistics [19] indicate that more than 3.2 million people are involved in some form of online education. The creation of online educational opportunities has contributed to lowering the digital divide and the educational divide for several classes of individuals (e.g., rural communities, individuals with motor impairments).

Modern LMSs are designed to provide sophisticated organization of the various components of a course. Unfortunately, this sophistication commonly maps to highly complex visual representations—e.g., pull-down menus, tables, charts, active components. These components create a further deepening of the digital divide for individuals with visual disabilities [2,6]. Even ignoring these technical aspects, the layout of information across multiple pages makes the process of locating specific knowledge hard without the aid of a continuous visual overview.

Different group of learners have different requirements and this requires providing them with learning experience adaptable to their needs [11]. Several accessibility issues are related with the use of LMS, and studies (e.g., [2,6,18]) have denoted the lack of adherence to accessibility guidelines (e.g., WCAG) in

K. Miesenberger et al. (Eds.): ICCHP 2010, Part I, LNCS 6179, pp. 376–383, 2010.

several LMSs. For example, some LMSs suffer from not providing the users with sufficient keyboard control over all the components of the online course. Other accessibility obstacles are related to graphical elements (e.g., images, frames, input fields) that do not have meaningful descriptive information.

The literature provides several proposals aimed at enhancing the accessibility of e-learning by improving the accessibility options offered by the LMS itself, e.g., by enhancing keyboard access and providing aural output. Relatively more limited is the literature aimed at improving the accessibility of the actual content of the online course, by adding semantic meaning/markups to different parts of the online course. We strongly believe that this second direction can have a more profound impact in facilitating the use of LMSs for visually impaired students.

Following a research trend that has developed in the last years, we explore the introduction of technologies drawn from the field of the *semantic web* to aid in the process of enhancing non-visual accessibility of LMSs. We rely on two principles: *ontologies* and *folksonomies*.

Ontology is one of the main elements of the semantic web. An ontology is used to formalize the *concepts* in a domain and to describe their mutual relationships [16]. Ontologies can be used to build adaptable e-learning systems: using ontologies, (human or software) agents can automatically understand the meaning of the e-learning content and process it appropriately [16]. For example, ontologies enable semantic-based search of e-learning content [4].

The process of *collaborative tagging* produces a set of tags that can be used to describe a resource [1]. This tagging process, made popular by sites like del.icio.us, can be employed to generate *grassroot ontologies*, commonly called *folksonomies*. Folksonomies add semantics to resources through a social markup process, enabling the use of tag clouds to describe entities and determine relevance. The use of folksonomies allows the addition of semantics without the aid of individual manual indexers or automated keyword generators [1].

The tagging process does not create a strict taxonomy for objects, but it enables the user to employ his own keywords to categorize objects. Gruber [7] mentioned that, in collaborative tagging, there is no explicit links between entities, and no standard form is used for presenting the data. This limitation requires introducing a formal ontology along with folksonomies to formalize tags.

In this work, we will address the problem of non-visual e-learning accessibility in the context of the Moodle system, one of the most popular LMSs. The short-term objective of the project is to enhance Moodle with semantic annotations; these annotations are used to associate a semantic classification to all components and content of a Moodle-based course. The long-term objective is to develop ways to use the semantic annotations to guide assistive devices (e.g., screen readers) to provide effective presentations of content. Contrary to most of the existing literature, we propose to develop an ontology for Moodle using a combination of two processes—a developer-provided upper-level ontology and a user-provided bottom-up folksonomy.

2   Background

We identify two main classes of approaches that have been proposed in the literature which apply the semantic web technologies to improve the accessibility of web contents.

Semantic Web to Transform Web Pages: An extensive literature exists on applying principles of the semantic web to present web pages in an accessible form. Harper et al. [9] presented a system that uses ontologies to convert web pages into a more accessible form for visually-impaired users. In particular, the system relies on ontologies for Cascading Style Sheets (CSS).

Specific domain ontologies can be used to assist users when they access web contents by offering meaning for the components of the web page. Chang et al. [4] use an ontology for "geometric figures" to help students in 8th grade to search efficiently in a math class. Henze et al. [11] introduce an approach for dynamic generation of hypertext structures and presentations using three types of ontologies (domain, user, and observation). In another work, [13] presents a transcoding system, called Aurora, which alters web content according to the user need. The customized web pages are generated on-the-fly using XML data which identifies different goals of the users (e.g., searching, bidding on an auction).

Semantic Web to Add Meaning: Adding more descriptions for different portions of a web page can enhance its accessibility. By making use of ontologies, the accessibility of information can be improved, facilitating search and guiding navigation [15]. An ontology can be used to guide the presentation of the contents in a meaningful way. Heiyanthuduwage and Karunaratne [10] define an ontology for learning objects to efficiently retrieve learning content. The semantic information stored in web pages can be used by assistive technologies (e.g., screen readers) when rendering the material to the users. Harper and Bechhofer [8] introduce a system which store markups inside web pages as a semantic information for navigation.

The information about user capabilities and limitations can be used to offer alternative modalities of presentation. Karim et al. [14] propose a framework that provides a general level accessibility using ontologies to describe features like type of disability, device profiles, related tasks to a specific domain, and their relations. Kim et al. [16] use semantic web technologies in e-learning to support students by sending and receiving different messages by agents to present different tasks to the students. Cooper [5] emphasizes that the sharing the information and the use of semantic web can be utilized to help students discovering new knowledge.

3   Methodology

We have developed the first stage of the project—the development of an ontology and infrastructure for the annotation of the course content in Moodle. The proposed ontology consists of activities and entities involved in the e-learning process (e.g., lesson, quiz, student). Also the ontology defines the relationships between different classes in the e-learning ontology (e.g., an assignment is solved by a student). The ontology can be collaboratively extended by the users of the system by introducing new classes that are associated with other pre-defined classes in the ontology.

The ontology is structured in two parts: an *upper ontology* and a *bottom ontology*. Intuitively, the upper ontology is used to describe the overall structure of a generic course in Moodle. The upper ontology describes the components of a course that are common across *all* courses; as such, this is a static ontology. The bottom ontology describes the components that are course-specific and domain-specific. It is an inherently dynamic ontology.

The fundamental idea is to get the help from sighted students in the class to introduce a taxonomy for a specific online course. Students participating in the same class are encouraged to annotated the course content and share such annotations with other students. The benefit from integrating the two approaches (i.e., bottom-up and top-down) is to create a comprehensive semantic structure of a course, which can be used by students to understand the content of the course and facilitate the job of assistive devices (e.g., screen readers).

We believe that student collaboration in an online course can be used to improve the accessibility of the course. Lee [17] indicates that the social nature of the tagging application affects the tagging behavior of the users. The students in an online class represent a form of social collaboration that can help other students in the course—especially students with disabilities. For example, a student who reads the online course material can add annotations to explain specific parts of the lecture notes (e.g., describe a figure or a mathematical formula) in the process of studying the material. These annotations can be used by other users; the tagging of a figure can, for example, provide a textual documentation that a screen reader can reproduce for a visually impaired student of the same course.

User Scenario: To understand how the system operates, let us consider a blind student, who wants to access an online course in Moodle to review lecture notes for a math course. The student depends on a screen reader to access the content of the course web pages. During navigation the student is able to listen to a cue that tells him this part of the page is tagged. The student can then listen to the tags and annotations (made by other students studying the same material) to obtain tags that label the different part of the notes and to get new information about the content (e.g., a mathematical formula is annotated with a link that explains it, or a paragraph in lecture notes is tagged as a potential quiz question).

The user can use the category of the tag to find its relation to other course materials (e.g., a specific part of the lecture notes is tagged as an explanation for a mathematical formula in the notes the student is browsing). When the student encounters graphical content in the page he could look for the annotations associated with it to get a textual explanation about its contents and how it relates to the content of the lecture notes (e.g., a graph for mathematical equation). The use of the taxonomy provided by the ontology can be seen when the student wants to access specific part of the page (e.g., geometry→area of a triangle).

The Top Ontology: We built different classes in the top ontology (Fig. 1) on the basis of various components of Moodle (e.g., quiz, homework). The `Activity`

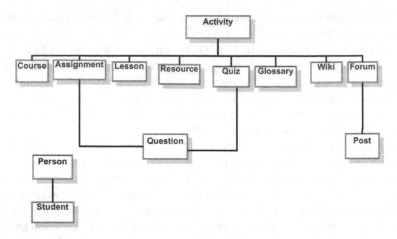

Fig. 1. Graph of a Fragment of the Upper Ontology

class is the super class of all the activities (`Lesson`, `Glossary`, `Assignment`, `Wiki`, `Forum`, and `Resource`) the student can perform in the e-learning system. Smaller components within the e-learning activity are defined (e.g., `Post` in a forum, `Question` in a quiz) to give a category for smaller components of the annotated information.

The interactions between different components in the LMS are presented as relationships between different concepts (e.g., `Quiz` *ConsistOf* `Questions`, `Assignment` *isSolvedBy* `Student`). The ontology concepts and the relationships between them are used to describe the structure of a course and as main concepts to be refined by the students with their bottom-ontology.

The Bottom Ontology: The user can tag a course component (e.g., a text fragment, an image, a formula) in the online course. The predefined set of upper ontology concepts can be used as the categories for the current annotated resource, or the user can define new concepts that will be used to refine and expand the upper-ontology. Each tag introduced by the student will be presented as an instance of the concept selected or defined by the student.

For example, a student can define a new concept (e.g., trigonometry formula) to annotate an equation in a math course note. The annotated equation will become an instance of this new concept. The user can add a tag or a set of tags (e.g., math, formula) to the annotated equations which are linked to the selected class via the *has-tag* relationship. As another example, the student can annotate a post in a forum as an explanation for a specific lesson; in this case, the annotated post will be treated as an instance of the `Post` class, and the connection between the `Post` and `Lesson` classes will be identified using the relationship defined between the two classes.

The various concepts introduced by the students, and the corresponding instances used to tag the actual course content, constitute folksonomies, that will be shared between students in the same class. For example, a trigonometry tag can be used by the students to find all the materials in the class tagged with this term.

Tagged content in the lecture notes

Accessible form to assign tag and category for the tagged content

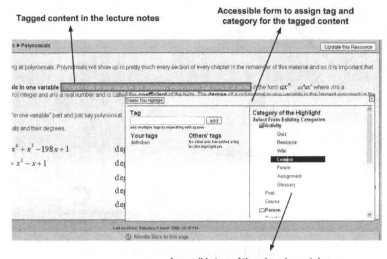

Accessible tree of the e-learning ontology

Fig. 2. A Screenshot of the Proposed System

Generating the Bottom Ontology: Collaborative tagging among different students of an online course can help in extending the upper-ontology and create new connections between different learning contents. Users are allowed to generate tag clouds, by freely tagging the content encountered in Moodle.

The tag cloud for a component of a Moodle class will provide domain specific classification of the elements of the course as well as the level of "agreement" across students concerning the description of the course entities. The tags frequency can be used as an agreement measure (based on the algorithm in [12]). The most agreed upon tags will flow into the bottom ontology, as new concepts. Using the proposed system (Fig. 2) the user can highlight a resource in the online course (e.g., text fragment) and then the tool interface can be used to select the category (concept) of the annotated resource or to create a new concept.

The construction of the tags and the expansion of the ontology is user-driven. The user can select the concept for the highlighted content and assign a tag for the content. T he user can navigate the tags (i.e., perform keyword search) in order to retrieve the set of items associated with that tag.

4 System Design

The first prototype of the system has been realized by including our ontology and annotation components (*accessible* OATS) into Moodle. In order to make the annotation process possible, our tool is included inside Moodle in a place visible to all web pages of the course. An accessible modified version of the *Open Annotation and Tagging System (OATS)* [3] has been developed. The new OATS has been made accessible, by replacing all user interactions with keyboard

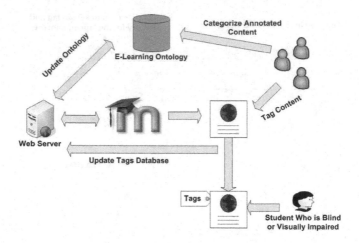

Fig. 3. The System Architecture

controls and aural messages to perform the highlighting and tagging. The e-learning upper-ontology is built-in into accessible OATS and available to the user for the annotation process.

The e-learning ontology provides the concepts taxonomy needed to classify the information (e.g., math→algebra→addition quiz) in the e-learning system. The relations defined in the ontology can be used to infer new information about the learning materials. For example, the **has_answer** relation between a quiz and a lesson can be used to imply a link between the instances of these classes. WordNet synonyms are used to infer concepts related to the students' tags. Synonyms are used to group tags as instances of the same ontology concept.

The system structure is depicted in Fig. 3. The implementation relies on several software components:

- **Connector between Apache and Tomcat:** to integrate Apache and Tomcat mod-proxy-ajp, a connector to connect Tomcat and Apache Httpd, is used.
- **REST web services (Servlets and AJAX):** a REST architecture is used to update the tagging and annotation system database.
- **JENA API:** this semantic web API is used to maintain the e-learning ontology.
- **WAI ARIA:** the different classes for Moodle ontology are displayed to the students using an accessible tree structure built using WAI ARIA.

5   Conclusion and Future Work

The proposed system uses collaborative tagging performed by the students in an online course to help other students, by relating different course components to each other, clarifying course materials by offering additional explanations, and providing connections between different course components.

In the future, we will use the proposed technology to guide assistive devices (e.g., screen readers) in a more effective navigation and presentation of course content. The SPARQL query language can be used to infer new information using the ontology. Visually impaired students will be allowed to pose natural language questions, which can be mapped to ontology-driven queries, providing a semantic-driven access to the course content.

References

1. Al-Khalifa, H., Davis, H.: Measuring the semantic value of folksonomies. In: Innovations in Information Technology, pp. 1–5 (2006)
2. Balasubramanian, V., Venkatasubramanian, N.: Adapting a multimedia distance learning environment for vision impairments. In: Int. Conf. Information Tech. (2003)
3. Bateman, S., Farzan, R., Brusilovsky, P., McCalla, G.: Oats: The open annotation and tagging system. In: I2LOR (2006)
4. Chang, B., Ham, D., Moon, D., Choi, Y., Cha, J.: Educational information search service using ontology. In: ICALT, pp. 414–415 (2007)
5. Cooper, M.: Accessibility of emerging rich web technologies: Web 2.0 and the semantic web. In: WWW, pp. 93–98 (2007)
6. Enagandula, V., et al.: BlackboardNV: a system for enabling non-visual access to the blackboard course management system. In: ASSETS, pp. 220–221 (2005)
7. Gruber, T.: Ontology of folksonomy: A mash-up of apples and oranges (2005), http://tomgruber.org/writing/mtsr05-ontology-of-folksonomy.htm
8. Harper, S., Bechhofer, S.: Semantic triage for increased web accessibility. IBM Systems Journal 44(3), 637–648 (2005)
9. Harper, S., Bechhofer, S., Lunn, D.: Sadie: transcoding based on CSS. In: ASSETS, pp. 259–260 (2006)
10. Heiyanthuduwage, S., Karunaratne, D.: A learner oriented ontology of metadata to improve effectiveness of learning management systems. In: Conf. e-Learning for Knowledge-Based Society (2006)
11. Henze, N., et al.: Reasoning and ontologies for personalized e-learning in the semantic web. Educational Technology and Society 7(4), 82–97 (2004)
12. Heymann, P., Garcia-Molina, H.: Collaborative creation of communal hierarchical taxonomies in social tagging systems. Tech. Rep. 2006-10, Stanford (2006)
13. Huang, A., Sundaresan, N.: A semantic transcoding system to adapt web services for users with disabilities. In: ASSETS, pp. 156–163 (2000)
14. Karim, S., et al.: Providing universal accessibility using connecting ontologies: A holistic approach. In: Univ. Access in HCI, pp. 637–646 (2007)
15. Karim, S., Tjoa, A.: Towards the use of ontologies for improving user interaction for people with special needs. In: Miesenberger, K., Klaus, J., Zagler, W.L., Karshmer, A.I. (eds.) ICCHP 2006. LNCS, vol. 4061, pp. 77–84. Springer, Heidelberg (2006)
16. Kim, T., et al.: On employing ontology to e-learning. In: ICIS, pp. 334–339 (2005)
17. Lee, K.: What goes around comes around: an analysis of del.icio.us as social space. In: CSCW, pp. 191–194 (2006)
18. De Marsico, M., et al.: A proposal toward the development of accessible e-learning content by human involvement. UAIS 5(2), 150–169 (2006)
19. Whitehead, J.: Challenges of online education (2009), www.articlesnatch.com/Article/Challenges-Of-Online-Education/115%265

Simple Browser Construction Toolkit

Osamu Miyamoto

Tsukuba University of Technology,
Kasuga 4-12-7 Tsukuba Science city, Ibraki, 305-8521, Japan
miyamoto@k.tsukuba-tech.ac.jp
http://www.tsukuba-tech.ac.jp/

Abstract. A special browser is a specialized browser designed only for a specific website, providing a very comfortable user interface for that website. However, it is usually necessary to update the special browser when there is a design change to the website. Therefore, a special browser should be easy to update. I propose such a browser here. The proposed browser also has robustness, meaning that it does not need to be updated for a small change to the website. *abstract* environment.

Keywords: Visually impaired person, Special browser, Web harvesting.

1 Introduction

1.1 What Is a Special Browser?

A special browser is a specialized browser designed only for a specific website, providing a very comfortable user interface for that website. Unlike a general-purpose browser[1], however, a special browser cannot access sites other than the specific site for which it is designed.

There are several examples of special browsers for visually handicapped persons in Japan, including those for accessing "NAIIV net" (a site where one can download Braille books, managed by a group of Braille libraries)[2], news sites[3][4][5], internet radio stations[6], train schedules[7]. These browsers are sold or are available for free.

Although there are even special browsers for sighted persons (for example, there is a browser that can access YouTube), special browsers are much more effective for visually handicapped persons.

Consider the case of learning how to use new software. A sighted user can easily use the software without referring to the manual, for example, by selecting from the menu bar, icons, etc. Even for more complex operations, a sighted user can make selections while referring to the manual. So for sighted users, there is little difference between a special browser and a general-purpose browser. On the other hand, in many cases visually handicapped persons cannot use the software until they have read the manual and completely memorized it. For this reason, special browsers are much more effective for visually handicapped persons than for sighted persons.

K. Miesenberger et al. (Eds.): ICCHP 2010, Part I, LNCS 6179, pp. 384–391, 2010.

Visually handicapped persons can use personal computers by making use of screen reader software, but this software is very difficult to use initially. The adoption of easy-to-use software should be extremely effective in improving the information literacy of the visually handicapped.

1.2   Comparison of General-Purpose Browser with Special Browser

To check the effectiveness of a special browser for visually handicapped persons, I examined the differences between a special browser and a general-purpose browser for a certain task. I download and read a Braille book from "NAIIV net" using both a special browser and a general-purpose browser, and I checked the number of keystrokes required. The general-purpose browser required 155 keystrokes, and the special browser required 36 keystrokes.

Screenshots for downloading and reading one Braille file from library with general browser

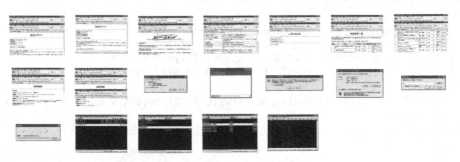

Screenshots for downloading and reading one Braille file from library with special browser

Fig. 1. Screenshots of downloading and reading a book with a general-purpose browser and a special browser

The best type of browser for a visually handicapped person to use depends on the situation. It is controlled by various factors, like the skill level of the user, the frequency of site updates, the availability of attractive content, and so on. The most popular special browser in Japan is probably the one designed for accessing NAIIV net.

1.3   Merits and Problems with Special Browsers
Merits of Special Browsers

- They are easy to use. They can have a friendly interface designed for visually handicapped persons, and they can be operated by using only the up and down cursor keys and the enter key.

- Support is straightforward. Visually handicapped persons can install, operate, and learn how to use the software by themselves.

Problems with Special Browsers

- If even a small change is made to the website design or layout, the special browser is likely to become inoperable.
- The ability to access sites other than the target site is non-existent or extremely limited.

1.4   Parameter Specification

A certain conventional browser[4] specifies a script called a "parameter file", which is written using regular expressions (RegEx). The aim of this script is to let the user follow updates to the website. However, this script is very difficult to make. List 1 is an example of a script file.

List. 1 An example of a "parameter file" for a conventional browser.

```
AllCategory=<a href="/([a-z0-9-_]+/update/[^.]+\.html)">
([^<]+)</a>(\(([0-9]{2}/[0-9]{2} [0-9]{2}:[0-9]{2})\)</li>){0,1}
Category9=
<a href="(\./editorial([0-9]{4}[0-9]{2}[0-9]{2}){0,1}\.html)">([^<]+)</a>
Category10=
<a href="(\./column([0-9]{4}[0-9]{2}[0-9]{2}){0,1}\.html)">([^<]+)</a>
```

1.5   Analogy with Spreadsheet Program

Consider making a calculation table. Making a program for calculating a table is not so difficult using a computer language such as BASIC or C. However, the program must be updated if a new item is inserted or another slight change is made.

On the other hand, rather than using a programming language, this updating is relatively easy using a spreadsheet program. However, it is very difficult to make an easy-to-use spreadsheet program.

The same thing can be said about a special browser for visually handicapped persons. It is not so difficult to make a special browser for the visually handicapped by using a programming language. However, every slight design change of the website must be tracked and reflected as changes to the browser program. Therefore, I consider that a more effective browser is needed, like a spreadsheet program for visually handicapped persons.

1.6   Thoughts of a Special Browser Developer

Author developed a special browser for the visually handicapped in 2001, and has continued to sell it since then. The development work was not so hard, but maintenance is extremely difficult. If a website design changes suddenly, the browser must be quickly updated. Such changes are an extremely common occurrence on most websites.

2   Proposed Solution

I propose a toolkit that can be used to easily construct a special browser for visually handicapped persons.

With currently available special browsers, the developer must update the software when design changes are made to the target website. On the other hand, the proposed browser can acquire update information by matching current web pages with older web pages.

The toolkit has two features: It is easy to make a specialized browser, and a browser made with this toolkit rarely causes rendering errors.

2.1   How to Construct a Special Browser

Reading (interface from computer to user). A general-purpose browser cannot recognize what information is important. Basically, a general-purpose browser speaks (i.e., text-to-speech conversion) all items on the web page. On the other hand, a special browser speaks the required information only. Advertisements should not be spoken. Also, the order in which items are spoken should be sorted by relevance or importance.

Thus, it is very important to easily specify the data to be read when the browser is constructed. In the proposed browser, the user specifies item to be spoken from a Document Object Model tree. A box is displayed on the web page corresponding to the item specified by the user. This makes the specifying task simple.

Fig3 shows an example of conversion from a table to a list box.

Selection (interface from user to computer). The proposed browser can handle links, push buttons, radio buttons, list boxes, text boxes, etc.

Fig4 shows examples of these items in a general-purpose browser. With a general-purpose browser, when there are many selectable items on the web page, the user must choose one item and use it. Usually, the user must memorize the locations of those selectable items. With a special browser, the browser lets the user use the selectable items one after another.

Fig.fig:ExampleOfFillIn shows example web pages containing a number of selectable items on the general-purpose browser and the special browser.

Text boxes for ID and password are typically filled in with the same information each time. Therefore, IDs and passwords could be stored in the program. Of course, the user can also fill them in each time.

- **Conventional Way 1.**

  Generic browser

 Difficult for beginner

- **Conventional Way 2.**

  Special browser

 Update is needed if site design is changed.

- **Conventional Way 3.**

  Special browser

 Script is hard to write

```
Example of part of script.

[NewsURL_RegExp]
AllCategory=<li><a href="/([0-9]{4}/[A-Z]+/([a-z]+/)
{0,1}([0-9]{2}/[0-9]{2})/[^/]+/index.html)">([^<]+)</a>
```

- **Proposed way**

  Special browser

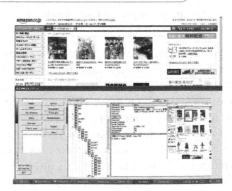

Fig. 2. Screenshots showing how to make a browser with the conventional approach and the proposed system

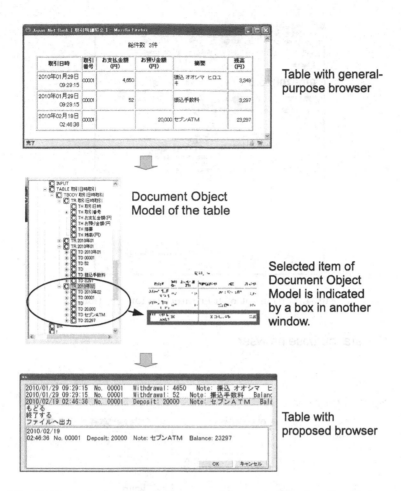

Fig. 3. Example screenshot of proposed browser (Construction Browser)

2.2   Matching Algorithm

The software saves previous editions of the website and then obtains the current edition of the website and matches the previous and current pages. This matching is done by dynamic programming.

3   Experiment

I made a special browser that can be used by visually handicapped persons to order items on Amazon. The basic usage of this special browser is as follows. The user scans the barcode of an item with a barcode scanner. The software obtains a detailed description of the item and speaks it to the user. If the user

Fig. 4. Screenshot of user interface for selection

General-purpose browser

照会期間: ☐ 年 ☐ 月

Special browser

2009

Enter YEAR to specify.

OK

5

Enter MONTH to specify.

OK

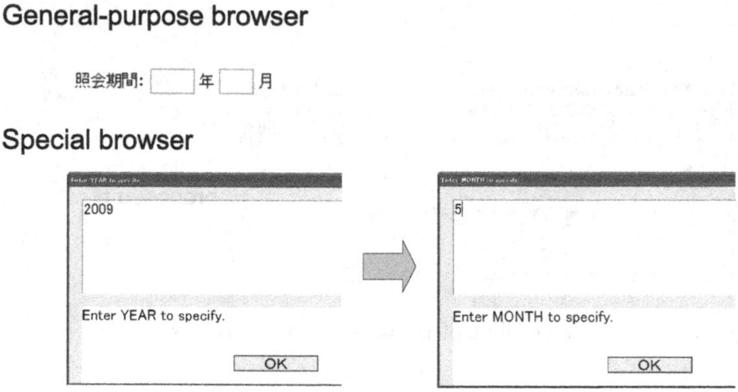

Fig. 5. Screenshot of user interface for selection

selects "Purchase" by pushing the enter key, the software orders the item from Amazon. When installing the software, it is necessary to set up 1-click ordering beforehand.

In this scenario, the user can find the names of items in the supermarket using a portable computer with a mobile internet connection. The user should scan the barcode on the commodity shelf, not the barcode attached to the item itself. Therefore, the browser has the ability to choose barcode databases other than Amazon's.

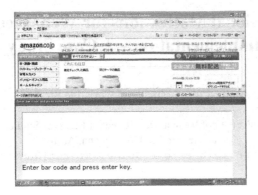

Enter bar code and press enter key.

Fig. 6. Screenshot of navigating with the proposed system

4   Conclusion

I proposed special browser construction toolkit for visually handicapped persons and showed its effectiveness. I believe that this toolkit will contribute to improving the life of visually handicapped persons.

References

1. Asakawa, C., Itoh, T.: User interface of a home page reader. In: Proceedings of the 3rd International ACM SIGCAPH Conference on Assistive Technologies (ASSETS 1998), pp. 149–156 (1998)
2. Enable Software Inc., "Naiiv Reader"
3. Kochi System Development, "MyNews", http://www.aok-net.com/
4. Katsuragi, N.: "Voice Popper", http://homepage2.nifty.com/oss/
5. Miyazaki, Y.: "MM news", http://www.am-corp2.com/
6. Miyazaki, Y.: "MM net radio", http://www.am-corp2.com/
7. Kochi System Development, "MyRoute", http://www.aok-net.com/

Organizational Motivations for Web Accessibility Implementation – A Case Study

Marie-Luise Leitner and Christine Strauss

University of Vienna, Department of Business Studies
Bruenner Str. 72, 1210 Vienna, Austria
{marie-luise.leitner,christine.strauss}@univie.ac.at

Abstract. Universal access to information and communication technologies represents an indispensable prerequisite for people with impairments' equal participation in societal life. Despite legal regulations and economic advantages, accessible web sites are rarely implemented in private sector organizations. This paper introduces a holistic, managerial approach to identify business experiences with web accessibility implementation in three industry sectors. The findings of this case study research include organizations' motivations for web accessibility implementation and therefore generate a sound basis for management decision recommendations.

Keywords: web accessibility, design for all, case study research, business approach, motivation, change management.

1 Introduction

Despite various efforts for the raise of awareness for web accessibility, its implementation in private sector organizations is still in its infancy. In Austria, public and governmental organizations face pressure due to legal regulations (e.g., Austrian e-Government Act) and a certain responsibility towards society. These drivers led to an increase in accessible web sites in public organizations in recent years. However, the motivations for managers implementing web accessibility are different. Mere social drivers do not suffice for organizations to consider accessible web sites; above all, new products or processes have to be promising in terms of profitability in order to be implemented in private sector organizations.

This contribution uses case study research for an exploratory analysis of motives for and against web accessibility implementation in the business-to-consumer (b2c) segment of three industry sectors and provides an initial knowledge base and facilitation for organizations intending to consider the implementation of web accessibility[1].

2 Background

Current Austrian legislation in terms of web accessibility does not only concern public and governmental web presences. The Austrian Equalization Act for People

---

[1] This contribution is part of the „Web Accessibility Quality Management" Project (Project Nr. 12461) funded by the Austrian National Bank.

K. Miesenberger et al. (Eds.): ICCHP 2010, Part I, LNCS 6179, pp. 392–399, 2010.

with Disabilities indicates that people with impairments must be granted equal rights for participation in societal life [1]. This act also holds for private sector organizations. The Austrian Equalization Act for People with Disabilities foresees a compulsory arbitration process before filing a lawsuit. In other words, in case of complaints by consumers due to inaccessibility of web presences, an arbitration process has to be conducted by the Federal Ministry of Social Affairs in order to achieve a settlement out of court. In Austria, several arbitration processes have already been executed, most of which with positive outcome[2]. This mechanism may support accessibility considerations in organizations because of possible negative media due to arbitration processes.

Despite legal requirements, business considerations may also provide arguments for an implementation of web accessibility in private sector organizations. It can be estimated that in the EU at least 50 million people, which is about 10% of the population, have some type of disability [2]. People with impairments may be more dependent on using the Internet as the main source of information, since other sources, like printed information or personal advice, may be difficult or even impossible to access.

Accessible web is also of high value for elderly people, a user group that is becoming increasingly important from an economic point of view. Many age-related conditions, such as vision impairments, hearing loss, motor skill diminishment, memory and processing problems are similar to those experienced by the disabled. The world population, particularly in developed countries, is aging rapidly; the EU estimates that by 2030, 24.7% of the EU population will be older than 65 years [3]. Currently, only 10% of people older than 65 years use the Internet [4]. In the near future, this number will increase dramatically, due to two developments: (i) an increase in the Internet penetration in this age group, and (ii) a more Internet-accustomed elderly generation in the years to come. Another user group that benefits significantly from web accessibility is the group of the mobile device users. In the age of smart phones and PDAs, these users are facing similar barriers as people with disabilities (e.g., they rarely use the mouse, they often do not or cannot load images). All the same, mobile internet use is becoming increasingly popular but still suffers from accessibility and usability problems [5].

In a nutshell, organizations with accessible web sites may profit at least in two ways: (i) they eliminate the risk of negative media and penalties that may result from arbitration processes, and more importantly (ii) they profit from an enlargement of their customer group as the web sites are accessible to people with disabilities, elderly people, and mobile device users.

3 Research Design

3.1 Methodology

Due to the exploratory nature of this research problem, case study research methodology was applied. Several theories on case study research have appeared in

---

[2] An overview of arbitration processes in Austria is available on an arbitration database at: http://www.bizeps.or.at/gleichstellung/schlichtungen
(last access 29/03/2010)

literature [6]. This research design is based on Yin's suggestions who defines a case study as an empirical method of analysis of "a contemporary phenomenon within its real life context" ([7] p. 13) taking into account multiple information sources (e.g., qualitative and quantitative data combination). Yin distinguishes four types of case study designs: holistic single-case, holistic multiple-case, embedded single-case, and embedded multiple-case design [7]. For reasons of validity, the embedded multiple-case design is chosen from these types as it addresses more than one case and permits multiple units of analysis.

Our model comprises the analysis of private organizations in the b2c segment of three industry sectors with high relevance in electronic business, representing day-to-day operations that provide facilitations for people with disabilities when performed online: (i) tourism, (ii) financial services, and (iii) information [8]. In each of the three sectors, the benefit of web accessibility is analyzed focusing on two polar types [6], namely organizations which have successfully implemented web accessibility and organizations which have failed in web accessibility implementation. Figure 1 shows the industry sectors investigated and their embedded units of analysis (UA).

Fig. 1. Embedded, multiple case study design for web site accessibility in three e-business-affine sectors

The purpose of the case study design outlined in Figure 1 is to monitor the motivations for organizations for web accessibility implementation in three selected sectors with high e-business affinity. The results will provide first insights in the business and managerial perspective of web accessibility and therefore constitute an important input for further (quantitative) research.

3.2 Research Instruments and Analytical Approach

Typically, in case study research, multiple data collection methods are combined in a so called triangulation process [6]. In this case study, both quantitative and qualitative data is involved that resulted from an application of various research instruments:

(i)   web site evaluations: 89 web sites in three industry sectors have been evaluated following a 3-step procedure: (a) selection of relevant organizations, (b) automated tests, and (c) manual tests. Automated tests have been performed with the help of the Total Validator tool. Sites having passed automated tests have been evaluated by manual tests (Lynx browser, Web Developer Add-on) [9].

(ii) industry information: sector specific information used for this case study included quantitative website evaluation, general industry information (fact sheets, business reports, search queries), and information about the accessibility in the three industry sectors.

(iii) interviewers' notes and meeting minutes.

(iv) semi-structured interviews: in total, 12 semi-structured interviews that lasted between 45 and 90 minutes have been conducted following a pre-determined guideline (cf. [10]) in order to ensure comparability across cases [11]. The interview transcripts have been analyzed using Atlas.ti software performing an iterative approach [12] that suggests going back and forward in data for an identification of common themes, a subsequent development of categories, and finally, of relationships between categories. Open and axial coding procedures were applied for this purpose [13]. Moreover, only patterns that continuously appeared in the data were considered in order to attain saturation [12].

4 Findings

The reasons for web accessibility implementation of all three cases analyzed are summarized in Table 1. The indication of the sector is given where the respective reason has been identified: tourism (T), financial services (F), information (I). Moreover, the reasons are classified into three different categories (economic, social, and technical motivations) and substantiated by selected quotations. Patterns across all three sectors can be derived as some of the reasons appear in every case analyzed (key personality, social commitment). Others are mentioned in two of the cases (e.g., web site quality, design for all, elderly customers) and others again turn out to be specific to one certain case (e.g., consumer consciousness, importance of web site).

Table 1. Categorization of motivations for web accessibility implementation

Motivation	Reasons for implementation	Sector	Selected quotation
Economic	Differentiation	F	*"We tried to be the first to implement accessibility in order to be different from our competitors".*
	Elderly Customers	F,I	*"Our website is being used by elderly people above average".*
	Fear of negative image	F	*"We cannot afford negative headlines".*
	Importance of website	T	*"Every guest will see our web page first, judge it, and then decide if he wants to come or not".*
Social	Consumer consciousness	F	*"Ethical criteria are more and more being included in the purchase decision process".*
	Design for all	T,F	*"Our main reason was 'simple and for all'; the simpler the better and the more customers will understand and buy the product".*
	Key personality	T,F,I	*"The technical department colleague's girlfriend has a hearing impairment; he had first suggestions about the issue".*
	Social commitment	T,F,I	*"We have always had awareness for social issues. In this case, implementation of web accessibility is easier; when the awareness already exists".*
	Top management support	F	*"We had the advantage that one member of the management board was 150% web affine; this made it easier to convince him".*
Technical	Website quality	T,I	*"Nobody was satisfied with the old website. It did not look good, did not work satisfyingly, and did not have enough traffic".*

T=tourism, F=financial services, I=information

4.1 Economic Motivations

First, the implementation of web accessibility in an organization can be initiated out of *economic motivations*. In this case, organizations focus on customer orientation and customer satisfaction and implement an accessible web site as a means to increase turnover, image, and customer base. Organizations with Internet presence (both "click and mortar" companies with an additional offline presence and pure online companies) face the problem of lower switching costs of customers compared to traditional ("brick and mortar") companies. Thus, the importance of customer satisfaction and loyalty increases tremendously [14]. At the same time and out of similar reasons, competition and, thus, the need of differentiation gains in importance. Web accessibility implementation can provoke competitive advantage due to differentiation from direct competitors which is mentioned as one of the economic reasons for its implementation.

The ongoing demographic shift and the continuing trend of elderly people using the Internet constitute other economic motivations for web accessibility implementation. Elderly people are a rapidly growing segment of the Internet economy [15] with significant purchasing power [16] and may dispose of mobility limitations similar to people with disabilities. Thus, for organizations with accessible web presences elderly people represent a new customer group.

The "design for all" aspect of accessible web sites implies not only the consideration of people with disabilities and elderly, but the inclusion of any Internet user group. Simplicity, usability, and high web site quality of accessible web presences entail advantages for every user. Design for all has been identified as a major economic reason for accessible web presences.

Prospective image amelioration through web accessibility is a major motivation for organizations. This aspect is closely linked to the differentiation aspect and has also a strong relationship to the social reasons for web accessibility implementation (e.g., social commitment). The way how an organization is perceived by its customers influences customer loyalty which is, in turn, strongly related to a firm's profitability [17]. As a consequence, image enhancement due to web accessibility implementation may result in an increase of a company's profitability.

4.2 Social Motivations

Second, *social motivations* may be the trigger for web accessibility implementation. In this case, web accessibility efforts are merely targeted to people with disabilities. Social aspects, such as equality, ethical behavior, social commitment, and responsible attitude towards society represent the main drivers for web accessibility implementation. Organizations that dispose of elaborate social values due to a corporate social responsibility strategy and corporate culture will rather implement web accessibility out of social reasons. Additionally, organizations in crisis-ridden business sectors (e.g., financial services sector in times of the economic crisis) focus on image amelioration by social instruments. These reasons may especially be the case for large organizations which usually dispose of corporate social responsibility strategies.

The degree of social commitment of an organization is closely linked to its corporate culture. A study shows that social responsibility of organizations represents one of the central motives for corporate culture [18]. The important role of corporate culture in conjunction with web accessibility implementation out of social motivations becomes obvious. Moreover, corporate culture is identified as the most important reason for driving innovation [19]. Besides other factors, organizational culture is influential on the readiness of employees for organizational change [20]. In their "Competing Values Framework", Quinn and Rohrbaugh (1983) put forth four culture types and conclude that the culture focusing on human relations and morale has a higher readiness for change [21]. Drawing on these assumptions, the change process of web accessibility implementation can be facilitated in a culture based on social commitment.

Therefore, the organizational background may play an important role in the implementation of web accessibility. An extensive social commitment of an organization and a corporate culture that includes social values may facilitate web accessibility implementation. The awareness for social issues is present in organizations with an elaborate corporate social responsibility strategy. Thus, the need for web accessibility as a social instrument is perceived important in organizations that dispose of such a background.

Social commitment as a reason for web accessibility implementation has been identified across all three sectors. However, traditionally, mostly large organizations dispose of a clearly defined corporate social responsibility strategy. Jenkins points out that "the power and resources of large companies produces responsibility to use that power and develop those resources responsibly" [22]. Despite recent trends of CSR for small and medium enterprises [23], large organizations are more likely to define and implement CSR strategies than SMEs [24].

Moreover, some business sectors seem to be especially concerned for their reputation towards customers. In the financial services sector, this has particularly become obvious. The ongoing financial crisis led to the fact that banking institutions are eyed on suspiciously which – in turn – has forced them to focus on social issues. Many interview partners have expressed the need to be perceived as a "decent bank" that "cares for others" as a reason for web accessibility consideration.

In a nutshell, organizations that dispose of elaborate social values due to a corporate social responsibility strategy and corporate culture will rather implement web accessibility out of social reasons. Additionally, organizations in crisis-ridden business sectors (e.g., financial services sector in times of the economic crisis) especially focus on image amelioration by social instruments. These reasons may especially be the case for large organizations which usually dispose of corporate social responsibility strategies.

4.3 Technical Motivations

Third, web accessibility implementation can be initiated out of *technical motivations*. They encompass the intention of an organization to improve the web site from its technical point of view in order to obtain a stable, secure, high quality site. This is the reason why the implementation of web accessibility out of technical motives is often initiated by IT experts who know about the advantages of accessibility in terms of quality of web pages. The poor web site quality of existing sites is a major reason for the consideration of accessibility, as it comprises several elements that lead to an increase in simplicity, clarity, usability, download speed, and web site quality. The usage of structural elements (e.g., headings, lists) contributes to a clearly arranged web presence, the separation of content and layout reduces code and provokes a reduction of download times, and the consistent navigation and layout for the whole web presence causes an increase in usability. In short, accessible web sites dispose of a higher web site quality than inaccessible sites.

The mere focus on the aesthetic design of a web site goes at the expense of its usability and may therefore cause frustration by the customer [14]. Moreover, web sites with many design elements tend to be more voluminous and thus slower in their download times. This is a crucial issue, given the fact that convenience and speed are the main reasons why customers prefer the Internet over traditional "offline" firms. Fast download times of a web site are therefore decisive for the success of the firm. Cox and Dale (2002) identify six key quality factors for web sites: clarity of purpose, design, accessibility and speed, content, customer service, and customer relationships. Additionally, they classify accessibility as the "most critical factor for any web site" [14]. The increasing use of mobile devices for Internet access further enforces the use of accessible web sites which provide device independency.

Compared to the tourism and financial services sector, the information sector was more concerned about the stability and quality of their web sites. Technical reasons were among the major motivations for web accessibility implementation in this sector because of a high fluctuation of web site contents especially in the online media branch. The improvement of web site quality may concern every sector analyzed. However, its importance increases with the importance of the web presence for the organization. Additionally, web sites where content is subject to high fluctuations will be more interested in web accessibility implementation.

5 Conclusion and Perspective

The findings of this exploratory case study indicate that three different kinds of motivations for web accessibility implementation may occur in organizations: (i) economic, (ii) social, and (iii) technical motivations. The type of motivation why organizations implement web accessibility depends on various factors, e.g., the size and complexity of the organization, the business sector, the corporate culture and degree of readiness for change, and the purpose and degree of complexity of the web site. For instance, complex organizations in the financial services sector rather implement web accessibility out of social motivations. By contrast, small organizations in the information sector rather draw on technical motivations.

This contribution uses case study research for an exploratory analysis of motivations for web accessibility implementation in three industry sectors with high e-business affinity and provides an initial knowledge base and facilitation for organizations intending to consider web accessibility implementation in the near future.

References

1. Austrian Equalization Act: Österreichisches Bundesgesetz über die Gleichstellung von Menschen mit Behinderungen (Austrian equalization act for people with disabilities) (2005)
2. European Disability Forum: Facts and figures about disability (2001), http://www.edf-feph.org/Page_Generale.asp?DocID=12534 (last accessed 12/02/2010)
3. VID: Vienna institute of demography: data sheet (2006)

4. Europe's Information Society: (2008) eInclusion: helping older people to access the information society,
   http://ec.europa.eu/information_society/activities/einclusion/policy/ageing/index_en.htm (last accessed 27/03/2010)
5. W3C: Mobile web initiative (2009), http://www.w3.org/Mobile/About (last accessed 29/03/2010)
6. Eisenhardt, K.M.: Building theories from case study research. The Academy of Management Review 14(4), 532–550 (1989)
7. Yin, R.: Case study research - design and methods, 3rd edn. Sage Publications, Thousand Oaks (2003)
8. European Commission: The European e-business report. Luxemburg (2007)
9. Leitner, M.-L.: Business Impacts of Web Accessibility. Frankfurt/Main, Peter Lang (2010)
10. Leitner, M.-L., Strauss, C.: Exploratory case study research on web accessibility. In: Miesenberger, K., Klaus, J., Zagler, W.L., Karshmer, A.I. (eds.) ICCHP 2008. LNCS, vol. 5105, pp. 490 497. Springer, Heidelberg (2008)
11. Miles, M.B., Huberman, A.M.: Qualitative data analysis: an expanded sourcebook, 2nd edn. Sage Publications, Thousand Oaks (2005)
12. Glaser, B., Strauss, A.: The discovery of grounded theory. de Gruyter, New York (1967)
13. Strauss, A., Corbin, J.: Basics of Qualitative Research. In: Grounded Theory Procedures and Techniques. Sage Publications, Newbury Park (1990)
14. Cox, J., Dale, B.J.: Key quality factors in website design and use: an examination. International Journal of Quality and Reliability Management 19(7), 862–888 (2002)
15. Trocchia, P.J., Janda, S.: A phenomenological investigation of internet usage among older individuals. Journal of Consumer Marketing 17(7), 605–616 (2000)
16. Reisenwitz, T., et al.: The elderly's internet usage: an updated look. The Journal of Consumer Marketing 24(7), 406–418 (2007)
17. Reichheld, F.F.: Loyalty and the renaissance of marketing. Marketing Management 2(4), 10–21 (1995)
18. Schmid, K.-H.: Planung von Unternehmenskultur. Dt.-Univ. Verlag, Wiesbaden (1995)
19. Yu, L.: Measuring the culture of innovation. MIT Sloan Management Review 48(4), 7 (2007)
20. Jones, R.A., Jimmieson, N.L., Griffiths, A.: The Impact of organizational culture and reshaping capabilities on change implementation success: the mediating role of readiness for change. Journal of Management Studies 42(2), 361–386 (2005)
21. Quinn, R.E., Rohrbaugh, J.: A spatial model of effectiveness criteria: toward a competing values approach to organizational analysis. Management Science 20, 363–377 (1983)
22. Jenkins, H.: Small business champions for corporate social responsibility. Journal of Business Ethics 67(3), 241–256 (2006)
23. Murillo, D., Lozano, J.M.: SMEs and CSR: an approach to CSR in their own words. Journal of Business Ethics 67(3), 227–240 (2006)
24. Perrini, F., Russo, A., Tencati, A.: CSR Strategies of SMEs and Large Firms. Evidence from Italy. Journal of Business Ethics 74(3), 285–300 (2007)

Using Collaborative Learning to Teach WCAG 2.0

Fernando Alonso, José L. Fuertes, Ángel L. González, and Loïc Martínez

Facultad de Informática, Universidad Politécnica de Madrid, Spain
{falonso,jfuertes,agonzalez,loic}@fi.upm.es

Abstract. Version 2.0 of the Web Content Accessibility Guidelines (WCAG) was published in December 2008. WCAG 2.0 has a different language, a different structure and a different rationale to WCAG 1.0. All of these influence how to teach web accessibility. In this paper we present an innovative approach that we have followed in a web accessibility module that is taught at the UPM's School of Computing as part of the BEng degree in Computer Science. Our approach combined several teaching methods: traditional lectures, collaborative learning sessions, a short exercise on web site evaluation and, finally, a short project consisting of the development of an accessible web site. In the paper we describe the methods used and the results.

1 Introduction

Version 2.0 of the Web Content Accessibility Guidelines (WCAG) was published in December 2008 [1]. This new version of WCAG had two main goals: it aimed to be technology-independent and it was to be testable.

Given these two goals, WCAG 2.0 has a different language, a different structure and a different rationale to WCAG 1.0. All of these influence how web accessibility should be taught. Here we present an innovative approach that we adopted in a web accessibility module taught at the School of Computing of the Technical University of Madrid (UPM) as part of the BEng in Computer Science.

The content of this paper is as follows. Section 2 will provide a short overview of WCAG 2.0. Section 3 will describe our teaching approach. Finally, Section 4 will provide the results and some conclusions.

2 WCAG 2.0 Overview

WCAG 2.0 contains three layers of guidance [1]. The four *principles* (perceivable, operable, understandable and robust) provide the foundation for web accessibility. Each principle contains one or more *guidelines*. These 12 guidelines provide the basic goals to be attained in order to make content more accessible. Testable *success criteria* are provided for each guideline. There are 61 success criteria with three levels of conformance: A (lowest), AA, and AAA (highest).

There is an external document that supplements WCAG 2.0: "Techniques for WCAG 2.0" [2]. This document is "informative" and provides three additional layers of guidance. *Sufficient techniques* provide guidance and examples for meeting the

K. Miesenberger et al. (Eds.): ICCHP 2010, Part I, LNCS 6179, pp. 400–403, 2010.

guidelines using specific technologies. These are not compulsory techniques, and other techniques could be used instead. *Advisory techniques* can enhance accessibility, but are not considered to be sufficient techniques for some reason as explained in [2]. And *common failures* are examples of bad practices that cause web pages to fail to meet the success criteria.

3 Our Teaching Approach

At the UPM's School of Computing, we have been teaching a module on Design for All and Accessible Web Design since 2003. This module is part of the 5th year of the BEng in Computer Science [3], [4]. The module is taught over a 15-week period of the winter semester from October until February.

The first opportunity we had to introduce WCAG 2.0 was in the 2009/2010 academic year, when we changed our teaching approach. In addition to traditional lectures and a short project (developing a small accessible web site), we incorporated two more methods: collaborative learning sessions and a short exercise on accessibility evaluation.

3.1 Lectures

The lectures are used for the introductory lessons about Design for All, diversity, assistive technologies, standards and legislation. Guest speakers also give lectures on independent living, media accessibility and telecare services.

3.2 Collaborative Learning: Jigsaw Sessions

The collaborative learning technique we used was jigsaw-based sessions [5]. Jigsaw sessions involve providing students with short pieces of documentation and having them work together to learn collaboratively as follows:

1. The students are divided into three-member groups. Each group member is given a different piece of documentation.
2. Each student reads his or her piece of the documentation individually.
3. Then all the students from different groups that have read the same documentation meet together and share their views on the document.
4. Each student individually prepares a short presentation of his or her document.
5. The groups meet to share information about the different documents. Each student presents his or her document to the other group members.
6. The session ends with oral presentations of the documents. The presenters of each document are students that did not read the respective document. The group is evaluated with respect to the presentations made by their members.

The collaborative learning period in our module lasted four weeks. Every week there was one two-hour jigsaw session, plus a one-hour session to discuss the content of the collaborative sessions with the instructor. The first week centered on principles, guidelines and success criteria and the other three weeks focused on different sets of sufficient techniques and common failures.

3.3 Short Exercise: Accessibility Evaluation

This year we also introduced a short exercise, where students were asked to evaluate how accessible a web page is. All the students were given the same page to analyze and a spreadsheet template to fill in with the results of their evaluation.

The students had to evaluate all the success criteria. For each criterion, the students had to provide a value (pass, fail, not applicable), a list of techniques and failures that support that value, a short commentary explaining the value and a degree of confidence in their own evaluation. In addition they had to provide a global commentary and an estimation of the time spent on the exercise.

At the end of the exercise, a session was held to compare the results of the students and the two instructors. Then, the students were asked to explain and discuss their decisions with their colleagues in order to reach a group agreement. The goal of that session was to harmonize criteria when evaluating the accessibility of web pages.

3.4 Short Project: Designing a Small Accessible Web Site

At the end of the module students are expected to develop a small-sized accessible web site (around 5 pages). The students were allowed to choose the subject of the web site, and they were asked to provide some diversity of content: text, images, tables, forms... Then the students had to evaluate the accessibility of their own web site, using the same template they used for the accessibility evaluation exercise.

4   Results and Conclusions

The students' final grade is based on attendance of lectures and guest lectures, participation in the jigsaws, the results of the accessibility evaluation exercise, and our evaluation of their web site. Fig. 1 shows the evolution of average final grades since we started to teach this module (03/04) until this year (09/10). The grades were ranked from 0 to 10, where 5 is the minimum grade required to pass the subject.

This year the final grades were slightly lower than in other years. To gain some insight into the reasons for the poorer results, Table 1 shows the four components of the final grade this year.

Student grades in the jigsaw sessions were low because many did not attend all of the sessions. Actually, if we only considered the sessions they attended, the result would be 6.13, and the resulting final grade would have been 6.33, much closer to the grade for other years. Attendance of lectures and guest lectures was also highly variable. The results of the accessibility evaluation exercise were quite good and not very variable, although our studies suggest that WCAG 2.0 is not testable for beginners [6]. Finally, the results for the web site design were quite low. The students averaged almost three failed level-A success criteria. There were two prominent failures: 83% failed 2.4.1 (skip blocks), and 67% failed 1.3.1 (information and relationships). Without these two mistakes, the results would have been much better.

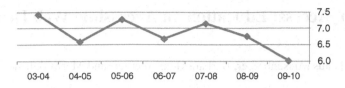

Fig. 1. Evolution of final grades

Table 1. Results for the 2009-2010 academic year

	Attendance	Jigsaw	Evaluation ex.	Web site
Average	6.33	3.97	7.36	5.35
Std. deviation	2.87	2.53	0.63	1.07

In conclusion, this year's results were poorer, but could have been worse if we had used the old evaluation of the final grade, which did not take into account attendance, jigsaw sessions and the evaluation exercise. There are several possible reasons for this. The two key difficulties we came up against were language (WCAG 2.0 was not available in Spanish at the time) and the unavailability of evaluation tools for WCAG 2.0: the students had to perform the accessibility evaluation manually, and this led to some mistakes. In addition, we found that two success criteria were difficult to apply at design time and will require more attention in coming years.

References

1. Caldwell, B., Cooper, M., Reid, L.G., Vanderheiden, G. (eds.): Web Content Accessibility Guidelines 2.0. W3C Recommendation (2008), http://www.w3.org/TR/WCAG20/
2. Techniques for WCAG 2.0, http://www.w3.org/TR/WCAG20-TECHS/
3. Benavídez, C., Fuertes, J.L., Gutiérrez, E., Martínez, L.: Teaching Web Accessibility with "Contramano" and Hera. In: Miesenberger, K., Klaus, J., Zagler, W.L., Karshmer, A.I. (eds.) ICCHP 2006. LNCS, vol. 4061, pp. 341–348. Springer, Heidelberg (2006)
4. Martínez, L.: La formación sobre accesibilidad electrónica en la UPM (in Spanish). In: European Conference EDeAN 2008, Training in Design for All: Innovative Experiences, León, Spain (2008)
5. Aronson, E., Patnoe, S.: The Jigsaw Classroom: Building Cooperation in the Classroom. Longman, New York (1997)
6. Alonso, F., Fuertes, J.L., González, A.L., Martínez, L.: On the testability of WCAG 2.0 for beginners. In: 7th International Cross-Disciplinary Conference on Web Accessibility. ACM Press, New York (2010)

Web_Access: Education on Accessible Web Design

Klaus Miesenberger, Barbara Hengstberger, and Mario Batusic

Institut Integriert Studieren, University of Linz,
Altenbergerstraße 69, 4040 Linz, Austria
{Klaus.Miesenberger,Barbara.Hengstberger,Mario.Batusic}@jku.at

Abstract. This paper presents the international study programme on accessible web design which has been developed by a multinational partnership in the framework of an EU – Erasmus Project. The paper will outline specific results and findings of the project, the curriculum and contents of the study programme, teaching and eLearning tools, the realisation and the additional benefit of the programme.

Keywords: Accessible Web Design, Education and Training, eLearning.

1 Introduction

The project 'web_access' [1] has set-up a comprehensive European module called 'Joint Programme on Accessible Web Design' which allows organisations interested in providing education on accessible web design to efficiently put together course or training offers respectively ranging from vocational seminars towards university courses.

The materials developed include a curriculum, course description, materials on the content oriented towards teachers to adapt it for specific teaching aims and public relation materials. All materials are made available using an eLearning platform and authoring tools supporting accessibility for learners and teachers.

The project 'web_access' started in October 2007 and has been finished in October 2009. It has been a multilateral project within the Erasmus sub-programme under the Action 'Curriculum development': Partners are:

- Johannes Kepler University of Linz, Institut Integriert Studieren, Austria
- Manchester Metropolitan University, Department of Information & Communications, UK
- Dublin City University, School of Computing, Ireland
- University of Pannonia, Department of Image Processing and Neurocomputing, HU
- Universitaet Karlsruhe (TH), Studienzentrum für Sehgeschädigte (SZS), DE
- Baobab Assosiation, Spain.

2 Background and State of the Art

Analysis of the state of the art has shown that [2].

K. Miesenberger et al. (Eds.): ICCHP 2010, Part I, LNCS 6179, pp. 404–407, 2010.

- Courses or modules on accessible web design do exist across Europe but they are offered locally and differ widely in scale and intensity. Almost all of them have problems making the programs sustainable or including them into mainstream.
- Accessibility needs to be addressed through more formal education and training throughout Europe, leading to a professional qualification, certificate or degree in accessible web design that is recognized by industry. This can be better achieved through international co-operation.
- A common European curriculum in the area of web accessibility to form the basis for a standard profile of a Web Accessibility expert on an academic level.
- There is growing need for education going beyond an in-depth knowledge on accessibility guidelines and application of corresponding techniques. The fast development asks for experts able to push accessibility forward, to do research and development and also to develop leadership.

3 Web_Access: Joint Study Programme on Accessible Web Design

The project set up a distance learning based programme addressed to teachers and educators to be adapted to diverse contexts. The target groups for the programme are web designers, students/graduates in computer science and related fields of study and those who have achieved equivalent knowledge and skills. Among them especially people with disabilities (PwD) are invited to participate because of both being experts for their own needs and enhancing their employability. Due to this accessibility of a) the eLearning platform, b) the content and materials but also c) the authoring tools have been taken into account. The following summarizes the products of the project [3]:

1. An elaborated and evaluated *curriculum on accessible web design* that has been evaluated by a panel of international experts in web accessibility; the curriculum is designed in a modular way to support reusability.
2. ICT based *teaching and training materials* supporting an easier and more efficient set up of targeted course courses.
3. *Guidelines* how to implement courses and programs based on 'web_access'.
4. Concepts for *business models* and different organizational frameworks for training and course programs both within the consortium and external.
5. *Public Relation materials* for dissemination and incentives for the take up of the 'web_access' results.
6. *Study skills materials* supporting students with a broad variety of backgrounds to prepare and benefit from the studying process.
7. An *accessible eLearning environment* including support for accessible content authoring.
8. *Accreditation* at two universities and expected accreditation at two more.

The curriculum of the Joint Study Programme on Accessible Web Design consists of content areas whereas each of the content areas contains appropriate courses.

Table 1. Table summarizing the Curriculum of the Study Programme [1,3]

Content Area	Course		ECTS
A. Fundamentals of Web Accessibility	A.1	Introduction to Accessible Web Design	3
	A.2	Societal Impacts and Effects of Accessible Web Design	2
	A.3	Technical Foundations	3
			8
B. Assistive Technology	B.1	Basics in Assistive Technology	1,5
	B.2	Categories of Assistive Technologies	4
			5,5
C. Guidelines and Legal Requirements	C.1	Web Accessibility Standards and Guidelines	3
	C.2	National and International Legal Framework	2
			5
D. Accessible Content Creation	D.1	Techniques for Accessible Web Design	3
	D.2	Evaluation and Repair Methodology and Tools	3
	D.3	Basics in Software Accessibility	3
	D.4	Rich Internet Applications and Multimedia Accessibility	3
	D.5	Authoring Tools and User Agents	3
	D.6	Accessible Document Design	3
			18
E. Design and Usability	E.1	Human Computer Interaction	3
	E.2	User Interaction Design	3
	E.3	Usability Engineering	1,5
			7,5
F. Project Development	F.1	Accessibility and Usability Audit	4
	F.2	Design and Redesign of Web Application in Practice	12
			16
Total	18 courses		60

4   Accessible Content Learning Management System

The content was made available in an eLearning system supporting the teachers to adapt it to their needs and contexts. To decide for a LCMS results and experiences from other EU projects (e.g. 'ALPE' [4], 'e-Learn VIP' [5], EU4All [6]) as well as own experiences made by the partners were used. Comparative analysis led to the decision to use the system ATutor [7]. The features of this learning content management system (LCMS) include:

- Public domain software
- An intuitive and clear design with good usability features
- The highest possible degree of accessibility available in this area
- Optimal teacher support by
  - Easy-to-manage course materials
  - Assessment tools
  - Integrated communications
- Optimal student support by
  - Using various learning objects
  - Elaborating exercises
  - Group work
  - And a good overview of the own work done or still to be done.

5 Additional Benefit of the Study Programme

'web_access' enhances and promotes *transnational mobility and flexibility* of students in the European Higher Education Area since it is implemented as a European curriculum and uses an extensively accessible eLearning tool for content provision. This represents an innovative structure when viewed in a global context and represents a clear benefit for participants with disabilities. The study programme causes a further increase in **awareness** towards the needs of PwD by offering accessible teaching and training materials. Moreover, it supports full access of PwD and older adults to an information and knowledge-based (European) society and therefore continues the European goal towards social, educational and economic inclusion. Further education in accessible web design is seen as a key requirement and opportunity for *labour market integration including PwD* themselves. By using an accessible and user centred design approach, labour market integration in this specific area is strongly supported. Content development and curriculum definition in such a dynamic field as ICT and web, and therefore also in accessible web design is in constant need of change and updating. The goal of 'web_access' has been establishing a comprehensive and stable body of knowledge. The design and outline of all materials underlines the need for adaptation to learners, cultural, national, regional contexts and situations. At the end of the project it should be added that time is also a factor that requires adaptation. The curriculum is outlined in a way which allows stability over several years, but asks for frequent adaptation of content.

References

1. Web Access Homepage, http://www.webaccess-project.net/
2. Hengstberger, B., Miesenberger, K., Batusic, M., Chelbat, N., Rodríguez García, A.: Joint Study Programme on Accessible Web Design. In: Miesenberger, K., Klaus, J., Zagler, W.L., Karshmer, A.I., et al. (eds.) ICCHP 2008. LNCS, vol. 5105, pp. 182–189. Springer, Heidelberg (2008)
3. Hengstberger, B., Miesenberger, K.: Distance Education and Training on Accessible Web Design. In: Emiliani, P.L., Burzagli, L., Como, A., Gabbanini, F., Salminen, A. (eds.) Proceedings of Assistive Technology from Adapted Equipment to Inclusive Environments, AAATE 2009. IOS Press, Amsterdam (2009)
4. ALPE project home page, http://adenu.ia.uned.es/alpe/
5. e-Learn Vip project home page, http://www.e-learn-vip.org/
6. EU4All project home page, http://www.eu4all-project.eu/
7. ATutor home page, http://www.atutor.ca/

Assessing WCAG 2.0 Conformance in Practice

Sylvie Duchateau, Denis Boulay, and Dominique Burger

INSERM – Université Pierre et Marie Curie
Association BrailleNet
9, quai Saint Bernard, 75252 Paris cedex 05, France
sylvie.duchateau@accessiweb.org, denis.boulay@accessiweb.org,
dominique.burger@upmc.fr

Abstract. On December 11, 2008, the W3C published the Web Content Accessibility Guidelines 2.0 as the new W3C recommendation. WCAG 2.0 aims to be more flexible and does not rely on a specific technology. Moreover W3C/WAI claims that WCAG 2.0 has been designed to be testable as to respond to multiple demands from stakeholders. However, few implementations have been completed yet providing enough feedback about WCAG 2.0 conformance systems over a long period. This paper will discuss the need for a methodology to ensure conformance to WCAG 2.0 that takes the new constraints of this standard into account. It will propose a process for developing this assessment methodology according to specific requirements. It identifies several steps that proved to be essential towards operational results. Finally, it discusses the possible benefits of such a methodology.

Keywords: WCAG 2.0, evaluation, conformance, accessibility, implementation, checklist.

1 Introduction

Over the past 15 years, the Internet and electronic information in general have been developing considerably. Public administrations, shops, banks, cultural entities, information media, provide content electronically in order to be available to all. As a matter of fact, the developing information society shall be accessible to all, in particular, to people with disabilities and aging people who can benefit from this new information media as a means for their better inclusion in the society. E-Accessibility has become a right for all citizens, now recognised in the UN convention for human rights in 2006 [1]. E-accessibility concerns not only the Web pages but also documents for download, computer and phone applications, digital TV …

The inclusion of E-accessibility in national and European policies was facilitated through WCAG 1.0, a standard published in 1999 by the World Wide Web Consortium (W3C). Since December 2008, version 2.0 of WCAG is the official W3C recommendation for Web content accessibility [2].

Many different stakeholders are concerned with the conformance to WCAG, such as content providers, quality managers, users and consumer organisations, like the European Disability Forum (EDF) but also European Standardisation Organisations or judicial authorities [3][4][5].

K. Miesenberger et al. (Eds.): ICCHP 2010, Part I, LNCS 6179, pp. 408–412, 2010.

2   The New Features of WCAG 2.0

WCAG 2.0 relies on four main principles: Perceivable, Operable, Understandable and Robust (POUR). Those principles focus on ultimate functional requirements, while 12 guidelines and 61 testable success criteria make it possible to reach conformance to them, "where requirements and conformance testing are necessary such as in design specification, purchasing, regulation, and contractual agreements".

In order to meet the needs of different groups and different situations, three levels of conformance are defined: A (lowest), AA, and AAA (highest)."

"Testable" is defined as "Either Machine Testable or Reliably Human Testable". The use of probabilistic machine algorithms may facilitate the human testing process but this does not make it machine testable."

Another innovation in WCAG 2.0 is that it is more flexible than WCAG 1.0 as it does not stick to a specific technology.

Principles, guidelines, success criteria, conformance and glossary are normative.

In order to support the implementation of the guidelines, W3C/WAI provides a rich documentation which is not normative as it is expected to change with technology evolutions. There are, How to meet WCAG 2.0, Understanding WCAG 2.0 and Techniques for WCAG 2.0.

Many countries and organisations have adopted the WCAG 2.0 immediately after their publication in December 2008. For instance, in its communication of December 1st, 2008, the European commission encourages all its Member States to adopt and implement those guidelines.

To summarise the impact of this new recommendation:

- The scope of WCAG 2.0 is much broader;
- The recognition of WCAG 2.0 in European and national policies should foster accessibility implementation;
- WCAG 2.0 provides a framework for conformance assessment;
- Tools that were relying on WCAG 1.0 shall be updated, and those tools shall be provided rapidly to encourage the real adoption of this standard.

3   Requirements for a Methodology to Assess Conformance to WCAG 2.0

As a standard, WCAG 2.0 proposes objectives and provides tools to achieve them. However, WCAG 2.0 doesn't provide a step-by-step methodology and leaves many degrees of freedom on how to reach those objectives. Such a methodology shall specify steps, checkpoints, tests to be performed, tools to be used, experts to be involved, etc ...

The analysis of WCAG 2.0, our experience in Web sites evaluation against WCAG 1.0, and discussions with Web professionals among a Web accessibility expert group in France, highlighted two types of expectations:

First, it shall generate a consensus among professionals about to apply it, i.e.:

- It shall fully match WCAG 2.0;
- People with various backgrounds or motivations should be able to easily understand it;

- It shall be unambiguous;
- It shall be coherent with other professional practices and methods;
- It shall be transparent and publicly exposed.

Secondly, this methodology shall be fully operational, which means that:

- It shall be applicable;
- It shall have a reasonable cost;
- It shall be reproducible;
- It shall be compatible with other requirements, like national standards.

Developing such a methodology is not a simple process, it takes time and has a cost. In the next section we propose an approach that appeared to be both affordable and successful.

4   A Process to Develop an Assessment Methodology

4.1   Set Up a Collaborative Task Force

This task force should be composed of knowledgeable experts with different professional and technical background, or representing different disability fields. Collaborative Web tools such as a wiki, a forum, a mailing list can be provided for making collaborative work easy.

4.2   Translate WCAG 2.0 in the Local Language

A preliminary task of the expert task force is to work out a translation of WCAG 2.0 which will forge a common conceptual understanding of the standard in countries where English is not the main language.

4.3   Collate Existing Methods and Best Practices

A good methodology is rarely built from scratch. The process for elaborating it must take into account pre-existing methods and best practices in an effort to incorporate them coherently in a new corpus of rules and procedures constituting the methodology.

4.4   Organise the Success Criteria According to Procedures

It may be useful to group several success criteria in a broader category. For instance, an inspection may be organised according objects categories like images, frames, tables, links... Success criteria can also be merged in a higher level rule. For instance, success criteria 1.3.1 "info and relationships" and 1.4.1 "use of color" which read : "1.3.1 *Info and Relationships: Information, structure, and relationships conveyed through presentation can be programmatically determined or are available in text.*" And "1.4.1 *Use of Color: Color is not used as the only visual means of conveying information, indicating an action, prompting a response, or distinguishing a visual element."* can be usefully integrated in a rule stating " *In each Web page, information shall not be provided by colour attributes only. Is this rule respected?* "

Once such rules have been formulated they may have to be split into several single tests in order to make them operable and provide a series of Yes/No answers. We have found that the rule above could be checked by 6 unique tests.

Structure the documentation following a progressive complexity, so that people with different profiles can access them at a level that correspond them better.

4.5 Make the Methodology Fully Compliant with WCAG 2.0

The tests shall cover the whole WCAG 2.0 recommendations. The methodology shall provide a mapping with the three conformance levels, namely A, AA and AAA.

4.6 Make the Methodology Compliant with Other Requirements

There may be other constraints related to other Web accessibility regulations or standards. If those are based on WCAG 2.0, check how the methodology matches those constraints. Establish cross correspondence between the methodology and other sets of compliance rules based on WCAG 2.0, as to be able to publish easily several reports and prove the multiple conformance.

4.7 Follow an Interactive Writing Process

Documents elaborated in the task force must regularly be confronted to various expertises. This can be done internally among the experts or by public call for comments. Also testing methods shall be exposed to real Web pages before they are validated.

5 An Example of Application of This Process : AccessiWeb 2.0

Since 2003 we have been developing and maintaining a Web accessibility assessment methodology based on WCAG, called AccessiWeb [6], from a version 1.0 based on WCAG 1.0 to a version 2.0 based on WCAG 2.0, published in December 2009. The developing process described above has been followed for this evolution:

- A group of knowledgeable professional experts has been constituted, currently counting more than 350 members;
- Translation committee of 43 organizations from 5 countries has been constituted and agreed by W3C. This committee has established the French Authorized Translation of WCAG 2.0;
- AccessiWeb 2.0 ensures a full correspondence with WCAG 2.0;
- It contains 300 unique tests allowing to validate the conformance to WCAG 2.0 success criteria;
- Three conformance levels have been defined, namely Bronze-Silver-Gold, with exact correspondence to A-AA-AAA;
- AccessiWeb 2.0 is structured in object categories that can be understood by all (images, frames, colors, tables, links…) and has several reading levels;

- It has been developed, discussed and iteratively updated within GTA expert group; A public call for comments has been processed; It has been validated through the evaluation of several Web sites;

It has been developed to allow the mapping with any set of success criteria based on WCAG 2.0, which has been done successfully with the mandatory requirements published by French administration, RGAA [7].

6   Conclusion

The process we have proposed for developing assessment methodologies has been applied for updating AccessiWeb, which led to a new set of criteria for Web pages fully coherent with two different accessibility reference documents, namely WCAG 2.0 and RGAA. This process will be continued with for methodologies assessing the accessibility of documents, multimedia, all based on WCAG 2.0. An important side effect is that this process has created a expert community in France and other French speaking countries.   We now plan to follow the same process for updating the Euracert certification schema [8].

References

1. Convention on the Rights of Persons with Disabilities,
   http://www.un.org/disabilities/convention/conventionfull.shtml
2. http://www.w3.org/TR/WCAG20/
3. European Commission: Expert meeting on web accessibility in Europe and the implementation of Web Content Accessibility Guidelines (WCAG) 2.0, Brussels, March 23 (2009)
4. European Commission - DG ENTR/D4 - 7th December 2005 - Mandate M376: Accessibility requirements for public procurement of products and services in the ICT domain (2005)
5. Waddell, C.D.: Update on Accessible Web & Electronic Book Litigation. In: CSUN 2010, San Diego, CA, USA (2010),
   http://www.icdri.org/CynthiaW/accessweb_kindle.htm
6. http://www.accessiweb.org
7. RGAA,
   http://references.modernisation.gouv.fr/rgaa-accessibilite
8. http://www.euracert.org

Is the Accessibility Audit Dead?

Joshue O. Connor

NCBI Centre For Inclusive Technology (CFIT), National Council for the Blind of Ireland,
Dublin, Ireland
joshue.oconnor@cfit.ie

Abstract. The Accessibility Audit has long been a staple of the usability professional and web accessibility specialists' toolkit. An audit is where problematic issues that limit the accessibility of a web site or application can be highlighted in a granular fashion, solutions outlined and statements of conformance to accessibility guidelines, like WCAG, teased out. However, in practice is the accessibility audit really the right tool for the job? As a methodology does it efficiently help to advance the cause of improving the accessibility of web sites and applications? Or effectively raise awareness of inclusive design amongst developers? Or is it merely an inert rubber-stamping exercise that could be replaced or enhanced by more progressive methods? [1]

Keywords: (e)Accessibility and Usability, eGovernment, eInclusion, Policies and Legislation, User Centered Design and User Involvement.

1 Methodology

The paper aims to critically assess the effectiveness of the auditing process and ask if other methods are needed to replace the accessibility audit or to compliment the process, thereby improving the quality of outputs for both the auditor and the client. It is based on the authors experience as an accessibility auditor.

1.1 Introduction

The birth of the accessibility audit came about after the development of the Web Accessibility Initiative's (WAI) first iteration of the web content accessibility guidelines. This established a methodology by which accessibility conformance could be assessed. [2]

These kinds of metrics were sorely needed. At the time there were other evaluation guidelines in the software world, and user interface/ergonomics realms, but advocating for quality design on the web was often entirely down to one or two lone voices that were champions of what would later become known as the 'user experience'.

Even for the user groups who could be considered to occupy the imagined 'normal' part of the curve, advocating for the needs of the regular user was in itself an uphill struggle. Never mind when we come to the 'outliers' such as blind, vision-impaired users and other user groups. The general mood was that these groups do not represent a significant target market and can be comfortably ignored. So what changed? In

K. Miesenberger et al. (Eds.): ICCHP 2010, Part I, LNCS 6179, pp. 413–416, 2010.

tandem with the ashes of the browser wars and the adoption of CSS by major browsers vendors, came improved understanding of the importance of semantic markup – for both SEO and Assistive Technologies (AT). All of which has had a positive impact on the digital lives of people with disabilities. This synergy of the Web Standards movement, the increasing impact of the WAI, the writings of Zeldman, Clark and the birth of the WCAG 1.0 - finally changed the landscape for good. The age of choice has also had a huge impact on the need to take the quality of the user experience far more seriously. [3] [4] [5] [6]

2   The Accessibility Audit – A New Way

Many organisations, sensing a sea change, quickly adopted a stance that they needed to accommodate the needs of people with disabilities so the accessibility audit soon became an established part of the new paradigm. To successfully be able to undertake an audit requires a diverse and complex set of skills. The auditor needs to have (non-canonical):

1) A good grasp of the technical fundamentals of HTML, CSS, JavaScript, as well as an understanding of dynamic web application development.
2) A strong visual design sense and aesthetic.
3) Good problem solving skills.
4) Ideally "real world" experience of the needs of people with disabilities.
5) A grasp of the esoteric WCAG guidelines themselves and an awareness of where they work and where they should not be taken as absolute.
6) The ability to be supportive whilst being critical – to be able to be the bearer of bad news about the reality of a web site's quality (or lack of) and still leave the meeting on good terms.
7) To be able to recognise when designers and developers know what they are doing, and when they don't and how to impart the necessary knowledge either way.
8) Understand how various kinds of AT works: from complex screen reader functionality, the Off Screen Model, buffer inconsistencies, DOM updates - to single switch access and all in between. [7] [8]

There is also the need to keep informed of emerging trends and how they related to the guidelines. For example, understanding Web 2.0 and AJAX and how they related to WCAG 1.0 was a challenge. Also, the emergence of JavaScript as a useful part of the toolkit (from the shadows as a pariah), to the dawn of WAI-ARIA and HTML 5. As an accessibility practitioner there is a lot to understand and then be able to effectively translate, and provide best practice advise for others. [9] [10] [11]

2.1   The Right Tool for the Right Job?

The audit is of itself a static, dull report. It is often very technical, long, verbose – full of code, screenshots and narrative opinion outlining how to 'fix' things. Personally, I have been doing audits for government agencies, public bodies and private companies for 6 years. Myself and my colleague, Mark Magennis, put a lot work and thought into designing an effective auditing service that:

1) Would meet the needs of our clients.
2) Illuminated the main problems, provided solutions and engaged them in the process of inclusive design.
3) Was not scary, intimidating and/or useless.

2.2 Après Audit

Following this stage there may be some user testing. We always recommend that the audit results are implemented first and then the user testing that follows (with 8-12 users that represent various user groups) shows us any improvement in the quality of the user experience. User testing is certainly a fantastic way of assessing how well the accessibility auditing process has improved the user experience. It is very effective as a part of an iterative design process. In short, for the results of the audit to be in any way qualitatively assessed there must be a follow on user test and/or some method of assessing the audits effectiveness.

2.3 No User Test, No Point?

A user test is a very different experience for many designers and developers. They may never have had any experience being around people with disabilities. There is often an epiphany, and they can leave a user test 'changed' – this is a very positive and useful experience.

So my question is, without the user test or other assessment methodology does the audit have any value? If so, how? Without some method of evaluation that can provide data outlining the differences between 'before' and 'after'? How can you be sure that an audit is worth it? Are there better ways to achieve improved accessible interfaces and do we need frameworks to establish metrics where we can be sure the results of our endeavours are actually implemented? Audits are often just abandoned to gather dust on a shelf. Over time organisational politics, communication breakdowns between departments, loss of motivation or a sense of urgency etc erode any potency it may have had. Many undertake audits as a rubber-stamping exercise of 'compliance' regardless of the outcome – they are seen to act. Can we effectively counter this attitude and improve the accessibility of the application and raise awareness via other methods?

2.4 Summary

Auditing can often be a time consuming process and I suggest more work is needed to help us critically evaluate the effectiveness of the auditing process and to help give us a greater understanding of complementary or alternative methods that will make the best use of our energies. Some research has shown that the accessibility audit is of benefit. However, I feel it is important to get a clearer idea of exactly what its role is today and ask are there other complimentary methods that could be adopted or replace the audit altogether? [12]

References

1. Web Content Accessibility Guidelines (WCAG),
   http://www.w3.org/WAI/intro/wcag.php
2. Web Accessibility Initiative, http://www.w3.org/WAI/
3. Microsoft and the Browser Wares, http://heinonline.org/HOL/
   LandingPage?collection=journals&handle=hein.journals/
   conlr31&div=45&id=&page
4. Lessons from the Browser Wars,
   http://dialnet.unirioja.es/servlet/articulo?codigo=2310150
5. Building Accessible Websites by Joe Clark,
   http://portal.acm.org/citation.cfm?id=975095
6. Designing with Web Standards by Jeffery Zeldman,
   http://portal.acm.org/citation.cfm?id=1177309&coll=GUIDE&dl=
   GUIDE&CFID=88258503CFTOKEN=64965267
7. Non-visual presentation of graphical user interfaces: contrasting two approaches (Mynatt, Weber) Conference on Human Factors in Computing Systems archive. Proceedings of the SIGCHI conference on Human factors in computing systems: celebrating interdependence table of contents, Boston, Massachusetts, United States, pp. 166–172 (1994) ISBN:0-89791-650-6
8. Lemon, G., Connor, J.O.: Managing Multiple Updates in Dynamically Driven Web Applications. In: Proceedings of the 2nd International Conference on Automated Production of Cross Media Content for Multi-channel Distribution, University Leeds. Firenze University Press (2006) ISBN 88-8453-526-3
9. HTML5 A vocabulary and associated APIs for HTML and XHTML,
   http://www.w3.org/TR/html5/
10. WAI-ARIA, http://www.w3.org/WAI/intro/aria.php
11. Dynamic Accessible Web Content Roadmap,
    http://www.w3.org/WAI/PF/roadmap/DHTMLRoadmap040506.html
12. The Effectiveness of the Web Accessibility Audit as a Motivational and Educational Tool in Inclusive Web Design by David Sloan,
    http://www.computing.dundee.ac.uk/staff/dsloan/phd.htm

Evaluating Conformance to WCAG 2.0: Open Challenges

Fernando Alonso, José L. Fuertes, Ángel L. González, and Loïc Martínez

Facultad de Informática, Universidad Politécnica de Madrid, Spain
{falonso,jfuertes,agonzalez,loic}@fi.upm.es

Abstract. Web accessibility for people with disabilities is a highly visible area of work in the field of ICT accessibility, including many policy activities in several countries. The commonly accepted guidelines for web accessibility (WCAG 1.0) were published in 1999 and have been extensively used by designers, evaluators and legislators. A new version of these guidelines (WCAG 2.0) was published in 2008. In this paper we point out the main challenges that WCAG 2.0 raises for web accessibility evaluators: the concept of "accessibility supported technologies"; success criteria testability; technique and failure openness, and the aggregation of partial results. We conclude the paper with some recommendations for the future.

Keywords: Web accessibility, Web accessibility evaluation.

1 Introduction

The web is an essential component of the information society, and as such has attracted special attention from the promoters of accessibility for people with disabilities.

The commonly accepted guidelines for web accessibility are the Web Content Accessibility Guidelines (WCAG) 1.0, published in 1999 by the World Wide Web Consortium (W3C) [1]. These guidelines have been in use for several years by designers, evaluators and legislators, and there is an arguably large consensus among practitioners about how to interpret and evaluate them.

A new version of WCAG has been under development for several years, and was published in December 2008 as WCAG 2.0 [2]. This new version had two main goals. Firstly, it aimed to be technology-independent, so it could be applied to current and future web technologies from either the W3C or other sources. Secondly, it was to be testable, that is, practitioners should agree about how to evaluate the conformance of a web site with WCAG 2.0.

WCAG 2.0 has a different language, a different structure and a different rationale. All of these influence how the evaluation of conformance to WCAG 2.0 is to be performed in the future, either manually or with the support of evaluation tools [3].

In this paper we present some challenges that we think are currently present when evaluating the accessibility of web sites with respect to WCAG 2.0. This discussion is based on our experience in teaching and evaluating web accessibility [4], [5], [6].

The content of this paper is structured as follows. Section 2 will provide an overview of WCAG 2.0. This is followed by four sections describing what we consider to be the key challenges: a) the concept of "accessibility supported technologies";

K. Miesenberger et al. (Eds.): ICCHP 2010, Part I, LNCS 6179, pp. 417–424, 2010.

b) success criteria testability; c) technique and failure openness, and d) the aggregation of partial results. Finally, the paper concludes with some recommendations for the future.

2 WCAG 2.0 Overview

WCAG 2.0 is a W3C Recommendation [2] that contains three layers of guidance: principles, guidelines and success criteria.

- The *principles* provide the foundation for web accessibility. There are four principles: perceivable, operable, understandable and robust.
- The 12 *guidelines* provide the basic goals that web designers should work toward in order to make content more accessible to users with different disabilities. The guidelines are not testable, but provide the framework and overall objectives to help web designers understand the success criteria and better implement the techniques.
- For each guideline, testable *success criteria* are provided to allow WCAG 2.0 to be used where requirements and conformance testing are necessary such as in design specification, purchasing, regulation and contractual agreements. In order to meet the needs of different groups and different situations, three levels of conformance are defined: A (lowest), AA, and AAA (highest).

There are additional layers of guidance provided by an external document that complements WCAG 2.0 [7]. This document is "informative" and provides three additional layers, referred to as sufficient techniques, advisory techniques and common failures.

- The *Sufficient Techniques* offer guidance and examples for meeting the guidelines using specific technologies. These techniques are considered sufficient to meet the success criteria. Most success criteria list multiple sufficient techniques, and any of the sufficient techniques can be used to meet the success criterion. There may be other techniques not documented by the W3C that could also meet the success criteria. As new sufficient techniques are identified, they can be added to the listing.
- The *Advisory Techniques* can enhance accessibility, but did not qualify as sufficient techniques because they are not sufficient to meet the full requirements of the success criteria, they are not testable, and/or are good and effective techniques in some circumstances but not effective or helpful in others.
- The *Common Failures* are examples of bad practices that cause web pages to fail to meet the success criteria. Failures during evaluation are interpreted differently than for techniques: if a common failure is found in a web page, then that web page fails the respective success criterion.

In addition, there is another important part of WCAG 2.0: the conformance section. This section lists five requirements for conformance to WCAG 2.0: (1) one conformance level is met in full; (2) conformance is for full web pages; (3) all web pages in a process conform to the same level; (4) only accessibility-supported ways of using the technologies are relied upon to satisfy the success criteria; and (5) technologies that are used in a way that is not accessibility-supported do not interfere with the accessibility of the page.

The conformance section also gives information about how to make conformance claims, which are optional. Finally, it describes what "accessibility supported" means. This "accessibility supported" concept is the key to the first challenge for WCAG 2.0 conformance evaluation.

3   Challenge 1: Accessibility Supported Technologies

The first challenge is to apply the key concept "accessibility supported ways of using technologies". The fourth WCAG 2.0 conformance requirement states: "Only accessibility supported ways of using technologies are relied upon to satisfy the success criteria. Any information or functionality that is provided in a way that is not accessibility supported is also available in a way that is accessibility supported" [2].

According to W3C, a Web content technology is "accessibility supported" when users' assistive technologies will work with the Web technologies and when the accessibility features of mainstream technologies will work with the technology [8].

The problem is that this is an open definition and, in particular, the W3C does not specify which or how many assistive technologies a Web technology must support in order for it to be classified as accessibility supported. This is a complex, environment- and language-dependent topic. The W3C states in WCAG 2.0 that there is a need for an external and international dialogue on this point.

This is the first and main challenge: a definition of which technologies are considered to be "accessibility supported" in a given context is needed in order to get consistent evaluation results. This definition should be provided by organizations that are industry independent and should be internationally agreed upon to prevent market fragmentation.

This is especially important for web sites that are obliged to be accessible by law. For instance, the web sites of the public administrations are obliged to conform to WCAG 1.0 (and, in the future, to WCAG 2.0) in many European countries. Each country defining its own set of accessibility-supported technologies would lead to a fragmented market where a web site is considered to be accessible in one country and non-accessible in another.

4   Challenge 2: Testability of Success Criteria

The second challenge deals with the actual degree of testability of the success criteria. According to W3C, the success criteria are written as testable sentences.

W3C provides definitions of testability for techniques [9]: a technique is testable if it is either machine testable or reliably human testable. It is machine testable if there is a known algorithm (regardless of whether that algorithm is known to be implemented in tools) that will determine absolutely reliably whether or not the technique has been implemented. It is reliably human testable if the technique can be tested by human inspection, and it is believed that at least 80% of knowledgeable human evaluators would agree on the finding.

There was some debate about the implications of testability during the development of WCAG 2.0 [10], [11], but now that WCAG 2.0 is complete the real challenge is to find out whether the success criteria and the techniques are actually testable.

Many success criteria have a more precise and objective language in WCAG 2.0 (for example, the language used for success criteria 1.4.3 on color contrast is much more precise –providing exact values to check against– than WCAG 1.0 checkpoint 2.2). But it is not clear that this is true for all the success criteria.

During our course on web accessibility taught in March 2009 within the ATHENS Program, we used WCAG 2.0 for the first time. It was an intensive one-week course for international students, and they were set the exercise of evaluating the same web page according to WCAG 2.0. Given that at the time there were no automated tools providing support for WCAG 2.0, all the evaluations were done manually.

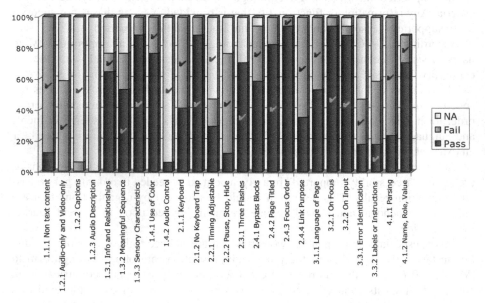

Fig. 1. Results of evaluating Level-A success criteria in an intensive web accessibility course

We examined our students' and our own results, and we compared the results for each success criterion. Figure 1 shows, for each success criterion, the number of times that each possible value (pass, fail, not applicable) appeared in the results provided by our students. It also shows what was considered to be the right result, that is, the result generated by the instructors, indicated by a check mark (✓), provided that at least one student entered the correct result. If a bar does not reach a value of 100%, it means that some students did no evaluate that success criterion. Of the 25 level-A success criteria (the ones that all the students were able to evaluate), only nine were reliably human testable, that is, 79% or more of the population agreed on the result (which is almost the 80% used in the W3C's definition). Agreement among evaluators was much less for the other 16 success criteria. The outcomes for some criteria, such as 1.3.2 (meaningful sequence of elements), 3.1.1 (language of page), 3.3.1 (error identification) and 3.3.2 (labels or instructions), were especially divergent [12].

In a repetition of the experiment on a recent non-intensive course (October 2009 to January 2010), better results were obtained. In this course, the students also had to evaluate the same web page (different to the one used in the previous experiment) according to WCAG 2.0. Figure 2 shows the results provided by the students. We examined our students' and our own results, and we compared the results for each success criterion. Of the 25 level-A success criteria, 17 were reliably human testable. The outcomes for some level-A criteria, such as 1.3.3 (sensory characteristics), 2.3.1 (three flashes), 2.4.3 (focus order) and 3.3.2 (labels or instructions), were especially divergent. In addition, of the 36 level-AA and level-AAA success criteria, 17 were reliably human testable, showing that students found the success criteria of these two levels were quite a lot harder to test reliably compared with level-A success criteria.

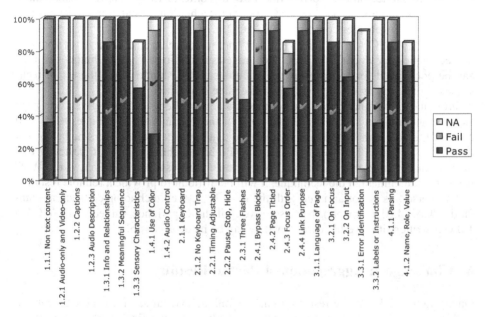

Fig. 2. Results of evaluating Level-A success criteria in a non-intensive web accessibility course

In addition, our experiments and results agree with Brajnik's experiment [13]. Some success criteria show up as being particularly weak in the studies: 1.3.3 (sensory characteristics), 2.1.1 (timing adjustable), 2.2.2 (pause, stop, hide), 2.4.1 (bypass blocks), 2.4.4 (link purpose in context) and 3.3.2 (labels or instructions). It would be interesting to see whether this trend keeps up in further experiments run to complement Brajnik's and our studies.

The detailed results that we have obtained led us to identify three sources of unreliability: comprehension, knowledge and effort [12].

Of course these are not conclusive experiments, but they point out that the testability of the WCAG 2.0 success criteria is not to be taken for granted for beginners and that support material and tools will be needed to help evaluators to provide consistent results in the future. Our experiments have been carried out by small groups of beginners

(17 and 14, respectively) and on non-diverse web pages, but we plan to repeat the experiments with more beginners and with a group of experts in web accessibility.

5 Challenge 3: Openness of Techniques and Failures

The third challenge is related to the openness of the techniques. The techniques belong to a non-normative document [7] that is intended to be a living document that will change as new techniques are defined, either inside or outside the W3C.

One reason for this incompleteness is that the W3C only documents techniques for non-proprietary technologies; the W3C hopes that vendors of other technologies will provide similar techniques to describe how to conform to WCAG 2.0 using those technologies. Another reason is that new web technologies will require new techniques to make web sites conform to WCAG 2.0.

In fact, the W3C acknowledges this fact and has established a process for updating the techniques document. The W3C encourages submission of new techniques so they can be considered for inclusion in the document. This should make the set of techniques maintained by the W3C as comprehensive as possible.

From the viewpoint of an evaluator this is a new challenge. If for a given web page element and a given success criterion, none of the documented techniques apply and none of the common failures apply, then the evaluator cannot decide whether or not the success criterion has been met. There could be a technique for that particular element in that particular case that makes the content accessible. However, if the W3C has not yet documented the technique, it will be difficult to provide a reliable result.

Of course this is not an issue with the most basic web technologies (such as standard HTML 4.01 elements), because, given all the experience gained since WCAG 1.0 was written, it is well known how they can be made accessible.

6 Challenge 4: Aggregation of Partial Results

Once evaluators know the result for each technique and failure for each element and each situation, how do they aggregate this result to get the final conformance result for the success criteria?

In WCAG 1.0 the situation was simpler because the checkpoints were restrictive: if one element fails to comply with one checkpoint, then this checkpoint fails for that page.

In WCAG 2.0 there are potentially different ways of making some specific element accessible. There are complex cases, where one of many different situations applies for each element, each situation includes several techniques, and several common failures are documented. In these cases, the evaluator first has to identify the situation that applies for each element, and then evaluate the sufficient techniques and common failures for that situation.

The complexity in WCAG 2.0 stems from the permissiveness of the techniques: if none of the documented techniques pass for any given element, the web page could still be accessible due to the application of a non-documented technique. And in a few cases, it is difficult to aggregate the values of the techniques because it is not clear if an 'or' or an 'and' operator should be used.

The challenge here is that the W3C has not documented how to combine the results of techniques, failures and situations to produce an aggregated result for each success criterion. This could lead to a situation where different evaluators use different aggregation strategies and thus produce different evaluation results. We are in the process of updating the Hera-FFX tool [6] to cover WCAG 2.0, and we have found that this is a real challenge that should be solved.

7 Some Recommendations for the Future

This paper has presented some challenges that, in our opinion, have to be faced when evaluating the conformance of web pages to WCAG 2.0. These challenges could explain why there are not many evaluation tools for WCAG 2.0 at present. In fact we are acquainted with just two tools: AChecker [14] and TAW [15]. As concluding remarks, we list the following recommendations for the future:

- When web accessibility is mandatory, public authorities should define the accessibility-supported ways of using technologies that apply in each context. Furthermore, this definition should be internationally harmonized to prevent market fragmentation.
- More experimentation is needed to assess the testability of techniques, failures and success criteria. This could help to create a common understanding and support material that could enable evaluators to produce consistent results. It could even lead to proposals of changes in the wording of some of the success criteria. We plan to work on further experiments, including comparisons between expert and non-expert evaluation, to gather more data and get more insight into success criteria testability.
- The W3C should provide recommendations about how to deal with the openness of techniques and about how to aggregate partial evaluation results to improve the consistency of evaluations produced by different tools and people.

Concerning the aggregation of partial evaluation results, we are currently developing an update of Hera-FFX [6] for WCAG 2.0. This tool considers six evaluation values for a given technique or failure: pass, fail, partial (i.e. "near pass"), not applicable, not verified (the evaluator has yet to examine the technique/failure) and don't know (the evaluator is unable to decide a value, typically due to disability).

The evaluation strategy for one element in one success criterion is as follows: first we look at the failures, aggregated using a "restrictive" approach in (1). This means that if one failure "fails" then the element fails for the success criterion. Only if the result of the aggregation of failures is "pass" or "not applicable" (i.e. the evaluator is sure that there is no failure) does the strategy look at the techniques.

[Restrictive] fail $\gg$ partial $\gg$ not verified $\gg$ don't know $\gg$ pass $\gg$ not applicable   (1)

The techniques for one situation are expressed as and/or trees that are evaluated combining the restrictive and permissive approach. We use the "permissive" approach in (2) for an "or" branch (any child is enough), and then they are combined using the "restrictive" approach in an "and" branch (all of the children are needed). In the "permissive" approach, one pass is enough for the corresponding group of techniques.

[Permissive] pass >> not verified >> don't know >> partial >> failure >> not applicable   (2)

Although WCAG 2.0 success criteria are hard to evaluate objectively [12], [13], everyday practice is showing WCAG 2.0 to be significantly better in flexibility terms than WCAG 1.0.

References

1. Chisholm, W., Vanderheiden, G., Jacobs, I. (eds.): Web Content Accessibility Guidelines 1.0. W3C Recommendation (1999), http://www.w3.org/TR/WCAG10/
2. Caldwell, B., Cooper, M., Reid, L.G., Vanderheiden, G. (eds.): Web Content Accessibility Guidelines 2.0. W3C Recommendation (2008), http://www.w3.org/TR/WCAG20/
3. W3C. Web Accessibility Evaluation Tools: Overview (2006), http://www.w3.org/WAI/ER/tools/
4. Benavídez, C., Fuertes, J.L., Gutiérrez, E., Martínez, L.: Semi-automatic Evaluation of Web Accessibility with HERA 2.0. In: Miesenberger, K., Klaus, J., Zagler, W.L., Karshmer, A.I. (eds.) ICCHP 2006. LNCS, vol. 4061, pp. 199–206. Springer, Heidelberg (2006)
5. Benavídez, C., Fuertes, J.L., Gutiérrez, E., Martínez, L.: Teaching Web Accessibility with "Contramano" and Hera. In: Miesenberger, K., Klaus, J., Zagler, W.L., Karshmer, A.I. (eds.) ICCHP 2006. LNCS, vol. 4061, pp. 341–348. Springer, Heidelberg (2006)
6. Fuertes, J.L., González, R., Gutiérrez, E., Martínez, L.: Hera-FFX: a Firefox add-on for semi-automatic web accessibility evaluation. In: 6th International Cross-Disciplinary Conference on Web Accessibility, pp. 26–35. ACM Press, New York (2009)
7. Caldwell, B., Cooper, M., Reid, L.G., Vanderheiden, G. (eds.): Techniques for WCAG 2.0 (2008), http://www.w3.org/TR/WCAG20-TECHS/
8. W3C: Understanding Conformance (2008), http://www.w3.org/TR/UNDERSTANDING-WCAG20/conformance.html
9. Cooper, M. (ed.): Requirements for WCAG 2.0 Checklists and Techniques (2003), http://www.w3.org/TR/wcag2-tech-req/
10. Sampson-Wild, G.: Testability Costs Too Much. A List Apart (2007), http://www.alistapart.com/articles/testability/
11. Smith, J.: Testability in WCAG 2.0. WebAIM Blog (2007), http://webaim.org/blog/wcag-2-testability/
12. Alonso, F., Fuertes, J.L., González, Á.L., Martínez, L.: On the testability of WCAG 2.0 for beginners. In: 7th International Cross-Disciplinary Conference on Web Accessibility. ACM Press, New York (2010)
13. Brajnik, G.: Validity and Reliability of Web Accessibility Guidelines. In: 11th International ACM SIGACCESS Conference on Computers and Accessibility, pp. 131–138. ACM Press, New York (2009)
14. AChecker: Web Accessibility Checker (2009), http://www.achecker.ca/
15. TAW tool (2010), http://www.tawdis.net/ingles.html?lang=en

Automatic Checking of Alternative Texts on Web Pages

Morten Goodwin Olsen[1], Mikael Snaprud[1], and Annika Nietzio[2]

[1] Tingtun AS,
PO Box 48, N−4791 Lillesand, Norway
morten.g.olsen@tingtun.no, mikael.snaprud@tingtun.no
http://www.tingtun.no
[2] Forschungsinstitut Technologie und Behinderung (FTB)
der Evangelischen Stiftung Volmarstein, Grundschötteler Str. 40
58300 Wetter (Ruhr), Germany
egovmon@ftb-net.de
http://www.ftb-net.de

Abstract. For people who cannot see non-textual web content, such as images, maps or audio files, the alternative texts are crucial to understand and use the content. Alternate texts are often automatically generated by web publishing software or not properly provided by the author of the content. Such texts may impose web accessibility barriers. Automatic accessibility checkers in use today can only detect the presence of alternative texts, but not determine if the text is describing the corresponding content in any useful way. This paper presents a pattern recognition approach for automatic detection of alternative texts that may impose a barrier, reaching an accuracy of more then 90%.

1   Introduction

The Unified Web Evaluation Methodology (UWEM) [1,2] has been presented as a methodology for evaluating web sites according to the Web Content Accessibility Guidelines [3]. The UWEM includes both tests which can be applied manually by experts and tests which can be applied automatically by measurement tools and validators.

All automatic tests in the UWEM are deterministic, which has some drawbacks. As an example, one of the automatic UWEM tests checks whether an image (`<img>` element) has an alternative text. There are no automatic tests checking the validity of such alternative texts. This means, for a web site to conform to the automatic UWEM tests, any alternative text is sufficient. People and applications such as search engines, who are unable to see images, rely on the alternative text to convey the information of non-textual web content. If this information is not present, or when the text does not describe the image well, the information conveyed in the image is lost to these users.

To make sure web sites are accessible, appropriate textual alternatives are needed in many places, such as in frame titles, labels and alternative texts of

K. Miesenberger et al. (Eds.): ICCHP 2010, Part I, LNCS 6179, pp. 425–432, 2010.

graphical elements [3,4,5].[1] In many cases, these alternative texts have either been automatically added by the publishing software, or a misleading text has been supplied by the author of the content. Examples of such include alternative texts of images such as "Image 1", texts which resemble filenames such as "somepicture.jpg" or "insert alternative text here". Most automatic accessibility checkers, including validators that comply with the automatic UWEM tests, check only for the existence of alternative texts. The above mentioned texts, which are *undescriptive* and are thus not considered accessible, will not be detected by those tests. Our data shows that 80% of the alternative texts are not describing the corresponding content well.

This paper proposes an extension of UWEM with tests for automatic detection of alternative texts which, in its context, is in-accessible using pattern recognition algorithms.

To the best of our knowledge using pattern recognition to test for *undescriptive* use of alternative texts in web pages has not been done previously. However, similar related approaches has been conducted. For example, the Imergo Web Compliance Manager [6] provides results for suspicious alternative texts for images. The algorithm is not presented in the literature.

Furthermore, a technique for automatic judging of alternative text quality of images has been presented by Bigham [7].[2] This approach judges alternative texts in correspondence with the images, including classification using common words found in alternative texts and check if the same text is present in any other web page on Internet. The classifier uses Google and Yahoo, and has in their best experiment an accuracy of 86.3% using 351 images and corresponding alternative texts. However, in the presented results 7999 images are discarded because the algorithm fails to label the images. It is evident that discarding 7999 images (95.8%) is undesirable and has a severe impact on the over all accuracy. Taking the discarded images into account, the true accuracy of the presented algorithm is only 3.6%.

Detecting *undescriptive* texts in web pages has many similarities with detection of junk web pages and emails where heuristics and pattern classification has been successfully applied [8,9,10,11].

It is worth noticing that descriptiveness of a text could be seen in correspondence with the content. For example, if there is an image of a cat, an appropriate alternative textual description may be "cat" while "dog" would be wrong. In order to detect these situations image processing would most likely be needed in addition to text classification. Even though this could increase the over all accuracy, it is a much more challenging task which also includes significant increase in computational costs [12]. Image processing is not within the scope of this paper.

---

[1] All types of textual alternatives are in this paper referred to as alternative texts. An alternative text is *descriptive* if it describes the corresponding content well, and *undescriptive* if it does not.

[2] Note that this is limited only to alternative texts of images, while our approach includes several types of alternative texts.

2   Approach

This paper presents a method for detecting *undescriptive* use of alternative texts using pattern recognition algorithms. The paper follows traditional classification approach [13]: Section 3 presents the data used for the classification. From this data features are extracted in section 4. The classification algorithms and results are presented in section 5; Naïve Bayes in section 5.1 and Nearest Neighbor in section 5.2. Finally, section 6 and 7 present the conclusions and further work.

3   Data

The home page of 414 web sites from Norwegian municipality were downloaded. From these, more then 11 000 alternatives texts were extracted (more than 1700 unique alternative texts) and manually classified as either:

Descriptive: The alternative texts describes the corresponding content well and imposes no accessibility barrier.
- **Undescriptive**: The alternative texts does not the correspond to the content well and is a potential accessibility barrier.

All web pages have been deliberately chosen to be from only one language to avoid possible bias due to language issues such as; the length of words, which is language dependent [14], or words that are known to be *undescriptive* which will differ between languages [15]. Despite only using web pages from one language in this paper, the algorithms presented are not expected to be limited to only Norwegian. The algorithms can be applied to any language as long as appropriate training data is used.

Note that frequent problem of absence of *descriptive* texts [16] has deliberately been removed from these experiments. Testing for the presence of such *descriptive* texts are already present in UWEM as a fully automatable test [1,2] and is thus not addressed in this paper.

4   Feature Extraction

Several features of *undescriptive* texts in web pages have already been presented in the literature [7,15].

Slatin [7] found that file name extensions, such as .jpg, is a common attribute of *undescriptive* alternative texts of images. Additionally, the study indicates that a dictionary of known *undescriptive* words and phrases can be useful for such a classification.

Craven [15] presented additional features that characterizes *undescriptive* alternative texts. Most significantly, he found certain words/characters that are common in *undescriptive* alternative texts such as "*", "1", "click", "arrow" and "home". Additionally, he found a correlation between the size of the image and length of the alternative text. His empirical data indicates that images of small sizes are more often used for decoration and should because of this have an empty alternative text.

In line with literature [7,5,15], the following features where extracted from the collected data:

- Number of words in the alternative text.
- Length of the alternative text (number of characters).
- File type abbreviations such as GIF, JPEG and PDF.
- None alphabet characters such as *, 1, ..
- Words that are known to cause accessibility barriers such as "read more", "click here", "title".[3]
- The size of the image presented in the alternative text (INTxINT).
- HTML such as .[4]

Generally speaking, features will work well as part of classifiers as long as they have a discriminatory effect on the data [13]. This means, based on the properties of the features alone, it should be possible to separate the data which belongs to both the *descriptive* and *undescriptive* classes.

The features have different properties and distributions. The features "number of words" and "length of the alternative text" are represented by positive integer values $(1, 2, 3, ...)$. The discriminatory effect of these features are presented as density graphs in figure 1. Figure 1 shows that common properties for the *undescriptive* texts are shorter alternative texts and fewer words. Most noticeably, figure 1 shows that having only one word in the alternative texts is a common property of the *undescriptive* class, while having two or more words is a common property for the *descriptive* class.

The remaining features are represented by a boolean value. As an example, a file name extension is either present or not present in the alternative texts. Figure 2 shows the discriminatory effect of features represented by boolean values.[5] As an example, close to 50% of the *undescriptive* alternative texts had words which often cause accessibility barriers, while only 0.5% of the *descriptive* alternative texts had the same behaviour. Similarly about 2% of the *undescriptive* texts had file name extensions, while only 0.05% *descriptive* texts had filename extentions.

5 Classification

Essential for the algorithms is the actual classification. In this paper we have implemented and tested two well known classification algorithms; Nearest Neighbor and Naïve Bayes [17,13].

All algorithms have been tested with leave one out cross validation [18]; 1. Train with all data set except one instance. 2. classify the remaining instances. 3. Select next instance and go to 1. This ensures that the training sample is independent from test set.

---

[3] Norwegian translations of these words were used.
[4] In this study, all types of HTML is included. It is worth noticing that not every entity is problematic.
[5] Note that the y-axis is logarithmic.

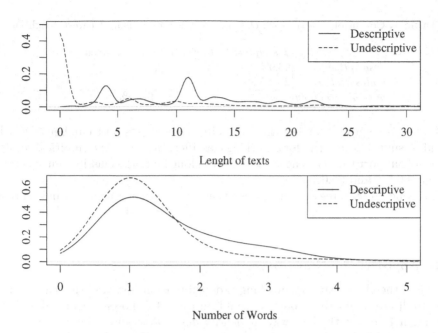

Fig. 1. Density Graphs for the features number of words and length of texts

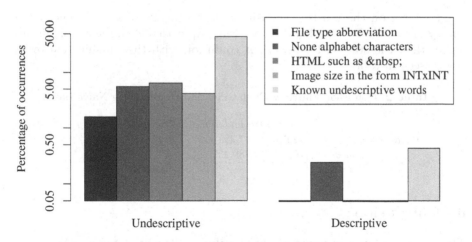

Fig. 2. Bar Charts with percentage of occurrence for features

5.1 Approach 1 - Nearest Neighbor

With the Nearest Neighbor algorithm, the data are added in multidimensional feature space where each feature represents a dimension, and every record is represented by a coordinate in the feature space. The euclidean distance is calculated between the item to be classified, and all items part of the training data. This identifies the nearest neighbors, and voting between the k nearest neighbors decides the outcome of the classification. In our experiments, k was chosen to be 1.

Table 1. Confusion Matrix with classification accuracy using Nearest Neighbor

	descriptive	undescriptive	over all accuracy
descriptive	93.9%	6.1%	
undescriptive	27.2%	72.8%	
over all accuracy			90.0%

Figure 1 suggests that length of the alternative texts and number of words could be sufficient features for a working classifier. However, the empirical results does not support this as using these features alone gives the classifier an accuracy of only 66.5% and 69.0%.

By using all features described in section 4 the classifier achieves an accuracy of 90.0%, which is significantly higher than the state-of-the-art [7]. A confusion matrix with the classification results can be seen in table 1.

5.2 Approach 2 - Naïve Bayes

How well the classification is working is dependant on how well the features are able to discriminate the classes. It could be that the chosen features described in section 4 are not the best way to identify *descriptive* and *undescriptive* alternative texts. The words themselves could have a significant discriminatory effect [19].

By relying on the words alone using a Naïve Bayes classifier, we get an accuracy of 91.9%. This is slightly more than Approach 1 and again significatly higher than the state-of-the-art [7]. A confusion with the classification results can be seen in table 2.

Table 2. Confusion Matrix with classification results using Naïve Bayes

	descriptive	undescriptive	over all accuracy
descriptive	92.6%	7.4%	
undescriptive	10.9%	89.1%	
over all accuracy			91.9%

6 Conclusion

This paper presents an approach for classifying alternative texts in Web pages as *descriptive* or *undescriptive*. *Undescriptive* texts are not describing the corresponding content well and may impose an accessibility barrier. The paper presents two approaches; classification based on well known properties of *undescriptive* texts presented in literature and classification using the texts alone. Both approaches have an accuracy of more then 90%, which is better than the state-of-the-art. Furthermore, in contrast to the state-of-the-art, this paper presents approaches that are independent from third party tools.

The findings in this paper gives a strong indication that *undescriptive* alternative texts in Web pages can be detected automatically with a high degree accuracy.

7 Further Work

Further work includes looking at alternative texts in comparison with the actual images. This would include adding image processing to improve the over all accuracy.

We could expect that the content of the alternative texts are related to the text of the page itself. We would like to explore to what extent *descriptive* text could be topicwise related content of the web page and how this can potentially part of the features.

This paper only presents an approach to detect *undescriptive* use of alternative texts. In the future we will explore how results from the tests can be incorporated with the existing UWEM framework.

Acknowledgements

The eGovMon project[6] is co-funded by the Research Council of Norway under the VERDIKT program. Project no.: VERDIKT 183392/S10. The results in the eGovMon project and in this paper are all built on the results of an exciting team collaboration including researchers, practitioners and users.

References

1. Web Accessibility Benchmarking Cluster: Unified Web Evaluation Methodology (UWEM 1.2) (2007), http://www.wabcluster.org/uwem1_2/ (Retrieved November 4, 2009)
2. Nietzio, A., Ulltveit-Moe, N., Gjøsæter, T., Olsen, M.G., Snaprud, M.: Unified Web Evaluation Methodology Indicator Refinement (2007), http://www.eiao.net/resources (Retrieved November 4, 2009)
3. World Wide Web Consortium: Web Content Accessibility Guidelines 1.0. W3C Recommendation (May 5, 1999), http://www.w3.org/TR/WCAG10/ (Retrieved November 4, 2009)
4. World Wide Web Consortium: Web Content Accessibility Guidelines (WCAG) 2.0 (2008) http://www.w3.org/TR/REC-WCAG20-20081211/ (Retrieved November 4, 2009)
5. Slatin, J.: The art of ALT: toward a more accessible Web. Computers and Composition 18(1), 73–81 (2001)
6. Web Compliance Center of the Fraunhofer Institute for Applied Information Technology (FIT): Web compliance manager demo. (2009), http://www.imergo.com/home (Retrieved November 4, 2010)
7. Bigham, J.: Increasing web accessibility by automatically judging alternative text quality. In: Proceedings of the 12th international conference on Intelligent user interfaces, p. 352. ACM, New York (2007)
8. Hershkop, S.: Behavior-based email analysis with application to spam detection. PhD thesis, Citeseer (2006)

---

[6] http://www.egovmon.no

9. Fetterly, D., Manasse, M., Najork, M.: Spam, damn spam, and statistics: Using statistical analysis to locate spam web pages. In: Proceedings of the 7th International Workshop on the Web and Databases: colocated with ACM SIGMOD/PODS 2004, pp. 1–6. ACM, New York (2004)
10. Yu, B., Xu, Z.: A comparative study for content-based dynamic spam classification using four machine learning algorithms. Knowledge-Based Systems 21(4), 355–362 (2008)
11. Kolesnikov, O., Lee, W., Lipton, R.: Filtering spam using search engines. Technical report. Technical Report. GITCC-04-15, Georgia Tech., College of Computing, Georgia Institute of Technology, Atlanta, GA 30332 (2004-2005)
12. Chen, Z., Wu, O., Zhu, M., Hu, W.: A novel web page filtering system by combining texts and images. In: WI 2006: Proceedings of the 2006 IEEE/WIC/ACM International Conference on Web Intelligence, Washington, DC, USA, pp. 732–735. IEEE Computer Society, Los Alamitos (2006)
13. Duda, R., Hart, P., Stork, D.: Pattern classification. Citeseer (2001)
14. Solorio, T., Pérez-Coutino, M., et al.: A language independent method for question classification. In: Proceedings of the 20th international conference on Computational Linguistics, p. 1374. Association for Computational Linguistics (2004)
15. Craven, T.: Some features of alt text associated with images in web pages. Information Research 11 (2006)
16. Gutierrez, C., Loucopoulos, C., Reinsch, R.: Disability-accessibility of airlines Web sites for US reservations online. Journal of Air Transport Management 11(4), 239–247 (2005)
17. Han, J., Kamber, M.: Data mining: concepts and techniques. Morgan Kaufmann, San Francisco (2006)
18. Wikipedia: Cross-validation (statistics) — wikipedia, the free encyclopedia (2010) (online accessed January 28, 2010)
19. Duchrow, T., Shtatland, T., Guettler, D., Pivovarov, M., Kramer, S., Weissleder, R.: Enhancing navigation in biomedical databases by community voting and database-driven text classification. BMC bioinformatics 10(1), 317 (2009)

OASES: Online Accessibility Self Evaluation Service – A Web-Based Tool for Education Institutions to Self-Assess the Accessibility of Their Practice

Simon Ball, Alistair McNaught, Sue Watson, and Andrew Chandler

JISC TechDis Service, Higher Education Academy Building, Innovation Way
York YO10 5BR, U.K.
{simon,alistair,sue,andrew}@techdis.ac.uk

Abstract. The JISC TechDis service identified a need to move institutions forward in their accessibility 'maturity'. An 'Accessibility Maturity Model' was developed to highlight the stages of development that different institutions were exhibiting. In order to move institutions forward an Online Accessibility Self Evaluation Service (OASES) was created. OASES allows key managers in education institutions to evaluate their own practice, and to benchmark that practice against the anonymised results of their peers. This information can then be used to affect institutional policy and strategy to move their institution to a higher degree of 'accessibility maturity'.

Keywords: Online, accessibility, inclusion, self-evaluation, benchmarking.

1 Introduction

JISC TechDis [1] is funded to provide advice and guidance on accessibility and inclusion through technology to Further Education (FE) and Higher Education (HE) institutions at no charge. JISC TechDis research between 2007-2009 explored the extent to which accessibility and inclusion principles permeated throughout education institutions beyond the 'pockets' of good practice readily identified by research programmes such as the HEAT Scheme [2] and Molenet [3].

This research indicated that most institutions were comfortable with accessibility in traditional 'learner support' areas, but struggled to embed it in broader institutional policies (marketing, libraries, networks etc). In response to the research findings, JISC TechDis published a series of senior manager briefings on accessibility and inclusion [4]. Subsequent evaluation showed that few of these briefings reached their intended destination, even when they had been sent to all institutions.

The difficulties in getting evaluation feedback appeared to be symptomatic of a culture where accessibility is regarded as a niche issue rather than a mainstream quality improvement indicator. This perception is asserted with "no evidence, based on an outmoded model of organisational values that defines excellence (or indeed quality) without consideration of value-added organisational processes (such as accessibility)" [5]. JISC TechDis recognised that the only way to get a holistic approach to accessibility was to help staff with different management roles understand the unique

K. Miesenberger et al. (Eds.): ICCHP 2010, Part I, LNCS 6179, pp. 433–436, 2010.

influences they had on the 'student life cycle' and the extent to which they were embedding inclusive practice. Once a problem is recognised and owned, getting interest in solutions is relatively easy.

Developing a short, online, role-focused self-evaluation exercise would allow anonymous benchmarking against other institutions. There appeared to be nothing of this kind already in existence, or even any other senior manager-oriented accessibility guidance at all, despite a wealth of excellent inclusive practice resources [1][6][7][8]. Careful survey design gave JISC TechDis the opportunity to present guidance on simple, role-relevant, affordable, mainstream accessibility practices – the same guidance that featured in the senior manager briefings. Six stakeholder roles were identified: senior managers; library staff; IT / network managers; marketing managers; learning technologists / staff developers; and disability / additional learning support officers.

2 Methodology

To understand good practice, JISC TechDis needed to understand general practice first and this was achieved by site visits, surveys of institutional websites, regional forums and online workshops with communities of practice.

The OASES pilot was created using the Survey Monkey online questionnaire generator. The questions were oriented around key issues identified in the research and covered in the senior manager briefings. Each of the six role-themed surveys contained around 20-25 questions and could be completed in about 30 mins, which in the pilots were within a synchronous, facilitated 90 minute online session. At the end of each pilot session the composite results were shared and discussed in real time. The experience gained in these sessions allowed JISC TechDis to refine the questions and the accompanying guidance to the point that video clips could be used to replace live facilitation, and present automated summaries of all previous responses (anonymised) for benchmarking purposes. This opens up many more options for participation as an individual (e.g. head of library), a regional community of practice (e.g. library forum) or an institutional cross-role management group (e.g. librarian with IT, disability advisor and marketing manager).

3 Results

Ninety-Eight different FE and HE institutions took part in the facilitated live pilot sessions. Reports on the role-related data from the pilots indicated a 'spiky profile' for practices - some areas of accessible practice, but most institutions inconsistent across the practices and policies surveyed. Many respondees were surprised at what they didn't know or couldn't find – in areas that were clearly under their direct influence. One of the key values of the work was in identifying areas where responsibilities genuinely overlapped and progress is only possible collaboratively. A significant proportion of participants, who believed their institution to be very advanced in terms of support for disabled learners, were surprised to find the gap between specific support and embedded practice. Also significant was the dearth of online training provision, despite a wealth of available free resources.

4 Discussion

It was evident from the original senior manager briefings that accessibility has not yet fully permeated institutions at policy level. This was supported by another piece of research [9] which showed that an inclusive culture can be most effectively implemented when there is coherence across different institutional policies. Therefore there needs to be a shift from policies that create and accommodate specific support for disabled people (to help them overcome institutional barriers) to policies that focus on reducing the institutional barriers in the first place and making mainstream provision and activities more accessible. A focus on reducing barriers requires a more strategic approach in which senior managers are the critical stakeholder - only they can ensure strategies are both joined up and pragmatic, involving practice as well as aspiration.

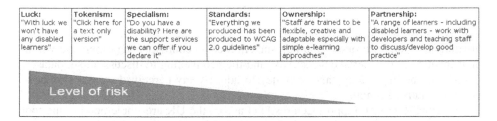

Luck:	Tokenism:	Specialism:	Standards:	Ownership:	Partnership:
"With luck we won't have any disabled learners"	"Click here for a text only version"	"Do you have a disability? Here are the support services we can offer if you declare it"	"Everything we produced has been produced to WCAG 2.0 guidelines"	"Staff are trained to be flexible, creative and adaptable especially with simple e-learning approaches"	"A range of learners - including disabled learners - work with developers and teaching staff to discuss/develop good practice"

Level of risk

Fig. 1. The Accessibility Maturity Model

The Accessibility Maturity Model describes the different institutional approaches to accessibility derived from the research. The OASES tool is designed to move the institutions towards the right hand side of the model by empowering key stakeholders who undertake the survey to recognise their role in embedding accessibility. This helps support disabled students, increases quality and flexibility of provision and reduces the risk of litigation.

The 'Luck' stage of development was commonplace prior to the UK Disability Discrimination Act (DDA) [10] and can be evidenced by the relatively small number of disabled students in UK higher education at that time. Following the DDA, many institutions moved to a 'Tokenistic' approach, providing generic alternatives for some disabled users but showing no subtlety or understanding of user need. Data from the pilot OASES projects suggests many UK institutions are still at the 'Specialism' stage. Students who declare a disability are provided with a range of support services, but this is usually at the expense of mainstream awareness and flexibility. Many institutions have moved to a 'Standards' approach, where accessibility measures are implemented against objective checklists rather than focusing on meeting user need. This approach may prove counter-productive; insisting on all resources being fully accessible means the value-added potential of partially accessible resources for specific users is lost. The most accessible institutions in the UK are now embedding the 'Ownership' level of maturity – all staff, whatever their role are being encouraged to consider their responsibilities in terms of accessibility, and mainstream teaching is being redesigned to accommodate as many user needs as possible. A few institutions are now beginning to develop a 'Partnership' level of maturity with disabled staff and students advising senior managers in developing key policies, and with those policies in turn embedding a culture of delivering fully inclusive mainstream education.

As the concept of e-maturity gains traction in UK education and online self assessment becomes a recognised quality assurance process (e.g. the Becta Generator), the role of tools like OASES becomes increasingly important at providing a reality check that is simultaneously able to signpost practical ways of embedding accessibility. Mature accessibility practice is good for all users, not just disabled ones.

5 Future Work

The OASES resource is being utilised by the six role groups and marketing activities have now begun to promote the resource to UK HE and FE institutions. There is no reason to assume that it would not also be beneficial to people working in institutions outside the UK. An early evaluation of the ways in which it is being used within institutions has shown that several institutions are already using OASES as a cross-institutional tool, with one of the key stakeholders encouraging the other five within their institution to undertake the survey, and then convening to discuss all six datasets in order to modify strategy and/or policy to address any perceived weaknesses or to build on relative strengths.

The JISC Regional Support Centres [11] across the UK are implementing the tool into their support programmes for the key stakeholder roles covered in the resource.

References

1. JISC TechDis, http://www.techdis.ac.uk
2. HEAT Scheme, http://www.techdis.ac.uk/getheatscheme
3. Molenet, http://www.molenet.org.uk
4. McNaught, A.: JISC TechDis Senior Management Briefings (2007),
   http://www.techdis.ac.uk/getbriefings
5. Williams, D.A., Berger, J.B., McClendon, S.A.: Toward a Model of Inclusive Excellence and Change in Postsecondary Institutions. One in a series of three papers commissioned as part of the Making Excellence Inclusive Initiative. Association of American Colleges and Universities (2005)
6. Simpson, A.: Teachability: Accessible Curriculum for Students with Disabilities. University of Strathclyde (2005), http://www.teachability.strath.ac.uk
7. BRITE: Beattie Resources for Inclusiveness in Technology and Education,
   http://www.brite.ac.uk
8. Open University: Making Your Teaching Inclusive (2006), http://bit.ly/arxmg3
9. Ball, S.: Technology Change for Inclusion: 12 Steps Towards Embedding Inclusive Practice with Technology as a Whole Institution Culture in UK Higher Education. JISC TechDis (2009), http://www.techdis.ac.uk/gettci
10. UK Disability Discrimination Act (1995),
    http://www.opsi.gov.uk/acts/acts1995/ukpga_19950050_en_1
11. JISC Regional Support Centres,
    http://www.jisc.ac.uk/whatwedo/services/as_rsc/rsc_home.aspx

Analysis and Evaluation of the Accessibility to Visual Information in Web Pages

Youssef Bou Issa, Mustapha Mojahid, Bernard Oriola, and Nadine Vigouroux

IRIT, Equipe IHCS, Université Paul Sabatier, 118 Route de Narbonne,
F-31062 Toulouse, Cedex 9
{bou,mojahid,oriola,vigourou}@irit.fr

Abstract. Blind persons do not get any information related to the visual arrangement or the design of objects in a web page. The objective of this paper is to identify this information and to prove that the lack of access to this visual information leads consequently to a lack of access to the informational content. We call "enhanced accessibility" accessibility to this type of information.

Keywords: Web Accessibility, visual information, enhanced accessibility, WCAG2.0.

1 Introduction

Many efforts that were made in the web accessibility focused on elaborating guidelines that must be considered in creating an accessible website and in testing it. The WAI (Web Accessibility Initiative) of the W3C (World Wide Web Consortium) published in this regard the WCAG2.0 (Web Content Accessibility Guidelines [3]). Among the requirements of these guidelines, webmasters should provide textual alternatives to all images, animations and non textual content in the purpose of revealing hidden visual information.

Nevertheless, we follow a different approach of accessibility: we define elementary visual objects those that are recognized using visual and/or lexical cues. Groupings of these visual objects are identified according to the principle of resemblance and difference [1] and using visual and/or lexical cues. The essential objective is to identify these objects (elementary or groups) and to define the contextual relations between each other (relations between objects inside groups and relations between groups).

The objective of this paper is to prove that the lack of access to this visual information (objects, cues, relations) leads consequently to a lack of access to the informational content. We call "enhanced accessibility" accessibility to this type of information.

Therefore, in our study, we focus on this level of web accessibility that is not totally taken into consideration by the W3C. In order to confirm our hypothesis we analyze a set of seven well formed websites that are compliant to the WCAG guidelines. The purpose of this analysis is to:

1. Identify the visual objects and visual cues in a web page;
2. Determine which might cause a problem in regards to our enhanced accessibility issue;

K. Miesenberger et al. (Eds.): ICCHP 2010, Part I, LNCS 6179, pp. 437–443, 2010.
© Springer-Verlag Berlin Heidelberg 2010

3. Validate our hypothesis by an experiment on these websites to see if this visual information is captured by the blind using a standard screen reader and to prove that access to these cues is essential to the overall comprehension of the web page.

The objective of this paper is to analyze and to evaluate the accessibility of the visual information contained in the selected seven tourism websites of five different European countries. This paper is divided into two sections: in the first section, we present the visual arrangement of the selected web pages in order to identify the visual objects and the visual groups in these pages that may present the problem of the enhanced accessibility.

The accessibility of these studied web pages has been verified according to WCAG standards using the WAVE tool [2] in order to study the visual objects that are still hidden to the blind, their properties, and the implicit visual and contextual relations that rely between these objects even in the W3C compliant pages.

Then, we present the experiment of these web pages with blind users. With this test, we can see if the visual cues are captured by the blind using common tools such as the screen reader Jaws. Finally, we will spot the essential visual objects necessary to the overall understanding of the page.

2 Accessibility Verification and Analysis of the Visual Content of Web Pages

We chose to analyze tourism websites. The choice is based on: (a) the accordance with European laws: tourism websites that are supposed to be accessible to the blind because it has become a requirement in all countries of the European Union to make their public websites accessible to everyone, especially people with visual impairments [3]; (b) the continuation of the psychological study of Etcheverry et al. (2007) [4] concerning the behavioral difference in navigation processing between French users with different ages. Therefore, these sites (Nice, Biarritz, Paris, Portugal, Germany, Britain, and Holland) [1]are supposed accessible according to the W3C guidelines (2008) [5]. We have reviewed these sites relatively to W3C guidelines in order to eventually move to a next level of accessibility not treated by the W3C. We have verified their accessibility with the help of WAVE free tool from webAim [2]. The version WAVE 4.0 helps to evaluates web page, referring to several recommendations of WCAG 2.0 and Section 508 (USA) [6]. The evaluation using WAVE showed that these websites are accessible with minor accessibility alerts that do not affect the overall accessibility of the websites.

We then analyzed the accessibility to the visual information in web pages in order to identify objects, cues, visual and contextual relationships that could pose a problem in regard to our "enhanced accessibility". We proceeded throughout a co-exploration phase between a sighted user and a blind who is expert in accessibility issues. The first objective was to determine whether the content read by Jaws matched the verbal

---

[1] Website of nice: http://nicetourisme.com, website of Biarritz: http://biarritz.fr, website of paris http://parisinfo.com, website of Portugal: http://visitportugal.com, website of germany: http://allemange-tourisme.com, website of Britain: http://visitbritain.com, website of Holland: http://holland.com

description, and above all, to see whether the blind could capture the visual object group that can be seen by the sighted person. The goal was also to see the shortcomings of Jaws in taking into account the visual presentation that clarifies or increases accessibility as intended by the author of the site.

This analysis has enabled us to detect problems that a blind person might be facing. This is particularly the essential information needed for understanding the overall structure of the page, the organization of visual groupings within the page, and the role of each group often distinguished by a visual character. As we said above, we made the study on seven different websites, but in the following, we illustrate it with examples from two of them (Germany and Britain). This study of the different websites, allowed discerning the objects and groups that constitute a web page, and the relations linking them.

2.1 Groupings

Sections of a web page are often visually arranged in groupings that have the same background color, the same text font family, and/or the same font size, so that they can be easily distinguished visually. For example we present the visual groupings in the home page of the visitbrain site. These groups are distinguished by common formatting and specific colors, Fig. 1. We consider the following groups:

Grouping A: contains the **main menu** at the top of the homepage: the objects of this group are text links. These objects are arranged linearly one beside the other, and are only distinguished from other elements **by visual indications**: the text color, the background color, the size and font of characters.

Fig. 1. Examples of Visual groupings in the home page of the visitbritain website

Grouping C: Content - animation of a series of images arranged one beside the other below the main image that is magnification (zoom) of an image of the series. Inside the main image, there is a text that ends with a link to another page of this site. A blind could not know that the main image is a **zoom** of an image **below**. These relationships between objects (an object is a **zoom** of the other, an object is **below** the other...) and the entire contents of this grouping are nevertheless important for understanding the overall structure of the page.

Grouping D: map of Great Britain: when we click on a region on the map, it is highlighted in a visual way. Note that regions are only distinguished by visual indications such as the different colors. The visual effect would not be perceived by users of screen readers.

Grouping F: Secondary drop down **menu** (*liens utiles*): it appears only when we click in the area of selection, but a standard screen reader would read it as part of the page. Its location would not be detected by the blind.

2.2 A Particular Case of Groupings: Menus

It may be the main menu of the page, or a sub-menu. The main menu is often visually arranged in an array of hyperlinks consisting of a row and several columns. The columns may have the same background color or colors. The sub-menu can be arranged horizontally or vertically as a drop-down menu. It can be distinguished from the main menu with the text color, background color, size or properties of the text (bold or not). Access to these menus present the problem of sequential read menus by the blind, with the difficulty of distinguishing between different levels of the menu since this distinction or the tree is done with visual properties such as color. For example, as we have seen in the site of Great Britain, the menu to the right has a tree form that could not be detected by a screen reader unless when using multilevel bullets. In fact, according to Rule 4.1 of WCAG, if the content is not structured syntactically via the markup language, then it is not accessible. For example, the distinction between

Fig. 2. Right menu of the homepage of the site visitbritain.fr

Boutique en ligne and *transport* is purely visual (Fig.2): different colors of text and background, and different sizes and fonts. Thus, a blind user perceives these two links in the same level, although visually they are of different levels. This would adversely affect overall understanding of the page.

Also, in the website of Germany, the main menu consists of items presented horizontally in a table with the same background color, but the lower side of each cell has different color than the others. This same color, but with a contrast, indicates that the cursor is placed on a given cell, Fig. 3.

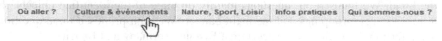

Fig. 3. Main menu of the website of Germany

2.3 Relations

Each object has neighborly relations with other objects. These relations can exist between objects inside a grouping or between the groupings. We can talk about visual geometric relations "left, right, top, bottom", objects containing several objects, two or more objects with an area of intersection. We can see that these relations are denoted by layout configurations and properties. These relations involve: (1) **implicit visual relations**: menus are visually broken down into menus and sub-menus with a visual tree, while for the blind side, no relation can be detected: The Grouping A of the Fig. 1 shows the items of the main menu that are visually broken into submenus; (2) **implicit contextual relations** (the text description of a certain image the Grouping E is a typical example concerning the contextual relations between the text and the image. As well for the Grouping D, in which there is a contextual relation between the text "London" and its corresponding position in the map).

3 Testing Access to the Identified Visual Information: The Observation

The analyzed web pages consist of several items and visual groups. We presume that the organization of these objects and their relations are essential to understanding the content. We then wanted to study the ability of the blind user to capture the visual information proposed by the author of a website, and this by using the screen reader Jaws. We also sought to test whether the blind can identify the geometric and contextual relations between these objects and see if he could identify them by the means of lexical or layout criteria.

The development of tasks to be performed by the blind required several steps before reaching the final form of the survey.

3.1 The Series of Tasks

The experiment was proposed to 5 blind subjects including 4 blind youth and a person of 59 years. They are experts on the use of computers, i.e. people who use computers and therefore the Internet to perform daily tasks (emails, online shopping, booking, consulting bank accounts, out of telephone bills ...). They are also experts in Jaws and its various features. These topics are most suitable for our experiment. We found that the number of 5 subjects is sufficient, since the answers converged. Indeed, as shown in the two studies by Nielsen [7], making the case study with a subject can address between 28 and 30% of problems. The more we repeated the test with additional subjects, the more we will get to increase the number of discussed problems. Five subjects could reach 85% of problems.

We have proposed a series of questions to the blind users. We avoided questions that require a memorization time and we eliminated the terminology not understood by the blind. We focused our questions mainly on three of the identified objects: the main menu items, groupings and the main banner. We then proposed three questionnaires, referring to the three websites: Great Britain, Germany and Biarritz.

3.2 The Results

The following tables present the main results of the experiment. We saw that the majority of the users could not identify the sub menu or the main banner, and could not determine any visual relation between objects.

Table 1. The results of the test with the blind subjects

Visual object	Totally identified (n/5)	Partially identified (n/5)	Relation	Identified (n/5)
Main menu	3	2	Implicit contextual relations	4
Sub menu	2	0		
main banner	0	0	Implicit visual relations	0

The spotted results allow us to assert that even if the web page conforms to the WCAG, accessibility to objects and visual groups is unclear. In addition to the recommendations of the W3C, one must consider a second level of accessibility that we have called "enhanced accessibility". This second level should take into consideration the visual information, the objects and their arrangement in the web page, which is essential for the understanding of the web page. Screen readers cannot enable the accessibility and the understanding of visual information. In fact, at the request of a web page, the visitor would face a number of important visual cues. Accessing such objects using the existing tools constitutes an information overload.

4   Conclusion

At the request of a web page, the Internet user, as we have seen, would face a significant amount of information. All objects, entities and relations constitute an overload of information. For a blind user, the field of perception is limited; this overload of data must then be taken into consideration. A solution would be to divide the information into two levels of details; we call the view displayed to the blind user as the First Glance (FG). The first level would contain the overall page structure, identification of objects with coordinates, shape, space an object occupies on the page, and the degree of importance of an object relatively to another. The second level would contain more detailed objects on the page, including a representation of implicit contextual relationships between objects. In the continuation, we propose a language to formalize the objects with features to make them explicit. The system will extract objects, their visual properties and relationships to make a formal endorsement to a more accessible page. The objective is to prepare the data to be compatible with several types of outputs and based on several forms: oral and tactile modalities in our study or the combination of the two methods, by creating rules for inter-modality [8].

References

1. Virbel, J.: The Contribution of Linguistic Knowledge to the Interpretation of Text Structure in Structured Docments. In: André, J., Quint, V., Furuta, R. (eds.). Cambridge University Press, Cambridge (1988)
2. WAVE4.0, Web Accessibility Evaluation tool, http://wave.webaim.org/
3. Support-EAM European program, supporting the creation of an eAccessibility Mark, http://www.support-eam.org/
4. Etcheverry, I., Terrier, P., Marquie, J.C.: 1. Recherche d'information sur internet, influence de l'âge et des tâches de navigation sur la mémorisation épisodique; Congrès de la Société Française de Psychologie (2007)
5. Web Content Accessibility Guidelines, W3C recommendation (December 11, 2008), http://www.w3.org/TR/WCAG20/
6. Section 508 Amendment of the Rehabilitation Act, United States of America, http://www.section508.gov/
7. Nielsen, J.: Estimating the number of subjects needed for a thinking aloud test. International Journal of Human-Computer Studies 41(3), 385–397 (1994)
8. Bou Issa, Y., Mojahid, M., Oriola, B., Vigouroux, N.: Accessibility for the Blind: Rendering the Layout of the Web Page for a Tactile Experience. In: European Conference for the Advancement of Assistive Technology in Europ. (AAATE 2009), Florence, Italie (2009)

User Testing of Google Reader and RIA Complexity – A Warning

Joshue O. Connor

NCBI Centre For Inclusive Technology (CFIT), National Council for the Blind of Ireland,
Dublin, Ireland
joshue.oconnor@cfit.ie

Abstract. There are many APIs and toolkits available in the wild today that allow developers to build rich sophisticated Web Applications. There are a variety of frameworks and toolkits at use in the wild. While these platforms - in
principle - offer the promise of greater functionality and more robust interoperability they also cast a potential shadow of greater complexity and how will
this complexity then impact on the user experience for people with disabilities?
In tandem, there are many guidelines designed to help make inclusive, accessible and usable designs a reality such as the principles of Universal Design, the
WCAG and other international usability standards. [1][2][3].

So how can we ensure that when we build complex Rich Internet Applications (RIAs) that they can be easily used by the widest possible audience,
including older people and people with disabilities? A well-established method
is to conduct a user test.

Keywords: (e)Accessibility and Usability, eInclusion, HCI and Non Classical
Interfaces, User Centered Design and User Involvement.

1 Methodology

The user test took place in the NCBI Centre for Inclusive Technology (CFIT) usability lab and is very informal. There is a combination of both a "Think Aloud" usability
methodology and "Co-discovery" methodology used in the test. [4] [5]

An RIA (Google Reader) was used therefore as a test case for an experienced
screen reader user to put through its paces in the NCBI Centre for Inclusive Technology (CFIT) usability lab. The aim was to examine the usability of this popular RIA by
a user of AT, in this case a screen reader.

1.1 Evaluation Criteria

The main evaluation criteria were:

1) Is the application basically usable by a blind screen reader user?
2) Are the main application controls easily discoverable?
3) Are all the main functions of the site usable by a blind screen reader user?

K. Miesenberger et al. (Eds.): ICCHP 2010, Part I, LNCS 6179, pp. 444–448, 2010.
© Springer-Verlag Berlin Heidelberg 2010

4) The complexity of coming to terms with use of the application and the level of cognitive load on the user.
5) Is the user experience pleasant?
6) Are there conflicts with current AT controls for web application?
7) *Will the user have to learn more complex ways of navigation or different modes of interaction? [6]*

So how did the application perform? Watch the video and find out! Download the "User Testing of RIA" Video [WMV, 104.5 Mb] from the NCBI Centre for Inclusive Technology website. [7]

1.2 The RIA Toolkit

WAI-ARIA, the Accessible Rich Internet Applications Suite, defines a way to make Web content and Web applications more accessible to people with disabilities. It especially helps with dynamic content and advanced user interface controls developed with Ajax, HTML, JavaScript, and related technologies. Currently certain functionality used in Web sites is not available to some users with disabilities, especially people who rely on screen readers and people who cannot use a mouse. WAI-ARIA addresses these accessibility challenges, for example, by defining new ways for functionality to be provided to assistive technology. With WAI-ARIA, developers can make advanced Web applications accessible and usable to people with disabilities. *[8]*

Authors Note:
While the purpose of the test was originally to explore the use of WAI-ARIA in the wild, in this case during the test it was found that the Google Reader contains only a very small amount of WAI-ARIA functionality. Therefore it is best to view the test really as an examination of the user experience for a blind screen reader user when using an RIA, and not solely as an exploration, or critique, of WAI-ARIA.

1.3 The AxsJAX Accessibility Framework

AxsJAX (a Google Accessibility Framework) injects accessibility enhancements as defined by W3C WAI-ARIA. In order to be able to use AxsJAX and WAI-ARIA you need:

1) A current Web browser that supports W3C ARIA.
2) Adaptive technologies that respond correctly to the accessibility enhancements introduced by W3C ARIA.
3) Also, many of the enhancements injected by AxsJAX depend on support for live regions a feature that enables adaptive technologies like screen readers and self-voicing browsers deal correctly with asynchronous updates to portions of a Web page.

Note: The Google Reader however does not contain any live regions. [9]

The test participant used JAWS 10, Internet Explorer 8 and Firefox version 3.5 and 3.2.

2 Test Outcomes and Observations

The following are observations from the user test by the author.

- Labeling of elements was generally poor. This is totally avoidable and also a surprise considering the sophistication of the interface and these basic accessibility errors are easily avoidable.
- Google reader is an interesting example of a great idea that is poorly executed. In terms of intuitive RIA usability it does not perform well. When the enhanced version is activated there is nothing to indicate what you have to do to access this extra functionality. Even if the link for *'Click here for ARIA enhanced interface'* had the extra instructive text similar to *'Press * for list of commands'* that would have made the whole experience much easier for the user by informing them that some extra action was needed from them in order to get the most out of the accessible interface functionality.
- However, once the user has climbed the steep learning curve and has been orientated the interface does come into its own – but that is a steep curve! Therefore, it cannot be considered to be very accessible or usable without great commitment on the part of the user. Most users would be likely to abandon the application in favor of a simpler solution.
- The keyboard command to give the user the list of short cut keys in Google Reader does not work with JAWS 10, in virtual PC mode. Or in the common mode used by many blind screen reader users. The user must de-activate the PC Cursor *(Insert+Z)* and toggle between different modes to successfully interact with the interface itself and to take advantage of the advanced functionality. This is far too complicated. It is very likely that the more inexperienced AT user will be put off using this kind of applications due to this switching of modes. However, is this the shape of things to come, as other RIAs follow suit? Or is this a singular example of how not to implement RIA functionality?
- There were problems with Help function. Pressing the JAWS help key *(Insert +F1)* is the usual way of accessing help information by added text to the buffer. In this case the text was not placed in virtual buffer- so the user tester was confused as to it was coming from. Therefore there is an inconsistency with how screen reader help and support works (with JAWS) and any other screen readers that use a virtual buffer.
- The user testers comments *"It's a different experience – turning off the virtual cursor"* and *"I would like to see a way of interacting with the virtual cursor"* were very interesting and gave an insight into how the user feels like he is moving into a new mode of browsing. The user was not notified that the Virtual Cursor had to be off in some instances, such as when using the advanced functionality.
- In Internet Explorer when the virtual cursor is off the enhanced features won't work. In Firefox it is working, but the buttons won't work properly with the Virtual Cursor on. The average user will just not be able to deal with changing Virtual Cursor – on and off – on top of the complexity of learning extra commands.

- There were also inconsistencies – in different browsers – and Virtual Cursor settings gave certain elements focus and others where ignored/invisible.
- JAWS didn't go into 'Forms mode' when the "add a subscription" button was activated in Firefox.
- Use of the text in the UI *"Add a subscription button on the left"* is useless and in breach of WCAG guidance.
- Focus issues – the screen reader user cannot read character by character easily, due to virtual cursor being turned off. This effects how the user can interact with content in a very disruptive way.
- Will the concept of layered commands be an option to deal with more complex Web Applications in the future (such as in JAWS 11)? [10]

2.1 Results

While viewing the results with the initial evaluation criteria in mind, we can come to the conclusion that while there are aspects of the application that are accessible, the usability of the RIA leaves a lot to be desired. What is interesting is that the test participant (my friend and colleague Stuart Lawler) is an expert power user, comparing his experience that what a user with a moderate or basic level of Assistive Technology may experience - really puts this test into context even though it is only illustrative of the potential complexity of poorly implemented accessibility features. It is by no means exhaustive, or conclusive but indicative.

This usability study is a classic example of where we searched for 'X' but found 'Y'. As we can see from the above highlighted issues, this research highlights the problems that could arise when technology does not successfully mediate complexity and is a salient warning of how not to build a UI that is to successfully cater for the diverse needs of people with disabilities.

What this very informal test does, is illustrate that even with the best of intentions, the latest API, and some cutting edge accessibility markup a design can still go horribly wrong and be virtually unusable to only the most persistent. What is disappointing is that AxsJAX is an explicit accessibility framework.

The test highlights the importance of user testing of RIAs, of constantly considering the diverse needs of users with disabilities and involving them in the development process.

References

1. Centre for Universal Design,
   http://www.design.ncsu.edu/cud/about_ud/about_ud.htm
2. Web Content Accessibility Guidelines (WCAG),
   http://www.w3.org/WAI/intro/wcag.php
3. International standards for HCI and usability,
   http://www.usabilitynet.org/tools/r_international.htm
4. Virzi, R.A., Sorce, J.F., Herbert, L.B.: A Comparison of Three Usability Evaluation Methods: Heuristic, Think-Aloud, and Performance Testing. Human Factors and Ergonomics Society Annual Meeting Proceedings, Computer Systems, 309–313

5. Buur, J., Bagger, K.: Replacing usability testing with user dialogueSource. Communications of the ACM archive 42(5), 63–66 (1999)
6. CFIT User Testing, http://www.cfit.ie/user-testing
7. User Testing Video Download, http://www.cfit.ie/video/Usability_RIAs_CFIT.wmv
8. WAI-ARIA, http://www.w3.org/WAI/intro/aria
9. AXSJAX Framework, http://code.google.com/p/google-axsjax/
10. Whats new in JAWS 11, http://www.freedomscientific.com/downloads/jaws/JAWS-whats-new.asp

Analyzing Effects of Web Accessibility – A Framework to Determine Changes in Website Traffic and Success

Rudolf Hartjes and Christine Strauss

University of Vienna, Department of Business Studies
Brünner Straße 72, 1210 Vienna, Austria
{rudolf.hartjes,christine.strauss}@univie.ac.at

Abstract. The potential of web accessibility to boost a website's traffic numbers and quality is believed to be a major motivation for website operators to implement web accessibility. In this paper we present a long-term framework for the measurement of such improvements, relying on multiple examination objects. This paper comprises a detailed specification of relevant key performance indicators, relevant traffic sources, a monitoring and evaluation schedule as well as an outlook on the strategic values of this framework.

1 Introduction

Despite various efforts to demonstrate the importance of web accessibility for the entire set of internet users, the benefits of an accessible website are primarily perceived in a social and ethical context [1]. Due to the lack of solid indicators for business-relevant implications of web accessibility only limited research on the economic benefits of accessible websites have been performed so far. Prior qualitative studies [2] have shown that, in order to implement web accessibility, decision makers are in need of motivations, may they be of technical, social or economical nature.

Furthermore, earlier quantitative/empirical research on short-term implications of a website's success due to accessibility implementation indicated significant improvements regarding search-engine generated traffic as well as visitor behavior [3].

However, as these quantitative findings were based on one single research object, the results were not applicable in a generalized context. Therefore, this paper presents a framework that enables systematic analysis for the measurement of changes in website success due to web accessibility implementation. The framework focuses on the analysis of both visitor and search engine indexing behavior, in order to provide solid key figures on a website's economical changes and as a consequence support transparency in decision making.

K. Miesenberger et al. (Eds.): ICCHP 2010, Part I, LNCS 6179, pp. 449–455, 2010.
© Springer-Verlag Berlin Heidelberg 2010

2   State of the Art

So far, the economical aspect of web accessibility has been covered from various viewpoints. For one thing, Heerdt et al. suggest estimated relative savings for accessible websites between 12% and 35% of the website's costs [4], taking into account the total accessibility costs depending on enterprise size and website complexity. For another thing, accessible websites are believed to increase a customers' positive perception of an organization due to increased trust and transparency [5], and therefore induce image ameliorations [6]. However, one of the most significant requirements for a website to be a successful one in economical terms is a high-quality visitor traffic, which enables companies to generate additional revenue by exploiting a larger market [7].

Thus, improvements in visitor behavior are likely to generate additional revenue, as improvements in search engine behavior are likely to generate more visitors. These improvements mostly rest upon the indexing of not just more but more *relevant* website content. For example, if a website holds several images which are correctly described via alternative text (ALT-Text), a blind user as well as a search engine are able to determine the image's content without actually *seeing* the picture. Prior research [3] suggests, that accessible website content is being indexed by search engines in a more loyal way regarding its' context, i.e., the website will be found more often and with an increased regularity by those users who will get exactly the information they intend to find by the use of a search engine.

3   Framework

3.1   Purpose and Design

The proposed framework supports decision makers with a detailed course of action to perform a systematic analysis to measure changes in website success due to web accessibility implementation. The framework aims at suggesting a concise and uniform approach to retrieve solid empirical data based on a time series analysis. Core elements of the framework are (i) three different traffic sources, measured by (ii) seven key performance indicators reflecting the behavior of visitors and search engines and (iii) an adaptable monitoring and evaluation schedule that allows a short term as well as a long term benchmarking.

3.2   Traffic Sources and Key Performance Indicators

Collecting relevant data aims at a comparison of web metrics before and after the implementation of web accessibility on a particular web presence. The proposed framework is based on two units of analysis (cf. [8]): the behavior of visitors (e.g., the duration of a visit, the users' activity during a visit or the overall bounce rate of visitors) and the behavior of search engines (e.g., the amount of indexed content or number of relevant keywords) before and after the implementation of

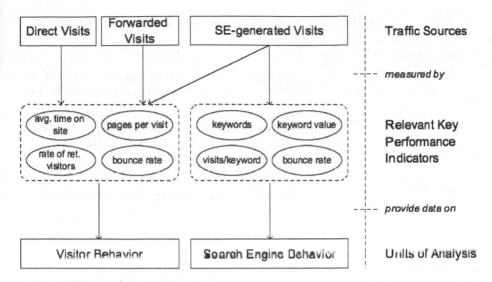

Fig. 1. Traffic sources and their relevant set of key performance indicators providing data on visitor and search engine behavior

web accessibility on a particular website. Both units of analysis are provided with data from several instances of key performance indicators and website metrics, respectively, which are partially overlapping; they were selected due to their quantitative and empirical nature.

Figure 1 describes the three different traffic sources (direct visits, forwarded visits and search engine generated visits) that provide data on the several instances of the key performance indicators. As direct and forwarded visits are generated without utilization of a search engine, they provide data on visitor behavior but not on search engine behavior. The third traffic source, search engine generated visits, serves both units of analysis.

Each traffic source is measured by its own set of relevant key performance indicators (KPI). For example, the KPI *pages per visit* would encompass three different values for each traffic source and apply to visitor behavior, whereas the KPI *keyword value* would solely encompass one value given by the source of search engine generated visits and therefore exclusively apply to search engine behavior. The KPI *bounce rate* (intersecting, as described in Table 1) would collect data from all three traffic sources and serve both units of analysis, as it is believed to provide insight on the context loyalty of search engine results, as well as on how direct and forwarded visitors experience their first impression of a website[1].

The distinction between the traffic sources was drawn in order to generate a variety of solid data, as well as to elaborate nuances in user behavior.

---

[1] The first impression of a website is often determined by factors such as navigation mechanisms, site structure, etc.

Table 1. Key performance indicators associated with each unit of analysis

Visitor behavior	intersecting	SE behavior	Use/Description
		Keywords	Amount of keywords entered by users in search engines that lead to a visit
		Keyword Value	Average position of the 10 most traffic generating keywords in search engine results
		Visits per Keyword	Average number of visits generated per average number of keywords
	Bounce Rate		Rate of visitors leaving the website on entry without navigating to any other page
Average Time on Site			Average time spent on website during a visit while performing several actions
Pages per Visit			Average number of pages accessed by visitors during their visit
Rate of Returning Visits			Rate of visits entering the website not for the first time

Table 1 lists the designated web metrics/key performance indicators and their relation to each unit of analysis, i.e., visitor behavior and search engine (SE) behavior.

As table 1 shows, most of the key performance indicators are referencing to the entity of a *visit* rather than to a visitor although the framework is focused on the visitor's behavior (beside search engine behavior). This differentiation was made due to the fact that the entity of a visitor is inconsistent with several key performance indicators. For example, if a visitor accesses a website and returns later for a second visit, he/she would be both, a new visitor *and* a returning visitor. This would lead to a falsified rate of returning visitors. Therefore the entity of a *visit* (performed by a visitor) allows a clear distinction and is expected to generate solid data.

The proposed framework focuses on the behavior of visitors and search engines rather than on the sole amount of visitors. Nevertheless, gaining insight into search engine indexing behavior (such as how the implementation of web accessibility affects a website's ranking on search engine result pages) enables decision makers to draw conclusions on how the number of visitors is likely to change after a successful accessibility implementation[2].

---

[2] The process of such an implementation results in a website complying with the Web Content Accessibility Guidelines 2.0 "Double A".

3.3   Monitoring and Evaluation Schedule

To provide reliable empirical data influences from seasonal or other external traffic volatility should be avoided or kept to a minimum. Therefore, the analysis of each case consists of three analysis phases (Figure 2)[3].

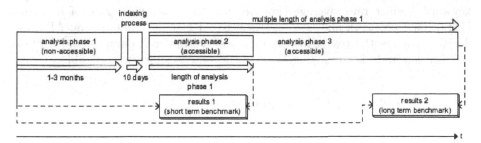

Fig. 2. Monitoring and Evaluation Schedule

During Analysis Phase 1 (AP1) data is collected from the non-accessible version of a website; the phase starts one to three months before (re)launching the accessible website. Three months is advisable but not a strict necessity due to the fact that AP1 is positioned at the very end of the inaccessible website's life-cycle, thus, at this point its content should already be extensively indexed by search engines.

In real applications the actual length of AP1 very often is determined by the duration of the accessibility implementation work but should not fall below a minimum length of one month to ensure that sufficient reference data is recorded.

Between the end of AP1 and the start of Analysis Phase 2 (AP2) a period of 10 days should be scheduled. Such duration is long enough to provide search engines with sufficient time to index first portions of the new website content but at the same time short enough to avoid seasonal traffic bias between AP1 and AP2. The length of AP2 should equal the length of AP1. Analysis Phase 3 (AP3) shares the same start time as AP2, but has a longer duration, due to the fact that the entire accessible content will be indexed by search engines not at once but rather as a continuous process over time, as prior research suggests [3]. The total length of AP3 (enclosing AP2) should be a multiple of AP1 and cover an entire seasonal cycle.

3.4   Results

Comparing the values of the key performance indicators during AP1 with those in AP2 enables the determination of first preliminary results that can serve as a benchmark for the evaluation of AP3 (Figure 2). Those results represent a quick

---

[3] The time intervals given refer to a medium sized website of a small/medium enterprise (SME); they are meant to provide a general approach that covers the majority of cases.

rough evaluation of the effects initiated by web accessibility. The comparison of AP1 and AP3 is expected to show long term developments in visitor and search engine behavior (see *results 2* in Figure 2) due to accessibility. The length of the observation phase after web accessibility implementation (AP3) enables detailed analysis of the quality development over time.

Furthermore, if restricted to relative key performance indicators (visits per keyword, bounce rate, average time on site, pages per visit, rate of returning visits) our framework allows comparison to AP1 at any time during AP3. For decision makers the results of the analysis provide transparency and support justification in decision making, e.g., on the expenses for the accessible website.

4   Conclusion and Perspective

Unlike inaccessible websites, accessible ones are found to require earlier and higher investments at the time of their creation [4]; hence decision makers are provided with data on how and when the additional investment will pay off. In order to generate solid empirical data, the proposed framework enables the comparison of seven websites' key performance indicators before and after an implementation of web accessibility regarding the behavior of visitors and search engines. The different key performance indicators are provided with data by three different sources of traffic, which enable our framework to aggregate more than one data instance per key performance indicator. Furthermore, the proposed timeframe for the analysis ensures a fast evaluation as well as a representative long term data aggregation and benchmarking.

In a next step, the presented framework is the basis for the creation of a systematic collection of cases in a public database containing relevant and empirical information on the improvements of a website's success due to accessibility implementation. Such a collection of show cases may support the dissemination of know-how on web accessibility effects. To provide representative data, an initial case base could comprise 15 show cases. As to the selection of relevant cases, prior research [9] on business impacts of web accessibility suggests categorization based on benchmarks, e.g., company size, number of employees, industry segment, or turnover.

To provide efficient support by representative show cases a three-level categorization (high-medium-low) with five cases per category based on the website's impact on a company's core business seems an appropriate selection criterion. For example, a company that distributes its products solely by the use of its web presence will be considered as high impact. Companies using their website to distribute products or services among other channels would correspond to a medium impact of their web presence. Hence, the category of low impact would apply to companies that only facilitate their website for company presentation but not for online revenue.

The strategic aspect of such a database lies in its potential to be enriched step by step with new cases and therefore provide aggregated information and decision support to any person or organization that might consider the implementation of an accessible web presence. Furthermore, solid empirical data on the traffic benefits of web accessibility implementation may enable further research on real-life economical effects, such as website revenue and benefit.

References

1. Neuhold, L., Wrann, G.: Studie: Barrierefreies Internet in Österreich (2003), http://www.henworx.de/de/downloads/studie_barrierefreiheit_in_au.pdf
2. Leitner, M.L.: Business Impacts of Web Accessibility - a Holistic Approach. Verlag Peter Lang, Frankfurt/Main (2010)
3. Hartjes, R., Leitner, M.L., Quirchmayr, G., Strauss, C.: Veränderter Website-Traffic bei Einführung von Barrierefreiem Web: eine Fallstudie. HMD - Praxis der Wirtschaftsinformatik (to appear, 2010)
4. Heerdt, V., Strauss, C.: A cost-benefit approach for accessible web presence. In: Klaus, J., Miesenberger, K., Burger, D., Zagler, W. (eds.) ICCHP 2004. LNCS, vol. 3118, pp. 323–330. Springer, Heidelberg (2004)
5. Puhl, S.: Betriebswirtschaftliche Nutzenbewertung der Barrierefreiheit von Web-Präsenzen. Shaker Verlag, Aachen (2008)
6. Ortner, D., Miesenberger, K.: Improving web accessibility by providing higher education facilities for web designers and web developers following the design for all approach. In: Proceedings of the International Workshop on Database and Expert Systems Applications, pp. 866–870 (2005)
7. Lazer, R., Lev, B., Livnat, B.: Internet traffic measures and portfolio returns. Financial Analysts Journal 57(3), 30–40 (2001)
8. Yin, R.: Case Study Research: Design and Methods, 4th edn. Applied Social Research Methods, vol. 5. Sage Publications, Thousand Oaks (2009)
9. Leitner, M.L., Strauss, C.: Exploratory case study research on web accessibility. In: Klaus, J., Miesenberger, K., Burger, D., Zagler, W. (eds.) ICCHP 2008. LNCS, vol. 5105, pp. 490–497. Springer, Heidelberg (2008)

Implementation Concept for an Accessible Web CMS

Dietmar Nedbal and Gerald Petz

Digital Economy, School of Management, Upper Austrian University of Applied Sciences,
Wehrgrabengasse 1-3, A-4400 Steyr, Austria
{dietmar.nedbal,gerald.petz}@fh-steyr.at

Abstract. The number of Austria's municipalities that maintain WAI-compliant websites is increasing. Even though the Web Content Management Systems (CMS) are able to generate accessible Web content, accessibility within the administrative backend itself is hardly considered. The paper describes an implementation concept for accessible Web CMS authoring tools. The implementation concept is derived from a criteria catalog that merged several accessibility and usability guidelines and a qualitative analysis of the Web CMS RiS-Kommunal. The paper includes the methodology used, the key findings of the analysis and the implementation concept.

Keywords: e-Government, accessible Web CMS, administrative backend, accessible software, WAI.

1 Introduction

1.1 Motivation and Initial Study

The asset "web accessibility" in general may be driven by social responsibility, legal requirements, and economic advantages [1]. Considering non-profit-making e-government websites, the incentive for creating an accessible website is often the need to fulfill legal requirements, but needs to be paired with social awareness of responsible people for maintaining the website [2]. Taking a look at the European legal landscape shows that the European Nations are becoming more and more aware of the importance of accessibility in their e-Government sites. In recent years several programs like the "eEurope 2002 Action Plan" and its successor-programs "eEurope 2005 Action Plan" and "i2010" have been launched by the European Commission. In Austria the "e-Government"-law [3] – which requires authorities to use the Web Accessibility Initiative (WAI) standards for their websites – was enacted in February 2004 and has now been in force since January 2008. As Fig. 1 illustrates, within the EU there are several guidelines, laws, quality marks as well as different procedures to assess WAI-conformity [1], [4], [5].

One possibility to determine the impact of these legal and awareness-raising actions across Europe is by the number of accessible governmental websites. Therefore the authors conducted a longitudinal study that reveals that the WAI-compliance of Austria's government websites is steadily increasing (see Fig. 2); the study was done through automated tests with the WAI-validator Cynthia

K. Miesenberger et al. (Eds.): ICCHP 2010, Part I, LNCS 6179, pp. 456–463, 2010.

Fig. 1. European Regulations, Laws and Quality Marks

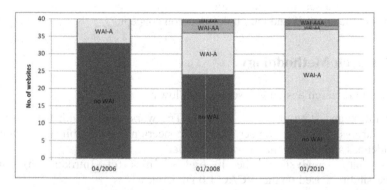

Fig. 2. Number of WAI-compliant Websites of Austria's 40 biggest cities

(www.cynthiasays.com) in April 2006, in January 2008 and in January 2010 and comprised the 40 biggest cities and local government authorities in Austria. To ensure compatibility with previous results, the validation used the Web Content Accessibility Guidelines (WCAG) 1.0.

1.3 Objectives

As stated above the number of municipalities that maintain WAI-compliant websites in the public sector is increasing – but how about the administrative "backend" tools for maintaining the public website? Several discussions (e.g. at scientific conferences like the ICCHP, ASSETS, or discussions in scientific papers like [6], [7]) emphasized the importance of accessible Web CMS (Content Management System) backends. Companies in general and public authorities in particular have to face "social responsibility" and hence it is useful and necessary to provide accessible Web CMS backends for authoring.

The initial study conducted only analyses of the frontend of websites and does not contain information about accessibility of the administrative backends. Despite increasing accessibility of the frontends the administrative backends have improved to a lesser degree: an analysis of some widely used CMS (such as typo3, Joomla, Drupal and Wordpress [8]) revealed that none of the administrative backends of these systems meet the WAI-criteria.

In this paper the Web CMS RiS-Kommunal is used for practical application of the results. It is already widely used by local government authorities in Austria, Italy and Germany – about 40% of Austria's municipalities maintain their websites based on RiS-Kommunal. More than 1,100 systems are hosted on a central platform; thus, the impact of upgrading the administrative backend of the CMS to conform to accessibility standards would be significant.

The main objectives of this paper are (i) to explore the requirements, and (ii) to establish a scientifically based implementation concept to create an accessible and user friendly administrative backend – exhibited on the Web CMS RiS-Kommunal. The paper discusses the methodology used in the research, followed by the key findings of the analysis and the implementation concept.

2   Research Methodology

The overall research design was set up as follows:

1. Literature and state-of-the-art research: The work started with literature research and analysis in the subject domain concerning accessibility (relevant laws, guidelines and quality marks were identified).
2. Comparative analysis of the 40 biggest cities (cf. Introduction) concerning accessibility, based on the WCAG 1.0 guidelines.
3. Consolidation of guidelines: Several guidelines and indices are common in the field of accessibility and usability; these guidelines and a qualitative questionnaire were merged together in order to develop a criteria catalogue as a basis for the evaluation of a Web CMS backend.
4. Qualitative analysis based on the consolidated guidelines, i.e. analysis of accessibility aspects, and analysis of usability aspects.
5. Conceptualization and consolidation: In this phase, the identified issues were clustered and consolidated into an implementation concept.

3   Main Results

This chapter discusses the main results of the research work: the key findings of the in-depth analysis of RiS-Kommunal that lead to the requirements catalogue and the implementation concept for an accessible administrative backend.

3.1   Consolidation of Checkpoints and Guidelines

As a result of discussions about validity and reliability of WCAG guidelines [9], different checkpoints, indices and guidelines regarding accessibility and usability were considered for evaluation. For usability evaluation the authors chose the Web Usability Index (WUI) ([10]) in combination with a qualitative questionnaire. For testing accessibility the authors aggregated the checkpoints from the latest stable and approved versions of the WCAG 2.0 guidelines ([5]) and the checkpoints of the Authoring Tools Accessibility Guidelines 1.0 (ATAG) ([4]). The ATAG Guidelines lead to a good understanding of how to design an accessible backend. Furthermore, some of the ATAG Guidelines contain references to WCAG-Guidelines, e.g. 1.3, 1.4, 3.1 – 3.3 and 4.1 – 4.2; these guidelines are aimed at providing support to authors to create accessible websites and developers to create accessible authoring interfaces. As the WCAG guidelines focus on how to make Web content accessible some of the checkpoints are rather inapplicable for a Web CMS backend, e.g.

- Guideline 1.2 "Time-based Media: Provide alternatives for time-based media" and the following sub-checkpoints, because editors administer these contents and should provide meta-information, but they do not consume these contents within the CMS backend
- Guideline 1.4.2 Audio Control (mechanisms to pause or stop the audio or to control audio volume): As stated at guideline 1.2 the backend is used to add and to describe these contents, rather than to consume.
- Guideline 2.2 "Provide users enough time to read and use content": It is not useful to implement time-dependent functions into the backend, because every user needs time to write an article, post news or edit pictures etc.
- Guideline 3.1 "Make text content readable and understandable": It is the task and the responsibility of the authors to write understandable texts and to provide mechanisms to recognize abbreviations. The backend of a CMS mainly contains controls to add and edit texts and graphical elements, and therefore this guideline is not applicable.

The resulting list of criteria ("criteria catalogue") provided guidance for all necessary components of the RiS-Kommunal backend which includes CMS tools that create Web sites dynamically from a highly structured content database, a what-you-see-is-what-you-get (WYSIWYG) editor, as well as tools for management of multimedia content (photo and video) and layout (CSS formatting).

3.2 Qualitative Analysis

An in-depth analysis of RiS-Kommunal revealed that already a lot of work has been done in increasing the accessibility of the frontend, resulting in good overall accessibility as it was redesigned with conformance up to WAI-AAA ([2]). On the other hand the qualitative analysis based on the criteria catalogue showed that the backend contained several critical accessibility and usability issues that are discussed in the following.

3.2.1 Accessibility
The analysis of the accessibility of the backend was carried out based on the list of ATAG and WCAG checkpoints. Some of the identified main problem areas are summarized in the following:

- Keyboard navigation: The functionality of the backend is operable through a keyboard interface, but not in a convenient way, because users have to use a lot of keystrokes to operate the backend.
- Navigation and search issues: The evaluation of the checkpoints regarding navigation revealed that the backend was originally not designed for visually impaired people. The navigation concept, the arrangement of input fields and buttons, etc. is obvious and understandable for non-visually impaired users, but the navigation has to be adapted completely to meet accessibility requirements.
- Input Assistance: The backend contained error messages as well as instructions on how to fix input mistakes, but these instructions are too superficial and do not provide adequate information.
- Support: The ATAG guidelines suggest supporting the creation of accessible content and accessible authoring practices; the evaluation highlighted weaknesses regarding the provision of this support.

3.2.2 Usability

In the first step, to measure the usability of the administrative backend, the Web Usability Index (WUI) was used. It is based on the Keevil Usability Index ([11]) and has a medium to high validity compared to other usability inspection methods [12]. The Web Usability Index includes 137 items clustered in five categories (navigation, interaction, quality, information, and accessibility) and was calculated both for the frontend and the backend. The WUI for the frontend was tested on a basis of four municipalities running RiS-Kommunal and the average was used to compare the results with the WUI of the backend. The average WUI of the frontend was 20.9% and the WUI of the backend was 49.8% (the lower the index the better). The only category with an acceptable overall WUI was "information and text design" (11.8%); the category with the worst index was "interaction and information exchange" (73.5%) followed by "navigation and orientation" (58%).

To get more insight and to validate the results of the WUI an additional questionnaire was send to all resellers of RiS-Kommunal. The distribution of the software is solely done by local resellers in their area. The resellers are also the first contact in support for the product, so they know best what users expect from or see as omissions in their backend system. Representatives of all nine resellers responded to the questionnaire by answering 20 questions concerning usability aspects of the backend. Besides rating the performance of the item they could prioritize their answers and provide an optional qualitative feedback. In summary, the questionnaire showed (in conformance to the results of the WUI) that orientation, navigation, as well as user interaction are critical parts that need to be improved.

Interdependence between usability and accessibility is discussed in several studies (e.g. [13], [14], [15]). Although the provision of technical web accessibility does not guarantee a better web usability, our analyses revealed deficiencies in both usability and accessibility of the backend, whereas applying the criteria catalogue to the frontend showed better results in both areas.

3.3 Implementation Concept

The final step included a consolidation of the accessibility and usability analysis. The resulting implementation concept includes a total of 71 instructions for implementing a more user friendly and accessible RiS-Kommunal backend. Table 1 contains an overview of the identified problem areas (groups), a short description and the number of instructions (i.e. improvements in accessibility and/or usability) per group.

Table 1. Overview of implementation instructions

Group	Description	Nr. of instructions
Navigation and Orientation	Navigation and orientation within the backend (e.g. keyboard navigation, breadcrumb, etc.)	25
Creation of accessible Content	Creation of accessible content and quality of created content (e.g. accessibility tests and forced accessible input)	7
Multimedia	Administration of multimedia-content (e.g. upload of pictures, videos, etc.)	5
Search and Filtering	Features about searching & filtering content within the backend	10
WYSIWYG Editor	Creation and administration of text-content with the help of a WYSIWYG editor	8
Help and Service	Help-functions and support of authors within backend	11
Miscellaneous	Several other features of the CMS backend	5

Table 2. Excerpt of implementation guidelines

Group	References	Implementation instruction (short)
Navigation and Orientation	WCAG 2.1.1	Let the user log in by pressing the Return key after input of the password (i.e. use a submit button), instead of using the mouse or the keyboard (Tab key followed by the Return key on the login button).
Navigation and Orientation	WCAG 2.4.2 WUI	Provide a descriptive and informative page title for each web page, e.g. Backend Mustergemeinde - Additional Modules - Official board - New entry
Navigation and Orientation	WUI QUEST 09	Always provide the format and file size for downloadable files.
Navigation and Orientation	WCAG 1.4.3 WCAG 1.4.4 WUI	As already implemented on the frontend offer the possibility to change the size and contrast of the backend system (and provide templates such as a high-contrast, graphic, text-only, or a large font version)
Navigation and Orientation	WCAG 3.3.1 WUI QUEST 11	Error messages have to be more precise and intuitive, (e.g. the message "you must not leave the field empty" is not enough!)
Quality of accessible content	ATAG 1.3 QUEST 14	The author has to be prompted for creating accessible content; for example when uploading a photo the alternative text should be a mandatory field (can be left blank at the moment).

Table 2 provides an insight into the implementation concept by listing some of the instructions. It shows the group as already mentioned in Table 1, the references and the actual implementation instruction. The reference may originate from both accessibility (WCAG, ATAG) and usability (WUI, QUEST) criteria, where QUEST is an abbreviation for the questionnaire carried out for testing usability; e.g. QUEST 09 corresponds to the 9th question "Error messages are adequate, i.e. you know where the problem is and how to fix it?", and WCAG 3.3.1 to the criteria "Error Identification" of the WCAG guidelines, etc.

4 Conclusions

Guidelines for accessibility have existed for several years, but are very sparsely implemented in the administrative backend of widely used Web Content Management Systems. The introduced methodology, criteria catalogue, and implementation concept serve as the basis for implementing an accessible and usable Web CMS backend. The results have already been adopted by the software vendor of RiS-Kommunal and the new accessible backend is scheduled to be released later this year. The impact on Austria's municipalities' staff is evident because of the broad utilization of RiS-Kommunal. Besides practical benefits, the results provide a sound basis for researchers and software engineers to design an accessible CMS backend.

Nevertheless, further research needs to address additional evaluation and proof-of-concept of the proposed criteria catalogue based on established guidelines and indices. In addition, the interdependence of accessibility and usability in authoring tools needs to be investigated on a broader scale. In the medium term accessibility features of new ("Web 2.0") technologies like Flash or AJAX, that are more and more used within authoring tools of a Web CMS have to be examined in more detail.

Acknowledgments. The authors thank the software vendor RiS GmbH, 4400 Steyr, and Patrick Brandtner for access to their data.

References

1. Leitner, M.-L., Strauß, C.: Exploratory Case Study Research on Web Accessibility. In: Miesenberger, K., Klaus, J., Zagler, W.L., Karshmer, A.I. (eds.) ICCHP 2008. LNCS, vol. 5105, pp. 490–497. Springer, Heidelberg (2008)
2. Nedbal, D., Petz, G.: A Software Solution for Accessible E-Government Portals. In: Miesenberger, K., Klaus, J., Zagler, W.L., Karshmer, A.I. (eds.) ICCHP 2008. LNCS, vol. 5105, pp. 338–345. Springer, Heidelberg (2008)
3. Bundesgesetz über Regelungen zur Erleichterung des elektronischen Verkehrs mit öffentlichen Stellen (E-Government-Gesetz - E-GovG), http://ris1.bka.gv.at/authentic/findbgbl.aspx?name=entwurf&format=html&docid=COO_2026_100_2_30412
4. Authoring Tool Accessibility Guidelines 1.0, http://www.w3.org/TR/ATAG10/
5. Web Content Accessibility Guidelines (WCAG) 2.0, http://www.w3.org/TR/WCAG20/
6. Frank, J.: Web Accessibility for the Blind: Corporate Social Responsibility or Litigation Avoidance? In: Proceedings of the 41st Hawaii International Conference on System Sciences (2008)

7. Waller, A., Hanson, V.L., Sloan, D.: Including Accessibility Within and Beyond Undergraduate Computing Courses. In: Assets 2009: Proceedings of the 11th international ACM SIGACCESS conference on Computers and accessibility, Pittsburgh, Pennsylvania, USA, pp. 155–162 (2009)
8. Shreves, R.: Open Source CMS Market Share (2008)
9. Brajnik, G.: Validity and Reliability of Web Accessibility Guidelines. In: Assets 2009: Proceedings of the 11th international ACM SIGACCESS conference on Computers and accessibility, Pittsburgh, Pennsylvania, USA, pp. 131–138 (2009)
10. Harms, I., Strobel, J.: Usability Evaluation von Web-Angeboten mit dem Web Usability Index. In: Proceedings der 24. DGI-Online-Tagung 2002 - Content in Context, pp. 293–292. Frankfurt am Main (2002)
11. Keevil, B.: Measuring the usability index of your Web site. In: SIGDOC 1998: Proceedings of the 16th annual international conference on Computer documentation Scaling the heights: the future of information technology; conference proceedings, pp. 271–277. ACM, New York (1998)
12. Othmer, A.: Ist der Web Usability Index ein brauchbares Instrument zur Evaluation von Webangeboten? Validierung eines expertenzentrierten Kriterienkatalogs zur Erfassung der Usability-Mängel von Websites durch einen nutzerorientierten Usability-Test (2006)
13. Arrue, M., Fajardo, I., Lopez, J.M., Vigo, M.: Interdependence between technical web accessibility and usability: its influence on web quality models. International Journal of Web Engineering and Technology 3, 307–328 (2007)
14. Theofanos, M.F., Redish, J.G.: Bridging the gap: between accessibility and usability. Interactions 10, 36–51 (2003)
15. Dey, A.: Usability and accessibility: best friends or worst enemies? In: Proceedings of the 13th VALA Biennial Conference and Exhibition (2006)

Requirements of the Vision Impairments for E-Government Services in Taiwan from Accessibility to Efficiency

Chi Nung Chu

China University of Technology, Department of Management of Information System, No. 56, Sec. 3, Shinglung Rd., Wenshan Chiu, Taipei, Taiwan 116, R.O.C

Abstract. According to W3C Web Content Accessibility Guidelines 1.0, there were 37 government department websites in Taiwan that were evaluated in this paper. Websites were investigated for the presence of various features dealing with information availability, service delivery, and public access. Features assessed include online publications, online database, audio clips, video clips, premium fees, user payments, disability access, security features, presence of online services, digital signatures, credit card payments, email address, and an English version of the website. The results of this survey provide suggestions for the development of e-government services in Taiwan.

Keywords: E-Government Program, Global e-Government Survey, Vision Impairments.

1 Introduction

The "E-Government Program" of Taiwan was initiated at the beginning of 1997 [1][2][3]. The annual Global e-Government Survey conducted by researchers at Brown University in the United States from 2002 to 2007 reported that Taiwan kept top 5 in the list of 198 countries around the world surveyed. In the meantime, one of the survey selected features in W3C Disability Accessibility was measured from 0 to 73. To promote e-government services in Taiwan, the Research, Development, and Evaluation Commission (RDEC) of Executive Yuan has been advocating four different levels of conformance for the websites of government department (Fig. 1) according to W3C Web Content Accessibility Guidelines 1.0.

conformance level "A"   conformance level "A⁺"   conformance level "AA"   conformance level "AAA"

Fig. 1. Four Different Levels of Conformance

K. Miesenberger et al. (Eds.): ICCHP 2010, Part I, LNCS 6179, pp. 464–467, 2010.

Access to the Internet has emerged as an integral part of human society. For the vision impairments in Taiwan, however, there are some requirements of accessibility and access efficiency faced with the assistive technologies that they use. This paper discusses the survey for the development of accessible and efficient e-government services implemented in the government department of Taiwan.

2 Method and Results

The data for our analysis consist of an assessment of 37 government department websites including executive offices, judicial offices, Cabinet offices and major agencies serving crucial functions of government, such as health, human services, taxation, education, interior, economic development, administration, natural resources, foreign affairs, foreign investment, transportation, military, tourism and business regulations. Websites are evaluated for the presence of various features dealing with information availability, service delivery, and public access. Features assessed include online publications, online database, audio clips, video clips, premium fees, user payments, disability access, security features, presence of online services, digital signatures, credit card payments, email address, and an English version of the website. Among the significant suggestions of the research are:

1) Guidelines for unified access key of widows positioning are needed

Access key of widows positioning is used to accelerate the information access of website such as Go Homepage, Sitemap, Group Hyperlinks in the upper area of website, Group Hyperlinks in the left area of website and so on. Unified access key can facilitate user accessing the websites.

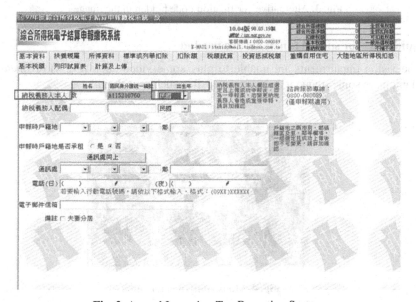

Fig. 2. Annual Incoming Tax Reporting System

2) 2-dimentional information uneasy to read

The screen reader functions in a linear way. It is hard for the vision impairments to keep going with the 2D information expression (Fig. 2).

3) Alternative verification code hidden in the image is needed

Screen reader is unable to sign in any website with verification code hidden in the image unless there is an alternative verification code such as aural or text description (Fig 3).

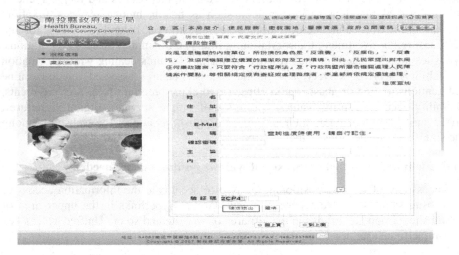

Fig. 3. Alternative verification code hidden in the image

4) Guidelines for special functions are needed

The vision impairments are unable to play some video clips (Fig 4) or uneasy to manipulate some frequent accessing websites such as webmail.

Fig. 4. Mouse only manipulation

5) Graphs with indeterminate alternative text can be eliminated

There are 54% of government department graphs with null or just "graph" description in the Alt attribute. These graphs are used for decoration in the websites. For accessing efficiency, these graphs can be eliminated.

3 Conclusion

The results of this survey were used for the development of e-government services. The satisfaction for the people is never full filled. In the future, the ongoing e-government services will be expanded to more government agencies and businesses. The availability of a broad range of accessible and efficient online services will be continually enhanced. The more we concern, the more quality of life the people with disability can get.

References

1. Executive Yuan: Note of the Executive Yuan Council No. 2557 Meeting (1997),
   http://www.ey.gov.tw
2. RDEC of the Executive Yuan: Introductory to the Electronic / Networked Government Program (1998), http://www.rdec.gov.tw
3. Data Communication Group of Chunghwa Telecom Co., Ltd.: Proposal for Government Service Network (GSN) of the Electronic/Networked Government Program (1998), http://www.rdec.gov.tw

Accessibility of eGovernment Web Sites: Towards a Collaborative Retrofitting Approach

Annika Nietzio[1], Morten Goodwin Olsen[2],
Mandana Eibegger[2], and Mikael Snaprud[2,3]

[1] Forschungsinstitut Technologie und Behinderung (FTB)
der Evangelischen Stiftung Volmarstein, Grundschötteler Str. 40
58300 Wetter (Ruhr), Germany
egovmon@ftb-net.de,
http://www.ftb-net.de
[2] Tingtun AS, PO Box 48, N−4791 Lillesand, Norway
{morten.g.olsen,mandana.eibegger,mikael.snaprud}@tingtun.no
http://www.tingtun.no
[3] University of Agder, PO Box 509, N−4898 Grimstad, Norway

Abstract. Accessibility benchmarking is efficient to raise awareness and initiate competition. However, traditional benchmarking is of little avail when it comes to removing barriers from eGovernment web sites in practice. Regulations and legal enforcement may be helpful in a long-term perspective. For more rapid progress both vendors and web site maintainers are willing to take short-term action towards improvements, provided that clear advise is available. The approach of the *eGovernment Monitoring project (eGovMon)* integrates benchmarking as a central activity in a user-driven project. In addition to benchmarking results, several other services and background information are provided to enable the users – in this case a group of Norwegian municipalities who want to improve the accessibility of their web sites – to gain real added value from benchmarking.

1 Introduction

Web sites of municipalities have evolved into an important means of interaction between government and citizens. However, many of those web sites are not accessible enough to allow all citizens to use them. An overview of eGovernment accessibility issues that arise at the different levels of service provision is given by Nietzio et al. [1]. Although the awareness about accessible eGovernment is fuelled by periodic benchmarking campaigns, several recent studies show that there is still much room for improvement.

The municipalities participating in the eGovMon project have expressed a strong demand for practical support. Often the web site maintainers are not aware of accessibility problems in their web sites or do not know how to resolve them. Therefore the eGovMon project is currently establishing a dialogue between content authors, software vendors, and web accessibility experts. In a

K. Miesenberger et al. (Eds.): ICCHP 2010, Part I, LNCS 6179, pp. 468–475, 2010.

collaborative effort they can analyse the nature of the accessibility barriers and determine who can address the barriers most efficiently.

The remainder of this paper is organised as follows. In Section 2 we discuss some recent accessibility studies and analyse the shortcomings of benchmarking. The eGovMon approach to overcome these shortcomings is presented in Section 3. Finally, results of the project so far and future plans are summarised in Sections 4 and 5.

2   State of the Art

The goal of improving web accessibility is addressed by a variety of measures. The two opposite ends of the continuum are *benchmarking*, which aims to inform and support policy decisions on the one hand and on the other end *technical knowledge* disseminated formally via university courses such as the "Joint European Study Programme on Accessible Web Design" [?] and vendor com mals; or rather informally through blogs and other dedicated web sites such as http://www.alistapart.com, http://www.webstandards.org, or http://www.456bereastreet.com – to name only a few. Whereas the former addresses mostly management and policy makers, the latter targets a technical audience of web designers and web developers. In between these two areas there is a gap. There are only few accessibility projects and initiatives addressing the needs of the people and organisations who run the web sites, such as maintainers of the Content Management Systems (CMS) and web editors.

2.1   Benchmarking

In the past few years a number of national and international studies on eAccessibility have been conducted. Some are covering mainly web accessibility, while others address a wider range of ICT products and services. The accessibility topic also found its way into eGovernment surveys such as the 2009 Capgemini study "Smarter, Faster, Better eGovernment" [3].

The "Assessment of the Status of eAccessibility in Europe" [4] and its followup from 2009 [5] present a policy survey, a status measurement based on a set of key indicators, and the results from questionnaires sent to stakeholder groups (ICT industries, user organisations, and public procurement officials). The main purpose of these studies was to follow up on previous studies and support the future development of European policy in the field of eAccessibility.

There are also national and regional benchmarking approaches that have been in operation for several years [6]. In general, the results are presented as a list of aggregated results which do not contain technical details and thus are not helpful for web site owners who want to improve the accessibility of their web sites. In Norway the annual survey carried out by the the Agency for Public Management and eGovernment (Difi) recently started to include additional information about the individual tests and their results [7]. However, none of the surveys we are aware of links the test results to practical advice for a specific content management system.

2.2 Barriers to Web Accessibility Improvements

Benchmarking, as well as other types of evaluation that are not commissioned by the subject of the study, often fail to have an impact. The results are published but are used neither by the site owners to improve their web sites, nor by CMS vendors to improve their software. This can have several reasons:

- The results are not detailed enough to be used as basis for implementing improvements.
- It is not clear in which part of the publication chain the barriers were introduced or who is in a position to fix them.
- The site owner does not have the resources to hire external consultancy to fix the accessibility problems; and the staff responsible for maintaining the web site doesn't have the knowledge.
- The known barriers are fixed in a one-off effort. But there are no quality processes in place so that the accessibility of the web site deteriorates rapidly because newly added content is still inaccessible.
- The benchmarking is carried out as one-off study, or indicators change frequently, so that progress can not be evaluated.

Local strategies for removing barriers have so far been limited to in-house guidelines [8] and best practices in user generated content [9]. The literature does not include actions to determine if the barriers are introduced by user generated content or if these are introduced by the content management systems, even though this is essential information when web accessibility barriers are to be removed.

Experience tells us that when web accessibility results are shown to web editors, they will blame the content management system. Similarly, the vendors will claim that the content authors are not using the system correctly.

3   The eGovMon Concept

In this section we present the eGovMon approach which aims to close the gap between high level benchmarking and accessibility improvements that are implemented as an isolated fix on a single web site by addressing the shortcomings outlined above. The concept is built upon several pillars: an on-line checker that provides detailed accessibility evaluations of single web pages; a community forum for web site maintainers from municipalities, web accessibility experts, and CMS vendors and developers; and finally the publication of regularly updated benchmarking reports, which allow the assessment of progress and improvements over time.

3.1   Detailed Test Results

The eGovMon project has developed an easy to use on-line tool that can check single web pages. The eAccessibility Checker[1] provides detailed information on the identified accessibility barriers and links to the potential solutions described in the eGovMon forum (see Section 3.2 for details).

---

[1] The eAccessibility Checker is available at http://accessibility.egovmon.no

The system contains 23 web accessibility tests, which are all derived from the *fully automatable* tests in the Unified Web Evaluation Methodology (UWEM) [10]. These tests are based on the Web Content Accessibility Guidelines (WCAG) [11]. Some restrictions apply when creating automatic measurements. Most significantly, many of the UWEM tests require human judgement. In fact only 26 of the 141 tests in UWEM are marked as automatable. As an example, automatic testing can find images without alternative text. However, to claim that an existing alternative text represents the corresponding image well, human judgement is needed. Thus, automatic evaluation can only be used to determine the existence of barriers, not to verify the absence of barriers needed to support and accessibility claim of a web page. Casado Martínez et al. [12] have shown that the automatic evaluation results can in some degree be used to predict manual evaluation results.

Figure 1 shows the result page of the eAccessibility checker with detailed background on a selected test. The results also include information on where in the HTML code the barrier was detected.

3.2 eGovMon Community Forum and Seminars

The municipalities participating in the eGovMon project have a lot in common: The organisations are often quite small without a full-time web site maintainer. They use one of a few CMS that are developed and marketed especially for municipalities in Norway. Therefore, it seems a natural step to invite them to a forum that enables the sharing and re-use of good practices, to make sure that isolated fixes can be applied by other users of the same system. Furthermore, the forum asks vendors and developers to provide examples of correct use of their software to produce accessible content.

The hints and tips are associated with the barrier messages of the eAccessibility Checker. It is also indicated if the solution is CMS-specific and which parts of the systems (usually some kind of template file) must be updated to remove a problem.

If a barrier is not caused by the template but was introduced by the web editor, the forum collects descriptions how to make sure that content added by web editors is accessible. For instance by documenting how alternative texts for images and other non-text content can be added in a specific CMS, or by explaining how to insert content as plain text to avoid that formatting instructions from word processing software affect the output of the CMS in an undesired way.

Template analysis. To get the forum started some CMS templates for different systems were analysed by web accessibility experts. The experts identified potential accessibility problems and described how to fix these within the functionality of the CMS.

Training seminars. To address the issue of missing accessibility competence of the staff, eGovMon is offering training seminars, which include an introduction to HTML and CSS, awareness raising for accessibility barriers, and techniques to improve accessibility.

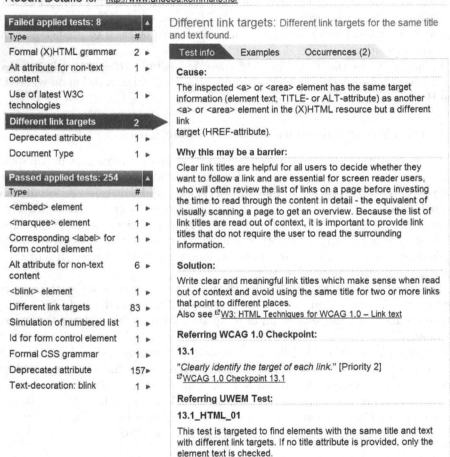

Fig. 1. Result page of the eAccessibility Checker

Quality processes. Web accessibility should be regarded as a process [13]. Therefore it is important to integrate it with the work flow of maintainers and web editors. eGovMon runs the on-line eAccessibility Checker that can be used to check single pages at any time, and also supports the municipalities in setting up tools and quality processes.

3.3 Regular Benchmarks

The eGovMon project conducts bi-monthly benchmarks of all Norwegian municipality web sites. The evaluations are carried out automatically with the eGovMon tool which consists of the following main components:

- **Crawler:** explores and detects 6000 web pages from each web site. If a web site is smaller than 6000 pages, the web site is exhaustively scanned.
- **Sampler:** randomly schedules 600 of the detected web pages for evaluation.
- **Web Accessibility Metric:** evaluates the HTML and CSS of the scheduled web pages according to the UWEM tests.
- **Database:** stores URLs of the pages detected by the crawler, evaluated by the web accessibility metrics, as well as aggregated information such as most common barriers, results per county, etc.
- **Web user interface:** presents the stored results as tables and figures. Figure 2 shows the results from Vestfold county.

Additionally, the Norwegian municipalities participating in the eGovMon project can trigger an evaluation of their web site at any time using an on-line web interface. These evaluations are carried out exactly as the the bi-monthly evaluations except that the result are sent out as a report in PDF format by email when the evaluation is completed.

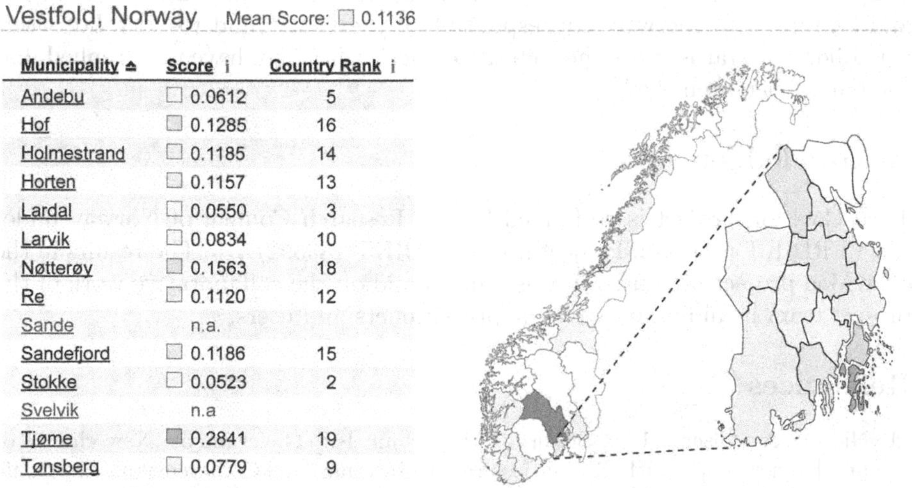

Vestfold, Norway   Mean Score: ☐ 0.1136

Municipality ⇕	Score i	Country Rank i
Andebu	☐ 0.0612	5
Hof	☐ 0.1285	16
Holmestrand	☐ 0.1185	14
Horten	☐ 0.1157	13
Lardal	☐ 0.0550	3
Larvik	☐ 0.0834	10
Nøtterøy	☐ 0.1563	18
Re	☐ 0.1120	12
Sande	n.a.	
Sandefjord	☐ 0.1186	15
Stokke	☐ 0.0523	2
Svelvik	n.a	
Tjøme	■ 0.2841	19
Tønsberg	☐ 0.0779	9

Fig. 2. Results from accessibility benchmarking of Norwegian municipality web sites. Example: Vestfold county (January 2010).

4 Impact

The first quality assured benchmarking results for the participating municipalities were published in December 2009. An on-line interface with enhanced visualisation and comparison features is currently under development.

All participating municipalities have reported that they use the eAccessibility Checker. Several of them use it frequently in their day-to-day work. At least three of them have engaged in a quality improvement dialogue with their vendors based on the results provided by eGovMon.

The eGovMon forum is organised in close collaboration with the Norwegian Agency for Public Management and eGovernment (Difi) to bring the relevant stakeholders together, to facilitate informal discussions on how measurements and reports are designed, and to enable further use of the results across all Norwegian municipalities.

5 Conclusion and Future Plans

The facilitation of a dialogue based on measurement results among the different stake holder groups involved in the quality improvement process is an essential outcome of the eGovMon approach. The different parts of the eGovMon approach address all of the shortcomings listed in Section 2.2.

In the future, we plan to encourage the use of the forum to turn it into a sustainable community. Another future development direction we intend to explore is the extension of activities to address also end users (citizens). Similar to the German "Abi Meldestelle"[2] and the Italian "Osservatorio per l'accessibilità dei servizi delle PA"[3] a service could be offered where end users can report accessibility barriers they encounter on public web sites. The complaints are analysed and forwarded to the web site responsible if they are found to be valid. Users can follow the status (were the web site owners contacted, have they replied, has the barrier been removed).

Acknowledgements

The eGovMon project is co-funded by the Research Council of Norway under the VERDIKT program. Project no.: VERDIKT 183392/S10. The results in the eGovMon project presented in this paper build on the collaborative work of the project team including researchers, practitioners and users.

References

1. Nietzio, A., Olsen, M.G., Snaprud, M., Brynn, R.: eGovernment: New chance or new barrier people with disabilities? In: 8th International Conference on Electronic Government: Proceedings of ongoing research and projects of EGOV 2009, Trauner Druck: Linz, Schriftenreihe Informatik (2009)

---

[2] http://www.webbarrieren.wob11.de/
[3] http://www.accessibile.gov.it/

2. Hengstberger, B., Miesenberger, K., Batusic, M., Chelbat, N., García, A.R.: Joint study programme on accessible web design. In: Miesenberger, K., Klaus, J., Zagler, W.L., Karshmer, A.I. (eds.) ICCHP 2008. LNCS, vol. 5105, pp. 182–189. Springer, Heidelberg (2008)

3. Capgemini: Smarter, Faster, Better eGovernment (2009), http://ec.europa.eu/information_society/eeurope/i2010/docs/benchmarjking/egov_benchmark_2009.pdf (retrieved February 1, 2010)

4. Cullen, K., Kubitschke, L., Meyer, I.: Assessment of the status of eAccessibility in Europe (2007), http://ec.europa.eu/information_society/activities/einclusion/library/studies/meac_study/index_en.htm (retrieved November 4, 2009)

5. Cullen, K., Kubitschke, L., Boussios, T., Dolphion, C., Meyer, I.: Study report: Web accessibility in European countries: level of compliance with latest international accessibility specifications, notably WCAG 2.0, and approaches or plans to implement those specifications (2009), http://ec.europa.eu/information_society/activities/einclusion/library/studies/docs/access_comply_main.pdf (retrieved January 28, 2010)

6. Snaprud, M., Sawicka, A.: Large Scale Web Accessibility Evaluation - A European Perspective (2007), http://www.springerlink.com/content/f017754512717k01/

7. Agency for Public Management and eGovernment (Difi): Quality of public web sites (2009), http://www.norge.no/kvalitet/

8. Greeff, M., Kotzé, P.: A lightweight methodology to improve web accessibility. In: SAICSIT 2009: Proceedings of the 2009 Annual Research Conference of the South African Institute of Computer Scientists and Information Technologists, pp. 30–39. ACM, New York (2009)

9. Martín García, Y.S., Miguel González, B.S., Yelmo García, J.C.: Prosumers and accessibility: how to ensure a productive interaction. In: W4A 2009: Proceedings of the 2009 International Cross-Disciplinary Conference on Web Accessibililty (W4A), pp. 50–53. ACM, New York (2009)

10. Web Accessibility Benchmarking Cluster: Unified Web Evaluation Methodology, UWEM 1.2 (2007), http://www.wabcluster.org/uwem1_2/ (retrieved November 4, 2009)

11. World Wide Web Consortium: Web Content Accessibility Guidelines 1.0. W3C Recommendation (May 5, 1999), http://www.w3.org/TR/WCAG10/ (retrieved November 4, 1999)

12. Casado Martínez, C., Martínez-Normand, L., Olsen, M.G.: Is it possible to predict the manual web accessibility result using the automatic result? In: Stephanidis, C. (ed.) HCI (7). LNCS, vol. 5615, pp. 645–653. Springer, Heidelberg (2009)

13. Brajnik, G.: Towards a sustainable web accessibility. In: Accessible Design in the Digital World, ADDW (2008)

Improving the Accessibility of Fabasoft Folio by Means of WAI-ARIA

Mario Batusic and Daniela Steiner

University of Linz, Institute Integriert Studieren
Altenbergerstrasse 69
A-4040 Linz, Austria
{daniela.steiner,mario.batusic}@jku.at
http://www.integriert-studieren.jku.at

Abstract. A lot of web applications already use AJAX to give the user the feeling of a desktop application. To make these applications more accessible for people with disabilities, the code can be enriched with WAI-ARIA roles, states and properties. This paper presents a practical case study, where an AJAX-based web application – Fabasoft Folio – has been evaluated and a solution through WAI-ARIA enrichment has been proposed and will be implemented for different widgets used in the application.

Keywords: AJAX, WAI-ARIA, Fabasoft Folio, Fabasoft eGov-Suite.

1 Introduction

There are already a lot of web applications that give the user the feeling of a desktop application. Many of these web applications are implemented with AJAX, which uses a combination of HTML and CSS for marking up and styling information and the DOM accessed with JavaScript to dynamically display and interact with the information presented. Data is exchanged asynchronously between browser and server to avoid full page reloads [1].

To make such web applications containing dynamic content and advanced user interface controls (widgets) developed with AJAX and related technologies more accessible to people with disabilities and users of assistive technologies, WAI-ARIA, the Accessible Rich Internet Application Suite [2] has been published by W3C/WAI. In order to provide proper semantics for custom widgets to make these widgets accessible, usable and interoperable with assistive technologies, W3C/WAI recommends to enrich the code of the modern web applications with the roles, states and properties provided in the WAI-ARIA Technical Specification [3].

This paper will present a practical case study, where WAI-ARIA enrichment has been implemented in the AJAX-based web application "Fabasoft Folio", a software product for Enterprise Content Management, Collaboration, agile Business Processes, Compliance Management and Information Governance, which supports the management of digital documents and allows cooperation between collaboration teams [4].

K. Miesenberger et al. (Eds.): ICCHP 2010, Part I, LNCS 6179, pp. 476–483, 2010.

2   Fabasoft Folio and Fabasoft eGov-Suite

Fabasoft Folio consists of three main areas: a portal header, a navigation area that is implemented as a tree, and the main application area (see Fig. 1).

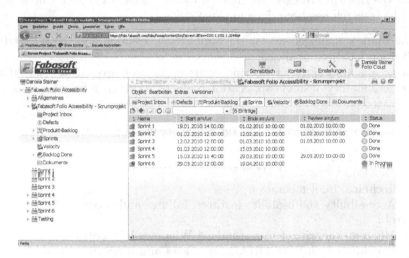

Fig. 1. Screenshot of Fabasoft Folio

As shown in Table 1, the main application area can be divided into several parts that can be mapped to different widget types. In addition, plenty of application functionalities are implemented as dialogs such as for example an attribute editor and a read properties dialog.

Table 1. Application areas and mapped widget types

Part of application area	Widget type
Breadcrumb path	toolbar
Standard functions	toolbar
Main application menu	menubar
List of tabs for the object list	tablist
Toolbar dependent on object list	toolbar
Object list headers	toolbar
Object list	table grid

Based on the Fabasoft Folio technology, the Fabasoft company has also developed the Fabasoft eGov-Suite, which is one of the leading products for electronic file and workflow management in the German-speaking countries. The product is used to increase the speed, efficiency and transparency of administrational processes in federal, regional and local authorities, and represents the backbone of citizen-oriented eGovernment processes [5].

3   Methodology

To improve the Accessibility of their products, the Fabasoft company has initiated a three-month scrum project in an agile software development process [6] with the Institute Integriert Studieren at the Johannes Kepler University of Linz. The research has been done in three steps:

1. The window management for the application selection and the selected application has been analysed,
2. the accessibility of the single window areas has been investigated, and finally
3. the accessibility of single application widgets and their interaction has been evaluated.

This last step was done sticking to the following methodology:

Widget analysis:
  − Function
  − Technical implementation
  − Accessibility and usability features, failures and needs
Research:
  − Mapping the widget to a standard Windows UI Control
  − Deciding which WAI-ARIA roles, states and properties should be used
Implementation:
  − Defining the keyboard layout for the widget
  − Defining the global taborder position of the widget in the application
  − Pointing out to an existing WAI-ARIA example, adapting an existing example or implementing an own example.

4   Results

In this chapter we want to present the main widgets that have been treated during the project, present the problems we have been confronted with, and describe our approach for solving the problems and implementing WAI-ARIA enrichment.

4.1   Application Role

To declare that a web appearance is not a simple web page, but a web application, WAI-ARIA offers the attribute `role="application"`, which should make it possible for screen reader users to utilise the application's own keyboard implementation in all application areas marked-up with this attribute. The problem is that – at the moment – most screen readers (including JAWS version 10) have no or only a very poor support for `role="application"`.

Nevertheless, the project team decided to lead the way into the future and to use `role="application"`. Because of lacking support of "older" assistive technologies, this decision implicates that the availability of all accessibility features worked out in the project is limited to the newest screen reader versions.

4.2   Navigation Tree

The navigation in the Fabasoft products is visualised as a tree (see Fig. 1). The requirement of the customer was to keep this tree and to enable the look and feel of Windows Explorer. The challenge was now to define a proper mapping between keys and their functionalities, and to enrich the code that generates the tree with the corresponding WAI-ARIA attributes.

An evaluation of the existing implementation came up with the following results and recommendations:

- The tree is already implemented as an unordered list (`ul`).
- If all tree items will be realised as child nodes (`li`) of the parent tree in the DOM, then a screen reader can automatically read and speak the correct nesting level. If this is the case, then all open- and close-images should get assigned `role="presentation"` in WAI-ARIA, in oder to exclude them from the screen reader scope.
  The synchronisation with WAI-ARIA has to work in all situations, even if there is not a direct mapping between mouse and keyboard events (as for example in the current implementation of the double click as open-/close-toggle). It is important that WAI-ARIA states, changes of tabindex and focus-handling will be done through using functions that can be called as handler for all mouse and keyboard events.

A prototypic solution has been developed which correctly implements keyboard navigation, focus visualisation and accessibility for screen reader users through use of WAI-ARIA roles, states and properties.

4.3   Menu

For a correct enrichment of a menu with WAI-ARIA, the implementation of the following roles, states and properties is recommended:

- Roles
  - `role="application"`: assigned to the surrounding `<div>`-container.
  - `role="menubar"`: container for the main menu items (should contain a reference to the element it affects by using the property `aria-controls`).
  - `role="menuitem"`: single menu item – can also include a pop-up menu or a submenu.
  - `role="menu"`: container for a pop-up menu or a submenu.
  - `role="menuitemcheckbox"`: if the menu contains an option that can be enabled/disabled.
  - `role="menuitemradio"`: if only one menu item can be chosen from a group of several menu items.
- States and Properties
  - `aria-haspopup="true"`: if an element with `role="menuitem"` offers a submenu that will be opened through activating the element.
  - `aria-disabled="true"`: for an inactive menu item (that nevertheless has to be focusable to reveal its existence to screen reader users.)

- aria-hidden="true": for a menu or menu item that is hidden with the CSS property display:none.
- aria-labelledby="*id of the element containing the menu header*": for clearly identifying the connection between menu item and menu header.

4.4 Toolbar

Toolbars offer a quick way to access the most important functions of a menu in a flat, non-hierarchical way. Therefore, toolbars are also very important for users of screen readers or users who work with the keyboard only.

The following WAI-ARIA roles, states and properties have been proposed for a correct toolbar implementation with WAI-ARIA:

- Roles
    - The toolbar should be surrounded by a <div>-container in HTML that gets assigned role="application".
    - The toolbar itself, e.g. implemented as an unordered list <ul> in HTML, should get assigned role="toolbar".
    - The single symbols of the toolbar should be ideally implemented in HTML as list items <li> that get assigned role="button".
- Properties
    - The function of the property aria-controls="*id of the table grid*" is to tell the assistive technology that activating this toolbar symbol can cause a dynamic change of the content of the table grid.
    - To make the connection between a toolbar symbol and the toolbar header clear for assistive technologies, the property aria-labelledby="*id of the element containing the toolbar name*" should be used.
    - The property aria-haspopup is used for buttons that open a submenu.
- States
    - If a symbol of the toolbar with role="button" is shown as inactive, it should get assigned the state aria-disabled="true".
    - If a symbol of the toolbar does not work as simple button, but as a toggle button, it should get assigned the state aria-pressed="true" or aria-pressed="false" respectively.

For users who cannot use the mouse, a proper keyboard layout as presented in Table 2 is of high importance.

4.5 Object List and Object List Header

The main working area in Fabasoft Folio is the so-called object list. Its standard appearance is a data table with its rows each presenting an object. The table has a customizable number of columns dependant on the type of listed objects as well as of the user's preference.

An additional accessibility problem concerning the object list results from the way it is implemented. The object list header is not integrated in the HTML table that presents the object data. It is only positioned on its visually proper place

Table 2. Keyboard layout for toolbar

Keys	Function
Tab and Shift-Tab	from outside: enter toolbar (set the focus on the toolbar); from inside: leave toolbar (move focus on next/previous element)
Left Arrow	move focus to previous symbol in the toolbar (circular)
Right Arrow	move focus to next symbol in the toolbar (circular)
Enter or Space	execute command and move focus back to working area

above the grid by means of CSS. This kind of tricking was necessary in order for the header to stay fix while the user scrolls through the data. Thus generated accessibility problem consists of separating the table data from their headers. To correctly render a data grid a screen reader program needs a complete data table – its data cells as well as header cells belonging to one and the same DOM parent – the table. And although WAI-ARIA provides the property aria-owns="*id of the virtual child element*", neither browsers nor screen readers support it at the current development stage.

So we were also forced to be tricky in our proposal for an accessibility solution here. We implemented the object list data table as a data grid with a visually hidden header, and the actual object list header with its controls as a WAI-ARIA toolbar. This practice ensures that a screen reader is able to correctly correlate every data grid cell with its column header.

The following WAI-ARIA roles, states and properties have been proposed for a correct data grid implementation of the object list:

- Roles
    - The data table is marked as grid: `<table role="grid">`
    - Every data cell is marked as: `<td role="gridcell">`
    - All column header cells is marked as: `<th role="columnheader">`
    - Each table row must be explicitely marked as: `<tr role="row">`.
- Properties
    - `aria-labelledby="`*id of the element containing the object list name label*`"`
- States
    - Every selected row will be marked as:
      `<tr role="role" aria-selected="true">`

The keyboard layout presented in Table 3 was proposed for the grid control.

4.6   Dialogs

Speaking of dialogs in the sense of WAI-ARIA always means speaking about "modal dialogs". It's about a way the software waiting for the user to make her/his decisions before proceeding with any other task. It is therefore important for the software to guarantee that the user is not allowed to activate any other actions letting the dialog open (unfinished).

Table 3. Keyboard layout for the data grid

Keys	Function
Tab and Shift-Tab	from outside: enter grid (set focus on the first grid cell or return focus to the previously focused cell); from inside: leave the grid (move focus to the next/previous control)
Left/Right Arrow	move focus to the left / right neighbouring cell
Up/Down Arrow	move focus to the up / down neighbouring cell
Home	move focus to the first cell in the current row
End	move focus to the last cell in the current row
Page Up	move focus to the first cell in the current column
Page Down	move focus to the last cell in the current column
Shift + Up/Down Arrow	Select more contiguous rows
Ctrl + Up/Down Arrows, then Space	Select additional non-contiguous rows

Fabasoft Folio offers dialogs primarily for creating and editing objects. This functionality in Folio is called "Attribute Editor (AE)". The accessibility solution for AE includes two layers as for all other widgets:

1. WAI-ARIA enrichment of the widget markup, and
2. keyboard support for the AE dialog.

As the main tool for configuring and editing object, the AE contains a large quantity of subwidgets for different types of simple and compound objects. Together with common HTML form fields such as single- and multiline text inputs, the AE comprises many proprietary Javascript driven controls such as

- Tri-state checkboxes with values: true, false and undefined,
- Token lists of enumerated values,
- Calendar date picker widget, etc.

We therefore had to propose a large number of roles, states and properties. It would be out of proportion of this paper to report all the WAI-ARIA markup proposed for Folio dialogs, but we present the most important ones.

- Roles
  - `role="dialog"` – markup for the utmost dialog container element,
  - `role="button"` – for all standard and non-standard dialog buttons,
  - `role="listbox"` – for token lists,
  - `role="option"` – for the selectable tokens in the lists,
  - `role="presentation"` – for excluding visual-only parts of the user interface from the scope of screen readers, ...
- Properties
  - `aria-labelledby="`*id of the element carrying the label for the control*`"`,
  - `aria-required="true"` – for all mandatory fields, ...

– States
  - `aria-checked="true|false|mixed"` – for the current state of a (tri-state) checkbox,
  - `aria-selected="true"` – for all selected tokens in a listbox,
  - `aria-invalid="true"` – for a field with a faulty user entry, ...

In addition to the specific keyboard support for all particular widgets within the dialog, Table 4 shows standard keyboard functionalities which have to be implemented in every dialog widget.

Table 4. Keyboard layout for dialog widget

Keys	Function
Tab / Shift+Tab	Bring focus to the next / previous dialog widget (circular); It is not possible to leave a modal dialog by tabbing out.
Enter	Activate default dialog action; dialog closes.
Escape	Activate the cancel action; dialog closes.

5 Conclusion

As all accessibility evaluations and improvements have been done in Fabasoft Folio, which the Fabasoft eGov-Suite is based on, the improvements will be part of the whole product line of the Fabasoft company and therefore have an impact not only in the eGovernment sector, but also in non-governmental organisations and companies using Fabasoft Folio throughout Europe.

References

1. Ajax (programming) - Wikipedia,
   http://en.wikipedia.org/wiki/Ajax_(programming)
2. WAI-ARIA Overview,
   http://www.w3.org/WAI/intro/aria
3. Accessible Rich Internet Applications (WAI-ARIA) 1.0 W3C Working Draft (December 15, 2009),
   http://www.w3.org/TR/wai-aria/
4. Fabasoft Folio - Products,
   http://www.fabasoft.com/folio/products
5. Fabasoft eGov-Suite - Overview,
   http://www.fabasoft.com/egov-suite/fabasoft-egov-suite/overview
6. Scrum (development) - Wikipedia,
   http://en.wikipedia.org/wiki/Scrum_(development)

Accessibility of Blended and E-Learning for Mature Age and Disabled Students and Staff: Introduction to the Special Thematic Session

Helen Petrie[1], Christopher Power[1], Carlos A. Velasco[2], and Jesus G. Boticario[3]

[1] Human-Computer Interaction Research Group, Department of Computer Science, University of York, Heslington, York YO10 5DD, United Kingdom
{Helen.Petrie,cpower}@cs.york.ac.uk
[2] Fraunhofer Institute for Applied Information Technology FIT, Schloss Birlinghoven, D53754 Sankt Augustin, Germany
carlos.velasco@fit.fraunhofer.de
[3] Dpto. Inteligencia Artificial, E.T.S. Ingeniería Informática, UNED, Calle Juan Del Rosal, 16, 28040 Madrid, Spain
jgb@dia.uned.es

Blended learning, the use of a combination of face-to-face and distance learning techniques, is becoming very common in all educational sectors. Almost all educational institutions now use websites to communicate with students, provide them with learning resources and, increasingly, allow students and staff to collaborate with each other. Many institutions use their own websites, others use virtual learning environments (VLEs) or learning management systems (LMSs). The transition of institutions to all learning being through electronic channels, or e-learning, is also becoming increasingly prevalent, particularly in the higher and further education domains. Even in primary and secondary school systems, the integration of virtual classrooms, multimedia resources and electronic whiteboards have further blurred the lines between the virtual and the physical world.

All of these innovations in learning provide opportunities and challenges for students with disabilities and mature age students and also for staff with disabilities. One needs to consider the accessibility of at least three layers of information and interaction: the accessibility of the basic units of content (e.g. blocks of text, mathematical or chemical formulae, pictures, diagrams etc); the accessibility of the medium in which this content is delivered (e.g. a Word or PowerPoint presentation, an specialist application such as SPSS or Mathematica); and finally the accessibility of the learning environment, such as the VLE or LMS. All of these can create their own accessibility barriers, which are different for each different student, staff member or even institution.

This STS addresses the needs of disabled students and staff at every level of education from primary school (the papers by Besio, Caprino and Laudanna and by Fuertes, Gonzalez, Mariscal and Ruiz), through secondary school (paper by Greene) to further and higher education (papers by Power, Petrie, Sakharov and Swallow, by Swallow, Petrie and Power and by Weiemair-Marki and Unterfrauner). A number of the papers address the needs of pupils and students (the papers by Besio, Caprino and

K. Miesenberger et al. (Eds.): ICCHP 2010, Part I, LNCS 6179, pp. 484–485, 2010.

Laudanna, by Fuertes, Gonzalez, Mariscal and Ruiz, by Power, Petrie, Sakharov and Swallow) and two address the needs of staff and institutions (papers by Swallow, Petrie and Power and by Weiemair-Marki and Unterfrauner).

Three papers discuss frameworks and guidelines for learning applications and ICT materials for disabled students. Fuertes, Gonzalez, Mariscal and Ruiz present a framework to support the development of learning applications for disabled children. They applied this framework in the development of accessible multimedia curriculum materials in the *Learn* and *Internet in the Classroom* Projects. Greene reports on her guidelines for the development of curriculum-focused ICT materials for a diverse range of Irish secondary school students. A range of materials was developed using these guidelines and assessed by teachers. Besio, Caprino and Laudanna report on the development of a novel robotic toy for disabled children. They also present guidelines for using robots in education and play therapy sessions for children with disabilities.

The other three papers in the STS are from the EU-Funded EU4ALL Project (European Unified Approach to Accessible Lifelong Learning). Swallow, Petrie and Power present highlights of their investigation of the needs of educational professionals in further and higher education in supporting students with disabilities and mature age students. The results are based on an online survey with 343 responses from educational professionals, as well as interviews, focus groups and an analysis of email discussion lists. Power, Petrie, Sakharov and Swallow investigated the accessibility of three major virtual learning environments (VLEs) for disabled students using both accessibility audits by experts and evaluations by disabled potential users of the systems. Finally Weiemair-Marki and Unterfrauner present a framework to describe the levels of preparedness of educational institutions in relation to meeting the needs of students with disabilities.

Understanding and Supporting the Needs of Educational Professionals Working with Students with Disabilities and Mature Age Students

David Swallow, Helen Petrie, and Christopher Power

Human-Computer Interaction Research Group, Department of Computer Science,
University of York, Heslington, York YO10 5DD, UK
{dswallow,petrie,cpower}@cs.york.ac.uk

Abstract. This study investigated the knowledge of educational professionals on the needs and preferences of disabled and mature age students in further and higher education. 102 Interviews and 6 focus groups were conducted in 4 European countries (Austria, Italy, Spain, and the UK) as well as in New Zealand and the USA. An online survey was publicised worldwide and 343 educational professionals from 21 countries responded. The results indicated a lack of standardisation in training and gaps in the knowledge and attitudes of educational professionals regarding how to appropriately support disabled and mature age in higher and further education. The use of e-learning technologies to address these issues is highlighted, as well as what is needed in future to better support not only disabled and mature age students but also the educational professionals who support them.

Keywords: Students with disabilities, mature age students, educational professionals, e-learning.

1 Introduction

Students with disabilities and mature age students are entering higher and further education institutions in increasing numbers. Members of staff in these institutions need a wide range of skills and knowledge about the needs and preferences of disabled and mature age students to be able to support them effectively. Members of staff who support disabled and mature age students include not only lecturers, other teaching staff, and disability support staff but also administrative staff, library staff, technical support staff and those who provide content for e-learning courses. This paper presents the results of an extensive investigation into the current levels of skill and knowledge amongst all these educational professionals in European and international educational institutions. It was carried out as part of the European Unified Approach for Accessible Lifelong Learning (EU4ALL) project, which aims to design, implement and evaluate a framework for accessible lifelong learning for students with disabilities and mature age students.

The experiences of over 450 further and higher educational professionals and 1,200 students from around the world were captured using a range of user requirements gathering methods. These included large-scale online surveys, in-depth face-to-face

K. Miesenberger et al. (Eds.): ICCHP 2010, Part I, LNCS 6179, pp. 486–491, 2010.

interviews, focus groups and an analysis of email discussion groups of disability officers in further and higher educational institutions. This range of methods allowed for triangulation of data between sources, which greatly increases the validity and robustness of the results; it also allowed a diversity of users, roles and environments to be explored.

Although the experiences of disabled and mature age students were of particular interest, the student survey was open to anyone who was currently taking a course (either for professional or leisure purposes) or had done so recently. Similarly, the professional survey was open to anyone working in education, regardless of his or her role or experience in working with disabled and mature age students. The interviews and focus groups were targeted more towards disabled and mature age students (although not exclusively so) as well as professionals who had experience of working with disabled and mature age students. Members of the email discussion groups comprised almost exclusively of disability officers and members of staff who have an interest in supporting students with disabilities.

The investigation on the whole covered a wide range of topics relating to the experiences of professionals and students in education. These included: disabilities and the use of assistive technologies; training; scheduling; communication; the use of learning materials; practical fieldwork; assessments; physical and virtual access; institutional knowledge; privacy and security; rights awareness; social inclusion; psychological support services; admissions; building access; procedures and policies; extra-curricular activities; as well as a number of role-specific questions.

This paper focuses upon the experience that educational professionals have gained in working with disabled and mature age students, either in their current role or previously. Knowledge of disability issues is explored, as well as the means by which educational professionals have attained this knowledge and how disability information is disseminated in their institution. Complaints that educational professionals have received from disabled and mature age students are examined in order to reveal the areas where support is lacking or where training has been insufficient. Finally, experiences of technology and, in particular, attitudes towards Virtual Learning Environments, are investigated and a novel application of e-learning technology is highlighted. It is hoped that by exploring the knowledge and attitudes of educational professionals, as well as the training and development opportunities that are available to them, this will provide an indication of how to improve the support of students with disabilities and mature age students.

2 Methodology

Prior to commencing formal data collection, a comprehensive review of existing services available to disabled and mature age students was carried out. As well as helping to understand what services were available, this process also identified a number of stakeholders, who were acknowledged as being important to the success of disabled and mature age students in education. These included: lecturers and teachers, disability officers, librarians and library staff, administrative personnel, notetakers, personal assistants, technical support staff, counsellors, and content producers. This informed the subsequent data collection activities, which were targeted at individuals from each of these professional groups.

The investigation initially focused upon the full range of sensory, physical and specific learning difficulties. However, based on feedback from disability officers and other educational professionals who work with disabled and mature age students, the scope was rapidly broadened to include the range of developmental (e.g. autism or Asperger's syndrome), mental health (e.g. depression, anxiety or stress) and chronic illness-related (e.g. diabetes or epilepsy) disabilities that are considered to be particularly important in further and higher education.

A combination of user requirements gathering methods was drawn upon in the data collection phase of the investigation, including: large-scale online surveys, in-depth interviews, focus groups and email discussion group analyses.

The online survey was used to engage a large number of educational professionals in questions concerning disability support in education. Approximately 60 questions long, the survey was administered using the online survey software, *QuestionPro*. All questions were optional and respondents were permitted to exit the survey at any time. In order to encourage participation, a prize draw for a limited number of €15 (or local equivalent) gift vouchers for the online store, *Amazon*, was offered. The survey was available in English, German, Greek, Italian, Spanish, and Portuguese languages and was carried out by 343 educational professionals over a period of one year.

Based on similar topics to the online surveys, the interviews and focus groups incorporated more in-depth, open-ended questions, often using the Critical Incident technique [1], to provoke more detailed discussion. The focus group schedule covered the same topics in a more general and discursive manner. Approximately 6-10 people took part in each focus group. Both the interviews and focus groups were designed to last no longer than one hour. 102 interviews and 6 focus groups were carried out with a range of educational professionals from institutions around the world.

Finally, in order to gain an objective understanding of the everyday problems facing educational professionals who work with disabled and mature age students, analyses were carried out on a number of UK- and USA-based email discussion lists for the support staff of students with disabilities. 666 posts were analysed from 2005 and 2006 and both relevant problems and requests for information were noted, as well as the responses that these appeals (sometimes) prompted. Where available, basic demographic data was collected in order to provide an indication of what problems were affecting what users at what stages of their educational careers.

3   Results

Experience of working with students with disabilities and mature age students was fairly high across all countries with a large proportion of respondents either currently working with or having previously worked with students from each of the different disability groups. Survey respondents felt significantly more informed about learning issues relating to students with visual and physical disabilities than to any of the other disability groups. Only 15-25% of respondents do not currently work with and never have worked with students from each of the different disability groups. A small number of respondents reported that they did not know whether they had worked with students from each of the different disability groups, however this may be explained by the large number of respondents from distance learning institutions who took part in the investigation.

Given that the majority of educational professionals reported working with students with disabilities, only 51.3% of respondents have received training in working with these groups. Even fewer respondents (28.3%) have received training in the needs of mature age students. Data from the interviews revealed a wide range of attitudes towards training and development. Some interviewees felt that their most significant training had been developed on-the-job through actually working with students with disabilities. Others felt that they did not need any training because they already have sufficient awareness of disability issues either through direct or indirect experience. Some interviewees felt they did not need any training whatsoever despite admitting that they knew very little about how to support students with disabilities.

The dissemination of information within institutions emerged in the interviews and focus groups as being rather problematic, with many communication problems arising from a lack of awareness over which member of staff or department is responsible for issues related to disabled and mature age students. Consequently, many members of staff are informed about disabled and mature age students either by being contacted directly by the student (53.6%) or merely by word-of-mouth (29.7%). Only 51% of respondents felt that the information that they receive regarding disabled and mature age students is adequate. This is reflected in the individuals and resources from whom respondents choose to seek such information, with many respondents looking outside of their institution, either from external online resources (35.3%) or members of external organisations (31.4%).

Despite many interviewees reporting that basic physical accessibility (e.g. wheelchair ramps) in their institution was adequate, the disability group from whom the greatest number of respondents (24.2%) reported receiving complaints was physically disabled students. The complaints received were varied and often specific to a particular student's situation, however, many concerned the poor accessibility of buildings and teaching room facilities. A similar disparity emerged with many complaints from students focusing upon a lack of provision, be it of services, of assistive technology, or of appropriate members of staff (e.g. sign language interpreters), despite staff satisfaction with the disability support services in their institution being generally high. One of the few areas in which educational professionals were less satisfied, however, was their own knowledge of assistive technologies and enhancements.

Technology, both mainstream and assistive, was reported to cause many problems for professionals and students, both in specific situations, such as assessments, as well as in everyday, general educational activities. Ensuring that assistive technologies are easily available, always working, and compatible with existing hardware and software, were frequently suggested improvements. Similarly, despite Virtual Learning Environments being introduced in many institutions, various problems and incompatibilities have led to a noticeable caution in placing complete dependence upon them. Even where the Virtual Learning Environment platform is compliant, consistent and satisfactory to its users, often the content is not or is difficult to find, with more accurate search facilities being highly desired.

4 Application

One of the ways in which the data from this investigation has already been exploited is in the creation of an e-learning course for support workers in further and higher educational institutions (see [2]). The state of knowledge and training for educational professionals in supporting students with disabilities and mature age students is evidently somewhat conflicted. Many respondents have also expressed a need for more complete information in order to better support students with disabilities and mature age students. Therefore, it was felt that an e-learning course could supplement the skills and knowledge of all educational professionals in disability-related issues and provide the desired awareness and information.

Following further consultation from a number of higher and further educational institutions as part of a participatory design process, an e-learning course was developed and is currently being piloted. Although initially targeted at the support workers of students with disabilities due to the diversity of support they provide, it is hoped that, if successful, the e-learning course will be extended to other groups of professionals and other institutions both nationally and internationally. This is just one example of the many ways in which this rich corpus of data could be exploited into order to support educational professionals and, ultimately, students with disabilities and mature age students.

5 Conclusions

Underlining many of the findings from this investigation is a need for greater information on how to support students with disabilities and mature age students in further and higher education. Educational professionals are extremely willing to provide such support and, indeed, the results of this investigation indicate that many already do or have done in the past, to varying degrees of success. The lack of information has led to many educational professionals losing confidence in their ability to support students with disabilities and mature age students. It has resulted in important knowledge being distributed word-of-mouth without any formal dissemination and has led to many professionals relying upon external resources and organisations in order to gather the information they need.

A degree of attitudinal change, at both the institutional and individual level, is necessary, particularly in relation to training and development. Institutions need to ensure that members of staff are offered training in the support of students with disabilities and mature age students, and consider innovative ways of achieving this, such as via e-learning. Individuals must also be receptive to ongoing training and development and willing to supplement their existing experiences with current best practices. There also has to be changes made to the technology that supports both students and professionals, not only in terms of usability and accessibility but also with regards to compatibility and reliability, particularly for assistive technologies and Virtual Learning Environments.

The purpose of the EU4ALL project from which this investigation emerged is to improve the accessibility of lifelong learning for students with disabilities and mature age students. In order to achieve this aim however, the educational professionals who provide this support must also be supported. This paper brings together the results of an extensive investigation, which drew upon a variety of method to solicit the experiences of over 450 further and higher educational professionals and 1,200 students from around the world. By highlighting the levels of knowledge, attitudes and needs of educational professionals in today's society, it is hoped that the situation for students with disabilities and mature age students will be greatly improved.

References

1. Flanagan, J.C.: The Critical Incident Technique. Psychological Bulletin 51(4), 327–359 (1954)
2. Power, C., Petrie, H., Swallow, D.: Who Supports The Support Workers? E-learning For Support Workers of Students With Disabilities. In: Jemni, M. (ed.) Proceedings of Second International Conference on Information and Communication Technologies, Hammamet, Tunisia (May 7-9, 2009)

Institutional Conditions for the Implementation of Accessible Lifelong Learning (ALL) Based on the EU4ALL Approach

Cäcilia Weiermair-Märki and Elisabeth Unterfrauner

Centre for Social Innovation, Linke Wienzeile 246, 1150 Vienna, Austria
{Weiermair,Unterfrauner}@zsi.at
www.zsi.at

Abstract. The project EU4ALL aims at researching and developing technologies and conceptual frameworks to make lifelong learning accessible to everyone. Within this project the conditions at higher education institutions necessary to introduce a service architecture as conceptual and technical framework such as the one developed within the project was studied. Beyond the project the results presented might be equally be applied to other innovations to be introduced in institutions in order to make lifelong learning more accessible while the introduction of the EU4ALL architecture might serve as example. Interviews with decision makers in Higher Education Institutions led to four different types of institutions with different levels of accessibility practice in place.

Keywords: Higher Education Institutions, accessibility, legal frameworks, social innovation, lifelong learning.

1 Introduction

Starting in autumn 2006 the four year EU funded project EU4ALL (European Unified Approach to Accessible Lifelong Learning) has been working on the development of an open service architecture to provide support services and technical infrastructure that enable teaching, technical and administrative staff of educational institutions to offer their teaching and services in a way that is accessible to disabled learners. EU4ALL is a standards based framework which consists of technological as well as conceptual parts. Besides the work on the technological framework research effort was put into the institutional conditions enabling educational institutions in general and higher educational institutions in particular to implement accessible lifelong learning (ALL) in general and the EU4ALL system in particular.

2 Typology of Educational Institutions

The findings are based on 35 interviews with (senior) representatives of Higher Education Institutions (HEI) across Europe (Austria, Greece, Italy, Spain and Great Britain) and beyond (Canada, Australia, USA). The in-depth analysis of the data

K. Miesenberger et al. (Eds.): ICCHP 2010, Part I, LNCS 6179, pp. 492–494, 2010.

resulted in a typology of institutions reflecting different levels of accessibility practice currently established in these institutions. Furthermore the results uncover that the types of institutions correspond very strikingly with general processes of social innovation in organizations. The concept of social innovations (c.f. [1]) implies that social change may take place alongside technological innovation and necessitates discourse in institutions about problems, values and objectives; actors perform new societal practice based on their intentions. This new societal practice is directed towards target groups and stakeholders. The underlying idea is diffused and institutionalized accordingly and unfolds impact on institutions which may be intended or not-intended. The process described is taking place in phases of social innovation. The characteristic phases of social innovation are intervention, institutionalization and professionalization. In the first phase the intervention is introduced similar to a pilot project, while no political programs exist and the resources and the benefits are unclear. Consecutively in the second phase, actions to institutionalize the new social practice are undertaken, cooperations are formed and communities (of practice) evolve, the benefit becomes visible through experience. Finally, the third phase of the social innovation process is characterized by professionalization, i.e. routine, the professional roles and the responsibilities are clear; benefits are formally evaluated. The four types of institutions are consequently presented according to their characteristics and location on the continuum of social innovation (c.f. Fig.1).

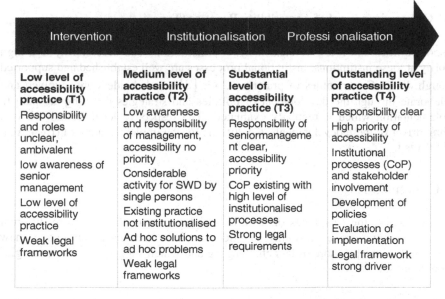

Intervention	Institutionalisation	Professi onalisation	
Low level of accessibility practice (T1)	**Medium level of accessibility practice (T2)**	**Substantial level of accessibility practice (T3)**	**Outstanding level of accessibility practice (T4)**
Responsibility and roles unclear, ambivalent	Low awareness and responsibility of management, accessibility no priority	Responsibility of seniormanageme nt clear, accessibility priority	Responsibility clear
low awareness of senior management	Considerable activity for SWD by single persons	CoP existing with high level of institutionalised processes	High priority of accessibility
Low level of accessibility practice	Existing practice not institutionalised	Strong legal requirements	Institutional processes (CoP) and stakeholder involvement
Weak legal frameworks	Ad hoc solutions to ad hoc problems		Development of policies
	Weak legal frameworks		Evaluation of implementation
			Legal framework strong driver

Fig. 1. Illustrates the connection of the implementation of EU4ALL with social innovation phases in organizations

2.1 Low Level of Institutional Accessibility Practice (Type 1)

In this type of institution the responsibilities and roles regarding accessibility of services are unclear. The (personal and institutional) awareness level of accessibility related issues is rather low and so is the level of existing services in place. These findings correlate with weak national legal frameworks. Conditions for the implementation of (EU4)ALL are hardly fulfilled.

2.2 Medium Level of Institutional Accessibility Practice (Type 2)

Type 2 is characterized by low level of awareness specifically at management level. Accessibility is not a priority on the institution's agenda. Although a considerable level of services for student with disabilities are offered, they depend on a single person. Existing practice are not institutionalized and ad-hoc solutions for ad hoc problems is the prominent strategy in place. Again these findings correlate with weak legal frameworks. Conditions for the implementation of (EU4)ALL are to some extent fulfilled.

2.3 Substantial Level of Accessibility Practice (Type 3)

In type 3 institutions the responsibility of senior management is clear and accessibility is high on the institutional agenda. Communities of practice exist with a high level of institutionalized processes and procedures. The legal frameworks support the institutionalization of accessible services through strong requirements. Conditions for the implementation of (EU4)ALL are to a large extent fulfilled.

2.4 Outstanding Level of Accessibility Practice (Type 4)

Responsibilities and roles are clear in type 4 institutions and accessibility is a high priority at these institutions. Institutional processes are well established and supported through divers Communities of practice (CoP, [2]). Stakeholders are involved and collaborate through the development of policies and strategies directing the path to implementation which is regularly evaluated. The respective legal framework is a strong driver of these developments. Conditions for the implementation of (EU4)ALL are fulfilled.

3 Conclusions

The results, i.e. the four types of institutions, demonstrate that there are different levels of institutional accessibility practice in place that make introducing new accessibility concepts more or less challenging and which suggest different strategies when doing so.

References

1. Nilsson, W.O.: Social Innovation: An Exploration of the Literature. Prepared for the McGill-Dupont Social Innovation Initiative. McGill University (2003),
    http://www.sig.uwaterloo.ca/documents/SocialInnovation.pdf
2. Wenger, E.: Communities of practice. Cambridge University Press, Cambridge (1999)

Design Guidelines for Developing Curriculum-Focused ICT Materials for Diverse Students

Cara Nicole Greene

National Centre for Language Technology, School of Computing,
Dublin City University, Dublin 9, Ireland
cgreene@computing.dcu.ie
http://www.nclt.dcu.ie/

Abstract. This paper presents design guidelines for developing curriculum focused Information Communication Technology (ICT) materials for diverse students with special needs in the inclusive secondary school setting. Mainstream and learning support teachers and students who developed these guidelines first took part in use of ICT questionnaires and took part in a three-month study investigating how these ICTs impacted on their classroom teaching. The teachers and students involved then took part in evaluation questionnaires and focus groups to develop design guidelines and good practice for developing curriculum-focused ICTs for diverse students. The guidelines were used to develop curriculum-focused materials for aspects of the Irish Junior Certificate (JC) English and History curricula [2]. English and History teachers and learning support teachers used the materials for three months with their classes and carried out an evaluation. Results showed that while mainstream teachers and students found the materials useful for enhancing the curriculum, the real benefit was for the learning support teachers and students.

Keywords: Specific learning difficulties, ICT, inclusive, second level, curriculum-focused, questionnaires.

1 Introduction

Section 2 introduces the background to this research. Section 3 briefly describes results from the initial ICT questionnaires and the study on how these ICTs are used in the classroom. This section goes on to describe the method used to formulate the design guidelines and the development and deployment of curriculum-focused Junior Certificate (JC) English and History ICT materials for diverse students. Section 4 presents the design guidelines developed by teachers and students and presents the results of the implementation of the curriculum-focused ICT materials. Section 5 highlights the contribution this research has made to the field. This is followed by conclusions and references.

K. Miesenberger et al. (Eds.): ICCHP 2010, Part I, LNCS 6179, pp. 495–502, 2010.

2 Background

The Irish National Council for Special Education (NCSE) [18] estimates that 18% of all children in Ireland have special educational needs. From this 18% the NCSE estimates that the prevalence of students with mild general learning disabilities is 1.5% and the students with moderate, severe and profound disabilities is 0.41%.

In Ireland, second level schools are working towards a fully inclusive environment so it is important for the curriculum to be fully accessible to all students. The National Council for Curriculum and Assessment (NCCA) has published teaching guidelines for teachers of students with general learning difficulties [15]. The guidelines point to the use of ICTs for certain learning outcomes such as presentation of class work. While the NCCA has published guidelines for teachers on ICT in the primary school curriculum [16], there has not been one for secondary level yet. The NCCA did publish a draft discussion paper on curriculum, assessment and ICT in the Irish context which includes second level [17].

Prior to undertaking this project, I worked as a learning support and resource teacher in a secondary school in the Republic of Ireland for a school year. This involved working with small groups of 13-16 year olds to support their classroom curricula and to work on literacy. Learning support teachers in the school relied heavily on general ICTs such as Microsoft Word [14]. Learning support teachers used literacy tools such as Read and Write Gold [19] that are aimed at younger primary level students because the content level was useful for their second level students who had literacy difficulties. I carried out a small pilot project to investigate the needs of a group of dyslexic students I was working with. The results showed the students wanted to use modules that were age-appropriate. In the school, there was no use of dedicated curriculum materials or tools along the lines of Scoilnet [20] to present the curriculum-focused materials to students with special needs.

Curriculum-Focused ICT Materials. Williams et al. [24] found that, although the literature shows a great number of ICT initiatives for people with all kinds of disabilities, there has been a surprising lack of research concerning those with specific learning difficulties. Computer-Assisted Learning (CAL) research has produced a number of projects aimed at students with special needs such as Korhonen's work on an adaptive spell checker for dyslexic writers [9] and Freda et al.'s paper on compensatory software which aids the mathematical learning process of dyslexic students [6]. Liu et al. [11] looked at how applications of ICT can be approached for people with special educational needs (SEN). The review of existing literature indicates a lack of attention to the application of ICT for people with special education needs, compared to other groups of disabled people such as visually impaired. Furthermore, the literature review carried out within this research showed that, of the small number of research projects developing ICTs for students with special needs, even less developed curriculum-focused ICT resources. Online curriculum materials such as Irish websites Scoilnet [20],

Teachnet [22] and Skoool.ie [21] have a wide range of curriculum materials available for the JC curriculum. Scoilnet and Teachnet materials are not aimed specifically at students with special needs. Can these materials be leveraged for use by teachers and students in learning support? Further research work in the area of designing ICTs to cater to second level students who have diverse abilities is needed.

3 Research and Methodological Approach

This paper presents design guidelines for developing curriculum-focused ICT materials for diverse students in the Irish second level inclusive school environment. In previous work reported in Greene (2008)[7] mainstream (MS)-, learning support- and resource teachers (LS) and diverse students from two secondary schools in the Republic of Ireland took part in questionnaires on the types of ICT tools that they use in the classroom or at home (Table 1).

Table 1. ICT Questionnaire Participants

Participant type	School A	School B	Total
MS teachers (MS)	27	18	45
LS teachers (LS)	7	6	13
MS students (MS)	163	261	424
LS students (LS)	18	25	43

The results point to three main ICT tool types being used by teachers and students in secondary schools today:

– General ICT tools (e.g. word processors)
– Special Needs-Focused Tools (e.g. text readers)
– Online curriculum-focused materials (e.g. Scoilnet curriculum materials)

Although the numbers involved in this survey are small, these questionnaire results have shown the gaps in the use of ICT in this context. They indicate a dichotomy between use for preparation and during class time. While 46% of students use computers and the Internet at home once a week to support homework, they are not using these resources in school. 80% of students are using online materials to support their homework but they are not using them in the classroom. 8% of MS teachers who are using online materials are printing the materials from these websites for use in the classroom but are not using the sites in the classroom (via overhead projectors for example). Teachers are printing work off for the students but they could actually be allowing the students to complete the work online as many of the students have the Internet at home and are using the sites frequently.

The results show that 50% of LS teachers and students rely on tool technology that is subject-independent. Only 4% of LS teachers and students are using curriculum-focused materials in school or at home. The findings show that there is an overall lack of curriculum-focused ICT materials for diverse students.

After this initial questionnaire, the teachers were invited to take part in a three-month study to analyse how these ICTs are being used in the classroom. The teachers and their students were split into three groups and each group was given one type of ICT:

- General ICTs (MS Word [14], MS PowerPoint [13], MS Excel [12])
- Focused ICT tools for special needs students (Kurzweil[10], Dragon Dictate[4])
- Online curriculum-focused materials (Scoilnet[20]; Teachnet[22], Skoool.ie[21])

Dragon Naturally Speaking is speech recognition software. Kurzweil is text-to-speech software. They are very expensive and schools can usually borrow them from the Irish Department of Educations Education Centres [3]. Teacher and student participants broken down the three types of ICT are shown in Table 2.

Table 2. Current impact of ICT project participant broken down by ICT type

Participant type	General ICTs	Focused Special-Needs ICTs	Online curriculum-focused ICTs	Total
MS teachers	12	12	12	36
LS teachers (LS)	4	4	4	12
MS students (MS)	119	120	124	363
LS students (LS)	13	14	14	41

Teachers and students then answered questionnaires and took part in focus groups to analyse how the ICT impacts on the curriculum teaching. Temkin [23] encourages the use of focus groups as the researcher can interact with the participants, pose follow-up questions or ask questions that probe more deeply. Results are broken down into General ICTs, Online Curriculum-Focused Materials and Focused ICT tools for students with special needs:

General ICTs. 46% of MS students and 18% of LS students said they used general ICTs such as Microsoft Word [14] for homework once a week already. During the project 100% of mainstream teachers set homework using general ICTs. 90% of mainstream students enjoyed the integration of the general ICT tools into classroom and homework activities. 75% of the mainstream teachers stated that the ICTs were most useful for project work or homework where students could work on their own. 100% of students stated they liked having PowerPoint [13] used in the class as they could present their own work and also have more interactive sessions with their teacher. 100% of LS teachers used Microsoft Word [14] and 56% of LS students liked using PowerPoint [13].

Online Curriculum-Focused ICT Materials. Results from the evaluation show that 100% of learning support teachers did not continue to use the available online curriculum materials (such as Scoilnet [20]; Teachnet [22]) for the three months because the content was not suitable to support key areas such as poetry and plays in the English curriculum. The content level was found to be too difficult and the materials were complicated to use and needed a lot of adaption for their students. 80% of learning support teachers stated that there was a lack of interactivity. It became evident that while mainstream teachers reported using online materials for revision and homework assignments and history project work, 100% of learning support teachers said they had to put significant effort into adapting the content to their students. Another problem that 25% of teachers reported was that it was always viable to use online materials due to websites/computers crashing and labs being unavailable for class-time.

Focused ICT tools for special needs students. 100% of learning support teachers reported finding both Kurzweil [10] and Dragon Dictate [4] very helpful for small group session or one-on-one session. 50% of mainstream teachers reported they found Dragon Dictate useful for project work. Students trained on the system and recorded themselves talking about a topic. The real benefit of this tools was for the learning support group for 100% of the mainsteam teachers and 60% of mainstream students found it interesting to integrate these tools into their classroom activities. While all of the learning support teachers had used a text reader, only 17% used one every day. 100% of learning support teachers reported it is very hard to get these tools as they are very expensive.

Design Guidelines and Development of Targeted Curriculum-Focused ICT Materials. The teachers and students then took part in focus groups to develop design guidelines for curriculum-focused ICT materials that cater to diverse students in inclusive mainstream second level schools.

The guidelines were used to develop curriculum-focused materials. In consultation with the Dyslexia Associate of Ireland (DAI) [5], I decided to use the History and English curricula and the tests subjects as the content level in these two subjects is regarded as the most difficult for students with literacy difficulties. I developed and tested (a) Online curriculum materials using HTML, PHP and Hot Potatoes [8] and (b) Clicker exercises [1] for aspects of the Irish Junior Certificate English and History curricula (Junior Cert 2010) over an initial period of two months. Clicker [1] exercises where the teachers can adapt the content were also developed. Clicker is a word processing software package that allows teachers to add pictures, videos and is very useful for creating mind maps for specific topics. English and History teachers worked with me to develop content for the online materials and Clicker exercises from their own teaching resources and curriculum texts.

English and History teachers and learning support teachers used the both sets of ICT materials for three months with their classes. Teacher and student participants in this deployment phase are shown in Table 3. Teachers and students

Table 3. Participants in deployment of curriculum-focused ICT tools project

Participant type	School A	School B	Total
English teachers	2	2	4
History teachers	2	2	4
LS teachers	7	5	12
MS students	64	67	131
LS students	17	24	41

answered questionnaires and took part in focus groups to analyse how the new targeted curriculum-focused materials impacted on their teaching and learning.

4   Findings

Mainstream and learning support teachers and students who developed the guidelines for designing curriculum-focused ICT materials for teenagers with special needs first took part in use of ICT questionnaires and took part in a three-month study investigating how these ICTs impacted on their classroom teaching.

Design guidelines for developing curriculum-focused ICT materials for teenagers with special needs included:

- Content level should be adapted depending on student literacy level
- Modules should cover one task only
- Age-appropriate material is vital
- Student should participate in design of materials
- Use dyslexia-friendly colours and fonts
- Keep text to a minimum
- Use pictures, graphs and videos to illustrate ideas
- Use exam question examples (exam paper wording)
- Materials do not need to be online due to problems with websites crashing
- Use mind-maps to reinforce material

The feedback from the focus groups on the initial ICT surveys, and the deployment and evaluation of those intial ICTs pointed to a lack of appropriate curriculum materials for teenagers in learning support. Mainstream teachers at the focus group said they benefited the most from available online curriculum-focused materials. 100% of learning support and resource teachers stated that the curriculum-focused materials online were not appropriate for their groups.

English, History and learning support teachers and students then took part in a three-month project to analyse how they used the new curriculum-focused materials developed within this project.

After the Clicker [1] materials and the online materials had been used in the schools for three months, the teachers evaluated how they had used the materials through questionnaires and focus groups.

Curriculum-Focused ICT Materials. 100% of the mainstream teachers said that the new English and History modules were better than the original Scoilnet [20] and TeachNet [22] materials as they did not have to adapt the content and it was in digestible chunks. 92% of mainstream students and 95% of stated that they found the History modules on the renaissance, viking settlements and ancient greece helpful for revision. 85% of learning support students stated they found the English module on poetry the most helpful. 85% of the learning support students said they would work confidently with the exercises on their own. 100% of the learning support and resource teachers who were involved throughout the whole project said they enjoyed working on the project and seeing their opinions reflected in the design of classroom materials. 100% of LS teachers stated that they could adapt the Clicker [1] materials very easily and create content-appropriate materials themselves. 75% the teachers preferred the Clicker [1] materials as both schools kept having Internet difficulties throughout the project so the online materials could not always be used. Conversely, 92% of learning support students and 80% of mainstream students preferred using the online materials and they could use in them in class as well as at home.

5 Contributions to the Field

This paper has contributed design guidelines to developers and teachers who want to create age-appropriate and content-appropriate curriculum-focused materials for diverse students at second level. A large group of teachers and students took part in this work and they are now using these materials.

6 Conclusions and Future Work

Teachers involved in this project undertook surveys on their use of ICTs in the classroom. They then used and evaluated different tools for three months. This feedback fed into design guidelines which were used to develop curriculum-focused materials. Teachers then evaluated these materials over a period of three months. Further subject materials could be developed in this area.

References

1. Clicker (2010), http://www.cricksoft.com/
2. Curriculum Online: Junior Certificate Cycle (2010),
   http://www.curriculumonline.ie/en/Post-Primary_Curriculum/Junior_
   Cycle_Curriculum/ http://www.curriculumonline.ie/en/Post-Primary_Curriculum/
   http://www.curriculumonline.ie/en/Post-Primary_Curriculum/Junior_
   Cycle_Curriculum/ Junior_Cycle_Curriculum/
3. Department of Education: Education Centres, http://www.education.ie/home/
   home.jsp?pcategory=49994&ecategory=38258&language=EN
4. Dragon Naturally Speaking, http://www.nuance.com/
5. Dyslexia Association of Ireland, http://www.dyslexia.ie/
6. Freda, C., Marcello Pagliara, S., Ferraro, F., Zanfardino, F., Pepino, A.: Dyslexia: Study of compensatory software which aids the mathematical learning process of dyslexic students at secondary school and university. In: Miesenberger, K., Klaus, J., Zagler, W.L., Karshmer, A.I. (eds.) ICCHP 2008. LNCS, vol. 5105, pp. 742–746. Springer, Heidelberg (2008)
7. Greene, C.: The Impact of Information Communication Technologies (ICTs) on Diverse Students and Teachers at Second Level. In: Miesenberger, K., Klaus, J., Zagler, W.L., Karshmer, A.I. (eds.) ICCHP 2008. LNCS, vol. 5105, pp. 207–214. Springer, Heidelberg (2008)
8. Hot Potatoes Half Baked FreeWare Software (2010), http://hotpot.uvic.ca/

9. Korhonen, T.: Adaptive Spell Checker for Dyslexic Writers. In: Miesenberger, K., Klaus, J., Zagler, W.L., Karshmer, A.I. (eds.) ICCHP 2008. LNCS, vol. 5105, pp. 733–741. Springer, Heidelberg (2008)
10. Kurzweil 3000 Scan and Read (2010), http://www.kurzweiledu.com/
11. Liu, Y., Cornish, A., Clegg, J.: ICT and Special Educational Needs: Using Meta-synthesis for Bridging the Multifaceted Divide. LNCS, pp. 18–25 (2007) 978-3-540-72589-3
12. Microsoft Excel (2010), http://www.microsoft.com/
13. Microsoft Powerpoint (2010), http://www.microsoft.com/
14. Microsoft Word (2010), http://www.microsoft.com/
15. NCCA: National Council for Curriculum and Assessment Guidelines for Teachers of Students with General Learning Difficulties (2010),
    http://www.ncca.ie/en/Curriculum_and_Assessment/Inclusion/
    Special_Educational_Needs/Download_Special_Educational_Needs_Guidelines/
    Guidelines_for_teachers_of_students_with_general_learning_
    disabilities.html
16. NCCA: Information and Communications Technology (ICT) in the Primary School Curriculum: Guidelines for Teachers. (2004a),
    http://www.ncca.ie/en/Curriculum_and_Assessment/ICT/#5
17. NCCA: Curriculum, Assessment and ICT in the Irish Context: A discussion paper (2004b),
    http://www.ncca.ie/uploadedfiles/ECPE/Curriculum%20AssessmentandICT.
    pdf
18. NCSE: National Council for Special Education Implementation Report: Plan for the Phased Implementation of the EPSEN Act 2004 (2006)
19. Read and Write Gold, http://www.edtech.ie/
20. Scoilnet Portal for Irish Education (2010), http://www.scoilnet.ie/
21. Skoool.ie portal (2010), http://www.skoool.ie/
22. TeachNet Ireland (2010), http://www.teachnet.ie/
23. Temkin, J.: How Focus Groups Work (2009),
    http://communication.howstuffworks.com/how-focus-groups-work.htm
24. Williams, P., Jamali, H., Nicholas, D.: Using ICT with people with special educational needs: What the literature tells us. In: Aslib Proceedings: New Information Perspectives, vol. 58, pp. 330–345 (2006)

A Framework to Support Development of Learning Applications for Disabled Children

José L. Fuertes[1], Ángel L. González[1], Gonzalo Mariscal[2], and Carlos Ruiz[2]

[1] Facultad de Informática, Universidad Politécnica de Madrid,
Boadilla del Monte, Madrid, Spain
{jfuertes,agonzalez}@fi.upm.es
[2] GI-CETTICO, Universidad Politécnica de Madrid, Boadilla del Monte, Madrid, Spain
{gmariscal,cruiz}@cettico.fi.upm.es

Abstract. Multimedia resources are an important tool that can be used by teachers in the classroom as a learning aid for learners with disabilities or by parents and children at home. However, disabled children are not always able to use existing assistive technologies because they are not experienced enough, suffer from medium/profound disability, or simply do not have the financial resources to buy commercial tools. Additionally, today's adapted tools are not always valid for a broad spectrum of disabled users and often focus on a user group. We claim that potential applications and resources for people with special needs must self-adapt to user capabilities and skills, reducing the use of external assistive technologies. In this paper, we present a guide for developers to create accessible applications and resources that reduce workload.

Keywords: Accessibility, human-computer interaction, education, assistive technology, children, special educational needs.

1 Introduction

The term 'special educational needs' (SEN) refers to people with learning difficulties or disabilities that make it harder for them to learn or access education than their peers [1]. Teaching SEN pupils is a complex task which involves implementing a teaching process and providing access to materials suited to learners' skills. In this context, digital media are a very useful tool to exploit in the classroom to educate SEN pupils.

The standards and guidelines for accessible software and Internet contents [2], [3] describe how applications should work to be used by disabled people with alternative devices and assistive technologies (ATs). The use of these standards benefits all users, as it equips systems for use by a broad spectrum of users.

There are several AT tools that can be used to adapt computer programs for people with special needs. They can be hardware or software based, and equally as wide-ranging and diverse as learners' capabilities and levels, and applications are. The selection of the best technology calls for a thorough and complex decision-making process to assure proper and effective use by each learner [4].

Moreover, an important consideration is that some ATs are complicated, difficult to set up and to learn. A non-proficient user may find it difficult to use ATs effectively

K. Miesenberger et al. (Eds.): ICCHP 2010, Part I, LNCS 6179, pp. 503–510, 2010.

or to combine a set of ATs. But what happens when the user is a child that has not yet learned how to use ATs like, for example, a screen reader or Braille display?

A lot of adapted tools reduce the development workload by just using ATs designed for a particular user type, even though multimedia tools only partially support some accessibility features. This decreases the number of potential users.

In this context, apart from conforming to the above standards, we claim that, despite the huge workload involved in developing a self-adaptive application, applications for SEN people should at least partially self-adapt to user capabilities and skills in order to improve use inexperienced AT users and solve this problem [4].

At first glance, managing all the alternatives suited to each user looks to be a complicated undertaking. We propose a development model and a framework to reduce the development workload of accessible self-adaptive applications.

Some of the features defined in the model and implemented in the current version of the framework are: indistinct use of mouse and keyboard, alternative text exposed to ATs for all graphical elements, descriptive text for all images, multilingual support, definition of direct accesses for each interactive system element, improving keyboard-mediated use and the use of concept keyboards, synchronized subtitling...

The remainder of the paper is organized as follows. In Section 2 we will look at existing solutions to the problem. In Section 3 we will present our solution and the platform implementation for Adobe Flash. Finally, in Section 4, we will present the results of applying the proposed Flash-based solution to a real-world problem.

2 State of the Art

Noteworthy tools with educational contents for children with SEN are "Hércules and Jiló" [5], CompuThera [6], "My Own Bookshelf" and "Running Start Books - Social Scripts"[1] [7]. E-learning software to help Down syndrome children to learn basic mathematical concepts and skills is described in [8].

Multimedia content is now a lot easier to author thanks to new tools, which have added the option of providing variable accessibility levels. US guideline-compliant accessible multimedia applications have been developed using Macromedia Flash MX since 2005. The Adobe Flash API offers a number of basic accessibility features, enabling communication with Microsoft Active Accessibility, but there are still accessibility gaps requiring programming or purchasing from another supplier [9].

Microsoft Silverlight [10] is a web application framework that offers a wide range of new accessibility enhancements: tabbing and tab order, focus and keyboard input, exposed Accessibility Tree for ATs, accessibility information written directly in XAML, notifications for high-contrast requirements...

Other approaches focus on adaptive course generation and adaptive e-learning platforms (Diogene and Intraserv [11], CEPIAH [12], eMEMORA [13]...). These generate contents automatically taking into account some metadata related to student profiles. The main weaknesses of these platforms are that a user profile has to be entered beforehand, and teachers have to provide a lot of information about all users.

---

[1] http://www.softtouch.com

Interactive multimedia authoring tool developers are investing a lot in improving the authoring of accessible materials. But all these tools come up short when users do not know how to use or cannot use some ATs. This applies to children with SEN, who, for age-related reasons, are unable to use some of the ATs recommended for users with a particular disability. For example, one pedagogical recommendation is to use recorded voices rather than screen readers with voice synthesis [14].

3   Proposed Solution

The solution is composed of a guide specifying the steps to be taken by the developer, including an implementation for the specific platform using the framework [15], [9].

3.1   Developing Steps

This phase is carried out during system design and analysis. Fig. 1 shows the required steps. The process starts after analysing the application. The first step is to define scenes. Scenes state a setting for interaction that is useful for establishing the right representation for each element and, in the case of educational resources, helps to define outcome assessment processes. It also improves the correlation between each scene and the learning objectives it addresses.

The next step is to analyse the interaction process and define a script for each scene. This step sets out a description of how to implement the interaction with the user.

The following step is to analyse the scripts. This analysis is helpful for determining the "actors" (interactive objects) and defining the actions that the user will be able to take, as well as useful information for understanding the scene (informational objects).

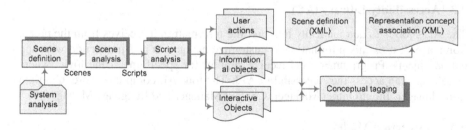

Fig. 1. Steps prior to framework use

The last step is conceptual tagging which enables the framework to represent and locate the materials required to render the scene, taking into account parameters like language, language proficiency, user abilities, etc. It associates a concept or identifier representing an element's purpose (interactive object, informational object, user action) to each input element within a scene. Also an XML document containing the relationship between the concept and its representation is generated [16].

3.2   The Model and Its Framework for Flash

The proposed solution models levels of conceptual abstraction [16]: conceptual definition of user actions, and of the interactive object and informational object.

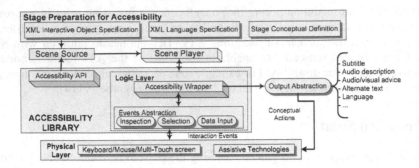

Fig. 2. Architecture overview

The mechanisms required to translate the AT input to a conceptually defined action or for use in system-user communications are provided by the Flash framework. The association of each interactive object and its scene with conceptual information enables this translation.

The defined model is shown in Fig. 2. Scene Player and Scene Source represent the scene player (in the model implementation for Adobe Flash 9.0) and the source code contains the scene implementation.

We described the Stage Preparation for Accessibility in the last section. The goal of the Scene Preparation for Accessibility is to generate the required data in XML format for the Accessibility Library (AL) to be able to do translation jobs, build components and execute actions based on the behaviour of the actors (interactive objects) in the scene.

3.3 Accessibility Library (AL)

The AL's job is to automatically interpret the information it receives from the preparation stage. It uses this information to customize navigation and interaction with application objects. Programmers will receive support for specifying scene logic, whereas developers can access the Accessibility API. The four AL components are: Configuration Manager, Input/Output Manager, Context Manager and Language Manager [9].

3.4 Abstraction Model

Actions in response to user events are simplified by means of an abstraction adapted from the model described in [16]. The model will be responsible for associating each interactive object with the necessary events and translating user actions into the respective conceptual action. All this is transparent to developers: an API takes charge of applying the abstraction to the objects defined in the XML file. Developers only need to define conceptual actions, e.g. "Help", "Play", "Move object", etc., without bothering about how users request the execution of the action (click on a button, gesture, menu option selection, etc.) or what device they use (a qwerty keyboard, concept keyboard, pointing device, etc.).

Programmers have to use concepts that represent the output information transmitted to the user. XML files, created in the last stage, will contain the output information. The chosen configuration will determine the media to be used to display the information.

3.5 Output Abstraction

This process is responsible for selecting the right media to represent the scene (Fig. 3). It requires user information, scene description and contextual information. This information is entered in the search engine to search for the required materials. The search engine uses a media repository. The media repository has been previously fed with the association between the concepts and representation defined in the preliminary 'Scene Definition' stage.

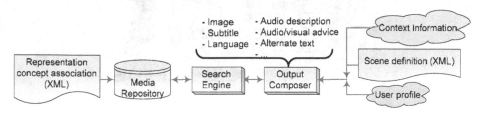

Fig. 3. Scene composition

As a result, the materials (image, audio description, descriptive text, etc.) required to represent the scene are assigned to the interactive objects and informational objects. The interactive objects and informational objects should also be registered as accessible elements. In the registration process, the information required for the scene to self adapt or be used with ATs, depending on user needs, is associated with these elements.

In our implementation for Adobe Flash 9, the search engine consists of an XML file set. The engine selects the XML file to extract the information based on the input parameters. Obviously, search engine complexity depends on problem requirements.

4 Applying the Framework: Learn and Internet in the Classroom

Based on this framework, we developed the Learn Project [15] and its continuation Internet in the Classroom[2] [9] (Fig. 4), funded by the Spanish Ministry of Education and Science. These projects involve generating many accessible multimedia materials associated with a curriculum especially designed for learners with SEN. These activities are developed by subgroups working separately but liaising with each other. Development is coordinated by the Higher Institute of Teacher Training and Networked Resources. The CETTICO research group was responsible for developing some of these materials in both projects.

Both projects are online educational resources targeting children with learning difficulties. The overall objective is to build up and develop the physical, cognitive and communicational skills of learners with SEN using new ICT to promote their personal autonomy and social integration. To achieve the overall objective, it is necessary to attain other general goals such as introduce ICT at primary and secondary schools, develop modified curriculums to meet learners' needs, and develop accessible contents to help teachers in the classroom.

---

[2] http://www.educacontic.es/recursos

Fig. 4. Screenshot from Internet in the Classroom project

The projects imply the integration of different professional profiles with clearly defined tasks and responsibilities. Apart from the coordination team, three profiles were established: *contents developers* (pedagogues and educators), whose mission is to prepare the contents; *graphics developers* produce the graphics and audiovisual material; and *technical developers* (software engineers and programmers) who develop the new adaptive tools, design web pages and schedule activities.

These projects were developed taking into account the learners' needs and skills to customize the resource. Thus, other specific objectives related to learners' skills are:

- To establish multimedia activities related to personal autonomy, everyday problem solving and decision making.
- For pupils to learn to live in society through knowledge of the rules of cooperation and participation.
- To develop understanding, knowledge, linguistic skills, memory, logical reasoning and everyday problem-solving.

The learning objectives are metaphors (worlds, scenarios, characters or objects) to make the contents more appealing. They are learning worlds and their contents are:

1. Learning to be: It develops personal skills (dealing with feelings and tension…). Scenarios are presented as a number of interesting places visited in daily life.
2. Learning to do: This module develops practical skills in which learners apply their knowledge to interact with the environment and acquire new competences.
3. Learning to live together: This module develops interpersonal skills, pointing out learners' ability to interact and work in groups. These lessons also develop empathy, courtesy, friendship, cooperation and teamwork.
4. Learning to know: This module develops cognitive skills, such as decision making and problem solving.

The projects were implemented as a website (level AA of WCAG 1.0) and a multimedia application (conforming to the software accessibility standard [2]).

5 Results and Conclusions

Educating people with SEN is a complex task even for experts and educators. Each learner's education should be individualized depending on his or her characteristics and abilities, enabling a more effective use of AT. Unfortunately, none of the previous research connects the whole teaching process.

The proposed solution takes into account all the steps in the teaching process for SEN (from design to implementation and evaluation). The presented model and its implementation for Adobe Flash 9 is able to reduce the workload involved in creating self-adaptive activities. To verify this point, we experimented on the 'Learn Project' and 'Internet in the classroom' taking measurements of the workload required to develop multimedia activities for groups with and without the technology described in this paper. We planned two experiments (see Table 1):

Table 1 Comparison of development times (days)

Work Group	Use Case 1	Use Case 2
Group 1	18.5	33.0
Group 2	19.0	34.0
CETTICO	16.0	25.0
Groups 1 & 2 Average	18.75	33.50
CETTICO Improvement	15%	25%

- Use Case 1: Development of an accessible learning object within the 'Learn' project. Development groups 1 and 2 each developed a very similar multimedia activity without using the framework or the AL. The CETTICO group developed a similar activity to the other groups but using the framework and the AL.
- Use Case 2: Development of an accessible and self-adaptive learning object within the 'Internet in the Classroom' project. Development groups 1 and 2 developed a similar multimedia activity without using the framework or the AL. The CETTICO group developed a similar activity but using the framework and the AL.

From the results in Table 1, we can conclude that our solution leads to a development workload reduction of about 15% for accessible applications and 25% if the application needs to be self adaptive. In addition, CETTICO developed 15 activities throughout the 2007-2008 project, of which 10 needed to be self-adaptive and the other five needed to be accessible and compatible with AT.

In order to assess the quality of results by accessibility and usability, the Spanish Ministry of Education's Institute of Educational Technologies (ISFTIC) applied an assessment process. The conclusion reached by ISFTIC is that the quality of accessibility and usability of the multimedia activities developed by the different teams was very similar.

References

1. DirectGov: What are special educational needs?, http://www.direct.gov.uk/en/Parents/Schoolslearninganddevelopment/SpecialEducationalNeeds/DG_4008600
2. ISO (International Organization for Standardization): ISO 9241-171:2008 Ergonomics of human-system interaction – Part 171: Guidance on software accessibility (2008)
3. W3C: Web Content Accessibility Guidelines (WCAG) 2.0, http://www.w3.org/TR/WCAG20
4. Poon-McBrayer, K.F., Lian, M.G.J.: Special needs education: children with exceptionalities. Chinese University Press (2002)
5. Lacerda, G.: Hércules y Jiló. Un Software Educativo para la Estimulación Matemática, Lingüística y Social de Niños con Deficiencia Mentas. Revista de Informática Educativa, 32–47 (February 2000)
6. Moore, M., Calvert, S.: Brief report: vocabulary acquisition for children with autism: teacher or computer instruction. Journal of Autism and Developmental Disorders, 359–362 (2000)
7. SoftTouch, http://www.softtouch.com
8. Ortega-Tudela, J., Gómez-Ariza, C.: Computer assisted teaching and mathematical learning in Down syndrome children. Computers, Mathematics, and Down Syndrome 22, 298–307 (2006)
9. Cantón, P., González, Á.L., Mariscal, G., Ruiz, C.: Building accessible Flash applications: an XML-based toolkit. In: Miesenberger, K., Klaus, J., Zagler, W.L., Karshmer, A.I. (eds.) ICCHP 2008. LNCS, vol. 5105, pp. 370–377. Springer, Heidelberg (2008)
10. Rideout, M.: Accesibility in Silverlight 2, http://archive.visitmix.com/blogs/Joshua/Silverlight-2-Accessibility-with-Mark-Rideout/
11. Sangineto, E., Capuano, N., Gaeta, M., Micarelli, A.: Adaptive course generation through learning styles representation. Universal Access Information Society 7, 1–23 (2008)
12. Trigano, P., Giacomini, E.: Toward a Web based environment for Evaluation and Design of Pedagogical Hypermedia. J. Educ. Technol. Soc. IEEE Learn. Technol. Task Force 7(3) (2004)
13. Benayache, A., Abel, M.-H.: Using knowledge management method for e-learning. In: Chiazzese, G., Allegra, M., Chifari, A., Ottaviano, S. (eds.) Methods and Technologies for Learning. WIT Press (2005)
14. Nass, C., Robles, E., Bienenstock, H., Treinen, M., Heenan, C.: Voice-based disclosure systems: Effects of modality, gender of prompt, and gender of user. International Journal of Speech Technology 6(2), 113–121 (2003)
15. Cantón, P., González, A.L., Mariscal, G., Ruiz, C.: Developing pedagogical multimedia resources targeting children with special educational needs. In: Miesenberger, K., Klaus, J., Zagler, W.L., Karshmer, A.I. (eds.) ICCHP 2006. LNCS, vol. 4061, pp. 536–543. Springer, Heidelberg (2006)
16. González, Á.L.: Modelo para la Generación y Gestión en Tiempo de Ejecución de Procesos de Interacción Hombre-Máquina a Partir de un Lenguaje de Especificación de Relaciones con el Usuario. PhD Thesis dissertation, Technical University of Madrid (2003), http://oa.upm.es/87/

Using Robots in Education and Therapy Sessions for Children with Disabilities: Guidelines for Teachers and Rehabilitation Professionals

Francesca Caprino, Serenella Besio, and Elena Laudanna

Università della Valle d'Aosta, Strada Cappuccini 2A,
11100 Aosta, Italy
{f.caprino,s.besio,e.laudanna}@univda.it

Abstract. Within the co-funded European pr4oject IROMEC (IST-FP6-045356), aiming at developing and experimenting an innovative robotic toy to be used in play intervention addressed to children with motor-based, cognitive and developmental disabilities, specific guidelines for using robots in educational and rehabilitation environments have been developed. The guidelines are addressed to therapists, teachers and researchers aiming to promote inclusion in play of children with disabilities and are meant as a tool to apply robotics in play-based intervention.

Keywords: Rehabilitation Robotics, Guidelines, ICF-CY.

1 Introduction

This paper presents one of the final results of the work carried out by the research group on robotics for children with special needs of the University of Valle d'Aosta within IROMEC, a project co-funded by the European Commission within the sixth Framework Research and Development programme (IST-FP6-045356). IROMEC developed and experimented an innovative robotic toy to be used in play interventions addressed to children with motor-based, cognitive and developmental disability. Moreover, the project carried out an extensive research on the state of the art robotics for play in relation to children with disabilities [1], [2], together with a methodological framework on robot-mediated play intervention in clinical and educational settings [3], [4].

Specific guidelines for using robots in educational and rehabilitation environment with children with disabilities have been developed as final methodological deliverable of the project [5]. The guidelines are addressed to therapists, teachers and researchers aiming to promote inclusion in play of children with disabilities and are meant as a tool to apply robotics in play-based intervention.

The primary goal of this paper is to summarize the methodology applied in the guidelines development and to describe the final result.

2 Motivation

Children with particularly severe disabilities are often unable to play like their peers. The differences are both qualitative (complexity of the games, type of skills

K. Miesenberger et al. (Eds.): ICCHP 2010, Part I, LNCS 6179, pp. 511–518, 2010.

demonstrated, ability to play with others) and quantitative (time that such activities entail). In the most severe cases play may not even be part of the child's behavioural repertoire. Joyful spontaneity, genuine fun, the electrifying experience of discovery the richness of social interaction associated with play may be partially or entirely precluded for children with autism or other severe diseases that limit their mobility, language, perception and thought.

There are many environmental and individual factors that prohibit a child from fully experiencing playtime activities in these cases. In addition to the child's physical impairments (motor-based, cognitive or sensorial), other factors not related to him/her – the lack of materials and accessible play areas, for example, or activities that are not compatible with the child's characteristics and potential – contribute to play deprivation which, in turn, because it compromises the child's full development, may generate secondary disabilities. Identifying and eliminating all these play barriers, where possible, is crucial for those who want, through play, to ensure full development, enhance involvement and improve the quality of life of children with disabilities. Selecting accessible play materials, adapting everyday toys, using assistive technologies for play: these are the strategies most often applied, in educational and rehabilitation environments, to improve the play activities of children with disabilities.

The new technologies, that provide clinicians and educators with an important resource for eliminating play obstacles, undoubtedly play the most important role in this sense. This is the case, among others, of the new robotic technologies, which, in recent years, have proven to be a resource capable of offering important play opportunities to children with even severe functional impairments [6], [7], [8]. Robots are real objects that exist and act in the real world: in fact, they can move in three-dimensional space and physically interact with users and with the surrounding environment. This aspect provides significant added value for users with physical disabilities for whom not being able to move or take action is one of the most powerful restrictions in their interaction with the environment: a robotic system, for example, can allow those with severe motor impairments to move in the play environment or manipulate objects independently, something that obviously a software system cannot offer. Then, a robot offers richer sensorial stimulation involving the visual and auditory channels, in addition to touch. This creates a much more significant perceptive experience than any virtual reality application developed to the present can provide.

Moreover robots seem to be more easily perceived as independent and intelligent agents. In other words, they are considered on the same level as persons rather than machines: in the case considered here, as playmates more than toys. The ability of some robots to simulate the behaviour of human beings has shown to promote social and affective development, especially in children with autism, guiding them within the complex world of social interactions [6]. But if robotic technologies continue to develop at breakneck speed, they also become obsolete just as fast. Choosing the most suitable technological tools to support play can be quite difficult for professionals not having up-to-date information. Furthermore, the availability of innovative technologies is not sufficient to ensure that children with disabilities will play effectively: to fully utilise the potential offered by robotic technologies it is also necessary to have a solid methodology which, starting from the real needs of children, makes efficient use of available tools.

3 Methodology

The Guidelines are the synthesis and the integration of the results of different research activities and apply theoretical knowledge to practical experiences in order to develop new methodological perspectives.

The first step has been a deep theoretical research and analysis of the critical factors – the most important variables and key-aspects – involved in robot mediated play activities addressed to children with disabilities for learning and therapy set-ups [1], [2]. The most important theoretical background of this work has been the International Classification of Functioning, Disability and Health – Children and Youth Version 2007 (ICF-CY) [9].

This theoretical research has then led to the development of a first methodological framework to introduce the IROMEC prototype in daily educational and rehabilitation activities. The framework, derived from existing instruments and methods for the assessment of Assistive Technology, has been intended mainly to support professionals, teachers and clinicians, in defining objectives of intervention, thus choosing the "best" scenarios from a limited set of pre-designed play activities [10] through the compilation of a step-by-step questionnaire [3]. This first version has been used to set up real experimental trials and has been then modified and improved on the basis of the observations and feedback collected from the professionals involved. As a consequence, a new version of the theoretical framework has been developed, now supported both from theory and experience [3], [4].

Another contribution to the Guidelines has been the theoretical research on play assessment procedures of children with disabilities. This study has led to two results: the proposal of some possible instruments to evaluate the outcomes of the play interventions with robots; the identification of the key aspects to take into account when defining the setting of intervention (role of the adult, play materials, presence and role of peers) [3]. Again the theory has been applied in real trials and an improvement of methods has been developed.

The final result of this process, the Guidelines [5], can be intended as the final synthesis of the knowledge acquired and developed within the IROMEC, applied to support education and rehabilitation professionals, but also families, in the planning process that from the child's needs leads to the choice and use of robots.

4 Results

The "Guidelines For Using Robots In Educational And Therapy Sessions For Children With Disabilities" describe:

- the role of play in educational and rehabilitation environments as a mean of motor-based, cognitive, communicative and social development and some possible interventions in a school or rehabilitation context;
- the experience of play in children with disabilities, namely their different play behaviours and different limitations in play (following the structure of ICF-CY), and how the application of robotics can overcome them;

- features of robots and possible matching of their features with the functioning of children with disabilities through play scenarios for play – based intervention
- case-studies, that is, real experiences with different robotic devices
- methodological approach for robot - mediated play intervention

4.1 Special Children at Play

The guidelines provide a description of functional limitations of three different categories of children with disabilities: children with motor impairments, children with cognitive disabilities and autistic children.

Children are described and clustered according to the ICF-CY, through their functional limitations (e.g. mobility, learning and applying knowledge, communication) and the consequences they have on the play activities described according to the ESAR classification system [11] (Exercise, Symbolic, Assembly, with Rules). (see Table 1 for a short example related to motor impairments)

The table below provides some examples of the comparison between children's limitations and the presence of dysfunctional play abilities.

Table 1. Influence of limitations in motor functions on play skills: on the left, the individual activities that are influenced by the impaired body functions for cases involving severe motor disabilities, and on the right the consequences they may have on play skills and opportunities

MOBILITY	
Limitations	**Consequences on play**
Limitations in remaining seated or remaining standing and in maintaining head position	Since the child cannot (or can hardly) maintain a stable position without any help, he/she cannot use standard play materials and interact with peers for a sufficiently long period of time
Limitations in using arms and hands to lift, to carry, to raise, to take, to push, to pull objects from one place to another, to reach, to turn and to throw objects	The child cannot interact with toys in a proper way, both in terms of exploratory aim (dropping or throwing them) and exercise aim (trying to send a ball or a little car in a precise direction). The following stages of assembly and symbolic play are affected too
COMMUNICATION	
Limitations	**Consequences on play**
Limitations in speaking	If the child cannot communicate through speaking, if he/she can hardly or cannot develop linguistic competences, he/she barely develops symbolic and pretend play activities or social interaction with peers in games with rules
Limitations in producing non-verbal messages (body gestures and facial expressions)	Facial expressions and body gestures are an important component of play interaction, both for symbolic play and for games with rules

GENERAL TASKS AND DEMANDS	
Limitations	**Consequences on play**
Limitations in undertaking, carrying out, completing one single simple task	These limitations affect play activities that require one single action repeated more than one time, such as assembling a tower of construction bricks or assembling a puzzle

LEARNING AND APPLYING KNOWLEDGE	
Limitations	**Consequences on play**
Limitations in touching and exploring using the mouth	The first stage recognized as play, sensory motor exploration using the mouth, is impossible or limited since the child cannot bring objects or his/her own hands and feet to his/her mouth
Limitations in using hands, fingers and other body parts to experience stimuli, such as touching and feeling textures	The child cannot easily explore the form and the surface of objects while handling them

For each disability's category and each play type the guidelines identify the possible role of robotic technologies in increasing play opportunities e.g. facilitating and motivating the children or assisting them in their physical and social interaction with the play environment, thus compensating for or substituting the impaired functions.

Information about the influence of environmental factors on play skills and play opportunities of children with disabilities are also supplied.

4.2 Robots for Play

The role of robotics is first described at large, also taking into account available products and technology for play (Assistive Technologies), robotic prototypes used for specific researches and adaptation of existing toy robots; then a separate section provides six concrete examples on the use of robotics in play interventions addressed to children with disabilities.

The characteristics of the existing systems (both robotic prototypes designed to be used with children with special needs and off-the-shelf toy robots) are then related to possible play activities and children's needs.

As any play-based intervention should always start from the needs and the abilities of the child, the features of the robot should be linked on the one hand to the scenario (activity) to be implemented and, on the other, to the child's functioning. In relation to the educational and rehabilitation objective(s), one or more scenarios (play activities) can be implemented and some particular features of the robot are required. The following logical sequence should be applied:

Child → scenario → robot

But also in relation to child functioning some adaptations might be necessary and another relationship is required:

Child → robot

Some of the existing relationships have been listed and analysed though several tables (see Table 2 for a short example) developed as a tool to understand if a "real" robot is suitable to carry out a pre-defined, play-based intervention, how it should be adapted

– if necessary – to the needs of a specific child, and in which context and play environment it should be used.

Some of the possible features of the robot have been clustered as follows:

- physical features and appearance (dimension, weight, appearance)
- movements of the body (mobility, speed, obstacle detection)
- sensing and user input interaction (light sensing, colour detection, sound detection, sound recognition, movement detection, touch detection, speech recognition, gesture recognition)
- input devices for controlling the robot (remote/on board, switches, scanning techniques, touch screen, keyboard, personal computer)
- feedbacks and output interactions (visual, tactile and auditory outputs, facial expression, upper limbs and head movements)
- complex functions (obstacle avoidance, following a moving target, executing patterns of movements and feedback, gripping objects, having proactive, reactive and physiological functions)

Table 2. Robots, scenarios and children: possible relationships of physical features

Robot	Scenario	Child
Dimensions	Small dimensions reduce the possible number of children that can play together (1 to 4) around a table or in a small area on the floor since the children should be near the robot in order to see and to interact. Bigger dimensions mean it is possible to work in a larger area, with more children.	Small dimensions require good visual functions and an adjustable setting if the child uses a wheelchair. Bigger dimensions associated to movements and speed, can scare young children, children with mental retardation or children who cannot autonomously move and run away.
Weight	Weight affects the place where the activity can be done. A heavy robot cannot be used for activities on a table, especially if it is a mobile robot that may fall off the table.	
Appearance	Anthropomorphic or zoomorphic appearance is required to induce physical appearance and to implement scenarios of symbolic and pretend play activities. The presence of limbs, tail(s), arms, legs, and overall face is fundamental to achieve this purpose.	The exterior appearance makes the first impression on the child so to enhance further interaction it should be appropriate to the age, the functioning and the preferences of the child. Young children, children with autism or cognitive disabilities usually like the appearance to be similar to toys (bright colours, simple appearance, not too small parts, not too many details), while older children can be attracted by a more technological look. An anthropomorphic or zoomorphic appearance can enhance communication and interaction.

4.3 Using Robots to Promote Play in Children with Disabilities

Finally, the guidelines illustrate a possible play-based methodology for using robots with children with disabilities. The proposed methodology arise from the application of theoretical studies developed within the IROMEC project to the experimental trials carried out with different prototypes. The intervention methodology considers:

- initial assessment (functional assessment of the child, play skills assessment)
- criteria for selection of the educational and rehabilitation objective(s) of the intervention (soundness of the objectives, identification of long, medium and short-term goals, definition of the success criteria)
- strategies to be applied to identify and describe possible play scenarios (actors involved in the play activity and their role, actions carried out by the various actors during play, characteristics of the play setting, duration and sequences of the play activity, play materials)
- possible roles of the adults involved in the play intervention (teachers, therapists, caregivers) and the level of the cognitive and physical support provided
- role of peers with or without disability involved in the play activity

5 Conclusions

"Guidelines For Using Robots In Educational And Therapy Sessions For Children With Disabilities" is a useful tool to efficiently and systematically implement robotic technologies in order to improve play skills of children with disabilities. Because of the continuous development of robotics, they can be considered only a first step in this field of studies, as they could be further improved with the inclusion of new systems and other experiences with children with disabilities.

The innovation brought by this work lies in the extensive research on the possible applications of robotics to play, in order to enhance the inclusion of children with different types of disability. This research is based on experimental investigation and periodic consultations with experts panels. The Guidelines for using robots in education and rehabilitation contexts with children with disabilities can be a useful contribution for researchers who aim at deepening this subject: they can find ideas to improve their prototypes, to develop new devices and to suggest new methodological approaches. The free electronic version of the Guidelines can be downloaded from the IROMEC Project webpages (www.iromec.org) or requested from the Authors.

References

1. Besio, S.: Analysis of Critical Factors Involved in using interactive Robots for Education and Therapy of children with disabilities. Uniservice, Trento (2008)
2. Besio, S., Caprino, F., Laudanna, E.: Profiling Robot-Mediated Play for Children with Disabilities through ICF-CY: The Example of the European Project IROMEC. In: Miesenberger, K., Klaus, J., Zagler, W.L., Karshmer, A.I. (eds.) ICCHP 2008. LNCS, vol. 5105, pp. 545–552. Springer, Heidelberg (2008)
3. Besio, S.: Methodological Framework to set up educational and therapy sessions with IROMEC. Uniservice, Trento (2009)

4. Caprino, F., Laudanna, E.: Methodological Framework to set up Educational and Therapy Sessions with Robotic Technology: the IROMEC proposal. In: Emiliani, P.L., Burzagli, L., Como, A., Gabbanini, F., Salminen, A. (eds.) 10th AAATE Conference, pp. 176–181. IOS Press, Amsterdam (2009)
5. Besio, S.: Guidelines for using robots in education and play therapy sessions for children with disabilities. Uniservice, Trento (2010)
6. Dautenhahn, K., Robins, B.: Learning and Interaction in Children with Autism. In: 6th IEEE International Conference on Development and Learning, London (2007)
7. Marti, P., Giusti, A., Rullo, A.: Robots as social Mediators: field trials with children with special needs. In: Emiliani, P.L., Burzagli, L., Como, A., Gabbanini, F., Salminen, A.L. (eds.) 10th AAATE Conference. Adaptive Technology from adapted equipment to inclusive environments, pp. 165–169. IOS Press, Amsterdam (2009)
8. Robins, B., Gelderblom, G.J., Kronreif, G.: Robotic Helpers: User Interaction, Interfaces and Companions in Assistive and Therapy Robotics. In: 3rd ACM/IEEE International Conference on Human-Robot Interaction, Amsterdam (2008)
9. World Health Organisation (WHO), International Classification of Functioning, Disability and Health, http://www.who.int/classifications/icf/site/
10. Robins, B., Ferrari, E., Dautenhahn, K.: Developing Scenarios for Robot Assisted Play. In: 17th IEEE International Symposium on Robot and Human Interactive Communication (RO-MAN 2008), Munich (2008)
11. Garon, D., Chiasson, R., Filion, R.: Le système ESAR. Guide d'analyse, de classification et d'organisation d'une collection de jeux et jouets. Electre, Paris (2002)

Virtual Learning Environments: Another Barrier to Blended and E-Learning

Christopher Power, Helen Petrie, Vasily Sakharov, and David Swallow

Human Computer Interaction Research Group
Department of Computer Science
University of York
Heslington, York, UK
{cpower,petrie,dswallow}@cs.york.ac.uk

Abstract. With online and blended learning now commonplace, it is surprising that the research regarding the accessibility of virtual learning environments and other collaborative learning management systems is relatively sparse. This paper provides an initial empirical investigation into the accessibility problems that are present in 3 different virtual learning environments. This investigation demonstrates that there are a number of places where virtual learning environments can present barriers to learning for students with disabilities.

Keywords: Accessibility, virtual learning environment, VLE, elearning, blended learning, empirical investigation.

1 Introduction

As education has moved from the traditional face-to-face learning of the classroom to the new frontier of digital resources, online lectures and remote collaboration, opportunities for students to learn have increased dramatically. For students with disabilities, there is a clear advantage to this new wholly online elearning model or blended learning model of education where the virtual is mixed with face-to-face experiences in that they can, in theory, access learning resources in adapted forms that are delivered according to their needs and preferences.

It is known that there are several layers of technology that can interfere with the student gaining access to such adapted resources. Conflicts with user agents, assistive technologies and the delivery format of the resources are the most commonly cited problems. However, before a student interacts with a learning resource, often they must first obtain that resource from an online location. In some cases, resources are made available on a website; but, in others the student must interact with a *virtual learning environment* (VLE) in order to gain access to learning resources.

Further, the VLEs are often used for communication with peers and with tutors, for sharing and collaborating on assignments and for assessments. As a result, the impact of an inaccessible VLE on a student's learning experiences could be very high.

This paper explores the issues surrounding the accessibility of virtual learning environments. First, it presents some of the previous work looking at virtual learning

K. Miesenberger et al. (Eds.): ICCHP 2010, Part I, LNCS 6179, pp. 519–526, 2010.
© Springer-Verlag Berlin Heidelberg 2010

environments and their context in blended learning and elearning. The examination of previous work has revealed that very little empirical work has been undertaken to determine the types of accessibility barriers that are common to VLEs.

This paper will then continue by presenting the methodology and results of an empirical investigation into the accessibility different VLEs. These evaluations include expert evaluations and user evaluations on three different platforms, including the commercial market leader *Blackboard* and the open source market leader *Moodle*.

The paper concludes with a discussion of the future work needed to ensure all students receive equal access to education.

2   Previous Work

In this section the literature regarding previous studies about the utility, usability and accessibility of VLEs is presented. The material review demonstrates that the accessibility, indeed even the basic design of virtual learning environment, is not terribly well understood or standardized in research or in practice. This is perhaps due to the fact that when VLEs were introduced in the late 1990s most of the web was still statically presenting information to the users and rich interactivity was rare. As such, the experience of the community in the types of interactions that were in VLEs were poorly understood from an accessibility point of view[1]. As such, it is important to first examine what functionality is provided by VLEs that presents challenges in accessibility.

The following are types of functionality that are typically available in virtual learning environments:

- Course/module outlines that provide a means of navigating through the material attached to a particular module
- Assessment and assignment pages that consist of both the downloading of contents for manipulation by a student, and integrated assessment questions that need to be completed online
- Email/contact facilities can sometimes be as simple as a link to trigger composition of an email or can be complex applications
- Student home pages that can be modified in a wide variety of ways to include structure and content that is independent of the module structure and content
- Content contribution tools that can take the form of content repositories or complete authoring applications.
- Synchronous collaborative tools (e.g. whiteboard, virtual classroom) and asynchronous message boards
- Metadata repositories to aid in search and retrieval of relevant learning resources

As can be seen, VLEs comprise most major tasks on the web. Indeed, since their inception they have included collaboration (both synchronous and asynchronous), user generated content and communication tools that are all now aspects of Web 2.0. As such, the accessibility of current VLEs, a mature technology, provides an interesting case study regarding the types of problems that can be encountered by users in current

---

[1] Indeed, it could be argued that we still have a long way to go in understanding interactivity on the web in terms of usability or accessibility.

web applications. In any accessibility evaluation, all of these different aspects must be examined, and as such user tasks and page sampling are of utmost importance.

Perhaps it is due to the complexity of VLEs that there are very few accessibility evaluations, or indeed usability evaluations, of them. Further, in those few that have been undertaken, the problems found are often similar to those on static web sites. For example Phipps et al. 7 point to the mismatches in needs and preferences of people with visual or hearing disabilities when accessing multimedia as being prevalent. These problems are compounded by poor navigational structure, colour contrast problems and major problems relating to mark-up conflicting with user agents and assistive technology. Similar, overlapping subsets of web design guidelines for people with disabilities are reported in: Sloan et al. 10, Pearson and Koppi 6 and Blankfield 1 Seale 9 rightly observes that when the above subsets are combined, the majority of the Web Content Accessibility Guidelines 23 apply to VLEs.

Unfortunately, many of these reports on accessibility in VLEs, such as Blankfield 1 and the more recent work by Hersch 5, are based on survey and interview data, not empirical results. Due to this, there is no indication about how prevalent, or how severe, accessibility problems are in practice today. As a result, it is difficult to make cases for improved awareness, training or procedures in accessibility at international education institutions.

This paper will now describe an empirical investigation conducted to collect such evidence.

3   Methodology

In this section, the methodology used in the empirical investigation of VLE accessibility is presented.

3.1   Platforms Evaluated

For the investigation three different virtual learning environments were chosen for evaluation.

Moodle² (version 1.9) is one of the leading open source platforms for e-learning. An installation currently in use in the Department of Mathematics at the University of York was used for purposes of the evaluations.

.LRN eLearning Platform³ (version 2) is an open source e-learning platform developed primarily at MIT. The installation at the Universidad Nacional de Educación a Distancia (UNED) was used for purposes of the evaluation.

Blackboard⁴ (version 8) is the current commercial leader in virtual learning environments. This is the primary VLE used at the University of York.

These platforms were chosen to provide a comparison of accessibility problems between two leading platforms of open source and commercial markets as well as another highly used VLE. All of these platforms were evaluated in September to December of 2008.

---

² http://moodle.org/
³ http://www.dotlrn.org/
⁴ http://www.blackboard.com/

3.2 Expert Evaluations

Accessibility audits were undertaken on each of the above platforms. These audits consisted of checking various pages of the VLEs against a subset of 10 checkpoints from the WCAG 1.0 guidelines (Chisholm, 1999). These 10 checkpoints were identified in the audits as capturing 80% of the accessibility problems on websites 48.

The accessibility audits were undertaken using a combination the automated testing, conducted with the Imergo 1.2 Web Compliance Manager, and semi-automated expert checks. The semi-automated checks used the Juicy Studio toolset.

In order to obtain an understanding of the overall accessibility of each VLE, a large variety of pages, in both their presentation and their functionality were sampled. In order to ensure that comparisons could be drawn between the VLEs, pages were chosen such that the functionality contained on the page was present in each VLE. The final sample of pages were:

- A login/authentication page
- A page presenting different aspects of a module being delivered through the VLE. For example, this could include, but is not limited to, accessing module notes and/or lecture slides or reading announcements.
- A calendar that is used to manage deadlines or events for students participating in a module.
- Discussion forums that allow for collaboration between students, their lecturers/tutors and their peers.
- A set of pages representing a workflow for submission of assignments/assessments for a module.

3.3 End User Evaluations

Expert evaluation is a necessary but not sufficient criteria for evaluating the accessibility of a web application. The expert evaluations were supplemented with user evaluations that consisted of four blind, screenreader users, who undertook a set of representative tasks in the VLE.

In order to provide comparable results across the VLEs, each VLE was set up in an identical manner with a module. A fictional module entitled *Design of interactive systems* was created and learning resources for it were prepared. These resources consisted of lecture notes, in PowerPoint presentation and PDF formats, an audio file, a jpeg picture and an assignment for the participants to undertake during the evaluation.

Every participant was required to undertake seven scenario-based tasks that involved interaction with each VLE. The tasks undertaken by all participants were:

T1. Find the number of events scheduled on a particular day in the module timetable.
T2. Update personal details, specifically a new email address and password.
T3. Download lecture material for the first lecture of the module
T4. Post a question on the module forum regarding the due date of an assignment.
T5. Submit the first assignment for the module.
T6. Download and listen to the module podcast.
T7. Check the marks assigned in the module

User evaluations were undertaken on a Windows XP personal computer equipped with the screenreader JAWS version 10.

Participants undertook the tasks using a concurrent verbal protocol that was recorded using the Morae suite of software[5].

4 Results

4.1 Expert Evaluations

For the expert evaluations, the audits performed produced the total number of checkpoint violations across all pages checked presented in Table 1.

Table 1. Number of checkpoint violations across all pages for each VLE, grouped by WCAG 1 priority level

Priority Level	.LRN Violations	Moodle Violations	Blackboard Violations
Priority 1 (P1)	7	7	10
Priority 2 (P2)	29	29	35
Priority 3 (P3)	17	15	10
Total	53	51	55

The total number of checkpoint violations found per VLE is quite similar. In .LRN 13.2% of all problems were Priority 1 (P1), 54.7% were Priority 2 (P2) and 32% were Priority 3 (P3). Moodle followed a very similar trend, a total of 51 problems of which 13.7% were P1, 56.8% were P2 and 29.4% were P3. Blackboard had the most checkpoint violation, with a large percentage of these problems being in P1 and P2.

The accessibility audit was performed using the 10 most critical WCAG 1.0 checkpoints as identified in the DRC and MLA audits. These checkpoints and the number of times they were violated across all 3 VLEs are presented in Table 2. From this table, it is clear that the two most violated checkpoints are 2.2 and 13.1, both of which are very easily detected and repaired.

4.2 User Evaluations

During the user-based evaluations, it was noticeable that participants struggled with Blackboard VLE more than with .LRN or Moodle. This was underlined by the amount of user-identified accessibility problems found in Blackboard, compared to the other two VLEs. Blackboard had 54% more user-identified problems than Moodle and 86% more user-identified problems than .LRN. These results are presented in Table 3.

---

[5] http://www.techsmith.com/

Table 2. Total number of checkpoint violations across all VLEs grouped by the violated checkpoint number

WAI WCAG 1.0 Guideline	Description	No. of times violated
1.1 (P1)	Text equivalents for every non-text element	7
2.2 (P2)	Good colour contrasts between background and foreground colours	15
3.4 (P2)	Ensure text size values are relative	7
6.3 (P2)	Pages are accessible when scripts and other objects are turned off or not supported	13
7.3 (P2)	Allow user to freeze moving content, avoid movement	0
10.1 (P2)	No pop-up windows which cannot be turned off	11
12.3 (P2)	Divide large blocks of information into manageable chunks	10
13.1 (P2)	Clearly identify target of each link	15
13.4 (P2)	Use navigational mechanisms in consistent manner	1
14.1 (P1)	Use clearest and simplest language appropriate for the content	4

Table 3. Number of accessibility problems encountered by users on each VLE

Task	Moodle Problems Encountered	.LRN Problems Encountered	Blackboard Problems Encountered
T1	2	5	8
T2	5	11	23
T3	16	4	2
T4	5	3	16
T5	4	6	2
T6	3	2	2
T7	0	0	1
Total	35	29	54

Clearly, task 7 was the easiest for all participants with only one problem encountered by one user. Updating personal information (T2) caused the most difficulty, but this is a seldom occurring tasks in the VLE. It is again T3 and T4, which frequent tasks that students will be undertaking on a day-to-day basis, that are of biggest concern. These proved to be very difficult, amounting to 39% of all accessibility problems found by users over the three VLEs.

5 Discussion

The evaluations presented in this paper demonstrate that there are some serious accessibility issues relating to the use of virtual learning environments in current practice. With only a small subset of WCAG 1.0 checkpoints tested, on a small subset of tasks, none of the three VLEs tested pass even Level A compliance.

Further, each VLE tested was demonstrated to have accessibility problems that interrupted the users when they were performing some of the most basic tasks in relation to a module.

For a variety of reasons, it is not possible to draw generalized conclusions from such an evaluation. First, this test was not comprehensive of major VLEs with a substantial share of the market. There are a plethora of other environments to which they can be compared. Second, each of these virtual learning environments had customized components and styles applied to them based on the institutions and departments in which they were deployed. Currently, there is no clear way to separate what is a problem associated with these 'in house' styles and what is a problem of the VLE itself. Indeed, there is the question as to whether it makes sense to even evaluate the two separately.

Finally, the user evaluations conducted here must be expanded beyond screen-reader users. In order to provide a true picture of the accessibility of any VLE environment, a comprehensive test with a broader, and larger, sample of participants is required.

Despite these issues, this work does show that there is a need to examine the topic of accessibility in VLEs more closely. When institutions mandate the use of a virtual learning environment, it is essential that they not only institute policies for staff regarding accessible contents, as is common practice, but that they also examine the platform that those staff members will be using for accessibility criteria.

These results demonstrate a need to educate the individuals developing, deploying and procuring these environments in institutions about accessibility and what criteria to apply when adopting a VLE.

References

1. Blankfield, S.: Supporting dyslexic students in effective use of online learning. Paper presented at Association for Learning Technology Conference, Sunderland (2002)
2. Caldwell, B., Cooper, M., Reid, L.G., Vanderheiden, G.: Web content accessibility guidelines 2.0: World Wide Web Consortium (2008)
3. Chisholm, W., Vanderheiden, G., Jacobs, I.: Web content accessibility guidelines 1.0: World Wide Web Consortium (1999)
4. Disability Rights Commission (DRC), The Web: Access and Inclusion for Disabled People. The Stationery Office, London (2004)
5. Hersch, M.: Accessibility and Usability of Virtual Learning Environments. In: Proceedings of the Workshop on Advanced Learning Technologies for Disabled and Non-Disabled People (WALTD); ICALT 2008: The 8th IEEE International Conference on Advanced Learning Technologies: Learning technologies in the Information society. IEEE, Los Alamitos (2008)

6. Pearson, E.J., Koppi, T.: Inclusion and online learning opportunities: designing for accessibility. ALT-J 10(2), 17–28 (2001)
7. Phipps, L., Sutherland, A., Seale, J.: Access All Areas: Disability, Technology and Learning. JISC TechDis Service and ALT (2002)
8. Petrie, H., King, N., Hamilton, F.: Accessibility of museum, library and archive websites: the MLA audit. Museums, Libraries and Archives Council, London (2005)
9. Seale, J.: Supporting The Development of E-Learning Accessibility Practices: New and Emergent Roles for Staff Developers. In: Crisp, G., Thiele, D., Scholten, I., Barker, S., Baron, J. (eds.) Interact, Integrate, Impact: Proceedings of the 20th Annual Conference of the Australasian Society for Computers in Learning in Tertiary Education, Adelaide (December 7-10, 2003)
10. Sloan, D., Rowan, M., Booth, P., Gregor, P.: Ensuring the provision of accessible digital resources. Journal of Educational Media 25(3), 203–216 (2000)

ICT for Persons with Disabilities: Bridging the Digital Divide in Bangladesh

Mahjabeen Khaled Hossain

Program Director, Institute of Hazrat Mohammad SAW
House 22, Road 27, Block K, Banani, Dhaka 1213, Bangladesh
ihmsaw@gmail.com
http://www.ihmsaw.org

Abstract. In the last two decades, the disability situation has undergone substantial change globally due to international initiatives supporting the UN declared World Decade of Disabled Persons. However, these progressive steps are yet to reach millions of disabled persons in rural Bangladesh. Around 13 million people in Bangladesh are physically handicapped of which 3 million are children. Disability is increasing with population growth and ageing. Disability on this scale represents not only a major health issue but also a prime cause of poverty and underdevelopment. Information and Communication Technology (ICT), opens up great opportunities to improve the quality of life of disabled people failing which will further the digital divide. This paper proposes to discuss the importance of ICT development and accessibility for persons with disabilities in Bangladesh and elaborate on how ICT has been utilized thus far and how we can further these initiatives towards development.

Keywords: Disability, Bangladesh, digital divide, poverty, ICT.

1 ICT for Overcoming Disabilities

ICT has opened up many new opportunities for citizens and consumers. It is imperative that people with disabilities are entitled equal access to education and employment, equal rights to parenthood, property ownership, political rights, and legal representation. Computers, adaptive technology and the internet can help disabled people take advantage of education and employment opportunities leading to sustainable long term empowerment opportunities.

For a developing country like Bangladesh which is home to over 13 million disabled persons, access to ICT remains a dream for many. A recent report from the Joseph Rowntree Foundation, UK states even if overall poverty falls, it is found to be increasing among disabled persons. Therefore, it is of no surprise that in Bangladesh, where most of its population is poverty stricken, people with disabilities are most neglected, marginalized and discriminated against. In these cases, creating self sufficiency and independence through the fruits of technology would play a pivotal role towards ensuring their basic rights and dignity.

However, there are some key barriers that disabled people need to overcome to make the most of opportunities available through information technology. Dr. Deepak

K. Miesenberger et al. (Eds.): ICCHP 2010, Part I, LNCS 6179, pp. 527–530, 2010.

Bhatia in his article 'Global Dialogue on ICT and Disability' published in the Development Gateway identified that there are six inter-related barriers to ICT for disabled people. These are lack of interest, lack of awareness, difficulty of access, high cost of ICT, lack of training, and lack of on-going support.

2 Existing Initiatives on ICT for Disabled Persons

Bangladesh is faced with the significant challenge of creating a 'Knowledge based Society' and ensuring that its citizens are equipped with required knowledge and skills to effectively use ICT. As a result the present Government's declaration of a vision to build 'Digital Bangladesh' by 2021 was received with warm appreciation by different sections of society.

With the declaration of 'Digital Bangladesh' campaign under a development vision for 2021, the government has incorporated ICT in the national development agenda. But it is unfortunate that the policy has vague or no mention of ICT for disabled persons. There is no clear cut program and no committee has been specially assigned for the task of bringing ICT to persons with disabilities.

Among current NGO initiatives, the Sight Savers International, a UK based International organization, has been working to empower the visually impaired people in Bangladesh. They have established a Resource Centre in the Central Library of University of Dhaka. Under the initiatives, the Resource Centre has been equipped with computers with necessary software such as Plextalk (DAISY Book Reader), Perkins Braille, Braille Printer, Braille Display and internet facility.

Volunteers Association for Bangladesh (www.vabonline.org), a USA based voluntary organization has taken an initiative to include ICT for the underprivileged persons. The New Jersey Chapter of Volunteers Association for Bangladesh initiated a project "Empowering Underprivileged Youths in Bangladesh through Computer Literacy" in late 2004 under the banner of Computer Literacy Program (CLP). This project aims towards developing facilities in rural areas for educating and training underprivileged disabled youths on ICTs

The Institute of Hazrat Mohammad (SAW) is a research and advocacy think tank which provides IT training for visually impaired persons. The Institute's work for persons with disability began since its inception in 2003. Its programs include classes on English Language and Computer Training. It aims to bring visually impaired students from the lower socio-economic stratum and give them opportunities to gain ICT training. The organization also provides its students further support in attaining jobs after completion of their trainings. The programs are aimed towards enabling disabled persons to build proficiency on English Language which in turn will stimulate their interest in ICT. The computer training is conducted in its IT lab which is equipped with talking computers and Braille printer. The Institute regularly conducts seminars and workshops to generate awareness on the rights of disabled persons and has been observing the UN International Days for Persons with Disability since 2006 with thematic programs. The programs of the Institute are offered free of charge. They are part of the Institute's commitment to uphold the rights of disabled persons and empower them with employable skills thereby enabling the disabled students to lead independent and dignified lives. Its current programs address the six barriers to ICT for disabled people by generating and sustaining their interest, creating access and offering affordability and convenience.

3 Recommendations

Although there has been some effort on part of the NGOs to raise awareness on the issue of ICT access for disabled persons and subsequently aid them, in order for this to be addressed on a larger scale, the Government of Bangladesh must take up initiatives and see to their implementation for one of the most neglected sections of the Bangladesh population.

Overcoming the six identified inter-related barriers to ICT for disabled people would be expensive especially for a resource constrained country like Bangladesh. Based on its experience in working with and for persons with disability, the Institute of Hazrat Mohammad SAW recommends the following for mainstreaming use and adoption of ICT for disabled persons:

- Literacy levels in Bangladesh are around 47% and it is much worse among the disabled population contributing to a serious lack of awareness on the benefits of technology in creating access to information, education and employment opportunities. This issue may be addressed through media campaigns and sensitizing the media on disability issues.

- More than 10% of Bangladesh's 150 million people suffer from some form of disability. This is an immense burden on a poor country like Bangladesh and it is imperative the government explores ICT-based cost effective solutions to make disabled persons more able and employable. Public-private partnerships may transfer some of the cost burden and specialized donor agencies may be approached. Other initiatives for disabled persons to gain access to ICT could include special account opening and operating facilities in Braille at banks and start of micro-credit programs by nationalized banks for people with disabilities.

- In a country like Bangladesh where institutions for the disabled can hardly afford computer labs, use of expensive speech software is an unthinkable notion. The Indian Institute for Technology has developed software called Multilingual Editor that makes computers talk not only in English but also in native languages of India. Moreover, this software is available free of cost for all Indian users. The Bangladesh government may take such initiative to develop similar software for speech delivery in Bengali and English.

  Bangladesh has a number of IT training centers. The Government may direct the large IT schools and training centers to have facilities for students with various forms of disability. Other incentives in the form of tax breaks, reduction in import duty for IT equipments could play a supportive role. Both home and abroad, Bangladeshis have excelled in the IT sector. It is our sincere conviction that the disabled persons in Bangladesh will do just as well or even better when they are provided access to information technology.

- The present government regards ICT as a thrust sector. It has developed a comprehensive plan for mainstreaming ICT throughout the country. The Government may scale up the current initiatives to address the special needs of disabled persons.

The cardinal concept of the Holy Quran is based on the principle that the ownership of everything belongs not to any person but to Allah, the universal Creator. This translates to the fact that every human being has the right to a means of living as God has created resources to benefit humanity in general. Persons with disability will only get the requisite social justice and resulting dignity when they are able to exercise their rights as people and as citizens and enjoy equal access to education, employment and empowerment.

References

1. The Holy Quran
2. Palmer, G.: Monitoring poverty and social exclusion in the UK, Joseph Rowntree Foundation, UK (2005)
3. Bhatia, D.: Global Dialogue on ICT and Disability, the Development Gateway (2002)
4. Khan, A.W.: Technology alone will not bridge knowledge divides. UNESCO Publications (2009)
5. Taking IT Global, http://www.tigweb.org

Success through Exchange:
The Higher Education Accessibility Guide (HEAG)

Andrea Petz and Klaus Miesenberger

Institute Integriert Studieren
Johannes Kepler University of Linz
Altenbergerstr. 69
4040 Linz, Austria
{andrea.petz,klaus.miesenberger}@jku.at

Abstract. This paper presents the work carried out within the HEAG framework amongst a joint European group of service providers for people with disabilities in Higher Education. Higher Education institutions from all over Europe were screened following a standardized questionnaire on their activities for students with disabilities and services provided. The gained data was published online and provides up to date information on studying in a specific country at a specific institution and has the potential to foster European exchange and students mobility even amongst students with disabilities, a group underrepresented in Higher Education mobility programs so far.

Keywords: Higher education, disability, mobility, exchange, support, service provision, survey.

1 Introduction

All over Europe, policy initiatives aim at increasing the numbers of students entering and completing higher education. This gets obvious at European level within the Council of Education Ministers' statements regarding participation within Higher Education as part of the 2010 Objectives for Education in Europe, also postulating targets and strategies to reach the Lisbon objectives that, following EU publications 2010 will only be reached in some side parts on time [1]. At National level different countries have different core areas for their initiatives to increase participation rates [2], one common area however being the increased participation of students from 'non-traditional' backgrounds, including students with disabilities and chronic illness.

Studies and research projects (e.g. the EU funded project HERN – Higher Education Reform Network [3], 2004) identified "accessibility" as general key to successful participation in Higher Education.

From applying to a specific study program or the general accessibility of a specific campus over the accessibility of study-related information / literature and eLearning platforms to support schemes, counselling, housing, transportation and funding possibilities – without proper information, especially students with disabilities will be left outside.

K. Miesenberger et al. (Eds.): ICCHP 2010, Part I, LNCS 6179, pp. 531–536, 2010.
© Springer-Verlag Berlin Heidelberg 2010

Therefore initiatives like Eurydice [4], HEAG – Higher Education Accessibility Guide [5] or "Study Abroad without Limits" [6] work on providing as much and as specific accessible information as possible in order to enable students from all over Europe to equally take part in Higher Education and get the chance to a successful career and finally integration in society corresponding to their personal skills, competences and preferences and independent from a possible disability or country of origin.

2   State of the Art

As realized in daily work, studies and research co-operations (HERN – Higher Education Reform Network; HEAG – Higher Education Accessibility Guide; "Study Abroad Without Limits") working to support students with disabilities in Higher Education, one core issue that serves as an example in this paper is the raising necessity (if not "condition sine qua non") of going abroad and learn within different cultural, social and educational frameworks – that asks, especially for students with a disability or a chronic illness for an intense preparation and organization phase and accurately fitting information before being able to "leave and learn".

Websites being set up to provide this information are already in use (e.g. Eurydice or HEAG website) that provides formal information (educational systems, funding, institutional contacts and general study framework), in case of HEAG for 29 European countries in 21 languages. The project "Study abroad used a totally different approach, enabling interaction and the informal information gathering by connecting trained peers from 5 different countries (Austria, Belgium / Flanders, Ireland, Sweden and The Netherlands) acting as experts "on site" with students interested in going abroad, asking for specific information best answered by students dealing with similar concerns and constraints every day, what might complement the more formal HEAG / Eurydice database to cover the full scope of issues to be sorted out before going abroad.

3   Methodology Used

This paper presents the work carried out within the European initiative HEAG, co-ordinated by the European Agency for Development in Special Needs Education [7], an independent and self-governing organization established by European member countries to act as a platform for collaboration regarding the development of provision for learners with special educational needs.

The European Agency for Development in Special Needs Education is maintained by the Ministries of Education in the participating countries (member states of the European Union as well as Iceland, Norway and Switzerland) as well as supported by the European Union Institutions via the Jean Monnet programme under the EU Lifelong Learning Programme.

Represented by National Agencies (located within the responsible ministries and national institutions / structures), the Agency facilitates the collection, processing and transfer of European level and reliable country specific information and offers the opportunity to learn from each other through different types of knowledge and experience exchange.

Those National Agencies appointed national experts working in the field of supporting students with disabilities or chronic illness in Higher Education.

In a starting meeting, those expert institutions were asked to identify the core topics and issues concerning studying (abroad) and the European Agency for Development in Special Needs Education presented the general framework for getting and providing relevant data that in the end should act as comprehensive Europe-wide repository for all interested countries, institutions and individuals – in English and the national language(s).

4 R&D Work and Results

Following the identified core topics, a questionnaire was designed in order to be sent out to national Higher Education institutions. This questionnaire was designed in English by the involved experts that additionally translated it into 21 national languages in order to facilitate the adaptation of the questionnaire to national realities and concepts.

The questionnaire covered the following categories:

- Key Data
  - o Contact information of the department / person filling in the questionnaire / supporting students with disabilities
- Available institutional support services (including those for students with special needs)
  - o From an office / person supporting incoming / outgoing students to support schemes for different possible disabilities
- Accessibility of the built environment
  - o From Campus over student halls to the provision of personal support
- Support for teaching and learning
  - o Asking for all possible support activities (Accessible study literature, sign interpretation, note taking till flexible timetables and study / exam schemes)
- Other information
  - o Asking for information on and availability of social network possibilities like students clubs, sport facilities, or community/NGO groups for people with disabilities on site

The adapted different versions of this questionnaire were implemented accessible and put online to the HEAG website. The national experts were asked to contact the national Higher Education institutions, send them the link to the questionnaire and validate the data filled in by the institutions in terms of completeness and appropriateness of information given.

As described above, 29 European countries (distinguishing between Flanders and Kingdom Belgium, including EU countries and Switzerland, Norway and Iceland) took part, providing 543 submissions from 490 different institutions.

Table 1. Countries, submissions and institutions taking part in the HEAG survey 2009, sorted alphabetically by country

Country	Submissions	Different institutions
Austria	17	17
Belgium (Vlanders)	13	13
Belgium (Royaume)	11	11
Croatia	62	30
Cyprus	1	1
Czech Republic	18	18
Denmark	41	41
Estland	6	6
Finland	38	36
France	48	48
Germany	30	30
Greece	3	3
Hungary	0	0
Iceland	4	4
Ireland	18	18
Latvia	8	7
Lithuania	30	30
Luxemburg	0	0
Malta	2	2
Netherlands	22	22
Norway	7	7
Poland	0	0
Portugal	42	41
Slovakia	0	0
Slovenia	21	4
Spain	19	19
Sweden	28	28
Switzerland	16	16
United Kingdom	38	38
Total	543	490

The submissions handed in range from information on faculty level up to information given for whole university campuses. Therefore the number of submissions might be different from the number of handing in institutions.

The power of this collection becomes obvious when one looks at the amount of data and information provided. In the moment it is possible to look up the support schemes of 490 different institutions in a most comprehensive variety of categories.

5 Impact on or Contributions to the Field

This huge collection of data – once consolidated – enables researchers and policy makers to compare support structures and funding schemes, benchmark the own institution and/or country and plan following reliable actual data.

As the survey ended in November 2009 and the website was put online (relaunched) in January 2010, the data are only available for nations / institutions – what means that interested individuals might look up specific institutions and their support structures but it is not possible to get an overall database to evaluate / benchmark support structures throughout Europe in the moment.

Also some countries are underrepresented or did not provide information, a fact that asks for a further investigation to get submissions in order to complete this first comprehensive and comparable educational and support map for students in Europe independent of a possible disability and/or wish to go abroad.

6 Conclusions and Planned Activities

Seen from researchers' view and as described above it will finally depend on the contributions from nations underrepresented or missing and on the availability of compiled, consolidated stable and reliable data what is possible with this huge data repository.

It will also depend on funding possibilities and the impetus brought in by European or National agencies and the national experts (in terms of involving missing institutions / countries, keeping the data actual and the network of experts alive) what research possibilities arise.

Seen from the view of structures / institutions supporting students with disabilities, this collection of data represents also a collection of showcases and best practise examples in supporting students with special educational needs.

Seen from the perspective of students with disabilities, these individuals get the chance for a one-stop-information repository at their fingertips, 24 hours a day, 7 days a week.

It would be most beneficial for students with disabilities when – as mentioned above – this "formal" data collection could and would be linked with the more informal and interactive peer support offer the website / project "Study Abroad without Limits" is able to provide, in order to complement this huge data collection with personal knowledge, experience and expertise giving a real incentive / kick to everyone thinking of studying abroad by connecting trained peers (that already were abroad and therefore know exactly what information / organisation and co-ordination actions might be necessary and beneficial) to interested young people with disabilities.

Acknowledgments. The work presented in this paper was initiated and supported by the European Agency for Development in Special Needs Education. We want to thank the Austrian National Agency for Development in Special Needs Education, the Austrian Federal Ministry of Education, Arts and Culture and the Austrian Federal Ministry of Science and Research for providing help and information.

References

1. Lisbon strategy and student mobility in education, http://ec.europa.eu/education/lifelong-learning-policy/doc1951_en.htm
2. Meijer, C.J.W., Soriano, V., Watkins, A. (eds.): Special Needs Education in Europe: Provision in Post-Primary Education. Middelfart: European Agency for Development in Special Needs Education (2006)

536   A. Petz and K. Miesenberger

3. Website Project HERN, http://www.hereform.net/
4. Website Eurydice,
   http://eacea.ec.europa.eu/education/eurydice/index_en.php
5. Website HEAG,
   http://www.european-agency.org/agency-projects/heag
6. Website, Study Abroad without Limits,
   http://www.studyabroadwithoutlimits.eu/
7. Website, European Agency for Development in Special Needs Education,
   http://www.european-agency.org/

Linking Instruments and Documenting Decisions in Service Delivery Guided by an ICF-Based Tool for Assistive Technology Selection

Emily Steel, Gert Jan Gelderblom, and Luc de Witte

Zuyd University Research Centre for Technology in Care, Nieuw Eyckholt 300, 6419 DJ Heerlen, Netherlands
{e.j.steel,g.j.gelderblom,l.de.witte}@hszuyd.nl
http://www.technologyincare.nl

Abstract. This paper demonstrates how information from existing instruments can be linked within a new framework and tool for AT selection, using the International Classification of Functioning, Disability and Health (ICF). A case study is presented to illustrate how this might work in practice, and describes the steps followed by practitioners using the tool and gathering assessment data through links to existing instruments. The potential added value of using the ICF in AT service delivery is discussed, and planned developments for the tool outlined.

Keywords: Assistive Technology, ICF, service delivery, framework, selection, instrument.

1 Introduction

The International Classification of Functioning, Disability and Health (ICF) introduced a new language and framework for disability in 2001 [1]. Assistive Technology (AT) is, from an ICF perspective, an environmental factor that can facilitate participation. This new paradigm has been adopted by the United Nations (UN) Convention on the Rights of People with Disabilities [2], and member states are obliged to promote the use of assistive technologies suitable for persons with disabilities where there are barriers to accessibility.

However providing AT solutions to meet individual needs is a complex process, for which practitioners require skills and strategies in addition to product information [3]. A European Commission study on Access to Assistive Technology in the European Union highlighted the variations in the AT provision processes among member states, and emphasised the need to improve, coordinate, and structure information and advice, and assessment procedures [4].

The political context requires that AT interventions and services demonstrate and communicate effectiveness in enhancing integration and participation of persons with disabilities. Attention has therefore already been given to the assessment of outcomes from AT interventions through the research and development of instruments [5]. The

K. Miesenberger et al. (Eds.): ICCHP 2010, Part I, LNCS 6179, pp. 537–543, 2010.

selection process also influences AT outcomes such as user satisfaction, use or non-use and cost-effectiveness [6]. The consideration of theoretical models and concepts in AT selection may increase the likelihood of positive outcomes from AT provision [7, 8], and guide evaluation to the most relevant domains by setting expectations based on user and service provider goals [5].

2   Assistive Technology Evaluation and Selection Tool (ATES)

A literature review to describe existing models and instruments for AT selection, and review their compatibility with the ICF, identified some instruments specific to AT selection [9]. Following the review, a sample of European AT practitioners were surveyed, reporting low use of theoretical frameworks and published instruments in clinical practice, and varied satisfaction with the process [6]. This apparent gap between theory and practice in the field of AT has been reported in research from the field of occupational therapy (one of the professions associated with AT service delivery), indicating some reluctance on the part of practitioners to consistently or systematically integrate theory into clinical practice [10]. Practitioners have highlighted their need for practical and concise tools and documentation methods, with the flexibility to adopt several theoretical models [11].

A tool was therefore developed (ATES, to be published), providing a structure for AT selection at a general level, for the purpose of broad application. It uses the ICF framework, linking concepts in a common language, with a concise format for documentation. As detail is required when selecting specific AT for individuals, the tool is intended to link to separate, specific instruments.

There are three steps in the tool, which is completed by the practitioner answering questions in a systematic order and documenting decisions and plans in each step. The information is built on in each step and, when completed, summarised in a report. Figure 1 illustrates the three steps and topics addressed.

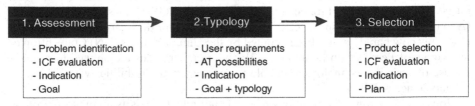

Fig. 1. The three steps of the Assistive Technology Evaluation and Selection tool (ATES).

A web page demonstrating the approach is publicly available (www.technologyincare. nl/ates) and studies testing the tool have commenced. Initial feedback on the development of the tool provided support for the approach, and indicated a need for links to other instruments and instructions, to support practitioners in adopting the new tool.

3 A Case Study Using the ATES Tool

To illustrate how the tool facilitates and structures the optional use of existing instruments, which objectify more detailed information required for sound AT selection, a case study is presented.

3.1 Angela: From Hospital Rehabilitation to Participation in Education

An 18 year old woman, Angela, is preparing to return to school 18 months after a traumatic brain injury which resulted in extensive hospital rehabilitation. The hospital rehabilitation team has referred her to the educational support unit in her community, and provided information through the WHO Disability Assessment Schedule II (WHO DAS II) [12] as a hospital discharge summary of her functioning.

3.2 Assessment

The education support officer (ESO) meets with Angela to discuss her educational goals and considers AT as a potential intervention. For a more detailed problem identification than the ATES tool provides, they choose to complete the full standardised version of the Individually Prioritised Problem Assessment (IPPA) [13].

Because the ESO knows little about Angela's experiences and expectations with technologies, they complete the Matching Person and Technology Survey of Technology Use (MPT SOTU) [14] together for additional information when considering the component of personal factors.

The key information from the three sources (WHO DAS II, IPPA, MPT SOTU) is compiled in the first step of the tool for consideration to decide on AT and parallel interventions, and form a goal and plan. The information is referred to the rehabilitation engineer for the next step of identifying appropriate computer AT for Angela.

3.3 Typology

The rehabilitation engineer works with Angela to explore her computer skills and difficulties and establish the most important functions required for use in the classroom and for home study. They establish a need for more concrete product information and browse different AT options through the online database EASTIN [15], then trial different computer joysticks and adjustments to Angela's wheelchair. They agree that positioning and training with the new AT will be important, and document this in the second step of the tool.

3.4 Selection

After several sessions trialling AT combinations with the rehabilitation engineer, Angela identifies the AT she prefers to use, and completes the Selection with the rehabilitation engineer and ESO. They choose the option of completing the modified Psychosocial Impact of Assistive Devices Scale (PIADS) [16] for more information about the expected impact of using the AT, and Angela and the rehabilitation engineer agree that going back to school and using AT will probably be rewarding but difficult. The evaluation suggests that the selected AT is well-matched to Angela's needs, but

---

Results and Interpretation of Assistive Technology Evaluation and Selection

Client: Ms Angela G   Age: 18
Practitioners: W Bean, education support officer (ESO); P Green, rehabilitation engineer

The Assistive Technology Evaluation and Selection (ATES) was completed with Ms G as a means of evaluating her needs, and identifying potential for modifying barriers to participation through the use of Assistive Technology (AT).

1: Assessment (completed 26/03/2010)
Ms G was interviewed to gain a better understanding of the current problems she experiences, and her capabilities and experience using technology.
Instruments used: IPPA: problem score 20; MPT Survey of Technology Use: score +14, neutral 11, -2

Ms G was offered a choice of interventions to address the identified barriers to participation. AT was identified as an appropriate intervention, with the parallel interventions of modification of the task or technique, modification of the environment, and personal assistance.
Goal: Ms G chose to work on the goal of using computer and software AT to enable participation in education.

2: Typology (completed 14/05/2010)
Ms G's requirements for AT were assessed, and the possibilities and accommodations for meeting the requirements.
Databases used: EASTIN

Ms G was offered a choice of alternative types of AT solutions. A wheelchair-mounted joystick for computer access and voice-operated software were identified as the preferred types of AT solution.

3: Selection (completed 27/05/2010)
X brand joystick with x-brand voice-operated software were selected for trial and evaluated for goal effectiveness, usability and anticipated impact for Ms G.
Instruments used: PIADS score +11

X brand joystick with x-brand voice-operated software were identified as appropriate for Ms G, to be used with a laptop computer and electric wheelchair (already in use).

Implementation and Evaluation
The following recommendations for delivery, follow-up and further intervention are:
1. ESO to follow-up with education department requests for classroom support worker and exam timing, and modifications to school accessibility.
2. Fortnightly AT training and adjustment for the first 2 months.
3. Evaluation to be completed at 3 months and 6 months using the IPPA, QUEST-2 and PIADS.
4. Copies of report to: Ms G, education department, school, rehabilitation team.

Fig. 2. The case study report generated from the ATES tool

that ongoing support is required, both in using the technology and keeping it up to date, and in ensuring that the classroom can be adapted when required (e.g. extra time in exams and use of personal support in class when required).

3.5 Report

A report is generated by the tool, illustrated in Figure 2, summarising the three-step process, decisions made, and recommendations for implementation and follow-up evaluation.

4 Discussion

The case study described shows one potential application of the ATES linked to other existing instruments, and its ability to incorporate information and results from multiple sources in to one structure that generates a concise report.

Use of different frameworks and instruments in assessment is part of routine clinical reasoning for practitioners when considering complex interventions such as AT [10]. Clinical practice without the obvious use of theory-based models or instruments is not indicative of poor decision-making, however the explication of what was done or recommended and why, is critical in a context of increased accountability for decisions and competition for health funds [17]. Communication of goals and plans is important for effective collaboration in service delivery, between the user and the multidisciplinary team and other stakeholders involved in AT provision [17, 18].

Use of the ICF in AT service delivery provides the added value of communication in what is becoming the common language of functioning, disability and health, from the level of practitioner to national and international policy and legislation [18]. The potential links to emerging and established instruments, databases and E-health applications are more easily made using the ICF, due to its increased application in rehabilitation and other settings [1].

Enabled links allow flexibility in the tool to adjust the process to different service provision contexts in Europe, and integrate more detail as required, thus increasing usability in practice. The basic structure of the tool may be perceived as a generic instrument that doesn't provide detail or answers for AT selection, but it retains relevance as a systematic and organising guide for novice or general practitioners providing AT. Given the time constraints in practice and apparent low use of instruments in AT selection, new and lengthy approaches to service delivery are unlikely to be adopted.

5 Conclusion and Planned Activities

AT selection is about working with individuals and finding solutions that will support or enhance their participation. Documentation and communication of processes and decisions based on theory, and in a common language, is one way that service providers can demonstrate this effect to justify resource allocation. The ATES tool has been developed to support practitioners in this purpose, without creating unnecessary tasks, and this paper has demonstrated one potential application of the tool.

Further work is indicated in the development of guidance to support practitioners in adopting the new tool and using it efficiently. A digital platform for the tool is being developed to enable data transfer within the tool and reduce duplication. Translation and further testing of the tool is required to determine its impact on service provision and user outcomes. Validation is expected to show the need for stronger linking of instruments and efficient ways to combine data from multiple sources into a coherent process.

Acknowledgments. The authors gratefully acknowledge financial support provided by the European Commission within the MURINET project (MRTN-CT-2006-035794) http://murinet.eu.

References

1. World Health Organisation: International classification of functioning, disability and health: ICF. World Health Organisation, Geneva (2001)
2. United Nations: Convention on the Rights of People with Disabilities (2006), http://www.un.org/disabilities/convention/conventionfull.shtml
3. Andrich, R., Gower, V., Caracciolo, A., Carbone, A., Agnoletto, A.: An On-Line System Supporting the Provision of Assistive Technology Products to Individual Users through the National Health Service. In: Emiliani, P.B.L., Como, A., Gabbanini, F., Salminen, A.L. (eds.) Assistive Technology from Adapted Equipment to Inclusive Environments, vol. 25, pp. 259–263. IOS Press, Florence (2009)
4. Marx, F.: Access to Assistive Technology in the European Union: European Commission Study. In: Assistive Technology - Shaping the Future (AAATE 2003), vol. 11, pp. 98–102 (2003)
5. Gelderblom, G.J., de Witte, L.P.: The Assessment of Assistive Technology Outcomes, Effects and Costs. Technology and Disability 14, 91–94 (2002)
6. Friederich, A., Bernd, T., de Witte, L.P.: Methods for the selection of assistive technology in neurological rehabilitation practice. Scandinavian Journal of Occupational Therapy (2010)
7. Roelands, M.A., van Oost, P., Depoorter, A.M., Buysse, A.A.: A Social-Cognitive Model to Predict the Use of Assistive Devices for Mobility and Self-Care in Elderly People. The Gerontologist 42, 39–50 (2002)
8. Wielandt, T., McKenna, K., Tooth, L., Strong, J.: Factors that predict the post-discharge use of recommended assistive technology (AT). Disability and Rehabilitation: Assistive Technology 1, 29–40 (2006)
9. Bernd, T., van der Pijl, D., de Witte, L.P.: Existing models and instruments for the selection of assistive technology in rehabilitation practice. Scandinavian Journal of Occupational Therapy 16, 146–158 (2009)
10. Ikiugu, M.N., Smallfield, S., Condit, C.: A framework for combining theoretical conceptual practice models in occupational therapy practice. Canadian Journal of Occupational Therapy 76, 162–170 (2009)
11. Edyburn, D.L., Smith, R.O.: Creating an Assistive Technology Outcomes Measurement System: Validating the components. Assistive Technology Outcomes and Benefits 1, 8–15 (2004)
12. World Health Organisation: WHO Disability Assessment Schedule (WHO DAS II). WHO (2010), http://www.who.int/icidh/whodas/index.html

13. Wessels, R., Persson, J., Lorentsen, O., Andrich, R., Ferrario, W., Oortwijn, W., van Beekum, T., Brodin, H., de Witte, L.: IPPA: Individually Prioritised Problem Assessment. Technology and Disability 14, 141–145 (2002)
14. Scherer, M.J., Craddock, G.: Matching Person and Technology (MPT) assessment process. Technology and Disability 14, 125–131 (2002)
15. EASTIN: European Assistive Technology Information Network, http://www.eastin.info
16. Jutai, J., Day, H.: Psychosocial Impact of Assistive Devices Scale (PIADS). Technology and Disability 14, 107–111 (2002)
17. Peterson, D.B., Murray, G.C.: Ethics and assistive technology service provision. Disability and Rehabilitation: Assistive Technology 1, 59–67 (2006)
18. Steiner, W.A., Ryser, L., Huber, E., Uebelhart, D., Aeschlimann, A., Stucki, G.: Use of the ICF model as a clinical problem-solving tool in physical therapy and rehabilitation medicine. Physical Therapy 82, 1098–1107 (2002)

Easy-to-Use Social Network Service

Niina Sillanpää, Sami Älli, and Timo Övermark

Finnish Association on Intellectual and Developmental Disabilities (FAIDD),
Papunet Web Service Unit
{niina.sillanpaa,sami.alli,timo.overmark,papunet}@kvl.fi

Abstract. Social media have become important tools for social networking. However, most services are too complicated for people with learning disabilities or cognitive impairments. The problems are mostly related to understanding the different concepts of the environment and related special terminology, but accessibility and usability problems common to all internet services also apply. To tackle these problems, a project was started, aiming to create an easy-to-use social network service for the abovementioned target group by applying user-centered design methods. This paper explains the rationale for starting the project and also describes the some of the implementation methods used.

Keywords: social media, social network services, accessibility, cognitive disabilities, facebook.

1 Social Media for People with Special Needs

Social media has become an important tool for social networking. Community-based social networks are extremely popular and will probably continue to be so.

This development offers new opportunities for people with special needs and much effort has been put into making, for example, Facebook more accessible [1]. Today, Facebook is fairly accessible for people using, for example, screen reader software [2]. As a technical feature, accessibility can be incorporated in practically any social media service. However, none of the existing social media services were originally developed for the needs of people with learning disabilities or cognitive impairments. For these special groups, technical accessibility is often not the main point, because for them, accessibility more or less equals to usability [3]. The same applies to senior citizens, as well [4].

There are simplified versions available for many of the popular social network services. However, these simplified versions were originally not intended for the above special groups but for visually impaired persons[1] or for people using the service over a slow network connection or on a mobile device[2,3,4]. Although the simplified version

---

[1] http://www.accessibletwitter.com/
[2] http://m.facebook.com/
[3] http://lite.facebook.com/
[4] http://m.myspace.com/

K. Miesenberger et al. (Eds.): ICCHP 2010, Part I, LNCS 6179, pp. 544–549, 2010.
© Springer-Verlag Berlin Heidelberg 2010

may be easier to use for people with special needs, it may lack some essential features and functions altogether. This applies to, for example, Facebook.

2 Social Media Is a Challenge for People with Learning Disabilities or Cognitive Impairments

The problems encountered by the above special needs groups in social media are mainly related to understanding the operating environment and the special terminology used. In addition to problems with the user interface and special terms, the new social networking environment in itself presents additional challenges. These problems are similar to the ones encountered in network services in general [5].

People with special needs may also fail to understand the risks involved in social networking: some may, for example, reveal confidential personal information to strangers. Others may feel that social network services are far too insecure and therefore decide to opt out completely. In general, many people using social media services have difficulties finding the right strategy for operating in the network environment [6]; for special needs groups, these difficulties are even more pronounced.

Currently, there are no community-based social network services that have been designed especially for people with learning disabilities, cognitive impairments or difficulties in reading or writing and very little research has been done into this subject. However, community-based social networks could provide invaluable tools for enhancing the social skills and participation of people with special needs.

3 Social Media to Support a Sense of Community

Social media could act as a significant tool for a new approach in the care disabled people. For decades, disabled people in Finland and generally in the EU have been put into various institutions. In the very near future, we are hoping to move more and more people from residential care to local communities [7]. Also people with intellectual and developmental disabilities should be able to participate in society as citizens. In order to achieve full participation, these people need to be empowered to assume responsibility for their own lives and to participate in decision-making as individuals and as members of society [8].

Social media could be one way for disabled people to network with each other, form groups and gradually learn to defend their rights as citizens. In social media, disabled people are able to encounter each other and other people without the presence of family members and staff. It is their very own space where they are in charge without family members or staff making decisions on their behalf. For those needing assistance to move from one place to another, social media makes it possible to meet people without leaving the comfort of your home.

In Finland, the government has made a decision to cut the number of people in long-term residential care from the current 2500 to about 500 by the year 2015. Also the 7000 disabled adults who continue to live with their parents are in need of various services [9]. According to the new approach, more and more people with intellectual or developmental disabilities would be able to live on their own with a personal assistant to help them when needed. The downside of living alone is often the feeling of loneliness. This may be alleviated by the chance to meet old and new friends on the net through a dedicated social media service.

4 The Easy-to-Use Social Network Service Project

In the spring of 2009, the Papunet network service unit of The Finnish Association on Intellectual and Developmental Disabilities (FAIDD) launched a project to create an easy-to-use social network service. The main target group for the new service were people having difficulties with using the existing network services. This includes, for example, disabled youths and adults and people with any kind of communication, attention control or guidance problems.

During the first year of the project, an easily accessible community-based network service was implemented by applying user-centred design methods. The user interface and the instructions for use were written in plain language.

Our network service includes all the typical features of any popular community-based network service, such as creating your own user profile, sharing pictures, blogging and keeping in touch with your friends. In other words, the focus is on managing and sharing the content produced by the user.

There were ten special needs students and their counsellors from Omapolku ry (Own Path Association) working in the project. These young media students have previously, among other things, produced animations and videos.

In the autumn of 2009, a total of six design meetings were arranged. The special needs students designed the layout and features of the service and outlined some of the modules, such as the image gallery. In addition to face-to-face meetings, there were a number of chat meetings with the people testing the service. The testing team included students from the Bovallius vocational institute for special needs and the network editor students from a class organised by the Finnish Association for Persons with Intellectual Disabilities.

5 Application Framework and User Interface

As interactive elements for web pages have gained popularity, there are some free applications available for the implementation of social media services. The assortment is not very wide, however, and most of the existing applications are designed for a single purpose. In addition to the application's features, our choice of application framework was affected by the ease of making modifications and the maturity of the application project. Out of the application frameworks evaluated, Elgg[5] seemed to provide the widest variety of features and the project was mature enough.

Elgg is a social networking framework aimed at developing web sites with social features, whether they will be social networking sites or static web pages with additional interactive elements. Elgg is open source software developed and maintained by an active online community. The software has a modular design, which makes it relatively easy to apply visual layouts and to add, alter or completely remove features

---

[5] http://elgg.org/

in the user interface. We took advantage of this during design meetings by having multiple versions of the same feature as plug-ins which we could switch "on the fly", letting the users compare which version worked best for them.

We started out by removing inaccessible elements and unnecessary clutter from the default Elgg user interface. The menu structure was simplified by removing drop-down menus and inserting icons to depict the various functions of the application. Various other unnecessary elements were removed from the user interface as well. We aimed at a fairly straightforward basic structure that could be used for testing the usability of individual functions. There was simply not enough time to start the design of the features and user interface of a social media service from scratch. Therefore, the basic structure and features of the service are similar to the existing social media services. This makes things easier for the users, as well, since some of them may have tried other social media services or may later move on to them. This way, an easy-to-use social network service may act as a stepping stone to other, more advanced services.

In the design team meetings, we focused on improving the user interface. In each session, we discussed a few chosen aspects of the service and experimented with different ways of implementing them. At the same time, we were able to spot the potential problems by observing the actions and feedback of the design team. The themes dealt with in the design team meetings included, for example, the suitability of the menu icons, importing photos, making a friend request, and the colour theme of

Fig. 1. Dashboard page of the prototype version of the easy-to-use social network service

the service. In addition to design meetings, we arranged polls on the prototype version to find out the opinions of design team members on certain features of the service.

During the project, the usability of the service reached a level where it was possible to let in new users, but there is still a lot of room for development. So far, we haven't had a chance to properly consider the overall structure of the service, but this is one of the issues requiring more attention as the number of users keeps growing.

6 Ideas for Further Development

The design and testing project made it absolutely clear that the main qualities of an easily accessible network service are simplicity and clarity. During the course of the project in 2009, we did our best to simplify the default user interface, but many users still have a hard time figuring out the various functions and concepts of the system. One way to further simplify the user interface would be to reduce the number of separate functions by combining them into the content views. This way you would only see the functions that are essential in the current context.

Another important observation has to do with interaction and communication. Some of the users had difficulties with writing, reading and reading comprehension. To overcome these problems, the network service allows you to choose from a set of ready-made greetings and phrases. In the chat room, some users prefer to use symbols for communication. This is an interesting aspect that we will further look into when developing the service.

One of the essential accessibility features is the use of a speech synthesizer to read, for example, the instructions. The next step would be to apply the speech synthesizer to the blog entries, messages and chat comments written by the users. Technically, it is possible to use the speech synthesizer to read the chat comments on real-time. This will probably be implemented in future versions of the service.

During the year 2010, the social network service will be further developed and opened for the public. The service will be open for everyone, but the user interface is available in Finnish only for the time being. Our presentation demonstrates the latest development version of the service.

References

1. Facebook, Help Center: Accessibility and Assistive Technology,
   http://www.facebook.com/help/?page=440
2. WebAIM: Screen Reader User Survey Results,
   http://www.webaim.org/projects/screenreadersurvey2/
3. NCDAE: Cognitive Disabilities and the Web: Where Accessibility and Usability Meet?,
   http://ncdae.org/tools/cognitive/
4. Arch, A.: Web accessibility for older users: successes and opportunities (keynote). In: Proceedings of the 2009 international Cross-Disciplinary Conference on Web Accessibililty (W4a), W4A 2009, Madrid, Spain, April 20 - 21, pp. 1–6. ACM, New York (2009)
5. Sevilla, J., Herrera, G., Martínez, B., Alcantud, F.: Web accessibility for individuals with cognitive deficits: A comparative study between an existing commercial Web and its cognitively accessible equivalent. ACM Trans. Comput.-Hum. Interact. 14(3), 12 (2007)

6. Strater, K., Lipford, H.R.: Strategies and struggles with privacy in an online social networking community. In: Proceedings of the 22nd British HCI Group Annual Conference on HCI 2008: People and Computers Xxii: Culture, Creativity, interaction, Liverpool, United Kingdom, September 01 - 05, vol. 1, pp. 111–119. British Computer Society, Swinton (2008)
7. European Commission. Directorate-General for Employment, Social Affairs and Equal Opportunities: Report of the Ad Hoc Expert Group on the Transition from Institutional to Community-based Care (2009)
8. Niemelä, M., Brandt, K. (toim.): Kehitysvammaisten yksilöllinen asuminen. Pitkäaikaisesta laitosasumisesta kohti yksilöllisempiä asumisratkaisuja (2007)
9. Valtioneuvosto: Valtioneuvoston periaatepäätös ohjelmasta kehitysvammaisten asumisen ja siihen liittyvien palvelujen järjestämiseksi (2010)

Standards Are Drivers for Accessibility and Usability: Introduction to the Special Thematic Session

Jan Engelen[1] and Christian Bühler[2]

[1] Katholieke Universiteit Leuven, ESAT-SCDocarch
Kasteelpark Arenberg 10 box 2442, B-3001 Leuven (Belgium)
jan.engelen@esat.kuleuven.be
[2] Faculty of Rehabilitation Sciences, Technical University of Dortmund
Emil-Figge-Straße 50, D-44227 Dortmund (Germany)
c.buehler@reha-technologie.de

Abstract. Standardisation of products and services developed with a Design for All or Universal Design perspective in mind has been a recurrent theme at the ICCHP conferences. Since the 2008 edition a special thematic session has been organised, bringing together the different contributions in this field. We will describe briefly the 2010 STS. Furthermore as this year's theme of the World Standards Day (organised by ISO, ITU and IEC) will be "Accessibility", some background information on this important issue will be given.

1 Introduction

In this contribution we will give an introduction to the presentations scheduled for this STS session. Due to its importance, ISO's World Standards Day 2010, focussing on accessibility will be covered also.

2 Themes within the Special Thematic Session

2.1 General

Jan Engelen will give an overview of the ongoing activities in the field of AT and DfA standardization, based on his research within the *DfA@eInclusion* project. The recently finished activities of the *Stand4All* consortium, that focused on the training of users and standardization committee members in the use of Guide 6[1] will be covered by Christophe Strobbe. Pitfalls related to the evaluation of user satisfaction about inclusive initiatives (e.g. the *Liberated Learning Project*) will be discussed by Ana Iglesias, Lourdes Moreno, Javier Jimenez and Pablo Revuelta.

Christian Galinski mentions in his contribution several ISO initiatives within the scope of federated repositories for all kinds of content items, as well as the fact that more and more solutions will require modularity, interoperability, multi-linguality and multimodality approaches. The interoperability of ontologies in the field of ambient assisted living (AAL) is given as an example.

K. Miesenberger et al. (Eds.): ICCHP 2010, Part I, LNCS 6179, pp. 550–552, 2010.
© Springer-Verlag Berlin Heidelberg 2010

2.2 Products and Services

The theme of accessibility and the possible need for redefining commonly held assumptions in this domain will be handled by Rui Lopes, Luis Carriço and Karel Van Isacker. Especially the trend of limiting accessibility testing to website accessibility only is criticized. In relation to website accessibility about ¾ of the respondents to a study, performed within the *Accessible Project,* have expressed their need for a conformity testing and certification solution.

Gill Whitney, Suzette Keith and Barbara Schmidt-Belz discuss the creation of specialized trainings on ICT Design for All and will give a short status report on the *CEN Workshop* "Curriculum for training professionals in Universal Design (CEN WS/UD-Prof-Curriculum)", initiated in the framework of the above mentioned DfA@eInclusion project.

2.3 Open Source Products

Andrea Gaal, Gerhard Jaworek and Joachim Klaus will discuss the barriers and conflicts encountered when standardizing Open Source software, taking the Linux *SUE project* (SUE = Screenreader and Usability Extensions) as an example.

3 World Standards Day 2010

World Standards Day [2] began as a celebration of the birth of the International Organization for Standardization (ISO), which held its first meeting in London on October 14, 1946. From an initial roster of 25 countries, ISO (based in Geneva, Switzerland) now has 123 member nations and has evolved into the global clearinghouse for all standards activities. Today, World Standards Day is sponsored annually by ISO; the International Electrotechnical Commission (IEC), which develops international standards for the electrical and electronics industries; and the International Telecommunications Union (ITU), an international organization responsible for the coordination, development, regulation, and standardization of telecommunications standards.

The goal of World Standards Day is to raise awareness of the importance of global standardization to the world economy and to promote its role in helping meet the needs of business, industry, government, and consumers worldwide. The international event pays tribute to the thousands of volunteers around the world who participate in standardization activities. Since its initial celebration in 1970, member countries commemorate World Standards Day by organizing special gatherings and events, ranging from conferences, exhibitions, and seminars to film shows, TV and radio interviews, and full "standards weeks" around mid October.

In 2010 the World Standards Day will be on 14 October 2010.

ISO, IEC and ITU have chosen *Accessibility* as the theme for the upcoming World Standards Day.

ISO has distributed following background information on the choice of this year's theme [3]:

> Accessibility is now a worldwide concern in the design of products, services and environments. According to the World Health Organization, about 650

million people have some limitations, more than 500 million of them in developing countries.

As able bodied people grow older, failing sight and hearing, reduced mobility and strength confront them with accessibility issues. Pregnant women, or mothers with baby carriages, can also experience reduced and time-limited accessibility.

The speed of technological innovations, particularly in information and communication technologies, can outstrip the capability of users, particularly the disabled and elderly, to benefit from access to e-mail, the Internet and mobile phones.

International Standards on designing products, services and environments with the disabled, elderly and disadvantaged in mind, on ergonomics and harmonized test methods can help to implement the aims of the 2006 United Nations Convention on the Rights of Persons with Disabilities.

Accessibility standards can also help to disseminate technological innovation to developing nations, to increase the market for new products and services, while meeting the generalized aspiration towards social responsibility. Finally, accessibility standards can facilitate access to transportation and buildings, as well as circulation in urban environments.

More details on how ISO itself will celebrate the event will be known only in July 2010.[4]

4 Conclusions

In this contribution we have given some insights in the talks that will be given within the STS session on Standardisation. Also background info on the ISO World Standards day has been provided.

References

1. Guide 6, the European version of ISO Guide 71, covers the knowledge that should be available within standardisation bodies willing to produce standards for accessible products. More details on, http://en.wikipedia.org/wiki/CEN/CENELEC_Guide_6
2. The World Standards Day (in fact a whole week in the US) is announced at, http://www.ansi.org/meetings_events/WSW10/fact_sheet.aspx?menuid=8
3. Press release of ISO in relation to the World Standards Day 2010 (2010), http://www.iso.org/iso/wsd_2010.htm
4. Updated information on the WSD can be found at the link above or at, http://www.iso.org/iso/events.htm

International AT and DfA Standardisation: What Is in the Pipeline?

Jan Engelen

Kath. Univ. Leuven – DocArch group – ESAT Dept. of Electrical Engineering,
Kasteelpark Arenberg 10, B-3001 Heverlee – Leuven (Belgium)
`jan.engelen@esat.kuleuven.be`

Abstract. In this contribution several recent actions in the field of Standardisation related to Assistive Technology and Design for All are reported. The main focus will be on several CEN initiatives, the status of Mandate 376 and the current EU Commission's plans for issuing a new mandate on the inclusion of "Design for All" in relevant standardisation initiatives.

1 Introduction

Standardisation of products and services supporting persons with special needs is an important aspect of the growing European unified market. In this contribution we will provide some details and pointers to the EU and global standardisation activities related to assistive technology and design for all solutions.

2 Guide 6, Guide 71 and beyond

In order to draw the attention of committee members in standardisation activities on the specific needs of persons with an impairment more than 10 years ago a special guideline was developed within ISO, the *"ISO/IEC Guide 71"* a document that was later taken over by CEN/CENELEC/ETSI as *Guide 6* [1]. Several follow up actions are currently under consideration. A few of them are detailed below.

2.1 The Need for Reworking Guide 6

During the trainings organized by the Stand4All project (cf. below, 5.2)) it became clear that Guide 6 (which dates from a pre-DfA period) has several shortcomings, a.o.:

1. No mention is made of combinations of handicaps
2. No "Design for All" approach is in place
3. The tables within the PDF version are not accessible for reading by people with disabilities (e.g. blind persons), even not with adapted computer software.

Items 1 and 2 require a thorough reworking by CEN and/or a new dedicated working group.

K. Miesenberger et al. (Eds.): ICCHP 2010, Part I, LNCS 6179, pp. 553–560, 2010.
© Springer-Verlag Berlin Heidelberg 2010

2.2 Collaboration with ISO Workgroup Involved in ISO/CEN Guide 71 & ISO/TR 22411:2008

The CEN Mechanism for Guide 6 follow up is rather fragmented and during the April 8, 2009 CEN workshop "Standardisation for All" it became clear that for Guide 71 a full supporting document: ISO/TR 22411:2008: *Ergonomics data and guidelines for the application of ISO/IEC Guide 71 to products and services to address the needs of older persons and persons with disabilities* was already in place since 2008 [1]. Due to ISO policy, the document itself can only be bought from National Standardization Bodies or directly from ISO (paid delivery via the web). It is therefore much less known by most user groups.

Although they would be very useful, currently no common meetings on follow-up procedures seem to be planned (cf. also 4.2).

3 Intersection of Policies and Standardisation: The Mandates

Up to now, it has been rather difficult to impose on a European scale any legal measures related to e-accessibility as social policy is still seen as a national affair. One of the possibilities the European Commission is exploring is to intervene in standardisation actions.

A "Mandate" from the Commission to the European Standardisation bodies – CEN, CENELEC & ETSI is a request for specific actions, paid from the EC budget.

3.1 Mandate 376

The 2005 EC Communication on Accessibility[1] stressed that Public Procurements in the ICT domain are an important lever for the deployment of eAccessibility as they have the potential to play a vital role in removing barriers to participation in the Information Society by disabled or older people. The underlying rationale is that, if companies have to produce accessible solutions in order to cope with the calls for tender, these solutions will also probably also be offered to the general public.

In the autumn of 2007 the work on the Mandate phase I had started. In charge were: CEN BT Working Group 185, Cenelec BT Working Group 101-5 and ETSI TC/HF (Technical Committee/Human Factors) that in practice acted via a Specialist Task Force (STF333).

We have reported on it during ICCHP 2008 and can provide now more practical details about phase II if the mandate work. This phase was supposed to start early in 2010[2].

---

[1] In full: The Communication from the Commission to the Council, the European Parliament, the Economic and Social Committee, and the Committee of Regions, regarding eAccessibility (adopted on 13 September 2005).
Link: http://europa.eu.int/information_society/policy/accessibility/policy/ com-ea-2005/a_documents/cec_com_eacc_2005.html
[2] But it has not at the time of writing (April 2010).

During 2009 two major steps have been put:

a) the acceptance of phase I work, first by the relevant working groups within CEN/CENELEC and ETSI, then by their boards and finally by the European Commission.

b) the negotiation about phase II work was finalised towards the end of 2009 so it might start in the second quarter of 2010. During a special standardization meeting, organised by the USEM project, following details about phase II work were provided[3].

Organisation of Phase II

- A Joint Working Group will be in charge of Phase II with:
    - ETSI member companies
    - CEN and CENELEC member representatives
- There will be 2 paid research teams (an ETSI STF and a CEN Project Team)
- Open consultation meetings will be held on interim and final drafts. One of them will be organised by DATSCG (Design for All and Assistive Technology Standardisation Coordination Group)
- the Joint Working Group approves TRs (Technical reports) or determines when the formal EN (European Norm) adoption process can start. The EN adoption process is a rather formal one: enquiry among all members, followed by vote.
- if adopted, this EN is published as "triple logo", i.e. a common document of CEN, CENELEC and ETSI

Planned deliverables (= outcomes of phase II): [4]

D1 - a European Norm (EN) specifying the functional accessibility requirements applicable to ICT products and services.

D2 - a Technical Report (TR) listing the standards and specifications used for the EN (D1).

The EN (D1) will be a stand alone document. This TR will provide additional explanation to assist users of the EN with clarifications and supporting information about measurement methods as well as identifying the sources for the EN content.

D3 - a Technical Report giving guidelines for award criteria

In a procurement process there is a difference between selection criteria such as a manufacturer's financial standing and the award criteria for the specific tenders that are eligible. This report will provide guidance on how the EN (D1) can be used for award criteria within the procurement procedure.

---

[3] This information is taken from the presentation by Luc Van den Berghe (CEN) at the USEM Network day (Oct 29, 2009). Information should be used with caution as long as the formal contract with the EC is not signed.

[4] **Warning:** this list cannot be taken as definitive as long as the official contract is not signed, which is still the case at the moment of this writing (April 2010).

D4 - a Technical Report on Conformity declaration

This TR contains (a) format template(s) for declaring conformity, as well as (b) the description of the conformity assessment methods that can be referred to by the procurer in his procurement. This TR will ensure that the procurer receives conformity statements from potential tenders that can be compared easily.

D5 - An on-line accessible toolkit (in English only)

Providing structured access to the full content of the EN (D1), the Technical reports (D2 & D3 & D4), and the additional guidelines and the guidance material (D6). Will be produced by a sub-contractor.

D6 – Additional guidance and support material for procurers, published as part of the on-line toolkit

User participation in Phase II

Special attention has been paid by the ESO's to user participation in phase II work. E.g. not only travel and lodging costs for selected stakeholders will be refunded but also for the personal assistants. This will definitely permit more users to contribute to the mandate work.

3.2 Mandate 420

Early 2008, it was announced that a follow-up mandate, called M420 on Accessibility of the Built Environment, was under preparation. In the context of public procurement, it would cover public buildings, public places, parking lots, roads, schools, hospitals, sports facilities etc. And also transport facilities such as airports, train/coach stations, ports etc. Liaison with the actors of M376 (cf. above) is also foreseen [3]. The mandate has been accepted [4] but not much details about outcomes seem to be available.

3.3 Mandate on "Design for All"

Early 2010 the European Commission (DG EMPL: Employment, Social Affairs and Equal Opportunities) initiated the procedure for a new mandate to the European standardisation bodies CEN, CENELEC and ETSI, this one being on techniques for imposing a Design for All philosophy when developing standards.

In April 2010 a plan for this new mandate was forwarded to the EC's "Standards and technical regulations consultative committee", also known as committee 98/34 which responsible for mandate work. At the time of writing this document (April 2010), the "98/34 Committee" had not yet agreed with the proposed text but it can be anticipated that following actions will be requested from the three standardisation bodies [5]:

(1) Identify the relevance of existing and future standardisation deliverables for people with disabilities and older persons.

This should lead to a report describing a process allowing to identify relevance of standardisation deliverables for people with disabilities and older persons and a report describing the main areas of standardisation to be reviewed in order to address the needs of people with disabilities and older persons.

(2) Develop a sustainable programme for reviewing and amending in the priority areas as identified above the relevant standardisation deliverables in order to address accessibility for person with disabilities following Design for all approach. This work should lead to a work plan with priorities and time schedule for addressing Design for all in standardisation items (new or for revision) starting with at least 2 work items per year and pursuing steps once the Mandate is finished.

(3) Apply the above plan to review and amend the identified standardisation deliverables starting with at least two of them per year.

(4) In order to support the manufacturing industry and service providers (public or private) to apply the new elements of accessibility in the standardisation deliverables, a new standard (or other deliverable as appropriate to be proposed by the ESOs and accepted by the European Commission), should be developed that describes how the goods manufacturing industry as well as public and private service entities in their processes can consider accessibility following a Design for all approach.

If available, updated information on this Mandate will be provided during ICCHP 2010.

4 CEN Activities

4.1 CEN Workshops

Several preparatory actions towards standardization are made in the so-called CEN Workshop structure, which is actually a series of workshops.

The two most important ones in the domain of Design for all are:

- the CEN Workshop on Certification, in full "CEN/ISSS Workshop on Specifications for a complete European Web Accessibility certification scheme and a Quality Mark **WS/WAC**" was initiated by the European Support-EAM project and lead to preliminary but somewhat controversial conclusions in 2008. A three year extension (till 2012) was recently granted in order to be able to cope with new certification ideas such as the ones that might come up in Mandate 376 Phase II.
- CEN Workshop on Curriculum development, in full "CEN Workshop on a curriculum for training of professionals in ICT industry in the "Design for All" (DfA) principles and methods - **WS/UDP**". From within the DfA@eInclusion project, several steps have been put during 2009 to start this new CEN Workshop. It is very likely that concrete work will start in 2010. More details can be found in the Business plan of May 2009 [6] and in deliverable "D5.4: White paper Recommendations for the development of eAccessibility training materials for the ICT industry" from the DfA@eInclusion project.

4.2 CEN Working Group on "Accessibility for All / Guide 6 implementation Mechanism"

The creation of this group by NEN (the Dutch National Standardisation organization) was announced during an ad hoc meeting in October 2008 [7].

A follow up meeting, organised by NEN (Dutch Standardisation Organisation) took place on April 8, 2009 in Brussels. During this meeting the relation between Guide 6 and ISO Guide 71 was discussed, as well as the different follow up mechanisms for both (otherwise identical) documents.

The group meanwhile has been renamed as: "CEN/CENELEC/BT/WG Guide 6 - Implementation mechanism". At the time of this writing (April 2010) it is not clear if and how much follow up will be given to the activities of this working group. '

5 Important Projects

5.1 TIRESIAS' Standardisation Overviews

Richard Hodgkinson, convener of ISO/IEC Joint Technical Committee 1/SC7/WG2 provides to the Tiresias archive a regularly updated list of ongoing Standardisation work related to accessibility of ICT systems on a global scale. Each time an overview is given on which standards are proposed and which ones are being developed or have been recently published. The main focus is on ISO and ETSI standardisation but also CEN and BSI (British Standards Institution) work is mentioned [8].

5.2 USEM and Stand4all Projects

USEM, User Empowerment in Standardisation[9] was a European project (it finished in November 2009)which aimed to facilitate, enhance and increase qualification and participation of disabled or elderly users and their respective organisations in the European standardisation process of IST. It organised a three day training course in Bonn (September 2008) and a special network day in October 2009.

Within the **Stand4all** project [10] focus was again on training, this time for user representatives and for committee members in standardisation. Part of the training consisted also of a practical role game (mimicking a standardisation meeting) where the opinions of both groups were confronted.

5.3 DfA@eInclusion Project

Within the DfA@eInclusion project [11], which was basically a support action for the European Design for All e-Accessibility network (EDeAN [12]), also special attention was paid to DfA & AT standardisation issues. Three reports on ongoing standardisation actions where produced in the course of the project [13].

In the framework of the Dfa@eInclusion project, also a large resource list on standardization (with summary texts) was made available within het Ariadne resource area of the EDeAN platform (January 2010).

This annotated bibliography provides, in about 100 documents, a rapid overview of the DfA standardization area[14]. All web entries have been critically checked in December 2009.

6 Conclusions

Within the different standardisation organisations a steady increase of awareness on the needs of persons with functional limitations can be seen, resulting in a growing number of new actions. The most recent ones are discussed in this contribution and pointers for further exploration of the field are given.

Acknowledgements

This research was supported by the EU USEM, STAND4ALL & DfA@eInclusion projects, the Katholieke Universiteit Leuven and LUCIDE: Leuven University Centre for Interdisciplinary Research on Difference and Equality [15].

References

1. ISO/IEC Guide 71 is available from ISO and ANSI (page charges do apply); Guide 6 can be, downloaded from,
   `ftp://ftp.cen.eu/BOSS/Reference_Documents/Guides/CEN_CLC/CEN_CLC_6.pdf`, Background information is available in the Wikipedia page (maintained by Ch. Strobbe of K.U.Leuven),
   `http://en.wikipedia.org/wiki/CEN/CENELEC_Guide_6`
2. Wikipedia article on CEN/CENELEC Guide 6,
   `http://en.wikipedia.org/wiki/CEN/CENELEC_Guide_6#cite_note-11`
3. Placencia, I., Sindelar, M.: The European Disability Action Plan and Accessibility Standardisation. Presentation made at the final COST219ter Conference, Vision in Action: Accessibility for All to Next Generation Networks, Brussels, February 7 (2008), Can be downloaded from:
   `http://www.tiresias.org/cost219ter/vision_action/sindelar.ppt`
4. Mandate 420 info on CENELEC wibsite,
   `http://www.cenelec.eu/NR/rdonlyres/144B7979-77EA-4D7D-93C4-0D116C65E6D3/2389/M420en.pdf`
5. Information based on CEN document N025-2010
6. The DfA@eInclusion deliverable D4.5 currently still is an internal document, Details about the planned Workshop can be found at,
   `http://www.cen.eu/cenorm/sectors/sectors/isss/workshops/businessplan2705.pdf`
7. The new CEN working group is referenced to at: `http://www.usem-net.eu/index.php?view=article&id=84%3Aaccessibility-for-all-meeting&Itemid=70&option=com_content`
8. Hodgkinson, R.: Report on International ICT Accessibility Standards proposed, Being Developed and Recently published, version 10 (June 2009),
   `http://www.tiresias.org/research/standards/report_10.htm`

9. USEM public website is at: `http://www.usem-net.eu`
10. Strobbe, C., Mosies, C., Bühler, C., Engelen, J.: The project is detailed in the ICCHP 2010 contribution, Stand4All: Promoting More Accessible Standards Through Training of Stakeholders, The STAND4ALL website can be found at,
    `http://www.stand4all.eu`
11. DfA@eInclusion's public website is at: `http://www.dfaei.org`
12. Info on the European Design for All Network can be found at:
    `http://www.edean.org`
13. The three reports mentioned can be downloaded from: Overview on ongoing standardization work (D2.2a): `http://www.dfaei.org/docs/D2.2a.pdf`,
    EDEAN-members' involvement in standardization (D2.4a),
    `http://www.dfaei.edean.org/deliverables/`
    `dfa@einclusion%20-%20Del2.4a.pdf`,
    EDEAN Contributions to new Standardisation actions (D2.4b),
    `http://www.esat.kuleuven.be/pub/bscw.cgi/d56873/`
    `D2.4b_2009_new_standardisation_items.doc`
14. The Ariadne document server is reachable via, `http://www.edean.org`
15. Katholieke Universiteit Leuven - Docarch group:
    `http://www.docarch.be/LUCIDE`, `http://www.kuleuven.be/lucide/`

Redefining Assumptions: Accessibility and Its Stakeholders

Rui Lopes[1,*], Karel Van Isacker[2], and Luís Carriço[1]

[1] University of Lisbon
Campo Grande 1749-016 Lisbon, Portugal
{rlopes,lmc}@di.fc.ul.pt
[2] Marie Curie Association
4023 Plovdiv, Bulgaria
projects@marie-curie-bg.org

Abstract. Accessibility is becoming more and more relevant in Information technologies, such as the Web and software applications, particularly due to the push on legislation to make public services accessible to everyone. While most accessibility issues are envisioned by the developer-user dichotomy, several stakeholders are responsible for the successful implementation of accessible software and services for all users.

In this paper we present an exploratory study on the current state of accessibility as perceived by its main stakeholders: developers, service providers, public bodies, accessibility assessors, and elderly and people with disabilities. By surveying more than 400 individuals, we have confirmed some of the expectations and results from other surveys, such as the perception about the lack of understanding and application of Web accessibility guidelines. We have found that this issue gets even worse outside the scope of the Web, for all stakeholders. Another eye-opening finding is that all stakeholders are welcome to the simulation of assistive technologies, in order to widen the perception and involvement of accessibility in the software development process.

Keywords: Accessibility, Stakeholders, Survey.

1 Introduction

Information and communication technologies (ICT) have profoundly changed people's lives. With the worldwide massification of technology, the user diversity landscape has widen, with more abilities and preferences to be taken into account. Thus, ideally, technology should be tailored to each one's needs [8,7]. While ICT products and services are *good enough* for the average user, people with mild or severe disabilities are hindered behind the inadequacy to their particular necessities, putting these users' goals at stake when interacting with them [8].

---

* This work is funded by the EU FP7 project ACCESSIBLE (http://www.accessible-project.eu), contract no. 224145, and by FCT through the SFRH/BD/29150/2006 grant and the Multiannual Funding Programme.

K. Miesenberger et al. (Eds.): ICCHP 2010, Part I, LNCS 6179, pp. 561–568, 2010.

To overcome these issues it is necessary first to grasp the understanding of accessibility by its stakeholders. While developers and people with disabilities are at the core of this issue, other user groups contribute to this situation [5]. In this paper we present our findings based on a survey conducted to 5 key stakeholders on accessibility issues – *Developers, Service Providers, Public Bodies, Accessibility Assessors*, and *Elderly and People with Disabilities* –, and discuss potential directions on accessibility research and outreach.

2   Related Work

Surveying the state of accessibility is not a novel task. With the increasing relevance of accessibility, some studies focus on understanding the perception of accessibility by its stakeholders. Lazar et. al [6] provide one of the first insights on the relationship of webmasters with accessibility. They cite project management issues and lack of time as the main reasons for poor Web accessibility support, and that only governmental websites tend to be accessible due to law enforcement. Accessibility-dependent end-users have also been the target of studies [9], citing accessible Web design as a critical need for the improvement of user interfaces.

On the developers' side, Freire et. al [4] confirmed that, for Web technologies, accessibility is seldom considered at project planning stages, mostly due to the lack of knowledge and communication among its stakeholders. Later work [3] surveyed academy, government, and industry, finding out that law knowledge and abidance is low due to the lack of training.

From what we could tell, surveys are mostly centred on Web technologies (most probably due to its pervasiveness). Consequently, they provide a limited picture of the general state of accessibility. Also, these surveys have insufficient, tangible goals to improve the state of accessibility. We propose to complete this with an umbrella view of accessibility for all stakeholders, with accompanying solutions. Next, we detail the methodology conducted in our survey.

3   Methodology

We created a specific methodology for the definition of questionnaires, by taking into account the particularities of stakeholders, as well as their relationships. As a starting point, we defined a specific rational on selecting the stakeholders with regards to this survey:

- *Developers* (software developers and designers) that will use tools for the development and testing of accessible software applications;
- *Accessibility Assessors* who are involved in assessing existing software solutions, and the accessibility of its user interfaces;
- *Public Bodies/Governmental Agencies* who are involved in policy making and provide the basis for future policies;

- *Service Providers* (public and private enterprises and organisations responsible for the content and graphic layout of Web products) who set (commercial) objectives and are key decision makers in Web accessibility development;
- *Elderly and Disabled Users* who benefit from enhanced accessibility and are the actual end-users of all developed solutions.

These questionnaires were tailored to each user group, encompassing preferred mediums (*online* vs. *paper*) and corresponding answering method (*self-answered* vs. *face-to-face interviews*). All questionnaires were made available in 7 languages (Czech, English, French, German, Greek, Italian, and Portuguese).

Regarding the content of the questions, they were categorised as follows:

- *Demographic data*: Required to identify significant connections between age and IT needs. Such can especially matter with elderly and disabled users;
- *Comprehension of accessibility*: Required to identify similarities and differences on how accessibility knowledge is being conveyed;
- *Working with accessibility*: Required to collect information on existing know how and on the willingness to a steady learning of the topic;
- *Expectation of accessibility*: Required to identify user needs which people might not be aware of;
- *Information on employment*: Required to create correlation between work situations, e.g. teamwork, decision authority and user needs;
- *Information on user behaviour on the Internet and computers*: Relevant for a possible market analysis on already existing accessibility of Web presence, software, etc.

To ensure a higher willingness on stakeholders' participation, we arranged the questions according to a *rising action*: general questions came before particular ones; familiar issues were addressed first than those that might be unfamiliar; difficult issues came after familiar (i.e., *simple*) issues; and any individual/personal issues were addressed only at the end.

Questions were presented sequentially with dichotomous and multiple response options. Additional half-open and open-field questions were used where it was believed that the answer categories were incomplete. *Don't know* answers were included for all questions. Nominal-scaled questions and ordinal-scaled questions were used to survey personal opinions and requirements.

4   Results and Discussion

The survey took place from April 2009 through July 2009 via both online submission forms and face-to-face interviews. It was agreed for interviews with developer and service providers to take place online, and to some extent also with public bodies and accessibility assessors. Interviews with elderly and people with disabilities were mostly undertaken face-to-face. The questionnaires were disseminated throughout different channels, such as specialised forums and conferences, in order to obtain a significant quantity of answers and as diverse as possible. A total of 408 individuals were surveyed (76.2% male).

4.1 Developers

254 development-related users participated in the survey. 25% were directors of a software division, while 65% were developers, and the rest either assistants or students. Around 30% of all those surveyed were acquainted with individuals who have a disability, either in the private (80%) or professional (20%) sphere. The meaning of accessibility for students is more heterogeneous than for individuals having an employment position. Students connect accessibility mainly to design for all (almost 90%) and platform independence (almost 50%). We hypothesise that this discrepancy is linked to the professional tasks developers and directors undertake on a daily basis, while students get faced with accessibility in a rather general manner.

Almost half of these indicated it did affect their daily work, acknowledging that they were already involved in accessibility related projects. Overall however, developers expressed the need for more knowledge about (combined) disabilities, functional limitations, and assistive devices (32%). There is awareness about accessibility standards and guidelines (40%), however this is more in a passive format.

A majority (85%) indicated a need for advanced education in the area of accessibility, especially for Web and mobile accessibility, accessible user interface aspects and (assistive) devices. The preferred type of advanced training and education was by working in project groups (67%), by participating in dedicated workshops (53%) and online training (34%). This need for advanced education corresponds to the rather low awareness of national and international guidelines and standards regarding accessibility as shown in Table 1:

Table 1. Familiarity with standards and guidelines

Guidelines, standards	Familiarity of students	Familiarity of directors, developers
WAI-ARIA	15%	65%
WCAG 1.0	65%	87%
WCAG 2.0	10%	45%
Section 508	4%	39%
ATAG	0%	7%

It must be highlighted here that for those that are being aware of standards, does not mean they actually know the standards and can implement this. This was rather bluntly put by one interviewee who stated: *"[...] do have a shelf of books on WCAG 1.0 and 2.0 issues, but hardly any of us uses it as we lack the time. What we all seek for is an embedded validator in our day to day developing tools such as Microsoft Visual Studio, Visual Basic .NET, Bluefish, Eclipse and Anjuta [...]"*. This evidences of an indication that they wanted embedded validators in development tools. While Integrated Development Environment (IDEs) are used by almost half, it is shown that few are aware of any embedded accessibility features. Regarding the preference for accessibility development tools, accessibility simulation and authoring tools were much preferred (70%), together with simulators of assistive technology. Still significantly wanted were accessibility assessment tools (48%). There was a clear preference (49%) to provide all tools online or as download.

4.2   Service Providers

A total of 41 individuals (of which 24 men) between 24 and 60 years of age were surveyed. They were primarily employed in the field of accessible website design and consulting, and mainly (over 90%) work in SMEs. 14 (34%) of the individuals surveyed have a disability. Since the early 2000s, accessibility guidelines have become more and more specialised, while an increasing demand (mainly from public institutions) has forced these providers to ensure they integrate accessibility within services. From the survey carried out, it looks like the individuals surveyed are fully aware of this (85%). They have a high awareness level of various accessibility standards and guidelines, especially WCAG 1.0 [2] (83%), with an interest towards WCAG 2.0 [1] (01%). While they have already access to various accessibility tools and methodologies, they are one of the most eager groups survey for further advancements in this area.

Surveyed individuals displayed a clear interest in further knowledge about Web (88%) and mobile accessibility (66%), and prefer to do so through real work in this area. Like developers, this user group prefers to be kept up-to-date on accessibility via online resources (83%). This is also the preferred channel to have access to new tools (93%).

All webmasters and designers indicated that their customers desire accessibility certification. However this is still limited to being, at most, W3C WAI-AAA compliant (90%).

They currently evaluate the accessibility of their developments mainly with assessment and simulation tools (66%), followed by the use of AT (32%) and the participation of potential users with disabilities (34%). They desired further usage of assessment and simulation tools (85%), both for accessibility and for AT.

4.3   Public Bodies

A total of 18 public servants and officials (aged 28 to 60, and 11 of them men) were surveyed. They work for public bodies and governmental agencies and corporations, such as public utility companies. While this sample is rather small, due in part to the difficulty in accessing the target group through the required official channels, it must be noted that accessibility of services provided by public bodies and governmental agencies is usually subject to European and national regulations. This means that obligations exist to make services such as websites, downloadable documents, and online forms accessible to all members of the general public. The individuals surveyed were all familiar with this aspect of accessibility, while over 75% associated accessibility also with making building constructions accessible.

Online access to information is also the main channel of accessibility knowledge (80%). This was the same for accessibility dissemination, despite most respondents being still keen on traditional printed media (50%). This has been an exception among all surveyed groups. We hypothesise that this might be based in a rather *traditional culture* that still survives in public bodies.

The unavailability of internal expertise was identified as being the main barrier regarding accessibility of delivered services (72%). Internal training were taking place (56%), but in most cases external expertise was still needed for assessments (50%). This also explains why the surveyed individuals were interested in accessibility related events and databases on accessibility experts to evaluate implementations.

Evaluation, assessment and simulation tools are the main support on ensuring accessibility of websites (67%), with hardly any involvement of end-users or AT. However, AT simulators were wanted by all of those involved in software development.

All indicated that the public bodies they work for do expect some kind of official accessibility certification of the services that they offer or develop (78%). If labels are applied, this is in most cases awarded by external assessors (organisations that were set up to test the accessibility of public websites), e.g., W3C AAA compliance labels.

4.4   Accessibility Assessors

The accessibility assessors user group encompasses advocators that intervene in all areas of society, in order to advance equal living conditions for people with disabilities. The questionnaire was completed by 37 individuals in this category (24 men and 11 women), between 23 and 54 years of age. As the accessibility assessors group does not correspond to a specific occupational group, the professional backgrounds of the individuals surveyed are distributed over a broad spectrum, from peer counsellors to university professors. Most (81%) have up to 12 years of work experience, and 9 of those surveyed have a disability (mobility and visual impairment). 11 individuals (among which are the 9 people with disabilities) are members of an organisation for people with disabilities.

They are highly aware of various accessibility standards and guidelines (81%), especially WCAG 1.0 since they often use a subset of it in the national guidelines. This group emphasised their active role in the accessibility assessment of Web (81%) and desktop applications (41%). As expected, they have shown a preference (90%) for online access to information to be kept up-to-date on accessibility issues.

Validators and simulation tools are mainly used to evaluate implementations, while there is strong interest in using disability (77%) and AT simulation (80%) tools. Equally, guidelines for the creation of accessible content (57%) and invitations to events about accessibility issues (63%) are of interest. The latter obviously as this is directly related with their role of accessibility advocators.

4.5   Elderly and People with Disabilities

A total of 67 individuals were surveyed (39 men and 28 women) between 19 and 75 years of age. Of this group, over 75% indicated they had a disability. We hypothesise that the remaining 25% accounts for elderly people.

All individuals 30 years of age indicated that they are disabled as did all individuals surveyed in the 40-49 age category. 91,7% of those individuals surveyed in the 30-39 age bracket indicated that they are disabled as did 84,6% in the 50-59 age bracket and 60% in the 60–69 age bracket.

It is however clear that these users are aware that the Web and increasingly also mobile applications are posing severe barriers to them (60%). Nevertheless, a majority uses the computer/laptop or mobile on an almost daily basis (75%). A wide variety of AT is used in order to access applications on both computer and mobile devices. Training is often taken for computer usage (60%), but proves to fall short of expectations. Users therefore often rely on friends to help them out (70%). This user group has expressively stated (73%) that the main improvement desired is the better compatibility between Assistive Technologies and Web pages.

5   Conclusions and Future Work

This paper presented a study on the current state of accessibility as perceived by its main stakeholders. Through the answers of more than 400 people surveyed, we have confirmed results from existing studies, such as the perception about the lack of understanding and application of Web accessibility guidelines. We have also confirmed the recurring need for assessment tools so that accessibility of Web, mobile and desktop interfaces can be assessed in an easier way. Summarising, the following set of recommendations for research and outreach for accessible software and services emerges from our study:

- There must be a higher spread of knowledge in what regards to WCAG 2.0, since most stakeholders are not sufficiently familiar with this new version of the guidelines;
- There is a willingness for more advancements on disability and AT simulation technologies;
- Developers desire for advanced IDE integration of accessibility assessment and simulation tools, instead of separate applications;
- Accessibility outside the scope of the Web is seldom taken into account, due to the shadowing of the extensive work on Web accessibility.

These results are playing a fundamental role on the definition of key use cases and requirements in the design and development of accessibility-aware software development tools in different application domains (Web, mobile, service description languages, etc.), the overarching goal of the EU FP7 ACCESSIBLE project.

References

1. Caldwell, B., Cooper, M., Reid, L., Vanderheiden, G.: Web Content Accessibility Guidelines 2.0. W3C Recommendation, World Wide Web Consortium (W3C) (December 2008), http://www.w3.org/TR/WCAG20/
2. Chisholm, W., Vanderheiden, G., Jacobs, I.: Web Content Accessibility Guidelines 1.0. W3C Recommendation, World Wide Web Consortium (W3C) (May 1999), http://www.w3.org/TR/WCAG10/
3. Freire, A.P., Russo, C.M., Fortes, R.P.M.: The perception of accessibility in web development by academy, industry and government: a survey of the brazilian scenario. New Rev. Hypermedia Multimedia 14(2), 149–175 (2008)
4. Freire, A.P., Russo, C.M., Fortes, R.P.M.: A survey on the accessibility awareness of people involved in web development projects in brazil. In: W4A 2008: Proceedings of the 2008 international cross-disciplinary conference on Web accessibility (W4A), pp. 87–96. ACM, New York (2008)
5. Kelly, B., Sloan, D., Brown, S., Seale, J., Petrie, H., Lauke, P., Ball, S.: Accessibility 2.0: people, policies and processes. In: W4A 2007: Proceedings of the 2007 international cross-disciplinary conference on Web accessibility (W4A), pp. 138–147. ACM, New York (2007)
6. Lazar, J., Dudley-Sponaugle, A., Greenidge, K.-D.: Improving web accessibility: a study of webmaster perceptions. Computers in Human Behavior 20(2), 269–288 (2004)
7. Obrenovic, Z., Abascal, J., Starcevic, D.: Universal accessibility as a multimodal design issue. Commun. ACM 50(5), 83–88 (2007)
8. Shneiderman, B.: Promoting universal usability with multi-layer interface design. In: CUU 2003: Proceedings of the 2003 conference on Universal usability, pp. 1–8. ACM, New York (2003)
9. Yao, D., Qiu, Y., Du, Z., Ma, J., Huang, H.: A survey of technology accessibility problems faced by older users in china. In: W4A 2009: Proceedings of the 2009 International Cross-Disciplinary Conference on Web Accessibililty (W4A), pp. 16–25. ACM, New York (2009)

Stand4All: Promoting More Accessible Standards through Training of Stakeholders

Christophe Strobbe[1], Charlotte Mosies[2], Christian Bühler[3], and Jan Engelen[1]

[1] Katholieke Universiteit Leuven, Kasteelpark Arenberg 10, B-3001 Heverlee-Leuven, Belgium
{christophe.strobbe,jan.engelen}@esat.kuleuven.be
[2] NEN, Vlinderweg, 2623 AX Delft, Netherlands
charlotte.mosies@nen.nl
[3] Forschungsinstitut Technologie und Behinderung (FTB), Evangelische Stiftung Volmarstein
(ESV), Grundschoetteler Strasse 40, 58300 Wetter (Ruhr), Germany
cb@ftb-volmarstein.de

Abstract. The Stand4All project is a response to a call for tenders by the European Commission's Directorate-General for Employment, Social Affairs and Equal Opportunities. Its goal is to increase the use of CEN/CENELEC Guide 6, which contains guidance on the inclusion of the needs of elderly persons and persons with disabilities during the standards development process. To reach this goal, the project consortium has developed and delivered training on standardisation in several locations in Europe and for two types of audience: persons with disabilities and members of standardisation committees. The training for persons with disabilities is meant to increase their effective participation in the standardisation process. The training for committee members is meant to increase their awareness and knowledge of accessibility issues faced by persons with disabilities.

1 Introduction

1.1 The European Disability Strategy

The European Union's long-term strategy on disability aims at enabling persons with disabilities "to enjoy their right to dignity, equal treatment, independent living and participation in society" [2]. One of the pillars of this strategy consists in "mainstreaming disability issues in the broad range of Community policies which facilitate the active inclusion of people with disabilities" [2]. One of the tools to reach this goal is standardisation. ISO Guide 71 [5] and its European equivalent CEN/CENELEC Guide 6 [1] provide guidelines for standards developers to address the needs of older persons and persons with disabilities. However, these target groups are not sufficiently involved in standardisation, especially at a European level. Call for tenders N°VT/2008/002, "Training of stakeholders on consultations on standardisation", by the European Commission's Directorate-General for Employment, Social Affairs and Equal Opportunities fits into the European disability strategy.

K. Miesenberger et al. (Eds.): ICCHP 2010, Part I, LNCS 6179, pp. 569–572, 2010.
© Springer-Verlag Berlin Heidelberg 2010

1.2 CEN/CENELEC Guide 6

The European Mandate M/283 pointed out that special needs were addressed in standards related to assistive technologies, but that there were no formal structures or procedures that ensure that the needs of elderly persons and persons with disabilities are taken into account during the standards development process [3]. As a result of this mandate, the European standardisation organisations CEN and CENELEC adopted ISO Guide 71 as CEN/CENELEC Guide 6 [1]. (ETSI uses ISO Guide 71.) "CEN/CENELEC Guide 6: Guidelines for standards developers to address the needs of older persons and persons with disabilities" is a document for participants in standardisation activities at CEN and CENELEC (technical committees, working groups, task forces, etcetera) and contains general guidance on how to ensure greater accessibility in products and services. However, the uptake of Guide 6 has been rather low, and this has led to new initiatives. One of these is the creation of CEN/CENELEC/BT/WG CEN/CENELEC Guide 6 Implementation Mechanism, an initiative by NEN (the Dutch standardisation body) supported by the consumer organisation ANEC. Another initiative is the European Commission's Call for tenders N°VT/2008/002 [4], which led to the Stand4All project.

2 Stand4All Goals

The Stand4All consortium consisted of the Dutch standardisation institute NEN (co-ordinating partner), the British Standards Institution (BSI), the Spanish standardisation institute AENOR, Vilans (the Netherlands), BAG Selbsthilfe (Germany), the Forschungsinstitut Technologie und Behinderung (FTB, Germany) and the Katholieke Universiteit Leuven (Belgium). The organisation for consumer representation in standardisation ANEC is also involved in the training session. Stand4All's goal was to develop training materials and deliver training to two types of trainees:

- training for (representatives of) elderly persons and persons with disabilities, in order to increase their effective participation in the standardisation process at a European level, and
- training for persons who have already been active in standardisation activities ("committee members"), in order to increase their awareness and knowledge of accessibility issues faced by persons with disabilities.

The ultimate goal was to increase accessibility in standardisation at a European level, in other words, the European standardisation organisations CEN, CENELEC and ETSI. The European Commission's call for tenders also required that the training should build on CEN/CENELEC Guide 6.

3 Related Work

The Stand4All project built on the knowledge and experience of the USEM project (User Empowerment in Standardisation, April 2007 – November 2009)[1], which was

---

[1] USEM: http://www.usem-net.eu/

run by a very similar consortium. USEM provided a training session to organisations that represent persons with disabilities; the goal was to provide a basic understanding of standardisation and to motivate trainees to get involved in standardisation. The focus was on ICT, not products and services in general. The project also formulated the "USEM concept", a set of six principles for end-user involvement in standardisation. These principles were derived from the seven principles formulated in the FOR-TUNE project (1999-2000[2]).

4 Stand4All Training Course

The training was delivered four times (Madrid, October 2009; Brussels, December 2009; London, January 2010; Dublin, March 2010). It was typically organised over the course of two days. The training for end users was spread over two days, while the training for committee members was covered in a single day, i.e. the second day of the training for end users. The first day of the training for end users covered the following topics. reasons why promoting the user perspective in standardisation is important, a general overview of standardisation at a European level, how consumers / end-users can contribute to the standardisation process, and an introduction to the use of CEN/CENELEC Guide 6. On the second day, the committee members received an introduction on reasons why promoting the user perspective in standardisation is important and an introduction to using CEN/CENELEC Guide 6. After this, the two groups of trainees were brought together for a role-play activity led by ANEC. This role-play simulated a committee meeting on the European standard EN 81-70:2003: "Safety rules for the construction and installation of lifts. Particular applications for passenger and goods passenger lifts. Accessibility to lifts for persons including persons with disability." The training concluded with a discussion on follow-up projects and activities.

5 Stand4All Trainees

The project wanted to recruit representatives from both organisations that represent persons with disabilities (for example, the European Disability Forum and its members) and organisations that represent older users (for example, Age – the European Older People's Platform[3] – and its members). However, only the former type of organisations responded to the recruitment.

The recruitment of committee members tried to persuade committee members with no prior knowledge of accessibility or CEN/CENELEC Guide 6, but many of these trainees were already aware of accessibility issues and some already had extensive knowledge and experience in this area.

6 Dissemination and Future Work

The Stand4All website at http://www.stand4all.eu/ hosts the project's deliverables and provides information on an e-learning module that can be used in conjunction

---

[2] FORTUNE: http://www.fortune-net.de/
[3] AGE: http://www.age-platform.org/

with training sessions in a blended learning approach. The platform that hosts the e-learning module also hosts a web-based network for trainees.

Acknowledgements. This publication is supported for under the European Community Programme for Employment and Social Solidarity (2007-2013). This programme is managed by the Directorate-General for Employment, social affairs and equal opportunities of the European Commission. It was established to financially support the implementation of the objectives of the European Union in the employment and social affairs area, as set out in the Social Agenda, and thereby contribute to the achievement of the Lisbon Strategy goals in these fields. The seven-year Programme targets all stakeholders who can help shape the development of appropriate and effective employment and social legislation and policies, across the EU-27, EFTA-EEA and EU candidate and pre-candidate countries.

References

1. CEN; CENELEC: CEN/CENELEC Guide 6: Guidelines for standards developers to address the needs of older persons and persons with disabilities (2002)
2. European Commission: Communication from the Commission to the Council, the European Parliament, the European Economic and Social committee and the Committee of the Regions - Situation of disabled people in the enlarged European Union : the European Action Plan 2006-2007 (COM/2005/0604) (November 28, 2005)
3. European Commission, M/283-EN: Mandate to the European Standards Bodies for a guidance document in the field of safety and usability of products by people with special needs (e.g. elderly and disabled),
   http://www.etsi.org/WebSite/document/aboutETSI/
   EC_Mandates/M283.pdf
4. European Commission. Specifications-Tender N° VT/2008/002: Training of Stakeholders on consultations on standardisation,
   http://ec.europa.eu/social/BlobServlet?docId=1331&langId=en
5. ISO; IEC. ISO/IEC Guide 71:2001: Guidelines for standards developers to address the needs of older persons and persons with disabilities (2001)

Standards-Based Content Resources:
A Prerequisite for Content Integration and Content Interoperability

Christian Galinski[1] and Karel Van Isacker[2]

[1] International Information Centre for Terminology (Infoterm),
Gymnasiumstrasse 50, 1190 Vienna, Austria
http://www.infoterm.info
[2] Marie Curie Association,
31 Osvobozhdenie avenue, Karina, 1st floor, ap. 4, Plovdiv 4023, Bulgaria
http://www.marie-curie-bg.org

Abstract. Standardized content repositories (and content repositories based on international standards) for structured content are becoming increasingly important for ICT-assisted communication among users, between users and their devices, and among these devices. Given the increasing ubiquity and pervasiveness of ICTs – especially in the communication with and around people with disabilities – it should be assured that ICTs are accessible and inclusive and that they and the standards-compliant data models used facilitate content interoperability. If not, remedial or additional programming may become necessary, which tend to be very costly or even impossible at times. Content interoperability (of structured content) as defined in this article also means – especially if the content itself is collectively developed and maintained on the basis of international standards – that effective methods and efficient tools can be conceived for verification, validation and certification.

Keywords: international standards, content repositories, structured content, standardized data models, standardized content, content interoperability, verification, validation, certification, accessibility.

1 Introduction

Different items of structured content – linguistic and non-linguistic ones – are increasingly combined with or embedded in each other (i.e. content integration at the highest degree of granularity). Therefore, a systemic and generic approach to data modelling and content management has become the order of the day. Content integration and content interoperability are the key concepts in this connection.

Going beyond semantic interoperability, content interoperability means the capability of content entities to be combined with or embedded in other (types of) content items on the one hand, and to carry enough *context* information for being extensively re-used (i.e. *re-usability* extended towards *re-purposability*).

K. Miesenberger et al. (Eds.): ICCHP 2010, Part I, LNCS 6179, pp. 573–579, 2010.

Content interoperability enhances the possibilities to search, retrieve, and recombine from different points of view. It also enhances the personalizability of ICT devices, which is especially important for people with disabilities.

Needless to say that the above-mentioned approach has a big impact on software development, as can be gathered from document MoU/MG/05 N0221[1], [1] which was adopted in 2005, and from document MoU/MG/05 N0222. [2] Modularity and comprehensive interoperability, capability for multilinguality and multimodality based on open standards are increasingly required.

This contribution tries to show how standards-based approaches for content standardization, content management, content related services and tools and their certification not only guarantee reliable content integration and content interoperability, but also are of particular benefit to ensure eInclusion for people with disabilities.

Particularly in the field of accessibility, the use and re-use of all kinds of content across different technical platforms is a must. On the other hand, today, strongly heterogeneous content is still more the rule than the exception. While in the past the development focus was on tools (i.e. devices, computer hardware and software), it is increasingly recognized today that "communication" ultimately is the most important issue, namely

- communication with and among impaired people (directly or through ICT devices),
- communication between impaired people and the devices they use and
- communication among these devices.

Therefore, metadata, data models, messages, protocols, conversion of all sorts, multilinguality (incl. cultural diversity), multimodality, design for all (DfA) etc. have become the objective of standardization efforts in industry, by specialized organizations or in public institutions. [3]

Since a number of years, the number of standards for services and structured content is growing exponentially. People with disabilities are among those who will benefit most from this development.

2 Definitions

2.1 Content Related Concepts

Structured content at the level of lexical semantics covers among others:

- Lexicographical data;
- Terminology and similar kinds of language resources, such as
    - o nomenclatures, taxonomies, typologies, glossaries, vocabularies etc.,
    - o terminological phraseology, morphology
    - o proper names, addresses and other items of all kinds of directories,
    - o graphical symbols and other non-linguistic representations,
    - o (product) properties, characteristics, attributes etc.,

---

[1] MoU/MG: Management Group of the ITU-ISO-IEC-UN/ECE Memorandum of Understanding on standardization in electronic business.

- Thesauri, classification schemes, keywords and other kinds of documentation languages (or controlled vocabularies);
- Encyclopaedic (knowledge) entries, covering among others
  o knowledge-enriched terminology entries and
  o (explained) proper names and other kinds of data closely related to proper names;
- Ontologies, topic maps and other kinds of knowledge-structuring systems;

which in reality in most cases are contradictory and not consistent. They are not based on proper metadata and data modelling methods, and therefore not possible to integrate, not reliable and full of deficits.

If needed in applications, which support people with disabilities, this is inacceptable, especially in our aging societies, where more and more people suffer from multiple impairments. It is getting clear that structured content of all sorts needs to be developed based on internationally standardized metadata and data models. ISO/IEC-JTC 1/SC 32/WG 2 *MetaData* is the Working Group that formulates the methodology standards on metadata and metadata registries. [4]

2.1.1 Content Management Related Concepts

In order to manage these different types of structured content (more and more web-based and in distributed form) – so that the best suited *stakeholder* for a given kind of content can ensure the maintenance, updating and versioning as well as quality assurance of the content in a most efficient way –, a number of additional elements are needed with respect to content interoperability, such as

- identification systems (with IDs) for individual pieces of information (such as ISO TS 29002-5 [5],
- standardized metadata (or data categories, as they are more precisely called in the field of terminology) and the respective metadata registries as well as
- standardized data models.

For the sake of completeness it should be mentioned that the above-cited approaches are increasingly applied also for the preparation and re-use of textual and other un-structured content, e.g. in technical communication, automatic and computer-assisted translation etc. No wonder that accessibility aspects are fairly recently discovered and developed also in such applications. [6]

In any case an efficient use and re-use of structured content can only take place if two fundamental principles of content management methodology are realized: *single sourcing* and *resource-sharing*.

2.1.2 Standardization Related Concepts

Standardization is an activity for establishing, with regard to *actual or potential problems*, provisions for *common and repeated use*, aimed at the *achievement of the optimum degree of order in a given context*. In particular, the activity consists of the processes of formulating, issuing and implementing standards – based on the consensus of the most important stakeholders. [7] Therefore, standards published by standardizing bodies are called *open standards* in contrast to *industry standards*, which

---

[2] Joint Technical Committee of ISO and IEC (International Electrotechnical Commission.

usually are proprietary. Huge efforts are undertaken to harmonize existing open standards at national, regional and international levels so that they do not contradict each other.

2.1.3 Certification Related Concepts

Certification is defined as a *procedure* by which a *third party* gives *written assurance* that a *product, process* or *service* conforms to *specified requirements.* [8] No doubt services can be certified. Certification involves a number of documented processes, arriving at a documented assessment result.

Data models and structured content should also be standards-compliant or standardized. Becoming (at least potentially) highly content interoperable they can be certified, which is new in this connection. Standards compliance would be assessed according to *validation/verification criteria,* [9] defined as policy, procedure or requirement used as a reference against which evidence is compared.

2.1.4 Quality Related Concepts

The above-mentioned concepts emerged in many years of discussion of standards-based quality management systems and their requirements. In this connection *quality* has been defined as the *totality of features and characteristics of a product or service* that bear on its *ability to satisfy stated or implied needs.* [10] The quality of data and data-related services and tools has only recently entered the radar of quality assessment and certification approaches. Needless to say that the potential for quality of data and related services and tools is higher than if they are not standards-based. In any case, the need for reliability of some data in accessible applications has to be much higher than that in many other content repositories. Therefore, the use of standards-based approaches here reduces risks and thus liability in cases of mishaps or accidents.

While quality assessment and certification through audits is relatively well developed in industry and services, the verification and validation of structured content and related services and tools is still in its infancy. Factual and physical properties based data can comparatively easily be validated. Other properties, e.g. those relating to *soft criteria,* such as functions, can probably only be validated, if validation is against a limited number of pre-defined values.

There is a need to develop standards that lay the basis for pertinent certification schemes and the required auditing procedures.

2.2 Special Case: Skills Certification in the ICT Field

eCertification (ICT certification) in Europe can be considered as the set of processes by which an individual gains a credential in a particular ICT skill or more generally a range of skills. Such credentials are usually granted by recognized bodies, themselves often but not always accredited by some governmental or official organization. [11][12]

While it can be recognized that certification provides value in both the labour and product segments of the ICT market, the HARMONISE report [13] describes over 600 often overlapping qualifications from over 60 providers as a "certification jungle", causing confusion to prospective users. The rapid growth in these industry qualifications has been driven by the market over recent years, indeed the market barely existed fifteen years ago. They usually relate to a more specific set of skills (including many for specific products), and are generally more practical in their approach than traditional academic qualifications.

As these market certifications [14][15] contrast and co-exist with the historic university based education system, leading to the phrase "parallel universe", there remains resistance, even hostility, in some academic quarters in some countries, to these certifications. "They are seen as developing skills not education, and product ability not underlying theory, little more than marketing aids to the commercial interests of the vendors. On the other hand, their global application contrasts with the national or even self-accreditation of most university degrees." [11]

Concerning the skills and qualifications necessary for implementing content interoperability – in particular with respect to Accessibility –, available training and studies are not sufficient (even if "certified").

3 Implementation Case: The EU-Project OASIS

OASIS (Open architecture for Accessible Services Integration and Standardization), an ongoing European large-scale Integrated Project within the 7th Framework Programme, started in January 2008 for a period of four years. OASIS aims at an open and innovative reference architecture, based upon ontologies and semantic services, which will allow plug and play and cost-effective interconnection of existing and new services in all domains required for the independent and autonomous living of the elderly and their Quality of Life enhancement (for this and the following see Bekiaris and Bateman, [16]).

OASIS development will provide an open source complementary solution to the direction now being pursued in the Semantic Web approach to ontology design: whereas in the Semantic Web re-usability is pursued across open ontologies, the OASIS solution will show how re-usability can be achieved by the OASIS hyperontology, which will demonstrate how interoperability can be achieved within strict modularity. Side effects in software design are a source of major system instability, development and maintenance costs – avoiding them for ontology design will therefore be a major innovative contribution of considerable benefit.

The OASIS Project aims to fill this gap by developing an open source Common Ontological Framework (COF), which will also be introduced into standardization. Needless to mention that COF will follow the MoU/MG recommendation of 2005, which states as basic requirements for the development of fundamental methodology standards concerning content interoperability the fitness for

-    multilinguality (covering also cultural diversity),
-    multimodality and multimedia,
-    eAccessibility (covering also eInclusion), and
-    multi-channel presentations,

which have to be considered at the earliest stage of software design and then throughout all software development cycles. [1]

4 Summary and Outlook

Content integration – whether in the form of virtual or real data integration – and content interoperability must be based among others on

- consistent methodology standards for data models and data modelling,
- coordinated standardization of several kinds of structured content,
- standardized identification systems for individual pieces of information,
- standardized transfer protocols and interchange formats, in order to be efficient and reliable.

At present, standardization in eBusiness is leading the field with highly generic methodology standards and the implementation of content repositories containing standardized structured content. OASIS attempts to combine the results of a number of past projects with best practices concerning structured content development and maintenance as well as with respect to content integration.

In certain cases there is a definite need for certification, validation or verification of data. The respective standardization efforts are still in their infancy. Some kinds of certification, validation or verification possibly can be done through web services. These and other kinds of certification should

- benefit also small content and service providers,
- be affordable and
- fit the kind of service, the technical state-of-the-art at the service providers' side and the expectations of the clients.

Coordination and harmonization efforts supported by the EU Commission have a positive effect on the development of technical, organizational and content interoperability standards as well as standards-based content repositories, which will benefit first of all people with disabilities.

Acknowledgments. This contribution was made possible by the EC FP7 project OASIS – Open architecture for Accessible Services Integration and Standardization, Grant Agreement No. 215754.

References

1. MoU/MG N0221:2004 Semantic Interoperability and the need for a coherent policy for a framework of distributed, possibly federated repositories for all kinds of content items on a world-wide scale (adopted in 2005),
   http://isotc.iso.org/livelink/livelink/fetch/2000/2489/
   Ittf_Home/MoU-MG/Moumg221.pdf
2. MoU/MG N0222:2004 Statement on eBusiness Standards and Cultural Diversity (adopted in 2006),
   http://isotc.iso.org/livelink/livelink/fetch/2000/2489/
   Ittf_Home/MoU-MG/Moumg222.pdf

3. ICTSB (ed.): Design for All. ICTSB Project Team Final Report (2000),
   `http://www.ictsb.org/Activities/Design_for_All/Documents/`
   `ICTSB%20Main%20Report%20.pdf`
4. ISO/IEC 11179 (series) Information technology – Metadata registries (MDR)
5. ISO/TS 29002-5:2009 Industrial automation systems and integration – Exchange of characteristic data – Part 5: Identification scheme (2009)
6. CEN CWA 15778:2008 Document Processing for Accessibility. In: CEN Workshop Document Processing for Accessibility. CEN/WS/DPA, Brussels (2008)
7. ISO/IEC Guide 2:2004 Standardization and related activities – General vocabulary (2004)
8. ISO 14050:2009 Environmental management – Vocabulary (2009)
9. `http://www.praxiom.com/iso-definition.htm#Quality`
10. ISO 9000:2005 Quality management systems – Fundamentals and vocabulary (2005)
11. CWA 16052: 2009 ICT Certification in Europe. In: CEN Workshop ICT-Skills (IT profiles and curricula). WS/ICT, Brussels (2009) (in print)
12. CEN CWA 15515:2006 European ICT Skills Meta-Framework – State-of-the-art review, clarification of the realities, and recommendations for next steps. In: CEN Workshop ICT-Skills (IT profiles and curricula). WS/ICT, Brussels (2006)
13. CEPIS (ed.): Survey of Certification Schemes for ICT Professionals across Europe towards Harmonisation (HARMONISE). Project of CEPIS Council of European Professional Informatics Societies, final report (September 2007), `http://www.cepis-harmonise.org`
14. Cedefop (ed.): ICT Skills Certification in Europe. Cedefop Dossier series 13. Office for Official Publications of the European Communities, Luxembourg (2006)
15. ISO/IEC 17024:2003 Conformity Assessment – General requirements for bodies operating certification of persons (2003)
16. Bekiaris, E.D., Bateman, J.A.: Content Interoperability Standardization. The open Reference Architecture of the OASIS Project with its open source Common Ontological Framework and related tools, Standardization. China, Beijing, pp. 41–44 (2009)
17. ISO/IEC TR 19759:2005 Software Engineering – Guide to the Software Engineering Body of Knowledge (SWEBOK) (2005)
18. ISO/IEC 24773:2008 Certification of software engineering professionals – Comparison framework, ISO 8000 (series) Data quality, ISO/IEC TR 20943 (series) Information technology – Procedures for achieving metadata registry content consistency (2008)

Standardization and Sustainability of Open Source Products
- Barriers and Conflicts Demonstrated with the Linux Screenreader SUE -

Andrea Gaal, Gerhard Jaworek, and Joachim Klaus

Study Centre for the Visually Impaired Students (SZS),
Karlsruhe Institute of Technology (KIT)
info@szs.kit.de
http://www.szs.kit.edu

Abstract. SUE is an open source screenreader developed for the graphical interface using Linux. The screenreader allows the visually impaired to work with Linux for typical office tasks and the desktop (GNOME) itself. A special training course will instruct teachers and pupils at institutions for the blind and the partially sighted in using the screenreader. This presentation will focus on SUE and screenreader solutions for Linux. In addition it will discuss the problems of sustainability and standardization in an open community.

Keywords: SUE, Screenreader & Usability Extensions, blind, partially sighted, low vision, accessibility, Open Source, GNOME, Linux, training programme, ECDL.

1 Introduction

Open Source is a popular concept when developing large software projects. The fact that everybody can adapt the software to their special demands and requirements makes it attractive for industrial and governmental solutions. In opposition to Microsoft and Apple applications which are strongly defined and closed systems, open source offers many alternatives and standards competing with each other. Keeping software accessible requires well defined accessibility interfaces and specifications.

The project SUE (Screenreader & Usability Extensions) deals with the development of an open source screenreader for Linux and its correspondent teaching concept. The project was funded by the German Federal Ministry of Labour and Social Affairs and ran from 2007 to June 2010. The aim was the integration of blind and partially sighted persons into the labour market by making Linux-based fields of work accessible. By means of SUE we want to point out problems in implementing enduring accessibility in open source projects.

2 State of the Art – Screenreader Solutions for Linux

In general Linux has two interfaces: the text console and the graphical one. The text interface is accessible for braille users for about 15 years now via BrailleTTY.

K. Miesenberger et al. (Eds.): ICCHP 2010, Part I, LNCS 6179, pp. 580–582, 2010.

BrailleTTY presents the text on various braille displays and supports speech output. The console is very useful when doing administration tasks with a Linux system. A second solution to make the console accessible is SBL, developed by openSUSE. The most common screenreader for the graphical interface is ORCA of Sun Microsystems [1]. It enables access to the Gnome desktop, OpenOffice.org and several other applications. It includes speech and braille output as well as basic magnification functionality. The main focus lies on speech output because in most countries the use of braille displays is not as popular as in Western European countries. The implemented braille functions in ORCA support only basic braille output; there is no off-screen model for structured braille-output implemented.

We decided to develop a new screenreader, because reading with braille displays is very common in Germany. Additionally, SUE supports the Compiz magnification, which is more powerful than Gmag. The adaptation of SUE is quite easy, because it is based on a very well structured object model of LSR [2].

3 The Screenreader SUE and the Training Programme

SUE bases on LSR, the former IBM screenreader work environment. LSR offers a well structured and defined object model of accessibility interfaces. SUE was developed on the Ubuntu/Linux distribution 8.04 – 9.04. We decided to use Ubuntu because this distribution wants to be "the Linux for all" - including people with disabilities. SUE enables the access to the basic functions of the graphical interface Gnome, of OpenOffice.org, Firefox and Evolution. It includes the free speech output engine eSpeak, an interface to BrailleTTY and magnification with the Compiz [3] window manager.

SUE was developed to enable basic office tasks like
  text processing with OpenOffice.org Writer,
  spreadsheet processing with OpenOffice.org Calc,
  E-Mailing with Evolution and
  Internet surfing with the browser Firefox.

Thanks to the efforts of volunteers, SUE is currently available in 9 different languages: English, German, Hungarian, Romanian, French, Dutch, Czech, Portuguese, and Swedish.

To teach the use of SUE and Linux training materials have been developed. The content of these materials is based on the 7 modules of the ECDL (European Computer Driving Licence [4]). ECDL is a certification attesting basic computer skills and exists in 148 countries. In Germany it is developed and distributed by the DLGI (Dienstleistungsgesellschaft fuer Informatik mbH [5]).

Training materials are available for free on the SUE project wiki [6], where they may also be downloaded as PDF. Most of the training material is in German, but there is one additional script provided in English [7].

4 Future of SUE

Sue is a 'never ending' screenreader project because the development of the supported applications is ongoing. At the moment SUE works quite well with Ubuntu 9.04, OOs 3.0 Writer and Calc. Firefox and Evolution require further development.

With the end of the project (6/2010) the development and adaptation of the screen-reader to the latest versions of Ubuntu and its applications has stopped. In the world of open source changes occur faster than in systems where companies define the standards and interfaces. This means that screenreader developers must react very fast to keep the system usable and up to date. The following changes are announced for the next Ubuntu version 10.04 and higher: the window manager Gnome 3 will be completely renewed; the handling concept, the programming languages and some interfaces will change. Therefore basic parts of the screenreader need to be reworked or entirely redeveloped. In the past Ubuntu changed the soundserver from Alsa to Pulse. The adaptation of SUE is still not fulfilled. The accessibility interfaces will change because Corba will be replaced by Debus and IAccessible2 becomes the new standard. Additionally the mail programme Evolution should be replaced by Thunderbird. Mozilla includes high accessibility for its software Thunderbird and Firefox. New concepts such as cloud computing set further pressure on developers. New trends in hardware also imply changes to the screenreader. One example is the rising use of touch screens. A screenreader with no community will not survive all these changes.

In opposition to the other existing Linux screenreader ORCA, SUE doesn't yet have a community to continue the work. Thus we want to encourage all to form and participate in such a community to bring SUE forward. We are especially looking for persons who are interested in the following tasks:

programming and developing the system

screenreader testers, to give feedback and suggestions

fundraisers

a company to take over the project

companies producing assistive technology and offering their devices for adaptation

institutions for visually impaired persons to teach and develop the training materials

The project is hosted by SourceForge.net [8] where those interested in our work will find current SUE releases including the source code, mailing list access [9], bug and feature request trackers, a wiki with all documentation, and more.

Our long-term goal is to establish a community of supporters – users, testers, developers – taking care of SUE's further development. Volunteers are more than welcome to join us at http://sourceforge.net/projects/sue/.

References

1. ORCA, http://live.gnome.org
2. LSR, http://live.gnome.org/LSR
3. Compiz, http://www.compiz.org/
4. European Computer Driving Licence (ECDL), http://www.ecdl.de/
5. Dienstleistungsgesellschaft fuer Informatik mbH (DLGI), http://www.dlgi.de/
6. SUE project wiki, http://www.sue-projekt.de
7. Training material in English,
   http://service.it-science-center.de/mediawiki/images/3/3b/
   Icc_schulungsskript.pdf
8. SUE, http://sue.sourceforge.net
9. SUE mailing list,
   https://lists.sourceforge.net/lists/listinfo/sue-list

The Challenge of Mainstreaming ICT Design for All

Gill Whitney[1], Suzette Keith[1], and Barbara Schmidt-Belz[2]

[1] The Design for All Research Group, School of Engineering and Information Sciences,
Middlesex University, London, UK
[2] Fraunhofer Institute for Applied Information Technology FIT, Web Compliance Center,
Schloss Birlinghoven, D-53754 Sankt Augustin, Germany
{g.whitney,s.keith}@mdx.ac.uk,
Barbara.Schmidt-Belz@fit.fraunhofer.de

Abstract. The education and training of ICT students and professionals with respect to Design for All is a vital part in the process of achieving eInclusion throughout Europe. This paper outlines the latest activity on the development of a curriculum in Design for All in ICT in higher education and professional development, and discusses some of the challenges of mainstreaming ICT Design for All. Concepts have been devised to introduce Design for All at bachelor-level of mainstream ICT education, to implement a masters degree in Design for All, and to provide training for professionals in ICT industry.

Keywords: Design for All, eAccessibility, eInclusion, Digital Inclusion, ICT (Information and Communication Technology).

1 Introduction

European society is changing; the population is ageing and the everyday tasks that people need to do require increasingly sophisticated e-skills. The future design of ICT products and systems will need to take into account the needs of all European citizens. Education and training of students and professionals working in Information and Communications Technologies (ICT) including computer sciences, information systems and web development is a vital part in the process of achieving eInclusion throughout Europe. Current and future researchers, developers, implementers of digital technologies and services as well as policy makers need a solid foundation from which to understand the wider needs of all technology users, creating opportunities for innovation and greater participation by all citizens.

The development of more accessible digital solutions have important economic and social benefits within Europe:

> "...bridging broadband and accessibility gaps, or improving digital competences, translates into new jobs and services. Initial estimates indicate that

K. Miesenberger et al. (Eds.): ICCHP 2010, Part I, LNCS 6179, pp. 583–590, 2010.
© Springer-Verlag Berlin Heidelberg 2010

benefits from e-Inclusion in the EU could be in the order of €35 to €85 billion over five years."[1]

The European eInclusion policies set out for 2010 identified six key themes, including eAccessibility, ageing, socio-cultural inclusion and geographic eInclusion. The policies set out where action was needed to avoid the risks of digital exclusion to those already at risk of social exclusion and isolation, for example as a result of disability, age related changes, social disadvantage and remote rural communities. Future policies for 2020 include a focus on social empowerment:

> "Empowering people in inclusive societies. The acquisition of new skills, fostering creativity and innovation, the development of entrepreneurship and a smooth transition between jobs will be crucial in a world which will offer more jobs in exchange for greater adaptability."[2]

As digital technologies and services continue to evolve rapidly it is economically and practically vital to adopt a pro-active strategy whereby the designers and developers of mainstream systems have the awareness, skills and competencies to adopt best Design for All practices. This paper outlines the latest activity on the development of a curriculum in Design for All (DfA) and considers some of the challenges of mainstreaming this within ICT programmes.

1.1 The Requirement for Design for All in ICT Courses

The IST Coordination Action "Design for All for eInclusion – DfA@eInclusion" contributed towards the advancement of eInclusion in Europe, building on its networks of excellence throughout Europe to raise awareness, and developing resources. Towards this end, DfA@eInclusion continued, extended and enhanced previous efforts targeted to the creation of a sound, interdisciplinary theoretical framework of reference and a set of proven engineering practices, by addressing the following strategic objectives:

- Support to existing European initiatives to promote Design for All and in particular the European Design for All eAccessibility Network (EDeAN);
- Enhancement of existing partnerships between academic, research, user, and industrial communities to promote eInclusion through adopting and promoting effective DfA practices;
- Facilitation of DfA knowledge spillovers across industry sectors and communities through appropriate mechanisms for knowledge transfer;
- Support the mainstreaming of accessibility in ICT products and services through a series of dissemination activities.

---

[1] COM(2007) 694Communication on e-Inclusion. Published by the Commission of the European Communities, Brussels http://ec.europa.eu/information_society/activities/einclusion/docs/i2010_initiative/comm_native_com_2007_0694_f_en_acte.pdf

[2] COM(2009)647 Commission Working Document, Consultation On The Future "EU 2020" Strategy. Published by the Commission of the European Communities, Brussels, 24.11.2009. Available from http://ec.europa.eu/dgs/secretariat_general/eu2020/docs/com_2009_647_en.pdf

The DfA@eInclusion project partnership represented 23 European countries. These partners helped to identify courses and programmes in ICT offering Design for All content. This review identified 50 courses offered by 35 course providers in 18 European countries. There were few specialised courses offering Design for All content, however it was possible to identify examples of hidden elements which were embedded in mainstream computing and technology programmes [1].

2 Why Europe Requires the Mainstreaming of Design for All Training

Within Europe there have been a number of initiatives and campaigns that serve to emphasis the need for training – improving the skills of users, addressing the needs of an ageing population and improving the understanding of the needs of these users by industry.

Most recently, the requirement for Europeans to acquire e-skills was reiterated in e-skills Week 2010, when Vice-President Antonio Tajani - Commissioner for Industry and Entrepreneurship, Neelie Kroes - Commissioner for the Digital Agenda and Androulla Vassiliou - Commissioner for Education, Culture, Multilingualism and Youth, issued a joint statement, stating that:

"Improving digital literacy is crucial to Europe's future. We must invest in the e-skills of all EU citizens to make sure that no one is left behind as the economy goes digital. Digital literacy and media literacy are crucial components of digital inclusion: people should be able to use computers and the internet, while understanding how the web actually works and how to assess the online information." [3]

Europe is also facing the social and economic effects of an ageing population. Viviane Reding, EU Commissioner for the Information Society and Media drew attention to the need for more accessible products and services:

"Europe's ageing population is a challenge for our job market, and its social and health systems. But it is also an economic and social opportunity. ICT will provide new and more accessible products and services that meet the needs of older people."[4]

In response to a report on "Ageing Well" it was announced that €1 billion would be spent between 2007 and 2013 in research and innovation for ageing well. The Ageing Well report noted that:

---

[3] e-skills: European Week 2010 underlines e-skills' potential to help Europe's economic recovery available from http://europa.eu/rapid/pressReleasesAction.do?reference=IP/10/220&format=HTML&aged=0&language=EN&guiLanguage=en

[4] IP/07/831 (2007) €1bn in digital technologies for Europeans to age well available from http://europa.eu/rapid/pressReleasesAction.do?reference=IP/07/831&format=HTML&aged=1&language=EN&guiLanguage=en

"Industry still has limited understanding of comparative user requirements, such as socioeconomic factors, gender needs and income levels that may impede access to ICT, personal attitudes and sensitivities to ICT, and even of lifestyles"[i]

The changes brought about by the rapid introduction of digital technologies and services and the ageing of the population affect both what skills are required by the population of Europe and the attributes of the population who need to be digital skilled. In the longer term, it requires that the technology developed by industry is designed in a way that enables the end user to understand and make use of the full functionality of the device and the services provided. The aim of this paper is to examine how designers and creators of future ICT systems can, as the results of better education and training in Design for All practices, contribute to the development of systems that are fully accessible and usable.

3 The Current Situation

The DfA@eInclusion project identified many pockets of excellence where committed academics and professionals passed on their skills and knowledge. But the situation is not uniform and small pockets of best practice knowledge will not be sufficient to ensure that the technology of tomorrow is accessible by the European citizen of tomorrow.

3.1 The Academic Approach

Over the life of the DfA@eInclusion project, the project partners reported concerns over the implications for mainstreaming versus specialist training. The argument for mainstreaming of DfA principles and practices is one of greatly increasing awareness to all ICT and design students and in parallel engaging multidisciplinary awareness in social sciences and humanities of the social issues.

The counter-argument for specialist programmes is increased professional recognition of the skills and knowledge needed to identify and solve complex problems. However, the argument against specialisation raised by the partners includes the risk factors for student and institution of becoming too specialised, diluting core technical skills and therefore limiting opportunities for employment – in effect the 'return on investment' for the student.

Progress in extending or developing bachelor and masters level modules with greater DfA content taking account of both specialisation and mainstream integration has been made. A recent survey of the DfA@eInclusion European project partners revealed new and extended courses:

- MSc Digital Inclusion validated to run at Middlesex University UK.
- Creation of a new module on accessibility to be introduced to new MSc Human Computer Interactions University of Siegen Germany (2010)

---

[5] COM(2007) 332 final Ageing well in the Information Society. Action Plan on Information and Communication Technologies and Ageing from http://ec.europa.eu/information_society/activities/einclusion/policy/ageing/launch/index_en.htm

- New course on Assistive technologies introduced in Czech Republic
- Planned introduction of new Masters in Web design at Linz, Austria
- Planned course opportunity within new MSc Health Informatics Engineering in Hungary.
- Planned expansion of MSc across Europe: interest has been expressed by partners in Greece, Austria, Malta and Finland

While progress is somewhat slow, these results are encouraging in gaining recognition of the many stakeholders: educational institutions, the academics responsible for course delivery, the student population, future employers in major industries and user representative organisations.

Curriculum guidelines have been prepared to support the development of new programmes and modules at bachelor and masters level (for more details of the curriculum guidelines see: www.dfaei.org). Particularly relevant to the argument for mainstreaming is the proposal for a short introductory module, equivalent to 2 ECTS, given to bachelor level students in their first or second year. This has the potential for reaching the greatest number of students, who may return to the subject at a later stage of their learning. The key objectives for this module are:

- To become aware of the rights and needs of all citizens to have equal access to the information society.
- To become aware of the opportunities and challenges in creating, developing and providing information technologies and services that are socially inclusive.

This could be delivered as a named module, so that it subsequently appears on the transcript of modules taken, integrated into a wider module on ethical and social issues of technology or even, as found in one example of best practice, fully integrated throughout the bachelor programme.

3.2 The Industry Approach

ICT industry needs short-term solutions when taking up new methods. Professionals who currently work in ICT industry need to acquire the necessary knowledge when taking up the challenge to implement Design for All principles in their development processes.

A survey among companies in the UK in 2006 revealed "lack of knowledge" as one of the top obstacles against implementing Design for All in commercial projects, next to lack of time and money [2].

We did a similar survey among those 27 professionals who had attended a training course "Introduction to eAccessibility" in Germany and Ireland, 2009. The top obstacle was lack of knowledge, followed by lack of time. This sample is too small to generalize the results, but it suggests that we still have not overcome "lack of knowledge" as an obstacle against Design for All. We also believe that lack of knowledge, from a company's economic point of view, is an equivalent to lack of time and/or lack of money.

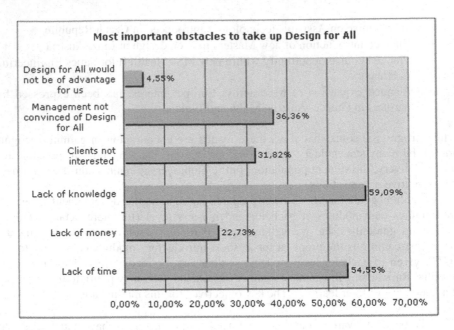

Fig. 1. Our survey confirms "Lack of knowledge" as a top issue when considering Design for All principles for ICT projects

The training of professionals has some specific requirements compared to training provided for university students. Typical training arrangements for professionals will allow them to stay in their full-time job, and indulge in a (short) period of non-formal learning, such as taking a tutorial, later continue to learn on the job in an informal way.

For the non-formal training of professionals, the DfA@eInclusion project has specified a comprehensive curriculum. It consists of 10 topics to be covered, each topic offered at three levels of granularity, and a recommendation for which professionals in ICT industry which levels would be appropriate. The specification of the curriculum is accompanied by references to available training material that matches each unit, and a list of recommended reading [3]. The curriculum and guidelines are the result of discussions among experts from research, industry and other stakeholders, e.g. during a 2-days workshop in Sankt Augustin near Bonn, in September 2007, and since May 2009 in a CEN workshop.

We investigated the current availability of teaching materials for these topics by asking our contacts in industry and other stakeholders for existing training material. Additionally, an extensive web search was undertaken. This search showed that there is training material available in the area of Web Accessibility, but not in all of the other topics. Thanks to the activities of the W3C group, and in particular the Web Accessibility Initiative (WAI), there exist very concrete, comprehensive guidelines on how to create accessible web sites. Based on this, several initiatives and companies have provided training material, such as online tutorials about web accessibility [4-6]. For other technologies, such detailed and concrete accessibility guidelines are often missing, and in consequence, there is a lack of training material addressing professionals in industry.

Table 1. These 10 topics should be covered by a Design for All training for professionals in ICT industry

Topic	Description
Design for All and Target User Groups	Awareness of users with impairments; principles and motivation for Design for All
User Interfaces	Accessible user interfaces; new paradigms
Back-end Technologies	Impact of back-end technologies on accessibility and adaptability
Web Applications	Accessibility of Web content, authoring tools, user agents and services
Consumer Electronics, Games	Accessibility of devices for entertainment and communication
User-Centred Design	Principles of human-centred design process as a frame for Design for All
Evaluation	Evaluation of qualities of use, in particular of accessibility
Assistive Technology (AT)	Assistive technology; the role of AT in a Design for All approach
Business Cases	Business cases of implementing Design for All in a company
Ethics, Legislation, Privacy	Legal and ethical basis of Design for All; legal aspects of user involvement in development and personalization of services

In order to provide more widespread support for the development of training materials for industry, the CEN workshop "Curriculum for training professionals in Universal Design" (CEN WS/UD-Prof-Curriculum)" was started in May 2009. A CEN workshop allows experts and stakeholders in an area to work towards a CEN workshop agreement, stating their common understanding and recommendations. A CEN workshop agreement on curricula for training ICT professionals in Universal Design shall ensure that training will be adequate, comprehensive and meets Industry needs. More information, including options to participate, can be found at: http://www.cen.eu/cenorm/sectors/sectors/isss/workshops/ws-ud-prof-curriculum.asp. The final CEN workshop agreement is expected in Autumn 2010.

4   Conclusion

In the future, Design for All training within European ICT academic and industrial courses needs to transform from a specialist element taught by committed experts for a limited number of highly motivated students, to become an essential part of all ICT courses. ICT, used within the mainstream, will increasingly allow older people to stay active and productive for longer; to continue to engage in society with more accessible online services; and to enjoy a healthier and higher quality of life for longer.

Technology education will need address the challenges of the social, economic and political contexts in which technology is used and the diversity of user requirements. The curricula produced by the DfA@eInclusion project can be used to facilitate this change. Many researchers in this area are becoming increasingly aware of the need to pass on their knowledge and need to be given the opportunity to deliver new and modified courses. Academics and trainers within ICT mainstream teaching will need to be encouraged and supported to integrate elements of DfA and eInclusion issues, highlighting the latest achievements and opening up opportunities for original research.

The curriculum guidelines provide the essential objectives and learning outcomes to be achieved. The DfA@eInclusion project and the EDeAN network calls on all experts within the ICT field to rise to the challenge of creating innovative programmes that will attract mainstream students in ICT, technology and design.

Further information about the training activities of the DFA@eInclusion project can be obtained at: http://www.dfaei.org.

References

1. Whitney, G., Keith, S.: European Developments in the Design and Implementation of Training for eInclusion. In: Miesenberger, K., Klaus, J., Zagler, W.L., Karshmer, A.I. (eds.) ICCHP 2008. LNCS, vol. 5105, pp. 156–161. Springer, Heidelberg (2008)
2. Goodman, J., Dong, H., Langdon, P.M., Clarkson, P.J.: Increasing the uptake of inclusive design in industry. Gerontechnology 5(3), 140–149 (2006)
3. Schmidt-Belz, B., Mohamad, Y.: White paper: Recommendations for the development of eAccessibility training materials for the ICT industry (2010),
   http://www.dfaei.org/downloads.html
4. W3C-WAI: Introduction to Web Accessibility (2008),
   http://www.w3.org/WAI/intro/accessibility.php (cited 2009)
5. Opera: Web Standards course,
   http://www.opera.com/company/education/curriculum/ (cited 2009)
6. WaSP: Curriculum on Web standards and best practice (2009),
   http://interact.webstandards.org/curriculum/ (cited 2009)

Evaluating the Users' Satisfaction Using Inclusive Initiatives in Two Different Environments: The University and a Research Conference

Ana Iglesias[1], Lourdes Moreno[1], Javier Jiménez[2], and Pablo Revuelta[2]

[1] Computer Science Department, Universidad Carlos III de Madrid,
Avda. Universidad, 30 – 28911 Leganés (Madrid), Spain
{aiglesia,lmoreno}@inf.uc3m.es
[2] Spanish Centre of Captioning and Audio Description,
Avda. Gregorio P. Barba, 1 - 28918 Leganés (Madrid), Spain
{jjdorado,prevuelta}@cesya.es

Abstract. This paper presents evaluation results of the user's satisfaction using the APEINTA project which main aim is to provide accessibility in education, in and out of the classroom. APEINTA is the Spanish acronym for "Aiming for an Inclusive Education based on Assistive Technology". The APEINTA project is focused in two main inclusive proposals: first, it deals with eliminating hard of hearing students' communication barriers in the classroom, providing them automatic real-time captioning and other mechanisms for making easy the communication with the teacher and others students; and second, it deals also in providing an accessible Web learning platform with accessible digital resources, so every student can access them in and out of the classroom.

Keywords: Inclusion, Web Accessibility, E-learning, Special Needs, Assistive Technology, Real-time Captioning.

1 Introduction

Historically, students with disabilities have experienced inadequate access to lecture materials in the classroom, and insufficient access to the academic resources necessary to sustain their progress. Sign Language interpreters have been traditionally used during the class for deaf students' inclusion. However, nowadays not every student with hearing disability uses Sign Language, thus signing does not provide deaf students full access to classroom information [1]. Nowadays, some researchers are working in lectures transcription based on Automatic Speech Recognition (ASR).

The Liberated Learning Project (LLP) is one of the most active initiatives, collaboration with IBM in developing the ViaScribe software based on the ASR ViaVoice (VV) software [2].

On the other hand, several research groups and organizations developed technologies and standards related to how to achieve accessible educational resources and how to develop Web platforms. For instance, the guidelines for developing accessible learning applications (IMS) [3], the World Wide Web Consortium (WC3) [4] and the

K. Miesenberger et al. (Eds.): ICCHP 2010, Part I, LNCS 6179, pp. 591–594, 2010.

Web Accessibility Initiative WAI [5] which play a leading role in promoting the importance of accessibility and developing guidelines which can help when developing accessible Web resources. These guidelines are useful for developing accessible Web resources.

There are other technologies as Learning Management Systems (LMS) or Learning Content Management Systems (LCMS) that include accessibilities issues as the dotLRN LMS [6] or the Atutor LCMS [7].

In this paper we evaluate the user's satisfaction using the APEINTA inclusive tools in two different environments: the University and a Research Conference.

2 The APEINTA Architecture

The APEINTA architecture shown in Figure 1 presents two well differentiated applications: a real-time captioning (using ASR technologies) and synthetic speaking multisystem (using Text-to-Speech technologies, TTS) in the classroom [8] in order to avoid communication barriers for hearing impaired students and students with speaking problems (see section 3); and a Web platform with accessible digital contents that can be used in and out of the classroom for students of all abilities, including benefits in their learning [9].

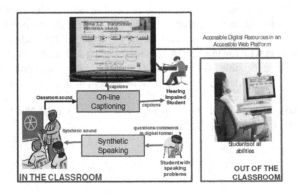

Fig. 1. APEINTA architecture

Firstly, the APEINTA project was designed and implemented in the educational environment (at University), but after the first evaluation process we realized the benefits that this initiative provide to people with temporal or permanent disabilities, older adults, foreign people or students with speaking problems, for instance. Subsequently this project was introduced and evaluated too during a talk in a research conference.

3 Evaluation of APEINTA

The evaluation of the users' satisfaction using APEINTA was carried out by surveying the users after using the inclusive tools.

The ASR and TTS services of APEINTA have been evaluated in 2009 during different classes of 50 minutes. These classes belong to Database Design signature in 3rd course of Computer Science degree at the Carlos III University of Madrid. Moreover, the APEINTA services were also evaluated during a 30 minutes talk in the ACAPPS (Federation of Families and Deaf People of Catalonia) Congress.

For the ASR evaluation, the orator trained the ASR software (Dragon Naturally-Speaking v.10) during 40 minutes approximately. The training was conducted by reading predefined texts (30 minutes) and adding new words to the vocabulary according to the subject specific vocabulary (10 minutes).

During the evaluation session (in both environments), the users could receive the captioning in a PDA, a Laptop and in a big screen in the auditorium (which size was calculated according to the size of the auditorium in each environment) overlapped with the lecture slides connected to the server. Moreover, they could use the PDA and the Laptop in order to write questions and comments and use the TTS service.

Five deaf and hard of hearing volunteers and two hearing volunteers participated in the evaluation of APEINTA during the conference talk. Moreover, 45 hearing students evaluated the APEINTA initiative in the classroom, 10 of them simulating hearing disabilities. Finally, three experts in captioning, usability and accessibility also evaluated the system in the classroom.

For this evaluation, surveys were distributed to the participants. All of them completed the survey voluntarily and some of them provided written comments about improvements and satisfaction to the inclusive initiatives. On the survey, the questions were measured using a 1 to 5 Likert-type scale [10], with 1 representing *Completely Disagree* and 5 representing *Completely Agree*. Furthermore, the experts in captioning, usability and accessibility were interviewed to gain a richer understanding of the feedback.

All participants were really satisfied with the pedagogical initiative (all of them answering 5 in the surveys). Related to the captioning service, most of them were globally satisfied with the captioning service. The average was 4.9 and the standard deviation was 0.37. Although the speech transcription was not completely correct (the average Word-Error-Rate measured was 10.4% during both sessions according to the Levenshtein Edit Distance) most of the participants answered that they could detect the errors and they could understand the global sense of the sentence (average of 4.55 and standard deviation of 0.79). Moreover, all of them were satisfied with the TTS service and the hearing students answered that the use of these technologies had not negative influence in their learning process.

On the other hand, the accessible Website including accessible pedagogical resources was evaluated in 2009 at University, but it was not implemented for the AC-CAPS congress. One hundred eighty-nine students participated in the survey (90 of them interacting with the accessible website), two persons with audio and visual disabilities and an accessibility human expert. The survey of the system showed how the accessible website presents pedagogical benefits to all the students and allows students who cannot assist to the classroom to pass the final exam of the subject. Additionally, the survey and the system monitoring showed that the system and its multimedia resources were accessible to all the students. It is important to underline that the e-learning platform and every interface used by the students in the APEINTA project offers a universal access for any typology of users, so Inclusive Methodologies and Universal Design Principles have been taken into account.

4   Conclusions and Further Research

The APEINTA project proposes to use two different inclusive proposals. In the classroom, the use of ASR and TTS services allows to avoid communication barriers among the speaker and the listeners. Out of the classroom, the use of accessible Websites and accessible digital resources provide benefits to all the users.

This paper presents evaluation results of the user's satisfaction using the APEINTA initiatives in two different environments: at University and during a talk in a Conference. Nowadays, we are working in evaluating the APEINTA project in a course where students with different levels of disabilities are enrolled and introducing these inclusive initiatives in other environments.

References

1. Marschark, M., Sapere, P., Convertino, C., Seewagen, R.: Access to Postsecondary Education through Sign Language Interpreting. The Journal of Deaf Studies and Deaf Education 10, 38–50 (2005)
2. Bain, K., Basson, S., Wald, M.: Speech Recognition in University Classrooms: Liberated Learning Project. In: Proc. of 5th Annual International ACM Conference on Assistive Technologies, pp. 192–196 (2005)
3. IMS guidelines for developing accessible learning applications, version 1.0 (2002), http://www.imsglobal.org/accessibility
4. World Wide Web Consortium, http://www.w3.org/
5. Web Accessibility Initiative (WAI), http://www.w3.org/WAI/
6. dotLRN LMS (Learning Management System), http://dotlrn.org
7. ATutor: The Adaptive Technology Resource Centre (ATRC) at the University of Toronto Atutor, http://www.atutor.ca
8. Revuelta, P., Jiménez, J., Sánchez, J.M., Ruiz, B.: Multidevice system for Educational Accessibility of Hearing-Impaired Students. In: Proceedings of the 11th IASTED Conference on Computer and Advanced Technology in Education (CATE), pp. 20–26 (2008)
9. Moreno, L., Iglesias, A., Castro, E., Martínez, P.: Using accessible digital resources for teaching database design: Towards an inclusive distance learning proposal. In: 13th Annual SIGCSE Conference on Innovation and Technology in Computer Science Education (ITiCSE 2008), pp. 32–36 (2008)
10. Brooke, J.: Sus: a 'quick and dirty' usability scale. In: Jordan, P.W., Thomas, B., Weerdmeester, B.A., McClelland, I.L. (eds.) Usability Evaluation in Industry, pp. 189–194. Taylor & Francis, London (1996)

ICCHP Keynote: Recognizing Silent and Weak Speech Based on Electromyography

Tanja Schultz

Cognitive Systems Lab, Karlsruhe Institute of Technology, Karlsruhe, Germany
tanja@ira.uka.de

1 Introduction

In the past decade, the performance of automatic speech processing systems, including speech recognition, spoken language translation, and speech synthesis, has improved dramatically. This has resulted in an increasingly widespread use of speech and language technologies in a large variety of applications. However, speech-driven interfaces based on conventional acoustic speech signals still suffer from several limitations. Firstly, acoustic speech signals are transmitted through air and are thus prone to ambient noise. Despite tremendous efforts there are still no robust speech processing systems in sight, which provide reasonably good results in noisy places. To overcome this problem we propose to capture and process the speech signal before it gets airborne and thus avoid to get affected by adverse noise conditions. Secondly, conventional speech interfaces rely on audibly uttered speech, which has two major drawbacks: it jeopardizes confidential communication in public and it disturbs any bystanders. Services which require the access, retrieval, and transmission of private or confidential information, such as PINs, passwords, and security or safety information are particularly vulnerable. The proposed Silent Speech Interface (SSI) allows to utter speech silently and thus overcomes both limitations: confidential information can be submitted securely and silent speech does not disturb or interfere with the suroundings. Last but not least, Silent Speech Interfaces might give hope to people with certain speech disabilities as the technologies allow the building of virtual prostheses for patients without vocal folds (Denby et al., 2009). Also, elderly and weak people may benefit since silent articulation can be produced with less effort than audible speech.

Our approach to capture speech before it gets airborne relies on surface Electro-MyoGraphy (EMG). This is the process of recording electrical muscle activity using surface electrodes. When a muscle fiber is activated by the central nervous system, small electrical currents in form of ion flows are generated. These electrical currents move through the body tissue, encountering a resistance which creates an electrical field. The resulting potential differences can be measured between certain regions on the body surface, i.e. at the skin. The amplified electrical signal obtained from measuring these voltages over time can be fed directly into electronic devices for further processing. Since speech is produced by the activity of the human articulatory muscles, the resulting myoelectric signal patterns allow for tracing back the corresponding speech. These signals are not corrupted or masked by environmental noise transmitted through air. Furthermore, since EMG relies on muscle activity only, speech can even be recognized when it is produced silently, i.e. mouthed without any vocal effort.

K. Miesenberger et al. (Eds.): ICCHP 2010, Part I, LNCS 6179, pp. 595–604, 2010.

We envision several application areas for Silent Speech Interfaces: (1) robust, private, non-distracting speech recognition for human-machine interfaces, such as silently speaking text messages, (2) recognition plus speech synthesis (at the remote side) for quietly accessing remote applications, such as speech or text-based information systems, (3) transmitting articulation parameters followed by articulatory synthesis for silent human-human communication, (4) speech prostheses, and (5) recognition of silent speech followed by text translation into another language followed by speech synthesis, which appears like speaking in a foreign tongue. In 2006 we successfully demonstrated a prototype of this last application at Interspeech (Jou et al., 2006) and CeBIT 2010 (see also http://csl.ira.uka.de/SilentSpeech).

2 State of the Art

While most efforts in the area of speech-driven technologies and applications to date were focused on the acoustic speech waveform as input modality, a significant body of research and technologies emerges on brain computer and silent speech interfaces that leverage off a variety of modalities arising from spoken communication: sensory data are acquired from the human speech production process ranging from the activity of articulators, their neural pathways, and the brain itself. We briefly summarize the types of technology that have been described in the literature so far (see (Denby et al., 2010) for a detailed review of Silent Speech Technologies).

Non-Audible Murmur (NAM), coined by (Nakajima et al., 2003), refers to very low amplitude sounds generated by laryngeal airflow noise and its resonance in the vocal tract. While the sound can barely be perceived by nearby listeners, it can easily be detected using a type of stethoscopic microphone attached to the skin (Nakajima et al., 2003). Several authors successfully applied NAM for robust speech recognition in noisy environments (Nakajima et al., 2006; Heracleous et al. 2007). Tran investigated speech transformation techniques to produce more natural sounding NAM-based speech synthesis, particularly useful for speakers with voice pathologies due to laryngeal disorders (Tran et al., 2010).

Analysis of glottal activity using electromagnetic (Titze et al., 2000; Ng et al., 2000; Tardelli Ed., 2004; Preuss et al., 2006; Quatieri et al., 2006), or vibration (Bos and Tack, 2005; Hansen et al., 2010) sensors with the goal of obtaining glottal waveforms that can be used for de-noising by correlation with an acoustic signal captured by standard close-talk microphones. The required waveforms may be obtained either via detectors which are directly sensitive to vibrations transmitted through tissue such as throat microphones, or from the interaction of glottal movement with an imposed electromagnetic field. Research in this area was propelled by DARPA's Advanced Speech Encoding Program, which provided funding to develop non-acoustic sensors for low bit rate speech encoding in harsh acoustic environments.

Electromagnetic Articulography (EMA): EMA systems aim to track the precise Cartesian coordinates of fixed points within the vocal tract as its shape is the most crucial part of speech production. Many investigated the method of implanted coils that are electrically connected to external equipment and are electromagnetically coupled to external excitation coils (Carstens, 2008; Schönle et al., 1987; Hummel et al., 2006). While conventional EMA is very inconvenient for the speaker, (Fagan et al., 2008) developed a less intrusive system which consists of permanent magnets glued to some points in the vocal apparatus that are coupled with magnetic sensors mounted on a pair of spectacles worn by the user. In laboratory conditions promising recognition results could be achieved on a small vocabulary (Fagan et al., 2008).

Ultrasound (US): Real-time characterization of the vocal tract using ultrasound and optical imaging of the tongue and lips (Denby and Stone, 2004; Denby et al. 2006; Hueber et al., 2007, 2010) developed a system that captures articulatory activity via ultrasound and video imaging and then transforms these multimodal observations of articulatory gestures into an audio speech signal based on a direct mapping between visual and acoustic features using Gaussian mixture models and alternatively based on an intermediate HMM-based phonetic decoding step to take advantage of a priori linguistic information. The resulting "silent vocoder" is particularly helpful to patients who have undergone a laryngectomy.

Surface electromyography (sEMG) of the articulator muscles or the larynx (Jorgensen et al., 2003; Maier-Hein et al., 2005; Jou et al., 2006; Jorgensen and Dusan, 2010; Schultz and Wand, 2010); While Jorgensen was first to prove the applicability of myoelectric signals for non-audible speech recognition on a small set of words, recent studies tackle large vocabulary speech recognition by removing the restriction of words or commands spoken in isolation and evolve toward a less limited, more user-friendly continuous speaking style (Maier-Hein et al., 2005); allowing for acoustic units smaller than words or phrases (Walliczek et al., 2006); Schultz and Wand, 2010); study the effects of electrode re-positioning (Maier-Hein et al., 2005) and more robust signal preprocessing (Jorgensen and Binsted, 2005; Jou et al. 2006); investigate real-life applicability, by augmenting conventional speech recognition systems (Chan, 2003), implementing alternative modeling schemes such as phonetic features to enhancing phoneme models (Jou et al., 2007); and to address coarticulation effects (Schultz and Wand, 2010); by examining the impact of speaker dependencies (Wand and Schultz, 2009); and by addressing size, attachment, and mobility of the capturing devices (Manabe et al., 2003; Manabe and Zhang, 2004).

Brain-Computer Interfaces: Interpretation of signals from electroencephalographic (EEG) sensors (Porbadnigk et al., 2009) and from implants in the speech-motor cortex (Brumberg et al., 2010). EEG-based brain computer interfaces (BCI) have become an increasingly active field of research. Overviews can be found in (Dornhege et al. Eds., 2007) and in (Wolpaw et al., 2002). Prominent examples of current BCIs, where the aim is to translate thoughts or intentions into control signals for devices, include the Thought Translation Device (Birbaumer, 2000) and the Berlin Brain Computer Interface (Blankertz et al., 2006). To avoid the time consuming learning process, and develop more intuitive silent speech interfaces, (Wester and Schultz, 2006) investigated a new approach that directly recognizes unspoken speech from EEG signals, i.e. speech imagined to be spoken but without actually producing any sound or moving any articulatory muscle. Also Suppes showed that isolated words can be recognized based on EEG and MEG recordings (Suppes et al., 1997) while a study by (Porbadnigk et al., 2009) indicates that temporally correlated brain activities may superimpose the signal of interest. DaSalla (DaSalla et al., 2008) proposed a control scheme for a silent speech brain computer interface using neural activities associated with vowel speech imagery. Recently, attempts have been made to utilize intracortical microelectrode technology and neural decoding techniques which have the potential to restore speech communication to paralyzed individuals (Brumberg et al., 2010; Bartels et al., 2008), or to restore written communication through development of mouse cursor control BCIs for use with virtual keyboards (Kennedy et al., 2000) and other augmentative and alternative communication devices (Hochberg et al., 2008).

3   Work and Results on Electromyographic Speech Recognition

Competitive performance in speech recognition was first reported by (Chan, 2001), who achieved an average word accuracy of 93% on a 10-word vocabulary of the English digits. A good performance could be achieved even when words were spoken non-audibly, i.e. when no acoustic signal was produced (Jorgensen, 2003), suggesting this technology could be used to communicate silently. Our recent work (Jou et al., 2006; Walliczek et al., 2006) successfully demonstrated that phonemes can be used as modeling units for EMG-based speech recognition by carefully designing the signal preprocessing front-end, paving the way for large vocabulary speech recognition. While a lot of progress was made over the last years, there are still major limitations which need to be overcome for the application of EMG to large vocabulary speech recognition. In particular, we see three major challenges. First, the impact of speaker dependencies, such as speaking style, speaking rate, and pronunciation idiosyncrasies needs to be investigated. Second, the EMG signal is affected by changes in electrode positioning, environmental conditions (temperature and humidity), and tissue properties (Leveau, 1992). These factors clearly favor the development of speaker dependent and often session dependent systems, i.e. systems in which training and testing is performed on data collected within the same recording session. Consequently, results known from the literature focus on a very small number of subjects. Third, little is known yet about the qualitative and quantitative articulation differences between silent and audible speech. Our experimental results in (Maier-Hein et al., 2005) and more recently in (Wand and Schultz, 2009c) suggest that EMG signals do significantly differ between silent and audible speaking mode. We assume that this is mainly due to the lack of acoustic feedback when speaking silently but further investigation will be necessary to continuously improve our silent speech interface. Nevertheless, we recently demonstrated the first speech recognition system that handles seamless switches between both speaking modes. In (Schultz and Wand, 2010) we focused on the issue of achieving reliable and robust models for large vocabulary speech recognition systems based on EMG and show that these models significantly improve the recognition performance, even when impacting factors such as speaker and session variabilities are present. For this purpose we collected over the last years a large database of EMG signals from 78 speakers, where the speakers produced audible and silent, i.e. mouthed, speech. This collection was done in a joint effort with colleagues from the Department of Communication Science and Disorders at University of Pittsburgh (Dietrich, 2008). Based on this EMG-PIT corpus, we implemented a new strategy of phonetic feature bundling for modeling coarticulation in EMG-based speech recognition and reported results on speaker-dependent and speaker-independent experimental setups (Schultz and Wand, 2010). We could show that the appropriate modeling of the interdependence of phonetic features reduces the word error rate of our baseline system by over 33% relative in the speaker-dependent case, and by about 28% in the speaker-independent system. With this approach we achieved an average word error rate of 31.5% and of 10% on the best performing speakers on a 101-word vocabulary task, bringing EMG-based speech recognition within useful range for silent speech applications.

Figure 1 shows the electrode positioning which gives best results for our silent speech recognition system. It uses five channels, numbered 1, 2, 3, 4, and 6. Channel five serves for experiments with different electrode positionings, however we did not use it for the experiments described here. Channels 1, 2, and 6 use bipolar derivation, whereas channels 3, 4, and 5 were derived unipolarly, with two reference electrodes placed on the mastoid portion of the temporal bone (right-most picture). The electrodes capture signals from the levator angulis oris (channels 2 and 3), the zygomaticus major (channels 2 and 3), the platysma (channel 4), the anterior belly of the digastric (channel 1) and the tongue (channels 1 and 6).

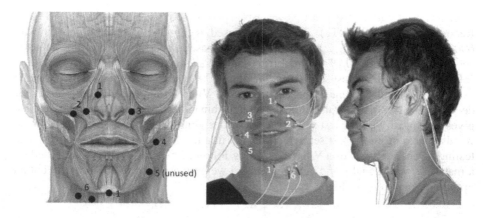

Fig. 1. Electrode Positioning

The baseline EMG-based recognition system uses 45 context-independent phoneme models and a silence model. Each phoneme is modeled using a three-state left-to-right hidden Markov model (beginning, middle, and end of the phoneme), silence is modeled by a single state. This results in 136 models, each of which applies Gaussian mixtures as emission probabilities. This modeling scheme follows the traditional setup for context-independent acoustic-based speech recognition. The amount of Gaussians is determined by a merge-and-split algorithm on the training data, resulting in roughly 2 Gaussians per model on average. In total the baseline system consists of 290 Gaussians. This small number is due to the very limited amount of training data. For the same reason our systems applies Gaussians with diagonal covariance matrices.

For feature extraction, we found that time-domain features gave optimal results. This feature extraction method follows (Jou et al., 2006): for any feature f, f' is its frame-based time-domain mean, Pf is its frame-based power, and zf is its frame-based zero-crossing rate. S(f,n) is the stacking of adjacent frames of feature f in the size of $2n + 1$ (-n to n) frames. For an EMG signal with normalized mean x[n], the nine-point double-averaged signal w[k] is defined as w[n]= 1/9 $\sum_{(n=-4)}$^4▓[v[n],where v[n]= 1/9 $\sum_{(n=-4)}$^4▓[x[n]]].

The rectified high-frequency signal is r[n] = |x[n] - w[n]|. Then the TD15 feature is defined as TD15 = S(f2, 15), where f2 = [w⁻, Pw, Pr, zr,r⁻]. On the EMG-PIT corpus, the stacking width of 15 frames gives the best results (Wand and Schultz, 2009). In these computations, we used a frame size of 27 ms and a frame shift of 10 ms. These values are reported as giving optimal results in our earlier work, therefore we adopted the same frame size and shift in the TD15 feature extraction. The TD15 feature is computed for each of the five electrode channels, then the final feature vector per frame is built by stacking the frame-based features of the five channels. After this procedure, Linear Discriminant Analysis is applied to reduce the dimensionality of the final feature vector from 775 to 32 coefficients per frame.

In order to initialize the EMG phoneme models, we require time alignments for the audible EMG training utterances. We obtain these time alignments by using the acoustic data which has been simultaneously recorded. These acoustic data are forced-aligned with a Broadcast News (BN) speech recognizer trained with the Janus Recognition Toolkit (JRTk). This HMM-based recognizer uses quintphones with 6000 distributions sharing 2000 codebooks. The baseline performance of this acoustic speech recognizer is 10.2% Word Error Rate (WER) on the clean speech condition (F0) of the official BN test set (Yu and Waibel, 2000). After the initial EMG phoneme models have been obtained, four iterations of Viterbi training are performed. For decoding, we apply a trigram language model trained on Broadcast News data, which gives a perplexity on the test set of 24.2. The decoding vocabulary is restricted tot he words appearing in the test set, which results in a test vocabulary of 101 words. The testing process consists of a Viterbi decoding followed by a lattice rescoring based on a matrix of word penalty and language model weighting parameters in order to obtain optimal recognition results.

4 Impact of Lack of Acoustic Feedback in Silent Speech

Recently, we investigated the impact on the EMG signal from the lack of acoustic feedback when speaking silently. The process of human speech production is very complex and subject to ongoing exploration, however it is widely accepted that acoustic feedback plays a major role in uttering intelligible speech (Guenther et al., 2007). Since silent speaking results only in a movement of the articulatory muscles, we hypothesize that the lack of acoustic feedback is compensated with a somatosensoric feedback. The speaker therefore makes more prominent use of his proprioceptive and tactile impressions of skin or muscles in order to correctly reach the desired articulatory targets. For this purpose we computed the power spectral density (PSD) of EMG signals to obtain a measure of the articulatory power. The PSD computation is based on Welch's method. We investigated the PSD of EMG signals of audible, whispered and silent speech. We split up the signals into frames with a length of 27ms and a frame shift of 10ms, which is the same setup as used by the EMG recognizer. The resulting frames can then be grouped according to the phonemes or phonetic features they represent. Clearly, the quality of this grouping depends on the quality of the underlying time alignment, which must be computed in advance Note that from the set of six available EMG channels, we picked channels 2 and 4 (see Figure 1) for our experiments since these electrodes are closest to the muscles which control the lips, and since we assumed that the lip movement is one major source of somatosensoric feedback while speaking. The difference between vowels and consonants is among the most fundamental distinctions of English phonology. Therefore, our first experiment compares the PSDs of consonants and vowels. We picked the designated phones from the according sessions and computed the mean audible, whispered and silent PSD over all sessions. Figure 3 shows the PSDs for consonants and vowels in channel 2 and channel 4. It can be seen in Figure 2 (left-hand side) that audible EMG in general has the highest spectral density. Whispered EMG seems to take the assumed role of an in-between of audible and silent speech, since the whispered PSDs are in the range between the other speech modes. While the PSD shapes of silent and audible consonants differ only little, there is a noticeable difference in the vowel PSD chart. A reason for the higher vowel PSD in audible EMG could be the fact that (English) vowels are syllable peaks and thus major articulatory targets. When the speaker lacks acoustic feedback while articulating, this might have the consequence that acoustic targets are not fully reached any more, thus causing a less intense vowel articulation.

The further experiments subdivide the classes of consonants and vowels. We performed these subdivisions according to the degree of somatosensoric feedback which we considered to be associated to the pronunciation of the respective phonemes. We fconsidered two groups of consonants, namely velar (i.e. 'g', 'k' and 'ng') and bilabial consonants ('p','b' and 'm'). Since bilabial phonemes are articulated by using both lips we hypothesize that a missing acoustic feedback may be compensated by the tactile feedback of closing the lips. This would imply that we can measure a relatively stronger articulation of bilabial consonants than of velar consonants, which are articulated with the back part of the tongue, nearly without somatosensoric feedback. Figure 2 (right-hand side) charts the PSDs of EMG channels 2 and 4. The result markedly shows that there is a significant difference between bilabial and velar consonants: While for velar consonants, we have the usual pattern of decreasing PSD from audible to silent speaking mode, this order is reversed for bilabial consonants, where the articulation power is much higher in silent speaking mode than in any other mode. Also note that the PSDs of bilabial and velar consonants in audible and whispered speaking mode are practically identical. This shows that bilabial consonants are indeed hyperarticulated in silent speech, emphasizing our hypothesis that a speaker makes use of an increased tactile feedback when speaking silently.

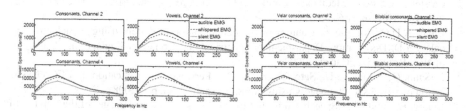

Fig. 2. Impact on EMG signal by lack of acoustic feedback

5 Conclusions

In this article we have described silent speech recognition based on Electromyography. With our approach we achieved an average word error rate of 31.5% on a 101-word vocabulary task, bringing EMG-based speech recognition within useful range for silent speech applications. Furthermore, we investigated the discrepancies between different speaking modes, analyzing the spectral densities of audible, whispered and silent EMG signals. While there is only little difference between whispered and audible speaking mode, we proved that in silent speech, phonemes whose articulation gives a strong tactile feedback are articulated relatively stronger than other phonemes. This result confirms our assumption that the speaker compensates the lack of acoustic feedback by focusing on the somatosensoric feedback—indicated by emphasizing those sounds which provide more somatosensoric feedback than others. With the given performance, we feel that several application areas for Silent Speech Interfaces come within reach: (1) robust, private, non-distracting speech recognition for human-machine interfaces, such as silently speaking text messages, (2) recognition plus speech synthesis (at the remote side) for quietly accessing remote applications, such as speech or text-based information systems, (3) transmitting articulation parameters followed by articulatory synthesis for silent human-human communication, (4) speech prostheses, and (5) recognition of silent speech followed by text translation into another language followed by speech synthesis, which appears like speaking in a foreign tongue.

References

1. Bartels, J.L., Andreasen, D., Ehirim, P., Mao, H., Seibert, S., Wright, E.J., Kennedy, P.R.: Neurotrophic electrode: method of assembly and implantation into human motor speech cortex. Journal of Neuroscience Methods 174(2), 168–176 (2008)
2. Birbaumer, N.: The thought translation device (TTD) for completely paralyzed patients. IEEE Transactions on Rehabilitation Engineering 8(2), 190–193 (2000)
3. Blankertz, B., Dornhege, G., Krauledat, M., Müller, K.-R., Kunzmann, V., Losch, F., Curio, G.: The Berlin brain-computer interface: EEG-based communication without subject training. IEEE Transactions on Neural Systems and Rehabilitation Engineering 14(2), 147–152 (2006)
4. Brumberg, J.S., Nieto-Castanon, A., Kennedy, P.R., Guenther, F.H.: Brain-Computer Interfaces for Speech Communication. Speech Communication, Special Issue on Silent Speech Interfaces (April 2010) (in press)
5. Carstens: Carstens Medizinelektronik (2008), http://www.articulograph.de/ (accessed November 6, 2008)
6. Chan, A.D.C.: Multi-expert automatic speech recognition system using myoelectric signals, Ph.D. Dissertation, Department of Electrical and Computer Engineering, University of New Brunswick, Canada (2003)
7. DaSalla, C., Kambara, H., Sato, M., Koike, Y.: Personal communication on EEG classification of vowel speech imagery using common spatial patterns (2008)
8. Denby, B., Stone, M.: Speech synthesis from real time ultrasound images of the tongue. In: Proceedings IEEE International Conference on Acoustics, Speech, and Signal Processing (ICASSP 2004), Montréal, Canada, May 17-21, vol. 1, pp. I-685 – I-I688 (2004)

9. Denby, B., Oussar, Y., Dreyfus, G., Stone, M.: Prospects for a Silent Speech Interface Using Ultrasound Imaging. In: IEEE ICASSP, Toulouse, France, pp. I365–I368 (2006)
10. Denby, B., Schultz, T., Honda, K., Hueber, T., Gilbert, J.: Silent Speech Interfaces. Speech Communication, Special Issue on Silent Speech Interfaces (April 2010) (in press)
11. Dornhege, G., del Millan, J.R., Hinterberger, T., McFarland, D., Müller, K.-R. (eds.): Towards brain-computer interfacing. MIT Press, Cambridge (2007)
12. Fagan, M.J., Ell, S.R., Gilbert, J.M., Sarrazin, E., Chapman, P.M.: Development of a (silent) speech recognition system for patients following laryngectomy. Medical Engineering and Physics 30(4), 419–425 (2008)
13. Guenther, F.H., Ghosh, S.S., Tourville, J.A.: Neural Modeling and Imaging of the Cortical Interactions underlying Syllable Production. Brain and Language 96, 280–301 (2007)
14. Heracleous, P., Kaino, T., Saruwatari, H., Shikano, K.: Unvoiced speech recognition using tissue-conductive acoustic sensor. EURASIP Journal on Advances in Signal Processing 2007(1), 1–11 (2007)
15. Hochberg, L.R., Simeral, J.D., Kim, S., Stein, J., Friehs, G.M., Black, M.J., Donoghue, J.P.: More than two years of intracortically-based cursor control via a neural interface system. In: Neurosicence Meeting Planner 2008, Program No. 673.15, Washington, DC (2008)
16. Hueber, T., Aversano, G., Chollet, G., Denby, B., Dreyfus, G., Oussar, Y., Roussel, P., Stone, M.: Eigentongue feature extraction for an ultrasound-based silent speech interface. In: IEEE ICASSP, Honolulu, vol. 1, pp. 1245–1248 (2007)
17. Hueber, T., Benaroya, E.-L., Chollet, G., Denby, B., Dreyfus, G., Stone, M.: Development of a silent speech interface driven by ultrasound and optical images of the tongue and lips. Speech Communication, Special Issue on Silent Speech Interfaces (April 2010) (in press)
18. Hummel, J., Figl, M., Birkfellner, W., Bax, M.R., Shahidi, R., Maurer, C.R., Bergmann, H.: Evaluation of a new electromagnetic tracking system using a standardized assessment protocol. Physics in Medicine and Biology 51, N205–N210 (2006)
19. Izzetoglu, K., Bunce, S., Onaral, B., Pourrezaei, K., Chance, B.: Functional Optical Brain Imaging Using Near-Infrared During Cognitive Tasks. International Journal of HCI 17(2), 211–227 (2004)
20. Jorgensen, C., Lee, D.D., Agabon, S.: Sub auditory speech recognition based on EMG signals. In: Proceedings of the International Joint Conference on Neural Networks (IJCNN), pp. 3128–3133 (2003)
21. Jorgensen, C., Binsted, K.: Web browser control using EMG based sub vocal speech recognition. In: Proceedings of the 38th Annual Hawaii International Conference on System Sciences, pp. 294c.1–294c.8. IEEE, Los Alamitos (2005)
22. Jorgensen, C., Dusan, S.: Speech interfaces based upon surface electromyography. Speech Communication, Special Issue on Silent Speech Interfaces (April 2010) (in press)
23. Jou, S., Schultz, T., Walliczek, M., Kraft, F.: Towards continuous speech recognition using surface electromyography. In: INTERSPEECH 2006 and 9th International Conference on Spoken Language Processing, vol. 2, pp. 573–576 (2006)
24. Jou, S., Schultz, T., Waibel, A.: Multi-stream articulatory feature classifiers for surface electromyographic continuous speech recognition. In: Proceedings of International Conference on Acoustics, Speech, and Signal Processing. IEEE, Honolulu (2007)
25. Kennedy, P.R., Bakay, R.A.E., Moore, M.M., Adams, K., Goldwaithe, J.: Direct control of a computer from the human central nervous system. IEEE Transactions on Rehabilitation Engineering 8(2), 198–202 (2000)
26. Maier-Hein, L., Metze, F., Schultz, T., Waibel, A.: Session independent non-audible speech recognition using surface electromyography. In: IEEE Workshop on Automatic Speech Recognition and Understanding, San Juan, Puerto Rico, pp. 331–336 (2005)

27. Manabe, H., Hiraiwa, A., Sugimura, T.: Unvoiced speech recognition using EMG-mime speech recognition. In: Proceedings of CHI, Human Factors in Computing Systems, Ft. Lauderdale, Florida, pp. 794–795 (2003)

28. Manabe, H., Zhang, Z.: Multi-stream HMM for EMG-based speech recognition. In: Proceedings of 26th Annual International Conference of the IEEE Engineering in Medicine and Biology Society, San Francisco, California, September 1-5, vol. 2, pp. 4389–4392 (2004)

29. Nakajima, Y., Kashioka, H., Shikano, K., Campbell, N.: Non-audible murmur recognition input interface using stethoscopic microphone attached to the skin. In: Proceedings of IEEE ICASSP, pp. 708–711 (2003)

30. Nakajima, Y., Kashioka, H., Campbell, N., Shikano, K.: Non-audible murmur (NAM) recognition. IEICE Transactions on Information and Systems E89-D(1), 1–8 (2006)

31. Ng, L., Burnett, G., Holzrichter, J., Gable, T.: Denoising of human speech using combined acoustic and EM sensor signal processing. In: Proc. Int. Conf. on Acoustics, Speech, and Signal Processing (ICASSP), Istanbul, Turkey, June 5-9, vol. 1, pp. 229–232 (2000)

32. Porbadnigk, A., Wester, M., Calliess, J., Schultz, T.: EEG-based speech recognition - impact of temporal effects. In: Biosignals 2009, Porto, Portugal, pp. 376–381 (January 2009)

33. Quatieri, T.F., Messing, D., Brady, K., Campbell, W.B., Campbell, J.P., Brandstein, M., Weinstein, C.J., Tardelli, J.D., Gatewood, P.D.: Exploiting nonacoustic sensors for speech enhancement. IEEE Transactions on Audio, Speech, and Language Processing 14(2), 533–544 (2006)

34. Schönle, P.W., Gräbe, K., Wenig, P., Höhne, J., Schrader, J., Conrad, B.: Electromagnetic articulography: Use of alternating magnetic fields for tracking movements of multiple points inside and outside the vocal tract. Brain and Language 31, 26–35 (1987)

35. Schultz, T., Wand, M.: Modeling coarticulation in large vocabulary EMG-based speech recognition, Speech Communication. Special Issue on Silent Speech Interfaces (April 2010) (in press)

36. Suppes, P., Lu, Z.-L., Han, B.: Brain wave recognition of words. Proceedings of the National Academy of Scientists of the USA 94, 14965–14969 (1997)

37. Tardelli, J.D. (ed.): MIT Lincoln Labs report ESC-TR-2004-084, Pilot Corpus for Multisensor Speech Processing (2004)

38. Titze, I.R., Story, B.H., Burnett, G.C., Holzrichter, J.F., Ng, L.C., Lea, W.A.: Comparison between electroglottography and electromagnetic glottography. Journal of the Acoustical Society of America 107(1), 581–588 (2000)

39. Tran, V.-A., Bailly, G., Loevenbruck, H., Toda, T.: Improvement to a NAM-captured whisper-to-speech system. Speech Communication, Special Issue on Silent Speech Interfaces (April 2010) (in press)

40. Walliczek, M., Kraft, F., Jou, S.-C., Schultz, T., Waibel, A.: Sub-word unit based non-audible speech recognition using surface electromyography. In: Proceedings of Interspeech, Pittsburgh, USA, pp. 1487–1490 (2006)

41. Wand, M., Schultz, T.: Towards speaker-adaptive speech recognition based on surface electromyography. In: Proceedings of Biosignals, Porto, Portugal (2009) (in press)

42. Wester, M., Schultz, T.: Unspoken speech - speech recognition based on electroencephalography, Master's thesis, Universität Karlsruhe (TH), Karlsruhe, Germany (2006)

43. Wolpaw, J.R., Birbaumer, N., McFarland, D., Pfurtscheller, G., Vaughan, T.: Brain-computer interfaces for communication and control. Clinical Neurophysiology 113(6), 767–791 (2002)

CanSpeak: A Customizable Speech Interface for People with Dysarthric Speech

Foad Hamidi[1], Melanie Baljko[1], Nigel Livingston[2], and Leo Spalteholz[2]

[1] Department of Computer Science and Engineering, York University, 4700 Keele St., Toronto, Ontario, Canada M3J 1P3
[2] CanAssist, University of Victoria, Victoria, BC, Canada V8W 3P6

Abstract. Current Automatic Speech Recognition (ASR) systems designed to recognize dysarthric speech require an investment in training that involves considerable effort and must be repeated if speech patterns change. We present CanSpeak, a customizable speech recognition interface that does not require automatic training and uses a list of keywords customized for each user. We conducted a preliminary user study with four subjects with dysarthric speech. Customizing the keyword lists doubled the accuracy rate of the system for two of the subjects whose parents and caregivers participated in the customizing task. For the other two subjects only small improvements were observed.

Keywords: Speech Recognition, Web Accessibility, Dysarthric Speech.

1 Introduction

For computer use, speech as an alternative input mode holds great potential for people with physical or motor disabilities for whom using conventional input devices such as the mouse or keyboard is difficult or impossible. However, despite considerable progress in the field of Automatic Speech Recognition (ASR), there are still important issues that hinder its use for many members of this community. One such issue is that motor disabilities can affect speech and often coexist with speech dysarthria. As a result, state-of-art ASR systems developed to recognize clear speech are unsuitable for these users [1]. We believe that key goals in the design of speech interfaces for people with disabilities are increasing system customizability and flexibility and minimizing the needed effort for initial setup.

Prior research has characterized dysarthric speech in terms of acoustic cue malformation and loss, as well as the introduction of erroneous acoustic cues [17]. In addition, prior work also demonstrated a high degree of intra speaker variation with respect to these parameters of dysarthria [1]. While modern systems have a wider tolerance for variations in utterances, they are still unsuccessful at coping with the greater degree of variation present in dysarthric speech [1, 15, 16]. Thus, the development of ASR systems that can effectively handle speech with these characteristics is hard because in addition to the complexity of automatically recognizing natural speech they have to handle the increased variance in the input.

K. Miesenberger et al. (Eds.): ICCHP 2010, Part I, LNCS 6179, pp. 605–612, 2010.

Most current ASR systems for dysarthric users are speaker dependant and require automatic acoustic module training. Automatic training requires considerable effort and the system may require many hours of training for persons with moderate to severe dysarthric speech [19]. Additionally, extensive training has adverse effects, such as fatigue and frustration [18, 20]. Furthermore, the purpose of the training phase is to establish a speaker-dependent acoustic model, which can become "outdated" if the user's speech changes significantly, due to, for example, effects of aging or changes in health conditions. However, there is evidence suggesting that undergoing speech therapy can improve the accuracy of ASR systems for dysarthric users [13].

The task of ASR with a closed domain, where the possible input is restricted, is clearly simpler, and thus more robust and accurate, than ASR with an open domain, where unrestrained speech is expected. Furthermore, ASR for individuals with dysarthric speech can be further simplified if the words in the closed domain are those that the individual is comfortable and relatively proficient at producing. Using this idea, we developed *CanSpeak*, a customizable speech interface for people with dysarthric speech. *CanSpeak* has a modular design that allows it to be integrated into any application that uses keyboard (or other discreet) input. We conducted user tests with four subjects with dysarthric speech.

2 Background

Using ASR has a long history in the field of assistive technology. In early systems, small vocabulary speaker dependant speech recognition was used to control wheelchairs, environmental controls and touch tone phones [3, 4].

In early systems, speech commands were used to replace keyboard and mouse input actions. In such systems, stored templates of spoken vocabulary were matched with user speech input to identify desired commands. In a test undertaken by two subjects with high-level spinal cord injuries and different degrees of dysarthria, only one of them achieved high accuracy rates (79% to 90%). The other subject was only able to achieve an accuracy rate of (45% to 60%) [6].

The STARDUST project implements a speech training system for users with dysarthria. It consists of an isolated word, small vocabulary, speaker dependent ASR system that uses a training algorithm designed to train the system on sparse dysarthric speech data. Two example applications, an environmental control system and a voice output communication aid, have been developed [8, 10, 11]. The environmental control system performed well with small vocabulary (10 words) in quiet settings [8]. However, for the voice output communication application the restricted number of recognized words posed challenges and translation schemes were needed to map them to a larger output that could be used for face-to-face communication [11].

In [14] an ASR typing system for an individual with severe traumatic brain injury was developed. The system uses the Dragon NaturallySpeaking platform. It was reported that the individual, who had mild dysarthria and cognitive-communication impairment was able to quickly learn and use the system and achieve an accuracy rate of approximately 80%. It was further reported that despite minimal differences, the texts produced using speech and a standard keyboard were qualitatively the same.

Previous research has also focused on developing algorithms for single digit recognition for dysarthric speech. In [2], a system was developed and tested with a subject with cerebral palsy and dysarthric speech and accuracy rates of 90% were reported after training. In another study, two different algorithms were compared in tests with three subjects with dysarthric speech with mixed results: while both algorithms worked for the subject with mild dysarthria, they each failed for one of the other two subjects with severe dysarthric speech [9].

3   The *CanSpeak* Interface

We have developed *CanSpeak*, a customizable speech interface for use by people with various degrees of speech clarity. The system does not require automatic training and stores a customizable list of keywords for each user. It is used as an intermediate interface between the user and any application that uses discreet input (e.g., from the keyboard or switches). The list consists of a small number of words specifically selected to be easy for the user to pronounce. Each of the keywords in the list is associated with a letter of the alphabet, a digit or a command. Each time a keyword is recognized the system sends a keystroke or command associated with it to the application that is using the interface. The application then interprets the input according to the interaction context. The number of keywords depends on the application and needs of the user. In our current implementation we use 47 keywords.

CanSpeak's user interface consists of the keyword list and associated letters of the alphabet shown alongside the interface of any other application that is using it. We have chosen to display only the keywords associated with commands and letters of the alphabet and not the keywords associated with the numbers, since the latter can be recalled easily. The interface is shown in the left hand side of Figure 1.

CanSpeak is written in Java and uses the open source Sphinx-4 speech recognition engine developed at the Carnegie Mellon University [22]. Although the system is capable of large vocabulary continuous speech recognition, we have configured it for recognizing a small vocabulary set: this simplifies the task of the engine and improves performance greatly. We have also limited the speech input to isolated words and phrases of less than three words, on the basis of evidence that people with severe dysarthria perform better with this type of speech than with longer utterances [19]. In previous research, the need to keep the recognition task simple is emphasized [5].

We used a modular design in *CanSpeak's* development that allows its integration into applications that use keyboard or other forms of discreet input. As an example, we have combined it with *KeySurf*, a keyboard-based Internet navigation application we have presented previously [21]. The resulting application, *WebSpeak*, is a multimodal Internet navigation interface that combines voice and keyboard input. The importance of this type of modular design is that it allows user-tailored modes of inputs (e.g., speech for one user but mechanical switches for another); this approach is particularly emphasized in assistive technology where the user population has varied needs and abilities [7, 12]. In terms of functionality, the interface simply replaces keystroke input from the keyboard with input from the speech module. Figure 1 shows the interface of *WebSpeak*.

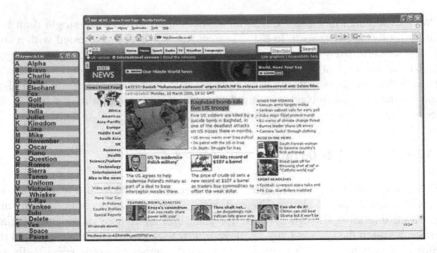

Fig. 1. The WebSpeech interface with CanSpeak's keyword list (left) and KeySurf's enabled browser (right)

The design of the keyword list presents several challenges. First, the keyword-command mapping should be intuitive and easy to recall. Second, the keywords themselves should be easily and clearly articulable by the user. Third, the differences among the keywords (in terms of acoustic confusability) should be above the threshold of ASR misrecognition. Thus, the selection of a suitable keyword list is not trivial. Our approach was to use a modified version of the NATO phonetic alphabet, in which some unfamiliar words were replaced with familiar ones, as the starting point and to allow the individual and his or her intervention team to make substitutions and modifications to this default setting as desired. Each keyword-command mapping is stored in each user's individual profile. We believe the best method for finding a good list is to take advantage of the user's own knowledge as well as feedback from people familiar with their speech such as his or her speech therapists, parents, teachers or caregivers about which words are easier for him or her to pronounce and for other listeners to understand. The results of the user study, presented in section 4, confirm this idea.

4   Evaluation

4.1   Subjects

We tested the program with four subjects all of whom have cerebral palsy and dysarthric speech. Three of the subjects are female and one male. The subjects' ages range from 19 to 35.

Subjects 1, 3 and 4 use computers on a regular basis. Subjects 1 and 3 usually use a regular keyboard to type but find typing fatiguing. Subject 4 uses his upper torso (head and lips movement) to type on a regular keyboard. All three subjects want to use speech input as an alternative input mode when they are tired from using their regular input routine. They are also interested in combining speech input with word prediction for writing. Finally, subject 2 does not have control of her hands and is not a regular computer user.

4.2 Procedure

The experiment consisted of two sessions, one done before and the other after the development of each subject's customized keyword list. The experimental task was to repeat each keyword after a recorded voice. Prior to each test session, the procedure was described and the subjects were given a chance to familiarize themselves with the system by saying a few words.

For the first session, after a brief warm up, subjects were prompted to say each of 47-words in the default list, described previously, in random order. The ASR system processed their input and recorded the prompts and recognized words in a log file.

Next, the experimenter spent four one hour sessions with each subject to refine their profile and identify problem words in the keyword list that needed to be replaced. All of the customization sessions were conducted by the same experimenter. During these sessions, the experimenter interviewed the subject and worked with him or her to identify candidate words to be included in the customized list. This phase differs from automatic acoustic model training in that, while the system was used to verify the recognition ease of candidate keywords, it did not attempt to adapt itself to the user automatically by analyzing a large training dataset but was customized utilizing the user's and his or her caregivers' knowledge directly.

The experimenter was able to consult with the parents, caregivers and teacher of subjects 1 and 2 and incorporate their suggestions into the customized list. For subjects 3 and 4, the experimenter only used suggestions from the subjects and himself. The engine was then tested with the new words to determine their suitability. These sessions resulted in a customized keyword list for each subject that was stored in a user profile. The new keyword list was then used in the second test that was identical in procedure to the first test and a second log file was created. The overall accuracy rates presented in the next section were derived from the log files created during the two tests.

5   Results and Discussion

Figure 2 shows the results of the experiment. Recognition accuracy improved remarkably for subjects 1 and 2 and improved marginally for subjects 3 and 4. The best results were achieved for subjects 1 and 2. The accuracy rate for both subjects doubled with the customized list (from 40.6% to 84.3% for subject 1 and from 37.5% to 75% for subject 2). The accuracy rates showed small improvement for subjects 3 and 4. They increased from 56.2% to 62.5% showing a 6.3% increase for subject 3 and from 28.1% to 34.3% showing a 6.2% increase for subject 4.

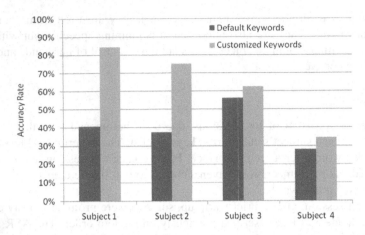

Fig. 2. Accuracy rates for the four subjects before and after keyword list customization

5.1 Discussion

The results show a dramatic improvement in accuracy rates for subjects for whom feedback from parents, caregivers and teachers was incorporated. However, in contrast, the improvements were marginal for subjects for whom this information was not available. This feedback when present helped create a better list and thus dramatically improve the performance. We believe that the keyword lists can be further improved by soliciting and incorporating input from speech therapists, parents, teachers and caregivers more systematically (e.g., by using questionnaires). Furthermore, the current customized words can be modified further over time when a larger number of problematic words are identified and replaced by better alternatives.

The selection of a suitable keyword list is a nontrivial problem. In this research, the customization of the word list for each subject was performed by trial and error. Moreover, the experimenter was not familiar with the subjects prior to the testing. We anticipate that this process will be more effective if a speech-language pathologist evaluates the user's speech in a short session and suggests a list of words that are easy for him or her to pronounce. This process can also be made more effective by incorporating suggested lists compiled by speech-language pathologists for each word.

In previous work, we tested the ASR engine using the same default list with subjects with clear speech and observed an average accuracy rate of 94% [21]. Compared to this accuracy rate, the rates for users with dysarthric speech are low. However, in assistive technology lower recognition rates are acceptable for applications in which error correction is not costly or speech can be supplemented by other input modes [19].

6 Conclusion and Future Work

We have presented *CanSpeak,* a customizable speech interface for people with speech dysarthria that does not require automatic training and provides an alternative to conventional input devices for discreet input such as the keyboard or switches. To use the system, the user says a small number of words that are customized to be easy for him or her to pronounce. The system associates each letter of the alphabet, digit or command to a keyword from the customizable set. The pronounced keyword is then mapped as keyboard input and used by applications.

We have conducted a user experiment with four subjects with severe dysarthric speech. The results show that customizing the keyword list can dramatically increase accuracy rates for some users. The main factor that affected the degree of improvement was the incorporation of suggestions from subjects' parents and teacher which doubled the accuracy rate when used. In the case of subjects for whom this input was not used, the improvements were small. This result shows the importance of involving people familiar with the user in the customization process.

In future, the keyword customization process can be improved by using candidate keyword lists, compiled by speech-language pathologists based on ease of pronouncement. A longitudinal study can examine how users can improve the keyword list with more use experience. Another longitudinal study can examine the effects of changes in the user's speech on the performance of the system.

Another area for future research is using this interface for speech therapy. The therapist can specify which words should be practiced by specifying them in the list. The patient can then use the interface in spelling games (e.g., Hangman or Spelling Bee) or other engaging tasks in between therapy sessions.

Acknowledgments. We would like to thank Madelene Levy at Participation House, Markham, for her valuable help and support.

References

1. Blaney, B., Wilson, J.: Acoustic Variability in Dysarthria and Computer Speech Recognition. Clinical Linguistics and Phonetics 14(4), 307–327 (2000)
2. Chen, F., Kostov, A.: Optimization of Dysarthric Speech Recognition. In: Proc. of IEEE/EMBS 1997, pp. 1436–1439. IEEE Press, New York (1997)
3. Clark, J.A., Roemer, R.B.: Voice Controller Wheelchair. Archives of Physical Medicine & Rehabilitation 58(4), 169–175 (1977)
4. Cohen, A., Graupe, D.: Speech Recognition and Control System for the Severely Disabled. Journal of Biomedical Engineering 2(2), 97–107 (1980)
5. Franco, H., Abrash, V., Precoda, K., Bratt, H., Rao, R., Butzberger, J., Rossier, R., Cesari, F.: The SRI EduSpeak System: Recognition and Pronunciation Scoring for Language Learning. In: Proc. of InSTL 2000, pp. 123–128 (2000)
6. Fried-Oken, M.: Voice Recognition Device as a Computer Interface for Motor and Speech Impaired People. Archives of Physical Medicine and Rehabilitation 34(3), 678–681 (1985)
7. Grammenos, D., Savidis, A., Georgalis, Y., Stephanidis, C.: Access Invaders: Developing a Universally Accessible Action Game. In: Miesenberger, K., Klaus, J., Zagler, W.L., Karshmer, A.I. (eds.) ICCHP 2006. LNCS, vol. 4061, pp. 388–395. Springer, Heidelberg (2006)
8. Green, P., Carmichael, J., Hatzis, A., Enderby, P., Hawley, M., Parker, M.: Automatic Speech Recognition with Sparse Training Data for Dysarthric Speakers. In: Proc. of EUROSPEECH 2003, pp. 1189–1192 (2003)

9. Hasegawa-Johnson, M., Gunderson, J., Perlman, A., Huang, T.: HMM-Based and SVM-Based Recognition of the Speech of Talkers with Spastic Dysarthria. In: Proc. of ICASSP 2006, pp. 1060–1063. IEEE Press, New York (2006)

10. Hawley, M., Enderby, P., Green, P., Brownsell, S., Hatzis, A., Parker, M., Carmichael, J., Cunningham, M., O'Neill, P., Palmer, R.: STARDUST:Speech Training and Recognition for Dysarthric Users of Assistive Technology. In: Craddock, G.M., McCormack, L.P., Reilly, R.B., Knops, H. (eds.) Assistive Technology – Shaping the Future, pp. 959–964. IOS Press, Amsterdam (2003)

11. Hawley, M., Enderby, P., Green, P., Cunningham, S., Palmer, R.: Development of a Voice-Input Voice-Output Communication Aid (VIVOCA) for People with Severe Dysarthria. In: Craddock, G.M., McCormack, L.P., Reilly, R.B., Knops, H. (eds.) Assistive Technology – Shaping the Future, pp. 882–885. IOS Press, Amsterdam (2003)

12. Kawai, S., Aida, H., Saito, T.: Designing Interface Toolkit with Dynamic Selectable Modality. In: Proc. of ASSETS 1996, pp. 72–79. ACM Press, New York (1996)

13. Kotler, A., Thomas-Stonell, N.: Effects of Speech Training on the Accuracy of Speech Recognition for an Individual with Speech Impairment. Journal of Augmentative and Alternative Communication 13(2), 71–80 (1997)

14. Manasse, N.J., Hux, K., Rankin-Erickson, J.L.: Speech Recognition Training for Enhancing Written Language Generation by a Traumatic Brain Injury Survivor. Brain Injury 14(11), 1015–1034 (2000)

15. Menéndez-Pidal, X., Polikoff, J.B., Peters, S.M., Leonzio, J.E., Bunnell, H.T.: The Nemours Database of Dysarthric Speech. In: Proc. of ICSLP 1996, pp. 1962–1965. IEEE Press, New York (1996)

16. Netsell, R., Abbs, J.: Acoustic Characteristics of Dysarthria Associated with Cerebellar Disease. Journal of Speech and Hearing Research 22, 627–648 (1997)

17. Patel, R., DiCicco, T.M.: Automatic Landmark Analysis of Dysartheric Speech. Journal of Medical Speech-Language Pathology 16(4), 221–224 (2008)

18. Raghavendra, P., Rosengren, E., Hunnicutt, S.: An Investigation of two Speech Recognition Systems with Dysarthric Speech as Input. In: Proc. of ISSAC 1994, pp. 479–481 (1994)

19. Rosen, K., Yampolsky, S.: Automatic Speech Recognition and a Review of its Functioning with Dysarthric Speech. Journal of Augmentative and Alternative Communication 16(1), 48–60 (2000)

20. Rosengren, E., Raghavendra, P., Hunnicut, S.: How Does Automatic Speech Recognition Handle Severely Dysarthric Speech? In: Porrero, P., Puig de la Bellacasa, R. (eds.) European Context for Assistive Technology, pp. 336–339. IOS Press, Amsterdam (1995)

21. Spalteholz, L., Lin, K.F., Livingston, N., Hamidi, F.: KeySurf: A Character Controlled Browser for People with Physical Disabilities.. In: Proc. of WWW 2008, pp. 31–39. ACM Press, New York (2008)

22. Walker, W., Lamere, P., Kwok, P., Raj, B., Singh, R., Gouvea, E., Wolf, P., Woelfel, J.: Sphinx-4: A Flexible Open Source Framework for Speech Recognition. Technical report, Sun Microsystems (2004)

Adding Voice to Whisper Using a Simple Heuristic Algorithm Inferred from Empirical Observation

Rüdiger Heimgärtner

Intercultural User Interface Consulting (IUIC)
Lindenstraße 9, 93152 Undorf, Germany
ruediger.heimgaertner@iuic.de

Abstract. The aim of the work described in this paper is to allow people that are enforced to use "whispery voice" to be endowed with "voiced voice". A very simple method and algorithm obtained by empirical observation of corresponding speech signals is presented and discussed. Only well-known methods like FFT, interpolation, normalization, and formant shifting are used. It turned out that the quality of the processed speech signal is adequate to be understood by hearers. The approach can also be used to replace normal speaking or singing voices.

Keywords: whisper, voice, speech signal, vowel, speech processing, phonetics, converting speech signals, HCI, voiceless, formant analysis, FFT, singing.

1 Introduction

The main objective of the presented project is to pass back "voiced voice" to people who are forced to speak with "whispery voice". However, it is not trivial to recognize voiced phonemes out of unvoiced speech signals because the carrier wave is not available and the signal is very noisy because of the strong air stream in whispering. Voiced phonemes ("vocals") can only be distinguished by virtue of its formants, because formants emerge also in very noisy regions. However, voiced phonemes like nasals or fricatives have high frequent formants and multifold spread frequencies over the noise area. Nevertheless, to help handicapped people, it is necessary to bypass the problems and to bring barrier free products to market as soon as possible. Therefore, it is necessary to use easy and cheap methods concerning algorithm complexity (as e.g. proposed by [1]) and financial effort to quickly develop products that can be paid by the people who need them. Even there are many elaborated methods for speech processing; they have not been used for the mentioned purpose for a long time (cf. [2]). Only now, [3] is working within the Bionic Voice Project on voiced speech from whispers for patients lacking the larynx partly or totally using very complex algorithms trying to restore natural speech. State-of-the-art-products to support whispering people to be heard in usual surroundings only amplify the whisper (cf. [4]). Probably, the well-known algorithms are too expensive to be used in cheap products. This seems to be one important reason why there is no commercial device

K. Miesenberger et al. (Eds.): ICCHP 2010, Part I, LNCS 6179, pp. 613–620, 2010.

converting whispered speech signals to voiced speech signals up to day (even if there is e.g., a patent from 2008 describing "a device and method for converting whisper into normal voice" [5] or some first prototypes as suggested in e.g. [6]).

2 Method Used

In contrast to the suggested mostly complex methods in research and patented devices (cf. e.g., [7]), in the approach proposed in this paper, only basic low-cost and already well-known methods in the field of speech recognition are used like Fast Fourier Transformation (FFT). In addition, it is not intended to recognize whispered speech, i.e. the syntax or even the meaning of the utterances (cf. [8]), but only to replace unvoiced areas of the speech signal that should be voiced using the voiced areas of another (prerecorded) speech signal. First, the spectrogram of the speech signal is generated using FFT. The traces of at least the first and second formant show the voiced areas of the speech signal (e.g. vowels or voiced consonants like a, e, i, o, u, m, n, etc.). In the second step, these areas are analyzed in more detail regarding the kind of vowel or voiced consonant as well as their amplitude, frequency, length etc. Then the fitting voiced consonant or vowel is retrieved out of a table containing the original parts of an arbitrary prerecorded voiced speech signal – hopefully the speech signal of the person of destination before losing the voice (cf. [9]). Finally, those parts of the unvoiced speech signal that should be voiced are substituted by the corresponding voiced consonants or vowels by interpolating their margins to avoid crunchy sound and by normalizing different amplitudes within the processed speech signal. The analysis of the spectrograms of speech signals with "whispery voice" supported the fact that it is possible to recognize formants, and thereby the parts of the whispered speech signal that should be voiced despite of lacking the fundamental frequency and having strong noisy disturbances (cf. figure 1).

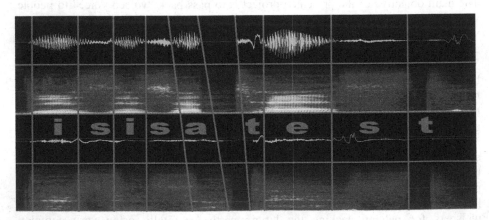

Fig. 1. Normal speech signal and its spectrogram (top) and whispered speech signal and its spectrogram (bottom) representing the utterance "This is a test"

3 Results

In areas of the whispered speech signal with vowels or voiced consonants, the recognition of the formant frequency is very stable. In contrast, the formant frequencies are totally varying in unvoiced areas of the speech signal. Stable formant frequencies indicate the areas of the whispered speech signal that should be voiced. Therefore, it is not necessary to replace other areas of the unvoiced speech signal than those that should be voiced (mainly vowels and voiced consonants). Rather it is sufficient to adapt the amplitude of the rest of the original speech signal (i.e. unvoiced areas containing, e.g., voiceless consonants, fricatives, plosives etc.) to the voiced parts of the newly generated (i.e. processed) speech signal, because there is no significant loss of the original speech signal as well as of the meaning of the utterances. Furthermore, for a first step, it is sufficient only to substitute the vowels because they represent the voiced areas of a speech signal that appear most often, most long, with high amplitude, and hence, contribute the most significant part for understanding the voiced part within a speech signal. A very simple heuristic algorithm to replace vowels is presented in figure 2.

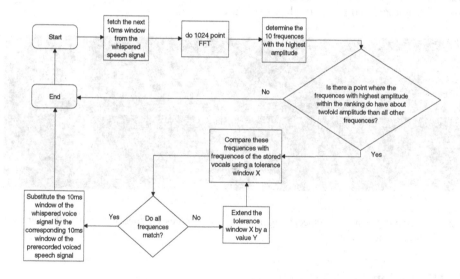

Fig. 2. Very Simple Heuristic Algorithm for Replacing Vowels

In addition, to keep it as simple as possible, in a first step, only the centre frequency of the formants for the target user group are used. Table 1 shows these frequencies according to the vowels e.g. for the German language as well as the corresponding phonetic signs defined by the international phonetic association (IPA) – also depicted in the articulatory vowel trapeze in figure 4.

Table 1. Formant Centres of German Vowels

Vowel	IPA	Formant F1 [Hz]	Formant F2 [Hz]
U	u	320	800
O	o	500	1000
å	ɑ	700	1150
A	a	1000	1400
ö	ø	500	1500
ü	y	320	1650
ä	ɛ	700	1800
E	e	500	2300
I	i	320	3200

The empirical comparison of human whispered and voiced speech signals, the replacement of relevant whispered parts by the corresponding parts of the voiced speech signal as well as auditory evaluation of the processed speech signal by some test persons showed that the method mentioned before is working properly. This is indicated by the fact that the formants are strongly amplified in the processed speech signal (cf. the linear white areas in the bottom part of figure 3). Thereby, they are easily recognized and understood by the hearer.

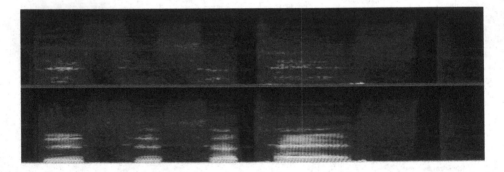

Fig. 3. Originally whispered speech signal (top) and processed speech signal with averaged formant frequencies (bottom)

4 Discussion

4.1 Problems of the Mentioned Approach

The most obvious problem in real time processing is that the used algorithms do not fulfill the required task within the given time. Another problem is the necessary processing delay between original and processed signal, which can be very disturbing within communication processes. However, this effect disappears, if the delay is lower than about 20 milliseconds (I do not have a reference here – it is my subjective impression – furthermore common analyzing windows in digital audio processing are about 10ms) because then the delay is not recognized by the hearers. This short delay neither disturbs the process of speech production of the speaker nor the process of speech recognition of the hearers. The delay can be reduced accordingly using fast hardware and adequate software employing simple algorithms that avoid high processing load. Another problem is the quality of the processed speech signal and its acceptance by the hearers. However, in my opinion, it is better to get back a loud "voiced voice" even if this voice is not the original one or has not yet the desired quality than to avoid communicating at all, e.g., because of lacking the possibility to express ones personality using loud voice or because of bad quality of simply amplified whisper. The quality of the output speech signal and its hearer acceptance must be improved by optimizing the applied algorithms based on the results coming from usability tests.

4.2 Ideas for Optimization

The average value of the amplitudes of all frequencies within the spectrogram is low for voiceless areas and high for voiced areas. An additional cue for voiced areas is the fact that the most significant frequencies in the spectrogram are below about 5 kHz representing the vowel formants. Furthermore, to recognize the kind of vowels, the analyzed windows can be compared with the prerecorded voiceless vowels from the same whispery speech signal to learn the whispered vowels and the position of their corresponding formants. Moreover, interpolation, FFT, and formant shifting are reasonable methods to get corresponding vowels from original ones by adapting the kind of vowels and their intonation. Thereby, it should be sufficient to use 5-13 voice samples taken from the edges and the center of the vowel trapeze to recognize the vowels within whispered voice and to adapt the corresponding parts of the prerecorded normal voice in frequency, length, and amplitude (cf. figure 4). Figure 5 shows the resulting speech signals examples when applying this method manually.

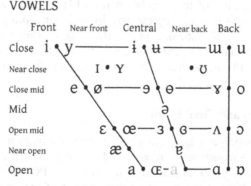

Vowels at right & left of bullets are rounded & unrounded.

Fig. 4. Articulatory Vowel Diagram/Trapeze according to IPA, cf. [10]

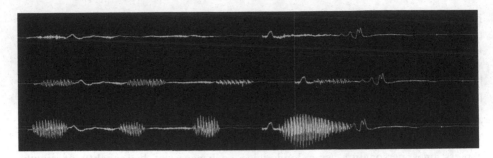

Fig. 5. Whispered speech signal (top), processed speech signal (mid) substituting vowel areas by prerecorded voiced signals and optimized (normalized, interpolated, and formant shifted) speech signal (bottom)

4.3 Impacts and Contributions to the Field

The approach described in this paper is very useful in various respects. As mentioned before, people that are enforced to use "whispery voice" can be endowed with "voiced voice". An additional positive aspect of this approach is that the users can choose the kind of the "voiced voice". If records of their original "voiced voice" exist, even their original voice can be restored. Second, the branch of industry for apparatus for voice generation might be extended. For instance, amplifiers for whispered speech signals may not only amplify the whispered speech signal but can also be facilitated with the feature of adding voice to the whispered speech signal. Thereby, arbitrary voices can be used. Besides whisper2voice also voice2voice (spoken and sung) is applicable. In music industry this effect can be used to imitate voices, which strongly contributes to joy of use. Everyone can speak or sing with the voice of another person (if the person agrees). Thereby, basic research concerning the processing of human speech and singing using electronic devices must be taken into account (cf. e.g. [11] and [12]). Finally, the recognized vowel (e.g., represented by a red point) can be displayed within the articulatory vowel trapeze (cf. figure 4) to visualize the kind of the vowel and the quality of its articulation (cf. [13]) to learn and train the correct articulation of the vowel (e.g., represented by a green point) within the desired language or dialect by the speaker or by the singer. Thereby, also people with articulation problems and even deaf people will benefit from such a training (cf. [14] and [15]) using a software or hardware device that has implemented the approach described above.

4.4 Demonstrators and Final Product

It is intended to develop at least three kinds of demonstrators to prove the described approach. The first demonstrator is represented by software that does not provide real time processing. It uses an algorithm that works on PC fed with a prerecorded whispered (unvoiced) input speech signal. The output of the algorithm is the voiced speech signal. It is intended to develop a second software demonstrator that will work in "real-time" with a maximal delay of 40 milliseconds between input and output signal. If the algorithm is elaborated enough, it can be implemented into a demonstrator embracing a digital signal processor developed using an adequate implementation chain like Matlab or Simulink to get the models into fast hardware (e.g., a field-programmable gate array (FPGA)). The final end-user product for converting whisper to voice (or replacing voice by voice) should be a very small and barrier free device (containing a processor, an amplifier, a loudspeaker, and a battery) that can be placed anywhere in the clothes using methods of ambient intelligence. A wireless microphone in contact with the device can be situated near the mouth (cf. [16]). To take into account aspects of universal design, it has to be checked, if the whispered (unvoiced) speech signals can be taken directly from outside or even inside the throat or mouth (cf. e.g. [17]) or using combinations (cf. [18]), so that finally the device is totally invisible representing the ultimate objective of universal design (cf. [19]).

5 Conclusion and Planned Activities

Up to day, there is no commercial device turning a whispered speech signal into a voiced speech signal. However, using a simple heuristic algorithm can be useful to efficiently and rapidly develop a device that replaces "whispery voice" by "voiced voice" simply by "adding" and adapting voiced parts of voiced speech signals to whispered speech signals. Therefore, the final product should have good value for money and because of its simplicity it should be easily usable by the end-users to support the people that already demand for this technology as soon as possible. The next steps are to evaluate a prototype doing usability tests as well as to optimize the quality of the processed voiced speech signals from the whispered speech signals. Even if much research is left, the mid-term objective is to turn the software prototype into a hardwired device applying the principles of universal design to offer an "invisible" but efficient product taking into account methods of ambient intelligence.

Acknowledgments. I thank Mr. Professor David Howard from the department of electronics at the University of York for several valuable hints and proof reading.

References

1. Jim: Voice Recognition Analysis. In: Welcome, Science, Applications. Machine Intelligence Technologies (2009), http://www.machineinteltech.com/ (last access 01/31/2010)
2. Howard, D.M., Murphy, D.T.: Voice Science, Acoustics, and Recording. Plural Publishing, Inc. (2007)
3. Sharifzadeh, H.R., McLoughlin, I.V., Ahamdi, F.: Voiced Speech from Whispers for Post-Laryngectomised Patients. IAENG International Journal of Computer Science, IJCS 36(4), 13 (2009)
4. Examples of state-of-the-art products: http://www.axistive.com/voice-amplifier-by-falck-vital-as.html, http://www.cordlessworkz.com/index.asp?PageAction=VIEWPROD&ProdID=1860, http://www.brucemedical.com/adkitplfepro.html (last access 01|31|2010)

5. CN000101188637A (DAPTISNET-Recherche,
   http://depatisnet.dpma.de/DepatisNet/depatisnet?window=1&
   space=main&content=treffer&action=treffer&so=asc&sf=vn&
   firstdoc=1 (last access 04/03/2010)
6. Fukumoto, M., Tonomura, Y.: Whisper: a wristwatch style wearable handset. In: Proceedings of the SIGCHI conference on Human factors in computing systems: the CHI is the Conference on Human Factors in Computing Systems archive, Pittsburgh, Pennsylvania, United States, pp. 112–119. ACM, New York (1999)
7. Jou, S.-C., Schultz, T., Waibel, A.: Whispery Speech Recognition using Adapted Articulatory Features. In: Proceedings of the IEEE International Conference on Acoustics, Speech, and Signal Processing, ICASSP 2005, Philadelphia, Pennsylvania (2005)
8. Acero, A., Alleva, F., Beeferman, D., Huang, X., Hwang, M.-Y., Mahajan, M.: From CMU Sphinx-II to Microsoft Whisper: Making Speech Recognition Usable (1994)
9. Orchard, T.L., Yarmey, A.D.: The effects of whispers, voice-sample duration, and voice distinctiveness on criminal speaker identification. Applied Cognitive Psychology 9(3), 249–260 (2006)
10. The IPA 1989 Kiel Convention Workgroup 9 report: Computer Coding of IPA Symbols and Computer Representation of Individual Languages. Journal of the International Phonetic Association 19, 81–82 (1989)
11. Disley, A., Howard, D.M., Hunt, A.D.: Further spectral correlations of timbral adjectives used by musicians. In: 4th joint meeting of the Acoustical Society of America and the Acoustical Society of Japan, Honolulu, Hawaii, vol. 3277 (2007)
12. Howard, D.M.: Human Hearing Modelling Real-Time Spectrography for Visual Feedback in Singing Training. Folia Phoniatrica et Logopaedica 57(5/6), 328–341, 1021–7762 (2005)
13. Ladefoged, P.: Elements of acoustic phonetics. Univ. of Chicago Press, Chicago (1998)
14. Eekhof, J.-A., de Bock, G.-H., de Laat, J.-A., Dap, R., Schaapveld, K., Springer, M.-P.: The whispered voice: the best test for screening for hearing impairment in general practice? Br. J. Gen. Pract. 46(409), 473–474 (1996)
15. Pirozzo, S., Papinczak, T., Glasziou, P.: Whispered voice test for screening for hearing impairment in adults and children: systematic review. BMJ 2003, 327(7421), p. 967 (2003), doi:10.1136/bmj.327.7421.967
16. Menzer, F., Buchli, J., Howard, D.M., Ijspeert, A.J.: Non-linear models of vowel fold vibration for pitch breaks and electrolaryngograph waveform output. LogopedicsPhoniatricsVocology 31(1), 36–42, 1401–5439 (2006)
17. Tsunoda, K., Ohta, Y., Soda, Y., Niimi, S., Hirose, H.: Laryngeal adjustment in whispering: Magnetic resonance imaging study. The Annals of Otology, Rhinology & Laryngology (January 1, 1997)
18. Erzin, E.: Improving throat microphone speech recognition by joint analysis of throat and acoustic microphone recordings. IEEE Transactions on Audio, Speech, and Language Processing archive 17(7) (2009)
19. Center for Universal Design: The Principles of Universal Design, Version 2.0. North Carolina State University, Raleigh, NC (Retrieved July 12, 2007),
   http://www.design.ncsu.edu/cud/about_ud/udprinciples.htm

LIPPS – A Virtual Teacher for Speechreading Based on a Dialog-Controlled Talking-Head

Hermann Gebert[1] and Hans-Heinrich Bothe[1,2]

[1] Technische Universität Berlin, D-10623 Berlin, Germany
[2] Danmarks Tekniske Universitet, DK-2800 Kgs. Lyngby, Denmark
h.gebert@xlp.de, hhb@ieee.org

Abstract. People with decreasing hearing ability are more dependent on alternative personal communication channels. To read the visible articulator movements of the conversation partner is one possible solution for understanding verbal statements. After giving an introduction to the principals of speech, visual speech & speechreading, we demonstrate the conception and implementation of a language laboratory for speechreading that is meant as an effective audio-visual complement and extension of classroom teaching. Further we show results of evaluation experiments and explain the functionality and interaction of the modules, the interaction between student, teacher, and virtual teacher and the structure of the pedagogical approach to teach speechreading with the help of a virtual teacher.

Keywords: speechreading, lipreading, language tutor, embodied conversational agent, facial animation, audio-visual, training-aid, hard-of-hearing, deaf, sudden deafness.

1 Speech and Visual Speech

Speech is the product of an arbitrary, rule-based movement of the speech apparatus [1, 2]. Those rules have to be learned up from early infancy. The motor development of speech production is coordinated by feedback, both on the acoustic path and on the kinesthetic path. If this feedback is partly missing, the acquisition of language is reduced by normal means.

Hearing-impaired people are not a homogeneous group. There are hard-of-hearing people, deaf people, and people with sudden deafness. Hard-of-hearing people have a residual hearing that in many cases allows for learning an acoustic language. Speech perception occurs mostly over the auditory pathway and can be supplemented by speechreading. Adults and children with a severe hearing loss but some residual hearing may use technical hearing devices as hearing-aids or cochlear implants to gain more listening experience. Together with a special education or training, those can help to understand and to learn an acoustic language.

K. Miesenberger et al. (Eds.): ICCHP 2010, Part I, LNCS 6179, pp. 621–629, 2010.

Profoundly deaf people are born without or with very low ability to hear, or they lost this ability prior to full language acquisition. The low amount of speech they might understand is not sufficient for correct language acquisition. They often use sign language for conversation, which is a combination of gestics (dynamic hand signs) and mimics, and body posture and movement. It is a fully accepted language with its own grammatical rules, which are very different from the grammar of the respective acoustic language of a country; but for communication with normal-hearing persons, profoundly deaf persons depend on speechreading.

A person belongs to the group of people with sudden deafness, if language acquisition is completed before the hearing loss occurs and the person has gained a high level of spoken language skills. The main problem in this case is that the person is not able to understand the acoustic language anymore, nor the sign language or any other alternative method to communicate. This often leads to a separation from the circle of friends and family because all of them are used to share the acoustic language. Also, the place of work might become improper and needs to be changed. A fast improvement of speechreading skills is therefore indispensable for these persons. Our virtual teacher explicitly addresses them as a potential clientele.

2 Speechreading

One major problem with speechreading is that the spoken language is not fully distinguishable by reading the lips; a huge amount of information has to be guessed. This is mostly done by following the context and by drawing conclusions from prior spoken sentences, which can be utterly exhausting. Speechreading is also not only done by reading lips, it involves the whole face, respectively the eyebrows, the eyes, the cheeks and the area around the mouth. Also normal hearing people are speechreading subconsciously. People with prelingual deafness have never learned the acoustic language and do therefore not know any of the used visemes. They have to learn speechreading by a holistic educational training, which makes the process much more difficult.

The acoustic language is based on a combination of sounds (phonemes) that can visually be perceived as specific face and mouth movements (visemes). There is a many-to-one relation regarding the mapping of phonemes to visemes, which leads to a bad best visual intelligibility of below 30%. The real intelligibility is dependent on the context, the practical competence, and the vocabulary of the speechreading person.

The ability to speechread is strongly dependent on a huge number of further factors, with the manner of speaking being one of them. On one hand the speaker should articulate well enough and should not mumble, on the other hand he should not over-articulate. The speaker should not speak too fast but also not too slow. It is very helpful and improves speech recognition when the speechreader knows the topic or at least the scope of the conversation. It is therefore helpful for any speechreading training to embed the relevant utterances in a context and to allow the dialogue partner to correct errors. It is also helpful when the speaker escorts his speaking with mimics and gestics to underline the spoken words. For the hearing-impaired person himself it is important to follow a set of simple rules regarding location and position of the conversation. It is very important that the speechreader can see the face and the lips of the counterpart clearly without any surrounding light reflections. Hence it is much better for the conversation partner or teacher to sit in the light across from a window or a lamp, so that the face is clearly visible and the speechreader has the light in the back. If the speechreader has some residual hearing and is able to understand parts of a conversation, then it is important to find a silent place with as little background noise as possible.

3 Pedagogical Concepts

There are different concepts used to teach speechreading, employing a human teacher requesting specific tasks from the hearing-impaired person in a dialog situation or making use of a standardized set of utterances that allow for using a video recorder with pre-recorded material. Our virtual teacher for speechreading is a technical training-aid on a PC, designed for open dialog situations with abilities similar to a real teacher, and many of the existing pedagogical concepts can be integrated.

1. Some members of "Deutscher Schwerhörigenbund" (DSB e.V.) are, for example, supporting the work of Willibald Wagenbach, who was an experienced speechreading teacher with a late hearing loss, using a hearing aid by himself. His method describes mouth shapes for single sounds and increases difficulty step by step. A starting approach for his method is to describe the position of jaw, chin, teeth, and lips for each letter of the alphabet. Thereafter, he teaches syllables, suffixes, and prefixes that are often used in the colloquial speech up to small words.

2. Lindner in [3] follows a somewhat related approach, enhanced by the meaning of body posture. Other concepts follow this scheme and add simple texts where one characteristic word is repeated very often or the whole dialogue is concerned about a given topic, for example the names of the months.

3. Pöhle's "Absehlehrgang für Schwerhörige und Spätertaubte" [4] is using the following stages: Simple words that are embedded into simple sentences. The specific word is repeated very often and shall practice a special viseme. Multiple similar words are integrated into one utterance, for example "Water", "Waterfall", "Watergate", "Water wall", "Water pipe", short stories about a special given topic (car, kitchen, post office, etc.), interrogative sentences (What's your name?, Where do you live?, etc.), or times and numbers, pre-and suffixes, confusable words, and abbreviations.

4. Eisenworth et al. [5] are combining the above mentioned approaches. They add tasks for counting words or syllables in a sentence or related to how often a specific vowel occurs in a word.

5. A totally different approach uses a video recorder with pre-recorded video material. The above mentioned pictures of mouth position or the spoken sentences are not presented by a real life teacher, but by a recorded motion picture. This has the advantage that the student is able to repeat the unit as often as he likes. Another big advantage is that he can train, where and when he likes, which enables an extended training at home. The major disadvantage is the work that is necessary to build those motion pictures. An expensive camera and lights equipment is necessary and the recorded data is static. Using pre-fixed data material leads to the point that the student is only learning a much reduced subset of what is used in the "real world".

6. This disadvantage is eliminated by the use of facial avatars. Facial avatars are computer animated faces (or talking heads), which look similar to a real human. Speech output is generated by a human speech production model and, often driven by text input in orthographic or phonematic transcription. The input text is synthesized and the facial expression is adapted to the speech output by mathematical algorithms. After software development and integration of the training data, the system is still extendable by the end-user. Our virtual teacher uses such a facial animation system in combination with a speech synthesis system and thus, allows for huge flexibility.

4 Technical Concepts and Implementation

Our virtual teacher is based on cooperative work within the Thinking Systems project and specifically, the ThinkingHead framework [6]. The main aim of this large project is to build a plug-and-play research platform, allowing users to test their related software without the overhead of building a complete system, and to create a standardized Thinking Head for the related cooperative community, which can improve human-machine interaction by integrating 'natural' human attributes. The ThinkingHead framework is designed in a very modular way (see Fig. 1). Two central modules, the active *Event Manager* and the passive *Synapse*, are responsible for any data distribution. All modules connect to one or both of them to communicate with other modules. The ThinkingHead framework contains several other modules, e.g., for speech recognition, dialogue management, facial animation, or text-to-speech synthesis, which we used or modified and integrated into the virtual teacher. The existing dialogue management module was, for example, adapted for the human teacher to implement his preferred pedagogical model. Two new modules were added, the input/output modules for human teacher and student.

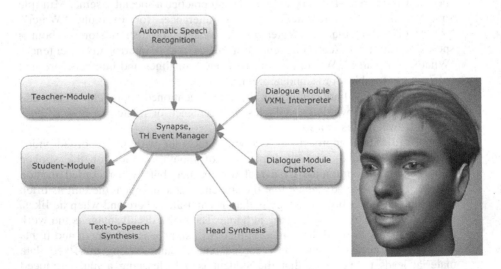

Fig. 1. Structure of the software and 3D virtual teacher with exemplary illumination

5 The Dialogue Modules

There are at least two possible ways to have a dialogue. The first one is using an artificial intelligence or machine learning tool, which controls the dialog, yielding an open and dynamic dialogue – which might be sensible or not. The second one is to build a deterministic or guided dialogue with a fixed grammatical structure and fixed questions with possible answers.

In our virtual teacher we implemented both, guided and open dialog communication. The possibility to have an open dialogue was implemented in form of an A.L.I.C.E chatbot [7], which reads and analyzes the user input on base of keyword-related decomposition rules. The chatbot mainly addresses students with a deeper knowledge of speechreading, who want to train their skills in more detail and depth. The system is mostly asking questions related to the last statements of the user, which in turn, the user can answer, then initiating a new question. The open dialogue is simulating an open dialogue as it could happen in the real world, centered on some given topics. The student can learn speechreading by using the resulting question-and-answer situations interactively. The 'correctness' of any given answer cannot be proven by teacher feedback but rather, the student may ask further questions or make further statements.

In the guided dialogue approach, the questions and answers are pre-given, thus yielding the possibility to evaluate the correctness of any given response. This is a critical point because immediate and direct feedback is very important for 'beginners', which is only possible when the system knows a correct answer. The guided training-aid approach could be seen as a virtual teacher for words, utterances or short sentences, who embeds these utterances in questions, which can be answered with the utterance itself. We employed *VoiceXML* to realize more complex dialogues in a simple way instead of being stuck in yes/no or true/false feedback situations; so our virtual teacher enables the human teacher in the background to implement all pedagogical methods mentioned above with low effort. Further, an electronic variant of the Leitner System [8] was integrated, which uses spaced repetition and can improve the learning progress significantly and quickly.

6 The Teacher and Student Modules

The teacher module is a direct interface between the human and the virtual teacher. The human teacher can create situations for new students, units or their respective hints, modules, new sceneries that can be assigned to a module or to assemble all the above to build completely new topic-related lessons. Since environmental variables are very important factors for the success of the speechreading task and must be considered, the teacher can superimpose noise, music or speech or scale the size or turning of the head, vary the light intensity or light source position, or integrate some distraction with the help of a background image or video.

The teacher module thus, allows the creation of different sceneries that are composed of appropriate backgrounds (e.g. kitchen, post office, etc.), related background sounds, or typical lighting conditions. Thereby, it is possible to create an adapted scene (e.g. a restaurant scene with a background image of a restaurant and some kitchen noise for a lesson about dishes on a menu). The virtual teacher is then capable of changing appearance and voice in real-time in order to match realistic prospects. The human teacher may, for example, build the scenery of a restaurant lesson by creating some units for the words *spoon*, *fork*, or *knife*. These units could contain hints like "Can you name the complement of a knife? (It is a fork!)" that would be presented by the virtual teacher and partly displayed in the subtitles as "Can you name the complement of a knife? Is it a ....?". Finally we can combine the restaurant scene and all units to build a learning module that is added to the lesson of an individual student. This lesson can be selected by the student with the help of the student module, which acts as a control dialogue and is used to enter the answers and to choose between a lesson and the unguided free dialogue. It contains the facial animation, synchronized with a speech synthesis system, and represents the virtual teacher.

7 Evaluation of the Virtual Teacher

The goal of the short evaluation is to find out if our virtual teacher can serve to improve a real person's ability to speechread rather than the quality of the facial animation, of the synchronized speech synthesis, or more generally, the effectiveness of the drilled repetition learning against free conversation learning.

The following audio-visual intelligibility test was conducted, using a text corpus with numbers between 21 and 99. The experiment was running five days in series taking about one hour for each test (audio only, audio-video). The audio-only test was only done on the first and on the last day and serves as a reference for possible memory effects. The audio-video test was done every day. To find-out what role an adaption to noise plays in the total improvement of the hit-rate, the audio-only test from the last day was compared to the one from the first day. Each number was used only once and only for one day. On the next day, a new set was created with new numbers to avoid any memory effect. The tests were always taken at the same time of the day on subsequent days.

The subject heard a set of numbers that are superimposed by a speech-shaped noise signal. The noise level was individually adapted for each subject such that it was marginally above the level of the just-intelligible signal. The respective signal-to-noise ratio (SNR) was used as a reference for tests with four adjacent SNR levels, two below and two above (± 4dB, ± 2dB) the just intelligible level. The order of the presentation was randomized to avoid a correlation between the hit-rate and the presentation order of the noise level.

During the test, the virtual teacher presented 15 words, each word three times and superimposed by one of the above SNR. This was repeated for every available SNR, yielding a total of 225 spoken words per session. The order of the words was randomized to avoid memory effects. After each spoken word, the subject was asked to enter the recognized number into an answer field. The test program waits for the answer as long as necessary; only for the audio-visual test, an audio-visual feedback is given to the subject.

The presented numbers and the given answers were at first transcribed into phonemes and then into the corresponding visemes, and thereafter compared. Doubly occurring visemes were interpreted as a single one. The viseme-strings were compared with each other with the help of the Levenshtein distance. The final result is a comparison of the perceived lip movements related to the articulation of two numbers. The distance was then compared with the maximal possible distance, which represents to what extend both strings match. This value was averaged across all numbers and interpreted as the percentage of (viseme-based) correct numbers (hit-rate [%]). Fig. 2 shows data for the - 4 [dB] SNR where the numbers were absolutely not recognizable by the subjects. This situation may reflect the circumstances in which the virtual teacher may likely be used.

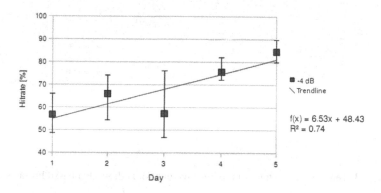

Fig. 2. Average recognition rate and trend, S/N -4 dB

The curve indicates that the recognition is increasing from day one to day five by nearly 28%. All detailed values can be seen in Table 1. The improvement of the mean recognition rate for the three situations {-4, -2, 0} [dB] is about 21%. The highest average improvement is stated for the worst listening situation (-4[dB]), the highest individual improvement is 34.22%, lowest one is 13.73%. Fig.3 shows the temporal trend lines, which are calculated by linear regression of the data from the whole week.

Table 1. Improved recognition rate from day 1 to day 5

S/N Ratio	Day 1	Day 5	Improvement
-4 dB	56.71%	84.57%	27.86%
-2 dB	64.81%	82.07%	17.26%
+0 dB	75.18%	93.01%	17.83%

They show steady improvement of the recognition rate with a gradient nearly independent on the SNR. The trend lines for the lowest SNR run almost parallel. Some subjects had a decreasing trend line for such signal-to-noise ratios, for which they could sometimes clearly understand the numbers. It can be assumed that the facial and lip movements of the facial animation system are not perfect, sometimes yielding a somewhat unnatural articulation of the virtual teacher, thus an unnatural perception and intelligibility of the numbers. When assuming that the speechreading skills generally improve during the test, then these 'wrong' artifact movements would corrupt the perception more for trained persons than for untrained ones, and the total hit-rate should in fact decrease over time.

The recognition rate for the poor SNR in the audio-only test is almost stable, only the -4 dB line is increasing slightly. Therefore we draw the conclusion that the improved recognition rate in the audio-video test is not conditional on an adaptation to the noise signal and is most likely caused by the virtual teacher.

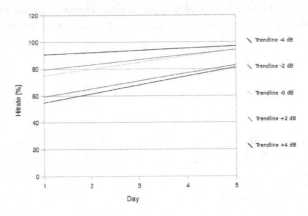

Fig. 3. Temporal trend lines of the improvement of audio-video-based hit rates

8   Conclusions

We designed and implemented a dialog-based virtual teacher for speechreading, which can employ forms of guided or free dialog. The virtual teacher is basically a 3D computer animation on a computer screen, developed within the ThinkingHead project with larger parts implemented at University of Adelaide/AU or University of Western Sydney/AU. The head is synchronized with a speech synthesis and controlled by a teacher or student module. First evaluations show that the virtual teacher can increase the ability to speechread from the computer animation; in further tests it will be investigated to what extend the ability to speechread from natural conversation partners can be improved.

Acknowledgement

We cordially like to thank the teachers Ute Dörfer at Berlin School for Hard-of-hearing Children, Berlin/D, Lothar Grahl at German Association for Hard-of-Hearing Persons, Frankfurt an der Oder/D, and Ulrike Witt at EAE School for Deaf Children in Berlin/D for their help and assistance concerning sensible pedagogic concepts for the training of speechreading. Further, we like to thank Trent Lewis and Martin Luerssen from Flinders University in Adelaide/AU for intensive and detailed help with some of the extremely voluminous ThinkingHead software, in particular the HeadX system we used, and Benjamin Weiss and Christine Kühnel from Technical University of Berlin/D for discussions on quality measurements for the ThinkingHead performance.

References

1. Flanagan, J.L.: Speech Analysis, Synthesis and Perception, 2nd edn. Springer, Heidelberg (1972)
2. Blauert, J.: Kommunikationsakustik II: Audiokommunikation und virtuelle Realität. Lecture Notes at Institut für Kommunikationsakustik. Ruhr-University, Bochum (1994)
3. Lindner, G.: Absehen - der andere Weg zum Sprachverstehen. Luchterhand (1999)
4. Gehörlosen- und Schwerhörigen-Verband der DDR: Absehlehrgang für Schwerhörige und Spätertaubte. Letters for Teachers and Students (1998)
5. Eisenwort, B., Viehhauser, G.: Ablesetraining. J. Groos-Verlag, Heidelberg (1992)
6. Burnham, D., Dale, R., Stevens, K., Powers, D., Davis, C., Buchholz, J., Kuratate, K., Kim, J., Paine, G., Kitamura, C., Wagner, M., Möller, S., Black, A., Schultz, T., Bothe, H.: From Talking Heads to Thinking Heads: A Research Platform for Human Communication Science (December 2009), http://thinkinghead.edu.au/
7. Wallace, R.S.: A.L.I.C.E. Artificial Intelligence Foundation (December 2009), http://www.alicebot.org
8. Leitner, S.: So lernt man lernen (how to learn to learn). Freiburg Im Breisgau (1972/2003)

Easy-to-Web:
Introduction to the Special Thematic Session

Cordula Edler[1] and Birgit Pebök[2]

[1] inbut, Integrative Consulting and Support, Teckstraße 23, 73119 Zell u.A., Germany
cordula.edler@t-online.de
[2] Competence Network Information Technology to support the Integration of People with
Disabilities (KI-I), Hafenstraße 47-51, 4020 Linz, Austria
birgit.peboeck@ki-i.at

Abstract. The needs of people with cognitive and learning disabilities are still underrepresented in the current scientific discussion. The STS Easy-to-Web tends to find a remedy. It aims to bring together web accessibility experts and experts for accessible information in order to bring together guidelines on Easy-to-Read and web accessibility guidelines. The main goal is a better integration of guidelines for accessible information to the World Wide Web, especially considering the needs of people with learning disabilities.

1 Introduction to the Special Thematic Session on Easy-to-Web

Web accessibility has gained worldwide awareness and attention over the last decade; according guidelines, legislation and tools are in place supporting better access for people with disabilities.

Web accessibility by nature has a focus on interoperability with Assistive Technologies and other end user devices. This leads to a predominant role of accessibility in a more technical sense related to display, navigation and interaction techniques [1].

Of course access for people with cognitive and learning disabilities is taken into account and general recommendations to use a language style which is understandable are integrated ("Easy-to-Read"). But it has to be outlined that there are no comprehensive and supportive guidelines and tools helping web designers and developers and in particular content providers to design and display textual and illustrative information in a way which would better suit the needs to support people with cognitive and learning disabilities.

Even more, a state of the art analysis shows that easy to understand information on the web is very seldom addressed as a research topic. This contradicts to potential of the web using a different style of designing and presenting information which much better could suit the needs of people with cognitive and learning disabilities and would lead to a better understandable web in general. It is time for **"Easy-to-Web"**!

K. Miesenberger et al. (Eds.): ICCHP 2010, Part I, LNCS 6179, pp. 630–633, 2010.
© Springer-Verlag Berlin Heidelberg 2010

2 Who Is the Target Group of Easy-to-Web?

The target group of Easy-to-Read and thus easy-to-use web applications in the broadest sense is called people with special educational needs. The primary target group are people with cognitive and learning disabilities[1]. The secundary target groups are:

- people with other disabilities, e.g. deaf people
- people with restricted education
- people with severe social problems
- people from abroad (migrants)
- elderly people

There are many types and an even wider variety of interests and capabilities of the users who have these disabilities. Cognitive and learning abilities are more or less complex and vary very between individuals. These people may have problems in memory, problem solving, attention, reading, linguistic, and verbal comprehension, mathematical comprehension and visual comprehension.

Some people need more time to understand new or difficult information or to learn practical skills. Other people may need plenty of support. Some have difficulties in understanding the language of the country they are living in. They all have different needs and skills and they all are (potential) target groups of "Easy-to-Web".

3 Motivation

A few years ago the question was "How can computers and inclusive education help people with cognitive and learning disabilities?" Back then they were excluded mainly from ICT use. Today - five years later - the questions must be "How become proven requirements functional specification of interface design for them?" or "How to use WebX.0 to enhance quality of life for people with cognitive and learning disabilities?"

2007 the United Nations Convention on the Rights of Persons with Disabilities sets an internationally recognised benchmark for the human rights of people with disabilities [2].

The motivation to find solutions for an inclusive participation of all in the information society not only arises from this directive. It is also caused by the demand of the target group (keyword "Empowerment") as well as a lot of positive experience in learning and using ICT by people with cognitive and learning disabilities.

Literacy, digital inclusion and digital technology can facilitate the self-advocacy of the (Easy-to-Read) target group by providing them a medium through which they are able to indicate their needs, wishes and abilities (e.g. via personal profiles in the form of web pages and multimedia presentations). The usage of assistive technology may help them to get more autonomy and independence.

---

[1] Remark: The group of people with cognitive and learning disabilities is larger than the group with physical and sensory disabilities combined.

4 How to Enhance Web Usability for People with Special Educational Needs as Design for All?

Our vision of inclusive web design aims to find ways to include also people with special educational needs. Improving web accessibility asks for research about easy-to-understand information, clear information design and simplification for the various target groups of "Easy-to-Web". Improving web accessibility for the target groups mentioned will improve access for all.

5 Structure of This STS

This Special Thematic Session will present results of some initiating scientific studies on guidelines for easy-to-web as well as ongoing research, (practical) experiences, concepts and approaches ("good and bad practice") related to this field.

The STS will open with a presentation of research findings regarding the needs of people with cognitive and learning disabilities using websites as well as some general concepts to support this target group. Next it will look at implementations of functions, software or platforms especially for people with cognitive and learning disabilities.

The need for Easy-to-Read information on the web is discussed by Ulla Bohman (Easy-to-Read Commission Services at the Centre for Easy-to-Read Centrum för lättläst, Sweden). She will also describe their experiences in working with Easy-to-Read on web sites.

Kerstin Matausch (Institute of Integrated Studies, Johannes Kepler University, Austria) and Birgit Peböck (Competence Network Information Technology to support the Integration of People with Disabilities, Austria) will give a description of their study about how people with cognitive and learning disabilities can be supported on using the internet. The study was part of the project "EasyWeb" in Upper Austria 2007. The study provided the basis of Easy-to-Read standards for print and web information in Upper Austria.

Harald Weber (Institute for Technologie and Work, University of Kaiserslautern, Germany) and Cordula Edler (inbut, Integrative Consulting and Support, Germany) will present a test setup to survey the needs of young people with cognitive and learning disabilities with regard to additional functions that could support their use of the web.

Markus Erle (Wertewerk - Barrierefreies Kommunikationsdesign, Germany) and Stephan Bergmann (Ximix, Germany) will discuss the needs of an easy search function on web sites for people with cognitive and learning disabilities and a possible implementation.

Chi Nung Chu (Department of Management of Information System, China University of Technology, China) will describe the design of a reading browser which can support people with reading difficulties to focus on the meaning of the text. This reading browser is designed with dynamic alternative text multimedia dictionaries for the Chinese language.

Finally, Emma Millard, Simon Ball, Andrew Chandler and John Sewell (JISC TechDis Service, United Kingdom) will present an open source e-portfolio system with flexibility for various colleges and the needs of various types of learners. A key feature is an accessible log in system which supports students with cognitive and learning disabilities.

References

1. W3C/WAI, Web Content Accessiblity Guidelines 2.0 (2008),
   http://www.w3.org/TR/WCAG/
2. UNO, Convention on the Rights of Persons with Disabilities (2007),
   http://www.un.org/disabilities/convention/conventionfull.shtml

The Need for Easy-to-Read Information on Web Sites

Ulla Bohman

Easy-to-Read Commission Services at the Centre for Easy-to-Read
Centrum för lättläst, Sweden
www.lattlast.se

Abstract. Internet as a media for transmitting information requires higher reading skills from the user than information presented on paper. Therefor it is a great need of easy-to-read information on web sites in order to make the internet accessible for people with reading problems. For the web-information to be accessible, it must be easy to find, the web site easy to navigate and the text must be readable and understandable. The information should be in easy-to-read language and presented in a separate web-room.

Keywords: Accessibility, Usability, Easy-to-Read, Web-room, Reading Problems, Target Groups.

1 Introduction

Approximately 25 per cent of Swedish adults have reading problems, according to The International Adult Literacy Study – IALS – of 1994.[1] Their reading skills do not reach the level expected of a pupil graduating from the nine-year compulsory school. These adults have difficulties in reading – and profiting by – a text on the level of news reports in a daily newspaper. The percentage that have difficulties with general information from state authorities regarding taxes, social security plans, insurances, new legislation etc are even higher.

Since the 1990´s there has been an ongoing work in Sweden with "Klarspråk", a Plain Swedish Language. A group was appointed by the government to encourage state authorities all over Sweden to start plain language projects in order to make the information to the citizens less bureaucratic. From July 2006, these activities were taken over by the Language Council (Språkrådet).[2] Focus for the work with Klarspråk is a reader with no reading problems - the 75 per cent of the adult population in Sweden with reading skills required by graduating from compulsory school. Focus is not the adult with reading problems. The group of 25 per cent needs information more easy-to-read than klarspråk.

Reading problems may be caused by many things. A disability, for example, might impair the ability to read, interpret and understand text and pictures. Intellectual disabilities, dementia, dyslexia or aphasia may make reading, interpreting and comprehension of text more difficult. People who are untrained readers, are poorly

---

[1] Grunden för fortsatt lärande, Skolverkets rapport nr 115.
[2] www.sprakradet.se

K. Miesenberger et al. (Eds.): ICCHP 2010, Part I, LNCS 6179, pp. 634–640, 2010.

educated, have social problems, concentration problems or immigrants also often have a need for the easy-to-read text.

In the year of 2000 the Swedish Parliament decided upon a strategy how people with disabilities are to enjoy the same rights and obligations as others. This strategy includes the rights to information. In order to make information more accessible for all, the different Swedish National Agencies focused on improving their web sites and the development of various e-services. The e-guidelines developed for the authorities had mainly a technical focus.[3] This progress was very positive for people with good reading skills, but for people with reading problems this increased accessibility was not a reality. Finding and reading information on internet is difficult and requires good reading skills. Very little was written in the guidelines and few recommendations were given regarding how the information should be presented for people with reading difficulties and the level of the language.

Therefor the Centre for Easy-to-Read in Sweden started working with how to make internet more accessible and easy-to-read for people with reading problems.

2 About Easy-to-Read on the Internet

Internet as a media requires higher reading skills than information presented in a brochure or on paper. The whole idea of internet is that there is no limit to how much information you can store in cyberspace – the information is there for you to find, read and share. The skilled reader master the search for information, including to use the web site´s search-function. He or she also manages to scan information and quickly sort out the relevant information – i.e. which one of the 40 different hits that actually is the information looked for. And, once finding the right information it has to be readable and understandable. A difficult text is not accessible just because you can reach it via internet.

The crucial questions for information presented on the internet is therefore:

1. is the information possible to find?

2. is the information readable and understandable?

These two questions has not been given enough focus from the weak readers´ point of view when web sites have been developed. The internet-user in focus has been the skilled reader with no special needs, or the skilled reader with special technical needs. The need of the less skilled and often very slow reader has most of the time been ignored.

2.1 The Reader Must Be Able to Find the Easy-to-Read Information

An easy-to-read text on the internet needs to be easy to find. Many Swedish web sites have an easy-to-read version of some information, but often this alternative version is hidden deep down in the web-structure impossible for the weak reader to find. Therefore all the information on easy-to-read language should be organized in a easy-to-read web-room, a separate part of the site parallel to the regular site. This way of organizing the web is similar to the structure many web sites have when it comes to

---

[3] Vägledningen 24-timmarswebben, 2006, VERVA.

offering the reader a version in a foreign language. The foreign language alternative is still, in the year of 2010, much more common than the alternative of an accessible version for poor readers!

2.2 The Easy-to-Read Web-Room

On the first page of a web site, there should be a link called "Easy-to-Read". The link takes the reader to the easy-to-read web-room where all the published information is in easy-to-read language.

Example 1: Piteå – small community in the north of Sweden

www.pitea.se (web site of community)

www.pitea.se/lattlast (easy-to-read part of same web site)

This example shows an easy-to-read web-room with about the same content as the regular site. It is a reflection of the regular community site and the visitor basically get the same information but summarized, and the visitor has access to the same service as via the regular web. Approximately 60 of the 290 Swedish communities has information in easy-to-read on their web sites and you find this information in a separate web-room. But so far, only a handful give broad information about the community´s service to citizens. A majority has focused their easy-to-read information mainly on information regarding service for people with special needs.[4]

2.3 Structure and Navigation Are Equally Important

It is important that the weak reader easily can find the easy-to-read information. It is also important that the risk of navigating back to the regular web by mistake is minimal. Therefore, the web sites must be easy to navigate and the structure must be simple to grasp. The structure should also easily communicate to the reader where to go, where to read.

Depending on the structure of the regular site, the easy-to-read web-room can have a similar structure or the structure needs to be modified. People with Swedish as a second language might be good readers and experienced internet-users in their native language. But, they need information in easy-to-read Swedish – some of them until they have conquered the new language, some of them forever. As a service to these readers, the community of Södertälje has chosen an additional way on their web to make the information in easy-to-read language more accessible. All the information in easy-to-read language can be found via the regular structure as well as in the easy-to-read web-room.

Example 2: Södertälje – neighbouring community of Stockholm

http://www.sodertalje.se/Kommun-demokrati/Politik-och-paverkan/

http://www.sodertalje.se/Sprak/Lattlast/Kommun--demokrati/Att-paverka-politiken/

---

[4] Kommunundersökningen 2009, Centrum för lättläst 2009.

The first link is to a web-page of the regular site. Above the text there are links which show alternative language versions of the specific information: Lättläst (easy-to-read), English, Suomi, Arabic. If you choose "Lättläst", the easy-to-read version of this text will open up in the regular web structure. It is the same easy-to-read text as you find when you are visiting the easy-to-read web-room. This is a good way to increase the accessibility. But, it had not been accessible for the vast majority of the weak readers if the easy-to-read versions where to be found only within the regular web site´s structure.

2.4   The Text in Easy-to-Read Language

To be a weak reader generates problems with finding information, difficulties with managing an extensive text, poor understanding of unusual or complicated words or structure of sentences and problems with grasping content of long sentences. Many of the weak readers have a more limited vocabulary compared to the advanced readers and some of them also have a limited general knowledge about society. The writer of the easy-to-read text should have a pedagogical approach to the writing of the text.

The text itself for this target group must be written simple and understandable, but at the same time in an adult and varied manner. To achieve this you have to take into consideration the content of the text, the language, pictures and the graphic layout. An easy-to-read text should have concrete content and the language should also be concrete. Long, unusual words should be avoided, as well as concepts that may have two meanings. Metaphors should be avoided since they must be interpreted. Many weak readers might interpret a metaphor literally. The expression "I´m just pulling your leg" doesn´t have anything to do with your legs. It means that I am teasing you. With metaphors there is also a big risk that the reader and the writer might not share the same frame of reference. The frames of references depend on age, gender, cultural background etc. The risk of mis-communication is big. The text often needs to give the background information that the weak reader might lack as well as explain context and specific words. A useful approach to the text is: The reader should get all the information that he or she needs to understand the text from the text.

Weak readers are also often slow readers. It takes a long time to read even a short paragraph and it is a mental as well as a physical effort. Therefore easy-to-read text should be as short as possible, without loosing the substance of content.

2.5   The Layout in Easy-to-Read

It is important for form and layout to be well thought through. It is easier for the reader to absorb information if text and pictures are presented as clearly and with as much space as possible. Running text written with CAPITAL LETTERS or in *italics* is difficult to read.

Many readers have difficulty in noticing full-stops and in reading long lines. An easy-to-read text is thus often written with line-feeds at the end of each phrase. A new line starts at a natural point in the sentence, and always after a full stop. The reader can then make a pause at the proper place. This is how the previous paragraph looks like when written in easy-to-read line feeds:

Many readers have difficulty in noticing

full-stops and in reading long lines.

An easy-to-read text is thus often written

with line-feeds at the end of each phrase.

A new line starts at a natural point in the sentence,

and always after a full stop.

The reader can then make a pause

at the proper place.

The line-feeds give the text a light and airy impression. To the weak reader the text does not look difficult nor massive. The text signals it is easy and possible to read.

The length/amount of information is a problem for people with reading problems. Therefore it is important to try to keep the information short. This is extra important for information on the internet where the reader is reading on a screen. Ideally you should not have to scroll - the whole text should fit on the screen. For the weak reader it is difficult to find the line/sentence where the information continues after having to scroll down the text. It might take a long time to find the right place, often too long and the weak reader gives up. Or, he or she by mistake skips one or several sentences and consequently misunderstands the information.

Since the information on the web-page should be kept short, there will not be room for all the information. Prioritize and always give information about who to contact if the reader wants to ask questions, needs more information.

2.6 Up-Date the Easy-to-Read Information

Very often the information in the easy-to-read part is static, sometimes even incorrect due to changes. This part of the web needs to be up-dated regularly as well as the rest of the site.

If the regular web offers services for the citizens like e-application for childcare, the same service should be accessible in the easy-to-read web-rum. The easy-to-read web-room should have the same content as the regular web and not only information regarding service for people with special needs.

2.7 Evaluate the Easy-to-Read Web-Room

In order to improve the web site and to make sure it is accessible for persons with reading problems, evaluate! At the Centre for Easy-to-Read in Sweden we have worked together with adult education, handicap organisations, training centres for people with Swedish as second language, centres for adults with intellectual disabilities evaluating easy-to-read information on web sites.

3 Our Experience Working with Easy-to-Read on Web Sites

Throughout the years we have been asked to help national agencies, municipalities and organizations to re-write information in easy-to-read Swedish. Since the year

2005 the amount of information for web-publishing has increased tremendously. But, there is a huge dilemma with this development; people with reading problems are generally not good internet-users.

The structure of internet requires that the user can manage a large quantity of information, of text. As an internet-reader you must know how to find information, how to sort out and select information. There is a general idea that if information is published on the internet you have made the information open and accessible for all.

The guidelines for accessibility on the internet that the Swedish National Board VERVA produced,[5] said very little about language and structure for people with reading problems. Neither has there been any studies in Sweden on accessibility on the internet for weak readers. Therefore we at the Centre for Easy-to-Read have been learning by doing, made into practice our long experience producing information for this specific target group.

We have made several small studies on how to find information on the National Agencies web sites, in each study 50-100 people have participated. High school students, elderly, immigrants and people with intellectual disabilities have participated in the studies – all representing the 25% of the IALS-study. We have used both individually written questionnaires and interviews. In the studies we have combined questions where the participant is asked to find a specific information at a specific web site, with general comments regarding structure, navigation, content, language and presentation.

Each study has given more or less the same results. Generally we can say that for the 25%-group:[6]

1. to find information on a web site is difficult
2. it is easy to get lost on a web site
3. if you find the information you are looking for, the information is not always understandable.

We have long known and can clearly see the need for information in easy-to-read Swedish on web sites, but there is also a great need of an easy-to-read structure. There has been many good initiatives taken regarding producing important information in easy-to-read. But the information has then been published somewhere hidden deep down in the web-structure, impossible to find for a person with reading problems.

Therefore we recommend and have developed a separate part of the web site in easy-to-read, where all the information is written in easy-to-read language.

4 Conclusion

Accessible information on internet is definitely not only about technical matters. In order to make internet accessible for people with reading problems you also need to focus on structure, navigation, language and the presentation of the information. These aspects must be included in guidelines regarding accessible internet. More research and studies on this topic needs to be done in this aspect.

---

[5] Vägledningen 24-timmarswebben, 2006, VERVA.
[6] http://www.lattlast.se/pub/5255/Rapport%20-%20Lättläst%20på %20webben.pdf

5 Centrum för lättläst – The Centre for Easy-to-Read

The Centre for Easy-to-Read is a resource and competence centre. The Centre can provide easy-to-read material or offer assistance in various questions relating to easy-to-read material. The Centre publish books and a newspaper "8 PAGES" under the slogan: "Easy to read and easy to understand".

References

1. Skolverket, Grunden för fortsatt lärande, Rapport nr. 115 (1996)
2. The national Language Council, http://www.sprakradet.se
3. VERVA, Vägledningen 24-timmarswebben (2006)
4. Centrum för lättläst, Kommunundersökningen 2009 (2009), http://www.lattlast.se
5. Centrum för lättläst, http://www.lattlast.se/pub/5255/

EasyWeb – A Study How People with Specific Learning Difficulties Can Be Supported on Using the Internet

Kerstin Matausch[1] and Birgit Peböck[2]

[1] University of Linz, Institute Integriert Studieren, Altenbergerstr. 69, 4040 Linz, Austria
`kerstin.matausch@jku.at`
[2] Competence network information technology to support the integration of people with disabilities (KI-I), Hafenstraße 47-51, 4020 Linz, Austria
`birgit.peboeck@ki-i.at`

Abstract. This paper presents a study on Easy-to-Read and its impacts on the support of people with specific learning difficulties. Research unveiled a lack of scientific research concerning Easy-to-Read but various scientific issues which interrelate with the underlying topic. Although having based on heuristic experiences the study represents a deep investigation concerning Easy-to-Read principles for print and online materials and what is more represented a signal for ongoing ambitious efforts to involve people with specific learning difficulties to all areas of life.

Keywords: Easy-to-Read, learning disabilities, learning difficulties, internet usage of people with learning disabilities, Easy-to-Read and WCAG.

1 Introduction

People with cognitive disabilities, people with learning disabilities and people with specific learning difficulties are named as the main target groups of Easy-to-Read (E2R). These terms are nearly equivalent in meaning. The following paper will use »people with specific learning difficulties (SPLD)« to name the main target group of E2R. It stands for all groups of people who have a lack of reading and understanding abilities. Access to societal activities and thus to information as part of societal interaction and knowledge transfer, however, can be seen as a right for everyone as to see in i.e. the Austrian e-Government Act Part I [3] and the Austrian Disability Discrimination Act [2].

A lot of information and services are provided on the web which makes it more and more necessary to deal with the internet. For years one discussed the needs of people with disabilities and the internet, yet the needs of people with specific learning difficulties and the internet had not been taken into account for a long time. Web accessibility and usability allow access to information for (almost) all. People with specific learning difficulties only benefit in parts from it. They additionally need content which is easy to understand. This can be supported by using the method of Easy-to-Read even on the internet.

K. Miesenberger et al. (Eds.): ICCHP 2010, Part I, LNCS 6179, pp. 641–648, 2010.

The study and its results which are presented in the following paper discuss the possibilities and the limits of a conflation of web accessibility and Easy-to-Read. It was carried out on behalf of the Upper Austrian Government during the project EasyWeb. The project had the following goals: 1.) an identification of Easy-to-Read standards and an accompanying know-how building, 2.) a definition of E2R guidelines for Upper Austria. The proposed guidelines should compass of principles for print and online documents. 3.) Prototyping: the proposed web principles on Easy-to-Read should provide their evidence by being implemented on the internet by means of a prototype. Finally, it should represent a signal for ongoing ambitious efforts to involve people with specific learning difficulties to all areas of life.

2   State of the Art

Research unveiled a lack of scientific research for Easy-to-Read (E2R) guidelines. Previous existing guidelines are predominantly based on heuristic experiences. They usually ask how to conduct accessible information and commonly are implemented by institutions supporting people with specific learning difficulties (SPLD) such as i.e. the Easy-to-Read Foundation Sweden, Lebenshilfe Germany, Mencap Ireland, Enable Scotland [6], Capito Austria. As far it is known due to a worldwide investigation no scientific research on this specific topic existed till EasyWeb was carried out.

Moreover hardly any guideline exists on how to accomplish Easy-to-Read on the internet [7, 12]. Following the importance of the internet for i.e. social interaction, information gathering, learning and e-Government, it is about time to deal with E2R and web applications.

In general, a huge number of Easy-to-Read materials can be detected. An investigation led to the assumption that countries with a low level of E2R development predominantly provide materials with a close life-oriented approach (i.e. concerning the vocational environment or how to deal with money). Countries with a high developed level of E2R and frequently a longer experience in producing easy reader materials provide a more sophisticated Easy-to-Read offer including what to do when being a witness in court [4], how to vote [8], laws concerning people with disabilities [2] and usual news from all over the world [17].

Finally, the current situation, especially in Austria, was and still is characterized by little existing knowledge but an increasing interest concerning Easy-to-Read implementations. This is proven by a raising number of requests from organizations. In general, an implementation of E2R on the internet is still very underdeveloped in Europe. Only a few provide easy readable information on the internet and even less are presenting it in a way which accords to the W3C WAI guidelines [15]. Austria's current situation is indeed characterized by the existence of a number of persons who are able to counsel regarding accessible web design, but there is a lack of persons who are able to give counselling on the interrelation of Easy-to-Read and accessible and usable web design [11].

3   The Main Results of the Study

Basically, the findings of the underlying study are based on the principles of accessibility, usability and Design for All. The methodology used comprises expert interviews and a desktop research conducted worldwide regardless an undeniable European focus. The research focused on Easy-to-Read initiatives, organizations dealing with print and digital easy reader materials as well as on a deep research concerning E2R and its implementation on the internet.

3.1 Additional R & D Which Has an Impact on Easy-to-Read Applications

As presented above a lack of scientific research concerning E2R does exist which makes an analysis in the underlying field of research more challenging. Nevertheless, there are other fields of research which interrelate with Easy-to-Read and which can be applied as a scientific dimension to E2R:

3.1.1 Gestalt Principles of Form Perception

The Gestalt Principles of Form Perception are useful in the context of E2R. They can support an easier comprehension of text structure. The following part will give a short description of those principles which benefit comprehension and usage of Easy-to-Read:

- The Law of Prägnanz: People tend to order their experience in a manner that is regular, orderly, symmetric and simple. So the gestalt law says that in a group of shapes especially those with a different appearance will be perceived. Important parts can thus be pointed out and perceived easier if its appearance is different to the rest. People (with specific learning difficulties) can be thus supported concerning an identification of important parts by means of the Law of Prägnanz.
- Law of Closure: People tend to ignore gaps and complete contour lines of an object to perceive it as unit. Lines which coherently border a space will be recognized more easily as a unit than incoherent lines. It represents additional cognitive effort to close the lines to a unit. Following this, one can support people (with specific learning difficulties) concerning a deep understanding of objects if contour lines are closed.
  Example: Important related information can be presented in a box with closed contour lines. The user will more easily perceive this information as related.
- Law of Similarity: Elements will be grouped perceptually if they are similar to each other.
  Example: Items of an unnumbered list with consistent bullets will be perceived as a group. Text with the same background color will also perceived as belonging together.
- Law of Proximity: Objects which are positioned close to each other tend to be grouped together. Adequate space between areas causes automatic distinction between those areas. Otherwise it causes automatic recognition of an area as such. [9]

3.1.2 Cognitive Text Processing

People with specific learning difficulties experience challenges at different levels and maybe at several levels of cognitive text processing. In the following the levels of cognitive text processing are described and it is discussed how the various level of cognitive text processing can be supported by using E2R-patterns.

- Basal processing: This level represents the level of word recognition, characters are identified and composed to words.

  Easy-to-Read principles such as clear fonts, a clear typeface and enough contrast will support this level of text processing. Moreover, short words can be recognized much easier.

- Semantic-syntactic processing: On this level words get connected to parts of phrases or to complete sentences. The coherence between words and the meaning of sentences becomes clear.

  Familiar wording, using always the same word for the same thing, and short sentences alleviate the semantic-syntactic processing and represent a relation with Easy-to-Read at the level of semantic syntactic processing.

- Elaborative processing: At this level text will be combined with previous knowledge. A cognitive visual presentation of the text is formed.

  This level of text processing interrelates with E2R by matching text processing an previoues knowledge of the target group. Examples and pictures support text processing at this level.

- Reductive processing: At this level the whole text is reduced to the essential information.

  A summary supports on the level of reductive processing.[1]

3.1.3 Readability Formulas (i.e. Flesch Reading Ease)

Readability formulas are mathematical procedures to determine the simplicity of a written text. They use measures (e.g word length and sentence length) and weight them or set them into relations. Such formulas can only be used in the language they are designed, they do not work in other languages.

They can be used for a first impression but not for a comprehensive evaluation because they can only measure simplicity in syntax and not in semantics. Building coherence or simplicity in grammar cannot be evaluated by readability formulas. Furthermore, readability formulas do not pass the test of validity. This means, two formulas usable in the same language do not necessarily result in the same simplicity. [5, 13, 14].

3.1.4 Hamburg Comprehensibility Concept

The Hamburg Comprehensibility Concept says that text with the following four characteristics of comprehensibility is easy to understand:

- Linguistic simplicity: This characteristic relates to wording and syntax. Usage of common words, simple and short sentences and explanation of difficult and unusual words makes information easier to understand.

- Arrangement structure / cognitive structure: Internal order and outside structure of a text are the main points of this characteristic. A meaningful order of information, clear clustering as well as highlighting the major information helps to make information accessible.

- Concision: This characteristic discusses the length of a text in relation to the information target. Information should be presented neither to short nor to long winded.

- Motivation: This characteristic refers to stimuli which can cause the interest and sympathy of readers. This principle can be implemented by using examples which are in touch with the reality of the audience, which directly address the users but also a humorous wording.

Advantages for editors:

- The search for structure and order clears own thoughts
- Effort to make information concise sharpens the view at the essence

Advantages for readers:

- Ability to understand information
- Keep information better in mind
- Positive feeling with reading and understanding [10].

3.2   Combination of Easy-to-Read and WCAG

Accessible internet needs both a technical accessibility and an accessibility of content. Technical accessibility can be achieved by following the WCAG 2.0 (Web Content Accessibility Guidelines) [16] from WAI (Web Accessibility Initiative) [15]. For that reason knowledge about WCAG 2.0 is important. But WCAG is insufficient for people with SPLD as the accessibility of content requires a strong usability aspect. So, accessible web design and usability are crucial in the context of E2R web applications. This asks for a comprehensive expertise in all these areas when dealing with E2R and the internet.

E2R stands not in opposition to the internet but represents a meaningful completion of usability and accessibility specifications. Usability research tells us i.e. to use short sentences and to concise text. E2R guidelines show how to do this and how to improve readability and understandability so that either people with SPLD are able to understand the content. Usability enhances the ability to achieve the required content. E2R helps to understand the offered content.

Following history, E2R guidelines were primarily developed for print materials and cannot be implemented one-to-one to the internet. Some print guidelines are suitable for internet requirements such as the following ones:

- *»Use sans serif fonts.«*
- *»Use short sentences.«*
- *»Speak to people directly.«*
- *»Never use a picture or a pattern as a background.«*

Some conform to internet requirements with restrictions:

- *»Always use large writing. You should use writing which is at least the size of Arial 14pt.«:* However, accessible web design requires scaleable font size. The combination should include a presetting of medium or large font which is scaleable.
- *»Where possible, one sentence should fit on one line. If you have to write a sentence on two lines, cut the sentence where people would pause when reading out loud.«:* On the internet the end of a line can reach out of the current view,

depending on the screen, on individual system settings and on the adjusted font size. Therefore predetermined breaks have to be defined with respect to a clear arrangement of information and non-text elements.

Finally, there are print guidelines which are not suitable for internet requirements such as the following one:

— *»Avoid cross references.«*: Yet, the internet subsists on hyperlinks. A combination with E2R makes sense i.e. concerning dictionaries defining terms.

It is advisable to consider those wide differences between print and digital media. The implementation of Easy-to-Read on the internet asks for a further development of Easy-to-Read guidelines so that they match the characteristics of the internet and refer to the needs of the target group. This leads to the following issue dealing with the »amount« Easy-to-Read is »claiming« at a website.

3.3 Implementation Options of Easy-to-Read on the Internet

The implementation of E2R on websites can take place in different ways at various levels of accessibility for the target group.

- Option 1: The whole website is available in E2R only – the whole website is accessible for the target group.
- Option 2: The whole website is available in both E2R and "normal" text – the whole website is accessible for the target group, but the costs are higher than in any other option.
- Option 3: The whole website is available in "normal" text and a part of this is additionally available in E2R – only parts of the website are accessible for the target group. The costs are higher than in option 1 and 4 and lower than in alternative 2.
- Option 4: Parts of the website are in "normal" text and other parts in E2R – only parts of the website are accessible for the target group [11].

The decision concerning the proportion of E2R and Non-E2R text is a indication for the necessity of accessible content considered as necessary, socio-integrative and ethic as well as financial aspects. The latter aspects point out some challenges one has to deal with when publishing Easy-to-Read. Further challenges are discussed in the following.

3.4 Common Challenges

Moreover, the study [11] revealed a number of challenges which have to be solved in future:

- The acceptance of Easy-to-Read material in general public is still low. People without SPLD are not aware of the importance of materials in E2R or decline to read information presented in E2R. Otherwise, people with SPLD sometimes refuse to be stigmatized by using E2R material. This challenge has to be considered if easy-to-read material is offered.

- An appropriate education for editors of E2R materials is still missing.
- A lack of information on the target group does exist. It is inhomogeneous and ranges from dyslexia to grave forms of cognitive disabilities. So, a detailed statistical background is required.
- A detailed knowledge is lacking regarding the strategies of people with SPLD concerning information search and information processing as well as concerning their »surf the internet« behavior.
- Large font, short lines, enough space between lines and paragraphs and longer explanations of complex information results in an increasing number of pages for print materials or long text sections on the internet. This asks for an advanced handling of usability and E2R.
- The quality of E2R material is hard to deduce. Although there are a number of signs labeling E2R materials, only some are accompanied by a standardized creation and testing process which is indeed important in order to reach high quality E2R materials.
- A final challenge is the collaboration between organizations dealing with E2R at a national and a European level (European network) concerning an adaptation and enhancement of E2R guidelines.

4 Impact and Contributions to the Field

As mentioned above the WAI guidelines WCAG 2.0 [17] do partially implement guidelines for people with SPLD. These guidelines which are obligatory by law in some countries could push forward accessible information for people with specific learning difficulties if E2R guidelines were included to a large extent.

The study "EasyWeb" proposed a scientific approach regarding Easy-to-Read and its execution on the internet. It led to the establishment of a »translation agency« and consulting centre for E2R in Upper Austria. This office provides for the first time a chance for Austrian organizations to be counseled in detail concerning the interrelation of E2R and the internet and to get support regarding E2R implementations on the web. Following this we assume that the augmenting request will lead to an increased execution of E2R on the internet and thus an increased accessibility of information for people with specific learning difficulties on the web.

Moreover, the results of the study "EasyWeb" do play an important role during discussions at a transnational level. One can detect an increasing interest on how to implement E2R on the internet at the level of the German language network for Easy-to-Read ("Netzwerk Leichte Sprache") which is a platform for a further E2R development in the German spoken area. Particular interest can be identified with respect to research regarding this topic. We assume that these discussions will lead to a growing public awareness concerning the connection of E2R and the internet as well as an initialization of follow-up studies in the sector of E2R which will be indeed worth for a further scientific debate concerning Design for All in information delivery.

References

1. Ballstaedt, J.P.: Wissensvermittlung, Die Gestaltung von Lernmaterial. Psychologie Verlags Union, Wennheim (1997)
2. Austrian Disability Discrimination Act 2006 (2006), http://www.ris.bka.gv.at/Dokumente/BgblAuth/BGBLA_2005_I_82/BGBLA_2005_I_82.html
3. Austrian eGovernment Act 2004 (2004), http://www.bka.gv.at/DocView.axd?CobId=31191
4. ENABLE, I am a Witness in Court, http://www.enable.org.uk/info.php?tid=6&sectiontype=0&sid=21&ssid=47
5. Hochhaus, S.: Der verständliche Text - Perspektiven auf die Textoptimierung. Schriftliche Hausarbeit für die Magisterprüfung der Fakultät für Philologie an der Ruhr-Universität Bochum (1998), http://www.yauh.de/files/magisterarbeit.pdf
6. ILSMH European Association, Make It Simple, http://www.osmhi.org/contentpics/139/EuropeanGuidelinesforETRpublications2.pdf
7. Inclusion Europe, Information for all European standards for making information easy to read and understand, Brussels (2009) ISBN 2-87460-110-1
8. Inclusion Ireland, Guide to Voting, http://www.choices.inclusionireland.ie/live/book.asp?bid=2&sid=1&pid=0
9. Katz, D.: Gestaltpsychologie. Schwabe Verlag, Basel (1969)
10. Langer, I., Schulz v. Thun, F., Tausch, R.: Sich verständlich ausdrücken, Ernst Reinhardt. GmbH & Co KG, Verlag, München (1999)
11. Matausch, K., Peböck, B.: Information Center on Accessible Information. In: Miesenberger, K., Klaus, J., Zagler, W.L., Karshmer, A.I. (eds.) ICCHP 2008. LNCS, vol. 5105, pp. 763–766. Springer, Heidelberg (2008)
12. Mencap, Making your web site accessible for people with a learning disability, http://www.intrasolutions.co.uk/website_accessibility.pdf
13. Readability Formulas, http://www.readabilityformulas.com/flesch-reading-ease-readability-formula.php
14. Wagener, R.: Kompetenzsimulation. In: Barrierekompass (2005), http://www.barrierekompass.de/weblog/index.php?itemid=303
15. W3C WAI, http://www.w3.org/WAI/
16. WCAG 2.0, http://www.w3.org/TR/WCAG20/
17. 8SIDOR, 8sidor.lattlast.se/

Supporting the Web Experience
of Young People with Learning Disabilities

Harald Weber[1] and Cordula Edler[2]

[1] Institut für Technologie und Arbeit (ITA), Gottlieb-Daimler-Str. Geb. 42,
67663 Kaiserslautern, Germany
harald.weber@ita-kl.de
[2] inbut, Integrative Consulting and Support, Teckstraße 23, 73119 Zell u.A., Germany
cordula.edler@t-online.de

Abstract. The paper describes a test setup to survey the needs of young people
with learning disabilities with regard to additional functions that could support
their use of the web. Via an HTML mock-up, different iconic representations of
buttons to invoke these additional functions as well as different placements of the
buttons were explored. Results with N=34 indicate that study participants
preferred button locations on the right side of web pages and prefer icons with
associative symbols and analogy symbols for text sizing functions and low-iconic
images, associative symbols and arbitrary symbols for text reading functions.

Keywords: Learning disabilities, special educational needs, SEN, button design,
button placement.

1 Introduction

1.1 Access for People with Learning Disabilities

It is widely acknowledged that information and communication technology (ICT) can
play a major role in empowering disadvantaged groups towards better participation in
society. However, people with learning disabilities are rarely benefitting from ICT. For
many years accessibility issues have been dealt with in numerous projects, activities and
large-scale initiatives, but the centre of gravity has been on providing access to ICT for
motor or sensor impaired users. Guidelines for designing accessible ICT still become
vague, when the target group of people with learning disabilities is addressed. Although
usability aspects have migrated slowly into common guidelines for accessibility, they
have been often dealt with as "optional". But for people with learning disabilities poor
usability can inhibit the use of ICT, while other user groups might find ways of working
around usability flaws. Good usability, hence, needs to be upgraded to a high-priority
accessibility requirement for people with learning disabilities.

1.2 Research Activities in the Field of ICT Accessibility

A multiplicity of projects and initiatives has focused on accessibility of ICT for
people with disabilities in the previous 15 to 20 years. In Europe, the Telematics

K. Miesenberger et al. (Eds.): ICCHP 2010, Part I, LNCS 6179, pp. 649–656, 2010.

Applications programme as part of the 4th Framework Programme (1994 – 1998), e.g., included the 'Technology / Telematics for the Integration of Disabled and Elderly people' initiative. Later, accessibility and the inclusion of the requirements of people with disabilities in ICT research and development projects were highlighted as obligatory for all projects to be funded.

There are only few resources available that provide empirical evidence on guidelines issued by experts to support the web experience of people with learning disabilities. Key problem issues that need to be addressed were identified in a project that tested an interactive multimedia learning environment with the target group [1] and came up with the following areas: accessibility, navigation, pedagogic structure, aesthetics, games and screen properties. Authors also claim that there is still a need for a more holistic approach to maximizing the role of the Web in enabling disabled people to access information, services and experiences including those with learning disabilities [2].

Some projects of interest to this area are for example ON-LINE [3], a European learning project to offer new ways of access to multi-media learning for people with special educational needs (SEN), the ECDL for people with disabilities [4] that aimed at adapting this ECDL certificate to the needs of people with disabilities, and ACCESSIBLE [5] that started 2008 and aims at researching and developing an assessment simulation module in order to fully support and incorporate accessibility approaches for the design and development of accessible new applications.

1.3 Target Group

Problematic with regard to the comparison of results of different activities is that there is still no internationally agreed disability terminology available. Hence, statistically comparable data are also missing to estimate the dimension of the target group. And because national definitions are often broad and not well-defined, the group of people with learning disabilities, who will be in the focus of the study, needs some further explanation. The target group comprises of people with learning / cognitive disabilities (IQ lower than 70) including people with autism, or deaf and blind people with cognitive problems, yet without people who are mentally ill. Spoken in terms of the WHO's ICD-10, the target group encompasses people with moderate mental retardation (IQ 35 – 49) and mild mental retardation (IQ 50 – 69). (The IQ, however, is not necessarily a reliable measure, as many of people's abilities and strengths do not show up well in IQ assessments. In fact, levels of learning disability are points on a spectrum, without clear dividing lines between them [6]). Within the study we aim at reaching people, who are able to communicate by spoken language, but their cognitive ability like attention, cognition, perception, conclusion, memory, abstraction or logic is limited by the disability.

2 Methodology

When surveying the needs of people with learning disabilities and of people with motor or sensor impairments, the knowledge base with regard to ICT accessibility seems to be disproportionate compared to the number of people who belong to these groups. While there is a multitude of experiences, tools, surveys and research outcomes available in the field of visually and motor impaired ICT users, users with learning disabilities are hardly covered. Most often, easy to understand language as well as clear navigation is recommended. Within this study, it is aimed to go a step further and to explore *how* and *where* additional functions should be made available for web browser users with learning disabilities.

For target group specific reasons, only a limited number of additional functions will be explored in the study. Often, people with learning disabilities have a limited span of attention. The introduction of too many new functions could be confusing and tiring to them. Therefore, two functions (*increase/decrease text size, start/stop reading aloud*) will be explored, and other functionality will be tested in additional studies later on.

As a lack of suitable content resources for the target group has been reported all over, the first step for setting up the study was to make available an information resource that both is interesting to the target group as well as is offered in easy to read. This information resource provided an easy to read version of the UN Convention on the Rights of Persons with Disabilities in German, implemented with an additional focus on the ease of navigation and use (see conference contribution by Erle & Bergmann). The pre-test scenario to check, whether the UN Convention is written as well as implemented in an understandable and fully accessible form, has been extended to address the study questions.

The target group to participate in this study was in the role of user experts. In advance to their participation, they received information on the project and on the purpose of their potential participation in understandable language, and at any stage of the project they could decide not to participate (anymore), without any negative consequences for the user.

3 Research and Development Work

From observations it was assumed that people with learning disabilities use the same web browsers like anybody else. The two most widely used web browsers in Germany are Mozilla Firefox (60%) and Internet Explorer (27%). Consequently, the navigation bar of the Mozilla Firefox web browser had been replicated in HTML to allow easy addition and modification of buttons, and the navigation bar of the browser engine underneath was hidden such that only the simulated bar remained.

Study participants were asked about their perceived level of own ICT experience (e.g. tools / applications they use when they are online) and about their knowledge of menus and navigation buttons. For each of the new functions (i.e. *increase font size, decrease font size, start reading aloud, stop reading aloud*) they were asked to select one icon from a set of 12 icons that best represent the function to the study participant. While Figure 1 groups these icons according to their level of graphical abstraction, the participants were offered a mix of 12 icons per function.

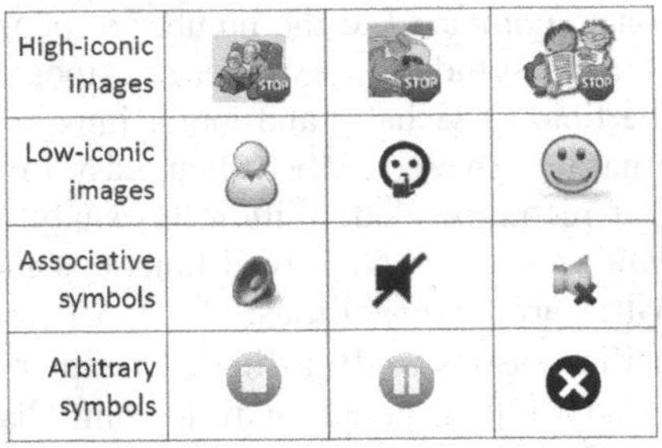

High-iconic images			
Low-iconic images			
Associative symbols			
Arbitrary symbols			

Fig. 1. Classification of icons (here: *stop reading aloud*) by level of graphical abstraction

After the selection of one of the presented icons, each new function was represented by a button that used this icon. Yet, the same button was placed at three different locations at the same time (see Figures 2 and 3). The first location was the top of the page menu which often is located left-hand side. The assumption for this location was that the main menu attracts a lot of attention, so the new function's location would be in the focus of the user's attention. The second location was at the far right-hand side in an area free of content. A vertical menu with functions like *print*, *sitemap* and *contact* was extended by the new button(s). The underlying assumption was that a button placed there does not need to 'compete' with other information for the user's attention. Finally, a position in the browser's navigation bar, just between the icons and the address bar was chosen. The assumption was that the browser's navigation bar always stays visible even on long pages where users might need to scroll down.

The aim was to observe where study participants naturally expect a new function to appear, and to monitor which of the three locations was selected when users were asked to use the new functions. As to minimize the influence of other factors, the icon / button selection area was placed equidistant to the three locations, and the size of the browser's navigation bar was slightly increased such that navigation buttons matched the size of the buttons for the new functions.

4 Results

The study was performed March 2010 with 34 young participants (20 male, 14 female) aged between 11 and 23 years in four different educational institutions. Three of these institutions were secondary schools, while the fourth was a pre-vocational institution. All participants were informed about the study and its purpose and agreed to contribute.

More than 60% of the study participants do have a computer at home, and more than 56% have internet access at home as well. Accordingly, the participants scored their own IT experience above average (3.5 on a scale from 1 '*not at all*' to 5 '*very good*'). Being asked of how often per week they go online the participants responded with 3.2 times per week in average. Preferred activities online were: watching videos (65%), listening to music (53%), gaming (47%), chatting (29%), writing / reading e-mails (29%), reading (18%) and searching for photos (15%).

4.1 Icon Design Preferences

To elicit the participants' icon design preferences, a web-based search for "real-world" examples for the four functions (*increase / decrease font size* and *start / stop reading aloud*) was performed. The rationale for searching icons instead of designing completely new ones was that real exemplars have some likelihood that users might encounter them while browsing the web.

In general, icons can be grouped into categories of high-iconic images, low-iconic images, associative symbols, ideomorphic symbols, isomorphic symbols and arbitrary symbols. However, for the functions *increase* and *decrease font size* no suitable high-iconic images could be found, while no suitable analogy symbols could be found for the functions *start* and *stop reading aloud*. Per icon category 3 icons were chosen, resulting in 12 icons presented to the participants per function.

Table 1 and Table 2 summarize the results of the study with regard to icon design preferences. The data imply that associative symbols and analogy symbols are quite well known and appreciated as self-explanatory enough to represent the two functions *increase / decrease font size* (see Table 1). For *start reading* low-iconic images and associative symbols seem to be preferred, while for *stop reading* the preferences are spread quite similar over the three categories low-iconic images, associative symbols and arbitrary symbols (see Table 2).

Table 1. Proportion of users who selected an icon considered most self-explanatory for the respective function (*increase / decrease font size*) from 4 different icon categories (N=34)

	Increase font size	Decrease font size
Low-iconic images	18 %	12 %
Associative symbols	33 %	21 %
Analogy symbols	33 %	48 %
Arbitrary symbols	15 %	18 %

Table 2. Proportion of users who selected an icon considered most self-explanatory for the respective function (*start / stop reading aloud*) from 4 different icon categories (N=34)

	Start reading aloud	Stop reading aloud
High-iconic images	13 %	16 %
Low-iconic images	34 %	29 %
Associative symbols	38 %	26 %
Arbitrary symbols	16 %	29 %

4.2 Button Location Preferences

After each icon selection, buttons were automatically generated using the icons as its graphical representation. Three copies of the same button were placed on the web site as described in section 3. The functions *increase* and *decrease font size* were included in a side menu on the right side of each page, in the left main menu and in the navigation bar (see Figure 2). 68% of the users selected the button placed right, 24% the button on the left, and no user the button placed in the navigation bar. 8% of the users did not find any of the three buttons.

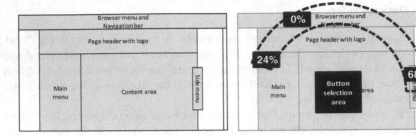

Fig. 2. *Left*: Basic structure of web page; *Right*: placement of buttons equidistant from the button selection area and percentage of users who selected each respective location. 8 % of users did not succeed in finding any of the buttons (N=34).

The test for the *start* and *stop reading aloud* function was quite similar. Yet, it was observed that on many web pages the button to invoke this function was placed behind the headline of the content area. In consequence, the button position formerly located in the right side menu was shifted slightly top-left to respond to this observation. The results are displayed in Figure 3. While 3 participants did not find any of the buttons for the other two functions, now 4 participants did not succeed (12%). This means that one participant who found the *increase / decrease font size* buttons on the right did not find the *start / stop reading aloud* buttons any more. In total, 62% of the participants used the buttons on the right, 26% the buttons on the left, and again no participant used the buttons in the navigation bar.

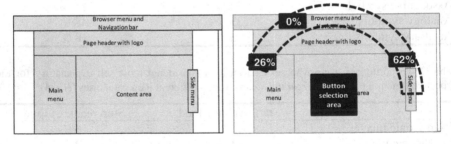

Fig. 3. *Left*: Basic structure of web page; *Right*: placement of buttons equidistant from the button selection area and percentage of users who selected each respective location. 12 % of users did not succeed in finding any of the buttons (N=34).

As to get further information on why the navigation bar location was the least favored, all participants were also asked about their knowledge of menu items and navigation bar functions. While 50% of the users knew at least one menu item under the *File* entry, only few knew other functions under other menu items (see Figure 4). 65% of the participants knew the *Back* button, 56% the *Forward* button, 6% the *Reload* button and 9% the *Home* button.

Fig. 4. *Left*: Browser menu and navigation bar; *Right*: Percentage of users who knew at least one of the functions of menu items or of the respective navigation bar icons (N=34)

5 Discussion

First of all, the group of study participants was in no way representative for the target group. The study aimed at younger volunteering participants as those are more likely to have web experiences. Second, the selection of icons used within the study was based on subjective grounds. The perceived frequency of occurrence triggered the decision to use an icon in the study. In general, high-iconic images would benefit from larger presentations than buttons provide. The study researched existing icon designs but did not explore own designs yet. However, the study results provide some insights which icon category seems to be suitable to be selected in future design.

An interesting issue was observed during the study. The web page contained a search field whose search button showed a magnifying glass. However, 52% of the participants selected an icon with a magnifying glass to represent the function *increase font size*, and 33% used an icon with a magnifying glass to represent the *decrease* function. Accordingly, only 23% of the participants found the search field without help. Obviously, this points out an area of potential conflicts.

Assumptions about the right placement of buttons on a web page were based on typical design decisions when setting up new web sites. As a new idea, a button location within the navigation bar was explored as well. This aimed at including the web browser into the discussion of 'practical usability', as users experience the combination of interactive elements in the web pages and of the web browser, which might create an overall complexity, resulting in barriers for the target group.

The results, however, show that users with learning disabilities, although quite web-experienced, prefer a location for additional functions which is not addressed accordingly by web designers yet. Buttons in the navigation bar were obviously placed in areas of low interest and presumably low attention accordingly. Study participants were also asked whether they could guess the functionality behind some additional buttons: 94% would expect a printing function behind a button with a simplified printer as an associative symbol, 50% would expect a mailing function behind a button labeled with a simplified letter, but only 14% expected a help function behind a button labeled with a question mark. Buttons that contained their function in writing (e.g. the "send" button) were recognized by all study participants. Research by Davies et al. [7] who modified web browsers supports these findings. Their modifications resulted in significantly improved performance data and user satisfaction levels. Sevilla et al. [8] consequently eliminated the menu in a modified browser and used only simplified buttons such as *Back* and *Home*.

The meaning of arbitrary symbols needs to be learnt, as it cannot be derived from its visual presentation (e.g. currency symbols). From the study's target group it was expected to have participants with limited cognitive abilities in the area of memory (for recognition of symbols) or in the area of conclusion and logic (for inferring that if a symbol works in one situation it could have the same function in another situation).

Surprisingly, arbitrary symbols ranked high to represent the function *stop reading aloud*. The symbol used for that is one often found on remote controls or music players ('pause', ❙❙), so it can be assumed that study participants were familiar with those interaction elements. This outcome highlights the relevance of training aspects and calls for a standardization of key interaction elements to support learnability of new applications as well as of explorability of web sites for the target group.

Study data suggest that the users hardly pay any attention to the navigation bar and thus are not aware of changes that take place within that area. This is possibly a strategy to cope with complexity, or to focus on areas that are useful to them. In fact, most web pages can be operated without the need to use navigation bar items. It could be worth exploring whether the location for buttons in the navigation bar will attract more attention if the other functions provided there are really useful for the users.

Future activities resulting from these outcomes include studies with people with learning disabilities aged 25 or older to cross-check whether age or ICT experience has an impact on the results, exploring the redesign of the browser standard buttons and layout to see whether user interaction improves, and discussing how web page content including navigation and browser design could be synchronised such that overall complexity can be prevented or at least reduced.

References

1. Brown, D.J., Powell, H.M., Battersby, S., Lewis, J., Shopland, N., Yazdanparast, M.: Design guidelines for interactive multimedia learning environments to promote social inclusion. Disability and Rehabilitation 24, 587–599 (2002)
2. Sloan, D., Heath, A., Hamilton, F., Kelly, B., Petrie, H., Phipps, L.: Contextual web accessibility - maximizing the benefit of accessibility guidelines. In: Proceedings of the International Cross-Disciplinary Workshop on Web Accessibility. W4A 2006, vol. 134, pp. 121–131 (2006)
3. ON-LINE, http://www.on-line-on.eu
4. ECDL-PD, http://ecdl.com/publisher/index.jsp?p=932&n=777&a=1054
5. ACCESSIBLE, http://www.accessible-eu.org/
6. British Institute of Learning Disabilities, http://www.bild.org.uk/
7. Davies, D.K., Stock, S.E., Wehmeyer, M.L.: Enhancing independent internet access for individuals with mental retardation through use of a specialized web browser: a pilot study. Education and Training in Mental Retardation and Developmental Disabilities 36(1), 107–113 (2001)
8. Sevilla, J., Herrera, G., Martinez, B., Alcantud, F.: Web accessibility for individuals with cognitive deficits: a comparative study between an existing commercial web and its cognitively accessible equivalent. ACM Transactions on Computer-Human Interaction 14(3), 1–23 (2007)

Easy-to-Web Search for People with Learning Disabilities as Part of an Integrated Concept of Cognitive Web Accessibility

Stephan Bergmann and Markus Erle

Wertewerk
Aixer Straße 12, 72072 Tuebingen, Germany
erle@wertewerk.de
www.wertewerk.de

Abstract. Accessible web for people with cognitive or learning disabilities doesn't only mean easy-to-read and font size magnification. Every interaction has to be reflected according to the needs of this target group. This paper describes the first step towards an easy-to-web search user interface which helps people with learning disabilities to start a query with a correct written and meaningful search word. It is also a suggestion how the guideline 3.3 "Input assistance" of the WCAG 2.0 could be fulfilled in the field of search function and cognitive accessibility.

Keywords: cognitive accessibility, cognitive disabilities, easy-to-read, learning disabilities, search user interface, spelling mistakes.

1 Search Function and People with Learning Difficulties

A useful search function is crucial for every kind of user in order to find web content fitting to its own interest. Useful search results depend on various factors relating to the stages of a search process:

1. The query
2. The mechanism or algorithm of the search engine itself
3. The presentation of the search results

People with learning disabilities also prefer to use a search function but they hardly succeed in finding useful results. They often already fail in typing correct text into the search box.[1]

According to the guideline 3.3 of the WCAG (Web Content Accessibility Guideline) 2.0 users should get help in order to avoid or correct mistakes. This also applies to search input fields. People with some disabilities have more difficulty creating error-free input. Although the WCAG 2.0 doesn't say a lot about the needs of

---

[1] Smith (2009) emphasizes two issues according to the problems of people with learning disabilities using a search function: misspelled search words and difficulties to select the search result fitting best to the user's interest.

K. Miesenberger et al. (Eds.): ICCHP 2010, Part I, LNCS 6179, pp. 657–660, 2010.

people with learning disabilities, input assistance is important especially for them. The reason is: often they are not able to notice their error or to understand what they should do to correct it.

Therefore we focused on finding a support mechanism during query specification which is able to compensate spelling mistakes typically made by people with learning disabilities.

2 Our Approach

In a first step we had a look at common strategies to avoid input mistakes and their applicability for people with learning disabilities. In a second step we analyzed typical input mistakes made by them. In a third step we developed a "search before the search" based on syntactic similarity of the typed in search word to words of a manual edited index. We didn't change the standard search engine with its full-text search.

2.1 State of the Art of Fault-Tolerant Search Functions

There are two main strategies of fault tolerant search functions:

1. Auto completion:
   The user types the first letters of a search word, the system suggests completed words. Disadvantage: the first letters of a search word have to be written correctly. Users with learning disabilities often type wrong letters even at the beginning of a search word.
2. Did you mean: xyz?
   The user types a misspelled search word, the system only suggests one alternative if at all. This is a standard support feature of google in case of an average wrong typed search word. Disadvantage: For tested misspelled search words written by people with learning disabilities the google search didn't lead to useful results. For example: the German word for contact is "Kontakt". A typical spelling mistake is to write "Kontat". In that case google didn't suggest "Kontakt".

Conclusion: Both main strategies are not enough for the needs of web user with learning disabilities, spelling difficulties or bad literacy.

2.2 Typical Spelling Mistakes Made by People with Learning Disabilities

Through analyzing typical mistakes of people with learning disabilities we discovered that:

- they often write as they speak
- they forget a letter sometimes even at the beginning of the word
- they change letters
- they add one letter or more

Especially the first two typical mistakes are not compensated by standard mechanisms mentioned above.

3 The Search Before the Search

The easy-to-web search is based on two success criteria:

1. A mechanism which can compensate misspelled search words by suggesting meaningful alternatives of words that really can be found in the content of the website.
2. A user interface which is easy to use for people with learning difficulties and makes it easy to find the correct search word.

3.1 The Compensation Mechanism

Core function is a combination of some simple algorithms in order to find syntactic similar words to the typed in word based on an manual edited index.

The similarity of a word is evaluated through:

- the number of same letters
- the word length
- the same first letter counts more but is not essential

For every index word the similarity points are evaluated. The amount of points determines the size of the suggested search words.

3.2 The User Interface: The Word Cloud

People with learning disabilities often have special limitations according to perception, memory and attention. Therefore they need a search user interface which leads them to useful results in only a few steps without overcharging their capacity of information processing. Therefore we tried to design a very simple and clear user interface by adapting the cloud concept.

The easy-to-web search generally offers the possibility to determine, if the user wants to get 3, 5 or 10 suggestions of similar words.

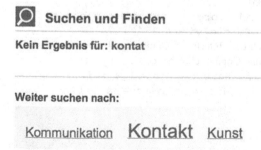

Fig. 1. The most similar search words are displayed as a word cloud. The word cloud is sorted alphabetical but the most similar word is displayed bigger than the less similar words. So it is very easy to recognize the write spelled word and to select the correct search word.

4 Work and Results

The easy-to-web search is developed for an easy-to-read version of the UN convention on the rights of persons with disabilities and available on the German website www.ich-kenne-meine-rechte.de. It enables an alternative access to this difficult but important content.

The improved search function is even usable for blind users (who also sometimes make spelling mistakes because the checking is difficult to them).

4.1 Evaluation

It was very important to catch user feedback during the development period because in the field of usability of search functions for persons with learning disabilities only very few research results are available.

In a pilot study 9 of 34 people with learning disabilities could use the easy-to-web search without assistance.

5 Conclusion

Based on common and widely spread technologies like PHP it is possible to develop functions especially answering to the needs of persons with learning disabilities. The strategy consists in combining available solutions in a smart way. An example is the easy-to-web search.

So in near future it is possible not only to present easy-to-read web content but also easy-to-web functions which are very necessary in order to realize an integrated concept of cognitive web accessibility.

References

1. Aula, A., Käki, M.: Less is more in Web search interfaces for older adults. First Monday 10(7) (2005),
   http://firstmonday.org/htbin/cgiwrap/bin/ojs/
   index.php/fm/article/view/1254/1174
2. Hearst, M.A.: Search User Interfaces. Cambridge University Press, Cambridge (2009)
3. Smith, J.: Insights into Cognitive Web Accessibility (2009),
   http://www.slideshare.net/jared_w_smith/
   insights-into-cognitive-web-accessibility

Adaptive Reading: A Design of Reading Browser with Dynamic Alternative Text Multimedia Dictionaries for the Text Reading Difficulty Readers

Chi Nung Chu[1] and Yao-Ming Yeh[2]

[1] China University of Technology, Department of Management of Information System,
No. 56, Sec. 3, Shinglung Rd., Wenshan Chiu, Taipei, Taiwan 116, R.O.C.
[2] National Taiwan Normal University, Information & Computer Education, 162, Sec. 1,
Hoping East Rd., Taipei, 106 Taiwan

Abstract. The effectiveness of reading comprehension on a Reading Browser with Dynamic Alternative Text Multimedia Dictionaries was explored in this paper. Students with text decoding difficulty (N=62) were randomly assigned to one of three modes: auditory mode, pictorial mode, 5 full functions mode. A quasi-experimental design was used to measure reading comprehension. Although differences were not significant among all of the modes, the findings indicate that all modes of Reading Browser with Dynamic Alternative Text Multimedia Dictionaries were successful in promoting reading.

Keywords: Reading Browser with Dynamic Alternative Text Multimedia Dictionaries, Text Decoding Difficulty, Adaptive reading Mode.

1 Introduction

Reading is an exceptionally demanding cognitive task. For readers with text decoding difficulty, the demands are extraordinary. The process of reading requires reader decode the text to obtain meaning [1]. The whole reading process involves two separate but highly interrelated areas - word identification and comprehension [2], [8],[12]. It requires readers familiar with letters of the alphabet and phonemic awareness. If a reader has difficulties in automatic word recognition significantly, that will affect the reader's ability to effectively comprehend what they are reading [10], [15]. Development of phonemic awareness is necessary to learn how to map speech to print. However written Chinese is a logographic orthography that differs greatly from alphabetic writing systems. The orthography–phonology relationship in alphabetic scripts is transparent [9], [17]. It is even harder for the text decoding difficulty readers to develop Chinese phonological ability.

Studies showed that phonological awareness facilitates reading. Success with phonemic awareness is a strong predictor of later reading success. However children with text reading difficulty do not always acquire skills in the normal developmental sequence. Therefore the barrier to prohibit them from reading comes heavier [5], [11] [14].

K. Miesenberger et al. (Eds.): ICCHP 2010, Part I, LNCS 6179, pp. 661–664, 2010.

The nature of text is changing. Digital text and the ability to read it well are necessities in the digital times. Hypertext environment provides different ways to approach information content. Readers with different cognitive style are normally free to make their own reading structure and sequence [3], [4], [7]. The non-linear characteristics of hypertext facilitate the non-sequential retrieval of information and allow different individuals to interact with the same information through different reading processes. This permits a reader to choose a path through the text that will be most relevant to his or her interests. With the development of digital technology, better reading environment can be created for different style readers with the opportunities of multi-sensory interaction [6], [13], [16]. It is a good remedial way to read in multi-sensory strategies. Text reading difficulty readers can use both their visual and verbal sensors retrieving, organizing and storing incoming information.

Adaptive Reading model proposed in this study accommodates a comprehensive range of individual preferences with regard to the reader's text cognition abilities to communicate necessary text-based information effectively. In the reading model, readers can get converted digital text into spoken words. It also allows readers to engage with text-based information aurally and visually and enables slow readers to process text more quickly and efficiently. The reading model with such mechanism tries to make the texts accessible. While decoding the actual words, readers can focus their attention on what the text actually means. Without the burden of decoding, the reader is free to think about and gain. Readers can thus derive more benefit from activities in which they actively participate. In such design, the readers with text reading difficulty will have greater opportunities for independence than ever before.

2 Reading Browser with Dynamic Alternative Text Multimedia Dictionaries

The Reading Browser is a reader with multimedia dictionary importing function to read digital documents from the Internet or client folders. It can provide any text matched from the multimedia dictionary as reader requests by selecting a number key from 1 to 5 (Figure 1). Adaptive Reading model proposed in this study accommodates a comprehensive range of individual preferences with regard to the reader's text cognition abilities to communicate necessary text-based information effectively. In the reading model, readers can get converted digital text into spoken words. It also allows readers to engage with text-based information aurally and visually and enables slow readers to process text more quickly and efficiently. Reader can request 5 different assisted modes (auditory vocabulary, pictorial vocabulary, oral glossarial, animation of stroke order for Chinese characters and animation of Chinese phonetic transcription) for redundant presentation of textual information.

Multimedia dictionary editor (Figure 2) provides the customized dictionary editing functions of alternative vocabulary which includes pictorial, verbal, oral glossarial, animation of stroke order for Chinese characters and animation of Chinese phonetic transcription. The Adaptive Reading is a way of thinking about digitized reading model that emphasizes alternative presentation and interpretation of text for readers who have text decoding difficulties. It is intended to develop any digitized text-based reading to provide compatibility with a variety of additionally alternative presentation and interpretation of text which can be perceived by readers with text cognition limitations.

 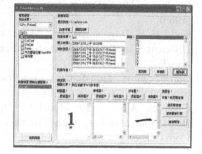

Fig. 1. Reading Browser with Dynamic Alternative Text Multimedia Dictionaries

Fig. 2. Multimedia Dictionary Editors

3 Analysis Module

The participants with text decoding difficulty in reading achievement were randomly assigned to one of the three versions of Reading Browser with Dynamic Alternative Text Multimedia Dictionaries (auditory vocabulary mode, pictorial vocabulary mode, 5 full functions mode), interacted with one of them and attempted to solve ten articles in reading comprehension.

During the post-test, the participants filled out a different set of 5 multiple-choice questions and a user perception survey. There were two versions of the test, such that the post-test was counterbalanced with pretest.

When the pre-test scores were examined, there were no significant differences among the tutoring conditions. As posttest scores were examined, we found that all the versions of Reading Browser with Dynamic Alternative Text Multimedia Dictionaries produced significant reading comprehension; posttest scores (M =.60, SD =.18) were significantly better than pretest scores (M = .46, SD = .19), $F(1, 129) = 141.17$, $p < .001$. Although there was no overall significant effect of tutoring conditions on posttest scores. All in all, Reading Browser with Dynamic Alternative Text Multimedia Dictionaries produced significant reading comprehension. The posttest scores (M =.56, SD =.19) were significantly greater than pretest scores (M = .39, SD = .20), $F(1, 93) = 87.73$, $p < .001$.

4 Conclusion

The Adaptive Reading model using Reading Browser with dynamic alternative text multimedia dictionaries for the text reading difficulty readers tries to make the texts accessible. While decoding the actual words, readers can focus their attention on what the text actually means. Without the burden of decoding, the reader is free to think about and gain. Readers can thus derive more benefit from activities in which they actively participate. In such design, the readers with text decoding difficulty will have greater opportunities for independence than ever before.

References

1. Baker, E.L., Atwood, N.K., Duffy, T.M.: Cognitive Approaches to Assessing the Readability. In: Davidson, A., Green, G.M. (eds.) Linguistic Complexity and Text Comprehension: Readability Issues Reconsidered, pp. 55–83. Lawrence Erlbaum Associates, Inc., Hillsdale (1988)
2. Catts, H.W., Hogan, T.P., Fey, M.E.: Subgrouping Poor Readers on the Basis of Individual Differences in Reading-Related Abilities. Journal of Learning Disabilities 36(2), 151–164 (2003)
3. Calcaterra, A., Antonietti, A., Underwood, J.: Cognitive Style, Hypermedia Navigation and Learning. Computers & Education 44, 441–457 (2005)
4. Chen, S.: A Cognitive Model for Non-Linear Learning in Hypermedia Programmers. British Journal of Educational Technology 33(4), 449–460 (2002)
5. Cornwall, A.: The Relationship of Phonological Awareness, Rapid Naming, and Verbal Memory to Severe Reading and Spelling Disability. Journal of Learning Disabilities 25, 532–538 (1992)
6. Fredericksen, E., Pickett, A., Shea, P., Pelz, W., Swan, K.: Student Satisfaction and Perceived Learning with Online Courses: Principles and Examples from the SUNY Learning Network. Journal of Asynchronous Learning Networks 4(2) (2000)
7. Gauss, B., Urbas, L.: Individual Differences in Navigation between Sharable Content Objects: An Evaluation Study of a Learning Module Prototype. British Journal of Educational Technology 34(4), 499–509 (2003)
8. Kieras, D., Just, M.: New Methods in Reading Comprehension Research. Erlbaum, Hillsdale (1984)
9. Lowe, C.C.: How to Improve the Instruction of Vocabulary Learning. Mandatory Education 35(3,4), 15–18 (1994)
10. Lyon, G.R.: Towards a Definition of Dyslexia. Annals of Dyslexia 45, 3–27 (1995)
11. Majsterek, D.J., Ellenwood, A.E.: Phonological Awareness and Beginning Reading: Evaluation of a School-Based Screening Procedure. Journal of Learning Disabilities 28, 449–456 (1995)
12. Mercer, C.D., Mercer, A.R.: Teaching Students with Learning Problems. Merrill Prentice Hall, Upper Saddle River (2001)
13. O'Dwyer, L., Carey, R., Kleiman, G.: A Study of the Effectiveness of the Louisiana Algebra I Online Course. Journal of Research on Technology in Education 39(3), 289–306 (2007)
14. Strattman, K.H., Hodson, B.: Variables that Influence Decoding and Spelling in Beginning Readers. Child Language Teaching and Therapy 21(2), 165–190 (2005)
15. Torgesen, J.K., Rashotte, C.A., Alexander, A.W.: Principles of Fluency Instruction in Reading: Relationships with Established Empirical Outcomes. In: Wolf, M. (ed.) Dyslexia, Fuency, and the Brain. York Press, Timonium (2001)
16. Vonderwell, S., Liang, X., Alderman, K.: Asynchronous Discussions and Assessment in Online Learning. Journal of Research on Technology in Education 39(3), 309–328 (2007)

In-Folio: An Open Source Portfolio for Students with Learning Disabilities

Simon Ball, Andrew Chandler, Emma Millard, and John Sewell

JISC TechDis Service, Higher Education Academy Building,
Innovation Way, York YO10 5BR, U.K.
{simon,andrew,emma}@techdis.ac.uk

Abstract. In-Folio is an Open Source e-Portfolio application developed to address the specific needs of the Independent Specialist Colleges sector. This sector caters for students with wide ranging learning difficulties and disabilities, often profound and multiple, and while currently available applications do address accessibility well they were not felt to be suitable for this group of learners. An e-Portfolio application that would meet the specifications of this sector was developed, with further modifications in process.

Keywords: accessibility, e-portfolio, e-learning.

1 Introduction

In-Folio is an Open Source e-portfolio system developed for JISC TechDis by the Rix Centre at the University of East London, UK. It is designed to meet the very specific needs of learners with wide ranging learning difficulties and disabilities (often profound and multiple disabilities) at Independent Specialist Colleges. Many of these colleges are small, residential organisations, offering extended curricula and high levels of care to their learners [1].

In 2007, JISC TechDis launched the second round of the Learning and Skills Council's (LSC) Innovation Fund [2], inviting Independent Specialist Colleges to bid for funding to use technology and e-learning in innovative ways for the benefit of staff and students. Several colleges identified the need for an e-portfolio system tailored to the needs of learners from this sector to build on work that was already underway in a number of colleges. For example, the Home Farm Trust used Microsoft® PowerPoint to collate multimedia materials created by learners to illustrate their life history and interests (*Life Stories*)[4]. Staff felt that this led to an improvement in communication skills and an increase in self confidence. Other colleges used technologies such as digital video cameras to enable individuals to record their progress and CDs, given to learners when they left college, as a tangible record of their time there.

A system was required that would allow students to record their work and achievements, accounting for the fact that learner achievements within the Independent Specialist Colleges sector could be very different compared to achievements in mainstream Further Education and may include a large amount of multimedia evidence

K. Miesenberger et al. (Eds.): ICCHP 2010, Part I, LNCS 6179, pp. 665–668, 2010.

(for example videos of learners cooking to demonstrate life skills as part of an extended curriculum). Crucially, learners must be able to take ownership of the material, organising and uploading it independently and in a style that suits them, rather than relying on help from staff and working to a set structure. They must also be able to take their e-portfolio with them to further study and employment when they leave.

2 The State of the Art

It was decided to combine similar proposals and develop a solution that could be employed across this sector, and eventually to learners with disabilities and learning difficulties across the wider education sector. This would mean an alternative and more sustainable outcome than having each college develop their own ad hoc system. Consultations between the four colleges collaborating on this project and the Rix Centre resulted in a list of objectives for the e-portfolio, which would essentially allow learners to upload and organise multimedia materials independently. Learners would need to retain ownership of the materials developed so that they could, for example, control 'read access' to the contents of their individual e-portfolios. They would also require continued access to their e-portfolios on leaving college.

The Rix Centre was commissioned to research current e-portfolio systems (both commercial and Open Source) and their suitability for use within Independent Specialist Colleges. They initially collated a list of forty existing applications that could form e-portfolio systems, ranging from blog applications to modules built into the Moodle VLE. Feedback from colleges highlighted the requirement for a specialised, discrete e-portfolio system, interoperable with existing platforms such as VLEs and Management Information Systems. This review led to a shortlist of two commercially available systems; PebblePad [5] and People and Places [6]. These products were demonstrated and reviewed by representatives of the colleges – their findings were:

- PebblePad is a robust and flexible system and the developers are working to ensure that it can be used with assistive technologies. However, at the time of reviewing, this work had not been completed and therefore there would be barriers for a number of users within the target group.
- People and Places, developed by CDSM, is targeted more specifically at the student target group and the developers have a track record of usability testing and work on interoperability. CDSM were invited to demonstrate People and Places directly to the college representatives, who raised some concerns about the social networking aspect of the application, the interface structure (which is organised chronologically, with a large amount of text and a number of links on each page) and a lack of an adjusted user interface for switch users with severe and profound intellectual disabilities.

3 The Alternative

It was therefore not feasible to use an existing application and so three options were identified:

1. Approach the suppliers of the existing products with a request for a bespoke installation for these colleges.
2. Develop a product that would meet the functional requirements.
3. Build an application around an existing Open Source framework.

College representatives chose option 3, basing the solution around the existing Elgg framework [7]. At each phase of development, the prototype system was demonstrated to the four core colleges, who were given the opportunity to trial the system and feed back to the developers.

4 The Result

In-Folio has been developed to offer significant flexibility to colleges so that it can be tailored to their learners' needs. The simplest option provides learners with one folder to store materials, with a more complex structure of multiple folders available if appropriate. Materials can be uploaded by learners to their individual e-portfolio, or by staff to a shared gallery accessible to all learners in a college. The tab-based interface allows learners to easily organise their materials. Because it is web-based, the portfolio is also available to learners from anywhere, even after leaving college.

A key feature of In-Folio is that it offers an accessible system of logging in. The following options are available to In-Folio users:

- A text-based username and password.
- Symbol log-in – users are presented with a range of symbols. Passwords arc set by selecting a specific combination of symbols.
- Image log-in – users upload an image and set their password by selecting particular areas of the image in a specified order.

This range of options enables learners to set their own passwords and log-in independently.

5 The Impact and Evaluation

In-Folio was launched at the 2009 NATSPEC Annual Conference and piloted by six colleges during Summer 2009. The pilot colleges hosted a series of roadshows to which representatives of all Independent Specialist Colleges were invited, to demonstrate In-Folio and enable it to be rolled out in time for the 2009/10 academic year. In addition to showcasing In-Folio, staff from the Rix Centre created training materials on collecting multimedia portfolio evidence - this is available on the In-Folio blog [8]. These events were attended by thirty-nine colleges and in November 2009, forty colleges had created In-Folio accounts, representing 57% of Independent Specialist Colleges. These colleges are continually feeding back and further developments are being made, and a formal evaluation will take place following the first full year's usage.

In-Folio has also been used by the Rix Centre in several schools and community-based projects in London, including the Setting Your Sites project, a local employment initiative. While the focus is primarily on creating a stable and usable platform for

Independent Specialist Colleges, there has been interest in In-Folio from mainstream Higher Education and particularly from Adult and Community Learning. As it is an Open Source product, In-Folio could potentially have a much wider impact across the education sector.

6 Future Work

In-Folio is currently hosted by the Rix Centre. A third round of the Innovation Fund launched in October 2009 offers colleges the chance to bid for an In-Folio package which includes a server with In-Folio installed and a year's technical support. The installation will also include Xerte (the Open Source Learning Object Development Tool) [9]. This should enable colleges to have more control of In-Folio and improve its security for users. It is also a more sustainable model, as space on the Rix Centre's servers is limited, although hosting will still be available if colleges require it.

This round also invited collaborative bids for further development of In-Folio, with the aim of improving its functionality in response to needs identified by the sector. As a result, the following developments scheduled for later in 2010 are underway:

- Training materials to enable parents to use In-Folio with their child, so that progress can be recorded when the learner is away from college.
- A community of In-Folio users, to stimulate further use and development.
- An application within In-Folio to track learner progress.

References

1. National Association of Specialist Colleges (UK), http://www.natspec.org.uk
2. The Innovation Fund, http://www.techdis.ac.uk/getinnovation
3. Kickstart Programme, http://www.techdis.ac.uk/index.php?p=2_3_14
4. Home Farm Trust,
   http://www.hft.org.uk/What_we_do/Assistive_technology
5. PebblePad, http://www.pebblepad.co.uk
6. People and Places, http://www.cdsm.co.uk/products/pandp/index.htm
7. Elgg, http://elgg.org/
8. In-Folio training materials, http://www.in-folio.org.uk/blog/?page_id=89
9. Xerte, http://www.techdis.ac.uk/getxerte

Author Index